A COMICS STUDIES READER

A COMICS STUDIES READER

EDITED BY JEET HEER AND KENT WORCESTER

University Press of Mississippi
Jackson

www.upress.state.ms.us

The University Press of Mississippi is a member of the Association of American University Presses.

First printing 2009
∞
Library of Congress Cataloging-in-Publication Data

A comics studies reader / edited by Jeet Heer and Kent Worcester.
    p. cm.
  Includes bibliographical references and index.
    ISBN 978-1-60473-108-8 (cloth : alk. paper) — ISBN 978-1-
60473-109-5 (pbk. : alk. paper) 1. Comic books, strips, etc.—
History and criticism. I. Heer, Jeet. II. Worcester, Kent, 1959–
  .C667 2008
  741.5'69—dc22
                                    2008016893

British Library Cataloging-in-Publication Data available

CONTENTS

CONTENTS

ACKNOWLEDGMENTS

We would like to express our thanks and gratitude to our contributors, as well as to Nic Bannon, Walter Biggins, Eddie Campbell, Lawrence Klein, Guy Lawley, Dan Nadel, Ken Fisher, Donald Rooum, Art Spiegelman, and Chris Ware. We would like to give special thanks to Robin Ganev, Jennifer Scarlott, and Julia Worcester. This book is dedicated to Seetha Srinivasan.

INTRODUCTION

Over the past two decades, intelligent and informed writing about comics, hitherto an endeavor with a long but often marginal history at the periphery of scholarly and intellectual worlds, has flourished as never before. Both the quantity and quality of scholarly writing on comics has increased enormously. More importantly, there is a sufficient accumulation of well-crafted work to inspire a sense of shared purpose and momentum among comics-minded scholars, essayists, and critics. The study of comics has become a lively field of inquiry and is no longer merely a topic area.

The burgeoning of comics studies is testified to by a wide array of evidence: impressive new biographies and monographs; the construction of a scholarly infrastructure (archives, conferences, journals, listserv groups, and so on); greater theoretical ambition and sophistication; the internationalization of comics scholarship (facilitated by the web); the recovery of lost classics; and the growing audience for talks, books, and articles on the history, aesthetics, craft, and politics of comics. Scholars interested in comics enjoy access to an expanding range of reference works, specialized terminology, and research opportunities. While the best of the new comics scholarship is eclectic, in approach and foci, it consistently returns to certain core themes: the history and genealogy of comics, the inner workings of comics, the social significance of comics, and the close scrutiny and evaluation of comics. Not coincidentally, these are the four themes we highlight in this book.

The rise of comics studies is concomitant with the increased status and awareness of comics as an expressive medium and as part of the historical record. This revaluation is testified to by the commercial and critical success of the graphic novel; the greater attention comics are receiving in museums, galleries, and libraries; and the growing interest in teaching comics in the classroom. A cohort of graphic novels, including *Maus, Persepolis, Jimmy Corrigan, American Born Chinese*, and *Fun Home*, have become standard items on college and university syllabi for courses on memoir, cultural history, postmodern literature, and area studies. The notion that comics are unworthy of serious investigation has given way to a widening curiosity about comics as artifacts, commodities, codes, devices, mirrors, polemics, puzzles, and pedagogical tools. Comics are no longer a byword for banality; they have captured the interest of growing numbers of scholars working across the humanities and historically oriented social sciences.

The study of comics has benefited from what our contributor W. J. T. Mitchell has termed the "pictorial turn" and an awakened interest in a broader range of visual articulation than has traditionally been embraced by the academy. The emergence of cultural studies in the postwar period opened up space for studying popular culture in general and comics in particular. The more recent near-canonization of specific works and cartoonists by critics and scholars has also helped legitimize comics studies. As a field concerned with a medium that simultaneously manufactures genre and facilitates self-expression, comics studies embraces both mass entertainment and the avant-garde. The phrase "teaching comics" itself has a dual connotation. An increasing number of faculty are integrating graphic literature into their existing courses. At the same time, more and more courses are being introduced on different aspects of comics. While the present collection is designed for use in courses *on* comics, it is also aimed at readers who are curious about where comics sit in relation to other kinds of materials that might usefully be assigned in art history, communication arts, design, history, literature, political science, and sociology.

The burgeoning of comics scholarship is an exciting and much belated development. If we accept the emerging consensus that Rodolphe Töpffer's work from the 1830s and 1840s provides a paradigmatic example of the form, comics have been around for well over 150 years. Over the intervening decades there has been an outpouring of writing about comics, starting with Töpffer's meditations on his craft. Yet much of this literature, while filled with insights that warrant revisiting, is improvised and impressionistic in its approach. Some of it is deeply polemical. The emergence of a research-driven scholarly corpus, informed by the regular exchange of ideas, information, and findings, is a relatively recent occurrence. By contrast, the secondary literature on film, a younger art form, has been from the early twentieth century onwards much larger, more systematic, and more culturally respectable and prominent.

Given the energy and ferment of contemporary writing on comics, this strikes us an ideal moment to step back and survey the terrain. Our anthology is intended as a starting point for defining comics studies as well as a springboard for further investigation. The book features twenty-eight noteworthy contributions to an expanding and intrinsically interdisciplinary field. It is aimed at students, faculty, curators, librarians, and general readers. Our interest is in addressing readers who are engaged by comics of all kinds and from multiple vantage points, whether as product, construct, language, argument, or aesthetic.

In preparing this volume, we have kept three broad goals in mind: first, to highlight the rich diversity of approaches to the investigation of comics; second, to locate comics in a multiplicity of contexts (historical, artistic, spatial, commercial); third, to showcase the remarkable new wave of comics scholarship. Taken together, the essays map the major approaches to the history, form, impact, and assessment of comics. Rather than privileging any single genre, framework, or style, the volume is informed by an appreciation for the diversity of forms and roles that comics inhabit, as well as for the divergent roads that scholars, critics, and essayists have taken in thinking and writing about comics.

The collection introduces readers to the debates, fault lines, and points of reference that continue to shape the field. The fact that the volume has pieces on Carl Barks, Superman, EC Comics, Chris Ware, Art Spiegelman, Alan Moore, and Charlie Brown is hardly accidental, given their cartooning landmark status. Similarly, certain lines of demarcation are reflected in the book's very organization, with some scholars focusing on the history of the medium, others concerned with the form's inner logic, and still others using comics as a social-historical mirror. These differences both reflect and influence choices about methodology and subject matter. Disciplinary and institutional locations, area studies interests, and theoretical commitments can also inspire and reinforce lines of demarcation in comics studies. Individual authors may work across as well as within various intellectual tendencies, but the camps themselves lend depth and coherence to scholarly deliberations.

At the heart of comics studies are a series of questions that are both historical and theoretical in nature:

- What are the definitional boundaries of comics? What is distinctive or unique about comics?
- What constitutes excellence, and how is it measured? (And is this the right question?) Should comics scholars establish canons, jettison the concept, or deconstruct the canon-making impulse?
- How do comics figure in the history of printing, reading, and mass entertainment? How have creators, publishers, consumers, and anti-comics campaigners influenced the development of the medium?
- What is the relationship of reading comics to other forms of literacy? Are comics primarily a literary medium (to be read), a visual medium (to be viewed), or a hybrid medium that requires distinctive reading strategies on the part of the reader?
- How does the experience of producing, distributing, and consuming comics vary from country to country, region to region, and across time?
- How do the combination and juxtaposition of words and pictures work? How do comics achieve *meaning*, for readers, subcultures, and societies?

As these questions suggest, the term "comics" is itself filled with ambiguity. In everyday language the term can refer to comic strips ("I was reading today's comics"), comic books ("I store my comics in the attic"), or even people who tell jokes. The term suggests a humorous intent that is inconsistent with the actual content of many, perhaps most, comic strips, comic books, and graphic novels. Comics scholars have consequently devised a variety of labels, from graphic narrative, graphic storytelling, the ninth art, and *bande dessinée*, to capture their target. They have wrestled with the surprisingly difficult task of defining comics, as well as tracing their genesis and excavating their antecedents. Just as importantly, scholars have sought to distinguish comics from (and to connect them to) neighboring phenomena, such as animation, caricature, children's books, posters, and illustration. The pieces reprinted here adopt divergent stances on how to talk about comics and whether the term itself is useful or valid.

It will quickly be evident that we have applied a broad rather than narrow interpretation of "comics." For our purposes, the term most often refers to comic strips, comic books, manga, and graphic novels, but also encompasses gag cartoons, editorial cartoons, and *New Yorker*-style cartoons. While web comics are beginning to stimulate informed criticism, our emphasis is on illustrated print. Our collection showcases a full range of methods and disciplinary influences, from historical survey, biography, and empirical investigation, to theoretical exegesis, comparative study, and formal analysis. Most but by no means all of our contributors are academics. Freelance critics, amateur historians, and cartoonists have produced outstanding comics scholarship, a fact that is reflected in this reader.

Aside from the pioneering writings of Rodolphe Töpffer, the earliest writing on comics mainly emanated from journalists and book critics who used the topic as a jumping off point for larger cultural concerns. Our collection *Arguing Comics: Literary Masters on a Popular Medium* (University Press of Mississippi, 2004), features essays from the late nineteenth century and the early-to-mid twentieth century that castigate illustrated storytelling on behalf of established literary values. We also included works by more sympathetic voices, such as Thomas Mann and Dorothy Parker, as well as Gilbert Seldes, who vigorously championed *Krazy Kat* and other comic strips. For Seldes, comics were part of a distinctively American vernacular that deserved respect rather than approbation. Seldes' cultural tolerance was challenged by mid-century authors such as Irving Howe, Gershon Legman, and the psychiatrist Fredric Wertham, who all invoked comics to illustrate the deleterious effects of mass culture. The history of the medium is marked by recurrent backlashes against comics as well as by the efforts of creators and publishers to reinvent existing genres, tap new markets, expand artistic boundaries, and/or satisfy the expectations of core audiences.

The mid-century campaign against comics helped catalyze a counter-reaction that was marshaled by fans and cartoonists rather than academics. Provoked in part by Wertham's best-selling critique, a small bookshelf's worth of insider studies emerged that was rich in anecdotes and craft lore. The superhero and horror genres provided a special locus for fan criticism and creator memoirs. Fan culture continues to generate in-depth interviews, comics business journalism, and statistical data, and remains an underrated resource for research-driven knowledge-building in comics studies.

In the academy, pioneering comics scholarship by such authors as Arthur Asa Berger, Thomas Inge, Donald Ault, and Umberto Eco found inspiration in literary studies, film theory, and semiotics. (Eco's incisive 1962 essay on Superman provides the final chapter of our *Arguing Comics* volume.) These writers often paid close attention to the textual elements of comics and, in particular, their storytelling conventions and narrative devices. The most recent generation of comics scholarship, which coalesced in the 1990s, has benefited substantially from the research and mentorship of this generation. It has also had the advantage of greater resources, numbers, and academic respectability. Significant innovations include the establishment of the International Comics Art Forum (ICAF) in 1995, the launching of the *International Journal of Comic Art* (IJCA) in 1999, the founding of the Comic Art and Comics area of the Popular Culture Association in 1992, and the more recent emergence of online journals, including *Image and Narrative*, *ImageText*, and *Signs: Studies in Graphical Narratives.*

The new comics scholarship has pursued multiple lines of inquiry, from business history and poststructural theory to oral history and the rediscovery of primary texts. It has paid special attention to the formal aspects of comics. Will Eisner's *Comics and Sequential Art* (1985), and Scott McCloud's *Understanding Comics* (1993), are touchstones for this formalist turn, as are the contemporaneous essays by cartoonist Art Spiegelman and essayist/cartoonist R. C. Harvey. One feature in particular distinguishes the current wave: a fresh appreciation for the distinctive properties that set comics apart from other mediums. Previously, comics had been sometimes treated as an offshoot of other art forms (usually literature or film). Recent scholarship on comics has helped demarcate what is distinctive to comics as against other expressive media. However, valuable work continues to be undertaken on the full range of research questions identified earlier, from definitional boundaries and evaluative criteria, to national cultures and periodical history.

A Comics Studies Reader is divided into four main sections: *Historical Considerations; Craft, Art, Form; Culture, Narrative, Identity;* and *Scrutiny and Evaluation.* Each section is prefaced by a short overview that situates the individual essays in a broader context. The first section explores the prehistory of comics, the genesis and development of the comic strip and comic book, and the anti-comics campaigns of the 1950s. Rather than imposing a single narrative, this section provides room for nuanced scholarship, informed essays, biography, and historically resonate polemics. The following section takes up the language, constituent elements (panels, gutters, word balloons, and so on), and vocabulary of comics—its rules, tools, shortcuts, and hidden logic(s). Also addressed are definitional issues and the boundaries that comics may or may not respect.

The third section shifts the discussion away from formal mechanisms and devices to fictional stories and personal histories. It includes pieces on autobiographical comics, the cultural meaning of comic book heroes, the nexus of biography and storytelling, and readers' responses to individual comics. Once again, rather than attempting to manufacture a synthetic account of comics as a cultural and (inter-) subjective phenomena, we have created space for diverse voices. Not all of these voices sing in harmony. The concluding section provides a sampling of scholarship on individual creative works and comics phenomena. The artists highlighted in this section are associated with very different styles, agendas, and audiences. Yet all of them enjoy an impact on cartooning that transcends any single story, title, or character.

A Comics Studies Reader speaks to the major research questions that are shaping the field. It also spotlights the intellectual richness that characterizes the field of comics studies.

JH
KW

A COMICS STUDIES READER

Why Are Comics Still in Search of Cultural Legitimization?

THIERRY GROENSTEEN

Although comics have been in existence for over a century and a half, they suffer from a considerable lack of legitimacy.

To those who know and love it, the art that has given us Rodolphe Töpffer and Wilhelm Busch, Hergé and Tardi, Winsor McCay and George Herriman, Barks and Gottfredson, Franquin and Moebius, Segar and Spiegelman, Gotlib and Bretécher, Crumb and Mattotti, Hugo Pratt and Alberto Breccia, not to mention *The Spirit*, *Peanuts* or *Asterix*... in short, comic art, has nothing left to prove. If its validity as an art form appears self-evident, it is curious that the legitimizing authorities (universities, museums, the media) still regularly charge it with being infantile, vulgar, or insignificant. This as if the whole of the genre were to be lowered to the level of its most mediocre products—and its most remarkable incarnations ignored. Comic art suffers from an extraordinarily narrow image, given the richness and diversity of its manifestations. Furthermore, its globally bad reputation jeopardizes the acknowledgment of its most talented creators. Comic art's continuing inability to reap the symbolic benefits of its most accomplished achievements is particularly striking and merits elucidation. This is the subject I would like to reflect upon today. Some of the points I will make concern the specific history and situation of French comics and cannot be applied to other national situations without some adaptation.

I will start by evoking some of the paradoxes of the history of the 9th art.

Modern (printed) comics appeared in the 1830s—in the form of Rodolphe Töpffer's pioneering work[1]—which makes them more or less contemporary with the invention of photography. And yet, it was not until the 1960s that the French language found a permanent name for this mode of expression—that was, by then, over a hundred years old. During this long period, comics were known, not as *bandes dessinées* (literally strips that have been drawn) but, successively or indiscriminately, as *histoires en estampes*, which is Töpffer's own term (stories told in prints), *histoires en images* (picture stories), *récits illustrés* (illustrated tales), *films dessinés* (films made of drawings) and of course, comics.

Translated by Shirley Smolderen. Reprinted by permission from Anne Magnussen and Hans-Christian Christiansen, eds., *Comics and Culture: Analytical and Theoretical Approaches to Comics* (Museum Tusculanum Press, 2000), 29–41.

Since coming into existence, comics have twice changed their readership and their form. Readership first. During the nineteenth century comics were intended for adults, only to be relegated, at the beginning of the twentieth century, to the pages of the children's press. So it is in the illustrated youth magazines that France first discovered the great American series (*Brick Bradford, Flash Gordon, Mandrake, Popeye*, and so many others), whereas on the other side of the Atlantic, they were originally published in the daily newspapers. The re-conquest of the adult readership—begun in the 1960s by *France Soir, Pilote, Hara-Kiri, Charlie hebdo, Chouchou*, and *Charlie mensuel*, as well as by the innovating publisher Eric Losfeld—is finally accomplished in 1972 when Gotlib, Bretécher and Mandryka launch *L'Echo des Savanes*, the first "adults only" comics magazine, so putting an end to an historical parenthesis of almost three quarters of a century.

Concerning the form given to comics, after having originally appeared in book form (Töpffer's, Cham's, Doré's and other founders' albums), comics in the 1870s had become a press phenomenon. For more or less a century, only the most popular works were given the honor of being released as albums after pre-publication in the press. Tens of thousands of other pages (often mediocre, but sometimes by undeniably talented artists) were to fall into oblivion after having been "consumed" in the press. But in the 1970s, the production of albums suddenly increases exponentially and in the next decade stabilizes at a very high level: around six hundred new albums are printed in French every year. At the same time, the illustrated press goes into decline, many "historic" magazines cease to exist (*Tintin, Pif, Pilote, Charlie, Metal Hurlant* . . .). In this way, a second loop is formed: after having won back its adult readership, comic art operates a return to its original form, the book.

The history of comics that I have just roughly sketched needs to be written in more detail and is still widely misunderstood, even, in my opinion, by self-proclaimed "specialists." By celebrating the so-called Centenary of Comics in 1996, some of these have simply chosen to ignore everything that was published between 1833—when Töpffer printed *Monsieur Jabot*—and the release of the Yellow Kid. Over half a century of French, English, German, Dutch, Spanish, and even American comics denied existence because they weren't mass-produced!

The fact that the birth of comics is still a subject of discussion and disagreement shows just how retarded the study of the 9th art is. As a cultural phenomenon and art form, comics (until the 1960s) were surrounded by a quite deafening silence. They simply were not regarded as such; there was a complete absence of critical, archivistic, and academic attention. After the *Essai de Physiognomonie* in 1845, in which Töpffer proposes the foundations for a theory of comics, a hundred and ten years passed before another book in French appeared on the subject—*Le Petit Monde de Pif le chien* by Barthélémy Amengual, in 1955. In this long interval books on cinema and photography were published by the dozen!

However, when comics turned to a readership of teenagers and children, they began to draw attention from one particular sector of society, the educators. For decades, they held the monopoly of discourse on the subject—a genre suspected of having a great influence on the morality of young people. Because they were the first to comment on comics, their ideas, of course, pervaded future thought on the matter. As late as 1964, the most widely read French dictionary, the *Petit Larousse illustré*, gave the following

4

phrase as an example of the use of the verb *salir* (to dirty, to soil): *ces illustrés salissent l'imagination de nos enfants* . . . ("these comics soil the imagination of our children").

You might say all this was a sort of double punishment for comics: deprived of their adult audience, comics were confined to the ghetto of youth magazines and reserved for children, but comics' massive introduction into these magazines provoked the hostility of educators, who untiringly denounced them as "bad for children." Comics are thus blacklisted for corrupting their already restricted audience.

In her study of the years 1919 to 1931, the art historian Annie Renonciat declares that "as soon as they appeared, these publications alarmed educationalists"[2] and prints various quotes to illustrate this prompt mobilization. As early as 1907, Marcel Braunschwig, author of an essay on esthetic education, wrote: "At the present time, we are engulfed by popular magazines for the use of children, against which it is high time to undertake a vigorous campaign in the name of the common sense and good taste they offend with impunity."[3]

Paul Winskler, who published the *Journal de Mickey*, *Robinson*, and *Hop-là*, was to become the main target of these attacks in the second half of the 1930s, but before that the Offenstadt brothers' publications were in the line of fire: *L'Epatant* (where the adventures of the famous trio "les Pieds Nickelés" were printed), *Fillette*, *L'Intrépide*, *Cri-Cri*, and *Lili*. The general "vulgarity" and "insanity" of these popular and cheap publications was constantly denounced and the characters that appeared in them presented as bad examples. For Alphonse de Parvillez (working for *l'Union Morale*, the *Revue des Lectures*, and the *Revue des Jeunes*), *L'Espiègle Lili* (Lili the Imp) is "the perfect handbook for rotten kids," and Abbé Bethléem, a sort of conscience for the *Revue des lectures* (Journal of Reading), denounces the use of "excessive caricature, filthy slang, the language of prisons and sleazy bars . . ."[4] in *L'Epatant*.

The vague fears inspired by comics can be explained in part, by the fact that they belong to a new culture that is on the rise. The sociologist Irene Pennacchioni explains: "In France, a cultural 'resistance' is growing up against the barbarous invasion of nickelodeons, cinema, tabloids (*Paris Soir*), radio (*Radio-Cité*), American funny characters. This new . . . mass culture reaches France in the thirties."[5]

Opinions on upbringing and education and society's understanding of children were not the same between the two wars as they are today. There was no talk of the rights of children but only of their protection. There was an absence of teenage culture; even the age group was hardly recognized in its specificity. Lastly, a concept inherited from the nineteenth century meant that children were usually assimilated to the least educated strata of society—the lower classes, "people of primitive intelligence, whose knowledge is sparse if not inexistant, in whom imagination is stronger than reason."[6] For the educators of the first half of the twentieth century, that which is popular is necessarily vulgar. Comics are seen as intrinsically bad because they tend to take the place of "real books," an attitude which crystalizes a double confrontation: between the written word and the world of images, on the one hand; between educational literature and pure entertainment on the other.

Children's books and magazines had always been intended to educate and moralize; to support and complete the work of parents and teachers. But the illustrated press, comic albums, and popular serialized novels turn their backs on this mission; their sole aim is to amuse and entertain. This was, not surprisingly, disturbing for specialists in education. Their conviction was that children have feeble minds and naturally bad instincts that need rectifying. These specialists aimed their attacks at the image. The more attractive it was, the more harmful it would be to children.

The following quote is representative of many others and is taken from a special issue of the Communist Party magazine *Enfance* (childhood) printed in 1954: "All the effects (of comics) are extremely excessive, in verbal expression as in graphic representation. These flashy colors, wry faces, twisted in hate or terror, this sensuality, these longing embraces, everything speaks to the imagination in the most brutal manner, all is suggestive and evocative . . ."[7]

An anthology of what was written about comics between the beginning of the century and the sixties would be extremely boring. From the thirties on, the arguments are always the same, and are often singularly lacking in perspicacity. It is rather surprising, for example, that the aesthetics of comic art should be systematically condemned as a whole, as if they were a single entity! From the point of view of morality, magazines were frequently labeled either "good" or "bad," whereas no distinctions were made on the artistic level between the different authors. Among the American comics that were most popular in France were works such as *Flash Gordon, Terry and the Pirates, Popeye, Bringing up Father, Tarzan,* and *Dick Tracy,* whose artists—who are all very different from one another—are now placed among the most respected masters of the 9th art. Blinded, no doubt by the urgency of their mission, the censors of the period did not differentiate between these masters and the more obscure drudges who worked for the same sort of magazines. Comics as a whole were indiscriminately written off as aggressively ugly.

From the thirties on, the speech balloon, which gradually replaced text located under the image, was a central target for educators and for those taking sides with the written word. The procedure was thought to be of American origin, which would have sufficed, if not to disqualify it, at least to make it an object of suspicion. Apparently, no one remembered that the balloon had been used in medieval times, and, more recently, in eighteenth-century European caricatures. It is true that, at that time, balloons were particularly popular in England, and already held in low esteem by the French.

As Annie Renonciat points out, "for the French, the balloon presents . . . various disadvantages: first, they place the text inside the image, thus imprisoning the verbal content within the visual system; then—most importantly—they limit the text to simple dialogues and direct enunciation, drastically reducing the amount of description and 'literary' expression." The same author goes on to say: "It also appears that publishers—and even some authors—thought a child could not properly understand a story in pictures without the help of words. This is confirmed by the presence of numerous redundancies in the captions to their pictures. . . ."[8]

A work whose verbal content is confined to "simple" dialogues is nothing scandalous in itself: it is the case of movies and the theatre. But films and live shows present them aurally, whereas in comics they must be read. Because they are printed, comics seem to be more closely related to literature; furthermore, in addressing children, they are expected to make a contribution to their education by helping them learn to read, encouraging them to love "beautiful texts" and "great authors." The imprisonment of verbal expression in

6

the visual system—to use Annie Renonciat's words—constitutes a symbolic revolution, a complete reversal of the commonly accepted hierarchy between semiotic systems. The champions of a culture which postulates the supremacy of the written word over all other forms of expression could only take this inversion as an attack.

The two last complaints most frequently made against comics by educators concern their violence and escapism. This quote is from the communist critic Georges Sadoul: "Everywhere, at every page, we found exaltation of brute force, assassination, violence, war, spying, banditism, and, at the same time, escape into the most stupid irreality."[9]

I will not talk in length about violence, which is not specific to comics. The violence inherent in adventure stories has always been condemned in the name of the protection of children—wherever it is found. The arguments used against comics in the twenties, thirties, and forties hardly differ from those brandished against television, video games and manga in more recent times. What has been, and still is, targeted by these critics is the corrupting power of the image, always capable of "striking the imagination." An image, they believe, invites the spectator to project onto the characters represented and identify with them.

More interesting—to me—is the fact that the "irreality" of comics was for a long time considered intrinsically stupid. Animals that speak, imaginary machines, time travel, supermen, and other fantasies have been blamed for cutting a child off from reality and making him or her lose all notion of it. Once again it is the power of the image that is feared, especially its capacity to abuse the credulity of young readers. La Fontaine, Lewis Carroll, and Jules Verne had not been victims of such censorship of the imagination. But Tarzan, king of the jungle, living half-naked among the animals was often singled out as one of the most harmful incarnations of this irrealism.

Previously blamed for all the sins of the world, comics would finally gain acceptance by educators. A book by Antoine Roux, for example, was published by Editions de l'Ecole in 1970 under the "slogan": "Comics can be educational." In time, some child specialists came to rely on comics as the last stand against illiteracy and a teacher's best aid in the teaching of reading (now threatened mainly by television).

From then on, the debate could focus on aesthetic and cultural questions. Comics were no longer accused of harmfulness, but the stigma of artistic mediocrity would stick—and has been reactivated in the context of the debate on the "confusion of artistic values" supposedly characteristic of the end of this century. To illustrate this, it will suffice to mention the title of a French television program presented in 1984 by Michel Polac in the series *Droit de réponse* (Right to reply): "*Asterix* versus the *Mona Lisa*."

Rather than entering into the details of this conventional debate over "high" and "low" art, I would like to propose a more general explanation of the fact that comics appear to be condemned to artistic insignificance. It seems to me that comic art suffers from a four-fold symbolic handicap. 1) It is a hybrid, the result of crossbreeding between text and image; 2) Its storytelling ambitions seem to remain on the level of a sub-literature; 3) It has connections to a common and inferior branch of visual art, that of caricature; 4) Even though they are now frequently intended for adults, comics propose nothing other than a return to childhood.

No doubt prejudice against comics cannot be reduced to these four charges. But it seems to me that these four form a basis for all the others. Even though they may not always be spelt out as such, they inform and guide the opinions of the cultural referees who are invested with the power to judge artistic merit.

However, when examined one by one, the 9th art's four original sins quickly reveal the academic preconceptions they are based on. Let us look at each one in turn.

Almost eight hundred years after the golden age of illuminated manuscripts, the juxtaposition of text and image on a printed page continues to be seen by some as an unnatural alliance. I will not go back to the subject of the balloon and the fact that the image appears to "swallow" the text. The origins of the scandal go deeper, to the mix of text and image itself.

Here is the opinion of one of our "great French writers," Monsieur Pascal Quignard: "Literature and the image are incompatible. . . . The two forms of expression cannot be juxtaposed. They are never apprehended together. . . . When one is readable, the other is not seen. When one is visible the other is not read. Whatever the proximity imposed upon them, the two media remain parallel, and it must be said, that these two worlds are, for eternity, impenetrable to one another. . . . The reader and the spectator will never be the same man at the same moment, leaning forward in the same light to discover the same page."[10]

This objection, which comics readers' experience apparently refutes, must be taken into consideration, as it is an integral part of occidental culture. "To show and to name; to represent and to describe; to reproduce and to articulate; to imitate and to signify; to look at and to read": such, according to Michel Foucault, are "the oldest oppositions in our alphabetical civilization."[11] Forgetting that for the ancient Greeks a single word, *graphein*, meant "to write" and "to paint," our alphabetical culture quickly became logocentric, subordinating visual forms of expression to language. Philosophers continually repeat that the image tricks and troubles us, acting on our senses and exciting our emotions, and that reason is on the side of the word.

Yet, our culture is the only one that harbors this opposition and hierarchy. They must therefore be relativized. They do not exist, for example, in China and Japan, where the stroke of the brush unites writing and drawing: calligraphic signs and representative lines are executed by the same hand with the same instrument. East Asian painters often insert whole poems in their images.

Moreover, it is virtually certain that western civilization itself is in the process of changing its conception of the relation between text and image. In the day of multimedia, the age-old opposition is somewhat obsolete. Modern humans, to whom the computer transmits text, sound, still and animated images, are subjected to an unprecedented range of sensory stimulations, and learn—from a very early age—to coordinate them.

But this theoretical objection is often accompanied by an aesthetic condemnation. If the marriage of text and image is not impossible, it would at least inevitably distort and weaken both of them. To illustrate this attitude, I will quote the former curator of the Prints department of the National Library of France. According to Michel Melot, the comics artist "produces illustrated literature more than narrative images. Current output is distressing poor, and so monotonous, that I doubt a solution exists. There is nothing in it for either literature or images, and no new, original genre emerges."[12] The same author points out, further on, that the sin of comic art is that of schematization:

"For the sake of readability, comics artists are drawn into an involuntary regression which explains the mediocrity of most of their work."

It is difficult to refute the aesthetic argument without showing that the criteria for appreciation of drawing in comics are not quite the same as those used for art drawings. They are, unlike other drawings, narrative and not illustrative, executed on a very small surface and destined to be reproduced. Are Hergé, Crumb, and Moebius mediocre artists? Most certainly not, but artists whose excellence in their domain cannot be compared to that of Da Vinci, Rembrandt, or Picasso in theirs.

The question is: why should two of the most respected forms of human expression, literature (the model for all narrative arts) and drawing (the foundation of all fine arts), be dethroned and debased as soon as they are side by side in a mixed media. . . ? Some will answer that comics have taken from literature and drawing their least noble parts: from the former stereotyped plots and over-referenced genres, and from the latter caricature and schematization. Founded or not, these complaints seem to be secondary to the fundamental aesthetic question: is it not the very fact of using text and image together that reputedly taints and discredits both of them?

In effect, comic art, just like the cinema, which is also a hybrid genre, goes against the "ideology of purity" that has dominated the West's approach to aesthetics since Lessing. In art, our modernity has never ceased preaching the deepening, by each discipline, of its own specificity. Music, literature, painting have turned inwards to their own domains. This means that they have eliminated or marginalized melody, subject, representation, narration, and signification, in favor of working on form and basic materials (sound, color . . . etc.) in their search for pure music, pure poetry, pure painting. It is conceivable that this ideology of purification has led contemporary art to a dead end. That however, is another story. I only wish to show the extent to which comics (where text and drawings contribute to the same narrative project) dispute the validity of the dominant trend of thought and therefore could not do otherwise than to provoke the disdain and contempt of the defenders of official culture. Moreover, the ideology of purity has given rise to an ever-increasing gulf between erudite culture and popular culture, the latter being naturally dedicated to fiction and entertainment.

In fact, the second sin attributed to comics is, precisely, their lack of narrative ambition. Comics are supposed to be easy literature because they are based on repetitions, and *Childre,* therefore more readable. They are also constantly being assimilated with what is known as paraliterature, a badly defined set of popular genres that includes adventure stories, historical novels, fantasy and science-fiction, detective novels, erotica, and so on.

The first important French seminar on paraliterature took place in Cerisy, in September 1967. The attendees (among whom were Francis Lacassin and Evelyne Sullerot) treated comics as a "category" of paraliterature on the same footing as spy novels or science fiction.[13] Thirty years later, this conception is still active. There exists in Belgium, for instance, a "Centre for Paraliterature, Comics and Cinema" (in Chaudfontaine). The radio program *Mauvais genres* on France Culture looks at detective novels, fantasy, and . . . comics. The *Monde des Livres* (literary supplement of the daily newspaper *Le Monde*) has a column which treats comics, science fiction, and detective novels in turn.

This placing of comics on the same plane as the various genres of paraliterature needs examining. It is evident that comics cannot be considered a genre in that sense, as they englobe and traverse many different genres: there are science-fiction comics, sentimental, erotic or autobiographical comics, detective stories, and westerns in the form of comics. . . . Comic art is an autonomous and original medium. The only things it has in common with literature are: that it is printed and sold in bookshops, and that it contains linguistic statements. But why should it be systematically lowered to the level of para- or sub-literature?

That it is, is mainly due to the fact that the comics market obeys the rules of commerce. The saleability of the product seems to be more important than the intrinsic worth of the art. Comics, like paraliterature, operate on a system of series, that orchestrates the constant revival of the same characters, who accumulate adventures ad libitum. The interchangeability of artists, who, one after the other, perpetuate the career of the most popular heroes reinforces the sentiment that comic art is an industrial form of literature.

How can we defend comic art against this accusation which disqualifies it as an art? Remind the accusers that serialization has its nobility? Evoke *Little Nemo* or *Tintin*—fine examples of how tremendous a series can be when handled by a creative genius? Encourage a wider diffusion of works by true authors, of comics free of commercial constraints, and of avant-garde comic art? My opinion is, that here, once again, defense of comics depends on recognition of the fact that they cannot be judged by the same criteria as are generally applied to literature.

In his diary, the writer Renaud Camus made this comment: "Certain films would make poor books, even though they are good, or even excellent films. This superiority is due to the actors—that by definition, we wouldn't have in the books."[14] In the same vein, many comics would make poor novels, though they are acceptable comics, and in this case, the difference is due to the drawings. The reader of comics not only enjoys a *story-related pleasure* but also an *art-related pleasure*, an aesthetic emotion founded on the appreciation of the exactness and expressivity of a composition, pose, or line. There also exists, in my opinion, a *medium-related pleasure*. It cannot be reduced to the sum of the other two, but is related to the rhythmic organization in space and time of a multiplicity of small images. Comic art is the art of details, and as such encourages a fetishistic relationship.[15]

Comics' third symbolic handicap is their relationship with humor, caricature, and satire. Since Ancient Greece, humor has been regarded as the opposite of harmony and of the sublime. It is not compatible with beauty and constitutes an inferior genre, barely legitimate. Humor is negative, it depreciates, renders ugly; satire belittles instead of glorifying. The French Romanticists, mainly in the shape of Jules Champfleury, attempted to rehabilitate caricature, but academic prejudice was never totally dispelled. Without going so far as to recall that for the Nazis, "degenerate art" was the art that put caricature in the place of ideals, it will suffice to note the rarity of studies on humor and comical effects—at least in France—in order to verify that the seriousness of critics and teachers excludes any playful or funny contribution to artistic creation.

Lastly, the fourth symbolic handicap is the link between comics and childhood. Far from trying to combat or contradict this objection, I am inclined to lay claim to it. I recalled earlier that between the start of the twentieth century and the sixties, comics had been captured by the children's press. Most modern commentators were not aware of the earlier history of picture stories (in the nineteenth century) and genuinely thought they were originally intended for children. They took them for a variety of illustrated children's books which was belatedly trying to gain its autonomy by taking advantage of a promising trend: pop-culture—or of what we call, in France, *contre-culture* (counter culture).

But these considerations on the birth and growth of the medium are hardly relevant today. Comics still have a privileged relationship with childhood because it is in childhood that each of us discovered them and learnt to love them. In a certain sense, we can agree with the sociologist Irene Pennacchioni when she says that "pictures are for the illiterate, as they correspond to 'naive' pleasures from before learning to read, before culture."[16] Many adults, in particular those who occupy a dominant position in the world of culture, take themselves very seriously . . . many adults have forgotten or rejected childhood pleasures in favor of more sophisticated, supposedly more noble, pleasures. Now, comics have a way of giving rise to some strongly nostalgic emotions. Psychoanalysts have shown that our attitude to drawings has a certain similarity to our relationship with our mother. Roland Barthes spoke somewhere of the "childhood passion for huts and tents: shut yourself in and settle down."[17] It is a reminiscence of this "existential dream" that a reader experiences when he plunges into the world of small pictures. One cannot avoid seeing that so many of our paper heroes prolong the little boy's fantasies of freedom and omnipotence, and offer us the chance to act them out . . . vicariously.

Yes, why not admit it? All of us here in Copenhagen, delivering our clever papers, are probably doing nothing more than holding out our hands to the kids we used to be.

NOTES

1. For further details, see Thierry Groensteen and Benoit Peters, *Töpffer: l'invention de la bande dessinee* (Paris: Hermann, 1994).

2. Annie Renonciat, *Les livres d'enfance et de jeunesse en France dans les années vingt*, thesis [History and Semiology of Text and Image] (University of Paris 7–Denis Diderot, 1997).

3. Marcel Braunschwig, *L'art et l'enfant* (Toulouse: Edouard Privat; Paris: Henri Dither, 1907): 327.

4. Quoted in Annie Renonciat, *op. cit.*, supplement 16.

5. Irene Pennacchioni, *La nostalgic en images* (Paris: Librairie des Méridiens, 1982): 121.

6. André Balsen, *Les illustris pour enfants* (Tourcoing: J. Duvivier, 1920). Quoted in Annie Renonciat, *op. cit.*, supplement 16.

7. *Enfance, 5: Les journaux pour enfants* (Paris: Presses Universitaires de France, 1954): 403.

8. *Les livres d'enfance et dejeunesse en France dans les années vingt, op. cit.*, 484.

9. George Sadoul, *Ce que lisent vos enfants. La presse enfantine, son evolution, son influence* (Paris: Bureau d'Edition, 1938.

10. Pascal Quignard, *VIle Traiti: sur los rapports quo le texte et l'image n'entretiennentpas* (Maeght, 1990). Reprinted in *Petits traités* I, "Folio" 2976: cf. 134–35.

11. Michel Foucault, *Ceci n'est pas une pipe* (Fata Morgana, 1973): 22.

12. Michel Melot, *L'ceil qui nt. Le pouvoir comique des images* (Fribourg: Office du Livre, 1975): 146.

13. Cf. *Entretiens sur la paralittérature* (Paris: Plon, 1970): 106 and 253.

14. Renaud Camus, *Laguerre de Transylvanie* (Paris: POL, 1996): 45–46.

15. For further details, see Thierry Groensteen, "Plaisir de la bande dessinée," *9e Art 2* (Angoulême: CNBD, 1997): 14–21.

16. Irene Pennacchioni, *La nostalgic en images. op. cit.*, 122.

17. Ronald Barthes, "Nautilus et bateau ivre," *Mythologies* (Paris: Seuil, 1957).

HISTORICAL
CONSIDERATIONS

The writing of the history of comics has been plagued by questions of definition and continuity: what constitutes a comic and what is the relationship between the proto-comics of the past (everything from Egyptian hieroglyphics and the Bayeux Tapestry to the sequential prints of William Hogarth) and subsequent comics. In this section, as through the rest of the book, the selected essays emphasize the diversity of both the scholarly literature and also the comics being studied. "Comics," as these essays make clear is very much an umbrella term which brings together a cluster of related forms: nineteenth-century illustrated stories, gag cartoons, comic strips, comic books, and many other branches of the same family tree. Because comics come in a wide variety, historians often have to address formalist questions as much as theorists do.

Early histories of comics tended to be popularly written books rich in enthusiasm and anecdote but lacking in primary scholarship based on archival research. The pioneering studies of the tireless art historian David Kunzle changed all that by going well past twentieth-century North American sources. Following in the footsteps of his teacher, the polymathic intellectual E. H. Gombrich, Kunzle authored a massively researched and encyclopedic two-volume *History of the Comic Strip* (1973, 1990), which covered countless European artists who did sequential visual stories from the end of the Middle Ages to the end of the nineteenth century. The upshot of Kunzle's work was to emphasize the pivotal role of Swiss writer and artist Rodolphe Töpffer (1799–1846) as both an artist and theorist. Much more so than his precursors, Töpffer integrated the element of time into his stories; equally important, he wrote extensively on how sequential images work and how they differ from other art forms.

In this section, we excerpt from Kunzle's *Father of the Comic Strip*, where attention is given to Töpffer's aesthetic theories as precursors to modernist thought. According to Kunzle, the Swiss cartoonist "rebutted the fundamental (traditional, classical) idea that the function of art is to imitate and idealize nature" and "anticipated the modernist idea that art transform nature, does nature over, transcends and bypasses it, and that it obeys its own laws independent of nature." This challenge to classical ideas, deepened by Töpffer's theory of caricature which emphasized the expressive richness of pictorial language, allows us to see comics as a distinctly modern art form, one that came of age in the era of mass printing and broke from traditional aesthetic norms.

R. C. Harvey, a gifted historian of comics with a formalist bent, takes the story from Töpffer to the early twentieth century, showing how the illustrated cartoons that appeared in nineteenth-century magazines evolved into twentieth-century gag cartoons and comic strips. As a theorist of comics, Harvey's great contribution has been to emphasize the importance of the "verbal-visual blend" as a characteristic feature of comics. In this essay, he carefully shows that a major artistic innovation of early twentieth-century comics involved a smoother fusion of words and pictures. In emphasizing the importance of words, Harvey's essay is pointedly challenging a famous definition of comics articulated by the cartoonist Scott McCloud, who wrote in his book *Understanding Comics* (1993) that comics are "juxtaposed pictorial and other images in deliberate sequence, intended to convey information and/or to produce an aesthetic response in the viewer."

As Harvey shows, the newspaper comic strip in North America emerged as a popular form in the late nineteenth century, borrowing from techniques developed by European artists working in the tradition of Töpffer but bringing a new populist vitality to comics. Harvey tells the story of the origin of these early comics strips, which first appeared in newspapers owned by Joseph Pulitzer and William Randolph Hearst, the most disreputable of American publishers. Eventually, comic strips became a respectable feature in most North American daily newspapers and inspired the birth of the newer form of the comic book (pamphlet-form publications that reprinted newspaper strips as well as original material). Paralleling the development of the comic strip and comic book is the more upscale form of the gag cartoon, which flourished in magazines.

Harvey's essay offers a crisp survey of nearly a century of history but no less than Kunzle, this work is guided by a concern for aesthetic theory. In tracing the history of the gag cartoon, the comic strip, and the comic book, Harvey is carefully to emphasize the role of words as well as pictures. As Harvey writes, "It seems to me that the essential characteristic of 'comics'—the thing that distinguishes it from other kinds of pictorial narrative—is the incorporation of verbal content."

To the extent that intellectuals noticed comic strips at all, they tended to dismiss them as typical products of the yellow press. The writer who did the most to break this tradition of genteel disdain was Gilbert Seldes (1893–1970), a pioneering modernist. While other intellectuals feared comic strips as a threat to established cultural hierarchies, Seldes, writing in the 1920s, celebrated the form for its liveliness and ability to mimic modern life and speech patterns. In effect, Seldes was arguing that comics were modern and American, an effective strategy in gaining a level of acceptance for the form. A metropolitan intellectual with a passion for movies and popular music, Seldes celebrated those cartoonists who depicted the sporting life, that early twentieth-century masculine milieu of gambling, boxing, horseracing, and pool playing. The cartoonists to whom he is most favorably inclined (Bud Fisher, Clare Briggs, Tad Dorgan) all celebrated the sporting life in their work. By contrast, Seldes is much less favorably disposed to those cartoonists whose work centers on domestic life, notably Frank King and Sidney Smith.

As comic strips became more respectable, a new form of comics became a source of cultural anxiety: comic books—periodicals sold at the newsstand, often to children, and featuring lurid stories influenced by pulp literature. In the late 1940s and early 1950s, the moral panic was fueled in part by the work of psychiatrist Fredric Wertham, who argued that the violent content of comics contributed to a deadening of moral sensibility in children.

Wertham's book not only shaped popular and elite perception of comics. It also had a real historical impact in North America (and to a lesser degree in Europe and Asia). Although Wertham himself was no believer in censorship, as a result of his writing, comic publishers in the United States instigated a stringent self-regulatory code limiting the contents of comics. The anti-comics movements of the postwar years have been the subject of much mythmaking among comic book fans. In their careful articles, Amy Kiste Nyberg and John A. Lent carefully document how multifaceted the anti-comics debate was. Nyberg provides a detailed history of the battle over the controversial EC horror comics, which were criticized not just by Wertham but also from within the comic book industry. While comics were being criticized by outside forces like Wertham and politicians in the U.S. Senate, the push for self-regulation also came from within the industry itself, both to placate the critics and also to limit competition from smaller publishers. By emphasizing the role of publishers, Nyberg complicates a story that has often been rendered in melodramatic terms as a battle between free speech and censorship.

Lent surveys the global terrain and demonstrates how international the anti-comics movements were. The move to restrict comes took place in nations as far flung as Britain, Canada, Australia, Japan, the Philippines, and Taiwan. While the debate in each nation followed a local trajectory, certain common themes recur: a focus on the dangers comics pose to kids, the reliance on experts like Wertham, and the calls for an increased role by the state to either regulate comics publishers or encourage them to self-regulate.

From the first appearance of Superman in 1938, the superhero genre has been a key component of the North American comic book industry. Peter Coogan provides an internal history of the genre, one that is attuned to the rules and conventions that govern superhero comics. Coogan argues "for a definition of the superhero comprising mission, powers, identity, and generic distinction." Coogan's internalist approach can be usefully compared to the externalist approach taken by Nyberg and Lent. Whereas Coogan emphasizes the narrative innovations found in comics, Nyberg and Lent are much more concerned with the social context in which comics are produced. Coogan's approach to superhero history is rooted in the tradition of fan scholarship, which is alert to the storytelling conventions and narrative traditions of various genres. As such, it offers a useful alternative to Nyberg and Lent.

As a form of historical analysis, the biographical approach has only recently come into maturity among comics scholars. Early biographies of cartoonists tended to be anecdotal and heavily dependent on recycled newspaper clippings. In the last two decades, however, the field has been enriched by heavily researched and wide-ranging biographies of Winsor McCay, Milton Caniff, and Charles Schulz. M. Thomas Inge's "Two Boys from the Twin Cities" is a pioneering and provocative application of biographical analysis to the life of *Peanuts* creator Schulz, juxtaposing the cartoonist's life with the sometimes parallel career of novelist F. Scott Fitzgerald. In situating Schulz and Fitzgerald as both sons of the Twin Cities of St. Paul and Minneapolis, Inge helps explain Schulz's lifelong fascination with Fitzgerald's *The Great Gatsby*. The comparisons and contrasts that Inge draws serve to link Schulz's distinct achievement with the wider currents of American culture. As Inge notes, "If Gatsby is the supreme romantic American hero, tainted by his tragic flaws, Charlie Brown belongs to another tradition in our culture—the figure of the lost soul, the little man, or what Charlie Chaplin called the Little Fellow."

The strength of the historical approach is that it is valuable in and of itself but also lays the foundation for other modes of inquiry. With these historical essays as a background, readers can understand the main issues that comics scholars will confront in other sections of the book: what are the formal properties of comics, how do comics relate to social conditions, and what aesthetics can we use to evaluate the work of cartoonists.

Rodolphe Töpffer's Aesthetic Revolution

DAVID KUNZLE

The graphic and aesthetic revolution that Rodolphe Töpffer (1766–1847) pioneered and argued for was to be won in the twentieth century. His *Essai de physiognomonie* and his numerous essays on art, written serially over a dozen years beginning in the 1830s and gathered by Dubochet under the title *Reflexions et menus-pro pos d'un peintre genevois* (*Reflections and Small Talk of a Genevan Painter*, first edition 1848, constantly republished since), contain many of the seeds of aesthetic theory that have flowered in our own times. A modern critic has called them "the finest essays on aesthetics in French."[1] Charles Baudelaire, who fails to mention Töpffer in his printed essays on caricature, knew of the Swiss,[2] probably through Theophile Gautier, the friend he called his master. Gautier's careful appreciation of Töpffer's *Reflexions* in the *Revue des deux mondes*[3] begins with a strenuous correction of Sainte-Beuve's disparagement of the comic albums, published six years before in the same magazine, and must have aroused attention.

The aesthetic ideas of Töpffer and Baudelaire have much in common, notably in rebutting the fundamental (traditional, classical) idea that the function of art is to imitate and idealize nature. Both anticipated the modernist idea that art transforms nature, does nature over, transcends and bypasses it, and that art obeys its own laws independent of nature. The Swiss does not go as far as to claim, with Baudelaire, that art may contradict nature. But art, being *independant* of nature, obeys its own laws. "Le beau de l'art est absolument indépendant du beau de la nature," was Töpffer's lapidary pronouncement.[4] But never for a moment, for Töpffer, still the Calvinist Swiss, was art to be independent of morality, that is social morality, and here Baudelaire parted company from him. While Töpffer took a polemical stand against the idea of "art for art's sake" (*l'art pour l'art*, of which Gautier's preface to *Mademoiselle de Maupin* [1835] is the manifesto), he and Baudelaire shared the aesthetic of negligence, of spontaneity—and particularly of *flânerie*, which may be translated, in Töpfferian terms, as casual mental zigzagging around. This is attested by the very form of Töpffer's meandering, digressive art criticism, as well as of the dreamlike flow of the picture stories and the "zigzag" philosophizing in the *Voyages en Zigzag*, themselves conducted in reality, as far as was practical, as semi-organized *flânerie*. Töpffer is the Montaigne of aesthetic reverie.

Reprinted by permission and adapted from David Kunzle, *Father of the Comic Strip: Rodolphe Töpffer* (University Press of Mississippi, 2007), 113–19.

Töpffer's ideas were rooted, more than he would have cared to admit, in Romantic attitudes. The notions of caprice, chance, instinct, and the unconscious which inform both theory and comic album; the insistence that all artistic signs are conventional rather than more or less close approximations of nature; the special expressive value attached to naïve, crude, childish, and incomplete but "essential" forms, harking back (and over) to non-Western "primitive" art; the law by which any doodled face, "unable to exist without having an expression, must indeed have one" ("Töpffer's Law")—these ideas, although familiar now, were new then. Couched in a casual flow that seemed to resist being taken seriously, they have found a central place in E. H. Gombrich's analysis of physiognomic perception as a fundamental aspect of artistic illusion and representation.[5] The idea of the doodle as it were an act of nature herself may be traced back to Töpffer's discovery as a boy watching a cockchafer (*hanneton*) that had dipped its terebra in ink crawl magically about the page of an exercise book. In a famous passage from his partly autobiographical *Bibliotheque de mon Oncle*, he watched it make delicate traceries of lines, and taught it, with guidance from a wisp of straw, over a period of two hours, to write his name "a masterpiece."

Töpffer is bubbling with theories that he cannot take seriously. He cannot, above all, imagine the reader taking him seriously for long. Like Goethe having to read *Cryptogame* bit by bit, he fears getting an indigestion of ideas, and losing the reader who may have wandered off on his own by now, or gone to sleep. The essays, which ramble on for three hundred pages, are wonderfully self-indulgent. Yes, Töpffer wrote and drew primarily to amuse himself. He will not attempt to define Beauty. Book 7, chapter 1 of the *Reflexions* declares that to require him to do so would be to deny him liberty, and "try to strangle in my scrap of string this proteus of infinite transformations."[6]

The ugly, the monstrous are aesthetic criteria, after all. In his chapter entitled "Where we deal with doodles" (*Où il est question de petits bonhommes*), he praises, as he did elsewhere, graffiti ancient and modern. He then goes on to evaluate the effect of statuary that very few people had ever seen, and was very little known: that of Easter Island, only discovered and reproduced in engravings in the late eighteenth century. He calls the statues "misshapen grotesques which in their rough breadth and deformed proportion hardly resemble anything but themselves, which resemble nothing . . . [they show] cruel, hard, superior creatures, brutal divinities, but divinities after all, of grandeur and beauty. They live, they speak, they proclaim."[7]

The preference for the primitive, to use the title of Gombrich's last book, is deeply embedded in the rise of modernism, and is surely linked closely to Töpffer's theories, probably more indirectly than directly. The loose, incomplete touch became that of Impressionism; the appropriation of the childish, crude, and ugly became a norm of twentieth-century art; the rejection of the academic, the systematic, of rules became the rule. Caricature, and comic strip as its narrative form that gave this style of draughtsmanship unheard-of popularity, blended into modernism, as did the fantastic, the surreal, the dreamlike. The tenuous line of social theory in the *Reflexions* purports to serve as justification for Töpffer's "graphic follies." Being reproducible, they have a large potential audience, being simple-looking—and thus aside from their sophisticate content—they appeal to the "simple man," the masses of unlettered folk; conceived like

Essai de Physiognomonie, title page, 1845.

Hogarth's engravings with a moral purpose, even if that is not always as clear as with the great English precursor, they serve social improvement. Unlike Salon painting, which is for the rich, and unlike *l'art pour l'art*, an absurdism leading to amoralism and anarchy,[8] Töpffer's "engraved literature" serves the people. While the citizen militates against it, the artist, *malgré lui*, speaks for democracy.

ESSAI DE PHYSIOGNOMONIE

Published, with *Albert*, in January 1845, handwritten and drawn in auto-lithography, the *Essai de Physiognomonie* is as methodical, systemic, and rigorously logical as the *Reflexions* and *Small Talk of a Genevan Painter* is randomly discursive, playful, and anti-systemic. The tone is also simply more serious, even solemn, scientific—as if his thoughts and theories about an essentially whimsical and entirely original invention demanded it, in a way his aesthetic theory in general did not. The fundamental importance of the *Essai* as an analysis of the very language or semiotics of art was first recognized by Gombrich in his pioneering *Art and Illusion: A Study in the Psychology of Pictorial Representation* (1960), in several pages of the chapter on "The Experiment of Caricature." Töpffer thereby took his proper place in the history of art theory, but unlike the often reprinted *Small Talk*, the *Essai* was not reprinted until our own times.[9]

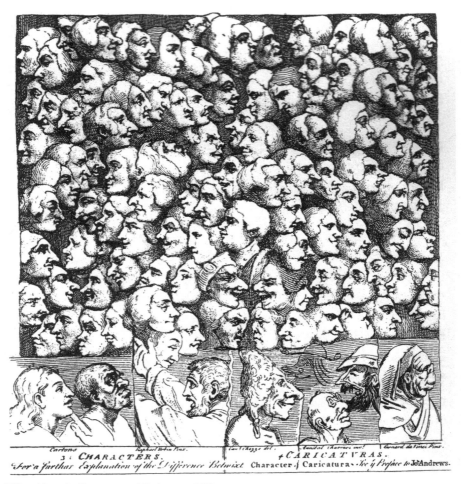

William Hogarth, *Characters and Caricatures*, 1743.

The point of departure was a polemical one recurrent in his thinking about narrative art: the moral usefulness of the hybrid form of pictorial literature which, practiced in the right, Hogarthian way, could act as a moral counterbalance to all the vicious literature of the Romantic school, of Sand, Balzac, and Sue. Töpffer himself, disingenuously, wishes (thinking back to the mild criticism of Goethe, perhaps), that his own picture stories had been more directed to serious moral concerns. He wants a picture story in praise, for instance, of marriage, to counterbalance all the immoral seductions offered by the French writers named. Töpffer was too much the Calvinist to find adultery matter for artistic entertainment, although he must have recognized that Hogarth did just this in his six-part *Marriage A-la-mode*, which he mentions by name (and enlarges to "ten to twelve plates"). Töpffer imagines that Hogarth really spoke to the lower classes, as he believed the moralizing picture story should, to inoculate them against the poisons of Sue and company; his own clearly did not.

There is a final irony here. The very method that Töpffer proposes depended on an auto-lithographic technique excluded from popular imagery, which for economic reasons relied on woodcut. Töpffer's *Essai* is, moreover, written on a high intellectual level and is not the kind of text read by the simple makers of *imagerie populaire*. They were moreover under strict surveillance of a censorship quick to suppress anything politically untoward. Töpffer's stories really bear no relationship to the tepid folktales peddled to the masses.

The *Physiognomonie* booklet is, like the *Essai d'Autographie*, a how-to-do-it treatise, an appeal to the amateur who does not need to know how to draw in order to be able to draw. Simple contours allow for easy development and recognition of forms; artistic signs are conventional and need not depend upon nature, especially when linear (there are no lines in nature). Expressions may be arrived at by doodling, that is, allowing the free-flowing pencil, accident, and chance (we would say the unconscious) to take over, and interrogating random scribbles for expressive effects. Hogarth insisted he was in the business of drawing credible characters and not grotesque caricatures. But Hogarth is also, in this plate, doodling and varying like Töpffer, but in his own, more finished way, while Töpffer allows himself the barest signifiers, flicks of the pen. Broken lines are sufficient to render expression and character, and have the advantage of inviting what Gombrich called "the beholder's share." We supply character or feeling, be the face never so crude, for merely by existing in lines on paper, a face must have an expression; it cannot indeed *not* speak to us, if only we listen. This is what Gombrich brightly codified into "Töpffer's law."

In a series of demonstration drawings Töpffer shows and explains how doodled faces can be systematically varied to suggest an infinite range of moods and characters, how changing proportions of different parts of the face relate to each other, and to a part of the face kept constant, which thereby itself changes; proving that we react to a gestalt, a pattern. Expressive facial types may be contradictory and incomplete. The artist distinguishes between the permanent and nonpermanent signs, the former being variable and fallible indices of character, the latter revealing reliable evidence of the emotions of the moment—what was called pathognomics. Here Töpffer returns to the critique he made in *Crépin* of phrenology, which is based on the assumption that the shape of the skull, particularly the upper part surrounding the brain, infallibly reveals character and even destiny. Physiognomics, the science of reading character and feeling from the signs, fixed or mobile, inscribed on the face, is "profound, subtle and mysterious;" phrenology, in theory and practice, was totally fallible, not even the beginnings of the science it set itself up to be. Töpffer skirts the fact that Lavater's *Physiognomic Fragments*, published in German, French, and English over the last quarter of the eighteenth century (and in a new French edition the year Töpffer's *Physiognomonie* came out), and deploying phrenological and physiognomic theory as it were divine truth, became a treasure trove of examples and stimuli for caricaturists and artists generally.

The face of *Crépin*, as we have seen, happened by chance, and was then briefly interrogated until a character and future blossomed forth. The doodled face thus allowed for the unfolding of a destiny—such a face on such a man was bound to give him wife—and children—trouble. Can we not add here that the physiognomic broken line which encouraged the beholder's share found its counterpart in the narrative broken

"And note well that the least practiced eye supplies the gaps in imitation, with a facility and above all truthfulness which turn entirely to the advantage of the artist. There they are, heads, a gentleman and a lady who present broken lines in the highest degree, discontinuities of contour not a little monstrous . . ." (*Essai de Physiognomonie*, 1845).

line, with open space for a succession of accidents and unpredictables—the share of the artist himself as beholder, or that of a boy observing him at work, the share of the artist's unconscious? Töpffer does not say what I intuit here as the logical consequence of his graphic method, which, drawn out into the time dimension, creates unpredictable patterns of incident and non sequitur. Or, like temporary physiognomic marks on the permanent signs of character, the pattern may be varied by circling back to "permanent" comic refrains such as Albert getting kicked in the pants, or Vieux Bois changing his shirt, or the dunking of the Rival on the waterwheel.

FRAMES AND CAPTIONS

The only place where Töpffer mentions his method of framing is in letters to Dubochet wanting the *filets tremblotants* (the trembling frame lines) introduced into the album edition of *Cryptogame*. This kind of frame actually complements the perfect unity of text and drawing design. Philosophically, Töpffer was averse to the straight line, to rules and rulers. When hiking, too: he disliked the "ribbons" (*rubans*) carved straight through the Alps to facilitate the horse-drawn vehicles; they were boring and unnatural.

In his first sketched versions, Töpffer drew the vertical lines between scenes and horizontal ones to separate the captions freehand. In the lithographic versions, I would guess, he used a ruler as a rough guide for the maintenance of vertical and horizontal, but ran his pen loosely beside it, and often cast aside the ruler to allow for in- and out-dents necessitated by the overrunning caption, or letters like *p* or *j* that dropped below the line. He allowed the frames, like his characters, to take on a spontaneous life of their own, in squiggles, curlicues, and faces. Like his use of handwriting instead of typeface, the trembling, quirky frame line establishes continuity between image and word: in *Crépin*, the frame grows a skull in sympathy with those being thrown at the phrenologist in the picture above, while in *Vieux Bois* 44 the bottom frame line seems to vocalize the squealing of a cat just above, as it sees Vieux Bois's dog appearing in the chimney. The frame becomes pictorial, and in so doing suggests a fluidity of time between scenes.

In another view, Töpffer's peculiar frame lines, in denying the convention that multiple vignettes in a print should be boxed on a page as pictures are on a wall, aspire to the convention that paintings, when exhibited to the public, had a right to individualized framing. The squiggles become sighs and twitchings of discomfort and protest. At other times, Töpffer seems to be imitating the effect of a manuscript torn at the edges—as if in preemption of his schoolboy readers' mistreatment in handling the pages.

Playing with the frame has become a hallmark of avant-garde art today. Comic strip art has long been aware that the convention of the tight grid of boxes is only a convention, observed to be sure for much of the twentieth century, but now something to be varied, ignored, and joked with. This is part of the maturation of the genre. The mathematical regularity of the grid is satisfying, especially, it seem to children. This may or may not have something to do with the custom of cutting out scenes and pasting them in to a book or on a screen, or it may respond to the feeling of the psychoanalyst and comic strip author Serge Tisseron, who as a child found happiness and safety in "space and time solidly partitioned: to every image, its frame, to every text, its balloon; each panel caught in the double embrace of its line and column."[10]

"Which comes first, text or picture?" is the question always asked of makers of comic strips. The answer is, as a rule, text, as in medieval illuminated manuscripts. But with Töpffer the captions were evidently composed or written after the drawing was done, with their overruns, crowding, blank spaces, and awkward word breaks, despite the many signs revealed by the sketchbooks of careful plotting of the scenario in advance. The pictures drive the narrative. If the round table at which the Crépin family sit in the valedictory scene impedes the normal rectangularity of caption frame, well, let the caption curve to table, and to rotundity of toast.

All this adds to the impression of spontaneity. It is not contrived; the author is letting us in on his creative process, where he himself does not know what will happen next. There are many small, easily correctable errors (notably the "Jaques" for "Albert," 25), and Töpffer makes no attempt to normalize his idiosyncratic handling of diacriticals. There is even a significant omission in a picture that it was left to plagiarist Aubert to make good: the missing hole in the roof in *Vieux Bois* (39). Rodolphe's son François, when he came to copy, by tracing, his father's designs for Gamier in 1860, is able to make the caption boxes look less crowded by writing them slightly smaller; he also smoothes out irregularities, corrects poorly defined accents, and generally enlarges the scenes sideways to equalize proportions, for which he adds bits of wall, furniture, architecture, and foliage where necessary. But he does not alter the eccentricity of the frame lines. The imposition of black boxes in certain German Töpffer editions (Nef 1887, and, even less excusable, Meizer 1975, copying Nef) condemns them outright.

Throughout the history of the nineteenth-century comic strip we find a deliberate, comic discordance between caption and drawing. This discordance reaches its apogee in Doré's 1854 *History of Holy Russia*, where the "straight," official historiography (caption) is made to collide with and contradict the cruel and cynical reality (drawing). Töpffer too plays on a discordance between the often stiff, solemn, banal, formal (and even archaic) phrasing of the caption (as it were, the official version of the mini-epic) against the spontaneous absurdity of the drawings (visualization of the imagined truth). It is the difference between what should be and what might be. The balance is perfect. There is here—as has been said of Wilhelm Busch, whose solemn moral platitudes in the verse highlight and contradict the author's evident delight in the mischief of the pictures—duel as well as duet.

NOTES

1. Marie Alamir-Paillard, "Rodolphe Töpffer: Critique d'art . . ." in Lucien Boissonnas et al, *Töpffer* (Geneva: Skira, 1996), 67.

2. Wolfgang Drost, "Rodolphe Töpffer et Charles Baudelaire Esthéticiens—affinités et influences—et le rôle de Théophile Gautier," in Danielle Buyseens et al, *Propos Töpfériens* (Geneva: Société des Études Töpffériennes and Georg, 1998), 173, who delves deeply into this topic, says that it is not only plausible that Baudelaire knew Töpffer, but "impossible" that he did not. We may add evidence that Baudelaire did intend to write about him, from a letter he wrote to the *Revue des deux mondes* (where Sainte Beuve had earlier praised Töpffer), with notes for a reworking of his essay on caricature, and a list of twenty-one artists' names, including Töpffer [sic], Cham, and Nadar. See Charles Baudelaire, *Oeuvres Complètes*, vol. 2. Edited by Claude Pichois. (Paris: Gallimard/Bibliothèque de la Pléiade, 1976), 1343–134.

3. "Du Beau dans l'art," *Revue des deux mondes*, September 1847, 887–908.

4. Cited by Drost, 181.

5. E. H. Gombrich, *Art and Illusion: A Study in the Psychology of Pictorial Representation* (London: Phaidon, 1960), 336–42; Ellen Wiese, trans. and ed. *Enter: The Comics: Rodolphe Töpffer's Essay on Physiognomy and the True Story of Monsieur Crépin* (Lincoln: University of Nebraska Press, 1965), chapter 5.

6. Töpffer, *Reflexions*, 288.

7. Ibid., Book 6, chapter 20.

8. Ibid., Book 5, chapter 24.

9. An interesting English edition (the first) is that of Ellen Wiese, with connections to ancient theories of rhetoric, film theory (of Eisenstein), and modern linguistics. For the latter, see also Philippe Junod, "Actualité de Rodolphe Toepffer: un precurseur de la sémiotique visuelle?" *Études de Lettres* 4 (1983): 75–84.

10. Serge Tisseron, *Psychoanalyse de la bande dessinée* (Paris: Presses Universitaires de France, 1987), 7.

How Comics Came to Be

Through the Juncture of Word and Image from Magazine Gag Cartoons to Newspaper Strips, Tools for Critical Appreciation plus Rare Seldom Witnessed Historical Facts

ROBERT C. HARVEY

In our stampede to elevate Scott McCloud's definition of comics to the status of holy writ, we may have overlooked the most conspicuous shortcoming of his concoction. While "juxtaposed pictorial and other images in deliberate sequence" can include verbiage (those "other images" can be written words), McCloud maintains that comics do not have to contain words to be comics (McCloud, 8). But words are clearly an integral part of what we think of when we think of comics: words as well as pictures. McCloud's definition is simply too broad to be useful as anything except as a springboard to discussion (which is one of the chief purposes he hoped it would serve). By his definition, the Bayeux Tapestry and Mexican codices are comics. So is written Chinese. McCloud's definition includes what we call comics just as "quadruped" includes horses. But dogs are not exactly horses even though dogs also have four legs. A more accurate definition of each contains other distinguishing characteristics that make it possible for us to tell a dog from a horse. Clearly, when we think about "comics," an image of the Bayeux Tapestry is not the first that leaps up before the mind's eye, and we need a definition that acknowledges this commonplace quirk of the mental process.

It seems to me that the essential characteristic of "comics"—the thing that distinguishes it from other kinds of pictorial narratives—is the incorporation of verbal content. I even go so far as to say that in the best examples of the art form, words and pictures blend to achieve a meaning that neither conveys alone without the other. To McCloud, "sequence" is at the heart of the functioning of comics; to me, "blending" verbal and visual content is. And the history of cartooning—of "comics"—seems to me more supportive of my contention than of his. Moreover, the evolution of the modern so-called "gag cartoon" (the humorously intended single-panel drawing with verbal

Part of this essay is adapted from Robert C. Harvey, "Comedy at the Juncture of Word and Image," in Robin Varnum and Christina T. Gibbons, eds., *The Language of Comics* (University Press of Mississippi, 2001), 75–96.

caption beneath) contains within itself the most vivid demonstration of the reason for that evolution—namely, the emergence of a superior humorous effect that is realized only with the economy of expression achieved by verbal-visual interdependence.

I realize that the gag cartoon falls outside McCloud's definition because it is not a sequence of pictures. In fact, gag cartoons fall outside most definitions of comics. But not mine. In my view, comics consist of pictorial narratives or expositions in which words (often lettered into the picture area within speech balloons) usually contribute to the meaning of the pictures and vice versa. A pictorial narrative uses a sequence of juxtaposed pictures (i.e., a "strip" of pictures); pictorial exposition may do the same—or may not (as in single-panel cartoons—political cartoons as well as gag cartoons). My definition is not a leak-proof formulation. It conveniently excludes some non-comics artifacts that McCloud's includes (a rebus, for instance); but it probably permits the inclusion of other non-comics. Comics, after all, are sometimes four-legged and sometimes two-legged and sometimes fly and sometimes don't—and, to employ a metaphor as mixed as the medium itself is, defining comics entails cutting a Gordian-knotted enigma wrapped in a mystery, a task somewhat beyond our present scope. But leak-proof or not, this proffer of a definition sets some boundaries within which we can find most of the artistic endeavors we call "comics." Even pantomime, or "wordless," cartoon strips—which, guided by this definition, we can see are pictorial narratives that dispense with the "usual" practice of using words as well as pictures. But that doesn't make the usual practice any the less usual. Pantomime cartoon strips are exceptional rather than usual. Usually, the interdependence of words and pictures is vital (if not essential) to comics, and the vitality of that yoking is readily apparent (and handily exhibited) in an examination of the history of the gag cartoon.

In tracing the history of cartooning, we don't need to go very far back. Humans doubtless began scrawling pictures on cave walls before the dawn of history as we know it, but we need go no further into the dim recesses of the past than the emergence of the modern use of the term "cartoon." Gag cartooning probably began in the eighteenth century with the publishing of broadsides, single-sheet publications displaying caricatures or vignettes of moral import—the work of such irrepressible British wags as William Hogarth (1697–1764), James Gillray (1756–1815), and Thomas Rowlandson (1756–1827) and the Spanish painter Francisco Goya (1746–1828), to mention a few. This custom was perpetuated and refined in weekly and monthly humor magazines in the nineteenth century. In France, gadfly caricaturist Charles Philipon (1806–1862) started a thoroughly political weekly, *La Caricature*, in 1830, adding the more literary *Le Charivari* to his productions two years later and employing the work of such satirical artists as Honoré Daumier (1808–1879) and Jean Grandeville (1803–1847). In England, *Punch* (subtitled "The London Charivari") was launched in 1841, and "cartoon" was first employed in the modern sense in this magazine.

"Cartoon" comes from the Italian *cartone*, meaning "card." Italian tapestry designers and fresco painters and the like drew their designs on sheets of cardboard at full scale before transferring those designs to the cloth or walls they were intended for. These designs were called by the name of the material upon which they were drawn—*cartones*, or "cartoons." Later, the word "cartoon" was applied to any preliminary study for a final work, and it is here that we meet the modern usage of the term.

John Leech, *Substance and Shadow*, 1843.

The modern usage of "cartoon" began in London in the 1840s. The Houses of Parliament had been all but destroyed in a fire in 1834. The building that took the place of the gutted relic was called the New Palace of Westminster and was built over the next decade. By the early 1840s, it had been determined that the New Palace would contain various murals on patriotic themes, and a competitive exhibition was held to display the cartoons (in the ancient sense) submitted as candidates for these decorations. *Punch*, then only a couple years old, entered the competition on its own, publishing in its pages a series of five satirical drawings about government and calling them "Mr. Punch's cartoons." The first of these appeared in the weekly issue dated July 15, 1843, and was greeted (we are told) with howls of joyous appreciation (Thompson, 116).

Identified in the magazine as "Cartoon No. 1," the drawing by John Leech depicts a motley collection of London's downtrodden and threadbare street folk who are viewing the exhibition of the cartoons submitted to the Parliamentary competition, an array of portraits of regal personages. Entitled "Substance and Shadow," the irony gains additional impact from a caption: "The Poor Ask for Bread, and the Philanthropy of the State Accords—an Exhibition." Even in this, the first modern example of "cartoon," the words give meaning to the picture and vice versa.

At first, *Punch* called its humorous drawings "pencilings." Eventually, it applied the term "cartoon" to any full-page politically satirical drawing (and most "cartoons"—but not all—in these earliest years were what we would term "political cartoons" rather than simply humorous). But to the man in the street, any funny drawing in the magazine after the summer of 1843 was termed one of "Punch's cartoons," and by this route, the word came into use for any comical drawing, of which, as time went on, there were more and more of the apolitical kind. By the time Americans launched their imitations of *Punch* in the mid-1800s, "cartoon" was well on its way to being established in the modern sense. And so was "cartoonist."

Punch inspired many imitators on this side of the Atlantic—*Wild Oats, Phunny Phellow*, and others, most of which failed after a few issues or months. Among those that lasted were the weekly humor magazines *Puck, Judge*, and *Life*, all introduced in the 1880s.

By this time, magazine cartooning had branched into the two categories to which I've already alluded—the political and the purely comic (the latter, eventually termed "gag cartoons" by cartoonists). Typically, the political cartoons were given the greater play: they appeared on the covers (front and back) and sprawled across the double-truck of the center spread. Other cartoons often honed a political axe or two, but they, and the strictly humorous cartoons, were spotted throughout the magazines amid paragraphs of light-hearted prose and verse. Some of the drawings were half-page in size; others, quite small. Virtually all of these efforts were captioned with several lines of text in type. Usually the text was itself comedic and self-contained: the reader didn't need the picture to understand the joke.

Until the 1920s, magazine gag cartoons were mostly illustrations of this sort. Lee Lorenz, long-time cartoon editor at the *New Yorker*, calls the earliest of these specimens "illustrated anecdotes" because the captions were sometimes two or three paragraphs in length (48); the drawings did no more than illustrate the situation to which the text applied. The text was gradually refined: first, it was transformed into a sort of conversation among the several persons depicted in the drawing; soon, the dialogue was reduced to a verbal exchange between two persons. These are the "multiple-speaker captioned cartoons" (the fondly recalled "he-she" cartoons in which He says something; then She responds with something funny—or vice versa). Here's a sample:

> *Wife: How many cigars a day are you smoking now?*
> *Husband: Oh, just enough to show the doctor his advice was wrong.*

In cartoons like these (of which there were millions from about 1880 until 1920), the pictures contributed almost nothing to the joke. We don't need the picture in order to see the humor in the dialogue. Cartoonists of the day called these specimens "illustrated jokes," betraying their belief that the humor was contained in the prose not the pictures (Kunkel, *Letters*, 70). In some cartoons, however, the pictures provide the setting that makes sense of the caption—for instance:

> *Uncle: Poor girls, so few get their wages.*
> *Flapper: So few get their sin, darn it.*

They are walking along a street in front of a theatre on the door of which is a sign advertising the latest film: "The Wages of Sin." Without the scene-setting picture, the cartoon isn't very funny. (This cartoon, incidentally, was published in the first issue of the

UNCLE: *Poor girls, so few get their wages!*
FLAPPER: *So few get their sin, darn it!*

Ethel Plummer, *The Wages of Sin*, 1925.

New Yorker.) But most cartoons of the earliest vintage are essentially verbal witticisms that are funny without their accompanying illustrations.

When, at the close of the nineteenth century, the great metropolitan daily newspapers (particularly in New York) sought to increase circulation by publishing Sunday supplements that included imitations of the comic weekly magazines, cartooning evolved in a second direction. In newspapers, cartoonists started creating short narratives by arraying their pictures in storytelling sequences ("comic strips")—to which we'll return for more anon. In magazines meanwhile, cartoonists continued pretty much as before, but in striving for ways of creating comedy, they also exploited the capacity of the medium for visual puns. Visual punning emphasized the importance of the pictures to the comedy in single-panel cartoons. Perhaps from this development—sporadic and occasional as it was amid the usual array of "illustrated anecdotes"—cartoonists began to realize that the comedic impact of their work would be much enhanced if the meaning or significance of the words under their pictures could be understood only by comprehending the role of the picture. And vice versa.

Whatever the cause, by the 1920s, a new style of gag cartoon was evolving. Cartoonists had discovered that all cartoons—not just visual puns—were funnier if the humor arose from joining picture to words in such a way that the one "explained" the other. In this form, gag cartooning achieves its apotheosis when neither the picture nor the words have humorous meaning alone. The picture sidles into a reader's consciousness as a kind of visual puzzle, meaningless until reading the caption "explains" it. The picture likewise "explains" the caption. Either way, as comprehension dawns—in the flash of an instant—the humor is revealed, and the revelation, coming, as it does, suddenly, gives comic impact to the combined "meaning" of the visual-verbal blend. In effect, the joke's impact derives from the "surprise" that is sprung upon the reader when he or she understands the full import of the picture or the caption. The hilarity is further enhanced if

Ellison Hoover, *He Burned His Britches Behind Him*, 1920s.

HE BURNED HIS BRITCHES BEHIND HIM.

only one of the characters in the picture is speaking: this maneuver effectively heightens the importance of blending picture to words to achieve an economy in expression that increases the "surprise" inherent in the blend—and, hence, the humor of the joke. And so emerged the "single-speaker captioned cartoon," the modern gag cartoon.

Because the modern gag cartoon is more economical in the deployment of verbal and visual resources, it is more focused and therefore has greater impact. Employing the same economy, cartoonists achieve similar impact in comic strips, too, and the best funny book artists also strive to yoke pictures and words in tandem for narrative sense. But the blend is more demonstrably evident in the relatively simple gag cartoon.

A classic cartoon of this breed is one by Peter Arno for the *New Yorker*. The picture shows several military personnel aghast at viewing, in the distance, the crash of an airplane, obviously one of theirs. A parachute hovering over the crashing plane reassures us that no lives have been lost in the tragedy. Emerging from the crowd and coming toward us is a mousy-looking man who is grinning and rubbing his hands and saying, "Well, back to the old drawing board."

The picture makes absolutely no comedic sense without the caption; and the caption is not at all humorous without the picture. It may be debated whether there is any humor in the grim situation depicted, but the expression on the face of the mousy man shifts our orientation from a possible tragedy to the comedy that always lurks at the edge of ordinary human self-absorption.

My choice, here, of a *New Yorker* cartoon is not altogether casual. In his *New Yorker* article celebrating the magazine's seventieth anniversary, Charles McGrath says flatly that Harold Ross invented the modern single-speaker gag cartoon (184). Well, yes and no.

Without a doubt, no history of gag cartooning could overlook Harold Ross, the world's most unlikely candidate for editor-founder of the nation's most sophisticated magazine of humor and urbanity. A frontier kid with only a tenth-grade education, he was born November 6, 1892, in Aspen, Colorado, then a mining camp. When he left

"Well, back to the old drawing board."

Peter Arno, *Well, Back to the Old Drawing Board*, 1941.

town as a teenager, he became a slovenly tramp newspaperman who spent his years before World War I roving from one newspaper to another, a common type in those years. During the war, he worked on *Stars and Stripes*, the armed forces newspaper, and he fell in with a convivial crew, and after the war, they all landed in New York, where they encouraged Ross to launch, after a false start or two, the *New Yorker*.

The magazine struggled in fiscal red ink for years, but Ross never wavered in pursuit of his vision. He couldn't articulate it, but he knew what he wanted. Slowly, he assembled writers (E. B. White, James Thurber, Janet Flanner, Katharine Angell White, Frank Sullivan) and cartoonists (Arno, Rea Irvin, Helen Hokinson, Charles Addams, George Price) who gave the publication its distinctive flavor.

But Ross remained throughout his life the same—a rowdy, gangly, mussed-up hick-looking *wight* with a gap-toothed grin, a droll sense of humor, and a profane vocabulary. In his uncouth eccentricity and sheer doggedness, Ross was without equal in American journalism. And his magazine became a beacon to cartoonists, beckoning to modern times. It became a showcase for gag cartoonists, but the single-speaker captioned cartoon wasn't invented there, whatever the oft uttered claims of cartoon mythology.

The single-speaker gag cartoon was in fairly widespread use in the old humor magazines *Life* and *Judge* (not to mention that child of the 1920s, *College Humor*) long before Ross launched the *New Yorker* in 1925. Cartoonists still did mostly multiple-speaker cartoons, but single-speaker cartoons were not hard to find.

Peter Arno was often credited with inventing the single-speaker cartoon at the *New Yorker*, but he specifically denied it (in his introduction to *Peter Arno's Ladies and Gentlemen*).

"I like to think that I did," Arno wrote, "and I have been given credit for it; but nothing so basically simple could be 'invented.' It must be as old as Confucius, or older. It was just lying there all the time, waiting to be picked up. I gravitated toward it naturally, and was one of the first to use it consistently, so that it became more or less a trademark. . . . I suppose it appealed to me because my English grandfather, who was the light of my boyhood years, had taught me that brevity was the soul of wit. . . . As with a smoking-room story, the shortest caption, if it hits with a wallop, brings the loudest guffaw; the kind that warms my heart" (7).

Clearly, one person did not invent the notion of the single-speaker cartoon. Not Peter Arno. Not Harold Ross. But Ross gets the credit because his magazine lasted; the others that used cartoons did not. If *Life* and *Judge* had lasted (both, for all practical purposes, expired in the 1930s), they would doubtless have used the single-speaker cartoon as consistently as the *New Yorker* did. And then not any one of them would be able to claim the invention of the genre. But Ross's magazine outlasted its rivals. And because the gag cartoon had evolved into a single-speaker captioned cartoon in which the words and the pictures (in the best of them) were "interdependent" (to use Arno's phrase [2]) and because the *New Yorker* used lots of gag cartoons, Ross and his cartoonists are credited with having invented the form.

Doubtless Ross's eccentric literalism contributed to the evolution of the modern gag cartoon. He insisted, for instance, that he, as a reader, should be able to tell at a glance which of the persons in the drawing was speaking. Here, he was rebelling against the old multiple-speaker illustration: depicting several speakers, the old time cartoonists didn't have to worry about which of the persons had his or her mouth open. Either they all did; or none of them did. But when there is only a single speaker, the reader must know which of the persons in the picture is that speaker.

Ross's insistence on this seemingly trivial matter doubtless helped to focus his cartoonists' efforts in the direction of the single-speaker cartoon because only in such cartoons did you need to discern which of the people depicted was speaking. And so by such indirections might Ross be said to have nudged the magazine cartoon into its modern manifestation. But Ross also realized that the kind of cartoon he wanted in the *New Yorker* was different from the "illustrated joke" of the previous generation of humor magazines. He had difficulty, however, in translating his notions into very precise guidance. In the summer of 1925, an advisory letter to contributors called for cartoons that were "illustrative of ideas" (Lee, 165) rather than of situations. In her book *Defining New Yorker Humor*, Judith Yaross Lee argues that this vague notion soon evolved into the "idea drawing," the "key discovery" of which was "the ironic relations between image and text" (202)—in other words, a cartoon in which the words and pictures blend to achieve a meaning neither is capable of alone without the other.

By 1932, Ross had a pretty firm grasp of what he was after in cartoons. Writing to cartoonist Alice Harvey, he discussed his convictions:

Before *The New Yorker* came into existence . . . the editors [of humor magazines] bought jokes, or gags, or whatever you want to call them, for five dollars or ten dol-

*"No sense timin' it, pa; she ginally cackles about three minnits, then the egg'll
be biled."*

Edward Winsor Kemble, *No Sense Timin' it Pa*, 1922.

lars, [and] mailed these out to artists. . . . The result was completely wooden art. The
artists' attitude toward a joke was exactly that of a short story illustrator's attitude
toward a short story. . . . Now, this practice led to all humorous drawings being "illustrations." It also resulted in their being wooden, run-of-the-mill products. The
artists never thought for themselves and never learned to think. They weren't humorous artists; they were dull-witted illustrators. A humorous artist is a creative person,
an illustrator isn't. At least they're not creative so far as the idea is concerned, and in
humor, the idea is the thing. . . . Unless an artist takes a hold of an idea and does more
than "illustrate" it, he's (she's) not going to make a humorous drawing. . . .

I judge from your letter that you apparently don't realize that you are one of the
three or four pathfinders in what is called the new school of American humor [in car-
tooning]. Your stuff in *Life* before *The New Yorker* started might well be considered
the first notes of this new humor. I remember seeing it and being encouraged by it
when I was thinking of starting *The New Yorker* (Kunkel, *Letters*, 70).

But Alice Harvey didn't invent the single-speaker caption cartoon any more than Ross
did. The canny editor was doing what he often did to cajole performance from his contributors: he was flattering her into submission. As I've said, other cartoonists were doing the same thing earlier than Harvey's work appeared. And they were producing such
cartoons long before the *New Yorker* debuted. But Ross's magazine *established* the form
as the most effective for the single panel cartoon.

In his history of cartooning at the magazine, Lorenz edges up to the question of the invention of the single-speaker gag cartoon, but, understandably, he cannot identify any single person as the inventor. He reports that William Steig and George Price among others told him that they realized that the single-speaker captioned cartoon as it emerged was a different kind of cartoon.

"Just how it came about seems impossible to establish sixty-five years after the fact," Lorenz continues. "I suspect it was the result of the increasing sophistication of the gag writers rather than the cartoonists themselves." But he also says that "the single-line caption required a new subtlety on the part of the artist: the less told in the caption, the more one had to tell in the drawing" (49).

I think the cartoonists themselves saw the enhanced comedic impact of a picture and its caption when the drawing and the words were inextricably linked in the most economical way possible—with the caption being the utterance of a single speaker. Cartoonists (almost by definition in my book) create in visual-verbal terms. Through the first three decades of this century, they became more and more accustomed to contriving comedy that arose from the blend of words and pictures. It would be natural in the normal progression of things for cartoonists to realize the superiority of the comedy inherent in the economy of single-speaker cartoons. And I think those who wrote or polished captions saw the same thing. They all worked to create better cartoons in this new mode. And Ross with his eccentricities and cloudy comprehension of what he was looking for elbowed them along in the same direction.

The gag cartoon proliferated and evolved a little more, continuing to establish verbal-visual blending as the vital aspect of the form. Following the *New Yorker's* lead, such magazines as the *Saturday Evening Post, Collier's*, and *Look* began using more and more cartoons, and the cartoons were soon exclusively of the "single speaker" type. In less than a half-dozen years after the *New Yorker's* launch, the venerable "he-she" cartoon disappeared from the landscape of magazine cartooning.

In the fall of 1933, *Esquire* was launched, inaugurating the next phase in the evolution of the magazine cartoon: the full-color full-page cartoon. *Judge* and *Life* had occasionally published a cartoon in color, but *Esquire* made it a regular practice. (*Collier's* also eventually published cartoons in color but not as full pages.) At the *New Yorker*, Ross continued printing cartoons in black-and-white, and when he was urged to consider doing color cartoons, he responded with a typical Ross-ism: "What's funny about red?" (Kramer, 287).

During the heyday of magazine cartooning, which lasted, by my calculation, from the mid-1930s until the 1960s, the major weekly magazines used over two hundred cartoons a month. Adding in such monthly magazines as *True* and *Argosy*, the monthly market probably devoured more than five hundred cartoons. And when *Playboy* appeared on the newsstands, the market expanded by another dozen or so a month.

The last step in the evolution of the gag cartoon was taken by Virgil Franklin Partch II. Born in 1916, Partch signed his cartoons VIP (a distortion of his initials which he began affixing to his work while in high school) and may have single-handedly jolted the genre of the gag cartoon out of its verbal complacency in the 1930s and into its most imaginative era, roughly the 1940s and 1950s.

"He's almost human."

Virgil Partch, *He's Almost Human*, late 1940s.

Partch began working at Disney Studios in the early thirties, but by the dawn of the next decade, some of his cohorts there had convinced him to try freelancing cartoons to magazines (Ketcham, 54). He sold his first to *Collier's* (which published it February 14, 1942) and gave up animation. His work was distinguished by its highly visual content: the joke usually depended upon a bizarre picture which made the caption comic. At a restaurant, a woman is shown with a fork-full of spaghetti on her head as she asks her male companion across the table, "How do you like me as a blonde?" In a hotel lobby, a score of identical men are milling around and one accosts another, saying, "Your face is familiar, but I don't recall your name." His reliance upon his pictures to do more than simply set the scene demonstrated vividly the narrative value of the visual element of a cartoon.

As celebrated as his wacky sense of humor was his zany rendering style that displayed a certain nonchalance about ordinary anatomy. A frequent objection was made to his unabashed disregard for the number of fingers that are customarily issued with each human hand. To this carping criticism, Partch responded patiently: "I draw a stock hand when it is doing something, such as pointing, but when the hand is hanging by some guy's side, those old fingers go in by the dozens. And why not? At Disney, I spent four years drawing three fingers and a thumb. I'm just making up for that anatomical crime" ("Partch"). When the magazine market began drying up in the late 1950s, Partch turned to newspaper syndication with *Big George*, a panel cartoon (1960–1989).

With the virtual collapse of the great general interest weekly magazines in the sixties, an enormous market for magazine gag cartoons evaporated. Or, rather, dissipated into sundry special interest magazines. There, the gag cartoon continues to flourish, a verbal-visual blend combining brevity and clarity in order to precipitate an abrupt arrival of complete comprehension—and a laugh. A vivid demonstration of the mutual importance of words and pictures in the art form, the modern gag cartoon is the haiku of cartooning, and no definition of the medium can be complete without embracing it.

To conclude this anatomical analysis of the origins of comics by exploring the medium's history, we now return to the aforementioned newspaper comic strip, which, like the modern gag cartoon, is a lineal descendant of the same humorous drawings that appeared in weekly humor magazines like *Puck*, *Judge*, and *Life* in the 1880s. Toward the end of the century, great metropolitan newspapers battled for readers, and, in the attempt to attract readers and build circulation, they began publishing extravagant Sunday supplements. The most famous of these circulation wars took place in New York, and comic drawings were on the frontlines of the battlefield.

The potential of the Sunday newspaper as a profitable venture was first demonstrated in New York by Joseph Pulitzer who invaded the city in 1883, purchasing the *World* with the profits from his St. Louis *Post-Dispatch*. Pulitzer fleshed out the Sunday supplement idea by concentrating entertainment features in the *Sunday World*—material for women and young readers and for sports enthusiasts, the offerings of literary syndicates, and humorous drawings and other illustrations. Pulitzer had run comics in the supplement as early as 1889, but when he acquired a four-color rotary press in 1893, new vistas opened. Morrill Goddard, who headed the Sunday staff, saw in the new technology a spur to circulation: he proposed to capitalize upon the popularity of the weekly humor magazines by imitating them but to improve upon the original by adding color. Goddard did just that and inadvertently perverted his native language forever.

Offering comical drawings and amusing short essays and droll verse, *Life*, *Judge*, and *Puck* were dubbed "comic weeklies" in common parlance—or, even, "comics." So when the *World* launched its imitation "comic weekly" in November 1894, it was lumped together in the popular mind as another of the "comics." And then, once the *World* had shown the way, papers in other cities began publishing humorous Sunday supplements full of funny drawings in color and risible essays and verse. In a relatively short time, obeying the dictates of demand, newspapers eliminated the essays and verse and concentrated on comical artwork, which was increasingly presented in the form of "strips" of pictures portraying hilarities in narrative sequence. It was but a short step to the use of *comics* to designate the art form (comic strips) as distinct from the vehicle in which they appeared (the Sunday supplement itself). Once that bridge was crossed, meaning deteriorated pretty rapidly. Storytelling ("continuity") strips arrived soon after, and even when the stories they told were serious, they were called "comics" because they looked like the art form called *comics* and they appeared in newspapers with all the others of the breed.

The comic weekly that Goddard produced was intended, like the magazines that inspired it, for a general audience, adults—chiefly male, but also the rest of the family, women and children. Children alone were not the target readers. Never had been. Not on Sundays. Not on weekdays either. The compulsions and vacillating fortunes of Bud Fisher's racetrack tout, A. Mutt, as we shall soon see, were scarcely of the sort that children would find amusing. But adults would. As the twentieth century dawned, various groups of concerned parents expressed alarm at the possible negative effect on their children of exposure to the vulgarity of the physical pranks of the Katzenjammer Kids and others of their ilk in the comics. Cartoonists subsequently kept juvenile readers in mind as well as adults when crafting their product and avoided material that might corrupt the youth of the nation. But comics, as a genre, were never aimed solely at youngsters.

Among Goddard's comic artists was Richard F. Outcault, who, in his weekly drawings occasionally burlesqued city life by focusing on its slums. Outcault's squalid tenements, bald-earth backyards, and cluttered alleys were infested with a manic assortment of raggedy urchins, juvenile street toughs, and enough stray dogs and cats to start a pound. In the midst of these nondescript ragamuffins, one waif stood out: he had a head as round and naked as a billiard ball, surmounted on either side by giant ears that could have been pitcher handles, and his only raiment was a long, dirty nightshirt on which Outcault often lettered some comment about the mayhem at hand. The kid, whose name was Mickey Dugan, began sporadic appearances on February 17, 1895, but soon after January 5, 1896, he became a full-time resident in the *Sunday World*. On that day, the kid's nightshirt was colored yellow, and Mickey Dugan forthwith disappeared in the mists of journalistic time. Thereafter, he was known only as the Yellow Kid. He quickly became a star attraction of the *World*. No matter what the disturbance in Hogan's Alley, the Yellow Kid was there, his vaguely Oriental visage baring its two teeth at the reader in a grin at the same time vacuous and knowing—the capstone above whatever irreverent commentary was emblazoned on the signal flare of his yellow billboard shirtfront. So popular was the Yellow Kid that he became the first merchandised comic character, appearing on buttons, cracker tins, cigarette packs, ladies' fans, and a host of other artifacts of the age. His omnipresence could scarcely escape the notice of young William Randolph Hearst, who was just beginning to build his newspaper empire.

Hearst had arrived in New York in the fall of 1895, buying the *Morning Journal* and immediately inaugurating a price war with Pulitzer. The papers fought for readers with screaming headlines that sensationalized the news. Journalism became a shrieking, gaudy, sensation-mongering enterprise, distorting facts to provide howling newsboys with whatever hawked best at street corners. Seeing the popularity of the Yellow Kid, Hearst hired Outcault away from the *World* to draw the cartoon for his *Journal*. But Pulitzer at the *World* hired another artist to draw the Yellow Kid, and for quite some time, the most visible combatant in the circulation battle between the two press lords was the Yellow Kid: delivery wagons for both publishers took newspapers around the city with posters on their flanks bearing the grinning visage of the Yellow Kid. The *World* wagons had the Kid; and so did the *Journal* wagons.

Bemused observers on the sidelines of the conflict sometimes referred to the two papers as "the Yellow Kid journals." Or just "the yellow journals." From which usage, we derive that expression customarily used to denigrate the sensational newspapering practices of Hearst and Pulitzer—"yellow journalism." This legacy of the Yellow Kid is a mixed blessing, a triumph whose tawdry connections tainted the future of the comics medium even while asserting its riveting appeal. That the first great character of American comics should have his chromatism appropriated by a journalistic movement was ample testimony to the powerful appeal of the comics. But because that movement was wholly commercial, embodying reprehensible ethics and questionable appeals to baser emotions, the new art form was associated with only the lower orders of rational endeavor—a circumstance that cast a shadow for a long time over any claims made for artistic merit and intellectual content in comics. How could anything that first surfaced in the jaundiced columns of the sensational press have any interest for respectable, thinking readers?

The Yellow Kid occupies his niche in the history of U.S. newspaper cartooning not because he was actually the first newspaper comic character (he wasn't) but because he was the first newspaper comic character to prove he could sell newspapers. And the buyers were adults, as they have ever been. It was the man of the house who bought the paper. Everyone in the family read the paper that the *pater familias* brought home, but he had to be persuaded to buy it to begin with. The Yellow Kid was an effective persuader, and he established, beyond doubt, the commercial power of newspaper comics. And for that, he deserves the hallowed place he has in the history of the medium.

In the wake of the Yellow Kid's success, the comics enjoyed a prized position in news-papering. They were an active ingredient in a newspaper's circulation-building strategy for at least the next half-century. And the reason is not hard to discover. Most cities were served by several daily newspapers, and the only thing that distinguished one from another was its editorial point-of-view and its feature content. The most conspicuous of the features were the comics. For a time, the headlines and the lead stories from paper to paper were different. But as newspapers began to seek accuracy and comprehensiveness in their coverage of the events of the day and as national wire services began to supply much of the content of every issue, the news in one paper in a city was pretty much the same as the news in another. Only the features—and the comics—were different. And editors exploited that difference. As testament to the circulation building power of comics, the compendious Sunday editions of most metropolitan newspapers began to be wrapped in the comics section. The comics advertised the Sunday edition: they appeared as its distinctive, gaily colored cover on all newsstands.

The comics that proliferated in the Sunday supplements as the nineteenth century drew to a close were not always comic strips: some, like Outcault's *Hogan's Alley*, the title of the Yellow Kid's domicile, were stand-alone humorous drawings. Although the Sunday comics sometimes displayed smaller drawings showing an action in sequence, the regular use of sequential panels was rare until Rudolph Dirks made it standard practice in his *Katzenjammer Kids*, beginning December 12, 1897. At first, words, when used, appeared under Dirks' pictures, not within them. But by the turn of the century, the combination of elements that constitutes the comic strip form appeared regularly in various places. When Frederick Opper's *Happy Hooligan* appeared in 1900, the comic strip had taken its definitive form: a narrative told by a sequence of pictures with the dialogue of the charac-ters incorporated into the pictures in the form of speech balloons. Opper's strip summed up all the previous experimentation and combined all the basic elements from its start.

The prototype of the comic strip—parades of pictures with text underneath—had appeared here and there throughout the nineteenth century. Perhaps the first of these prototypes was done by a Swiss artist, Rodolphe Töpffer, as early as 1827. Describing his new storytelling technique, Töpffer wrote: "The drawings without their text would have only a vague meaning; the text, without the drawings, would have no meaning at all. The combination of the two makes a kind of novel." The modern comic strip emerged when the text beneath the pictures disappeared. From that point forward, most of the words in comics were confined to speech balloons. But the words and the pictures are still yoked in tandem to tell stories: the verbal and the visual blend to achieve a meaning that neither is capable of alone without the other. Indeed, in the best examples of the art, the words (or the pictures) taken by themselves are, as they were to Töpffer, virtually meaningless because the best comic strips exploit fully the dramatic economy of which the verbal-visual blend is capable.

The technical hallmarks of the comic strip art—the things about it that make it unique—are speech balloons and narrative breakdown. Speech balloons breathe into comic strips their peculiar life. In all other static graphic representations, characters are doomed to wordless pantomime. In comic strips, they speak. And they speak in the same mode as they appear—the visual not the audio mode. We see and read the words of the characters just as we see the characters themselves and "read" their actions. Films are made in a hybrid mode—audiovisual. Comic strips are all visual, a seamless optic engagement.

Moreover, including puffs of dialogue within the pictures gives the words and pictures concurrence—the lifelike illusion that the characters we see are speaking even as we see them, just as we simultaneously hear and see people in life. In my own cartooning efforts (sporadic and itinerant as they are), the inclusion of speech balloons in any drawing has always seemed to change substantially the nature of the drawing. I've probably drawn hundreds of pictures of characters posturing and cavorting about, but however animated and vivid those drawings may be, it isn't until I join a speech balloon to one of the characters and make him or her talk that the drawing begins to live. Once a speech balloon points its "tail" to its speaker, that character seems more alive. Partly that's because the words spoken begin to shape the character's personality; but it is also the simultaneity and proximity of words and pictures—and their unified mode of presentation—that bring the characters uniquely to life for me.

If speech balloons give comics their life, then breaking the narrative into successive panels gives that life duration, an existence beyond a moment. Narrative breakdown is to a comic strip what time is to life. In fact, "timing"—pace as well as duration—is the result of the second of the unique ingredients of comic strip art. The sequential arrangement of panels cannot help but create time in some general way, but skillful manipulation of the sequencing can control time and use it to dramatic advantage. The sequencing of panels controls the amount and order of information divulged as well as the order and duration of events. Managing these aspects of a story creates pace, suspense, mood, and the like. Ordinary mainstream literary prose does all of this, too; comics differ in that the pictures as well as the words manipulate time. For instance, action can be slowed down by sequences of pictures that focus minutely on each aspect of a developing action in the manner of a slow motion camera.

During the new century's first decade, the comic strip made the transition from the Sunday supplements to the newspaper's daily pages, Bud Fisher leading the way with a strip that eventually became the famed *Mutt and Jeff.* This legendary strip attests to the visual power of the comic strip. The eponymous duo long ago ascended to the pantheon of American mythology: in common parlance, the names (seemingly forever linked) always denote a visually mismatched pair, a tall person and a short one. But as a comic strip, *Mutt and Jeff* enjoys another distinction: it established the appearance of the medium, its daily format.

Other cartoonists (Clare Briggs, George Herriman) may have strung their comic pictures together in single file across a newspaper page before *Mutt and Jeff* debuted on November 15, 1907, but *Mutt and Jeff* lasted. Its importance in the history of the medium is secured by what Coulton Waugh in his watershed history, *The Comics,* called "the Columbus Principle." The Columbus Principle works like this: the Vikings may have been the first Europeans to tread the beaches in the Western hemisphere, but Columbus inspired others with his visit and thereby gets all the credit. Ditto the Yellow Kid. Ditto *Mutt and Jeff.* Its comic "strip" predecessors were flashes in the pan—here today, gone tomorrow. But *Mutt and Jeff* kept coming back every day, tomorrow and tomorrow and tomorrow, seven days a week. The strip's regular appearance and its continued popularity inspired imitation, thus establishing the daily "strip" form for a certain kind of newspaper cartoon.

Until *Mutt and Jeff* set the fashion, newspaper cartoons usually reached readers in one of two forms: on Sunday, in colored pages of tiered panels in sequence (some, like Winsor McCay's *Little Nemo in Slumberland*, intended chiefly for children to read); on weekdays, collections of comic drawings grouped almost haphazardly within the ruled border of a large single-frame panel (directed mostly to adult readers). The daily cartoons were often found in a paper's sports section and featured graphic reportage and comic commentary on the doings of diamond, ring, track, and other arenas of athletic competition. Harry Conway "Bud" Fisher was a sports cartoonist on the *San Francisco Chronicle*, and so, not surprisingly, the comic strip he launched that became *Mutt and Jeff* focused on a preoccupation of the sporting crowd—namely, betting.

Most accounts of the cartoonist's life report that Fisher was born in Chicago on April 3, 1884, but in a 1915 news release prepared by Wheeler Syndicate, Fisher is quoted as saying he was born in San Francisco, April 3, 1885, ". . . but I didn't stay there long. We moved about rather rapidly on account of my father's business. My mother and father lived in Portland, Oregon, and Chicago and Milwaukee before I was seven years old." He was in Chicago by the time he was a teenager: he says he graduated from Hyde Park High School. Fisher attended the University of Chicago for a few months in 1903 and in 1904, but, according to the Wheeler release, "he did not remain in college, being too busy drawing." The Wheeler report is based entirely upon Fisher's testimony, quoting him extensively, and the cartoonist, by then world famous, reveals himself as a shameless embellisher and something of a blowhard. In a 1938 issue of *Editor & Publisher* (early February), an article by Stephen J. Monchak suggests that Fisher left Chicago (and, perhaps, the University of Chicago) because his family moved to Reno, Nevada, whereupon Fisher "kept right on traveling to San Francisco."

After some hand-to-mouth weeks drawing pictures for store windows, Fisher landed at the *Chronicle*, and soon thereafter, he, like most early cartoonists, was assigned to the sports department, where, for the next couple years, he did layouts and occasionally drew pictures celebrating in humorous imagery what proper society then regarded with disdain—the dubious prowess and feats of professional athletes, their trainers, managers, promoters, and hangers-on and other alleged riffraff. Then on that November day in 1907, Fisher made history by spreading his comic drawings in sequence across the width of the sports page. And when his editor consented to this departure from the usual practice, the daily comic strip format was on its way to becoming a fixture in daily newspapers.

Fisher scarcely imagined that he was establishing an art form. "In selecting the strip form for the picture," he once wrote, "I thought I would get a prominent position across the top of the sporting page, which I did, and that pleased my vanity. I also thought the cartoon would be easy to read in this form. It was" (Fisher, 11). But Fisher's editor had been a reluctant participant in the experiment. Two years earlier, John P. Young had turned down Fisher's suggestion for a similar "strip" because, he is alleged (by Fisher) to have said, "it would take up too much room, and readers are used to reading down the page and not horizontally."

By way of introducing and describing his cast, Fisher called his strip *A. Mutt.* "Mutt" was short for "muttonhead"—a fool (Eric Partridge in *Slang Today and Yesterday* even credits Fisher with inventing the clipped version of the term). And Augustus Mutt was indeed something of a fool: he was a compulsive horse-player, a "plunger." And at first the strip concentrated almost exclusively on his daily quest for the right horse to bet on and for the wherewithal to place the wager. We saw Mutt's wife every once in a while—and his young son, Cicero. But no Jeff. Jeff didn't come along until later.

Fisher's genius included business acumen: he had the foresight to copyright *A. Mutt* in his own name—and, later, to apply for a trademark on the title. The strip was his and no one else's. And Fisher fought in court to establish his ownership beyond question.

In 1913, Wheeler Syndicate (later Bell) offered Fisher a better syndication deal than Hearst was giving him. Hearst was then paying Fisher $300 a week; Wheeler offered the cartoonist $1,000 a week or 60 percent of the revenue, whichever was greater. It was a staggering sum, and once persuaded that Wheeler could make the weekly guarantee, Fisher left Hearst. Hearst hired another cartoonist (either Ed Mack or Billy Liverpool; sources vary) to draw *Mutt and Jeff.* And Fisher sued, prosecuting the issue to a final legal resolution: the strip and its characters belonged to Fisher not to Hearst or his paper. After winning his case, Fisher hired Ed Mack as his assistant, and Mack drew the strip until he died in about 1932. Mack's assistant, Al Smith, inherited the job and drew the strip until he retired, long after Fisher's death in 1954.

The soaring popularity of *Mutt and Jeff* made Fisher rich beyond his most extravagant fantasies. By 1916, popular magazine articles were reporting that he earned $150,000 a year; five years later, Mutt and Jeff animated cartoons and merchandising as well as the constantly growing circulation of the strip had increased his annual income to about $250,000. Fisher was without a doubt the profession's richest practitioner. He was also famous. And he quickly habituated himself to enjoying both wealth and renown.

The strip that made Fisher a wealthy celebrity graduated from pedestrian racetrack touting to classic comedy when the tall and gangling Mutt acquired his diminutive sidekick: Mutt had encountered Jeff among the inmates of an insane asylum in late March 1908, but it wasn't until a year or so later that Fisher brought Jeff back into the strip as a regular cast member. The skinny tall man sort of adopted the short fellow, and the historic team was born. By then, the strip was appearing in Hearst's *New York American,* well on its way to national distribution. Even before Jeff's arrival, however, Fisher had pioneered another of the medium's conventions—narrative that continues from one day to the next.

Fisher had recognized at once the potential of the daily comic strip for bringing readers back day after day after day. The central device of *A. Mutt* virtually forced the cartoonist into day-to-day continuity. Mutt places a bet one day; the outcome is reported the next day. And Mutt promptly places another bet. To learn whether Mutt won or lost, we must buy a paper every day. But Fisher soon began to bait his hook with other tidbits.

In early January 1908, Fisher insinuated another storyline into the daily ritual. Mutt's wife divorces him, and Mutt begins paying court to another woman. Even in the throes of courtship, however, the plunger makes his daily dash to the betting window. Despite his addiction, he wins the lady's hand—only to lose her once and for all when he deserts her at the altar in order to place a wager on a horse named Lazell running in the Third

Race that day. Subsequently, Mutt's wife takes him back, telling him that the divorce had been faked, a tactic she cooked up with a judge to jolt Mutt into dependable domesticity. The scheme, clearly, didn't work. They resume their marriage, Mutt as devoted to the track as ever.

Obviously, Fisher's strip was aimed at adult readership. Wagering is an adult diversion. Thus, when Fisher launched *A. Mutt*, he defined the new genre almost at birth. *A. Mutt* presented itself as a "strip" of pictures, its narrative was continued from day-to-day, and it was aimed deliberately at an adult audience. At this late date in the study of comic strips, it may come as a surprise that the first of the breed burst upon the pages of a San Francisco newspaper with virtually all of the medium's conventions in place at the very onset. On reflection, though, it is not quite so astonishing. As Samuel Johnson said of Jonathan Swift's *Gulliver's Travels*, "When once you have thought of big men and little men, it is very easy to do the rest." With newspaper cartoons, once the decision had been made to format them in "strips" and run them daily, the rest—continuity, even adult readership—follows logically. And these elements were not the last of Fisher's innovations. He continued to play with the medium, and over the next two years, he explored many facets of the form—including political satire—that others would take up again in later years.

The political satire emerged during a February–March 1908 sequence in which Mutt is tried for stealing money in order to place bets. Fisher used characters in the legal and law enforcement professions that referenced actual San Francisco politicians lately caught in civic corruption.

The trial is of interest for yet another reason: it brought us to the immortal Jeff. Mutt's sanity is brought into question during the proceedings, and as soon as he is released from jail, he finds himself committed to a local insane asylum. (Fisher skimps on the reasons for this development; and so, therefore, must we.) In the "bughouse," Mutt meets such historic personages as Shakespeare, George Washington, the Czar of Russia, and assorted millionaires, poets, kings, and captains of industry. Among these deluded souls is a short bald fellow with mutton-chop whiskers who believes he is James Jeffries, the heavyweight boxing champion of contemporary notoriety (particularly on the sports pages where *A. Mutt* appeared). Little Jeff at last has arrived, wandering on stage March 27, 1908.

Jeff did not immediately become Mutt's sidekick and comic factotum. He disappears from the strip until that summer when the 1908 Presidential campaign began heating up. Mutt is the Bughouse Party nominee for President, and Jeff is the other half of the ticket. This may be the first time a comic character ran for the U.S. Presidency (and *Mutt and Jeff* will do it again several times). Jeff makes periodic re-appearances over the next months, eventually proving himself the ideal foil for Mutt. By mid-1909, Jeff is a regular cast member, appearing frequently, and in July, according to historian Allan Holtz in *The Early Years of Mutt and Jeff*, the strip was officially entitled *Mutt and Jeff*. As if to confirm the christening, when a booklet reprinting a selection of 1910 strips was published that year, the booklet was called *The Mutt and Jeff Cartoons*.

With the emergence of Little Jeff as Mutt's partner, the strip acquired the humane dimension that made it a classic: it ceased to be solely a daily chorus about crass money-grubbing and became a cautionary tale about the human condition. Mutt remained the scheming conniver that he'd always been as a horse-player: his role in the strip was to come up with ways to make a buck. Jeff's seeming mental deficiency made him the perfect innocent, the ideal foil for Mutt the Materialist. And the strip's comedy soon took its vintage form with Mutt's avaricious aspirations perpetually frustrated by Jeff's benign and well-intentioned ignorance. Foiled by the little man's uncomprehending bumbling, Mutt often responds with classic vaudevillian exasperation: the strips' punch lines are frequently precisely that, punches. In the best slapstick tradition of the stage, Mutt lets his pesky partner have it in the face with a pie, a dead chicken, a brick, or whatever object he happens to have in his hand when he realizes the little runt had scuttled yet another scheme with his literal-minded stupidity. Being beaned with a brick was a classic *Mutt and Jeff* finish long before George Herriman took the same device and turned it into poetry in *Krazy Kat*. But we always root for Jeff: visually, the short guy is the underdog, and most American readers cheer for the underdog out of cultural habit.

The comics could have been tailor-made for syndication: they were an entertaining feature that could easily be produced without topical or local references, making them ideal for distribution and sale to newspapers anywhere in the country. The market was clearly ready for syndicated comics. Over 5,000 new papers had started in the decade 1870–1880; and from 1880 until 1890, newspapers multiplied at the rate of two new publications a day. Many were small operations that could scarcely afford a staff artist let alone a cartoonist. But by paying a syndicate a modest weekly or monthly fee, these papers could publish comics just like the big city papers with their populous art departments. And the accumulation of hundreds of such small weekly or monthly fees netted huge financial rewards for the syndicates—and for the cartoonists whose work sold best.

Comics went into syndication almost as soon as they had demonstrated the kind of appeal that increased circulation. Comics were a part of the Hearst syndicate's package at the beginning; in 1898, the *World* was selling its comics to other papers although it didn't set up a separate syndication operation until 1905. By 1906, comics were in nationwide circulation: even small town papers were offering weekly comic supplements in full color. Syndication proved a bonanza for cartoonists, but—more importantly—it stimulated the growth and refinement of the comic strip medium.

Until the advent of syndication, a cartoonist's earning power was limited to the salary his paper paid him. Whopping salaries were paid, naturally, to those cartoonists whose work was deemed vital to maintaining and building circulation. But the earning power of a syndicated cartoonist was, by comparison, nearly unlimited: over and above a guaranteed annual salary, cartoonists were paid according to the number of papers that bought his comic strip. Both the cartoonist and the syndicate stood to gain by increasing a feature's circulation. In the usual arrangement, the syndicate fielded a sales force to sell the feature to papers across the country, and it also distributed the feature (supplying mats or proofs) and kept the books. After the costs of distribution were deducted, the syndicate split the profits—whatever amount exceeded the cartoonist's salary—with the cartoonist.

In return for the financial commitment it made to sell and distribute a feature, a syndicate took ownership of the feature. This policy protected the syndicate's interests: if the cartoonist of a popular strip died, say, or failed to produce his work on a deadline schedule, the syndicate could continue to supply the feature to its clients by installing another cartoonist. But the policy made the cartoonist, in some sense, a hired hand.

Contractually, a syndicate could dismiss a cartoonist at whim. But few, if any, ever did: it was clearly in the best interests of the syndicate to retain the services of a cartoonist of a popular feature since it was his creative imagination that made the feature popular.

Syndication was mutually beneficial, but it pinched both parties to the arrangement. In the hope of great financial return, the syndicate risked its resources in a double gamble that a new strip would sell and, having sold, that the cartoonist would continue to produce; in order to reap the initial rewards, the creator of a comic strip had to give up all rights to his creation—including, usually, any share in revenue generated by merchandising his characters. Once the merchandising mill began to grind for a popular strip, this inequity grated more and more, leading ultimately to fairer contracts. (Today, most comic strips are copyrighted in the cartoonist's name.) Uneasy though the relationship might have been, it was better for most cartoonists than working in a single newspaper's art department, their niche before the era of syndication.

The compensation from syndication had other implications than the purely financial for a cartoonist and for the medium. Non-syndicated cartoonists in the early days of comics were usually required by their papers to produce a great variety of comic illustrations. They may have produced a regular full-page feature for the Sunday edition, but the rest of the week, they drew sports cartoons, editorial or political cartoons, column decorations, ads, and miscellaneous fillers and features of all kinds. Once syndicated, a cartoonist escaped this gamut of illustrative labors and could devote his whole energy to the feature that was syndicated. With his creative energy thus focused—even confined—in a single enterprise, the cartoonist was bound to improve the product: his imagination and invention had no other outlet.

Syndicates were the forcing bed, too, for the growth of the medium. The exclusive nature of the syndicate's contracts with their client papers encouraged a proliferation of comic strips. Not only did a given syndicate need a variety of strips to satisfy the array of needs newspaper editors imagined for their readers, but syndicates had to have offerings similar to the most popular strips distributed by their rivals. When *The Gumps* proved so popular in the *Chicago Tribune*, for example, other syndicates came up with their own "family" strips to sell in Chicago to the *Tribune's* competitors. Thus, we find *The Nebbs* offered by Bell Syndicate, beginning May 22, 1923; and *The Bungle Family*, by McNaught in 1925. Eventually, every major syndicate felt it had to have a science fiction strip (in imitation of *Buck Rogers*), a cops and robbers strip (*Dick Tracy*), a young marrieds gag strip (*Blondie*), and so on. Some of the imitations were but pale reflections of original conceptions that were, in the last analysis, inimitable. But a few—like *Barney Google* (which began as a strip about a racing tout, following in Fisher's *A. Mutt* footsteps) and *Flash Gordon* (King Features' answer to *Buck Rogers*)—were classics in themselves. Without the competition among syndicates, comic strips would never have multiplied as they did, and the art form wouldn't be nearly as rich in invention and variety as it is.

To fully appreciate the importance of the comics in newspapers during the early days, we must imagine life without radio or television. Until the advent of the broadcast media, the newspaper was a family's major source of outside information and amusement in the home. It was an anodyne: by informing, entertaining, and distracting its readers, it soothed and comforted. The daily newspaper gave people something to do between dinner and bedtime. And the voluminous Sunday editions furnished a leisure day's amusement for the entire family. The comics were integral to the recreational function of the paper. Comics sections may have kept the kids from bothering their parents on their day of rest, but the humor in many of them would be lost on all but adult readers.

WORKS CITED OR CONSULTED

Arno, Peter, *Peter Arno's Ladies and Gentlemen* (New York: Simon and Schuster, 1951).

"Bud Fisher: His Life Story." Wheeler Syndicate Press Release. Photocopy of typescript obtained through R. S. Craggs, who prefaced the piece by saying: "Here is a biography of Bud Fisher. This article has been in my files for 65 years and was originally released in 1915. Fisher was 30 years old at the time."

Fisher, Bud, "Confessions of a Cartoonist," *Saturday Evening Post,* July 28 (10–11, 76, 78, 81); August 4 (26, 28, 110, 113–14, 117); August 11 (28, 30, 78, 83); August 18, 1928 (31, 90, 95, 99).

Gill, Brendan, *Here at* The New Yorker (New York: Random House, 1975).

Ketcham, Hank, *The Merchant of Dennis the Menace* (New York: Abbeville Press, 1990).

Kramer, Dale, *Ross and the New Yorker* (New York: Doubleday, 1952).

Kunkel, Thomas, ed., *Letters from the Editor: The New Yorker's Harold Ross* (New York: Modern Library, 2000).

———, *Genius in Disguise: Harold Ross of* The New Yorker (New York: Random House, 1995).

Lee, Judith Yaross, *Defining New Yorker Humor* (Jackson: University Press of Mississippi, 2000).

Lorenz, Lee, *The Art of* The New Yorker: 1925–1995 (New York: Knopf, 1995).

Maugham, Somerset W., "Preface," *Peter Arno's Cartoon Revue* (London: Robert Hall, 1942), v–vi.

McCloud, Scott, *Understanding Comics: The Invisible Art* (Northampton: Tundra, 1993).

McGrath, Charles, "The Ross Years," *The New Yorker,* February 20 & 27, 1995: 180–90.

Monchak, Stephen J., "Fisher Clicks Again with 'Mutt and Jeff.'" *Editor & Publisher.* A clipping, dated, based upon internal information in the article, approximately January or February 1942.

"Partch, Man and Boy." Dust jacket copy. Virgil Partch. *It's Hot in Here.* New York: McBride, 1945.

Shikes, Ralph E., *The Indignant Eye: The Artist as Social Critic in Prints and Drawings from the Fifteenth Century to Picasso* (Boston: Beacon Press, 1969).

Sloane, David E. E., ed., *American Humor Magazines and Comic Periodicals* (New York: Greenwood Press, 1987).

Thompson, Ross, and Bill Hewison, *How To Draw and Sell Cartoons* (Cincinnati: North Light Books, 1985).

Thurber, James, *The Years with Ross* (Boston: Little, Brown, 1957).

Vincent, Howard P., *Daumier and His World* (Evanston: Northwestern University Press, 1968).

Yagoda, Ben, *About Town: The New Yorker and the World It Made* (New York: Scribner, 2000).

The "Vulgar" Comic Strip

GILBERT SELDES

Of all the lively arts the comic strip is the most despised, and with the exception of the movies it is the most popular. Some twenty million people follow with interest, curiosity, and amusement the daily fortunes of five or ten heroes of the comic strip, and that they do this is considered by all those who have any pretentions to taste and culture as a symptom of crass vulgarity, of dullness, and, for all I know, of defeated and inhibited lives. I need hardly add that those who feel so about the comic strip only infrequently regard the object of their distaste.

Certainly there is a great deal of monotonous stupidity in the comic strip, a cheap jocosity, a life-of-the-party humour which is extraordinarily dreary. There is also a quantity of bad drawing and the intellectual level, if that matters, is sometimes not high. Yet we are not actually a dull people; we take our fun where we find it, and we have an exceptional capacity for liking the things which show us off in ridiculous postures—a counterpart to our inveterate passion for seeing ourselves in stained-glass attitudes. And the fact that we do care for the comic strip—that *Jiggs* and *Mutt-and-Jeff* and *Skinnay* and *The Gumps* have entered into our existence as definitely as Roosevelt and more deeply than Pickwick—ought to make them worth looking at, for once. Certainly they would have been more sharply regarded if they had produced the counterpart of Chaplin in the comic film—a universal genius capable of holding the multitude and exciting the speculations of the intellectuals. It happens that the actual genius of the comic strip, George Herriman, is of such a special sort that even when he is recognized he is considered something apart and his appearance among other strips is held to be only an accident.

It is by no means an accident, for the comic strip is an exceptionally supple medium, giving play to a variety of talents, to the use of many methods, and it adapts itself to almost any theme. The enormous circulation it achieves imposes certain limitations: it cannot be too local, since it is syndicated throughout the country; it must avoid political and social questions because the same strip appears in papers of divergent editorial opinions; there is no room in it for acute racial caricature, although no group is immune from its mockery. These and other restrictions have gradually made of the comic strip a changing picture of the average American life—and by compensation it provides us with the freest American fantasy.

In a book which appeared about two years ago, *Civilization in the United States*, thirty Americans rendered account of our present state. One of them, and one only, mentioned the comic strip—Mr Harold E. Stearns—and he summed up the "intellectual" attitude perfectly by saying that *Bringing Up Father* will repay the social historian for all the attention he gives it. I do not know in what satisfactions the social historian can be repaid. I fear that the actual fun in the comic strip is not one of them. *Bringing Up Father*, says Mr Stearns, "symbolizes better than most of us appreciate the normal relation of American men and women to cultural and intellectual values. *Its very grotesqueness and vulgarity are revealing*" (italics mine). (Query: Is it vulgar of Jiggs to prefer Dinty's café to a Swami's lecture? Or of Mrs Jiggs to insist on the lecture? Or of both of them to be rather free in the matter of using vases as projectiles? What, in short, is vulgar?) I am far from quarrelling with Mr Stearns' leading idea, for I am sure that a history of manners in the United States could be composed with the comic strip as its golden thread; but I think that something more than its vulgarity would be revealing.

The daily comic strip arrived in the early 'nineties—perhaps it was our contribution to that artistic age—and has gone through several phases. In 1892 or thereabouts Jimmy Swinnerton created *Little Bears and Tigers* for the San Francisco *Examiner*; that forerunner has passed away, but Swinnerton remains, and everything he does is observed with respect by the other comic-strip artists; he has had more influence on the strip even than Wilhelm Busch, the German whose *Max und Moritz* were undoubtedly the originals of the *Katzenjammer Kids*. The strip worked its way east, prospered by William Randolph Hearst especially in the colored Sunday Supplement, and as a daily feature by the Chicago *Daily News*, which was, I am informed, the first to syndicate its strips and so enabled Americans to think nationally. About fifteen years ago, also in San Francisco, appeared the first work of Bud Fisher, *Mr Mutt*, soon to develop into *Mutt and Jeff*, the first of the great hits and still one of the best known of the comic strips. Fisher's arrival on the scene corresponds to that of Irving Berlin in ragtime. He had a great talent, hit upon something which took the popular fancy, and by his energy helped to establish the comic strip as a fairly permanent idea in the American newspaper.

The files of the San Francisco *Chronicle* will one day be searched by an enthusiast for the precise date on which Little Jeff appeared in the picture. It is generally believed that the two characters came on together, but this is not so. In the beginning Mr Mutt made his way alone; he was a race-track follower who daily went out to battle and daily fell. Clare Briggs had used the same idea in his Piker Clerk for the Chicago *Tribune*. The historic meeting with Little Jeff, a sacred moment in our cultural development, occurred during the days before one of Jim Jeffries' fights. It was as Mr Mutt passed the asylum walls that a strange creature confided to the air the notable remark that he himself was Jeffries. Mutt rescued the little gentleman and named him Jeff. In gratitude Jeff daily submits to indignities which might otherwise seem intolerable.

The development in the last twenty years has been rapid, and about two dozen good comics now exist. Historically it remains to be noted that between 1910 and 1916 nearly all the good comics were made into bad burlesque shows; in 1922 the best of them was made into a ballet with scenario and music by John Alden Carpenter, choreography by

Adolph Boim; costumes and settings after designs by George Herriman. Most of the comics have also appeared in the movies; the two things have much in common and some day a thesis for the doctorate in letters will be written to establish the relationship. The writer of that thesis will explain, I hope, why "movies" is a good word and "funnies," as offensive little children name the comic pages, is what charming essayists call an atrocious vocable.

Setting apart the strip which has fantasy—it is practised by Frueh and by Herriman—the most interesting form is that which deals satirically with every-day life; the least entertaining is the one which takes over the sentimental magazine love-story and carries it through endless episodes. The degree of interest points to one of the virtues of the comic strip: it is a great corrective to magazine-cover prettiness. Only one or two frankly pretty-girl strips exist. *Petey* is the only one which owes its popularity to the high, handsome face and the lovely flanks of its heroine, and even there the pompous awkwardness of the persistent lover has a touch of wilful absurdity.

Mrs Trubble, a second-rate strip unworthy of its originator, is simply a series of pictures dramatizing the vampire home-breaker; I am not even sure she is intended to be pretty. When nearly everything else in the same newspapers is given over to sentimentality and affected girl-worship, to advice to the lovelorn and pretty-prettiness, it is notable that the comic strip remains grotesque and harsh and careless. It is largely concerned with the affairs of men and children, and, as far as I know, there has never been an effective strip made by, for, or of a woman. The strip has been from the start a satirist of manners; remembering that it arrived at the same time as the Chicago World's Fair, recalling the clothes, table manners, and conversation of those days, it is easy to see how the murmured satiric commentary of the strip undermined our self-sufficiency, pricked our conceit, and corrected our gaucherie. Today the world of Tad, peopled with cake-eaters and finale-hoppers, the world of the *Gumps* and *Gasoline Alley*, of *Abie the Agent* and *Mr and Mrs* serve the same purpose. I am convinced that none of our realists in fiction come so close to the facts of the average man, none of our satirists are so gentle and so effective. Of course they are all more serious and more conscious of their mission; but—well, exactly who cares?

The best of the realists is Clare Briggs, who is an elusive creator, one who seems at times to feel the medium of the strip not exactly suited to him, and at others to find himself at home in it. His single pictures: *The Days of Real Sport* and *When a Feller Needs a Friend*, and the now rapidly disappearing *Kelly Pool*, which was technically a strip, are notable recreations of simple life. Few of them are actively funny; some are sentimental. The children of *The Days of Real Sport* have an astonishing reality and none are more real than the virtually unseen Skinnay, who is always being urged to "come over." They are a gallery of country types, some of them borrowed from literature—the Huck Finn touch is visible—but all of them freshly observed and dryly recorded. Briggs' line is distinctive; one could identify any square inch of his drawings. In *Kelly Pool* he worked close to Tad's *Indoor Sports*, and did what Tad hasn't done—created a character, the negro waiter George whom I shall be sorry to lose. George's amateur interest in pool was continually being sub-merged in his professional interest: getting tips, and his "Bad day . . . ba-a-ad day" when tips were low is a little classic. Deserting that scene, Briggs has made a successful comedy of domestic life in *Mr and Mrs*. No one has come so near to the subject—the grumbling, helpless, assertive, modest, self-satisfied, self-deprecating male, in his contacts with his sensible, occasionally irritable, wife. As often as not these episodes end in quarrels—in utter blackness with harsh bedroom voices continuing a day's exacerbations; again the reconciliations are mushy, again they are genuine sentiment. And around them plays the child whose one function is to say "Papa loves mamma" at the most appropriate time. It is quite an achievement, for Briggs has made the ungrateful material interesting, and I can recall not one of these strips in which he has cracked a joke. Tad here follows Briggs, respectfully. *For Better or Worse* is considerably more obvious, but it has Tad's special value, in sharpness of caricature. The surrounding types are brilliantly drawn; only the central characters remain stock figures. Yet the touch of romance in Tad, continually overlaid by his sense of the ridiculous, is precious; he seems aware of the faint aspirations of his characters and recognizes the roles which they think they are playing while he mercilessly shows up their actuality. The finest of the *Indoor Sports* are those in which two subordinate characters riddle with sarcasm the pretentions of the others—the clerk pretending to be at ease when the boss brings his son into the office, the lady of the house talking about the new motor car, the small-town braggart and the city swell—characters out of melodrama, some, and others so vividly taken from life that the very names Tad gives them pass into common speech. He is an inveterate creator and manipulator of slang; whatever phrase he makes or picks up has its vogue for months and his own variations are delightful. Slang is a part of their picture, and he and Walter Hoban are the only masters of it.

Ketten's *Day of Rest* is another strip of this genre, interesting chiefly as a piece of draughtsmanship. He is the most economical of the comic-strip artists, and his flat characters, without contours or body, have a sort of jack-in-the-box energy and a sardonic obstinacy. The Chicago School I have frankly never been able to understand—a parochialism on my part, or a tribute to its exceptional privacy and sophistication. It pretends, of course, to be simple, but the fate of every metropolis is to enter its small-town period at one time or another, to call itself a village, to build a town hall and sink a town pump with a silver handle. The Gumps are common people and the residents of Gasoline Alley are just folks, but I have never been able to understand what they are doing; I suspect they do nothing. It seems to me I read columns of conversation daily, and have to continue to the next day to follow the story. The campaign of Andy Gump for election to the Senate gave a little body to the serial story—he was so abysmally the ignorant Congressman that he began to live. But apart from this, apart from the despairing cry of "Oh, Min," one recalls nothing of the Chicago School except the amusing vocabulary of Syd Smith and that Andy has no chin. It is an excellent symbol; but it isn't enough for daily food.

The small-town school of comic strip flourishes in the work of Briggs, already mentioned, in Webster's swift sketches of a similar nature, and in Tom MacNamara's *Us Boys*. The last of these is an exceptional fake as small-town, but an amusing and genuine strip. It is people by creation of fancy—the alarmingly fat, amiable Skinny, the truculent Eaglebeak Spruder, the little high-brow Van with his innocence and his spectacles, and Emily, if I recall the name, the village vampire at the age of seven. Little happens in *Us Boys*, but MacNamara has managed to convey a genuine emotion in tracing the complicated relations between his personages—there is actual childhood friendship, actual worry and pride and anger—all rather gently rendered, and with a recognizable language.

It is interesting to note that none of these strips make use of the projectile or the blow as a regular *dénouement*. I have nothing against the solution by violence of delicate problems, but since the comic strip is supposed to be exclusively devoted to physical exploits I think it is well to remark how placid life is in at least one significant branch of the art. In effect all the themes of the comic strip are subjected to a great variety of treatments, and in each of them you will find, on occasions, the illustrated joke. This is the weakest of the strips, and, as if aware of its weakness, its creators give it the snap ending of a blow, or, failing that, show us one character in consternation at the brilliance of the other's wit, flying out of the picture with the cry of "Zowie," indicating his surcharge of emotion. This is not the same thing as the wilful violence of *Mutt and Jeff*, where the attack is due to the malice or stupidity of one character, the resentment or revenge of the other.

Mutt is a *picaro*, one of the few rogues created in America. There is nothing too dishonest for him, nor is there any chance so slim that he won't take it. He has an object in life: he does not do mean or vicious things simply for the pleasure of doing them, and so is vastly superior to the Peck's Bad Boy type of strip which has an apparently endless vogue—the type best known in *The Kaizenjammer Kids*. This is the least ingenious, the least interesting as drawing, the sloppiest in colour, the weakest in conception and in execution, of all the strips, and it is the one which has determined the intellectual idea of what all strips are like. It is now divided into two—and they are equally bad. How happy one could be with neither! The other outstanding picaresque strip is *Happy Hooligan*—the type tramp who with his brother, Gloomy Gus, had added to the gallery of our national mythology. *Non est qualis erat*—the spark has gone out of him in recent years. Elsewhere you still find that exceptionally immoral and dishonest attitude toward the business standards of America. For the comic strip, especially after you leave the domestic-relations type which is itself realistic and unsentimental, is specifically more violent, more dishonest, more tricky and roguish, than America usually permits its serious arts to be. The strips of cleverness: *Foxy Grandpa*, the boy inventor, *Hawkshaw the Detective*, haven't great vogue. *Boob McNutt*, without a brain in his head, beloved by the beautiful heiress, has a far greater following, although it is the least worthy of Rube Goldberg's astonishing creations. But Mutt and Jiggs and *Abie the Agent*, and *Barney Google* and *Eddie's Friends* have so little respect for law, order, the rights of property, the sanctity of money, the romance of marriage, and all the other foundations of American life, that if they were put into fiction the Society for the Suppression of Everything would hale them incontinently to court and our morals would be saved again.

The Hall-room Boys (now known as *Percy and Ferdy*, I think) are also picaresque; the indigent pretenders to social eminence who do anything to get on. They are great bores, not because one foresees the denunciation at the end, but because they somehow fail to come to life, and one doesn't care whether they get away with it or not.

Abie and *Jerry on the Job* are good strips because they are self-contained, seldom crack jokes, and have each a significant touch of satire. Abie is the Jew of commerce and the man of common sense; you have seen him quarrel with a waiter because of an overcharge of ten cents, and, encouraged by his companion, replying, "Yes, and it ain't the principle, either; it's the ten cents." You have seen a thousand tricks by which he once sold Complex motor cars and now promotes cinema shows or prize fights. He is the epitome of one side of his race, and his attractiveness is as remarkable as his jargon. Jerry's chief fault is taking a stock situation and prolonging it; his chief virtue, at the moment, is his funny, hardboiled attitude towards business. Mr Givney, the sloppy sentimentalist who is pleased because someone took him for Mr Taft ("Nice, clean fun," says Jerry of that), is faced with the absurd Jerry, who demolishes efficiency systems and the romance of big business and similar nonsense with his devastating logic or his complete stupidity. The railway station at Ammonia hasn't the immortal character of *The Toonerville Trolley* (that meets all the trains) because Fontaine Fox has a far more entertaining manner than Hoban, and because Fox is actually a caricaturist—all of his figures are grotesque, the powerful *Katinka* or *Aunt Eppie* not more so than the Skipper. Hoban and Hershfield both understate; Fox exaggerates grossly; but with his exaggeration he is so ingenious, so inventive that each strip is funny and the total effect is the creation of character in the Dickens sense. It is not the method of *Mutt and Jeff* nor of *Barney Google* in which Billy de Beck has done much with a luckless wight, a sentimentalist, and an endearing fool all rolled into one.

These are the strips which come to life each day, without forcing, and which stay long in memory. I am stating the case for the strip in general and have gone so far as to speak well of some I do not admire, nor read with animation. The continued existence of others remains a mystery to me; why they live beyond change, and presumably beyond accidental death, is one of the things no one can profitably speculate upon. I do not see why I should concede anything more to the enemies of the strip. In one of *Life's* burlesque numbers there was a page of comics expertly done by J. Held in the manner of our most popular artists. Each of the half dozen strips illustrated the joke: "Who was that lady I seen you with on the street last night?" "That wasn't a lady; that was my wife." Like so many parodies, this arrived too late, for the current answer is, "That wasn't a street; that was an alley." Each picture ended in a slam and a cry—also belated. The actual demolition of the slam ending was accomplished by T. E. Powers, who touches the field of the comic strip rarely, and then with his usual ferocity. In a footnote to a cartoon he drew *Mike and Mike*. In six pictures four represented one man hitting the other; once to emphasize a pointless joke, twice thereafter for no reason at all, and finally to end the picture. It was destruction by exaggeration; and no comic strip artist missed the point.

At the extremes of the comic strip are the realistic school and the fantastic—and of fantasy there are but few practitioners. Tad has some of the quality in *Judge Rummy*, but for the most part the Judge and Fedink and the rest are human beings dressed up as dogs—they are out of Aesop, not out of La Fontaine. But the Judge is actually funny, and I recall an inhuman and undoglike episode in which he and Fedink each claimed to have the loudest voice, and so in midwinter, in a restaurant, each lifted up his voice and uttered and shouted and bellowed the word "Strawberries" until they were properly thrown into the street. This is the kind of madness which is required in fantasy, and Goldberg occasionally has it. He is the most versatile of the lot; he has created characters, and scenes, and continuous episodes—foolish questions and meetings of ladies' clubs and inventions (not so good as Heath Robinson's) and through them there has run a wild grotesquerie. The tortured statues of his *décors* are marvelous, the way he pushes stupidity and ugliness to their last possible point, and humour into everything, is amazing. Yet I feel he is *manque*, because he has never found a perfect medium for his work.

Frueh is a fine artist in caricature and could have no such difficulty. When he took it into his head to do a daily strip he was bound to do something exceptional, and he succeeded. It is a highly sophisticated thing in its humour, in its subjects, and pre-eminently in its execution. His series on prohibition enforcement had infinite ingenuity, so also his commentaries on political events in New York City. He remains a caricaturist in these strips, indicating, by his use of the medium, that its possibilities are not exhausted. Yet for all his dealing with "ideas" his method remains fantastic, and although he isn't technically a comic-strip artist he is the best approach to the one artist whom I have only mentioned, George Herriman, and to his immortal creation. For there is, in and outside the comic strip, a solitary and incomprehensible figure which must be treated apart: The Krazy Kat that Walks by Himself.

Excerpt from *Seduction of the Innocent*

FREDRIC WERTHAM

The Superman group of comic books is superendorsed. A random sample shows on the inside cover the endorsement of two psychiatrists, one educator, one English professor and a child-study consultant. On the page facing this array is depicted a man dressed as a boy shooting a policeman in the mouth (with a toy pistol). This is a prank—"Prankster's second childhood." In the story there is a variant of the comic-book theme of a girl being thrown into the fire: "Her dress will be afire in one split second! She'll need Superman's help!"

In another story a tenement building is set afire—also to be taken care of by Superman after it is afire. Until near the end of the book, attempts to kill people are not looked upon askance, and are not to be prevented apparently by humans but only by a superman. Then the lesson that after all you should not kill is expressed like this: "You conniving unscrupulous cad! Try to murder Carol, will you!" This is scarcely a moral condemnation. The lawyer who does not share in a million-dollar swindle is praised by Superman because he "remained honest." In fact this honesty is rewarded with a million dollars! A gun advertisement with four pictures of guns completes the impression that even if you can't become Superman, at least you can rise above the average by using force.

This Superman-Batman-Wonder Woman group is a special form of crime comics. The gun advertisements are elaborate and realistic. In one story a foreign-looking scientist starts a green shirt movement. Several boys told me that they thought he looked like Einstein. No person and no democratic agency can stop him. It requires the female superman, Wonder Woman. One picture shows the scientist addressing a public meeting:

"So, my fellow Americans, it is time to give America back to Americans! Don't let foreigners take your jobs!"

Member of the audience: "He's right!"

Another, applauding: "YEAHHH!"

The Superman type of comic books tends to force and superforce. Dr. Paul A. Witty, professor of education at Northwestern University, has well described these comics when he said that they "present our world in a kind of Fascist setting of violence and hate and destruction. I think it is bad for children," he goes on, "to get that kind of recurring diet . . . [they] place too much emphasis on a Fascist society. Therefore the democratic ideals that we should seek are likely to be overlooked."

Reprinted by permission from *Seduction of the Innocent* (Main Road Books, 2004 [1954]), 33–40.

Actually, Superman (with the big S on his uniform—we should, I suppose, be thankful that it is not an S.S.) needs an endless stream of ever new submen, criminals and "foreign-looking" people not only to justify his existence but even to make it possible. It is this feature that engenders in children either one or the other of two attitudes: either they fantasy themselves as supermen, with the attendant prejudices against the submen, or it makes them submissive and receptive to the blandishments of strong men who will solve all their social problems for them—by force.

Superman not only defies the laws of gravity, which his great strength makes conceivable; in addition he gives children a completely wrong idea of other basic physical laws. Not even Superman, for example, should be able to lift up a building while not standing on the ground, or to stop an airplane in midair while flying himself. Superwoman (Wonder Woman) is always a horror type. She is physically very powerful, tortures men, has her own female following, is the cruel, "phallic" woman. While she is a frightening figure for boys, she is an undesirable ideal for girls, being the exact opposite of what girls are supposed to want to be.

We have asked many children how they subdivide comic books. A thirteen-year-old boy, in a letter to a national magazine commenting on one of Sterling North's excellent articles on the subject, named five groups of harmful comics: "Fantasy comics, crime comics, superman or superwoman comics, jungle comics (the worst, in my opinion) and comics which still pretend to be funny but throw in a lot of nudity to help them sell."

Many children have a simpler classification. They distinguish between "jokey" books and "interesting books." The latter they also call "exciting books" or "danger books." Very young children who supposedly read only harmless animal comic books often see others in the hands of their older siblings or in other places.

One Lafargue researcher asked a little six-year-old girl what comic books she liked and was told "corpsies." This baffled the researcher (that name would fit so many!). It finally developed when she produced the book that she meant "kewpies." It was one of the very few artistic comic books and had on its inside back cover a charming "Map of Kewpieville" showing Kewpie Square, Willow Wood, Mischief Grounds, Welcome Bridge, a Goblin Glen, Forsaken Lake, Blue Lake and a Snifflebrook. What was impressed on this child's mind, however, were the "corpsies" she had seen in the crime comic books of her friends.

Of course there are also super-animal magazines, like Super Duck. In one of them the duck yells: "No! I kill the parents [of the rabbits]. I am a hard guy and my heart is made of stone!" The scene shows a rabbit crying and begging for mercy, the duck poised to kill him with a baseball bat.

Just as there are wonder women there are wonder animals, like Wonder Ducks. In one such book there is a full-page advertisement for guns, "throwing knives" and whips, and a two-page advertisement for "Official Marine Corps knives, used by the most rugged branch of the armed forces, leathernecks swear by them."

There are also super-children, like Superboy. Superboy can slice a tree like a cake, can melt glass by looking at it ("with his amazing X-ray eyes, Superboy proves the scientific law that focussed concentrated X-rays can melt glass!"), defeats "a certain gang chief and his hirelings." Superboy rewrites American history, too. In one story he helps George Washington's campaign and saves his life by hitting a Hessian with a snowball.

54

George Washington reports to the Continental Congress: "And sirs, this remarkable boy, a Superboy, helped our boys win a great victory."

One third of a page of this book is a picture of Washington crossing the Delaware—with Superboy guiding the boat through the ice floes. It is really Superboy who is crossing the Delaware, with George Washington in the boat. All this travesty is endorsed by the impressive board of experts in psychiatry, education and English literature.

Comic books adapted from classical literature are reportedly used in 25,000 schools in the United States. If this is true, then I have never heard a more serious indictment of American education, for they emasculate the classics, condense them (leaving out everything that makes the book great), are just as badly printed and inartistically drawn as other comic books and, as I have often found, do not reveal to children the world of good literature which has at all times been the mainstay of liberal and humanistic education. They conceal it. The folklorist, G. Legman, writes of comic books based on classics, "After being processed in this way, no classic, no matter who wrote it, is in any way distinguishable from the floppity-rabbit and crime comics it is supposed to replace."

A writer of children's books, Eleanor Estes, has said of these comics (in the *Wilson Library Bulletin*), "I think that worse than the comic books that stick to their own fields are the ones that try to rehash the classics. They really are pernicious, for it seems to me that they ruin for a child the fine books which they are trying to popularize."

David Dempsey, writing in the *New York Times Book Review*, has said of the comic book *Julius Caesar* that it has "a Brutus that looks astonishingly like Superman. 'Our course will seem too bloody to cut the head off and then hack the limbs . . .' says Brutus, in language that sounds like Captain Marvel . . ." and he notes that "Julius Caesar is followed by a story called Tippy, the Terrier."

An adaptation from one of Mark Twain's novels has the picture of two small boys in a fight, one tearing the other's hair—a scene not the keynote of Mark Twain's novel. Inside, three consecutive pictures show a fight between two boys ("In an instant both boys were gripped together like cats") and the last picture shows one boy with a finger almost in the other's eye (the injury-to-the-eye motif again).

At the end of 1948 the 60-million-comic-books-a-month were split up between over four hundred comic-book titles of assorted types. All through 1948 the trend of the industry was toward crime comics. Experts of the industry were busy explaining to credulous parents that the industry was only giving to children what they needed and wanted, that scenes of crime and sadism were necessary for them, even good for them, and that the industry was only supplying a demand. But in the meantime my advice to parents had begun to take at least some hold. They had begun to look into crime comic books, and different groups and local authorities started to contemplate, announce, attempt—and even to take steps.

In direct response to all this the industry executed a brilliant and successful maneuver. Leaving their psychiatric and child experts with their explanations and justifications, they struck out on their own. The experts had said that what the children need is aggression, not affection—crime, not love. But suddenly the industry converted from blood to kisses. They tooled up the industry for a kind of comic book that hardly existed before, the love-confession type. They began to turn them out quickly and plentifully before their own experts had time to retool for the new production line and write scientific papers proving that what children really needed and wanted—what their psychological development really called for—was after all not murder, but love! In this new genre, shooting a girl in the stomach was out, though previously it had been so necessary.

There had of course been teenage comics before. But they were mostly not about love or kissing, but in large part about humiliations, a disguised kind of psychological sadism. The confession type, on the other hand, implies a love relationship. There are misunderstandings, jealousies and triangle troubles. The girl is either too shy or too sociable, the boy friend is either the wrong one altogether or he says the wrong things. In many of them, in complete contrast to the previous teenage group, sexual relations are assumed to have taken place in the background. Just as the crime-comics formula requires a violent ending, so the love-comics formula demands that the story end with reconciliation.

If we were to take seriously the experts of the comic-book industry, the psychology of American children completely reversed itself in 1949. In order to provide for the "deep psychological needs" of children, the industry had been supplying more and more comic books about violence and crime. Now suddenly it began producing dozens of new titles of love comics, to satisfy children's new needs. *Murder, Inc.* became *My Private Life*; *Western Killers* became *My True Love*. With the new and profitable policy of the industry, the needs of children had changed overnight. All this would be funny if the happiness and mental development of children were not involved.

Just as some crime comics are especially marked on the cover "For Adults Only" (which of course entices children even more), so some of the love-confession comics are marked "Not Intended For Children." And just as there were supermen, superwomen, superboys and super-ducks, so the industry now supplied a "super-lover." Studying these love-confession books is even more tedious than studying the usual crime comic books. You have to wade through all the mushiness, the false sentiments, the social hypocrisy, the titillation, the cheapness.

Every investigation has its dark moments. One day I received a letter from a highly intelligent and socially active woman who had taken great interest in the curbing of crime comics. She wrote me that in her opinion the love and confession comics may be in bad taste, but at least they do no harm to children although they "give a false picture of love and life." This letter gave me the first doubt that I could ever achieve any practical results from my time-consuming investigation. What more harm can be done a child than to give him "a false picture of love and life"?

It is a mistake to think that love comics are read only by adolescent and older children. They are read by very young children as well. An eight-year-old girl living in a very comfortable environment on Long Island said, "I have lots of friends and we buy about one comic book a week and then we exchange. I can read about ten a day. I like to read the comic books about love because when I go to sleep at night I love to dream about love."

Another confession comic book is the reincarnation of a previous teen-age book with an innocuous title. That one was, despite its title, one of the most sexy, specializing in highly accentuated and protruding breasts in practically every illustration. Adolescent boy call these "headlight comics." This is a very successful way to stimulate a boy sexually. In other comic books, other secondary sexual characteristics of women, for example the hips, are played up in the drawing.

The confession comic into which this one turned has a totally different style, the new love-comics formula. One story, "I Was a Spoiled Brat," begins with a big picture of an attractive girl looking at herself in the mirror and baring herself considerably. The dash of violence here is supplied by a hit-and-run driving accident and by the father's dying of a heart attack when he hears about his daughter's life. It all comes out right in the last picture: "But I did live down my past. Tommy is now a leading merchant in Grenville."

Flooding the market with love-confession comics was so successful in diverting attention from crime comic books that it has been entirely overlooked that many of them really are crime comic books, with a seasoning of love added. Unless the love comics are sprinkled with some crime they do not sell. Apparently love does not pay.

William Gaines and the Battle over EC Comics

AMY KISTE NYBERG

Comic book publishers, when investigated by the Senate Subcommittee to Investigate Juvenile Delinquency in 1954, eagerly embraced the committee's recommendation that the industry "clean house" and adopt a self-regulatory code. For them, the code represented an immediate solution to the bad publicity being generated about comics. The lone dissenting voice was William M. Gaines, who never believed that EC horror comics harmed their young fans. This chapter chronicles his battle against government and industry forces that sought to regulate comic books in the mid-1950s.

William Gaines, best known for publishing a line of horror comics in the 1950s and for *MAD* magazine, inherited the company from his father, Max Gaines, who has been called by many the father of the modern comic book. It was Max Gaines, along with Harry I. Wildenburg, who came up with the idea to produce and sell comic books. He decided to start a line of educational and strictly juvenile titles under the imprint Educational Comics. Although he published "wholesome" comic books that parents approved of, they were not popular with young readers. In 1947, Max Gaines was killed in a boating accident, and his twenty-five-year-old son inherited a company that was $100,000 in debt. William Gaines, then an education student at New York University and newly divorced, moved in with his mother, finished his studies, and took over as head of the failing Educational Comics.[1]

It was an uncertain time to be in the comic book business. When the circulation of the superhero comics that had been so popular during the war dropped off, publishers began to search for other genres that would appeal to their readers. Most of the comic book publishers had some background in the pulp magazine field, and it seemed only natural that the crime, mystery and horror themes that had served the pulps so well could be resurrected. By 1948, every fifth comic book sold was a crime comic. After the circulation of crime comics peaked, the industry added elements of horror and terror to keep reader interest high.[2]

One of William Gaines' first moves was to beef up his father's line of kiddie comics. He hired a new artist, Al Feldstein, and by the end of 1949, the company was producing crime and western comics.[3] His next step was to create, in 1950, a new line of hor-

Reprinted by permission from *Inks: Cartoon and Comic Art Studies* (February 1996), 3–14. Copyright © The Ohio State University.

ror comics. The company changed its name from Educational Comics to Entertaining Comics as *Crypt of Terror, Haunt of Fear* and *Vault of Horror* joined the EC lineup. The new magazines sold well, and within a year EC's financial problems were over.[4] Each title offered a collection of eight-page stories that followed what Harvey Kurtzman described as the classic short-story form—the punch ending.[5]

The EC horror line, like all successful comic book ideas, was copied by other publishers, and by 1954 there were more than forty horror titles a month being published.[6] Two events that year would signal the beginning of the end for the company that Gaines built. One was the publication of *Seduction of the Innocent*, an attack on the comic book industry by Dr. Fredric Wertham, a New York psychiatrist who, convinced that comic books were a contributing factor in juvenile delinquency, had been campaigning for legislation restricting the sale of comic books to children. The second was the announcement by the Senate Subcommittee to Investigate Juvenile Delinquency that it would hold hearings on the comic book industry as part of its broader mission to examine the effects of mass media on America's youth.

Throughout the late 1940s and early 1950s, Wertham had written articles for both the popular press and professional journals and served as an expert witness for various governmental bodies investigating comic books as he worked to halt the sale of comic books to children under sixteen. His campaign had resulted in little legislative activity. With his book, Wertham clearly hoped to rekindle interest in state and federal legislation against comic books. *Seduction of the Innocent* was written primarily to alert parents and others that crime and horror comics existed and were read by children. With public sentiment behind him, Wertham felt legislators would have to heed his calls for regulation of the comic book industry.

Seduction of the Innocent included graphic descriptions of the sex and violence found in comic book pages, complete with illustrations. The illustrations Wertham chose were single panels presented out of context, but they were powerful images nonetheless. Among the illustrations were several from EC publications. Wertham did not identify any of the publishers when he reprinted their work, but it was not difficult to track down the sources of the panels excerpted in *Seduction of the Innocent*.

Public response to Wertham's book prompted the Senate Subcommittee to Investigate Juvenile Delinquency to begin their investigation of the mass media with the comic book industry. In his opening remarks at the hearings on April 21, 1954, the chairman of the committee, Senator Robert Hendrickson, remarked: "From the mail received by the subcommittee, we are aware that thousands of American parents are greatly concerned about the possible detrimental influences certain types of crime and horror comic books have upon their children."[7]

The committee compiled a list of witnesses to testify at the hearings that included experts on children and delinquency, publishers, and distributors. The hearings were originally scheduled for just two days. Gaines appeared on a tentative list of witnesses and was scheduled to testify April 21st before the committee right before lunch. Wertham was to follow after lunch.[8] Gaines said he contacted the committee and volunteered to testify after his business manager, Lyle Stuart, suggested that someone should go before the committee to testify in favor of comic books.[9] On April 19th, the committee served Gaines with a subpoena ordering him to appear before them on April 21st. The committee had also prepared a subpoena for Lyle Stuart that was never served, apparently as a back-up if the U.S. deputy marshall was unable to locate Gaines.[10] The committee staff also drew up background statements on each of the witnesses indicating what position the committee could expect each to take on comic books. Gaines' statement read:

> Mr. William M. Gaines is the owner and Managing Editor of "Entertaining Comics Group," located at 225 Lafayette Street, New York City, N.Y.
>
> Mr. Gaines is known for having taken a bankrupt comic book company and made it a financial success by injecting horror into the crime comics. Some of the publications by Mr. Gaines are known as "Mad", "The Haunt of Fear", "Weird Science Fantasy", "Vault of Horror", "Shock Suspense Stories."
>
> The type of advertising in the Entertaining Comics Group is handled primarily by the company itself and they built up their mailing list by such devices as correspondence to "The E. C. Fan Addict Club, Room 706, 225 Lafayette Street, New York, N.Y." (Individual membership, 25 cents—Charter membership for groups of 5 or more).
>
> On December 22, 1953, there appeared the following news item in the New York World Telegram: "William Gaines said he would comply with the Massachusetts Attorney General George Finegold's demand to withdraw the comic "Panic" which contained a cartoon version of "The Night Before Christmas." The Attorney General had threatened criminal proceedings.[11]

During the morning session, Richard Clendenen, the executive director of the committee, presented a slide show and commentary about horror comics. Singled out in his presentation were the comic titles *Black Magic, Fight Against Crime, Mysterious Adventures, Crime Must Pay the Penalty, Strange Tales, The Haunt of Fear*, and *Shock SuspensStories*. The latter two were EC titles. Clendenen also showed the committee an advertisement published in the EC line, titled "Are You A Red Dupe?" The ad had been concocted in response to a four-part expose on the comic book industry that had just run in a Connecticut newspaper, the *Hartford Courant*. In one segment, reporter Irving M. Kravsow went to New York to interview publishers for an article that appeared 15 February 1954, with the headline: "Public Taste, Profit Used to Justify 'Horror' Comics." Kravsow interviewed two publishers, Stanley Morse, publisher of Gilmor Magazines, and William Gaines. In that article, Gaines defended his publication of horror comics by explaining that profits from the horror comics allowed him to underwrite the expense of publishing the less popular educational comics. Gaines pulled out the issue of *Panic* with the Christmas satire that had earned the distinction of being "banned in Boston," remarking, "There's nothing wrong with it." The reporter quoted Gaines: "We try to entertain and educate. That's all there is to it. A lot of people have the idea we're a bunch of monsters who sit around drooling and dreaming up horror and filth. That's not true as you can see." The next paragraph of the news story described Gaines' office as "decorated with framed paintings of characters from the horror books such as witches and ogres."[12]

Six weeks after the expose ran, the *Courant* reported it was still receiving letters on the subject, all favorable. The only unfavorable letter the newspaper received was from Gaines himself, who accused the *Courant* of presenting a biased picture. *Editor &*

Publisher, the newspaper industry's trade magazine, noted: "The same publisher hit back by running full page ads in his comic books declaring that the group most anxious to destroy comics are the Communists." The magazine also gave the *Courant's* response:

> Thus do the sellers of literary sewage justify their profits from the debauch of youth. . . . But the jig is now up for the panderers of dirty comic books, and this Red scare is a frantic rear-guard action from a discredited and soon-to-be deactivated phase of publishing. Their end is in sight and they know it.[13]

The ad was the brainchild of Gaines and business manager Lyle Stuart. The ads ran in all of his comics, and Gaines sent a tearsheet of the Red Dupe ad to anyone who wrote Gaines attacking his comics. Said Gaines: "It was all pretty dopey. I made the ad out of devilishness. It was supposed to be a spoof, but it didn't come off that way."[14]

Clendenen described the ad to the committee and read the call to action at the bottom of the ad:

> Now there is a message down at the bottom and it ends up by saying, "So the next time some joker gets up at a PTA meeting, or starts jabbering about 'the naughty comic books' at your local candy store, give him the once-over. We are not saying he is a Communist. He may be innocent of the whole thing! He may be a dupe! He may not even read the *Daily Worker*! It is just that he's swallowed the Red bait—hook, line, and sinker."

Clendenen commented: "So at the other extreme some people would make out anyone who raised any question whatsoever about the comics was also giving out Red-inspired propaganda."[15] Senator Estes Kefauver asked that the copy of the ad be placed in the record of the hearings. Kefauver reacted very negatively to being accused, however indirectly, of being a Communist, especially with charges being made by his opponent in the Senate race that Kefauver was "coddling Communists."[16]

Clendenen's presentation apparently ran on longer than expected, pushing Gaines' testimony until after lunch. But after the committee reconvened, Wertham appeared to testify, and the committee moved him ahead of Gaines. Wertham, too, illustrated his presentation with examples from the various horror comics, many of them published by Gaines. Near the end of his testimony, he mentioned one EC story that he claimed was teaching "race hatred." He noted the story repeated a derogatory term for Puerto Ricans twelve times, and summed up the story this way: "What is the point of the story? The point of the story is that then somebody gets beaten to death."[17]

Then it was Gaines' turn. According to his biography, Gaines was on diet pills, and one side effect of the medication was that when the drug began to wear off, a depressing fatigue set in. Unfortunately, that happened about midway through Gaines' testimony. He recalls: "At the beginning, I felt that I was really going to fix those bastards, but as time went on I could feel myself fading away. I was like a punch-drunk fighter. They were pelting me with questions and I couldn't locate the answers."[18]

Gaines began his testimony by reading a statement he and Stuart had written the night before. He listed his father's contributions to the industry and pointed out that the industry employed thousands of writers, artists, engravers, and printers as well as providing millions of hours of entertainment for children. He then turned to the subject of horror comics, telling the committee: "I was the first publisher in these United States to publish horror comics. I am responsible, I started them."[19]

Gaines then took issue with the testimony given by Wertham, refuting the charges that his comic books preached racial intolerance. He argued that the story was designed to show the evils of race prejudice and mob violence, and concluded: "This is one of the most brilliantly written stories that I have ever had the pleasure to publish. I was very proud of it, and to find it being used in such a nefarious way made me quite angry."[20]

He tried to draw a distinction between the "messages" that were deliberately incorporated into the stories and the suggestion on the part of the committee that children might be picking up on other unintentional messages about the use of violence to solve problems. In defending his story "The Orphan," where an abused child kills her father and frames her mother for the murder in order to go live with a kindly aunt, Gaines said: "No message has been spelled out there. We were not trying to prove anything with that story. None of the captions said anything like 'If you are unhappy with your stepmother, shoot her.'"[21]

Trying another tack, Herbert Hannoch, the chief counsel for the committee, asked Gaines: "You think it does them (children) a lot of good to read these things?" to which Gaines replied, "I don't think it does them a bit of good, but I don't think it does them a bit of harm, either." Then Herbert Beaser, Hannoch's assistant, asked Gaines: "Is there any limit you can think of that you would not put in a magazine because you thought a child should not see or read about it?" Gaines said, "My only limits are bounds of good taste, what I consider good taste." With that statement, Gaines set himself up for what would be remembered as the "the most infamous passage of the closely watched hearings." Senator Kefauver joined the fray, holding aloft a Johnny Craig cover from *Crime SuspenStories* and remarking: "This seems to be a man with a bloody ax holding a woman's head up which has been severed from her body. Do you think that is in good taste?" Gaines had little choice but to answer: "Yes, sir; I do, for the cover of a horror comic."[22]

That exchange signaled the turning point in Gaines' testimony. Reidelbach notes, "Public sentiment turned decisively against the young publisher, as television and print news reports widely quoted the severed head exchange."[23] The front page story in the *New York Times* focused on that part of the hearings and carried the headline: "No Harm in Horror, Comics Issuer Says."[24] Gaines, of course, realized things had gone drastically wrong. His biographer notes he "left the courthouse in a state of shock" and "took to his bed for two days with a painfully knotted stomach, most likely psychosomatic."[25]

Gaines received a routine letter from the chairman of the subcommittee, Senator Hendrickson, thanking him for his testimony. He fired back a reply, telling Hendrickson that the approach of the committee was neither impartial nor scientific and his treatment was unfair. He complained that he had been scheduled to testify in the morning, was told he would be the first witness in the afternoon, and was "shunted aside" when Dr. Wertham showed up and forced to wait until 4 p.m. before he testified. He noted his four-minute statement was rudely interrupted, commenting, "I need not tell you that this was far from the kid-glove patience accorded Dr. Wertham—who spoke for hours on end—much of his contribution being obvious gush designed solely to increase the sale of his book." He continued: "The headline-seeking carnival staged by your Committee has given fuel to those in our society who want to tar with the censor's brush. As a result, my business together with the entire comics industry has been severely damaged. Since this was so obviously an objective of your Committee, I trust it will give you some satisfaction."[26]

In a draft of a reply that was never sent, Senator Hendrickson wrote: "For some time I had before me your letter attacking the integrity of the Subcommittee to Investigate Juvenile Delinquency and charging it with bias in its investigation of the comic book industry. Had opportunity offered, I would have replied to it on the floor of the Senate." Hendrickson noted he did not believe Gaines spoke for the entire industry: "While you are falsely charging us with attempting to wreck an industry, other publishers and distributors are giving concrete evidence of the sincerity of their concern for youth by discontinuing the publishing and distribution of objectionable comics."[27]

The speech Hendrickson alluded to was written but never delivered. In that speech, Hendrickson wrote: "Recently, I received a vicious letter from one of the so-called comic book publishers who attacked the integrity of this subcommittee and who charged, among other things, that we are out to destroy the comic book industry."[28] He summarized the testimony Gaines had given at the hearings, concluding: "This is the calm, deliberate thinking of a so-called 'comics' book publisher who attacks a United States Senate Subcommittee that is under mandate to explore and shed light upon possible causes of juvenile delinquency in the United States." Next, Hendrickson took Gaines to task for encouraging youngsters to write to the Subcommittee in defense of comics. Hendrickson wrote: "Now, I do not object to youngsters writing to their Congressmen. In fact, I welcome it. But I do object to his inferring in this bulletin to thousands of young people that Congressional investigations are conducted because 'November is coming.' And I most strongly object to his deliberately misinforming these youngsters as to the opinion about crime comics of authorities in this field, including Doctor Robert H. Felix, Director of our National Institute of Mental Health. It's malicious, Mr. President, to attempt to discredit the integrity of the Senate in the eyes of American youth." Hendrickson concluded the draft of his speech by saying that no attack upon the subcommittee "by a publisher whose own product evoked consternation and revulsion at our hearings" would deter the committee from continuing its investigation into any facet of the media that may be contributing to the "juvenile delinquency scourge."

The bulletin Hendrickson was referring to was *The Fan-Addict Club Bulletin*, which began in November 1953 and was mailed to nine thousand charter members. The bulletin was "friendly, newsy, and innocuous. Births and marriages among EC's staff and freelancers were announced, and a trading post for old EC comics was set up." In the June 1954 issue of the bulletin, mailed to seventeen thousand subscribers, the address of the subcommittee was printed and fans were urged to begin a letter-writing campaign.[29] The *Bulletin* began: "*This is an emergency bulletin!* This is an appeal for action!" In describing the threat, the bulletin noted: "The congressmen get frightened. November is coming! They start an investigation. This wave of hysteria has seriously threatened the very existence of the whole comic magazine industry." That hysteria, the newsletter argued, is caused by a small minority who oppose comics, adding: "The voice of the *majority* . . .

you who buy comics, read them, enjoy them, and are not harmed by them . . . has not been heard!" It urged the readers to write "a nice, polite letter" and encouraged young-sters to get their parents to write or add a P.S. to the letter "as the Senate Subcommittee may not have much respect for the opinions of minors." The appeal was signed "Your grateful editors (for the whole EC Gang)."[30]

The same plea was published as an editorial that ran in the EC line, and the *Bulletin* and editorials generated an estimated three hundred to four hundred letters from chil-dren, teenagers and adults.[31] The subcommittee kept a separate tally of those who men-tioned the EC Fan-Addict Club in their letters. The list compiled included the name of the letter writer, state of origin, their age (if known), whether the letter favored or opposed horror comics, and relevant comments (usually who else in the family or neigh-borhood favored horror comics). On the list were 217 names of people writing in sup-port of horror comics and twenty-seven who were opposed to horror comics, but liked other comics.[32]

The major themes of these letters were that comic books do not cause juvenile de-linquency, that crime comics actually teach children that crime is bad, and that read-ers of comics should decide for themselves what to read. While there is a smattering of postcards in the files, most are long, handwritten letters. In some cases, the parent obviously wrote or typed the letter for the child to sign, and many parents followed the suggestion in the editorial, adding postscripts to their children's letters. Occasionally, a letter would be signed by an entire neighborhood group of children. They were mailed to the subcommittee in two waves. The first wave of letters came in response to the call to action in the *Bulletin* and were from younger readers. The second wave resulted from the editorials in the EC line of comics and included many adult readers.

Many of the letters rephrased the information given in the editorial, quoting the ex-perts and attacking the so-called "do-gooders" who wanted to rid the country of comic books. But other letters were more clearly the opinions of the writers. One young man from Idaho wrote the subcommittee: "Please do not crucify my favorite pass-time [sic] . . . How can anyone truthfully say that reading a magazine actually gives them an urge or an idea to kill? With all of the 'love magazines' being printed, I am surprised we aren't all professional lovers, if that's the case."[33] One mother offered her own explanation for the anti-comic book sentiment: "I think that the only thing they have against these comics is just that they can't get the kids to help around the house because they are too inter-ested in the comics and that the mothers get tired of picking up a bunch of books."[34] A young woman wrote that the comic books were the only entertainment that she and her young daughter could afford, and "the most enjoyment for us is to go to bed early in the evening and read a funny book or two."[35] A thirteen-year-old boy asked the senators to "let the kids read what they want and what they like" and concluded, "Besides, if you do take them off [the stands], you'll have every kid in the country on your back."[36] The impact of the Senate investigation was mentioned in quite a few letters by readers who were no longer able to find the comics they used to read on the newsstands; retailers had removed the controversial titles from their racks.

The letter writing campaign, however, was a lost cause long before the letters even reached the Senate subcommittee. Shortly after the hearings concluded in June 1954, the comic book publishers set to work on a self-regulatory code they hoped would appease critics and derail efforts to get legislation passed to regulate comic book content. Gaines may have inadvertently set this chain of events into motion as well. In May, he sent out a letter to the publishers urging them to organize and launch a public relations campaign to counter the bad publicity comic books were receiving and suggested involving the American Civil Liberties Union in the industry's battle against censorship. He began to meet individually with each publisher. The comic book business was highly competitive, and the men who ran it were not friends with one another, but they saw the wisdom of what Gaines was proposing and agreed to a meeting.[37]

Gaines' idea was to hire experts in the field of juvenile delinquency, and he had in mind the husband and wife research team of Sheldon and Eleanor Glueck of Harvard. They published an important study in the 1930s, *One Thousand Juvenile Delinquents*. In it they suggested that family disintegration was the most important factor in studying juvenile delinquency. Their two postwar works, *Unraveling Juvenile Delinquency* and *Delinquents in the Making*, develop their theories about family environment, rather than external influences, as a cause of delinquency.[38]

It was clear from the Senate subcommittee hearings that little scientific research had been done on the effects of comic book reading on children. Gaines believed that a research study done by the Gluecks would provide a definitive answer to the question of effects, vindicate the comic book industry, and business could continue as usual. But the other publishers were not interested in what they perceived as a long-term solution. They desired more immediate action in order to stem the tide of negative public opinion. Their solution, modeled on what had worked for other media, especially the film industry, was to adopt a code. While the exact wording of the code would need to be worked out, the consensus was that the horror and terror books would have to be sacrificed as proof that the industry meant business. Gaines would note years later:

> And it was always an ironic thing to me that I was the guy who started the damn association and they turned around and the first thing they did was ban the words weird, horror and terror from any comic magazine . . . those were my three big words.[39]

At the organizational meeting of the Comics Magazine Association of America August 17, 1954, the members of the new association heard a report on the activities of the Special Committee on Organization, headed by John Goldwater of Archie Comics. That special committee recommended the association be empowered to establish and enforce a code governing the industry in editorial and advertising content of comics magazines, that a symbol or seal be designed, and that a public relations campaign be undertaken to inform the public, the wholesalers and the newsstand dealers about the new steps taken for self-regulation. A code had already been drafted by the Special Committee but would not be made public until the association selected a "czar" to oversee its enforcement.[40]

When Fredric Wertham turned down the job, the association selected judge Charles F. Murphy and set the announcement for September 16, 1954. Murphy would take charge October 1, and the publishers promised a code would be in place by November 15th.[41] Two days earlier, knowing the formation of the CMAA would mean the end of his EC horror comics, Gaines announced he was discontinuing his line of comics "because this seems to be what American parents want." In reality, Gaines was told by his wholesalers that they simply would not handle the controversial EC horror titles any longer. To take their place, Gaines introduced seven titles he labeled his "New Direction" comics. They were *Aces High*, *Extra!*, *Impact*, *Piracy*, *Valor*, *MD*, and *Psychoanalysis*.[42]

Initially, Gaines refused to join the comics association. He was not the only hold-out. In a statement issued after the CMAA was formed, Dell Comics publisher George Delacorte noted that his line of comics had always been above reproach and he had no desire for the Dell Comics name "to be used as an umbrella for some of the inferior products" available. Gilbertson, publishers of *Classics Illustrated* comics, maintained that their publications were not really comic books, but adaptations of literary classics. The distributors, however, aware of Gaines' notoriety, refused to handle the EC line without the "Seal of Approval" on the cover, and Gaines joined the association.

The relationship was a stormy and short-lived one, Gaines was clearly unhappy with the way the association was being run. He met with several of the publishers individually, but they were apparently unwilling to buck the association. He pushed for greater accountability on the part of the association; the association agreed to meet more frequently "so members could be apprised of the activities of the association."[43] He publicly attacked the association, despite having an agreement with the CMAA not to do so.[44]

In August 1955, Lyle Stuart wrote a letter to James Bobo, who was currently serving as general counsel to the Senate Subcommittee to Investigate Juvenile Delinquency, asking the senators to investigate the CMAA, claiming the "autocratic, self-appointed group has subverted the good intentions of the Kefauver Committee into a monopolistic instrument" and suggesting that the association was working to destroy small publishers. Stuart told Bobo in his letter that there were publishers willing to testify about what the association had done to squeeze them out of business. The letter to Bobo was inspired, in part, by the latest dispute between Gaines and the CMAA reviewers. Stuart explained:

> Just today we had a story turned down. It was a harmless story for a science-fiction magazine. But in the story an automaton thinks and talks. Nobody is hurt. There is no violence. But the story was turned down because to suggest that an automaton can think is contrary to Judge Murphy's religious beliefs that only man was granted a soul and the ability to think by his Creator.
>
> The complete story was turned down. And this was a substitute story for another which was turned down. Thus, the book has been delayed to the point where we cannot bill our advertisers for the full rate because of the delay . . . and our art and editorial costs now make even a break-even sale seem unlikely.[45]

Another version of the story is that the substitute story, "Judgment Day," which was a morality tale about bigotry on other planets, featured a black astronaut with sweat on his brow. The code enforcer demanded the sweat be removed, apparently believing the depiction could constitute a violation of the code's prohibition against ridicule or attack on any racial group. Gaines refused, printed the story anyway, and promptly announced he was discontinuing all his comic books. He would instead turn all his attention to *MAD*, which, since it was now published in a magazine format, was exempt from the scrutiny of the CMAA.[46] The association included this terse comment in its minutes of

December 14, 1955: "On motion by Mr. Liebowitz [Jack Liebowitz of DC Comics], it was decided to accept the oral resignation of Entertaining Comics, made on Oct. 25, 1955, and the executive secretary was instructed to notify this firm of this decision."[47] The battle over EC Comics was officially ended.

NOTES

1. Maria Reidelbach, *Completely MAD: A History of the Comic Book and Magazine* (Boston: Little, Brown, 1991), 10–12.
2. Mike Benton, *Horror Comics: The Illustrated History* (Dallas, TX: Taylor Publishing, 1991), 9.
3. Frank Jacobs, *The Mad World of William Gaines* (Secaucus, NJ: Lyle Stuart, 1972), 64, 73.
4. Mike Benton, *Superhero Comics of the Golden Age: An Illustrated History* (Dallas, TX: Taylor Publishing, 1992), 17; Reidelbach, *Completely MAD*, 6.
5. Harvey Kurtzman, *From Aargh to Zap: Harvey Kurtzman's Visual History of the Comics* (New York: Prentice Hall, 1991), 28.
6. Kurtzman, *From Aargh to Zap*, 25.
7. Senate Subcommittee to Investigate Juvenile Delinquency, Juvenile Delinquency (Comic Books): Hearings before the Senate Subcommittee to Investigate Juvenile Delinquency, 83rd Cong., 2d sess., 21–22 April and 4 June 1954, 2.
8. "Tentative Proposed Witness List," 16 April 1954, Records of the Subcommittee to Investigate Juvenile Delinquency, Committee on the Judiciary, 1953–1961, Box 171, National Archives, Washington, D.C.
9. Reidelbach, *Completely MAD*, 26; Jacobs, *The Mad World*, 105–6.
10. Subpoena for William Gaines, Records of the Subcommittee to Investigate Juvenile Delinquency, Box 92, National Archives.
11. Background statements, Records of the Senate Subcommittee to Investigate Juvenile Delinquency, Box 170, National Archives.
12. Pamphlet, "Depravity for Children—10 Cents a Copy?" from the *Hartford Courant*, Records of the Subcommittee to Investigate Juvenile Delinquency, Box 167, National Archives.
13. Charles L. Towne, "Hartford Is Aroused by Comic Book Expose," *Editor & Publisher*, 10 April 1954, 11.
14. Jacobs, *The Mad World*, 104–15.
15. Hearings, Juvenile Delinquency (Comic Books), 58–59.
16. Joseph Bruce Gorman, *Kefauver: A Political Biography* (New York: Oxford University Press, 1971), 176.
17. Hearings, Juvenile Delinquency (Comic Books), 95.
18. Jacobs, *The Mad World*, 107.
19. Hearings, Juvenile Delinquency (Comic Books), 98.
20. Hearings, Juvenile Delinquency (Comic Books), 99.
21. Hearings, Juvenile Delinquency (Comic Books), 101.
22. Hearings, Juvenile Delinquency (Comic Books), 109.
23. Reidelbach, *Completely MAD*, 28.
24. Peter Kihss, "No Harm in Horror, Comics Issuer Says," *New York Times*, April 22, 1954, A1.
25. Jacobs, *The Mad World*, 110.
26. William Gaines to Robert Hendrickson, 21 May 1954, Records of the Subcommittee to Investigate Juvenile Delinquency, Box 168, National Archives.
27. Draft of letter from Robert Hendrickson to William Gaines (not sent), undated, Records of the Senate Subcommittee to Investigate Juvenile Delinquency, Box 168, National Archives.
28. This remark and the quotations from it that follow may be found in Robert Hendrickson, draft of speech to the Senate (not delivered), July 7, 1954, Robert Hendrickson Papers, Box 74, Folder titled "U.S. Senate

Committee: Judiciary Subcommittee to Investigate Juvenile Delinquency, Reports, Misc.," Syracuse University Library, Syracuse, NY.

29. Reidelbach, *Completely MAD*, 24, 28.

30. The *National E.C. Fan-Addict Club Bulletin*, No. 3, June 1954, Records of the Senate Subcommittee to Investigate Juvenile Delinquency, Box 168, National Archives.

31. Robert Hendrickson to Mrs. Mario Levi, September 29, 1954, Records of the Senate Subcommittee to Investigate Juvenile Delinquency, Box 169, National Archives.

32. "Survey of E.C. Fan-Addict Club Letters," undated, Records of the Senate Subcommittee to Investigate Juvenile Delinquency, Box 211, National Archives.

33. James Beard to Senate Subcommittee, September 26, 1954, Records of the Senate Subcommittee to Investigate Juvenile Delinquency, Box 169, National Archives.

34. Mrs. L. D. Thomas to Senate Subcommittee, September 23, 1954, Records of the Senate Subcommittee to Investigate Juvenile Delinquency, Box 169, National Archives.

35. Ruth Scheffer to Senate Subcommittee, September 8, 1954, Records of the Senate Subcommittee to Investigate Juvenile Delinquency, Box 169, National Archives.

36. Kenneth White to Senate Subcommittee, July 7, 1954, Records of the Senate Subcommittee to Investigate Juvenile Delinquency, Box 169, National Archives.

37. Lyle Stuart, remarks at William Gaines' memorial service, May 5, 1992, transcribed by John Tebbel.

38. Gilbert, *Cycle of Outrage*, 132–33.

39. William Gaines, interview by John Tebbel, New York City, August 4, 1986.

40. Minutes of the organizational meeting of the Comics Magazine Association of America, 17 August 1954, CMAA files.

41. Gilbert, *Cycle of Outrage*, 107; *New York Times*, September 17, 1954, A1.

42. Jacobs, *The Mad World*, 112–13; Reidelbach, *Completely MAD*, 30.

43. Minutes of a special meeting, 26 April 1955, CMAA files.

44. Minutes of Board of Directors meeting, June 23, 1955, CMAA files.

45. Lyle Stuart to James H. Bobo, 11 August 1955, Records of the Senate Subcommittee to Investigate Juvenile Delinquency, Box 168, National Archives.

46. Reidelbach, *Completely MAD*, 34–35.

47. Minutes of Board of Directors of CMAA, December 14, 1955, CMAA files.

The Comics Debates Internationally

JOHN A. LENT

There are a number of ancestors of the comic book, including nineteenth-century penny dreadfuls in England and the pulps about the same time in the United States. Almost from the beginning of American comic strips, before the turn of the twentieth century, the funnies were reprinted as books. They continued in this form through the 1930s, although some significant changes came about during that decade.

First, some new comics of the 1930s were done as magazines rather than books, running about thirty-two pages and fronted with a soft cover. In 1933, Eastern Color Printing Company of New York, at the urging of Max Gaines and Harry Wildenburg, published *Funnies on Parade* in this format. A thirty-two-page reprint of color comic strips, *Funnies on Parade* was a Proctor and Gamble giveaway. Gaines compiled two other giveaway collections and one meant to be sold, all three made up of newspaper strips and in the magazine style.

A second innovation that came out of the 1930s was the use of new material in comic books. In 1935, Major Malcolm Wheeler-Nicholson published *New Fun*, consisting of stories written specifically for that title. The next year, William Cook and John Mahon, through their Comics Magazine Company, brought out three titles dependent on original work. Sensing that a market for new comics stories was developing, Harry "A" Chesler opened his art shops to produce material for both Nicholson and Cook-Mahon.

A third breakthrough of the 1930s was the forging of the first single-theme comic book, which resulted when Nicholson and Harry Donenfeld formed Detective Comics Inc. and brought out a title by that name in 1937. Nicholson envisioned yet another publishing venture, *Action Comics*, but before its first number appeared in mid-1938, Donenfeld had forced him out. *Action Comics* No. 1 accounted for the fourth phenomenon of the decade, the advent of the superhero in the form of "Superman." As Jerry Robinson, one of the original Batman artists and the creator of the character "Joker," wrote, "The superhero—and the supervillain with the addition of the Joker—became the essential narrative framework for the next half century and the present."[1]

In the 1940s, other genres, such as jungle, war, and funny animal, debuted. By 1942, the first crime comic books had appeared, with Lev Gleason's *Crime Does Not Pay* heading

Reprinted by permission and adapted from John A. Lent, ed. "Introduction" to *Pulp Demons: International Dimensions of the Postwar Anti-Comics Campaign* (Fairleigh Dickinson University Press, 1999), 9–28.

the list. When superheroes lost some of their favor in the post–World War II era, crime, as well as romance, dominated comics sales. The earliest horror comic book, *Adventures into the Unknown*, was released in 1948 by the American Comics Group, and two years later, Bill Gaines and Al Feldstein made their Entertaining Comics the home of some of the grimmest horror comics and the chief target of anti-comics crusaders. Gaines first converted *Crime Patrol* into *Crypt of Terror* and after its success, he launched *The Vault of Horror* and *The Haunt of Fear*. These and most crime and horror comics were banned after the 1954 Kefauver hearings and subsequent Comic Book Code.

In neighboring Canada, American comics dominated to the extent that Canadian publishing efforts were usually thwarted. The only letups occurred when the Canadian government stepped in, usually for economic reasons. The first instance of such action was in December 1940, when the War Exchange Conservation Act was passed. Aimed at countries outside the sterling bloc, the act restricted the importation of nonessentials (including comic books) from the United States.[2] With lessened competition, Canadian publishers, by early 1941, released indigenous titles such as *Better Comics* by Maple Leaf and *Robin Hood and Company* by Anglo-American Publishing. Others, usually of the funny or hero genres, quickly followed in what was termed Canada's golden age of comics, 1942–46.

The war's end hastened the return of United States comics, the results being that Canadian comics companies folded and their artists left for the United States in search of work. Some publishers continued to reprint American comic books, and when an economic crisis put an embargo on their importation in 1947, these companies purchased the four-color mats from the Americans and paid a fee according to how many copies they printed.

Both U.S. and Canadian comic books came in for criticism in the mid-1940s as insidious threats to Canadian children. In 1948, a mass movement of parents and community and church groups, led by Eleanor Grey of the Victoria and District Parent Teacher Council and Member of Parliament E. Davie Fulton, pushed for the banning of comics. The result was passage of Bill 10 which, along with relaxation of the Foreign Exchange Conservation Act and a resultant deluge of American comics, sealed the fate of the Canadian comics industry.[3] One publisher, William Zimmerman, of Superior Publishing, lasted until 1956, although he issued his last horror comic the year before.

Britain's first comics magazines date to 1874 and 1884, with the publication of *Funny Folks* and *Ally Sloper's Half Holiday*, respectively. Other titles such as *Illustrated Bits* and *Comic Cuts* followed in style and form, using a mixture of cartoons, strips, and prose.[4] By the early twentieth century, a backlash against these tabloids set in; they were blamed for debasing culture and lowering literacy.

Throughout the 1920s, and most of the 1930s, Amalgamated Press led the comics field as it issued a flood of children's titles; but in the late 1930s, DC Thomson challenged Amalgamated's dominancy with two successful comics, *The Dandy* in 1937, and *The Beano* in 1938. The two companies engaged in a fierce circulation war until the 1950s, unhampered by U.S. comics which usually were not imported because of cultural prejudice.[5] In 1950, the first successful adventure comic book, *The Eagle*, made that genre commercially viable for the first time, and a number of imitations followed.[6]

Although not prevalent in Britain, by 1952, American comic books had nevertheless struck fear in the minds of some Britishers; and in 1955, they were banned by law, not permitted in again until four years later. During that time, British comic books reached a peak that they were never to achieve again after 1960, partly because of the competition for audience given television and other new media, partly because some genres, such as adventure which depended on World War II for themes, were passé by the 1970s. As in the United States, British comics were later rejuvenated.[7]

Comics in the form of strips have a long history in Germany, dating to at least 1865, when "Max und Moritz" was published in *Münchener Bilderbogen*. Also appearing in the late nineteenth century were humor and children's picture books, notable examples being *Struwwelpeter* and *Kasperlgraf*. Over the years, other comics-like materials, such as e.o. plauen's (Erich Ohser) pantomine strip of 1935, *Vater und Sohn*, were popular, but generally, the comics were not thought to be an important medium in Germany.[8]

When American soldiers occupied Germany at the end of World War II, comics rushed in, at first carried by the GIs, and rather quickly, reprinted by West German publishing houses. By the end of the 1940s, with considerable concern among Germans about borrowings from U.S. comic books, efforts were made to establish an indigenous industry. Munich publisher Rolf Kauka took famous heroes from popular books—such as Till Eulenspiegel, Baron Münchhausen, and Reineke Fuchs—dressed them in contemporary outfits, put word balloons in their mouths, and issued them as the comic series Fix und Foxi, successful to this day. At the same time, other books came out, including Reinhold Escher's *Mecki*, Carl Fischer's *Oskar*, and Manfred Schmidt's *Nick Knatterton*.[9]

Writing about the genesis of comic-picture books, which occurred about 1970, Dolle-Weinkauff said they resulted because of

> a weakening of basic educational reservations. The picture book author's successful confrontation with comics started at the time when the negative assessments in the West German public began to change. The fact that the comics in the guise of picture books rank with the most innovative examples of the genre is connected with the creative way in which many of the authors saw themselves; they did not care for a mere continuation of famous models.[10]

Dolle-Weinkauff contended that many comic artists in Germany dealt with characteristics of the art form ironically, in playful tones.[11]

Like those of the United States, Australian comic books evolved from newspapers strips, and strangely enough, at about the same time. The first such local comic book was the shortlived *Fatty Finnis Weekly*, in 1934. Two years later, the *Melbourne Herald* packaged American strips in a book called *Wags*; most early comic books contained only U.S. funnies.

The dumping of foreign comics in Australia ended rather quickly, after a series of events, partly prompted by Senator D. Cameron's 1939 presentation in Parliament about the plight of local artists. That year, the government began enforcing the Australian Industries Preservation Act (1906–1937), the Customs Tariff (1901–1936), and the Import Licensing regulation that controlled the amount of U.S. dollars that could be spent. From July 1940, the import of U.S. comics was banned in Australia.

All this, and the imposition of World War II economic sanctions, proved fortuitous for the development of Australian comic books. As John Ryan wrote, "It can be fairly said that had there not been a war there would never have been a local comic book industry."[12] First to publish original Australian comics was the NSW Bookstall Company, which started with *Jimmy Rodney on Secret Service*. Will Donald and Terry Powis, along with Edward Brodie-Mack, were responsible for the company's first two dozen comic books. Another regular publisher of wartime comics was Frank Johnson Publications. Most books were humor-filled; no adventure tradition yet existed.

In the postwar boom, foreign comics were allowed entry, and although the Australian Journalists Association and Black and White Artists' Club continued to agitate against imported comic books, there was nothing the government felt it could do.

By the early 1950s, comics were under scrutiny again, as some people objected to a number of books with anti-Communist slants, brought about by the Korean War and McCarthyism in the United States, and as a prominent cartoonist was convicted of rape and sentenced to death (commuted to fourteen years). The trial of Len Lawson in July 1954 attracted much unfavorable attention in the press, which highlighted that he was the comics artist who filled pages with violence and bosomy heroines. As a result, the Queensland Literature Board of Review—which in its first nine months banned forty-five publications, one-third of which were comic books—stopped Lawson's *The Lone Avenger*.

Comic books came to Asia mainly after World War II. In the Philippines, *Hulakhak Komiks* was first, in 1946, but it died after only ten issues. It took a publisher-artist team responsible for launching the country's first comic strip in 1928 to make a success of comic books. Ramon Roces, owner of a chain of magazines, persuaded Antonio Velasquez, creator of the first strip, "Kenkoy," to join him in starting Ace Publications; their first comic book was *Pilipino Komiks*, in 1947. In rapid succession, Ace Publications put out four other titles and for the next fifteen years led the *komiks* industry. The Philippines enjoyed its heyday in the 1950s, but it dimmed briefly before the industry had a renaissance in the early 1960s when other companies producing *komiks* were started.[13]

Taiwan's golden age of comics was also the 1950s, even though the first indigenous (as opposed to Japanese) comic book, *Hsun Hsien Chi* (Finding Paradise) did not appear until 1953. Cartoonists such as Yeh Hung-chia, Niu Ko, Liang Chung-ming, Chen Hai-hung, and Tsai Chih-chung created mostly adventure stories that kept comic books near the top of periodicals in circulation. In both Taiwan and South Korea, early comic book cartoonists were individuals already doing newspaper and magazine political cartoons and comic strips.

As happened in other countries, the euphoric period did not last long; in fact, the Taiwanese comic book industry almost dried up as key cartoonists left the profession when they could not cope with the general diminishment of quality and the censorship policies of the government. Cartooning's dismal period was also attributable to the competition for audiences intensified by the advent of television and the stronger control enforced by the government's National Institute for Compilation and Translation.[14]

Children's comic books were already popular, although irregularly published, in South Korea during the late 1940s. They did not gain a stable footing until after the Korean War, although some sixteen-page books by Kim Yong Whan (*Kojubu Tam Jung*, Detective Kojubu) and Shin Dong Hun (*Ung Ter Ri Mok Gong So*, Phony Carpenter) entertained Koreans during the conflict. Other titles served as propaganda for the South Korean military. In the post–Korean War era, comic books had a brief boom period with a few books of hundreds of pages published, usually made up of stories compiled from Korean children's magazines or from foreign sources. After a few years, children's comics lost some of their popularity and at that point, the industry switched from book store sales to rental shops.[15]

Japan's comics tradition is long, with cartoon magazines prominent in the late nineteenth century and the first serialized comic strip (Rakuten Kitazawa's *Tagosaku to Mokube no Tokyo Kembutsu*, Tagosaku and Mokube Sightseeing in Tokyo) appearing in 1902. By the 1920s, a form of comic book, printed sometimes in color and on pulp paper, was published monthly. These lasted into World War II.

In the postwar period, some children's comics reappeared, and small-scale publishing companies began issuing "red book" comics—inexpensive, with red-ink covers, printed on rough paper and sold in the streets. Also during this time, Osamu Tezuka began his career which would revolutionize manga. Tezuka applied cinematic effects in his books, a result being that some reached 500, even 1,000, pages.

Perhaps the severe competition among children's magazines in the mid-1950s helped create a better market for comic books. To improve their circulation, the magazines began giving their subscribers two or three small comic books. Obviously, this gimmick benefited manga, introducing them to thousands of children who previously perhaps had not given them much thought. The payoff was apparent by 1966, when *Shonen*, the first weekly devoted to comics, topped the one million circulation mark.[16]

COMMONALITIES OF ANTI-COMICS CAMPAIGNS

When reactions against comics set in during the late 1940s and early 1950s, the countries involved experienced similar phenomena—the issues were basically the same, as were the players, methods of handling the controversies, and solutions. Without trying to be exhaustive or equally representative of each country's situation, a few examples are offered.

The major issue, of course, dealt with what were perceived as the negative impacts of comics on children, the effects already discussed in this chapter. For the most part, the fear related to American comic books, although indigenous ones also came in for criticism.

Eighty percent of the comics circulated in Australia originated in the United States. They were described as un-Australian in speech and lifestyle and "responsible also, it was widely feared, for young readers being conditioned to regard violent crime as acceptable, as well as to approve of other delinquent activities."[17] As early as 1947, the Australian novelist Dal Stivins blasted these comics as a "narcotic, a depressant" which helps keep the majority of people in slavery, drugged from one day's work to another.[18] Certain British, German, and Canadian factions also were repulsed by American comics.

An article in Britain's *Picture Post* in 1952 used the same tact evident elsewhere: equating comic books to a narcotic:

These books depend on the administration of violent shocks to the nervous system, and just as the drug addict must progressively increase the dose to obtain the same effect, so, as sensibilities become dulled by the repetition of a particular kind of brutal act, the degree of violence must of necessity increase.[19]

Often, odd alliances made up the anti-comics factions. In Australia, civil liberties groups and commercial interests combined to support comics against the Communist Party, Catholic Church, women's groups, and educators, who, for various reasons, attempted to have the importation of comics banned. Some participants in the controversy were caught in a double bind: The Communist Party had a difficult time determining the proper line on comics, if it was to maintain its claim of representing the working class, and a major literary magazine, *Meanjin*, felt uncomfortable about the use of censorship but still called for control.[20] Similarly in Britain, the Communist Party, which along with parents, teachers, and church groups, played a major role in the crusade against comic books, had to revamp its strategy, especially when enthusiasm for the movement waned temporarily upon revelation of the party's participation. In late 1953, the CP became part of a more effective and less political-looking organization, the "Comics" Campaign Council.

The players in the controversy sometimes took their lead from, or had direct connections with, Wertham in the United States. Fulton and Grey, Canada's chief opponents of comics, had contact with the American psychiatrist, and Fulton appeared before the 1954 Kefauver committee. George Pumphrey and Peter Mauger, both at the forefront of the British campaign, referred to Wertham's work in reviews, speeches, and a booklet.[21] Gosta von Uexküll of Germany felt there was an "antidote" for crime, violence, and corruption in the person of Wertham. Wertham's *Seduction of the Innocent* was also a factor in raising the issue in Australia.

Some of the methods used to propagandize or otherwise handle the issues changed little from one country to another. In Britain and Australia, radio debates were set up to discuss the comics issues, similar to the 1948 Town Meeting of the Air in the United States. The British broadcast in 1953 featured the psychologist Dr. Alex Comfort, the children's author Enid Blyton, and others on the topic of horror comics, while the much earlier 1949 Australian Broadcasting Corporation debate pitted cartoonists Stan Cross and Jim Russell against the educator Donald McLean and psychiatrist Dr. John McGeorge on the subject, "Comic Strips—Good or Bad?" In the latter debate, all participants defended comic strips but labeled comic "booklets" the principal moral and social threat. Cross echoed the fears of parents when he said "the pernicious little gaudy booklets" emanated from big cities "where viciousness and vice are normal facts of life, and where, therefore, armed banditry and brutal brawling are acceptable factors in its fictional representation."[22]

Almost every country included in these chapters handled the comics controversy through government investigations and hearings. In the United States, the hearings occurred in April and June 1954, when the Senate Subcommittee on Juvenile Delinquency heard testimony about crime and horror comics; in its opening statement, the committee (often called the Kefauver Committee) indicated that it did not plan to be a censoring body. The committee was designed to meet its public duty to say something about the comics while, at the same time, protecting the medium in a free enterprise system. The final report called for self-regulation.

Like their counterparts in the United States, Canadian senators in the 1949 hearings showed sympathy for the businessman's position as long as the debate concentrated on intangibles such as freedom of speech and psychology. However, when William Zimmerman of Superior Comics, present to defend crime comics, showed examples, he sealed the fate of Bill 10 which outlawed crime and horror comics. Afterwards,

Zimmerman defied Bill 10, starting a racy crime comic book and acquiring rights to Bill Gaines's line of New Trend EC Comics.[23] The British Parliament acted similarly, passing a law, The Children's and Young Persons (Harmful Publications) Act (1944), which banned the importing or reprinting of crime and horror comics.[24]

Like the Americans, the Germans set up Voluntary Self Control for Serial Pictures after government investigations and action; the Australians, Koreans, Taiwanese, and Filipinos also instituted self-censorship, under varying circumstances and degrees of enforcement. Australian self-censorship, implemented by the largest distributor, Gordon & Gotch, and by comics publishers, was particularly harsh, As Ryan wrote, "The censorship imposed by Gordon & Gotch was similar to moves which saw the establishment of the Comics Code Authority in the U.S."[25] Starting with a local comic book, *The Scorpion*, the censors painted guns out of cowboys' hands, leaving the preposterous scene where "Indians were dropping in their tracks because the cowboys were pointing fingers at them," or rearranged heroes' positions when they held women in a "too suggestive and provocative manner."[26] Horwitz Publications, mainly a reprinter of U.S. comics in the early 1950s and producer of Australian titles at the end of the decade, followed the U.S. lead, in March 1954, issuing a *Code of Publishing Ethics* to all editors, artists, and authors. As Ryan explained:

> The Code had a particular reference to comics and spelled out the details of what could not be done. Plots had to be told simply in a way not to confuse even the youngest reader as to motive; sex was out in any shape or form; grammar had to be faultless; blasphemy, reference to the Deity, and profanity or suggested profanity was forbidden . . . ; at no time could a hero break a law, no matter how minor. Like its U.S. counterparts, Horwitz's Code was aimed at producing pap for the lowest common denominator.[27]

Korean industry officials, anticipating government intervention, created a self-regulatory body, but it was soon supplanted by one established by ministerial action. In Taiwan, the government was blamed for retarding comics with its stringent censorship policies, while in Japan, public outcries never moved the government and seldom shook the industry to clamp down on comic books. The Philippine situation was much like that of the United States, in that self-regulation and code-writing first started within an individual comics company and then an industry association.

NOTES

1. Jerry Robinson, *Introduction to Comic Books and Comic Strips in the United States: An International Bibliography*, John A. Lent, comp. (Westport, Conn.: Greenwood Press, 1994), xxiv.

2. John Bell, ed., *Canuck Comics* (Montreal: Matrix, 1986), 23.

3. Ibid., 33.

4. Roger Sabin, *Comics, Comix and Graphic Novels* (London: Phaidon, 1996), 15.

5. Ibid.

6. Ibid., 38.

7. Ibid., 131.

8. Bernd Dolle-Weinkauff, "German Contributions to 'Literature in Pictures,'" in *The Grandchildren of Max and Moritz: Comics and Cartoons Made in Germany* (Frankfurt: German Publishers and Booksellers Association, 1990), 1–2.

9. Ibid., 3.

10. Ibid., 4.

11. Ibid.

12. John Ryan, *Panel by Panel: An Illustrated History of Australian Comics* (Melbourne: Cassell, 1979), 154.

13. Cynthia Roxas and Joaquin Arevalo, Jr., *A History of Komiks of the Philippines and Other Countries* (Quezon City: Islas Filipioas, 1985), 11–12, 20–21. See also, John A. Lent, "Komiks: National Book of the Philippines," *Comics Journal*, May 1989, 79–84; John A. Lent, "Southeast Asian Cartooning: Comics in Philippines, Singapore and Indonesia," *Asian Culture*, Winter 1993, 11–23.

14. See John A. Lent, "The Renaissance of Taiwan's Cartoon Arts," *Asian Culture*, Spring 1993, 1–17.

15. See John A. Lent, "Korean Cartooning: Historical and Contemporary Perspectives," *Korean Culture*, Spring 1995, 8–19.

16. John A. Lent, "Japanese Comics," in *Handbook of Japanese Popular Culture*, Richard Gid Powers and Hidetoshi Kato, eds. (Westport, Conn.: Greenwood Press. 1989, 229–30); see also Frederik Schodt, *Manga! Manga! The World of Japanese Comics* (Tokyo: Kodansha, 1983).

17. Vane Lindesay, *Drawing from Life* (Sydney: State Library of New South Wales, 1994), 37.

18. Graeme Osborne and Glen Lewis, *Communication Traditions in 20th Century Australia* (Melbourne: Oxford University Press, 1995), 88.

19. Quoted in Sabin, *Comics, Comix and Graphic Novels*, 68.

20. Osborne and Lewis, *Communication Traditions*, 99.

21. Martin Barker, *A Haunt of Fears* (London: Pluto Press, 1984), 30, 82.

22. Lindesay, *Drawing from Life*, 38.

23. Bell, *Canuck Comics*, 32–33.

24. Sabin, *Comics, Comix and Graphic Novels*, 68.

25. Ryan, *Panel by Panel*, 206.

26. Ibid., 208.

27. Ibid., 209.

The Definition of the Superhero

PETER COOGAN

Superhero. A heroic character with a selfless, pro-social mission; with superpowers—extraordinary abilities, advanced technology, or highly developed physical, mental, or mystical skills; who has a superhero identity embodied in a codename and iconic costume, which typically express his biography, character, powers, or origin (transformation from ordinary person to superhero); and who is generically distinct, i.e. can be distinguished from characters of related genres (fantasy, science fiction, detective, etc.) by a preponderance of generic conventions. Often superheroes have dual identities, the ordinary one of which is usually a closely guarded secret.

In his 1952 ruling that Wonder Man copied and infringed upon Superman, Judge Learned Hand provided a succinct definition for the superhero. The characteristics of mission, powers, and identity are central to Hand's determination that Wonder Man copied Superman.

MISSION

Judge Learned Hand referred to both Superman and Wonder Man as "champion[s] of the oppressed" who combat "evil and injustice," thus summing up the heart of the superhero's mission. The superhero's mission is pro-social and selfless, which means that his fight against evil must fit in with the existing, professed mores of society and must not be intended to benefit or further his own agenda.

The mission convention is essential to the superhero genre because someone who does not act selflessly to aid others in times of need is not heroic and therefore not a hero. But it is not unique to the genre. Superman's mission is to be a "champion of the oppressed . . . sworn to devote his existence to helping those in need," i.e. to "benefit mankind" (Siegel, *Action Comics* #1 June 1938, 1). This mission is no different from that of the pulp mystery man Doc Savage, whose "purpose was to go here and there, from one end of the world to another, looking for excitement and adventure, striving to help those

Reprinted by permission from Peter Coogan, *Superhero: The Secret Origin of a Genre* (Monkeybrain Books, 2006), 30–60.

who needed help, punishing those who deserved it" (Robeson, *Man of Bronze* 1964, 4). Nor does Superman's mission differ materially from the missions of the dime novel or pulp and radio heroes of the late nineteenth and early twentieth centuries.[1] Without this mission, a superhero would be merely an extraordinarily helpful individual in a crisis (like Hugo Hercules, the eponymous superstrong hero of J. Kroener's 1904–05 comic strip, who might set a train back on the tracks or lift an elephant so that a lady could pick up her handkerchief), someone who gains personally from his powers (like Hugo Danner, the superpowered protagonist of Philip Wylie's 1930 novel *Gladiator*, who uses his super-strength to earn a living as a circus strongman), or a supervillain (if he pursued his interests at the legal, economic, or moral expense of others, like Dr. Hugo Strange, an early foe of Batman).

POWERS

Superpowers are one of the most identifiable elements of the superhero genre. Hand identifies Superman and Wonder Man as having "miraculous strength and speed" and being "wholly impervious" to harm. He cites instances when they each crush guns in their hands, rip open steel doors, stop bullets, and leap around the buildings of modern cities. He notes that each is designated the "strongest man in the world." These abilities are the heroes' powers—or superpowers, to emphasize the exaggeration inherent in the superhero genre—and they are the first area of real difference between Superman and his pulp and science fiction predecessors. Each of Superman's powers amplifies the abilities of the science fiction supermen who came before him. Hugo Danner in *The Gladiator* was fairly bulletproof and had super-strength and super-speed. In the first issue of *Action Comics*, Superman displays super-strength, super-speed, super-leaping, and invulnerability at only slightly greater levels than Danner does. Over time, though, Superman's powers went far beyond merely exaggerating the strength, speed, and toughness of ordinary human beings as SF supermen's powers had done.

IDENTITY

The identity element comprises the codename and the costume, with the secret identity being a customary counterpart to the codename. Hand notes that *Action Comics* and *Wonder Comics* portray characters with heroic identities—Superman and Wonder Man—who conceal "skintight acrobatic costume[s]" beneath "ordinary clothing." Hand here identifies the two elements that make up the identity convention of the superhero: the heroic codename and the costume. The identity convention most clearly marks the superhero as different from his predecessors. Characters like the Scarlet Pimpernel and Zorro established both the heroic and the secret identities that were to become hallmarks of superheroes. However, the heroic identities of these characters do not firmly externalize either their alter ego's inner character or biography. The Scarlet Pimpernel does not resemble the little roadside flower whose name he takes, except perhaps in remaining unnoticed in his Percy Blakeney identity; Zorro does not resemble the fox whose Spanish name he has taken, except perhaps in his ability to escape his pursuers. These minimal connections between heroic codename and character are not foregrounded in the hero's adventures, but those adventures did serve as models for the creators of superheroes in their portrayals of their heroes' foppish alter egos.

The connection of name to inner character or biography came with pulp mystery men like the Shadow and Doc Savage. The Shadow is a shadowy presence behind events, not directly seen by his enemies or even his agents; thus his name expresses his character. Doc Savage's name combines the twin thrusts of childhood tutelage by scientists—the skill and rationality of a doctor and the strength and fighting ability of a wild savage, thus embodying his biography. The heroic identities of Superman and Batman operate in this fashion. Superman is a super man who represents the best humanity can hope to achieve; his codename expresses his inner character. The Batman identity was inspired by Bruce Wayne's encounter with a bat while he was seeking a disguise able to strike terror into the hearts of criminals; his codename embodies his biography.

COSTUME

The difference between Superman and earlier figures such as the Shadow or Doc Savage lies in the element of identity central to the superhero, the costume. Although Superman was not the first costumed hero, his costume marks a clear and striking departure from those of the pulp heroes. A pulp hero's costume does not emblematize the character's identity. The slouch hat, black cloak, and red scarf of the Shadow or the mask and fangs of the Spider disguise their faces but do not proclaim their identities. Superman's costume does, particularly through his "S" chevron.[2] Similarly, Batman's costume proclaims him a bat man, just as Spider-Man's webbed costume proclaims him a spider man. These costumes are iconic representations of the superhero identity.

The iconicity of the superhero costume follows Scott McCloud's theory of "amplification through simplification" (30). In *Understanding Comics* (1993), McCloud argues that pictures vary in their levels of abstraction, from completely realistic photographs to nearly abstract cartoons. Moving from realism to abstraction in pictures is a process of simplification, "focusing on specific details" and "stripping down an image to its essential 'meaning'" (30). This stripping-down amplifies meaning by focusing attention on the idea represented by the picture. McCloud explains, "By de-emphasizing the appearance of the physical world in favor of the idea of form, the cartoon places itself in the world of concepts" (41). The superhero costume removes the specific details of a character's ordinary appearance, leaving only a simplified idea that is represented in the colors and design of the costume. The chevron especially emphasizes the character's codename and is itself a simplified statement of that identity. Pulp hero costumes do not similarly state the character's identity. The Shadow's face—the most common way the character is identified on pulp covers—while somewhat abstract because of the prominence of the hawk nose and burning red eyes, contains too many specific details to reach the level of the chevron's abstraction.

Color plays an important role in the iconicity of the superhero costume. In his chapter on color, McCloud shows the way the bright, primary colors of superhero comics are "less than expressionistic," but therefore more iconic, due to their simplicity. Specifically with reference to costumes, McCloud says, "Because costume colors remained exactly the same, panel after panel, they came to symbolize the characters in the mind of the reader" (188). To illustrate this point, he shows a boy reading a comic book with two thought balloons, each containing three horizontal blocks. In the first Batman is represented by blocks of blue, yellow, and gray; and the Hulk by blocks of purple and green.

The flatness of the colors in traditional four-color comics also has a "tendency to emphasize the shape of objects," thereby simplifying the objects (188). This simplification makes the superhero costume more abstract and iconic, a more direct statement of the identity of the character. The heroes of pulps, dime novels, and other forms of heroic fiction are not similarly represented as wearing such abstract, iconic costumes. The costume then, as an element of identity, marked the superhero off from previous hero types and helped to establish the genre.

Some pulp heroes stand as exceptions that test the rule that their costumes do not embody their identities, but they represent detours, and the connection of inner character, biography, and identity expressed in a costume did not become a convention for pulp mystery-men as it did for superheroes. Johnston McCulley's Crimson Clown (1926–31) wears a clown outfit as he robs criminals and wicked wealthy men of their ill-gotten booty; thus his costume does proclaim his identity. But wealthy socialite Delton Prouse, the Crimson Clown, did not grow up in a circus, nor did a clown jump through his window as he sought a disguise in which to practice wealth redistribution. He does not seem to have had a good reason for choosing the clown identity, but McCulley's characters rarely needed such reasons.

Both the Bat and the Black Bat wore bat costumes. The Bat (*Popular Detective* 1934), who may have also been created by Johnston McCulley, was Dawson Clade, a private detective framed for murder who faked his death in the electric chair and took up the Bat identity to gain revenge on the crooks who framed him. He wore a bat costume and wielded the ever-popular sleep-gas gun, as did so many of McCulley's heroes. The Bat's identity came to him when he sought a way to transform himself into a terror to gangland and a bat flew in his room and was silhouetted by a lamp. He saw the bat and adopted it as his totem just as Bruce Wayne would a few years later.

The Black Bat (*Black Book Detective* #1, July 1939), who premiered a month after Batman's first appearance, wears a black body suit and a scallop-edged cape with a bat cowl. Blinded by acid-throwing crooks, district attorney Tony Quinn adopts the Black Bat identity after training himself to peak physical condition and regaining his sight in a secret operation. His identity emerges from his biography—the acid left him blind as a bat, and his bat cowl expresses that identity. His costume is essentially a superhero costume, but crucially it lacks a chevron. The convention of the mystery-man genre was not to connect inner character or biography with the costume. Although the Crimson Clown, the Bat, and the Black Bat demonstrate that the costume could express inner character, biography, or heroic identity before the debut of Superman, they stand as exceptions to the general rule of mystery-man costumes.[3]

In contrast to most pulp-hero costumes, Superman's outfit does proclaim his identity. This difference between superheroes and mystery-men is immediately apparent on the cover of *Action* #1 with Superman in primary colors holding a car over his head and smashing it into an embankment. The "ridiculousness" of the scene on the cover so concerned publisher Harry Donenfeld that he banned Superman from the cover of *Action*, restoring him after five issues because of an increase in sales due directly to Superman's presence in the comic book (Benton, *Golden*, 17). The covers of *Action* #2–#5 show scenes of intense action, but none match the striking quality of the first one. The characters featured on these covers all fit into existing adventure genres and none feature so striking and particular an outfit as Superman does. Science fiction and hero pulps frequently featured scenes of outlandish action, and early comics share in this tradition. So the ridiculousness of *Action* #1 that struck Donenfeld had to be located in something different from the fantastic scenes of earlier pulps and comics. Most likely, it was Superman's costume in conjunction with the display of superpowers within the contemporary setting. This setting did not distance the action as a more exotic setting, such as an African jungle or an alien world, would have done. The costume was a crucial, early marker of the genre.

The importance of the costume convention in establishing the superhero genre can be seen in characters who debuted without costumes or with mystery-man costumes but went on to develop regular superhero costumes. In 1974 Martin Goodman, former publisher of Marvel Comics, and his son Charles started Seaboard Publications and inaugurated a short-lived line of comics under the Atlas banner. Atlas first attempted to break out of a sole focus on superhero comics, beginning its line with a variety of genres: superhero, war, horror, science fiction, barbarian, private detective, adventure, and teen humor. However, Atlas quickly moved toward the more commercially viable superhero genre. The Scorpion, created by Howard Chaykin, exemplifies this shift. The Scorpion's adventures were set just before WWII, and the character himself was a pulpy soldier of fortune with some science fiction elements. The Scorpion debuts without a costume, wearing a leather jacket, flight scarf, riding boots, and armed with pistols. A new creative team was brought on after the second issue, and the Scorpion was made over, appearing in the third and final issue in a blue-and-orange cowled affair sporting a large scorpion chevron.

Another Atlas title, *Targitt*, began as the formulaic story of a man seeking revenge against the Mob for killing his family. He dresses in ordinary clothing. With the second issue, he becomes "John Targitt, Man-Stalker," attired in a blue union suit with a full-face mask and a red, white, and blue target symbol as his chevron. The full-face mask changes into a cowl for the third and final issue. In its attempt to compete with Marvel, Atlas shifted toward the familiar superhero formula and did so specifically through the costume.[4]

The Sandman and the Crimson Avenger fit the second category, characters who begin with pulp-hero costumes and adopt superhero costumes. Both heroes first appeared between the debut of Superman and that of Batman, before the conventions of the superhero genre had been fully implemented and accepted by the creators. The Crimson Avenger begins with a Shadow/Green Hornet-inspired costume of a slouch hat, a large domino mask, and a red cloak. In *Detective Comics* #44 (October 1940), his costume changes to red tights with yellow trunks and boots, a smaller domino mask, a hood with a ridge running from his forehead backward, and a chevron of an eclipsed sun. He is present at the formation of the Seven Soldiers of Victory in *Leading Comics* #1 (Winter

1942), a superhero team designed to capitalize on the success of the Justice Society of America (Benton, *Golden,* 169). His ward and sidekick Wing acquires an identical costume with a reversed color scheme.

Sandman debuted in a double-breasted green suit, a purple cape, an orange fedora, and a blue-and-yellow gas mask.[5] When Jack Kirby and Joe Simon took over the character in *Adventure Comics* #69 (December 1941), his outfit was changed into a standard yellow and purple superhero suit. That both these characters debuted before the superhero genre had fully been established, that both were tied more to the style of the pulp mystery-men (Benton, *Golden,* 23, 27; Goulart, *Encyclopedia,* 13, 318), and that both moved into standard-issue superhero garb indicates that DC Comics felt that they needed to be in step with their counterparts and that costumes such as these signified superhero status.

GENERIC DISTINCTION

These three elements—mission, powers, and identity, or MPI—establish the core of the genre. But, as with other genres, specific superheroes can exist who do not fully demonstrate these three elements, and heroes from other genres may exist who display all three elements to some degree but should not be regarded as superheroes. This apparent indeterminacy originates in the nature of genre. In his attempt to define the genre of romantic comedy, Brian Henderson quotes Ludwig Wittgenstein's discussion of games to show that universal similarity is not necessary to define a genre. In *Philosophical Investigations,* Wittgenstein wrote:

> For if you look at [games] you will not see something that is common to all, but similarities, relationships, and a whole series of them at that [. . .] we see a complicated network of similarities overlapping and crisscrossing: sometimes overall similarities, sometimes similarities of detail [. . .]. I can think of no better expression to characterize these similarities than "family resemblances" (ellipses in Henderson 1986, 314).

The similarities between specific instances of a genre are semantic, abstract, and thematic, and come from the constellation of conventions that are typically present in a genre offering. If a character basically fits the mission-powers-identity definition, even with significant qualifications, and cannot be easily placed into another genre because of the preponderance of superhero-genre conventions, the character is a superhero.

For example, the Hulk can be said to be a superhero without a mission. At times he seems absolutely anti-social, and he frequently finds himself in conflict with the U.S. Army, which in the Silver Age was not presented as corrupt or malign but with the welfare of citizens as its motivating force. Stan Lee claims the Frankenstein monster as an inspiration for the Hulk, "He never wanted to hurt anyone; he merely groped his tortuous way though a second life trying to defend himself, trying to come to terms with those who sought to destroy him" (*Origins,* 75). The Hulk was Lee and Kirby's attempt to make a "hero out of a monster" (75). The green-skinned goliath's adventures do not arise from his attempts to fight crime or to improve the world. In early adventures,

Bruce Banner moves to stop the Metal Master and the invasion of the Toad Men, but as the Hulk, he offers to join forces with the Metal Master and once in control of the Toad Men's spaceship thinks, "With this flying dreadnought under me I can wipe out all mankind" (Lee, *Hulk*, 42). The Hulk eventually loses his calculating intelligence and wanders the planet primarily seeking solitude while being drawn, or stumbling, into the plans of supervillains. The Hulk fights primarily for self-preservation but inadvertently does good. He acts effectively as a superhero but does not have the mission or motivation to do so. His tales, though, are suffused with the conventions of the superhero genre: supervillains—the Leader, the Abomination; superhero physics—the transformative power of gamma rays; the limited authorities—General Thunderbolt Ross; a pal—Rick Jones; superteams—the Avengers and the Defenders; and so forth. These conventions keep the Hulk within the superhero genre.[6]

Regarding the powers convention, Batman was originally designed as a superhero without superpowers (Kane, *Batman and Me*, 99). His mission of vengeance against criminals is clear, and his identity—represented by his codename and iconic costume–marks him as a superhero. While he has no distinctly "super" powers, his physical strength and mental abilities allow him to fight crime alongside his more powerful brethren. As with the Hulk, Batman operates in a world brimming with the conventions of the superhero genre: supervillains—the Joker, the Penguin; the helpful authority figure—Police Commissioner Gordon; the sidekick—Robin; superteams—the Justice League and the Outsiders; and so forth.

The Fantastic Four illustrate how elements of the identity convention can be absent or weak and yet the characters remain superheroes. In the first issue of *The Fantastic Four*, the powers and mission conventions are clear. After their space ship is exposed to cosmic rays, each manifests a superpower. The ship's pilot, Ben Grimm, declares their mission: "We've gotta use [these powers] to help mankind, right?" (Lee, *Origins*, 32). The heroes then place their hands together and proclaim their superidentities: Mr. Fantastic, the Invisible Girl, the Human Torch, and the Thing. These codenames fit with the powers they have received and are expressions of the characters' personalities.[7]

The secret identity and costume elements of the identity convention are absent from the debut of the Fantastic Four. Stan Lee claims that he wanted to do away with these aspects of superheroes:[8]

> I was utterly determined to have a superhero series without any secret identities. I knew for a fact that if I myself possessed a super power I'd never keep it a secret. I'm too much of a show-off. So why should our fictional friends be any different? Accepting this premise, it was also natural to decide to forgo the use of costumes. If our heroes were to live in the real world, then let them dress like real people. (17)

The secret identity is a typical, but not necessary, convention for the genre. It clearly has great importance to the genre as its stable presence in superhero stories shows. Lee and Kirby were trying to be inventive and so chose to disregard aspects of the genre that they felt held them back. But the first issue of *The Fantastic Four* is clearly a superhero comic book, as is evident from the characters' powers and mission, the superhero physics, and the supervillain Mole Man with his plot to "destroy everything that lives above the surface" (42). And it is so without costumes. Significantly, although the Fantastic Four initially wore ordinary clothes, they quickly acquired costumes.

A CASE STUDY

Other definitions of the superhero overlook the idea of generic distinction, that is the concatenation of other conventions that Henderson calls family resemblance.[9] Generic distinction can be used to divide superheroes from non-superheroes. Basically, if a character fits the MPI conventions, even with some significant qualifications, and cannot be easily placed into another genre, the character is a superhero. On the reverse side, if a character largely fits the MPI qualifications of the definition, but can be firmly and sensibly placed within another genre, then the character is not a superhero. Typically, the identity convention (codename and costume) plays the greatest role of the three elements in helping to rule characters in or out.

Luke Cage serves as an excellent example of the importance of generic distinction in defining a character as a superhero and placing him within the genre.[10] Luke Cage clearly has superpowers. He is invulnerable and super strong. But such a character could operate a detective/security agency within a science fiction or horror/SF milieu and not be considered a superhero.[11] The editors and writers at Marvel Comics took great care to place Luke Cage within the superhero genre by surrounding the character with superhero conventions and foregrounding these conventions. These conventions mark Luke Cage as a superhero and not as a detective or adventure hero who has superpowers. The cover of the first issue proclaims it a "Sensational origin issue!"

Superheroes have origins, whereas characters in other genres may go through similar transformations but these are not referred to as origins. Lucas is a wrongly convicted prisoner at Seagate Maximum Security Prison, who volunteers for a medical experiment that, in formulaic fashion, goes awry and empowers him. After Lucas uses these powers to escape from prison, he works his way back to New York City and reflexively stops a criminal's getaway after the man robs a diner. The diner's owner proclaims "You dodged that shot an' nailed him like a real super-hero!" (Thomas, "Out of Hell," 21). This comment gives him an idea for a career, and he goes to a costume shop and rejects both a Captain America and a Captain Marvel outfit as too expensive, settling instead for an open yellow shirt, blue pants, blue and yellow boots, a steel headband and bracers, and a chain belt. This costume does not proclaim his identity as the costumes of Spider-Man or Batman do, but it is intended to be seen as a costume, and the chain embodies his biography by serving as a reminder of his prison days (Goodwin, 7). After changing into his new outfit, Cage muses, "Yeah! Outfit's kinda hokey . . . but so what? All part of the super-hero scene. An' this way when I use my powers, it's gonna seem natural" (Thomas, "Out of Hell," 22). As with the cover and the explanation of his actions, the idea of the costume as a convention of the superhero genre is here foregrounded by being identified as such in the text itself.

Cage's superpowers enabled him to escape from prison where he had been incarcerated for a crime he did not commit. His former best friend, Willis Stryker, framed him for the murder of a woman who was killed by a rival gang in an attempt to assassinate

Stryker. To revenge himself upon Stryker, Cage sets himself up as a hero for hire and begins to harass Stryker's underlings, a revenge-fantasy motif common to the overall action-adventure meta-genre. But Stryker is given the accouterments of a supervillain instead of those of an ordinary crime boss, again foregrounding the placement of this story within the superhero genre. Stryker is consistently depicted in a green snake-skin suit with a yellow shirt, and he goes by the name "Diamondback."

He has no explicit superpowers, but has trained himself in knifethrowing and possesses specially designed knives, which can deploy gas, give off damaging sonic waves, or explode. While Cage initially faces blaxploitation criminal types, he soon finds himself running up against opponents with powers, codenames, and costumes, such as Mr. Luck, Lion-Fang, and Stiletto. Costumes are again foregrounded as an element of the genre when two of Cage's prison buddies, "Comanche" and "Shades," escape in order to revenge themselve upon Rackham, a prison guard who has been fired for his brutality. In order not to be recognized while attacking Rackham, the escaped convicts steal costumes.

Comanche dresses in a masked outfit with a black muscle-shirt and a yellow "C" chevron, buckskin pants, and a candy-striped headband similar to the one he wore in prison; this costume is accented by two large knives, a bow, and a quiver full of arrows. Shades sports a big-collared white muscle-shirt, white boots, blue pants, oversized sunglasses, and carries two pistols in large red holsters. Ironically, although they adopt these costumes to disguise their identities, a stool-pigeon named Flea, who has read brief mentions of them in the journal kept by the scientist who transformed Cage, recognizes them easily, "Considering one wore dark goggles and the other had a big yellow 'C' on his chest" (Isabella, 3). In no other genre would wearing such costumes be presented as reasonable for escaped convicts seeking to hide their identities.

Continuity, another convention of the genre, is brought into play by showing Cage interacting with the rest of the Marvel Universe. Existing Marvel supervillains like the Owl and the Ringmaster's Circus of Crime face off against Cage. Other Marvel superheroes cross over into his adventures, such as Iron Man, Black Goliath, and the X-Men. Beginning with issue #17, Luke Cage takes on the cognomen "Power Man" because of a lack of coverage of his feats by the *Daily Bugle*, which covers the heroics of Spider-Man and Captain America. He wonders, "Why, blast it? What've they got that I don't? Super-powers? Nope—I got me those. A flashy costume? These threads'll do fine. A fancy name? A fancy . . . name? Yeah maybe that's it. Maybe 'Hero for Hire' just don't cut it" (Wein, "Rich Man," I). He comes up with his codename while facing off a villain who declares, after seeing him break into the advanced armored airship he is stealing, "This ship's construction makes what you've done impossible!" Cage responds, "Just chalk it up to black power, man."

He realizes that "Power Man" sounds good and settles on it for his new identity. Therefore, his codename arises out of an incident in his life, expresses his powers, and includes a racial subtext that has been present in the series since its inception. In fact, the cover of issue #17 (February 1974) proclaims him "The first and still the greatest black superhero of them all!" even though the Black Panther obviously preceded him at Marvel, which may be why the cover of issue #19 (June 1974) describes him as "America's first and most startling black super-hero!"[12] As with these other aspects, Marvel foregrounded the conventions of the genre so as to declare Hero for Hire a superhero comic book, distinct from other genres.

RULING IN AND RULING OUT

While generic distinction can be used to define some characters as superheroes, it can just as easily be used to establish that some characters are not. If a character to some degree fits the mission-powers-identity qualifications of the definition but can be firmly and sensibly placed within another genre, then the character is not a superhero. Typically the identity convention (codename and costume) plays the greatest role of the three elements in helping to rule characters in or out of the genre. While ruling characters in or out of the superhero genre is a bit of a parlor game, it has value in highlighting the superhero genre as a distinct genre of its own and not an offshoot of science fiction or fantasy.

A leading candidate for this sort of exclusion by genre distinction is Buffy the Vampire Slayer. Superficially, Buffy could be seen as qualifying as a superhero. She has a mission: to fight and slay vampires and other demons who threaten humanity. She has superpowers; her training raises her to the level of Batman in fighting ability and her strength is greater than the chemically enhanced strength of Riley Finn, an agent of the U.S. military's demon-hunting Initiative, or the supernaturally enhanced strength of Angel, a vampire. Buffy has an identity as the Slayer. But this identity is not a superhero identity like Superman or Batman. This identity is not separate from her ordinary Buffy identity the way Superman is from Clark Kent, whose mild-mannered personality differs greatly from Superman's heroic character. The Slayer is not a public identity in the ordinary superhero sense; even the well-financed and government-sponsored Initiative views the Slayer as a myth, a boogeyman for demons. Buffy does not wear a costume; and while such a costume is not necessary, it is typical.

Finally, and more importantly for the purpose of demonstrating that generic distinction is a crucial element of the superhero, the Slayer is a hero-type that predates the superhero, fitting firmly within the larger horror genre and specifically within the vampire sub-genre. Literarily, the vampire hunter descends from Dr. Van Helsing in *Dracula*. Historically, the hero-type descends from actual vampire hunters, including the *dhampir*, the supposed male progeny of a vampire who is particularly able to detect and destroy vampires. Thus, though the writers of *Buffy* draw on superhero conventions, the stories are generically distinct from the superhero genre.

Genre distinction can also be seen as playing a role in self-definition. The producers of *Buffy the Vampire Slayer* do not seem to regard it as a superhero show. They clearly draw on elements of the superhero genre and make references to it. They also make references to Scooby Doo and the show fits within the Scooby Doo formula. Perhaps more telling is that Buffy has an origin much in line with the superhero origin, but it is not identified as such as is usually the case in superhero comics. This lack of self-identification with the genre helps to establish that Buffy is not a superhero.

But Buffy is a super hero, as are heroic characters from other genres that have extraordinary abilities such as the Shadow, the Phantom, Beowulf, or Luke Skywalker. They are superior to ordinary human beings and ordinary protagonists of more realistic fiction in significant ways. When they are called super heroes, super is used as an adjective that modifies hero; but they are not superheroes, that is they are not the protagonists of superhero-genre narratives.

An excellent way to understand this distinction is through Northrop Frye's theory of modes. Frye sets up a system of classification of fiction "by the hero's power of action, which may be greater than ours, less, or roughly the same" (1957, 33). According to his scheme, in myth the hero is "superior in kind both to other men and to the environment" and is a divine being. In romance, the hero is "superior in degree to other men and to his environment" but is identified as a human being, and "moves in a world in which the ordinary laws of nature are slightly suspended" (33). The other categories are high mimetic—the hero, a leader, is "superior in degree to other men but not his natural environment"; the low mimetic—the hero is "one of us" and "superior to neither men nor to his environment"; and the ironic mode—the hero is "inferior in power or intelligence to ourselves" (33, 34). Thought of in this way, heroes who are super—all those characters who are referred to as super heroes but do not fit the generic definition of the superhero presented herein—are romance heroes. Referring to these characters as romance heroes, though, given the contemporary use of romance—stories of couples whose love relationship develops to overcome all obstacles—would be confusing; instead it makes sense to refer to them as super heroes.

A useful analogy is that *hero* is to *super hero* as *model* is to *supermodel*. A super hero is a hero who is super or superior to other kinds of heroes (typically by virtue of physical abilities), just as a super model is superior to other types of models (typically by virtue of superior attractiveness and charisma). The distinction between super hero and superhero is analogous to the distinction between every day (i.e. every single day) and everyday (i.e. ordinary). One might wear everyday clothing every day, so the two terms are related but they have distinct meanings.

This distinction gets muddied by characters from other genres who operate in a superhero universe, such as spy chief Nick Fury who occasionally teams up with established and clearly defined superheroes like Captain America, Spider-Man, or the Thing to battle some menace.

His mission is obvious from the name of the counter-intelligence spy agency he heads, S.H.I.E.L.D.: Supreme Headquarters, International Espionage Law-Enforcement Division. He has no superpowers, although another character with access to his stock of weaponry and equipment could operate as a superhero. He has no secret identity and no separate heroic identity, nor any costume that announces such an identity. Although he occasionally opposes the schemes of Marvel Universe supervillains, his enemies typically take the form of traditional spy villains, primarily similarly equipped organizations like Hydra or Advanced Idea Mechanics, who wear outfits more in line with those of Klan-influenced pulp villains than with inverted-superhero supervillain costumes.[13] Nick Fury fits neatly within the spy/secret agent genre, which has deep roots going back to the early twentieth century in characters like Operator #5 and the Diplomatic Free Lances.

A third example is DC Comics' spaceman Adam Strange, who might seem to fit into the superhero genre as a sometimes ally, but not a member, of the Justice League of America. In this allegiance, he is somewhat akin to "pal" characters, like Jimmy Olsen or Snapper Carr, who accompany superheroes and even help them to fight villains but are not superheroes themselves. Adam Strange's mission is to protect his adopted world, Rann, from alien invaders and other threats.

His jetpack and ray guns give him quite an offensive capacity. But he has no identity other than the one with which he was born. His red and white space suit does not announce his identity and it does not stand out from the futuristic clothing worn by everyone on Rann. More importantly, Adam Strange clearly falls within the science-fiction genre and was created in the mold of John Carter, Buck Rogers, and Flash Gordon. Like these three heroes, Strange finds himself transported to a strange and distant world where he fights unearthly monsters, madmen, and despots, and finds love with a beautiful maiden.

John Constantine, Hellblazer, is a straightforward trench-coat-wearing horror investigator, like DC's earlier hero Doctor Occult, characters out of H. P. Lovecraft's tales, or a non-governmental X-Files operative, and he exists within the DC Universe and therefore occasionally interacts with its superheroes. Like Nick Fury and Adam Strange, John Constantine's placement in a superhero universe might mistakenly be seen as marking him as a superhero. But to do so would be to overvalue the continuity convention and to undervalue the mission, powers, and identity conventions and also to ignore the importance of genre distinction.

Overlooked here is the existence of a liminal genre status, which includes characters that cross genres or fall at the borderline of the superhero genre and another one. It could be argued that Buffy, Adam Strange, and John Constantine should be considered cross-genre or genre-borderline superheroes because of the way Buffy's adventures contain significant elements of the superhero genre or the way Strange and Constantine operate in the DC Universe. But their strong ties with other genres, it can be argued, should exclude them from this cross-genre or borderline-genre status. As I have argued, the identity convention often works to signify whether a story with some superhero elements falls within the superhero genre or within another genre, and these heroes lack the identity convention. Strong identity markers are the clearest way to place a story within the superhero genre, although such markers need to be backed up by the presence of other equally clear conventions.

The most successful cross-genre superhero comic book series is the Legion of Super-Heroes. This feature blends the superhero and the science-fiction genres. It is set in the thirtieth century and features futuristic technology, space travel, alien races, other worlds, and a variety of other SF elements, the strength of which allow it to be considered SF. But it is clearly a superhero comic book as the title indicates. The characters all have super-powers, wear costumes, have codenames, and the group's founders sought to emulate the legendary twentieth-century heroes Superboy and Supergirl.

The Phantom Rider (originally the Ghost Rider, a 1967 revival of Marvel Enterprise's Ghost Rider of the 1950s) straddles the borderline between the superhero and Western genres. He has no powers, but like the Lone Ranger fights frontier crime and, unlike the Lone Ranger, wears a fairly unequivocal superhero costume. Without the costume—an all-white luminescent outfit with a fullface mask—he would clearly be considered a typical Western hero like the Ringo Kid or Kid Colt. But his villains occasionally have supervillain codenames and costumes, and therefore serve as inverted-superhero super-villains, one of most significant markers of the superhero genre. Additionally, the Phantom Rider's adventures have been retroactively included in the Marvel Universe, i.e. a publisher-certified genre signifier.

Ka-Zar is a bit more problematic than Adam Strange or Nick Fury. Although he clearly is a jungle hero, he interacts with superheroes and villains in a manner similar to Strange or Fury, but more directly. He is essentially a non-superhero adventure-hero who crosses genres. He was created as a pulp knock-off of Tarzan in 1936, but because Marvel had retained the rights to the character from their earlier incarnation as Timely, Ka-Zar could be introduced into the Marvel Universe (*X-Men* #10, March 1965). Like the Sub-Mariner and Atlantis, Ka-Zar fights to keep the Savage Land free of incursions from the outside world, and he fights to oppose the schemes of inverted-superhero supervillains like Magneto. His physical abilities allow him to interact as an equal with characters like the X-Men, Spider-Man, and Daredevil. Ka-Zar crosses genres, but also operates at the borderline of both the jungle and superhero genres.

The Punisher began as a vigilante, killing criminals, but gradually was transformed into a superhero as he became popular with readers. He fits directly into "aggressor" formula (Kettredge, xxix).[14] Unlike many of his brethren, he does not work for any government agency. This independent operating pushes him toward the superhero camp. He has no superpowers, but his level of weaponry and physical skills let him operate among superheroes like Spider-Man. Like Batman, his family was killed by criminals, which similarly supplies him with a mission.

He has both the costume and codename aspects of the identity convention. Within the Marvel Universe, he is fairly clearly a superhero, but his allegiance with the aggressor hero-type pushes him out of the center of the superhero formula. As he became popular in the 1980s and was featured in multiple series, the Punisher switched back and forth between the aggressor formula and the superhero genres depending on whether he appeared in his own comics or made guest appearances in superhero stories, that is, his definition as a superhero varied depending upon the concatenation of conventions in any particular story.

This ability to switch back and forth marks the current incarnation of Shang-Chi. As originally developed in *Master of Kung-Fu*, Shang-Chi was a martial arts hero operating in an older pulp-style universe as the son and enemy of Dr. Fu Manchu. But when he was revived for the Marvel Knights superhero team, he became a superhero, though a formula shift could throw him back into his original adventure genre. Shang-Chi can be thought of metaphorically as a planet orbiting a genre sun. In *Master of Kung-Fu* he was a pulp-hero, but the gravity of the Marvel Knights series pulled him toward the sun of the superhero genre.

A solar system can serve as a useful metaphor in thinking about genre-switching characters like the Punisher and Shang-Chi. At the center of the genre system, the formula burns hottest and the gravity is the strongest, keeping conventions and formulas rigid. At a comfortable distance—like Earth and Mars—the light and heat of the sun provide an environment conducive to life and evolution. As one moves out to the gas giants, the genre shifts and the formula carries less influence (just as Jupiter sheds more light on its moons than the sun does), but the stories are still recognized being within the genre. Some planetoids, such as Shang-Chi, are in empty space between solar systems or are part of another system, but get pulled by the gravity of writers and publishers into the superhero genre solar system and out of their own genre systems.

Man-Thing and Swamp Thing offer their own definitional challenges. Because of his mindlessness, Man-Thing is pretty clearly a monster character, unwittingly doing good. He interacts with superherocs, but cannot be said to be operating with much volition, thereby negating the mission convention. He does have superpowers, but no separate identity—his human self having been destroyed in the creation of the Man-Thing form, and his change from Ted Sallis to the Man-Thing fits more with the horror genre than with the transcendent transformation of a superhero origin. Primarily his lack of volition, which is similar to the Hulk's lack of mission, places him outside the superhero genre, but his presence in the Marvel Universe could arguably place him at the borderline.

Swamp Thing has powers and identity elements similar to those of Man-Thing, although his powers expanded when Alan Moore shifted the character away from being a human being whose body had taken on properties of the swamp to a plant that had taken on a dead human being's personality. His self-consciousness is unambiguous, so he has the potential for a mission. Depending on the interests of the writer, Swamp Thing falls more or less within the SF/horror genre or the superhero genre. Initially he pretty clearly fell into Cawelti's altered states meta-genre, which includes horror (*Adventure*, 47–49), albeit with some generous helpings of the adventure meta-genre, such as the revenge fantasy and the supervillain. Over time, Swamp Thing became more embroiled within the DC Universe and faced costumed opponents and interacted with DC's superheroes. Alan Moore took a more primal horror approach, retaining superhero elements because of his fascination with the artistic and storytelling possibilities of the DC Universe.

Another way to clarify the issue of cross-genre or genre-borderline category is to look at characters clearly identified with other genres or who are otherwise excluded from being superheroes, but who operate in a superhero universe. Detective Harvey Bullock, Gotham PD, is a police officer. He is a normal human being and falls into the "loose cannon" cop stereotype. If he accompanies Batman on a raid or even tracks down a supervillain like the Penguin on his own, does he suddenly become a superhero?

When Ben Urich, reporter for the *Daily Bugle*, shares information with Daredevil that helps the hero bring down the Kingpin, does that interaction transform him into a superhero? Does the ear-wiggling ability of Willie Lumpkin, the postal carrier whose route includes the Baxter Building, count as a superpower because he is a friend of the Fantastic Four and occasionally sees supervillains while delivering mail?

Are these interactions as transformative as radioactive spider bites? All these questions can be answered easily with a firm "No." The same is true for characters from the other genres that fit into the larger adventure meta-genre established by John Cawelti (*Adventure*, 39) and are sometimes found in superhero comics, such as spies, cowboys, knights, and ninja. Generic distinction marks these characters as non-superheroes even though they may have the missions and powers requisite to be superheroes, and might even possess elements of the identity convention.

CONCLUSION

In this chapter I have argued for a definition of the superhero comprising mission, powers, identity, and generic distinction. Clearly the superhero has been studied previously without this definition in place, so the question arises, why do we need it? The answer to this question is that we already have it and it is already in use. My definition brings forth the unstated assumptions that generally guide the study of the superhero and the production of superhero comics. As the ruling of Judge Learned Hand shows, recognition of the mission-powers-identity triumvirate as the necessary elements of a definition of the superhero existed very early in the superhero's history. Generic distinction merely accounts for the "family resemblances" of the other conventions that mark the superhero genre off from the rest of the adventure meta-genre. Another proof for the definition offered here is the way that the ages of superhero comics neatly parallel the stages of genre evolution set out by Thomas Schatz. In *Hollywood Genres*, Schatz puts forward a four-stage evolutionary cycle for any genre:

> A form passes through an experimental stage, during which its conventions are isolated and established, a classic stage, in which the conventions reach their "equilibrium" and are mutually understood by artist and audience, an age of refinement, during which certain formal and stylistic details embellish the form, and finally a baroque (or "mannerist" or "self-reflexive") stage, when the form and its embellishments are accented to the point where they are the "substance" or "content" of the work (Schatz, 37–38).

These stages match the progression of ages: Golden, Silver, Bronze, and Iron. This progression of stages and ages does not encompass the mystery-men pulps—which followed their own genre progression—science fiction, legends, epics, or any of the other source genres whose characters are proposed as superheroes but who fall outside the genre definition presented in this chapter. The neat fit between Schatz's theory of genre evolution and the ages of superhero comics bolsters the claim that superheroes debuted in 1938 with Superman at the start of the Golden Age and evolved in superhero comics, therefore reinforcing the mission-powers-identity-generic distinction definition.

This lengthy and detailed discussion is also necessary because of the nature of genre study. Genre tales are some of the most important of cultural products that promulgate cultural mythology (Cawelti, *Adventure*, 35–36). Genres have boundaries. Some are narrow, like the superhero, and others are broader, like science fiction or horror. A well-defined genre can be studied for the way the culture industry interacts with popular taste. It can be seen as a way of examining the resolution of cultural conflicts and tensions that audiences regard as legitimate. A poorly defined genre that includes characters from other genres as superheroes or fails to distinguish between the genre definition and the metaphoric use of superhero renders the term becomes meaningless as tool for genre criticism and analysis.

A parallel can be made with the Western. If the definition of the Western is limited to Cawelti's man-in-the-middle convention (*Six-Guns* 1984, 74), then *Casablanca* and *Slingblade* are Westerns as they both feature men standing between savagery and civilization who protect and advance the values of civilization through savage violence. If the definition is limited to the Western setting, then both *The Beverly Hillbillies* and *Frasier* are Westerns; additionally both feature characters from the East moving westward on voyages of personal discovery and renewal, a common convention of Westerns. If these examples were counted as Westerns, the whole project of Western scholarship would collapse because the broad range of examples would defy analysis of common elements.

A sloppy definition of the superhero makes it more difficult to examine the way the superhero genre embodies cultural mythology and narratively animates and resolves cultural conflicts and tensions. A tight definition enables scholars to focus specifically on the genre itself, separate it from related genres, and compare it with other genres.

NOTES

1. The superhero's mission does distinguish him from certain hero types, however. Many Western and science fiction heroes do not have the generalized mission of the superhero or pulp hero because they are not seeking to do good for the sake of doing good. Instead, many of these heroes reluctantly get drawn into defending a community. Superheroes actively seek to protect their communities by preventing harm to all people and by seeking to right wrongs committed by criminals and other villains.

2. I use chevron to indicate the costume insignia that superheroes employ. It is a more concise term than chest symbol, chest shield, insignia, icon, or any of the various terms used to indicate the iconic symbols that indicate superhero identities. It also enables one to discuss costume insignia that are not located on the character's chest, such as the Phantom's skull or Bullseye's target, although such examples are rare. Although the term carries the connotation of a v-shaped symbol, it also indicates rank or service in military and police uniforms.

3. The overwhelming majority of covers for *Black Book Detective* do not show the Black Bat costume, but instead feature a faded vignette of the Black Bat's cowled head in the background observing a scene of violence. Superhero comics typically show the hero and his costume in the foreground.

4. For excellent histories of the short-lived company, including a gallery of the covers of every issue Atlas published, see J. C. Vaughn's "Atlas Seaboard," *Comic Book Marketplace*, April 2000: 26–45. The December 2001 issue of *Comic Book Artist* focuses on the company.

5. The Sandman likely debuted in *New York World's Fair Comics of 1939* (April 1939), which was published before *Detective Comics* #27. See Steve Gentner's "Will the Real First Appearance of Sandman Please Stand Up?" *Comic Book Marketplace* #20, Dec. 1992: 62–63.

6. The Sandman's gas gun marks him as a pulp mystery man and has an ancient provenance, ancient in popular fiction terms. It derives immediately from the Green Hornet, but goes back to Johnston McCulley's heroes the Crimson Clown and Black Star.

7. The Hulk lacks a costume, but his body serves this function and was intended to do so.

8. The question of *What If* #6 (December 1977) is "What if the Fantastic Four had Different Super-Powers?" The series host, the Watcher, explains that the specific powers the four received from the bombardment of cosmic rays "were not a result of mere chance. No, for the effects of the cosmic rays had been influenced—by the very unconscious minds of these fantastic four . . ." (Thomas, *What If* 1977: 10).

9. With the minor caveat of Blythe and Sweet's inclusion of the "other conventional comic book types" that the superhero operates among (Henderson 1986, 185).

10. Luke Cage is inventional in a number of ways. He has a secret identity, but it is secret so that he can avoid going to jail. He invents the alias "Luke Cage" out of his real name, Lucas, and a remembrance of this time spent in prison. Cage only later acquires the name Power Man, and even then has no secret identity in the traditional sense, given that his business cards read Luke Cage. His mission is not selfless. He takes cases for pay instead of merely patrolling for crime. He is a poor black man instead of a middle-class or wealthy white man.

11. As Angel, the spin-off character from *Buffy the Vampire Slayer*, does. Angel is not considered a superhero nor should be.

12. Even this designation is incorrect as both John Stewart, the black Green Lantern (1972) and the Falcon (1969) predate Luke Cage.
13. An inverted-superhero supervillain follows the definition of the superhero but has an inverted mission, one that is selfish and anti-social. These characters can easily reform and become superheroes, as Hawkeye, the Scarlet Witch, and Quicksilver did.
14. The aggressor is an "active force for moral order. His crusade is not the result of a particular mystery, but of a sudden perception—usually caused by his victimization through an act of violence—that there is something pervasively wrong with society. His response is to set aside the question of individual guilt and innocence, and move unilaterally against the generalized source of corruption" (Kettredge, xxix–xxx). Kettredge marks Don Pendelton's Mack Bolan as the first fully realized aggressor detective in *War Against the Mafia* (1969). The Punisher is merely the transferal of the Executioner into the superhero genre.

WORKS CITED

Benton, Mike, *Superhero Comics of the Golden Age* (Dallas: Taylor Publishing, 1992).

Cawelti, John G., *Adventure, Mystery, and Romance: Formula Stories as Art and Popular Culture* (Chicago: University of Chicago Press, 1976).

———. *The Six-Gun Mystique* (Bowling Green: Bowling Green State University Press, 1984).

Frye, Northrop, *Anatomy of Criticism* (New York: Antheneum, 1957).

Henderson, Brian, "Romantic Comedy Today: Semi-Tough or Impossible?" in Barry Keith Grant, ed. *Film Genre Reader* (Austin: University of Texas Press, 1986).

Kettredge, William, and Steven M. Krauzer, eds., *The Great American Detective* (New York: New American Library, 1978)

Lee, Stan, *Origins of Marvel Comics* (New York: Simon and Shuster, 1974).

McCloud, Scott, *Understanding Comics* (Northampton: Tundra, 1993).

Robeson, Kenneth [Lester Dent], *The Man of Bronze* (New York: Bantam, 1964 [1933]).

Schatz, Thomas, *Hollywood Genres: Formulas, Filmmaking and the Studio System* (New York: McGraw Hill, 1981).

Siegel, Jerry, and Joe Shuster, *Action Comics* 1 (New York: DC Comics, 1938).

Thomas, Roy, "Out of Hell—A Hero," *Hero for Hire* 1 (New York: Marvel Comics, 1972).

Wein, Len, "Rich Man, Iron Man, Power Man, Thief," *Power Man* 17 (New York: Marvel Comics, February 1974).

Two Boys from the Twin Cities

M. THOMAS INGE

While F. Scott Fitzgerald and Charles M. Schulz grew up in distinctively different parts of the Twin Cities of St. Paul and Minneapolis, their experiences as children were not dissimilar. The older Fitzgerald was the product of recent immigrant families of common Irish stock. The maternal grandfather had begun as a bookkeeper and small businessman and became a prosperous grocery wholesaler after the Civil War in St. Paul. His daughter, Mollie, therefore was well educated and traveled and had some standing in the community. The paternal grandfather had kept a general store in Maryland but died when his son was only two years old. Edward attended college for a while but then went west to St. Paul to seek his fortune. There Mollie and Edward, Fitzgerald's parents, wed in a financially unequal but promising union.

The promise, however, was never realized. By the time Scott was born on 24 September 1896, his father's business as a furniture manufacturer was not prospering. He then became a grocery salesman for Proctor & Gamble, which required the family to move first to Buffalo and then to Syracuse, New York, only to lose his job in 1908 and return to St. Paul a failure at age fifty-five. While Mollie's family would see them through financially, he would remain unsuccessful and dispirited the rest of his life. The family moved almost annually to various apartments but always in the fashionable Summit Avenue section of St. Paul.

Schulz's father, Carl, was a German immigrant who settled in St. Paul to become a barber and met and married Charles's mother, Dena. While never prosperous, Carl Schulz was able adequately to provide for his family even through the Depression. As his son recalled, "I always admired him for the fact that he and my mother had only third grade educations and from what I remembered hearing in conversations, he worked pitching hay in Nebraska one summer to earn enough money to go to barber school, got himself a couple of jobs, and eventually bought his own barber shop. And I think he at one time owned two barber shops and a filling station, but that was either when I was not born or very small, so I don't know much about that" (Inge, 167).

Schulz was born 24 November 1922 in Minneapolis, and except for a year-and-a-half that the family spent in Needles, California, where his father pursued a misguided

Reprinted by permission from M. Thomas Inge, "Two Boys from the Twin Cities: Jay Gatsby and Charlie Brown," *Comic Art*, no. 6 (Spring 2004), 64–69.

version of Western life, he grew up in St. Paul, living at various times on Chicago Avenue, James Avenue, and Macalester Street, and finally at the corner of Snelling and Selby Avenues above his father's barbershop. Both the Fitzgerald and the Schulz families knew the difficulties and the privations of a penny earned.

Fitzgerald had the advantage of attending several private and Catholic schools in Buffalo and St. Paul and especially after 1908 St. Paul Academy, where he proved to be neither a popular nor particularly good student. As Matthew J. Bruccoli put it, "The outsider was not a loner who withdrew into his sense of uniqueness. Scott's desire for recognition required an audience and admiring companions" (26). Despite his boasting and his flirting with the girls, he made many fast friends and experienced the satisfaction of seeing his first story published in the school paper. Even with an indifferent high school record, including two years at Newman School in New Jersey, Fitzgerald made it into Princeton University in 1913.

Once again his bad study habits and pursuit of extracurricular activities prevailed, and he left Princeton four years later without graduating. Like many other young men his age during World War I, he entered the army in 1917 and was commissioned a second lieutenant. He was stationed in several campus in Kansas, Kentucky, Georgia, and Alabama, but the hostilities had ceased before he could be shipped abroad. It was at a country club dance in Montgomery that he met the love of his life, his golden girl, Zelda. After an on and off again courtship, and almost losing her, he won her hand in 1920 and thus began the fabulous pursuit of success and excess that would make them the best known and most discussed couple in American literary history. Living beyond their means in high style and pushing themselves to the edge of emotional and mental exhaustion, Fitzgerald nevertheless managed to produce a body of writing that has earned for him a permanent place in the pantheon of world-class authors.

Schulz too had a very undistinguished career in the public schools of St. Paul. Although he skipped two grades in elementary school, he failed every subject in the eighth grade. A shy, slender, and ungraceful young man, he experienced a good deal of the pain, insecurity, and failure that would become the staple of the humor in his comic strip work. He once recalled, "It took me a long time to become a human being. I was regarded by many as kind of sissified. . . . I was not a tough guy, but I was good at sports. . . . So I never regarded myself as being much and I never regarded myself as being good looking and I never had a date in high school, because I thought, who'd want to date me? So I didn't bother" (Inge, 168). On another occasion, he noted, "I wasn't actually hated. Nobody cared that much" (Inge, 5).

Although he was always interested in drawing, only an elementary school teacher encouraged his talent. He was invited to contribute drawings to his school yearbook, but not a single one of them was published. Schulz did have a small success in seeing a drawing of his dog published nationally in the newspaper feature Robert Ripley's Believe It or Not in 1937. He finished high school on time but was not inclined to attend college, so he enrolled in a correspondence course in cartooning with Art Instruction in Minneapolis with the financial and moral support of his parents.

While attempting to sell gag cartoons to magazines, in 1943 Schulz was drafted into the army during World War II. His mother died while he was in training at Fort Snelling in Minnesota, and he deeply felt the loss. He was shipped out from Kentucky to serve and see battle with the 20th Armored Division in France and Germany as an infantryman, staff sergeant, and machine gunner. Discharged from the Army in 1945, Schulz returned to St. Paul to do comic book work for a local publisher and teach at Art Instruction. There he met and fell in love with his golden girl, a young lady named Donna Wold, who eventually chose to marry another man. While he would marry twice and raise five children, Schulz never forgot his first disappointment in love and transformed her into Charlie Brown's unattainable ideal, an unnamed little red-haired girl. In the meantime, Schulz would take his cartoon feature called *L'il Folks*, sell it to United Features Syndicate, and with their encouragement turn it into *Peanuts*, the most successful comic strip in the history of the medium, which he would write and draw himself without assistance for a record run of almost fifty years. Before his death, Schulz would become the most admired, widely loved, and wealthiest comic artist in the world. The novel was already a respected art form before Fitzgerald turned his hand to fiction, but under Schulz's hand, the comic strip became an influential and versatile form of artistic expression, respected by academics and average readers alike.

Schulz was always a regular and omnivorous reader and counted among his favorite writers Sir Arthur Conan Doyle, Leo Tolstoy, Katherine Anne Porter, James Thurber, Flannery O'Connor, Carson McCullers, Thomas Wolfe, Margaret Drabble, and Joan Didion, and toward the end of his life he was reading such contemporaries as Anne Tyler, Elmore Leonard, John Grisham, and Don DeLillo. He also counted himself among the greatest admirers of Fitzgerald and *The Great Gatsby*. He began to read Fitzgerald in 1945 after the war while he was working as an instructor at the Art Instruction correspondence school. He wrote in a letter to the present writer on 2 February 1966, "Obviously *The Great Gatsby* is one of my favorite books, although it took about four readings before I understood it. I have certainly read almost everything Fitzgerald wrote, except maybe a few short stories."

Little wonder then that *The Great Gatsby* is the most frequently cited and quoted American novel in the fifty-year run of *Peanuts*. The earliest reference I have found to Fitzgerald occurs in the strip of 22 May 1980, when Charlie Brown is lying in bed and dreading a new day without his homework done. He recalls what was Schulz's favorite quotation from Fitzgerald: "In a real dark night of the soul it is always three o'clock in the morning." But he concludes, "When you have to get up at seven, and you still haven't written the English theme that's due today . . . six fifty-nine is the worst time of day." Then, in the opening panel of the Sunday strip for 22 July 1990, we find Snoopy reading to his little bird scouts on a camping trip from the final page of *Gatsby*, "I think of Gatsby's wonder when he first picked out the green light at the end of Daisy's dock." After a sigh and a sniff, they all retire for the night presumably having had the entire novel read to them.

But Gatsby becomes a more integral part of *Peanuts* and its narratives in a sequence beginning 30 May 1991. Charlie Brown's little sister, Sally, is teaching a Sunday school class and asks, "Can anyone tell me who hit Goliath in the head with a stone?" A new child in the class named Larry, a sober and scholarly looking boy with glasses, answers, "I know! The Great Gatsby!" Larry continues to provide such misinformation to the class on the next two days, much to Sally's frustration: "Gatsby stood by the Sea of Galilee, and picked out the green light at the end of Daisy's dock" (31 May) and "Gatsby had a mansion in Jericho, and he used to throw great big parties" (1 June). Finally when Larry claims on 3 June that Gatsby had parted the Red Sea, Sally loses his patience and banishes him from class. But the little boy can't leave because he is too short to reach the doorknob. When Sally asks Charlie on 4 June, "How can you teach someone who thinks the Great Gatsby was in the Old Testament?" she is floored to learn that Larry is the minister's son. At the conclusion of the class on 7 June, an unrepentant Larry leaves and comments, "Goodbye, ma'am. Whenever I think of you, I'll think of Gatsby and the green light at the end of Daisy's dock." Snoopy adds in a thought balloon, "So long, old sport!"

Larry would reappear six months later in the class at Christmas time and continue to confuse his stories. On 18 December he announces, "When he was little, Gatsby got a sled for Christmas, and he called it 'Rosebud'!" On 19 December, Sally asks the class, "Who can tell me why we put a star on top of our Christmas trees?" Larry responds, "Gatsby used to look across the street at the green star on top of Daisy's tree." Sally again loses her cool, despite the Christmas spirit. What these sequences suggest is that the sacred and the secular have become confused in Larry's mind, and so influential is his respect for fictional character of Jay Gatsby that he has moved the literary figure back into the great events of the biblical past and used him as a way of explaining some of the age-old traditions and beliefs of society. So powerful was the force of Gatsby that he might have proved a David or a Moses in another place or time rather than a corrupter of the American dream.

Schulz's love affair with Fitzgerald would continue a few years later. On 26 June 1995, Snoopy is sitting beneath a tree with Woodstock, in one of his philosophical moods, contemplating the canine condition. Using one of Fitzgerald's favorite themes, that people have a fixed amount of emotional capital that can be recklessly exhausted but not replenished, Snoopy ruminates, "You're emotionally bankrupt . . . Scott Fitzgerald was emotionally bankrupt . . . we're all emotionally bankrupt . . ." This is not surprising, coming from Snoopy, the great-unread American writer, author of "It Was a Dark and Stormy Night" and other unpublished classics, who obviously feels an alliance with another misunderstood genius. The strip too reflects the sometimes darker strain of thought that threads through Schulz's usually upbeat sense of humor.

As late as 1998, Schulz returned to *The Great Gatsby* as a source of quotations for Snoopy. While Charlie Brown tries to get up enough nerve to ask his eternally elusive red-haired girl to dance, Snoopy stands by the punch bowl imaginatively casting himself in the role of Gatsby, "trying to look casual and uninterested in the dancers," and quoting from the novel (21 May and 23 May). On 25 May when Charlie musters enough courage to approach the little red-haired girl, he finds he has been preempted by Snoopy. Since Schulz never actually portrayed the little red-haired girl, she appears only in shadow dancing with Snoopy, as he thinks, "Daisy and Gatsby danced . . . I remember his graceful conservative fox trot." On at least two subsequent occasions (21 January and 13 August 1999) Snoopy would bring thoughts of Gatsby into the strip.

It seems evident from these references and quotations that among the things Schulz admired about Fitzgerald was his way with words and his ability to capture the essence of an emotion or a fading memory in such succinct and poetic prose. Given Schulz's daily task of capturing a moment of humor within the close confines of a comic strip, he would naturally respect the brevity and conciseness of Fitzgerald's style as best displayed in *The Great Gatsby*. We do not have Schulz's reading copy of the novel, or at least it does not seem to be among the books in his library. We do have his copy of *The Short Stories of F. Scott Fitzgerald*, and it demonstrates his tendency to underline certain phrases and images that captured his fancy, for example: "trying to look casually at home and politely uninterested in the dancers" (147, paraphrased in the *Peanuts* strip of 21 May 1998 quoted above), or "He wanted not association with glittering things and glittering people—he wanted the glittering things themselves" (220–21). Like most readers of Fitzgerald, Schulz no doubt admired the sharp images and poignant phraseology that captured so well the romantic sense of longing that they shared thematically in their creative work.

While they both had a common interest in emotional loss and yearning, it also seems that they came down on opposite sides in their treatment of the American dream. This becomes evident when one compares their signal creations, Jay Gatsby and Charlie Brown. Gatsby is an embodiment of the failure of the American dream of success, the notion that one can rise from rags to riches through industry, ambition, self-reliance, honesty, and temperance. In this myth, inspired by Benjamin Franklin, Horatio Alger, and other self-made men, lies the genesis of what impels Gatsby, whose childhood dreams focused on self-improvement and personal development. But in an ironic reversal, by imitating the great American moralists, Gatsby rises to become a rich and powerful criminal. What we learn through the eyes of the narrator, Nick Carraway, is that pure will power, divorced from decency and rationality, leads to destruction, and that a merely selfish dream is insufficient to justify the enormous amount of energy and life expended by Gatsby.

It is that selfish dream, however, that makes Gatsby the ultimate arch-romantic. Because he lacked the wealth and timing, he missed marrying Daisy, the girl on whom he had focused what Nick called his "heightened sensitivity to the promises of life" (*Gatsby*, 2). After obtaining the wealth through corrupt means, he returns five years later to fulfill his "incorruptible dream" by attempting to repeat the golden moment of his life when he possessed that "elusive rhythm," that "fragment of lost words" which we all seek to recall in this mundane existence from a former lover, time, or world (*Gatsby*, 155, 112). When viewed against the moral decadence and cowardly conduct of the wealthy and privileged Buchanans, Gatsby's unassailable romanticism makes him appear almost heroic, but his mean and violent death reflects the degradation to which he has descended.

If Gatsby is the supreme romantic American hero, tainted by his tragic flaws, Charlie Brown belongs to another tradition in our culture—the figure of the lost soul, the little man, or what Charlie Chaplin called the Little Fellow. This seemingly inadequate hero came about in response to the overwhelming anxieties and insecurities of the technological society of the Industrial Revolution and includes such figures as James Thurber's Walter Mitty, Chaplin's Tramp, Walt Disney's Mickey Mouse, Buster Keaton's screen persona, and characters in the writings of Robert Benchley, E. B. White, Langston Hughes, and Art Buchwald. Like Woody Allen, who has continued the tradition, Charlie Brown is a particularly appropriate little soul because of his preoccupations with what has possessed all of us—anxiety over our neurotic behavior, the need to discover our own identities, the relationship of the self to society and the responsibilities that entails, and the desperate need to gain control of our destinies.

Schulz said himself that Charlie Brown was intended to represent "everyman":

> Readers are generally sympathetic toward a lead character who is rather gentle, sometimes put upon, and not always the brightest person. . . . No matter what happens to any of the other characters [in *Peanuts*], somehow Charlie Brown is involved at the end and usually is the one who brings disaster upon one of his friends or receives the blunt of the blow. Charlie Brown has to be the one who suffers, because he is a caricature of the average person. Most of us are much more acquainted with losing than we are with winning. Winning is great, but it isn't funny. (Schulz, 83–84)

The power of Charlie Brown, and the timid souls who preceded him, lies in his resilience, his ability to accept and humanize the dehumanizing forces around him, and in his eternal hope for improving himself and his options in life. One day the kite will fly and escape the clutches of the trees. Some year Lucy will not pull away the annual football at the last moment and allow him to kick it. Eventually he will get up enough nerve to approach the little red-haired girl. In his state of suspended pre-adolescence, everything remains possible. This is the kind of faithful innocence and stubborn resistance to repeated and demonstrable failure that sustains belief in the American dream. Corruptibility and cynical self-interest lie down the road beyond the eternal childhood of Charlie Brown and his friends. Theirs is indeed an "incorruptible dream."

In one of the more recent newspaper reprints of *Peanuts*, originally from 1990, we see the difference in attitude between Fitzgerald and Schulz (1 July to 10 August 2002). Charlie is away at summer camp and falls for a little girl named Peggy Jean. In his nervousness he tells her his name is Brownie Charles. When she offers to hold a football for him to kick, his bad memories of Lucy's annual trick prevent him from responding. When he is unable to act, she leaves because he doesn't trust her. Charlie is left with Snoopy, sitting at the end of a dock, regretting his loss, but with no green light across the bay to inspire him. Rather than abandon Charlie, Schulz brings Peggy Jean back and ends the story on a hopeful note, with a kiss and promise of future meetings. Charlie may never get the attention of the little red-haired girl, but he is allowed occasional moments of happiness in a world of frustration and romantic yearning.

F. Scott Fitzgerald and Charles M. Schulz are clearly among the most celebrated and admired native sons of the Twin Cities. The first, the son of an unsuccessful businessman, and the second, the son of a barber, demonstrated that despite a slow start in life, with talent and ambition, one can achieve fame and fortune. Neither was among the best of students, and coming of age during a World War, both served in the military. Returning home, they each fell in love with the girl of their dreams and, through those relationships, experienced the disappointment of an unattainable dream. A strong creative urge drove both to seek careers in popular literature, the novel and the comic strip respectively, as a way of expressing their sense of the American experience and capturing the anxieties of the twentieth century. Each contributed a major figure to popular mythology, Jay Gatsby as the corrupted romantic idealist and Charlie Brown as the discouraged but indomitable little man. Both have proven to be influential and profound commentators on the human condition and spoken to generations of Americans about the values necessary for survival in the modern world.

WORKS CITED

Bruccoli, Matthew J., *Some Sort of Epic Grandeur: The Life of F. Scott Fitzgerald* (New York: Harcourt, 1981).

Fitzgerald, F. Scott, *The Great Gatsby* (New York: Scribner's, 1925).

———, *The Short Stories of F. Scott Fitzgerald: A New Collection.* Edited by Matthew J. Bruccoli (New York: Scribner's, 1989).

Inge, M. Thomas, ed., *Charles M. Schulz: Conversations* (Jackson: University Press of Mississippi, 2000).

Schulz, Charles M., *Peanuts Jubilee: My Life and Art with Charle Brown and Others* (New York: Ballantine Books, 1976).

CRAFT, ART, FORM

The previous section offered a broad overview of the history of comics from a variety of perspectives but one of the contributors, R. C. Harvey, also raised the issue of form, which has increasingly come to the fore in comics scholarship. While early writings on comics were mainly focused on questions of content, either decried for its vulgarity or praised for its vitality, scholars are increasingly interested in the formal properties of comics. The formal turn has led to an increased attention to comics-as-a-language: what are the constituent elements that make up comics, how is the demarcation line separating comics from other art forms to be set, what are the codes used to make effective comics.

The essays in this section can all be seen as attempts at mapping and boundary setting. As we saw in the introduction to the previous section, cartoonist Scott McCloud gave a definition of comics that highlighted the use of sequential images. R. C. Harvey countered by suggesting that the verbal-visual blend was a crucial feature of comics that was obscured by McCloud's definition. In his essay on "Caricature," philosopher David Carrier offers a further challenge to McCloud's definition by noting that causality can be found even in single panel images.

Using Gary Larson's *The Far Side* as a jumping off point, Carrier shows how a single static image can contain narrative within it, implying past or future actions that will make a story. Larson, Carrier argues, possess a sadistic imagination of disaster, skilled at placing his hapless characters in harm's way. But these disasters are rarely shown; rather they exist implicitly in cartoons that imply future action. As Carrier notes, "Baudelaire follows the tradition in which interpreters understand a picture by "moving it, envisaging the next moment of a scene. . . . Larson's humor very often depends upon a viewer's expectation about how thus to move images." By calling attention to the implied causality of Larson's art, Carrier helps us see the linkage between single panel strips and sequential comics.

Word and pictures make up the elemental units of comics. Art theorist W. J. T. Mitchell complicates the usual bifurcation between words and pictures by arguing that even by themselves they are not pure forms. Offering a critique of the ideal of formal purity, Mitchell argues "it is also a fact that 'pure' visual representations routinely incorporate textuality in a quite literal way, insofar as writing and other arbitrary marks enter into the field of visual representation. By the same token, 'pure' texts incorporate visuality quite literally the moment they are written or printed in visible form." Words contain images and pictures have literary meaning. By complicating the distinction between words and pictures, Mitchell helps us see that comics can be seen as part of a larger spectrum that includes both the literary and the pictorial. The critique of purity is a valuable line of argument in comics scholarship because the hybrid nature of comics, the mixture of words and pictures, has been a continual site of controversy. (The term "imagetext," which Mitchell helped popularize, remains useful in highlighting the hybrid nature of comics and related forms.)

The most audacious interventions in comics theory have often come from France, where the influence of structuralism, poststructuralism, and semiotics has fostered unusually rigorous analyses. Thierry Groensteen's *The System of Comics* is perhaps the most theoretically ambitious book in this tradition. By sternly eliminating any definition of comics that is purely historical or contingent, Groensteen arrives at the notion of "iconic solidarity" as a foundational principal for defining the form. Iconic solidarity is defined as "interdependent images that, participating in a series, present the double characteristic of being separated . . . and which are plastically and semantically overdetermined by the fact of their coexistence *in praesentia*." (This can be seen as a more refined presentation of Scott McCloud's emphasis on sequential images.) Groensteen's argument can be usefully contrasted with David Carrier's essay, which discusses panels that offer little in the way of "iconic solidarity."

If Groensteen can be seen as overlapping with McCloud, Charles Hatfield is working in the tradition of R. C. Harvey in giving salience to the "verbal-visual blend" as a crucial component in the language of comics. While Harvey was careful to say that the "verbal-visual blend" is not a universal feature of all comics, he did find greater aesthetic pleasure in comics that cunningly combine words and pictures to achieve effects that could not be created otherwise. Charles Hatfield takes his cue from Harvey in focusing on the interplay between words and pictures. But whereas Harvey most often praises clarity of storytelling, Hatfield is interested in how the "verbal-visual blend" can make stories more complicated and dense. Influenced by W. J. T. Mitchell's critique of formal purity, Hatfield contends that "pictures are not simply to be received; they must be decoded."

By dealing with how an imagetext conveys meaning, analysts like Hatfield are implicitly dealing with the issue of reader response. Joseph Witek brings this implied reader to the fore by looking at the use of panel-numbering, arrows, and grid shape in early twentieth-century comics. He shows how these techniques were used to create a protocol for reading, so that the eyes that viewed the page would know how to follow a narrative along. By raising the issue of a reading protocol, Witek also helps shift the debate over the nature of comics away from a search for an all-encompassing definition towards a historically aware focus on strategies used by cartoonists to engage readers.

Witek suggests that "a consideration of two such intriguing and now-obsolescent features that once served as reading guides—the numbering of panels within the grid of the page in early comics strips, and the directional arrows which occasionally have been deployed to guide the eye of the reader to the proper panel in a narrative sequence—suggests that 'comicsness' might usefully be reconceptualized from being an immutable attribute of texts to being considered as a historically contingent and evolving set of reading protocols that are applied to texts, that to be a comic text means to be *read* as a comic." Witek's argument highlights the evolving nature of comics. If comics are a language, it is a language whose grammar changes over time.

The question of form can be approached from a macro-level (how words and pictures interact), but it can also be looked at from a micro-level. Breaking down the component parts of comics (e.g., panels, word balloons, lettering, and sound effects) and examining their functioning can yield great insight. Nothing on a comics page can be taken for granted, not even the space behind characters and between panels (as discussed by Pascal Lefèvre) nor the wide range of sounds found in manga (as examined by Robert S. Petersen). In calling attention to the way in which cartoonists place their characters within panels and place panels within a page, Lefèvre reinforces the arguments Hatfield and Witek made about the complex ways in which readers navigate through pages of comics. "Each reader is confronted with a particular extradiegetic space of the comic book itself, with a particular organization of the space on each page and with a particular representation of the fragmented diegetic space in a series of panels," Lefèvre concludes. "During his reading process the reader tries to cope with these various aspects of space and to make meaning of it all."

Petersen's essay is particularly insightful in showing how sound effects vary in different linguistic traditions. Situating manga sound effects both in Japanese cultural history and in the craft practices of manga artists (*mangaka*) Petersen argues that "the character of Japanese language has helped *mangaka* create new and exciting uses for sound in their manga. The effective use of sound in manga produces a drama and vitality to the work where the reader not only subvocalizes the sounds, but also becomes more attune to silences." In effect, he serves as a bridge between formalist concerns and a revived focus on culture and context that we will see in the third section.

Caricature

DAVID CARRIER

'Tis only causation, which produces such a connexion, as to give us assurance from the
existence of action of one object, that 'twas follow'd or preceded by another existence
or action.

DAVID HUME, *A Treatise of Human Nature*

While working in my third-floor study, I can sometimes see the postman coming along
my quiet dead-end street. And when then I run downstairs, I view the mail coming
through the slot and hear my daughter's dog, Brigston, rushing barking to defend the
house. I understand what is happening at any given moment by relation to what happens earlier or later. The mail appears in the door because the postman has arrived;
Brigston awakens because he hears the postman. I infer, as Hume noted, causal connections between those pairs of events.

This everyday experience tells something about how to look at an old-master visual
narrative. Viewing the *Nightwatch* in the Rijksmuseum, Amsterdam, I see the militia-
men, arranged around the man at the center, seeming to march forward toward me; "the
impression of action . . . is so persuasive that its admirers have long wondered whether
the painting does not depict some specific event."[1] That the painting is set on the far wall
of the room may encourage this illusion. Nowadays everyone is aware of the fallacies of
interpreting old-master pictures as if they were photographs. Since artists of Rembrandt's
time did not aspire to depict individual moments of ongoing actions, it would be anachronistic to identify moments before and after that instant they show. The general goal
of such artists was to create a self-contained, clear visual presentation. A photograph,
because it is of the world, necessarily shows one of a sequence of moments. A painting,
however naturalistic it may appear, does not have this relation to the visual world.[2]

In viewing some visual images, however, understanding the depicted scene does
require imagining an earlier or later moment of the depicted action. To understand
"Dropping the Pilot," a caricature discussed by E. H. Gombrich, we must see Bismarck,
on the ship's ladder, as descending.[3] Someone who thought that Bismarck, walking

---

Reprinted by permission of the publisher from David Carrier, *The Aesthetics of Comics* (Penn State University Press, 2000),
11–25.

Sir John Tenniel, "Dropping the Pilot," *Punch*,
March 29, 1890.

backward, was preparing to ascend would give a quite fallacious reading, though one consistent with the visual evidence. Just as understanding one of Poussin's esoteric subjects requires knowing his iconography, so the correct interpretation of this image demands some background information about German politics. The viewer needs to know why Bismarck was represented as a pilot, dropped off by Wilhelm II. Such background knowledge is required also by Edward Gorey's images, where "the moment depicted is the moment of maximum drama, just before the effect of disaster."[4] Anticipating that next scene, our laughter expresses pleasure at our imagining of disaster.

Just as what Danto calls a narrative sentence makes reference to a later moment, so too must these pictures refer to some such later moment. "During the French revolution, the father of the author of *The Painter of Modern Life* renounced his priesthood." That description of Charles Baudelaire's father could only be understood in the 1860s, when *The Painter of Modern Life* was published. Narrative sentences that "refer to at least two time-separated events, and describe the earlier event," Danto argues, thus form the basis of historical explanations, which, by connecting moments, tell how the world changes.[5] Visual narratives, analogously, refer to at least two such separated moments. Hume asks how is it that we imagine connections between events. If causal connections are known only through experience, then why do we believe that one event inevitably is followed by another? Comics theorists ask a similar question. What experience gives us warrant to place an individual picture within such an imagined sequence?

How does representation work? Aestheticians and art historians invoke such diverse concepts as "art as illusion," "seeing in," and "seeing as" to describe the way that pigment on canvas or ink on paper represents.[6] Some think this a problem calling for an adequate technique of description; others believe that semiotic theorizing provides the key; and some, myself included, are inclined to suspect that experimental psychology provides the best analysis. Gombrich's account, in which the history of representation making is treated as a story of discovery, like that of scientific theorizing, has the great virtue of showing how this activity can be the source of a master narrative, linking together the concerns of European artists ranging from Cimabue to Constable and the Impressionists.[7]

How is it that from one isolated image we envisage earlier and later moments of an ongoing visual narrative? Caricatures pose this equally interesting but much less discussed question. Gombrich's argument that making successful representations involves projection may also help to explain caricature. The artist's aim is to enable the spectator to form some hypothesis about what is depicted. If that process is successful, the spectator's hypothesis matches the artist's intention, and that viewer sees illusionistically represented what the artist desired to depict. When, rather, the artist's image is visually ambiguous—capable of more than one plausible interpretation—then he or she has failed to communicate. Thus we understand many caricatures by forming some hypothesis about the previous or the next scene of the action.[8] Seeing the world, I know that it existed a moment earlier and will continue to exist. A picture shows only how things appear at one moment. Seeing a picture, I need not imagine that the depicted scene existed before and after the moment depicted. Many representations—still lifes, portraits, some landscapes—do not appear to define temporal sequences. Usually I do not imagine how the man portrayed got into his sitting position, or how he will stand up after the portrait is completed. What nowadays makes thinking about images as moments in narrative sequences so natural is movies. Just as, so it has been argued, the development of naturalistic representaions made it possible to understand the first photographs, so perhaps the experience of caricatures and comics made the earliest films more accessible. "With a few rare exceptions, the comic strip gathered most of its basic expressive resources without recourse to the cinema, and often even before the later was born."[9]

Baudelaire gives a characteristically lively description of Daumier's great 1840 image *Le dernier bain*: "Standing on the parapet of a quay and already leaning forward, so that his body forms an acute angle with the base from which it is parting company—like a statue losing its balance—a man is letting himself topple into the river. He must have really made up his mind, for his arms are calmly folded, and a huge pavingstone is attached to his neck with a rope."[10] In an instant, this poor man will be underwater dying, unseen by the placid fisherman on the opposite riverbank. Logically speaking, many other alternatives are visually consistent with what we see. The man could detach the weight; what appears a weight could rather be a container filled with feathers; he could fall safely into a boat; an angel or a person with a flying suit like the one worn by Buck Rogers could rescue him. But, just as a Constable landscape "works" as a representation because we inevitably see the small white mark as a house and not any number of other possible things, so Daumier's success involves creating an unambiguous picture. Even before reading the title, we are sure that this man is about to drown himself.

Honoré Daumier, *Le dernier bain*, 1840.

Many caricatures, of course, do not work this way.[11] But some caricatures are pro-tocomics because understanding them requires imagining a later moment of the action. In his analysis of representation, Gombrich argues that projection can be understood by knowing what background information we bring to the picture. With caricatures, anal-ogously, how we interpret depends upon such knowledge. In the caricature of Bismarck, we require information about German history; in the Daumier, common-sense knowl-edge about the effects of gravity. These two caricatures are in this way ideologically neutral: whether you admire or detest Bismarck, whatever your views on suicide, you will see these images the same way.

Gombrich gives Rodolphe Töpffer's caricatures a key role in the history of modern-ism: "It needs the detachment of an enlightened nineteenth-century humorist to play with the magic of creation, to make up these playful doodles, and to question them for their character and soul as if they were real creatures."[12] Earlier, he suggests, it was not possible to handle aggressive images in this detached way. Caricature is inherently an art of exaggeration. The Neoplatonic tradition involves creating ideal beauty, finding that perfection realized only imperfectly in actual individuals; caricature (and the comic) involves deformation. Engraved images of modern life, Baudelaire observes, "can be translated either into beauty or ugliness; in one direction, they become caricatures, in the other, antique statues."[13] Manet painted modern beauty; Daumier had an altogether different concern. There are many obscene caricatures, and a great deal of sex in comics; but the characters are never ideal enough to be beautiful.[14]

As Baudelaire explained, Louis Philippe caricatured as a pear is a classic example of visual aggression.[15] "Philipon . . . wanted to prove . . . that nothing was more innocent than that prickly and provoking pear . . . in the very presence of the court, he drew a series of sketches of which the first exactly reproduced the royal physiognomy, and each successive one, drawing further and further away from the primary image, approached ever closer to the fatal goal—the pear!" When, in the course of writing *High Art: Charles Baudelaire and the Origins of Modernism,* I came to Baudelaire's essays on caricature, I was pleased that Michele Hannoosh's recent book dealt so thoroughly with this topic.[16] My own approach, providing a philosophically plausible reconstruction of Baudelaire's ideas rather than merely setting them in historical context, was not easy to extend to caricature. Hannoosh's admirably detailed discussion of the caricaturists discussed by Baudelaire provides a very full and convincing statement of the historical context of his thinking, but has little to say about the application of his ideas to present-day caricature. That is unsurprising, for this part of his aesthetic theory is grounded in highly traditional Catholic ideals.

Much (but not all) of Baudelaire's *Painter of Modern Life* can be read as a manifesto for modernist art, a prophecy of the tradition of art depicting urban consumer society, a tradition running from Manet and the Impressionists to Andy Warhol, the other Pop artists, and their successors in the 1990s.[17] "On the Essence of Laughter," like Baudelaire's account of Delacroix, seems centered on ideas now essentially of historical interest.[18] Baudelaire proclaims that our pleasure in laughter shows the importance of original sin. We laugh because we are sinners: "It is certain that human laughter is intimately linked with the accident of an ancient Fall. . . . In the earthly paradise . . . joy did not find its dwelling in laughter" (149–50). Christ experienced anger and tears; but "in the eyes of One who has all knowledge and all power, the comic does not exist" (149). It seems obviously difficult to extract his claims from this essentially theological context. When most modern-day unbelievers have great difficulty taking such claims literally, what remains of Baudelaire's theory of caricature?[19]

What then has caused me to reconsider this way of thinking has been more recent study of a contemporary caricaturist whose images exemplify this Baudelairean theory of humor in absolutely uncanny ways. Although in the 1980s Gary Larson became much more famous than anyone known only within the art world, his caricatures have not inspired much commentary, so far as I know, by art critics.[20] This is surprising, for his extraordinarily inventive images tell us a great deal about American culture of that era.[21] Larson employs repeated, even obsessive, development of a few central concerns; for every example I cite, many similar ones could easily be provided.

Totally apolitical—apart from his passionate support for animal rights—Larson hates change, which he thinks always brings disaster. Taking almost all his subjects from lower- or middle-class white American life, but not a chauvinist, his only significant foreign settings are African jungles, the Arctic, and rivers inhabited by headhunters. Borderlines between city and country, humans and animals, are blurred: deer are hunted in their own living rooms; dogs steal family cars; animals take photos on vacation and appear on quiz shows. Larson loves endless mindless repetition—people in hell doing five million leg lifts or discovering that cold fronts never arrive, and disasters that befall those stupid enough to eat potato chips or buy tropical fish in the desert (Heaven is of less interest to him than hell). He shows petty theft, minor crime, and, occasionally, homicide; menacing ocean scenes hold a special attraction for him. He adores sharks.

Larson's archaeologists are doomed never to learn about the past, his anthropologists to understand nothing of the "natives" they study. His animals mimic humans doing stupid things. Larson's world is oddly asexual in a preadolescent-male way. He loves toilet humor and human-animal couples, not as illustrations of bestiality but as just another variety of dumbness. His women would just as soon be married to animals—and why not, when all people are so stupid? Apart from such normal fascinations as dog-cat battles, his odd obsessions include cross-dressing cowboys, men with peg legs, and—what does this mean?—the erotic significance of chickens. His stupid, sadistic, and dysfunctional characters enjoy their lives. Gravely serious academic commentators have written much about "postmodernism" and the end of history. Larson's immense popularity—is there anyone who really dislikes his work?—shows that, at some level, very many people suspect that progress is finished. It is hard to imagine him showing the triumph of virtue.

The man at the blackboard who has discovered "the purpose of the universe"—an elaborate equation he works on sums up to zero—summarizes Larson's worldview. Living in a run-down universe can be fun. Scientists who play games instead of doing research, pilots who cannot read instrument-panel dials, a musician who tries to perform with only one cymbal: Larson's characters are happily, hopelessly incompetent. He really has only this one major theme, disaster. This is why encountering his pictures one by one in the newspaper was more fun than looking at the collections of his art. Humor of this sort is only occasionally a central concern in old-master art.[22] Unfunny paintings, calling for knowledge of esoteric texts, give their interpreters the sense that they are smart. Larson's cartoons make you feel as stupid as the characters he loves to depict; temporarily imagining being stupid, he shows, can be fun. Or as he puts it, quoting Mel Brooks: "Tragedy is when I cut my finger. Comedy is when you walk into an open sewer and die."[23]

The essence of such humor, Baudelaire claims, is to "produce in the spectator, or rather the reader, a joy in his own, superiority" (164). Seeing Larson's idiotic characters, we recognize our own modest superiority. I would never let my daughter's dog drive while I hung out the car window like a dog. A farmer meets extraterrestrials who are walking hands: "Inadvertently, Roy dooms the entire earth to annihilation when, in an attempt to be friendly, he seizes their leader by the head and shakes vigorously."[24] Why is Roy's action funny? Few people really desire that our planet be destroyed. And yet, the idea that it might be destroyed by aliens so dumb as to be offended by Roy is amusing. We laugh, flattered to be reminded that we are not as stupid as people who read manuals about snake identification while poisonous snakes bite them, or aliens who come all the way to Earth to steal chickens. Responding aesthetically, we enjoy imagining disaster. It may seem odd to speak of "an aesthetic response," for all of Larson's figures, even Jackie Onassis, are hopelessly ugly. And yet, what lucky people! Their ugliness does not disturb them, for they are found desirable by others. When "the elephant man meets a buffalo gal," they find each other ravishing.[25] In his apolitical way, Larson shows the problems with belief in the superiority of your own species.

Fascinated by religion, Larson is seriously skeptical of its claims. His characters frequently are scientists or inventors, but he rejects belief in technological progress entirely. It is surprising that nerds, one of his great subjects, love him. Everyone in his pictures looks old, even the children—they have no future. Bad as it presently is, our world could be even worse: that assertion is funny because we postmoderns fear that it might be true. Perhaps this is why technocrats seem especially to enjoy his work—this worry must be an occupational hazard for them. Larson appeals to those who don't much like modern art. When he shows Leonardo da Vinci learning to draw from a matchbook advertisement, you cannot but feel his populist ambivalence about high culture.

Need you be a closet sadist to laugh at Larson's fat woman calling for her dog to run into a blocked door, "Here, Fifi! C'mon! . . . Faster, Fifi!"?[26] When Amnesty International objected to his scenes of torture—"Congratulations Bob, Torturer of the Month" reads the slogan behind three bound victims—he said: "This group has at least raised my consciousness to this problem."[27] Like cat lovers who objected to showing the dog's tying up the new cat, these critics blur the line between appearance and reality. No doubt we all do that in responding to caricatures, but without some such temporary suspension of disbelief, cartoon art would be impossible. Could a man in a slowly sinking rubber life raft be watching a portable TV? Might a time machine run out of gas, leaving its inventor stranded among dinosaurs? Would deer tie up a hunter, leaving the hunting license stuck in his mouth? If you think too much, Larson's images cannot "come off." To understand his art, you must enjoy momentarily being stupid.

Comedy—this is the true cliché—is an inherently conservative artistic genre. It shows that nothing changes. You cannot "tell" a Matisse, for his art is essentially visual; but you can usually "tell" a Larson, for mostly his conceptions are verbal. What Baudelaire calls our "double nature" (165) consists in the capacity to enjoy imagining people being injured in disasters while ourselves remaining safe. God and advanced intelligences from other planets are no smarter than humans in Larson's anthropomorphic World, where the sun rises and sets, run by a man who operates a switch. Aliens intelligent enough to operate flying saucers crash because a bee enters their spacecraft or because they get too close to the Statue of Liberty. Even God is humanly stupid: he dials the wrong phone number; discovers that snakes are easy to construct; and when but only a child—who are His parents?—tries to make a chicken in his room.

Almost all Larsons are absurdly easy to interpret. (When it takes effort to understand his images, as in some few he himself analyzes, then he fails.) Very often commentary treats modernist museum art as personal expression, the artist's choice of subjects understood in relation to his or her politics and private life. When Larson shows scenes that almost everyone understands immediately, asking about his personal beliefs is irrelevant. Many accounts of populist culture, growing out of the Marxist tradition, propose to see through such images; today this condescending procedure is no longer satisfying. No doubt Larson expresses a childhood that his biographer might describe. But insofar as we value a Larson for what it tells us about our collective desires, fantasies, and fears, such analysis is essentially irrelevant. What constitutes the interpretation of a Larson is laughter. In thus interpreting, we learn about ourselves and our culture.

Larson almost always has a very simple iconography. Two men in a disheveled room peel open the venetian blind: "Roommates Elvis and Salman Rushdie sneak a quick look at the outside world."[28] To understand Larson's images you need only know about the culture's most famous heroes: Einstein (the would-be basketball player), Picasso, Superman, and people in the headlines, like the once notorious hijacker D. B. Cooper. "Only a one-liner"—what visual artist wants to be told that once you have "gotten it," there is nothing more to be said about his or her works? But Larson's entire oeuvre consists of but the pleasure of imagining disaster, which is perhaps why he retired early on—he seems to have been a one-theme artist.[29]

For a long time, Baudelaire's unoriginal theory of humor seemed to me obviously implausible.[30] Finding Baudelaire's odd antitheology absurd, it seemed a waste of time to analyze his argumentation. Some modern caricaturists play with Baudelairean pleasure in doing evil.[31] Edward Gorey's scenes of children's disasters belong to this somewhat precious self-consciously camp tradition. But unlike Gorey, Larson is genuinely popular. Baudelaire's irony, Hannoosh argues, implies that his account of humor should be interpreted, not as merely false, but metaphorically, as an ironizing that itself is "an example of comic art in the best sense."[32] To enjoy such visual jokes, we must pretend to take the doctrine seriously, while knowing that it is false, and not simply reject Baudelaire's theology or take it to be true. This kind of play is very naturally associated with Larson's caricatures, which are funny only for the viewer who can pretend to accept something like his view of sin. If you find Christian morality absurd (or offensive), then you can hardly make sense of joking scenes set in hell; if you believe the wicked are punished, then the idea that this hot place might temporarily be cooled by a boiler failure cannot be funny.

Only some of Larson's scenes play with theology in this way, but this attitude can be suggestively generalized to explain how he thinks of his nonreligious subjects. Very frequently he shows animals behaving like, or being mistaken for, humans. Denying that human beings are inherently different from animals, he thus touches upon religious tradition. To imagine that a cat could kill a bird by blowing up its cage, that a dog would play ventriloquist to a cat sitting on his knee, or that rowers on a slave ship could be entertained by a pianist playing *Row, Row, Row Your Boat*: this requires taking something like a former believer's attitude toward religion. What is comic for Larson is any situation that can be called absurd because it is neither simply the way things are nor just impossible to imagine. To speak in Baudelaire's terms, we laugh because "an artist is only an artist on the condition that he is a double man"—because "it is perfectly true that he knows what he is doing; but he also knows that the essence of this type of the comic is that it should appear to be unaware of itself" (164).

Frequently, modern attitudes toward theological tradition embody this essentially comic attitude. How funny it would be, a secular person can think, were such preposterous beliefs correct. A dying atheist who finds him- or herself in hell ought to be ready to laugh. In *High Art* I argue that Baudelaire's general aesthetic includes two very different accounts: a traditionally oriented way of thinking and an anticipation of radically original art of the city—a compromise expressed in his passionate admiration for both Delacroix and Guys. What makes his theorizing hard to grasp, I claim, is that it presents both these very different approaches without any attempt at synthesis. The same could be said about his theory of caricature, which both looks backward historically to religious tradition and, by treating that way of thinking ironically, expresses the skepticism associated with modernist secularization. When we laugh at Larson's images, we both take seriously religious ideas and refuse to take literally those out-of-date ways of thinking; to describe this situation in Hannoosh's ironical terms, the very doubleness of our divided nature appears when viewing one such image.

Why do we laugh at Larsons? *High Art* draws attention to the general way in which Baudelaire follows the tradition in which interpreters understand a picture by "moving it," envisaging the next moment of a scene. The difficulty of modernist visual art, I argue, is that insofar as it fails to indicate what will happen next, it threatens to be indecipherable. Larson's humor very often depends upon a viewer's expectation about how thus "to move" images. (This he probably learned from comics, in which that next scene is actually depicted.) Presented with one moment of an ongoing action, we imagine disaster in the next scene. As he explains, his images are funniest when, only implying "what is about to happen," they thereby heighten "the tension."[33] "Don't be alarmed folks. . . . He's completely harmless unless something startles him."[34] Imagining the next scene, when the door of a crowded elevator will close on this "harmless" lion's tail, is funny. Why do we project the next scene thus? There is, after all, nothing to prevent us from imagining that disaster is averted.

A model of the way we "move" such pictures is provided by the great Larson in which a hapless man walks unknowingly to face a sniper: "Misunderstanding his employees' screams of 'Simmons has lost his marbles,' Mr. Wagner bursts from his office for the last time."[35] Imagining the next moment when Wagner will be murdered, we laugh. (Is this Wagner the composer? The Germanic name may be part of the hostile joke.) The wordplay with the phrase "losing your marbles" is essential. Were the caption to read, "Misunderstanding his employees' screams of 'Simmons has a gun,' Mr. Wagner bursts from his office for the last time," the image would not be funny. That we seemingly freely choose the next scene reveals our double nature. We enjoy cruelly imagining disaster. There is nothing to prevent us from supposing that the sniper throws down his weapon or that Wagner, recognizing the danger, does not come forward. Unlike Baudelaire, I hesitate to draw theological conclusions. That we gain aesthetic pleasure from Larsons does not show that in life we, his admirers, are sadists. Perhaps one benevolent function of such art is to permit us to discharge our inevitable hostility in harmless ways. This disaster we imagine is not, so we hypocritically think, really our fault—we only pretend that it seems inevitable. Caught (in ways Freud analyzed in his discussion of verbal joking) in the pleasure of aggressive play, we would prefer to imagine Wagner's death. Such pictures are what Danto calls enthymemes, visual syllogisms with an obvious missing premise, which the reader must supply. This reader "is not, as a passive auditor, told what to put there; he must find that out and put it there himself."[36] Reasoning thus, we both acknowledge aggressive fantasy and disavow any such intention. Deceiving ourselves, we pretend that it is not our malice but only Larson's situation that inevitably will bring about disaster.

NOTES

1. Gary Schwartz, *Rembrandt: His Life, His Paintings* (New York: Viking, 1985), 210; see also David Carrier, *Principles of Art History Writing* (University Park: Penn State University Press, 1991), 197–200.

2. See Aaron Scharf, "Painting, Photography, and the Image of Movement," *Burlington Magazine* 10 (May 1962): 186–93, and William I. Homer, with John Talbot, "Eakins, Muybridge, and the Motion Picture Process," *Art Quarterly* 26, no. 2 (1963): 194–216.

3. See E. H. Gombrich, *Meditations on a Hobby Horse* (London: Phaidon, 1963), 131–32.

4. Karen Wilkin, "Mr. Earbrass Jots Down a Few Visual Notes: The World of Edward Gorey," in *The World of Edward Gorey*, by Clifford Ross and Karen Wilkin (New York: Abrams, 1996), 63; on the history of

caricature, see Irving Lavin, "High and Low Before Their Time: Bemini and the Art of Social Satire," in *Modern Art and Popular Culture: Readings in High and Low*, ed. Kirk Varnedoe and Adam Gopnik (New York: Abrams, 1990), 8–51.

5. Arthur C. Danto, *Narration and Knowledge* (New York: Columbia University Press, 1985), 1.

6. Richard Wollheim, *Painting as an Art: The A. W. Mellon Lectures in the Fine Arts* (Princeton: Princeton University Press, 1987), chaps. 1–2.

7. See David Carrier, *Artwriting* (Amherst: University of Massachusetts Press, 1987), chaps 1–2.

8. This argument is plausible quite apart from the ultimate critical judgment on Gombrich's theory of representation; unlike that account, a quasi-scientific testable theory, mine is a purely conceptual analysis.

9. Francis Lacassin, "The Comic Strip and Film Language," *Film Quarterly* 25, no. 4 (1972), 14. See also Donald Crafton, *Before Mickey: The Animated Film, 1898–1928* (Cambridge: MIT Press, 1982).

10. Charles Baudelaire, *The Painter of Modern Life and Other Essays*, trans. Jonathan Mayne (London: Phaidon Press, 1964), 176; see Michele Hannoosh, *Baudelaire and Caricature: From the Comic to an Art of Modernity* (University Park: Penn State University Press, 1992), 139–40.

11. In some special cases, a picture that appears an isolated still scene can, when properly analyzed, be revealed as essentially belonging to a narrative sequence. The drawing of his dream by Freud's patient the Wolf Man may be an example; see Whitney Davis, *Replications: Archaeology, Art History, Psychoanalysis* (University Park: Penn State University Press, 1996), chap. 11.

12. Gombrich, *Art and Illusion*, 342.

13. Baudelaire, *The Painter of Modern Life*, 2.

14. See Bob Adelman, with Art Spiegelman, Richard Merkin, and Madeline Kripke, *Tijuana Bibles: Art and Wit in America's Forbidden Funnies, 1930s-1950s* (New York: Simon & Schuster, 1997).

15. Baudelaire, *The Painter of Modern Life*, 172. See Elise K. Kenney and John M. Merriman, *The Pear: French Graphic Arts in the Golden Age of Caricature*, exhibition catalogue (South Hadley: Mount Holyoke College Art Museum, 1991).

16. Hannoosh, *Baudelaire and Caricature*.

17. A different approach is provided by Gérald Froidevaux, *Baudelaire: Représentation et modernité* (Paris: Jose Corti, 1989), chap. 5, "La caricature ou l'affirmation negative du beau."

18. Baudelaire, *The Painter of Modern Life*, 147–65; further references are incorporated into the text.

19. As Paul Benacerraf has pointed out to me, even on its own level this theory has obvious problems. Suppose that we are all fallen. Still, not everyone laughs at the same jokes. Appeal to our shared fallen condition cannot explain why we respond differently to jokes.

20. But see Bill Berkson, *Homage to George Herriman*, exhibition catalogue (San Francisco: Campbell-Thiebaud Gallery, 1997), and MaLin Wilson, "DemoKrazy in the American West," *Art Issues*, September/October 1997, 24–27.

21. My subject is Larson the cartoonist as revealed in his work, not the person, whom I have never met.

22. But see Paul Barolsky, *Infinite Jest: Wit and Humor in Italian Renaissance Art* (Columbia: University of Missouri Press, 1978).

23. Gary Larson, *The Prehistory of "The Far Side": A Tenth Anniversary Exhibit* (Kansas City: Andrews & McMeel, 1989), 5.

24. Gary Larson, *The Far Side Gallery 2* (Kansas City: Andrews & McMeel, 1988), 78.

25. Gary Larson, *The Far Side Gallery 4* (Kansas City: Andrews & McMeel, 1989), 109.

26. Gary Larson, *The Far Side Gallery 2* (Kansas City: Andrews & McMeel, 1986), 9.

27. Larson, *The Prehistory of "The Far Side,"* 164.

28. Gary Larson, *The Far Side Gallery 5* (Kansas City: Andrews & McMeel, 1995), 23.

29. His work has some affinities with James Thurber's, but otherwise it is hard to cite art-historical sources for Larson's art. He has, in obviously ironical ways, described the childhood sources of his art; see Gary Larson, *The Curse of Madame "C": A Far Side Collection* (Kansas City: Andrew & McMeel, 1994).

30. Larson's one exercise in Baudelairean Satanism, the scene of Christ, risen from the grave, wondering "what time it is . . . I feel like I've been dead for three days" (Larson, *The Prehistory of "The Far Side,"* 105) is, as he notes, not funny.

31. See David Carrier, "Introduction: Baudelaire's Metaphysics," in *High Art: Charles Baudelaire and the Origins of Modernism* (University Park: Penn State University Press, 1996).

32. Hannoosh, *Baudelaire and Caricature*, 283.

33. Larson, *The Prehistory of "The Far Side,"* 136.

34. Gary Larson, *The Far Side Gallery* (Kansas City: Andrews & McMeel, 1984), 192.

35. Larson, *The Far Side Gallery* 4, 142.

36. I borrow from Arthur C. Danto, *The Transfiguration of the Commonplace: A Philosophy of Art* (Cambridge: Harvard University Press, 1981), 170, on the rhetoric of visual images.

Beyond Comparison

W. J. T. MITCHELL

The best preventive to comparative methods is an insistence on literalness and materiality. That is why, rather than comparing this novel or poem with that painting or
statue, I find it more helpful to begin with actual conjunctions of words and images in
illustrated texts, or mixed media such as film, television, and theatrical performance.
With these media, one encounters a concrete set of empirical givens, an image-text
structure responsive to prevailing conventions (or resistance to conventions) governing
the relation of visual and verbal experience. Some plays (taking their cue from Aristotle)
privilege *lexis* over *opsis*, speech over scenery, dialogue over visual spectacle.[1] The film
medium has passed through a technological revolution involving a shift from a visual to
a verbal paradigm in the shift from silent film to the "talkies," and film theory invariably
confronts some version of the image/text problem whenever it attempts to specify the
nature of "film language."[2] The relative positioning of visual and verbal representation
(or of sight and sound, space and time) in these mixed media is, moreover, never simply
a formal issue or a question to be settled by "scientific" semiotics. The relative value, location, and the very *identity* of "the verbal" and "the visual" is exactly what is in question.
Ben Jonson denounced the spectacular set designs of Indigo Jones as degradations of the
poetic "soul" of the masque. Erwin Panofsky thought the coming of sound corrupted
the pure visuality of silent movies.[3] These are not scientific judgments, but engagements
in the theoretical praxis of representation. The image-text relation in film and theater
is not a merely technical question, but a site of conflict, a nexus where political, institutional, and social antagonisms play themselves out in the materiality of representation.
Artaud's emphasis on mute spectacle and Brecht's deployment of textual projections are
not merely "aesthetic" innovations, but precisely motivated interventions in the semio-
politics of the stage. Even something as mundane and familiar as the relative proportion
of image and text on the front page of the daily newspaper is a direct indicator of the
social class of its readership. The real question to ask when confronted with these kinds
of image-text relations is not "what is the difference (or similarity) between the words
and the images?" but "what difference do the differences (and similarities) make?" That
is, why does it matter how words and images are juxtaposed, blended, or separated?

Reprinted by permission of the publisher from W. J. T. Mitchell, *Picture Theory* (University of Chicago Press, 1994),
89–96.

The "matter" of the image-text conjunction matters a great deal in the work of William Blake, whose illuminated books seem designed to elicit the full range of relations between visual and verbal literacy. In his illuminated books, Blake constructed image-text combinations that range from the absolutely disjunctive ("illustrations" that have no textual reference) to the absolutely synthetic identification of verbal and visual codes (marks that collapse the distinction between writing and drawing).[4] It's not surprising, of course, that Blake's illuminated books, and the whole related genre of the "artist's book," would tend to exhibit flexible, experimental, and "high-tension" relations between words and images. The "normal" relations of image and word (in the illustrated newspaper or even the cartoon page) follow more traditional formulas involving the clear subordination and suturing of one medium to the other, often with a straightforward division of labor.[5] In the typical comic strip, word is to image as speech (or thought) is to action and bodies. Language appears in a speech-balloon emanating from the speaker's mouth, or a thought-cloud emerging from the thinker's head. (In the pre-Cartesian world of the medieval illuminated manuscript, by contrast, speech tends to be represented as a scroll rather than a cloud or bubble, and it emanates from the gesturing hand of the speaker rather than the mouth; language seems to co-exist in the same pictive/scriptive space—handwriting emanating from hand-gesture—instead of being depicted as a ghostly emanation from an invisible interior).[6] Narrative diegesis (cf. *Prince Valiant*'s "Our Story . . .") is generally located in the margins of the image, in a position understood to be "outside" the present moment of depicted action, scenes, and bodies.[7]

This is not to suggest that "normal" relations of word and image are uninteresting or that vernacular composite forms like the comic strip or the journalistic photo essay are incapable of experimentation and complex deviations from the norm. Gary Trudeau's anticinematic, talky cartoon sequences in *Doonesbury* defy the normal privileging of the visual image as the place "where the action is" on the cartoon page. *Doonesbury* is a kind of exercise in visual deprivation, rarely showing bodies in motion, often repeating an identical and empty image (a view of the White House, the back of a television set, a point of light above a presidential seal) in every frame, displacing all movement onto the bodiless voice indicated by the text. Postmodern cartoon novels like *Maus* and *The Dark Knight* employ a wide range of complex and self-reflexive techniques. *Maus* attenuates visual access to its narrative by thickening its frame story (the dialogue of a holocaust survivor and his son is conspicuously uncinematic in its emphasis on speech) and by veiling the human body at all levels of the visual narrative with the figures of animals (Jews are mice, Germans are cats, Poles are pigs).[8] *The Dark Knight*, by contrast, is highly cinematic and televisual, employing the full repertoire of motion picture and video rhetoric while continually breaking frames and foregrounding the apparatus of visual representation.

Similar observations might be made on the mixed medium of the photographic essay. The normal structure of this kind of imagetext involves the straightforward discursive or narrative suturing of the verbal and visual: texts explain, narrate, describe, label, speak for (or to) the photographs; photographs illustrate, exemplify, clarify, ground, and document the text.[9] Given this conventional division of labor, it's hardly surprising that an aggressively modernist experimental deviation like James Agee and Walker Evans's

Let Us Now Praise Famous Men would come into existence. *Famous Men* is a photo essay whose form resists all suturing of word and image: the photos are physically and symbolically separated from the text; there are also no captions on the photos, and few references to the photos in the text.[10] These deviations, moreover, cannot be fully accounted for by notions of "purifying" visual and verbal media. Or, more precisely, the "purist" strategies of Agee and Evans only make sense in relation to their sense of participating in a hopelessly compromised and impure representational practice, one for which the political and ethical conventions need to be challenged at every level.

How do we get from the study of media in which visual-verbal relationships are unavoidable—such as films, plays, newspapers, cartoon strips, illustrated books—to the traditional subjects of "interartistic comparison," the analogies and differences between poems and paintings, novels and statues? In some ways it should be clear that we ought never come back to this subject, that it is a non-subject without a real method or object of investigation. But in another sense it should be obvious that the subject of the image/text is just as unavoidable and necessary with these "unmixed" media as it is with mixed, composite forms. Interartistic comparison has always had an intuition of this fact, without really grasping its implications. The image/text problem is not just something constructed "between" the arts, the media, or different forms of representation, but an unavoidable issue within the individual arts and media. In short, all arts are "composite" arts (both text and image); all media are mixed media, combining different codes, discursive conventions, channels, sensory and cognitive modes.

This claim may seem counterintuitive at first glance. Surely, the objection will run, there are *purely* visual and verbal media, pictures without words and words without pictures. The extension of the concept of the composite imagetext to unmixed forms such as poetry or painting is surely a kind of figurative excess, extending a model that applies literally to mixed media beyond its proper domain.

There are several answers to this objection. The first focuses on the question of literal and figurative applications of the image/text division. It is certainly true that the division applies literally to mixed media like film, television, and illustrated books. But it is also a fact that "pure" visual representations routinely incorporate textuality in a quite literal way, insofar as writing and other arbitrary marks enter into the field of visual representation. By the same token, "pure" texts incorporate visuality quite literally the moment they are written or printed in visible form. Viewed from either side, from the standpoint of the visual or the verbal, the medium of writing deconstructs the possibility of a pure image or pure text, along with the opposition between the "literal" (letters) and the "figurative" (pictures) on which it depends. Writing, in its physical, graphic form, is an inseparable suturing of the visual and the verbal, the "imagetext" incarnate.[11]

But suppose we bracket for the moment the issue of writing. Surely, the objection might continue, there are visual representations in which no writing appears and verbal discourses (especially oral) which need never be written down. How can we deny the merely figurative status of visuality in an oral discourse, or the merely figurative status of textuality in a painting purely composed of shapes and colors, without legible, arbitrary signs? The answer is that there is no need to deny the figurative status of the imagetext, only to dispute the "merely" that is appended to it. To claim that a label only applies metaphorically, notes Nelson Goodman, is not to deny that it has application, only to specify the form of application.[12] Figurative labels ("blue" moods and "warm" colors) apply as firmly and consistently as literal ones and have as much to do with actual experience. That images, pictures, space, and visuality may only be figuratively conjured up in a verbal discourse does not mean that the conjuring fails to occur or that the reader/listener "sees" nothing. That verbal discourse may only be figuratively or indirectly evoked in a picture does not mean that the evocation is impotent, that the viewer "hears" or "adds" nothing in the image.[13]

Perhaps the best answer to the purist who wants images that are only images and texts that are only texts is to turn the tables and examine the rhetoric of purity itself.[14] In painting, for instance, the notion of purity is invariably explicated as a purgation of the visual image from contamination by language and cognate or conventionally associated media: words, sounds, time, narrativity, and arbitrary "allegorical" signification are the "linguistic" or "textual" elements that must be repressed or eliminated in order for the pure, silent, illegible visuality of the visual arts to be achieved. This sort of purity, often associated with modernism and abstract painting, is both impossible and utopian, which isn't to dismiss it, but to identify it as an ideology, a complex of desire and fear, power and interest.[15] It is also to recognize the project of the "pure image," the unmixed medium, as a radical deviation from a norm understood to be impure, mixed, and composite. The purist's objection to the image/text, and to the heterogeneous picture of representation and discourse it suggests, turns out to be a moral imperative, not an empirical description. It's not that the claim that all media are mixed media is empirically wrong, but that these mixtures are bad for us and must be resisted in the name of higher aesthetic values.

It would be easy to document a similar kind of resistance to visuality in literary discourse, in the name of a similar kind of utopian purification of language, and in response to a similar intuition about the composite, heterogeneous character of normal discourse.[16] My aim is not to dismiss the purists, but to redescribe the way their utopian projects invoke the metalanguage of the image/text, understood as a body of figures for the irreducible impurity and heterogeneity of media. Christian Metz demonstrated long ago that cinema cannot be reduced to the models of linguistics, that film is *parole* but not *langue*.[17] But suppose that language itself were not *langue*, that its deployment as a medium of expression and discourse inevitably resulted in its contamination in the visible? That is what it means, in my view, to approach language as a medium rather than a system, a heterogeneous field of discursive modes requiring pragmatic, dialectical description rather than a univocally coded scheme open to scientific explanation.

This decentering of the purist's image of media has a number of practical consequences. It clearly obviates the need for comparison, which thrives on the model of clearly distinct systems linked by structural analogies and substantive differentiations. It also permits a critical openness to the actual workings of representation and discourse, their internal dialectics of form understood as pragmatic strategies within the specific institutional history of a medium. There's no compulsion (though there may be occasions) to compare paintings with texts, even if the text happens to be represented directly (or indirectly) in the painting. The starting point is to see what particular form of textuality is elicited (or repressed) by the painting and in the name of what values. An obvious entry to the "text in painting" is the question of the title. What sort of title does the painting have, where is it located (inside, outside, or on the frame)? What is its institutional or interpretive relation to the image? Why are so many modern paintings entitled "Untitled"? Why the vigorous, explicit verbal denial of any entitlement of language in painting, the aggressive paradox of the title which denies that it is a title? What is being resisted in the name of labels, legends, and legibility?[18]

The question of the title is a literalist's entry point to a whole series of questions about the ways that words enter pictures. How, for instance, might we sort out the differences among the following kinds of textuality in painting: a picture that represents (among other objects) a text (like an open book in a Dutch painting); a picture that has words and letters, not represented in, but inscribed on its surface, as in Chinese calligraphic landscape or the large canvases of Anselm Kiefer; a picture in the mode of classical history painting that depicts an episode from a verbal narrative, like a still from a movie or a play; a picture in which the words "speak to" or disrupt the image, occupying an ambiguous location, both in and outside the image (like Dürer's signature monograms inscribed on plaques, or Magritte's inscription in "This Is Not a Pipe"); a picture whose entire composition is designed around a linguistic "character"—a hieroglyphic or ideogram, as in the work of Paul Klee; a picture that eschews all figuration, reference, narrative, or legibility in favor of pure, unreadable visuality. The investigation of these questions doesn't begin with a search for contemporary texts that betray structural analogies in some parallel literary institution or tradition. The starting point is with language's entry into (or exit from) the pictorial field itself, a field understood as a complex medium that is always already mixed and heterogeneous, situated within institutions, histories, and discourses: the image understood, in short, as an imagetext. The appropriate texts for "comparison" with the image need not be fetched from afar with historicist or systemic analogies. They are already inside the image, perhaps most deeply when they seem to be most completely absent, invisible and inaudible. With abstract painting, the appropriate texts may well be, not "literature" or "poetry," but criticism, philosophy, metaphysics—*ut pictura theoria*.[19]

In a similar way, the visual representations appropriate to a discourse need not be imported: they are already immanent in the words, in the fabric of description, narrative "vision," represented objects and places, metaphor, formal arrangements and distinctions of textual functions, even in typography, paper, binding, or (in the case of oral performance) in the physical immediacy of voice and the speaker's body. If it is hard to keep discourse out of painting, it is equally difficult to keep visuality out of literature, though the impulse to do so is adumbrated in the topos of the blind poet, literature's answer to painting as "mute poesy." Not that the situation of literature and visual art as mutual "significant others" is purely symmetrical. It seems easier for painting to represent and incorporate textuality in a quite literal way than for the reverse to happen. Language becomes "literally" visible in two ways: in the medium of writing, and in the utterances of gesture language, the visible language of the Deaf.[20]

The most damaging objection to the imagetext model for the analysis of either texts or images might be that, like the comparative method, it simply rearranges the deck chairs and reiterates existing dominant paradigms of analysis in the disciplines of literature and art history. The notion that images may be read as texts is hardly news in art history these days: it is the prevailing wisdom, the latest thing.[21] On the side of literary study, reading texts for the "imagery" is definitely not the prevailing wisdom: it is as old as the hills.[22] It is seen as an outmoded paradigm, a relic of psychologistic approaches to literary experience and of stultifying routines like motif-hunting, image-counting, and a disproportionate attention to figurative and formal analysis, at the expense of real cultural history.

NOTES

1. Aristotle's repudiation of *opsis* is so thorough that he is even willing to jettison performance itself, in favor of a narrative presentation of the action. "The plot should be so constructed that even without seeing the play anyone hearing of the incidents thrills with fear and pity as a result of what occurs. . . . To produce this effect by means of an appeal to the eye is inartistic and needs adventitious aid." (*The Poetics* XIV, translated by W. Hamilton Fyfe, 1927 [Cambridge: Harvard University Press, 1973]), 49.

2. See Christian Metz, *Film Language: A Semiotics of the Cinema*, translated by Michael Taylor (New York: Oxford University Press, 1974).

3. Ben Jonson, "An Expostulation with Indigo Jones," in *The Complete Poems*, edited by George Parfitt (New Haven: Yale University Press, 1975), 345–47; see Erwin Panofsky on space and time in cinema in "Style and Medium in the Motion Pictures," *Critique* 1: 3 (Jan.–Feb. 1947), reprinted in Gerald Mast and Marshall Cohen, eds., *Film Theory and Criticism* (New York: Oxford University Press, 1979), 243–63.

4. See Blake's *Composite Art* (Princeton: Princeton University Press, 1978) and W. J. T. Mitchell's *Picture Theory*, chapter 4, "Visible Language."

5. I am adapting here the concept of "suture" as developed in psychoanalytic film theory and am relying principally on Stephen Heath's article, "On Suture," in *Questions of Cinema* (Bloomington: Indiana University Press, 1981), 76–112. Suture might be described most generally in Lacan's words as the "junction of the imaginary and the symbolic" (quoted in Heath, 86), the process by which the subject (the "I") is constituted both as a division and a unity. "I," as Heath notes, is "the very index of suture." Film theory adapted the notion of suture to describe the construction of the spectator position in cinema (the "I/eye" as it were) and to analyze the specific characteristics of film discourse. Suture might be described as that which "fills in" the gaps between images and shots by constructing a subjective sense of continuity and absent positionality. Shot-reverse-shot, with its interplay of shifting spectatorial positions and self/other identifications, is thus the paradigmatic figure for suture in cinema. My adaptation of this notion to the "image/text" is very rough and preliminary, but not, I hope, completely unfounded. At the root of the idea in both psychoanalysis and film theory is the figure of a heterogeneous field of (self-) representation and the process by which its disjunctions are at once concealed and revealed. The specific form of that heterogeneity (for Lacan, the imaginary and the symbolic; for film theory, the transformation of the sequence of film images into a discourse) is already very close in its formulation to the problem of the image/text. Film theory's emphasis, not surprisingly, has been on the suturing of the image sequences and the construction of the subject as spectator. But the question of the image/text suggests, I hope, that the notion of suture might well be extended to include the subject as reader and listener, as Heath himself notes (107–8). On the interpellation and suturing of spectatorial subject and image more generally, see *Picture Theory*, chapter 2, "Metapictures."

6. I'm indebted to Michael Camille for this contrast between the medieval and post-Cartesian cartoon.

7. There's nothing to prevent the rearrangement of these conventional spaces, of course. Dialogue need not appear in voice balloons, but can simply run along the bottom edge of the frame (the normal convention of the single panel cartoon and of multiple-panel narrative cartoonists like Jules Feiffer). For a very useful insider's account of rhetorical and narrative devices in cartoons, see Will Eisner, *Comics & Sequential Art* (Tamarac: Poorhouse Press, 1985).

8. See Art Spiegelman, *Maus I: A Survivor's Tale: My Father Bleeds History* (New York: Pantheon, 1973). The effect of Spiegelman's brilliant animal caricatures is, of course, more complex than a simple "veiling" of the human form. The reduction of the Holocaust to a "Tom and Jerry" iconography is at once shocking in its violation of decorum and absolutely right in its revelation of a fitness and figural realism in the animal imagery. Spiegelman's images insist that the Jews really were "scared mice"; they really were treated as vermin to be hunted down and exterminated; they hid in cellars like and with rats; some of them were traitors and rats, notably when they organized themselves into the collaborationist institution of the "Judenrat" (Jewish Council). The Germans really are heartless predators, but feline and unpredictable, luxuriating in the pleasure of absolute power over abject victims. The Poles really are pigs, fattening themselves on the dispossessed goods of the Jews, sometimes goodhearted, but inevitably gross and unrefined. The hyperbole of the animal imagery enforces a mode of critical realism, while defending the viewer against (or preventing) an unbearable (or voyeuristic) access to the banal human forms of evil and abjection. For more on abjection and visual defense, see *Picture Theory*, chapter 6, "Narrative, Memory, and Slavery."

9. See Jefferson Hunter, *Image and Word: The Interaction of Twentieth Century Photographs and Texts* (Cambridge, MA: Harvard University Press, 1987), and *Picture Theory*, chapter 10, "Illusion: Looking at Animals Looking."

10. See *Picture Theory*, chapter 9, "The Photographic Essay," for an extended discussion of *Let Us Now Praise Famous Men* (first published in 1939; reprint: Boston: Houghton-Mifflin, 1980) and its relation to the genre of the photographic essay.

11. I take the equivocal status of writing as image/text to be one of the leading themes of Jacques Derrida's *Of Grammatology*, translated by Gayatri C. Spivak (Baltimore: Johns Hopkins University Press, 1977). See also *Picture Theory*, chapter 4, "Visible Language."

12. See Nelson Goodman, *Languages of Art* (Indianapolis: Hackett, 1976), 68–69. See also Derrida's discussion of "literal" and "figurative."

13. On the psychology of visual response in reading, see Ellen Esrock, *The Reader's Eye* (Baltimore: Johns Hopkins University Press, 1994). Esrock is the first to connect the "senses" (semantic or cognitive) in which readers might be said to visualize with a thorough survey of the psychological literature on the subject.

14. The classic argument for the purification of poetry and painting, and the strict segregation of them according to visual/verbal and spatial/temporal categories, is, of course, Lessing's *Laocoon* (1766), translated by Ellen Frothingham (New York: Farrar, Straus, and Giroux, 1969). For a critique of Lessing, see chapter 4 of Mitchell's *Iconology*.

15. The most notable modernist redaction of the "purity" argument is Clement Greenberg's essay, "Toward a Newer Laocoon" (1940; 23–38 of vol. 1 of *Collected Works*), with its self-conscious evocation of Lessing. For more on the modernist purification of media, see *Picture Theory*, chapter 7, "Ut Pictura Theoria."

16. See my essay, "Tableau and Taboo: The Resistance to Vision in Literary Discourse," *CEA Critic* 51: 1 (Fall 1988): 4–10.

17. See Metz, *Film Language*. "When approaching cinema from the linguistic point of view, it is difficult to avoid shuttling back and forth between two positions: the cinema as a language; the cinema as infinitely different from verbal language. Perhaps it is impossible to extricate oneself from this dilemma with impunity." (44) We need not accept Metz's ultimate valorization of narrative as the essence of cinema to see that film can never be explicated fully as a systematic language.

18. On titles, see Gerard Genette, "Structure and Function of the Title in Literature," *Critical Inquiry* 14: 4 (Summer 1988): 692–720. For more on the relation of label, object, and image, see *Picture Theory*, chapter 8, "Word, Image, and Object."

19. See *Picture Theory*, chapter 7, "*Ut Pictura Theoria*."

20. For more on gesture language, see *Picture Theory*, chapter 5, "Ekphrasis and the Other."

21. See Mieke Bal and Norman Bryson on "Semiotics and Art History," in *The Art Bulletin* (Vol. 73, no. 2, June 1991), which argues that the key move in semiotic versions of art history is the treatment of the

image as a sign or "visual text" (179): "Considering images as signs, semiotics sheds a particular light on them, focusing on the production of meaning in society . . ." (176). Although Bal and Bryson insist that they are proposing "a semiotic turn for art history" rather than "a linguistic turn," they underestimate, in my view, the extent to which semiotics privileges textual/linguistic descriptive frameworks. Far from avoiding "the bias of privileging language," semiotics continually reinstates that bias.

22. See *Iconology*, chapter 1, for a discussion of the attacks on the notion of literary imagery.

The Impossible Definition

THIERRY GROENSTEEN

The definitions of comics that can be found in dictionaries and encyclopedias, and also in the more specialized literature, are, as a general rule, unsatisfactory. It is easy to understand the reasons.

These definitions are of two sorts. The first, often concise, participates in an essentialist approach and looks to lock up some synthetic form of the "essence" of comics. This enterprise is no doubt doomed to failure if one considers that, far from verifying the long assumed poverty of expression and intrinsic infantilism, comics rest on a group of coordinating mechanisms that participate in the representation and the language, and that these mechanisms govern in their movements numerous and disparate parameters, of which the dynamic interaction takes on extremely varied forms from one comic to another. Whatever its successes on the plane of art, one must recognize that any comic:

1) is necessarily (constitutionally) a sophisticated structure
2) only actualizes certain potentialities of the medium, to the detriment of others that are reduced or excluded

Consequently, searching for the essence of comics is to be assured of finding not a shortage but a profusion of responses. In the brilliant essay by Alain Rey entitled *Les Spectres de la bande*, one thus reads that "the essential" of comics is in "the organized space that cheats between the two dimensions of the format and the perceptive suggestion of the world" (102); that "the exchange between the textual and figural values creates the essence of comics" (104); that from now on the medium characterizes above all "a creative battle between figuration and narrativity, not between image and text, this last assumes nothing but the most superficial aspect of the story" (200). These are many different and fertile suggestions, and no doubt it would not be difficult to find in this single book half a dozen other analogous formulas that suggest some part of the truth.

But one also meets definitions of comics that are longer and more articulated, better conforming to the definition of a *definition*: "An enunciation of attributes that distinguish something, that belongs in particular to the exclusion of all others" (Littré). These differing definitions are retained as pertinent for the number and the identity of their

Reprinted by permission from Thierry Groensteen, *The System of Comics* (University Press of Mississippi, 2007), 12-20.

attributes. Researchers have not failed to butt heads on this point, as one can see by looking at some clarifying examples.

The work of David Kunzle, *The Early Comic Strip*, launched a series intended to cover the entire history of comics. This first book examines the pre-Töpfferian period, from 1450 to 1825, grouping not only anonymous popular imagery but also painting and engraving cycles by artists such as Callot, Rubens, Greuze, and Hogarth, to name but a few. Kunzle formulates "four conditions" under which these stories in images can be considered proto-comics or, if one prefers, assimilated *a posteriori*:

> I would propose a definition in which a "comic strip" of any period, in any country, fulfills the following conditions: 1) There must be a sequence of separate images; 2) There must be a preponderance of image over text; 3) The medium in which the strip appears and for which it was originally intended must be reproductive, that is, in printed form, a mass medium; 4) The sequence must tell a story which is both moral and topical.[1]

Bill Blackbeard, another, and no less eminent, American researcher, is violently opposed to this view. Challenging, and not without some bad faith, each of the conditions proposed by Kunzle, Blackbeard formulated the following definition:

> A serially published, episodic, open-ended dramatic narrative or series of linked anecdotes about recurrent identified characters, told in successive drawings regularly enclosing ballooned dialogue or its equivalent and generally minimal narrative text.[2]

These two definitions are, to my understanding, both unacceptable. They are equally normative and self-interested, each made to measure in order to support an arbitrary slice of history. For example, the third of Kunzle's conditions only serves to justify the fact that he chose the invention of printing as a starting point for *The Early Comic Strip*. While Blackbeard's definition, which defends the thesis of the American origin for comics, applies only to printed comics and is destined to dismiss the entire field of comics that predates the appearance of the Yellow Kid in 1896.

In France, let us recall that Antoine Roux proposed a definition in six points in *La Bande dessinée peut être éducative* (Éd. de l'École 1970), a definition backhandedly swept aside (and, here again, in part unjustly) by Yves Frémion in *L'ABC de la BD*, where one reads: "In ten years, none of these criteria, although a priori serious, has withstood history."[3]

The difficulty of producing a valid definition of comics, a definition that permits discrimination in that which it is not but which excludes none of its historical manifestations, including its marginal or experimental visionaries (I am thinking, for example, of the works of Jean Teulé and of Martin Vaughn-James, where the reception can seem to be problematic), was indicated by Pierre Couperie in 1972:

> Comics would be a story (but it is not necessarily a story . . .) constituted by handmade images from one or several artists (it must eliminate cinema and the photo-novel), fixed images (in difference from animation), multiple (contrary to the cartoon), and

juxtaposed (in difference from illustration and engraved novels . . .). But this definition applies equally well to Trajan's Column and the Bayeux Tapestry.[4]

And Couperie adds that neither the framing of images, nor the use of the balloon, nor
the mode of distribution are determining criteria.

So great is the diversity of what has been claimed as comics, or what is claimed today
under diverse latitudes, that it has become almost impossible to retain any definitive
criteria that is universally held to be true. I want to demonstrate this for two of the
pertinent traits often erected as doctrinal elements:

1) the insertion, in the image, of verbal enunciations
2) the permanence, within the panels, of at least one identifiable character (a criterion
   notably insisted upon by Blackbeard)

Although used overwhelmingly, these elements must be seen to be contingent characteristics, suffering a number of exceptions. It follows that they can only produce reductive
definitions.

Here, first of all, are some authors who have produced "mute" comics, that is to
say, devoid of verbal enunciations, without dialogue or the narrational text (captions).
Coming from Germany, this particular narrative form was widespread at the end of the
nineteenth century with the pantomines of Caran d'Ache, K-Hito, or A. B. Frost, to
mention not a single French, Spanish, or American artist. One later finds works "without words" in every category of comics: the daily comic strip and/or independent pages
(*Adamson* by Oscar Jacobsson [1920]; *The Little King* by Otto Soglow [1931]; *Vater und
Sohn* by e.o. plauen [1934]; *Henry* by Carl Anderson [1934l; *Globi* by J. K. Schiefe and
R. Lips [1934]; *Professeur Nimbus* by André Daix [1934]; *M. Subito* by Robert Velter
[1935]; *Max l'explorateur* by Guy Bara [1955]; etc.); complete stories published in the
illustrated press (here the examples abound, recall only, among the successes, *Allô! il est
vivant* by Raymond Poïvet [1964]; *Sanguine* by Philippe Caza [1976]; many episodes
of *Ken Parker* by Milazzo and Berardi [mid-1980s]; *Magic Glasses* by Keko [1986]; or
again the sketches of the German artist Sperzel, such as those that can be found in recent
years in *U-Comix* and *Kowalski*); finally, in books, from Milt Gross (*He Done Her Wrong*
[1930]) to Thierry Robin (*La Teigne* [1998]), passing through Moebius (*Arzach* [1975]),
Crepax (*La Lanterne Magique* [1979]), Ana Juan (*Requiem*, with Gordillo [1985]), Avril
and Petit-Roulet (*Soirs de Paris* [1989]), Hendrik Dorgathen (*Space Dog* [1993]), Alberto
Breccia (*Dracula, Dracul, Vlad?, bah . . .* [1993]), Fabio (*L'Oeil du Chat* [1995]), Lewis
Trondheim (*La Mouche* [1995]), Anna Sommer (*Remue-ménage* [1996]), and Peter
Kuper (*The System* [1997]), and this list has no pretence to completeness.

The permanence—and the present vitality—of this tradition does not prevent some
researchers from asserting that "what distinguishes a comic from a cycle of frescoes is the
fact that the written words are essential to the understanding of the story."[5] An amusing detail—and indicative of his blindness—the author next produced, in support of
this observation, a *Krazy Kat* page in which the texts were masked, without seeming to
notice that, unfortunately for him, the narration, developed in eleven images, remained
perfectly intelligible despite the verbal amputation!

As for the presence of a recurrent character, there are diverse ways to bypass this. I will note six:

1) The first is radical: it is sufficient that no human being is depicted in the story; in this case, these works have the unique motor of a metamorphosis of a place or of a population of objects. Examples: *The Cage* by Martin Vaughn James (1975), *Intérieurs* by Regis Franc (1979), *A Short History of America* by Robert Crumb (1979).

2) The second case can be considered as an attenuation of the first. Although the recurrent character is not shown, his presence is suggested "in absentia" by the use of a verbal narration in the first person, and/or a focus of perception assumed by the images (a practice in cinema that is known by the expression "subjective camera"). André Juillard's contribution to the collective anthology *Le Violon et l'archer* (1990) illustrates this second case. One might also remember the famous page by McCay, in *Dreams of a Rarebit Fiend*, where the protagonist assists in his burial at the bottom of his coffin. (The series was published from 1904 to 1911, then restarted in 1913; the precise date of the particular page is not, to my knowledge, mentioned in any edition.) A neighboring case is one where the character is simply held permanently off-screen—one can hear him speak without seeing him—as in *Calma chicha* (1985), a short story by the Spanish artist Marti.

3) There is also, while present in the image, the character that is not physically identifiable, because the elements that form his identity (and, in the first instance, his face) are systematically evaded. The book *Carpets' bazaar* by Francois Mutterer and Martine Van (1983) rises to this challenge. A slightly different example would be *Unflip coca* by Edmond Baudoin (1984), where the features of the heroine are not revealed to the reader except in the last three pages of the book. (She is, until that point, depicted from the back or with her face covered by her hair.)

4) The "stability" of the character can also be given a pounding by incessant mutations of the corporeal envelope or by the graphic treatment that is reserved for him. An experimental book such as *John et Betty* by Didier Eberoni (1985) proposed an approximation of this practice. René Petillon used it in a humorous mode in depicting the "head of directory enquiries of Terra . . . one of these unstable class B14 mutants, which constantly change their heads" (*Bienvenue aux terriens* [1982], 25).

5) The character as a recognizable individual dissolves when all the characters resemble each other, ruining the very idea of identity. Within a population such as that of the Smurfs, the physical marks of individuation are extremely rare (initially reserved for Papa Smurf, Brainy Smurf, and, of course, Smurfette). Here, the process of naming (under a form of qualified epithet: Grouchy Smurf, Poet Smurf, Jokey Smurf, etc.) allows the story to adapt to the state that Bruno Lecigne has precisely baptized hyper-twinhood (*hypergemellite*). Certain stories by Francis Masse or by Florence Cestac have also come close to the total indifferentiation of the body.

6) Moreover the case of comics where the "actors" renew themselves from panel to panel, each seeing his role limited to a single, unique appearance. Several works by the Bazooka Group illustrate this tendency, as well as the five pages by Crumb entitled *City of the Future* (1967). The first chapter of *C'était la guerre des tranchées* by Jacques

Tardi (published in *[A suivre]* no. 50 [March 1982]) is not very far removed from this; its polyphonic structure attests to the collective nature of an outlook (the absurdity of war) that is not suitable to personalization, and which is under pains to reduce it.

Thus, two dogmatic criteria, retained for the most part in current definitions of comics, must be dismissed. The difficulty encountered here is not particular to comics. It arises in almost identical terms for the most part, if not completely, in forms of modern art, like the cinema, and for forms where the evolution over the course of a century has smashed the traditional definition (novel, painting, music) into pieces. For example, Roger Odin shows clearly that it is almost impossible to express a definition of cinema that also applies to animated films and to all the forms of experimental or "widened" cinema. The aporia that the semiotician necessarily unblocks is thus described:

> By what right do we exclude from cinema these productions when their authors present them explicitly as "films"? The fact that these productions do not enter into our definition of the "cinema," is that a sufficient justification for this exclusion? If not, must we revise our definition of cinema in a more generalizable manner in order to integrate these counter-examples? But if so, where do we stop this generalization: at the absence of the film? At the absence of the screen? At the absence of the projector? Won't we arrive at a sort of definition that tells us nothing about its object?[6]

Roger Odin suggests that it is necessary to surpass this immanent approach to cinema in order to take into account its social uses. No longer considering the "cinematic object" but the "cinematic field," he concludes (57) that "cinematic objects are definable objects, but variable objects in space and time."

ICONIC SOLIDARITY

If one wishes to provide the basis of a reasonable definition for the totality of historical manifestations of the medium, and also for all of the other productions unrealized at this time but theoretically conceivable, one must recognize the relational play of a plurality of interdependent images as the unique ontological foundation of comics. The relationship established between these images admits several degrees and combines several operations, which I will distinguish later. But their common denominator and, therefore, the central element of comics, the first criteria in the foundational order, is iconic solidarity. I define this as interdependent images that, participating in a series, present the double characteristic of being separated—this specification dismisses unique enclosed images within a profusion of patterns or anecdotes—and which are plastically and semantically overdetermined by the fact of their coexistence *in praesentia*.

No doubt giving the word "comics" such an extensive meaning is not without inconveniences. This is the danger noted by Pierre Couperie. From the steles, frescoes, and the ancient Egyptian books of the dead to the predellas of medieval painting, and from the Bayeux Tapestry to the polyptychs of every age, all the way to the pre-Colombian codex, the stations of the cross, the Emakimono (Japanese picture scrolls), storyboards for films and modern photo-novels, there are probably too many of these works of art that can find refuge in this potluck collection.[7]

Comics will encounter a problem similar to that which has long concerned the world of literature. Everyone admits that it is not sufficient to simply align words in order to make a literary work, for the reason that "of all the materials that humanity can utilize among others in the fine arts, language is perhaps the least specific, the least closely reserved to this end."[8] Resuming a debate begun in the time of Aristotle, Gerard Genette struggles to define the criteria of literarity, that is to say the conditions by which a text can be recognized as literary. I concede in the same way to the "essentialists" that it is not sufficient to simply align images, even interdependently, to produce a comic. Many other conditions can be legitimately debated, which would touch in priority, initially the "nature" of these images (their substance, their mode of production, their formal characteristics), followed by their mode(s) of articulation, eventually even the published form that they take, their distribution and the conditions of their reception—in short, everything that inscribes them in the specific process of communication.[9] But it is improbable that unanimity will be reached on any of these conditions.

In reality, research on the essence of comics is not quite on the same order as that of a definition of literarity. The point is, in the second case, to separate the literary discourse from all the other forms of discourse, starting with day-to-day language. Literature is characterized by "a rupture with the ordinary regime of the language." The clearly posed question from then on is to define "that which makes a verbal message a work of art," according to the formulation of Roman Jakobson recalled by Genette. For the latter, the rupture can be analyzed in terms of *fiction* (in so far as a work of fiction develops in the reader an "aesthetic attitude" and a relative "disinterest" with regard to the real world), or perhaps in terms of *diction*, that is to say by the observation of formal traits that are "facts of style." This opposition stretches to coincide with the division of the field of literature to "two great types: on the one hand fiction (dramatic or narrative), on the other lyric poetry, more and more often designated by the term poetry all told."[10]

Comics rest on a device that is not known from familiar usage. It is not noted that everything can be expressed by this means—even if the practice of comics is, technically and financially speaking, available to everyone, as is confirmed by the aptitude of those children who devote themselves to it. One cannot help but compare it with other forms of creation (those, notably, that we have enumerated above) that participate with complete rights in the domains of art or fiction. The comics are not based on a particular usage of a language, there is no place to define them in terms of diction. But neither are they bound exclusively with fictional forms, since there are examples of publicity or propagandistic comics, political and pedagogical comics, and, occasionally, comics journalism, where the concern is to inform or to testify. We can also add that the proliferation of autobiographical comics is a remarkable phenomenon of recent years, stemming from America, where the works of Robert Crumb, Art Spiegelman, and Harvey Pekar, notably, have opened the door. This plasticity of comics, which allows them to put in place messages of every order and narrations other than the fictional, demonstrates that before being an art, comics are well and truly a language.

But it is not necessary, at this stage of reflection, to push the concern for the delimitation of the medium further ahead. It will be enough for us that one cannot conceptualize comics without verifying the general rule, that of iconic solidarity. The necessary, if not sufficient, condition required to speak of comics is that the images will be multiple and correlated in some fashion.

This fact is empirically verified by whoever leafs through a comic book or comics magazine. What is put on view is always a space that has been divided up, compartmentalized, a collection of juxtaposed frames, where, to cite the fine formula of Henri Van Lier, a "multi-framed aircraft" sails in suspension, "in the white nothingness of the printed page."[11] A page of comics is offered at first to a synthetic global vision, but that cannot be satisfactory. It demands to be traversed, crossed, glanced at, and analytically deciphered. This moment-to-moment reading does not take a lesser account of the totality of the panoptic field that constitutes the page (or the double page), since the focal vision never ceases to be enriched by peripheral vision.

It is observable that the words for the French term *bandes dessinées* (drawn strips) itself implies a restrictive perception of the field that it is supposed to cover. The epithet, specifically assuming that the image will be the product of a drawing (*dessin*), seems to remove a priori all recourse to the photo, to typography, and even to painting. More seriously, the notion of the strip (*bande*) abusively privileges one of the components of the medium, the horizontal segment that sometimes constitutes a micro-story, sometimes nothing other than an ongoing continuing story, or only a portion of a page. If one believes Jean-Claude Glasser, the reign of this term is historically justified:

> It is truly in the buildings of the Agence Opera Mundi that the expression *bande dessinee* was formed [in the 1930s], then progressively imposed itself. . . . It remained to designate the daily strips . . . which explains why it is not found in the illustrated magazines (*illustrés*) of the age where the Sunday pages predominated. . . . It is only in the 1950s that it ceased to apply only to daily strips.[12]

But what was formerly nothing but a lexical generalization has become a veritable impropriety. Now that the book [*album*] is, in Europe, the preponderant vehicle for comics, it follows that the page is the technical unit, market and aesthetic reference.[13]

Iconic solidarity is only the necessary condition so that visual messages can, in first approximation, be assimilated within a comic. As a physical object, every comic can be described as a collection of separate icons and interdependent images. If one considers any given production, one quickly notices that comics that satisfy this minimal condition are naturally longer, but also that they do not all obey the same intentions and do not mobilize the same mechanisms. All theoretical generalizations are cognizant of the trap of dogmatism. Far from wanting to defend a school of thought, an era or a standard against others, or again to prescribe any recipes, I want to force myself to note the diversity of *all forms* of comics and spare my reflections from any normative character.

That is why I have chosen the notion of the system, which defines an ideal, as emblematic of this reflection. The comics system will be a conceptual frame in which all of the actualizations of the "ninth art" can find their place and be thought of in relation to each other, taking into account their differences and their commonalities within the same medium. In this meaning, the notion of the system, "an ensemble of things that are held" (Littré), advances the fundamental concept of *solidarity*.

NOTES

1. Paris: Minuit, "Critique," 1978.

2. David Kunzle, *The Early Comic Strip: Narrative Strips and Picture Stories in the European Broadsheet from c. 1450 to 1825* (Berkeley: University of California Press, 1973), 2.

3. Bill Blackbeard, "Mislabeled Books," *Funny World* 16, Michigan, 1974, 41.

4. Casterman, "E3" *Tournai*, 1983, 36. The third and fourth criteria advanced by Antoine Roux, "comics are a chain of images" and "comics are a rhythmic story," have not lost their pertinence in my eyes.

5. Cf. David Carrier, "Comics and the Art of Moving Pictures: Piero della Francesca, Herge and George Herriman," *Word & Image* 13: 4 (October–December 1997), 317.

6. Roger Odin, *Cinema et production de sense* (Paris: Armand Colin, 1990), 49–50.

7. I have intentionally mentioned only the forms where narrative is a natural slope or a possible application. There exists other series of fixed interdependent images that obey the principles of specific correlation. Thus, architectural drawings represent the same building, for which it is important that the outline, section, and elevation are in agreement. The images of a comic are not subjected to a referential solidarity of this order, except when the author makes this specific choice, with a concern for realism.

8. Gerard Genette, *Fiction et diction* (Paris: Le Seuil, 1991), 11–12.

9. Once again it must be seen that this is situated at the intersection of two distinct logics. Thus, to retain as a criterion of definition the fact that comics can be entrusted to printing creates the challenge of the original page, or its projection on a screen. It follows from this end, for me—but not, as we have seen, for David Kunzle—that an unprinted comic itself does not cease to be a comic. The system that I propose pays attention to the language of comics, not the institution.

10. This paragraph summarizes very schematically the first pages (7–21) of *Fiction et diction*, op cit, where all the citations are located.

11. Henri Van Lier, "La bande dessinee, une cosmogonie dure," in *Bande dessinee, recit et modernite*, ed. Thierry Groensteen (Paris: Futuropolis-CNBDI, 1988), 5.

12. Letter published in *Les Cahiers de la bande dessinee*, no. 80 (March 1988), 8.

13. Translator's note [Bart Beaty]: The situation that the author describes finds an analogue in the English language. The term "comics" originates in the early twentieth century as a description of daily or weekly strips in newspapers, the majority of which were humorous, and is akin to "funnies." The term has outlived its original meaning and is now used to encompass the entire range of expression in the medium. A cognitive dissonance can occur in instances where the term "comics" is used to describe works that take part in a variety of genres, such as tragedy, romance, or the epic. Similarly, the term "comic book" seems to refer to a collection of funny stories, but in fact describes all types of publications containing comics, most often in magazine, rather than book format.

An Art of Tensions

CHARLES HATFIELD

Comics raise many questions about reading and its effects, yet the persistent claims for the form's simplicity and transparency make it impossible to address these questions productively. Criticism, whether formalist or sociocultural in emphasis, will remain at an impasse as long as comics are seen this way—that is, as long as they are rhetorically constructed as "easy." In fact, comics can be a complex means of communication and are always characterized by a plurality of messages. They are heterogeneous in form, involving the co-presence and interaction of various codes. To the already daunting (and controversial) issue of reading, then, we must add several new complexities, if we are to understand what happens when we read comics.

From a reader's viewpoint, comics would seem to be radically fragmented and unstable. I submit that this is their great strength: comic art is composed of several kinds of tension, in which various ways of reading—various interpretive options and potentialities—must be played against each other. If this is so, then comics readers must call upon different reading strategies, or interpretive schema, than they would use in their reading of conventional written text.

The balance of this chapter will engage the fundamental tensions within comics, with emphasis on the kinds of judgment (or suspension of judgment) they demand of readers. I shall concentrate on questions of reader response, in the sense of participation and interpretation, rather than those underlying questions of reading process that properly belong to empirical study (for example, eye movement, working memory, or graphophonic competence). My aim is not to set forth an empirical model of comics reading but rather to establish the complexity of the form by broadly discussing the kinds of mixed messages it sends even to the most experienced of readers. This discussion will serve as a prospectus for the collective task of theorizing reader response in comics in a more general way.

Such theorizing, I will argue, must grapple with four tensions that are fundamental to the art form: between *codes* of signification; between the *single image* and the *image-in-series*; between narrative *sequence* and page *surface*; and, more broadly, between reading-as-*experience* and the text as material *object*. To demonstrate these tensions, I will draw on a range of examples, including alternative and mainstream, children's and adults', and European and American comics.

Reprinted by permission and adapted from Charles Hatfield, *Alternative Comics: An Emerging Literature* (University Press of Mississippi, 2005), 36–65.

CODE VS. CODE

Definitions of comics commonly (though not universally) depend on the co-presence and interplay of image and written text. Some critics regard this interplay as a clash of opposites: the image's transparency versus the written text's complexity. McCloud, for instance, though his own definition deemphasizes words, insists on this contrast: he speaks of pictures as received information, in contrast to words, whose meanings must be *perceived* (49). Such a distinction posits a struggle between passive and active experience, that is, between inert spectatorship and committed reading. By this argument, comics depend on a dialectic between what is easily understood and what is less easily understood; pictures are open, easy, and solicitous, while words are coded, abstract, and remote.

Yet in comics word and image approach each other: words can be visually inflected, reading as pictures, while pictures can become as abstract and symbolic as words. In brief, the written text can function like images, and images like written text. Comics, like other hybrid texts, collapse the word/image dichotomy: visible language has the potential to be quite elaborate in appearance, forcing recognition of pictorial and material qualities that can be freighted with meaning (as in, for example, concrete poetry); conversely, images can be simplified and codified to function as a language (see Kannenberg, "Graphic Text" and "Chris Ware"). McCloud himself notes this, arguing for comic art in which word and image tend toward each other (47–49, 147–51). This recognition renders McCloud's larger argument incoherent, as it belies his earlier distinction between perceived and received information. The distinction does not hold in any case, for, as Perry Nodelman points out with regard to picture books, "All visual images, even the most apparently representational ones, . . . require a knowledge of learned competencies and cultural assumptions before they can be rightly understood" (17). Though the image is, as W. J. T. Mitchell says, "the sign that pretends not to be a sign" (*Iconology,* 43), it remains a sign nonetheless, "as bound up with habit and convention as any text" (64). Pictures are not simply to be received; they must be decoded.

Still, responding to comics often depends on recognizing word and image as two "different" types of sign, whose implications can be played against each other—to gloss, to illustrate, to contradict or complicate or ironize the other. While the word/image dichotomy may be false or oversimple, learned assumptions about these different codes— written and pictorial—still exert a strong centripetal pull on the reading experience. We continue to distinguish between the function of words and the function of images, despite the fact that comics continually work to destabilize this very distinction. This tension between codes is fundamental to the art form.

PICTOGRAPHIC LANGUAGE

Comics can exploit the tension between picturing and writing without incorporating words per se, as the growing body of "mute" or "pantomime" (that is, wordless) comics attests. Such comics often rely on diagrammatic symbols, such as panels, speed or vector lines, and ideograms, to gloss or reinforce what's going on in the pictures. Nor does the "written" text within balloons or captions have to consist of words in a conventional sense. Indeed, in comics dialogue icons may take the place of words: the use of pictograms within balloons is a rich tradition, recently explored by such cartoonists as Hendrik Dorgathen and Eric Cartier. For example, Cartier's *Flip in Paradise* and *Mekong King*, told in miniature album format, use pictograms to suggest elaborate dialogues between the hapless picaro, Flip, and the inhabitants of the various lands he visits.

In *Flip in Paradise*, for instance, as the hero haggles over the price of a joint, his dialogue devolves into a cluster of visual non sequiturs—as if Flip is already beginning to succumb to the effects of dope. At first the pictograms in the balloons suggest bargaining, with ever-decreasing amounts of money, but as the balloons crowd together the dialogue's logic becomes harder and harder to grasp. Later in the same book a drunken Flip will teach a parrot some new words—all about killing and cooking the bird—as shown in a tête-a-tête in which man and bird spout the same pictograms. Cartier makes ingenious use of such visual symbols to dramatize Flip's struggles to communicate in strange lands (ironic, as these symbols allow the cartoonist's work itself to cross national and cultural borders).

Such visual "dialogue" may be drawn in a different style than the pictures used to establish the diegesis: typically, they are less particular, or more generic. Alternately, they may be of the very same style, just enclosed within balloons like regular dialogue. In François Avril and Phillipe Petit-Roulet's *Soirs de Paris*, for example, the story "63 Rue de a Grange aux Belles" uses elaborate pictograms to capture the conversations taking place at a cocktail party. The partygoers' dialogue balloons contain a range of pictures: from simple icons, as when a man asks a woman to dance; to cartoons in the same style as that used to depict the speakers (as when a would-be Romeo uses a series of balloons to itemize a woman's attractive features: her eyes, breasts, legs, and so on); to detailed swipes of images by such artists as Gauguin and Matisse, which indicate the topics of conversation among a group of cultured wallflowers. Such examples suggest that visual/verbal tension is not necessarily even a matter of playing words against pictures; it may be a matter of playing symbols against other symbols.

Such visual/verbal tension results from the juxtaposition of symbols that function diegetically and symbols that function non-diegetically—that is, the mingling of symbols that "show" and symbols that "tell." More precisely, we may say that *symbols that show* are symbols that purport to depict, in a literal way, figures and objects in the imagined world of the comic, while *symbols that tell* are those that offer a kind of diacritical commentary on the images, or (to use another rough metaphor) a "soundtrack" for the images. In most comics, the symbols that show are representational drawings while the symbols that tell are words, balloons, and a few familiar icons. (These icons are non-alphabetic symbols of a sort that many word processors now make available to writers: arrows, dotted lines, lightbulbs, stars, and so forth.) But the potential exists for comics creators to push this tension much further, even to incorporate representational drawings as "dialogue" and to blur the difference between alphabetic symbols and pictures. At its broadest level, then, what we call visual/verbal tension may be characterized as the clash and collaboration of *different codes of signification*, whether or not written words are used. Again, the deployment of such devices assumes a knowing reader.

SINGLE IMAGE VS. IMAGE-IN-SERIES

Most definitions of comics stress the representation of time, that is, of temporal sequence, through multiple images in series. The process of dividing a narrative into such images—a process that necessarily entails omitting as well as including—can be called *breakdown*, a word derived from "breakdowns," a term of art that refers to the rough drawings made in the process of planning out a comics story (Harvey, 14–15). The reverse process, that of reading through such images and inferring connections between them, has been dubbed (borrowing from gestalt psychology) "closure" by McCloud, in keeping with the reader-response emphasis of his *Understanding Comics*. In fact "breakdown" and "closure" are complementary terms, both describing the relationship between *sequence* and *series*: the author's task is to evoke an imagined sequence by creating a visual series (a breakdown), whereas the reader's task is to translate the given series into a narrative sequence by achieving closure. Again, the reader's role is crucial, and requires the invocation of learned competencies; the relationships between pictures are a matter of convention, not inherent connectedness.

At times this process of connecting, or closure, seems straightforward and unproblematic, as when strong visual repetition and/or verbal cuing make the connections between images immediate, or at least fairly obvious. For instance, Julie Doucet's self-referential vignette "The Artist" uses successive panels to capture the methodical, step-by-step provocation of a striptease. This striptease implicates the spectator in an unnerving way, for the artist ends by spilling her guts with a knife. The deliberate, incremental advances of the sequence, from one panel to the next, establish a rhythm and an expectation, and eventually this rhythm makes the unthinkable thinkable: the artist mutilates and literally opens herself before our eyes in calm, measured steps. This violent, self-destructive climax, accomplished through methodical breakdown, ultimately exceeds and beggars all expectations.

At other times, closure may require more active effort on the part of the reader, as demonstrated repeatedly in Jason Lutes's novel *Jar of Fools*. A quarter of the way into the novel, a two-page sequence depicts a day's work for Esther O'Dea, who serves customers at a coffee bar called the Saturn Café. In just twenty-four panels Lutes manages to evoke the tedium and sheer drudgery of seven hours on the job, showing both minute details and Esther's overall attitude toward her work. The breakdown of the action is characterized by several bold choices: for instance, Lutes challenges the reader by beginning from the inside out, with a close-up of Esther preparing a double espresso, rather than from the outside in, with an establishing shot of the café itself (here being introduced to readers for the first time). We see a larger image of the café interior only after Esther hands the espresso to a customer, and a shot of the exterior (specifying the location) only in the middle of the sequence. Thus Lutes frames the entire day from Esther's point of view, sticking close to the minutiae of her clockwork routine. The repeated use of close-ups throughout the sequence reinforces the repetitive yet discontinuous nature of her work.

After showing the interior of the café, Lutes builds the rest of the sequence around Esther's query, *Can I help you?*—a phrase she mechanically repeats throughout the day. One customer responds to this with a suggestive sneer and a verbal come-on, "In more

Jason Lutes, *Jar of Fools* (1997). Copyright © Jason Lutes. Used with permission.

ways than one, sweetheart," an overture which Esther repays with stony silence even as she imagines belting the man with a left hook (36). That she *imagines* this, but does not do it, is something the reader must figure out for herself: Lutes suggests this both by the unvarying rhythm of the sequence and by the subtle variation in panel bordering around the imagined punch (the latter a technique used previously by Lutes to set off dreams and memories—by this point the reader presumably knows the code). Yet the moment comes as a shock nonetheless, due in part to the repeated use of a single, unvarying image—Esther's taciturn face—to pace the sequence. We see her land a blow, yet nothing about her or around her changes to match this unexpected outburst. The reader must negotiate the larger context of Lutes's narrative to make this key distinction.

On the next page, as the hours crawl forward, Lutes repeats the image of a clock—along with Esther's *Can I help you?*—to suggest the slow, frustrating passage of time. Verbal and visual repetition (the clock, the coffee cups, Esther's face, *Can I help you?*) succeed in quickly evoking a sense of boredom and restiveness—no mean feat. The repeated close-up of the clock face, with changing times, finally gives way to the sight of Esther watching the clock from an oblique angle, as her spoken *Can I help you?* becomes an unspoken *Can I kill you?* (37). This is the moment when her shift ends, finally, and she can leave the café. In just a few panels, then, Lutes compresses a day's work into a montage of numbing,

Jason Lutes, *Jar of Fools* (1997).
Copyright © Jason Lutes. Used
with permission.

repetitive activity and emotional frustration. To follow this sequence, the reader must be mindful of Lutes's previously established habits as a storyteller—his approach to panel bordering, his interpolations of dream and fantasy into mundane reality, and so on—and take an active part in constructing a flow of events from discontinuous images.

At times achieving closure can be quite difficult, as when images seem radically disjointed and verbal cues are scant. For example, Art Spiegelman's wordless "drawn over two weeks while on the phone" (*Raw* 1) presents a series of disconnected panels with recurrent character types and situations but no narrative per se. Generic conventions—nods to film noir, for instance—are repeatedly invoked but without a linear rationale; motific repetition suggests at best a vague connection between otherwise disjunct panels. Certain characters and symbols are repeated: geometric symbols, for instance, which serve as pictographic dialogue, as decorative effects, and, in a droll reversal, even as characters. But the sought-for unity of the piece, finally, rests on the reader's recognition of the author's formal playfulness rather than on any coherent narrative. It takes much knowledge and careful attention to read Spiegelman's series as a sequence. The tension between single image and image-in-series is bound up with other formal issues, and therefore hard to codify. McCloud's *Understanding Comics* remains the strongest theoretical treatment (in English, that is) of comics sequencing; yet McCloud, perhaps because he does not consider visual/verbal interplay crucial to the form, neglects just how much the interaction of image and word can inform, indeed enable, the reading of sequences. Verbal cues do help to bridge the gaps within a sequence, as seen in common transitional captions such as "Later" or "Meanwhile" (devices that have fallen from favor as readers become more versed in reading comics, just as title cards, fades, irises, and other such transitional devices fell from favor in cinema). In fact verbal continuity can impose structure on even the most radically disjointed series. Witness, for instance, Spiegelman's oft-reprinted "Ace Hole, Midget Detective," in which the hero's nonstop narration (a spoof of hard-boiled fiction) serves to structure an otherwise nonlinear barrage of non sequiturs, visual gags, and stylistic swipes.

To some extent, then, the process of transitioning, or closure, depends not only on the interplay between successive images but also on the interplay of different codes of signification: the verbal as well as the visual. In other words, how readers attempt to resolve one tension may depend on how they resolve another. Verbal/visual interplay often muddies the pristine categories of transition that McCloud tries to establish in *Understanding Comics* (moment to moment, action to action, scene to scene, and so on). Words can smooth over transitions and unobtrusively establish a dramatic continuity that belies the discontinuity of the images. Two contrasting examples from Harvey Pekar's *American Splendor*, both scripted by Pekar and illustrated by Robert Crumb, illustrate this point:

In "The Harvey Pekar Name Story" (1977), the visuals pace and punctuate a verbal monologue, and the successive images are near-identical, so much so that a reader who held the book at arm's length and squinted would be hard-pressed to see any variation. (Lutes uses a similar strategy in the above example from *Jar of Fools*, but Pekar and Crumb use fewer variations and push the repetition much farther.) The story concerns the relationship between name and identity, and the near-sameness of the drawings both reinforces and subverts the speaker's preoccupation with self-definition, Here a man named "Harvey Pekar" (not to be confused with the author) addresses the reader in forty-eight equal-sized panels over four pages. His concern? His name—which, though unusual, turns out not to be unique, as he discovers by looking through the phone book, where he finds not one but two other "Harvey Pekar" listings. The deaths of these two other Pekars (Harvey Sr. and Harvey Jr., father and son) restore the narrator's sense of uniqueness, until a *third* Harvey Pekar appears in the directory, prompting the age-old question, "What's in a name?" On a more personal level, the narrator is left asking himself, and us, "Who is Harvey Pekar?"—a question he can answer only with silence, in the final, wordless panel.

Like Doucet's "The Artist," "The Harvey Pekar Name Story" relies on minute changes from panel to panel to convey a carefully timed sequence. Yet Pekar and Crumb take an even more deliberate approach, calling for a constant subject and point of view with only the minutest changes in gesture and nuance. Pekar's breakdowns invoke the rhythms of verbal storytelling or stand-up comedy, with occasional silent panels for pause and emphasis; the relationship between the speaker and the reader is everything, as the former confronts the latter in a frustrated attempt at self-affirmation. This attempt is fraught with irony: the consistent, even monotonous, point of view in every panel supplies the very appearance of stability that the narrator craves, but the serial repetition of his likeness (subtly varied by Crumb) erodes our sense of his uniqueness.

Both the story's rhythm and its themes depend on the unvarying vsuals, which force us to confront this "Harvey Pekar" in all his (thwarted) individuality even as they help us concentrate on the spoken text.

In contrast, Pekar and Crumb's "Hypothetical Quandary" (1984) merges words and pictures more dynamically, and asks more of the reader in her quest for closure. This story is inward-looking and nakedly autobiographical, focusing on thought rather than talk. Rendered in a bolder, brushed style, "Quandary" finds Harvey carrying on a dialogue with himself as he drives, then walks, to a bakery to buy bread: How would he react to success and fame? Would it blunt his writing by robbing him of his "working man's outlook on life"? Would it dilute his personal vision? This hypothetical dilemma (not entirely hypothetical, for Pekar has had brushes with fame, especially in the wake of the *American Splendor* film in 2003) occupies Harvey through his entire trip to the bakery; indeed, except for a single panel in which he buys the bread, all of Harvey's words occur in thought balloons, and the dark, lushly textured images position him within a fully realized world rather than vis-à-vis the reader in a full-on monologue.

Propelled as much by Pekar's text as by the subtle authority of Crumb's pictures, "Hypothetical Quandary" moves Harvey (and the reader) over a great distance, telescoping his Sunday morning expedition into three pages. Like the above example from Lutes's *Jar of Fools*, this story relies on words as well as common visual cues for its pacing. Driving, walking, buying bread, walking again—all of these happen while Harvey's internal dialogue carries on without interruption, until the last two panels find him savoring the bread's fresh smell, his quandary forgotten. The continuity of the verbal text disguises the discontinuity of the visual: Pekar's ongoing words, exploring all the twists and turns of Harvey's thinking, elide the gaps in the visual sequence, making this stylized evocation of his world seem naturalistic and unforced. Whereas "The Harvey Pekar Name Story" weds the author's text to deliberately repetitive breakdowns and a single, static composition, "Hypothetical Quandary" uses text to carry the reader from one locale to the next without ever losing continuity of thought. These contrasting examples point up the possibility that breakdown may depend on mixing the verbal and the visual. Thus the two tensions named so far, code vs. code and single image vs. image-in-series, interact to create a yet more complex tension, soliciting the reader's active efforts at resolution.

SEQUENCE VS. SURFACE

In most cases, the successive images in a comic are laid out contiguously on a larger surface or surfaces (that is, a page or pages). Each surface organizes the images into a constellation of discrete units, or "panels." A single image within such a cluster typically functions in two ways at once: as a "moment" in an imagined sequence of events, and as a graphic element in an atemporal design. Some comics creators consciously play with this design aspect, commonly called *page layout*, while others remain more conscious of the individual image-as-moment. Most longform comics maintain a tug-of-war between these different functions, encouraging a near-simultaneous apprehension of the single image as both momentum-sequence and design element. The "page" (or *planche*, as French scholars have it, a term denoting the total design unit rather than the physical page on which it is printed) functions both as sequence and as object, to be seen and read in both linear and nonlinear, holistic fashion.

This tension has been described in various ways. For instance, French scholar Pierre Fresnault-Deruelle, in a seminal essay, proposed the terms "linear" and "tabular" to denote the sequential and nonsequential functions respectively ("Du linéare au tabulaire"; see also Peeters, 39–40). "Tabular" perhaps conjures the traditional Western comics layout of a boxlike or gridlike enclosure, rather like a mathematical table, within which each panel acts as a discrete cell; potentially, though, it applies to any comics page, even one that abandons such rectilinear design. More generally, we can say that the single image functions as both a point on an imagined timeline—a self-contained moment substituting for the moment before it, and anticipating the moment to come—and an element of global page design. In other words, there is a tension between the concept of "breaking down" a story into constituent images and the concept of laying out those images together on an unbroken surface. This tension lies at the heart of comics design—and poses yet another challenge to the reader.

This tension can be illustrated through two contrasting examples from "Waiting," a series of single-page alternative comic book stories scripted by Linda Perkins and drawn by Dean Haspiel. The first in the series (from *Keyhole* 1, June 1996) uses a conventional design conceit, often called the "nine-panel grid" by comics readers, to suggest the repetitive, unvarying nature of a waitress's work. The strictly gridlike (3-by-3) configuration of the page imparts a constant, unyielding rhythm to the piece, one well suited to the patterns of repetition shown in the compositions. Of all the panels, only the middle one in each tier shows significant variation, as it depicts the face of yet another customer asking the same question (a question already answered in the menu). Panel four, showing the waitress outside (presumably outside the restaurant), implies seasonal variation through the use of snow, though, curiously, the waitress's outfit has not changed to suit the weather. The drastic elision of intervening time, and the static repetition of visual motifs—of exact images, in fact—emphasizes the numbing sameness of the waitress's work routine (not unlike the mood of the café scene in *Jar of Fools*). This routine is enlivened only by the comic grotesquerie of the customers. Here a rigid layout reinforces the air of tedium, frustration, and stasis (that is, of waiting, in two senses) conveyed in the repeated compositions.

If the first "Waiting" story conveys a sense of the tedium and repetition involved in waiting tables, the third (from *Keyhole* 3, January 1997) conveys a hectic, almost frantic impression of the hard work involved. Its more inventive and complicated layout reinforces the busyness and overwhelming sense of customer demand called for in the scenario: here the waitress is working very hard indeed, responding gamely to the simultaneous requests and comments of a large dining party. Perkins and Haspiel exploit the tension between page (*planche*) and panel to emphasize the stressful, even frenzied, quality of the dinner from the waitress's point of view.

The first three panels are page-wide oblongs, crowded with detail, which convey the entire dinner in synoptic fashion. Common questions and banal observations appear in tail-less word balloons, as if hovering over the party: *Where is the bathroom?*, *This would be the perfect place to bring Mom*, and so on. A man's request for a wine glass in the first panel leads to his cry for assistance in the second: "Hey!!! I spilled my drink!" (The

Linda Perkins and Dean Haspiel, "Waiting," *Keyhole* 1 (1996). Copyright © Dean Haspiel and Linda Perkins. Used with permission.

waitress, intent on taking another customer's order, responds by handing him a towel, without even turning to look.) In the third panel, the waitress balances several steaming coffee cups on her arm while the customers look on in the background, barely visible over the cups. A full-figure image of the embattled waitress overlaps these three panels, linking them, her six arms spread Kali-like (roughly speaking) to imply her haste and efficiency. Each hand holds a common tool: a menu, a peppermill, and so on. This full shot of the waitress not only provides an irreverent bit of visual parody but also serves to unite these horizontal panels in a single graphic conceit without arresting the sequence of events depicted. What's more, we are able to see the events from multiple perspectives at once, for the first panel appears to show the dinner party from the waitress's viewpoint, while the second and third depict the waitress herself, in medium and close-up shots respectively. Her overlapping figure in these three panels frustrates any sense of linearity, allowing for an impossible and provocative at-onceness.

The last three panels on the page, forming the bottom tier, are stunted verticals of equal size, much smaller than the images above. They depict a briefer sequence of events: a final exchange between the waitress and the man paying the bill. In reply to the skimpy tip (just $5 for a bill of $295), the waitress asks the man, "Was there something wrong with the service?" His response is simple and unequivocal, though seemingly irrelevant: "Yes. My wife burned my toast this morning." His grotesque, comically exaggerated features contrast with the idealized close-up of the waitress immediately above, lending a spiteful certainty to his accusation. Here there are no outsized images to violate or overlap the bordered panels; only three simple images in a deliberate rhythm, reminiscent of the gridlike regularity in the first "Waiting" story. Whereas the top three panels convey the almost desperate efficiency of the waitress's efforts, and show her earning what by rights ought to be a generous tip, the last three show her comeuppance, as masculine spite holds her responsible, by proxy, for another woman's failure to please. It is largely through the ingenious layout of the page that Perkins and Haspiel underscore the unfairness of the man's response.

The page divides into two design units—the three horizontal panels and the three verticals—to contrast the waitress's efforts with her scant reward. In the top three panels, the temporal sequence is confused, even collapsed, by the full figure of the waitress, an overlapping design element that functions tabularly to stress the frantic nature of her activity. The overlapping of images suggests the overwhelming demands of her work. In the bottom three, the uniform, unbroken panels, shorn of any elaborate design elements, establish a rhythm that leads to the strip's bitter punch line.

Uniting these two design units, the final image of the man's face stares at the reader as if seen from the waitress's point of view, a visual echo of the story's first panel (in which the man turns to get her attention). Moreover, the final close-up of the man contrasts with the close-up of the waitress directly above: she looks left, intent on her work, while he seems to be moving right, as if to leave; her face, an unblemished white, contrasts with his darker, more detailed features. Yet the two are linked by a strong vertical down the right-hand side of the page: in a tabular reading, the last cell relates directly to the cell above it, while in a linear reading it supplies the climax for the entire six-panel story. Linearly, the incident progresses from dinner, through dessert, to the final payoff, while, tabularly, the figures of the waitress and the man vie for position on the page. The Kali-

Linda Perkins and Dean Haspiel, "Waiting," *Keyhole* 3 (1997). Copyright © Dean Haspiel and Linda Perkins. Used with permission.

like waitress clearly dominates the surface, yet the man moves from right to center to right again, in an attempt to (re)assert his dominance. The layout of the entire page stresses the complete figure of the waitress, on the upper left, and the opposed close-ups of waitress and man, on the lower right. The fact that each panel functions both as a discrete part and within the larger context of the layout generates the tension that makes this vignette so effective.

From a reader's point of view, then, there is always the potential to choose: between seeing the single image as a moment in sequence and seeing it in more holistic fashion, as a design element that contributes to the overall balance (or in some cases the mean-ingful *im*balance) of the layout. The latter way of seeing privileges the dimensions of the total page/*planche*/surface, yet still invokes the meaning of the overall narrative sequence to explain why the page might be formatted as it is. Broadly, we may say that comics exploit *format* as a signifier in itself; more specifically, that comics involve a tension be-tween the experience of reading in sequence and the format or shape of the object being read. In other words, the art of comics entails a tense relationship between perceived time and perceived space.

TEXT AS EXPERIENCE VS. TEXT AS OBJECT

At a higher level of generalization, the tension *sequence vs. surface* is but one example of a larger relationship between (a) experience over time and (b) the dimensions of comics as material objects. The latter aspect, comics' materiality, includes not only the design or layout of the page but also the physical makeup of the text, including its size, shape, binding, paper, and printing. Like traditional books, but perhaps more obviously, long-form comics can exploit both design and material qualities to communicate or under-score the meaning(s) available in the text. Indeed, many comics make it impossible to distinguish between text per se and secondary aspects such as design and the physical package, because they continually invoke said aspects to influence the reader's participa-tion in meaning-making.

Material considerations influence not only the total design and packaging of a pub-lication but also matters of style and technique. The delineation of images, for instance, is always affected by the materiality of the text, for, as Eisner observes, comic art is nec-essarily rendered "in response to the method of its reproduction" (*Comics & Sequential Art*, 153). In fact style in comics is often profoundly influenced by technological and economic means, and many cartoonists develop highly self-conscious relationships with those means, relationships that, from a reader's point of view, can become fraught with significance. For instance, the European *Ligne Claire* (Clear Line) tradition of cartoon-ing, popularized in the much-loved *Tintin* series by Belgian master Hergé, privileges smooth, continuous linework, simplified contours and bright, solid colors, while avoid-ing frayed lines, exploded forms, and expressionistic rendering. A style of drawing linked with the flat color of *Tintin* and similar series, the *Klare Lijn* (so labeled by the Dutch cartoonist Joost Swarte) is marked by its traditional association with children's comics, yet has grown to embrace or at least influence a whole school of alternative cartoonists who work for adults as well as, or instead of, children. These cartoonists often treat its associations ironically, as if to question Herge's ideal union of style and subject (among many others: Swarte, Ever Meulen, Daniel Torres, the late Yves Chaland, and, in perhaps less obvious but still significant ways, Jacques Tardi, Vittorio Giardino, and the United States' Jason Lutes). In the work of such cartoonists as Swarte and Torres, the Clear Line carries an obvious ideological as well as stylistic burden: their comics not only parody racist stereotypes redolent of *Tintin*'s late-colonial ethos but also reveal a fascination with blurring the distinction between organic and inorganic form, a tendency perfectly realized in Swarte's cool, ironic work for both children and adults.

Often the Clear Line seems to deny the materiality of the comics page, relying on precise linework and flat colors to create pristine and detailed settings into which simply drawn characters are inserted. Though the settings are often much more complex than the characters, the two are equated through an unerring evenness of line: like the characters, the settings tend to be without shadow, except in the most diagrammatic sense, and also relatively textureless. The resultant tendency toward flatness produces what McCloud calls a "democracy of form," in which each shape has the same clarity and value, conferring the same authority on cartoon figures as it does on meticulous scenic detail (190). This tendency can of course be undercut, as in Swarte's strip "Torn Together" (*Samen gescheurd* in Dutch), which spoofs the democracy of forms and calls attention to the materiality of the page. Beginning with a panel whose upper left corner has deliberately been torn off, "Torn Together" goes on to depict a contretemps in which one man tears off the lapels of another's jacket, then tears off his ear, to which the other responds by tearing out the first man's right arm. (The dripping blood looks particularly incongruous in the *Klare Lijn*.) The second man proceeds to stuff the disembodied arm and ear into a vase to create a decoration, which he waters like a plant. This is an especially clear example of Swarte's interest in the confusion of living and unliving form: the flat coloring and pristine linework create an Herge-like scenario that ironically equates the tearing of paper with the tearing of people's bodies. The style is inextricably part of, and prerequisite to, the story's meaning.

In contrast to the Clear Line are more expressionistic styles that revel in the texture of the page, insisting on the materiality of the print medium. Gary Panter, for instance, hailed as "the Father of Punk Comics," has pioneered a raw, "ratty-line" approach at odds with the pristine illusionism of the clear line. Panter himself views his work in terms of "marks" rather than lines, a distinction that privileges expressiveness over clarity or precision (Groth and Fiore, 231–32). In contrast to the school of Hérge, which epitomizes the use of line as a means of definition and verisimilitude, Panter's mark-making emphasizes texture as a means of immediate, visceral expression. He privileges the raw gestural qualities of a drawing, as a record of physical activity, over its iconic or referential function. Panter's work—notably his occasional series *Jimbo*, which follows a punk everyman through various bizarre and fragmented episodes (for example, *Cola Madness, Jimbo in Purgatory*)—boasts a disorienting variety of graphic techniques, as well as an oblique and disjointed approach to language. The result is a ragged cartoon surrealism, often narrative in only the loosest sense, fusing the iconography of comics and animation with a painterly, fine-arts sensibility and the aggressive energy of punk. Indeed the humor of Panter's work depends in part on his use of rough, energetic marks to reconfigure characters lifted from television cartooning and children's comics, characters usually rendered with a slick consistency befitting industrialized cel animation. The approach recalls R. Crumb's anxious reinvention of cartoon icons in the late 1960s, but with an even greater emphasis on pure mark-making rather than figuration.

Many alternative comic artists, both in the United States and abroad, have followed in Panter's wake, drawing on the ironic tension between simplified cartoon vocabulary and roughhewn graphic technique. (Such disparate artists as David Sandlin, Jonathon Rosen, Julie Doucet, and Lloyd Dangle all qualify, as do such Europeans as M. S. Bastian of Switzerland and Max Andersson of Denmark.) This tension often serves to express a violent and absurdist worldview colored by apocalyptic anxieties, as in much of Panter's own work. In general, the post-Panter ratty-line (or "ugly art" or "comix brut") school subverts the cultural and ideological reassurances proffered by the Clear Line, and as such represents a visual argument about the implications of style. This argument foregrounds the active role of the reader in constructing meaning.

Beyond the bald ironies of punk, many other recent comics invoke the materiality of print by using suggestive styles based on tone and texture, just as the *ligne claire* is based on the precise delineation of form. Such styles (especially evident in the European avant-garde, with its *objet d'art* approach) tend to explore the relationship between figure and ground. For instance, French artist Yvan Alagbé often approaches figuration in a sparse, open, almost gestural way, despite a finely nuanced realism of expression; his pages pose indistinct or half- completed figures against blank, undifferentiated backgrounds, exploring the tension between positive and negative space. Simply put, Alagbé's characters seem constantly on the verge of dissolving into the page itself. His work thus reveals a profound faith in the reader's capacity for visual closure, as it calls on our ability to complete a process of figuration only begun by the artist. In such works as *Nègres Jaunes* (1995) Alagbé turns this daring graphic technique to cultural argument, thematizing the blackness and whiteness of ink and paper as signs of ethnic and cultural difference.

While Alagbé's work relies on traditional gridlike paneling to enclose and delimit its open spaces, German artist Anna Sommer (*Remue-Ménage/Damen Dramen*) allows series of images to spill freely across the undivided expanse of the page. She too displays great confidence in the reader's ability to construct meaning from fragments. Her fluid approach to *sequence vs. surface* mirrors her thematic interest in openness and surprise, in particular her exploration (as here) of the mutability of gender. This method goes beyond questions of layout to the interrogation of the physical page as surface and ground. Indeed, artists like Alagbé and Sommer call for a materialist criticism, one in which print-specific qualities such as drawing technique, tone, and surface can be interrogated for their narrative significance. Ditto those artists known for their painterly manipulation of texture, such as France's Jean-Claude Götting (who creates dense, dark imagery with a lithograph-like grain); Italy's Stefano Ricci (who sculpts thick, almost palpable tones by alternating drawing, erasing, and painting on fragile paper); the United States' Debbie Drechsler (who balances contour and texture through the mesmerizing buildup of delicate lines); and Switzerland's Thomas Ott (whose grim, often horrific fables are carved out of scratchboard, white on black—a perfect union of technique and subject). All of these artists are characterized by a keen grasp not only of comics as a narrative form but also of the relationship between narrative content and physical medium, that is, between the experience of reading and the material object. Calling attention to that relationship, these creators highlight the distance between text and reader, and foreground the reader's creative intervention in meaning-making. Their works bear out Pascal Lefèvre's dictum that "the materiality of a comic is essential. . . . The form of a drawing draws attention to the object represented in a way that deviates from ordinary perception" ("Recovering Sensuality" 142).

The above examples may seem exotic to American readers—but one need not look far afield to find invocations of the page-as-object. In Art Spiegelman's celebrated *Maus*, for instance, the page repeatedly refers to itself, as "objects" overlap the panels, creating at once an illusion of volume and a sense of intimacy (as if these found objects have been mounted in a diary or scrapbook). Maps, tickets, photographs—these commonplace items appear to have been laid "on top" of the page, as if to ratify the book's documentary nature as a family auto/biography. Early on, for example, Spiegelman conveys a key moment in the courtship between his father Vladek and his mother Anja by drawing a photograph of Anja into, and onto, the page (1:17). Anja's "photo" dominates the page, suggesting both the factualness of Spiegelman's account and Anja's growing importance in Vladek's reminiscence. This ironic appeal to the book's status as a physical object is complex and heavily fraught, as we shall see later on. Suffice to say here that the reader's awareness is called to the materiality of the book itself (albeit through an illusion), in such a way as to inflect her understanding of the narrative. This gambit is characteristic of Spiegelman, an artist for whom print is a privileged point of reference. Such self-reflexive commentary is in fact quite common in comics: beyond questions of texture and volume, the materiality of texts is often highlighted through embedded visual references to books, other comics, and picture-making in general—things and activities inevitably fraught with special significance for cartoonists and their readers.

WORKS CITED

Alagbé, Yvan, "Etoile d'Orient," in Yvan Alagbé and Olivier Marboeuf, eds., *Le Cheval san Tête 5: Nous sommes les Moures* (Wissous, France: AMOK, May 1998), 35–41.

Avril, François, and Phillipe Petit-Roulet, *Soirs de Paris* (Paris: Les Humanoïdes Associés, 1989).

Cartier, Eric, *Flip in Paradise* (Paris: Rackham, 1990).

Doucet, Julie, "The Artist," in *My Most Secret Desire* (Montreal: Drawn & Quarterly, 1993).

Eisner, Will, *Comics & Sequential Art* (Tamarac, FL: Poorhouse Press, 1985).

Fresnault-Deruelle, Pierre, "Du linéare au tabulaire," *Communications* 24 (Paris: Ed. Du Seuil, 1976), 17–23.

Groth, Gary, and Robert Fiore, eds., *The New Comics* (New York: Berkley, 1988).

Haspiel, Dean, and Josh Neufield, eds., *Keyhole* 1 (Kingston, RI: Millenium Publications, June 1996).

Harvey, R. C., *The Art of the Funnies: An Aesthetic History* (Jackson: University Press of Mississippi, 1994).

Kannenberg, Gene, Jr., "The Comics of Chris Ware: Text, Image and Visual Narrative Strategies," in Robin Varnum and Christina T. Gibbons, eds., *The Language of Comics: Word and Image* (Jackson: University Press of Mississippi, 2001); reprinted in this volume.

———, "Graphic Text, Graphic Context: Interpreting Custom Fonts and Hands in Contemporary Comics," in Paul C. Gutjahr and Megan L. Benton, *Illuminating Letters: Typography and Literary Interpretation* (Amherst: University of Massachusetts Press, 2001), 165–92.

Lefèvre, Pascal, "Recovering Sensuality in Comic Theory," *International Journal of Comic Art* 1:1 (Spring/Summer 1999): 140–49.

Lutes, Jason, *Jar of Fools* (Montreal: Black Eye Books, 1997).

McCloud, Scott., *Understanding Comics* (Northampton: Tundra, 1993).

Mitchell, W. J. T., *Iconology: Image, Text, Ideology* (Chicago: University of Chicago Press, 1986).

Nodelman, Perry, *Words About Pictures: The Narrative Art of Children's Picture Books* (Athens: University of Georgia Press, 1988).

Peeters, Benoit, *Case, Planche, Récit: Lire la Bande Dessinée*, Rev. ed. (Paris: Casterman, 1998).

Bob and Harv's Comics (New York: Four Walls, Eight Windows, 1996).

CSR 3-11

Comics originally for adults in 19th century somehow ending up for kids 20th cent.

149-156

The Arrow and the Grid

JOSEPH WITEK

Formalist analyses of comics often begin with an attempt to establish a comprehensive definition of comics by isolating a set of textual features that will constitute the irreducible essence of "comicsness." Like parallel historical efforts to unearth an originary "first comic," however, the search for some innate characteristics that will distinguish comics from other all visual and verbal forms has generated much more semantic quibbling than productive critical inquiry. Since visual narratives and word/picture combinations of various kinds are so plentiful throughout the history of human communication, and since the category of "comics" as ordinarily used contains such an array of heterogeneous specimens, in practice essentialist definitional projects often devolve into analytical cul-de-sacs and hair-splitting debates over an apparently endless profusion of disputed boundary cases and contradictory counterexamples. Of necessity, critics have adopted various rhetorical maneuvers in order to skirt the definitional roadblock, including the invention of new boundary terms ("proto-comics," for example) or the more-or-less arbitrary stipulation of some defining formal criteria (such as the presence of word balloons, the placement of verbal text within the picture plane, the creation of continuing characters, or the use of mechanical printing). Such pragmatic stratagems at least allow a given analysis to proceed while the ineluctable core of comics form remains a will-o-the-wisp.

Essentialist definitions assume that the textual features of comics can be divided into those that are indispensable and those that are disposable, and indeed any number of formal conventions that once were commonly used in comics have now nearly disappeared. But a consideration of two such intriguing and now-obsolete features that once served as reading guides—the numbering of panels within the grid of the page in early comics strips, and the directional arrows which occasionally have been deployed to guide the eye of the reader to the proper panel in a narrative sequence—suggests that "comicsness" might usefully be reconceptualized from being an immutable attribute of texts to being considered as a historically contingent and evolving set of reading protocols that are applied to texts, that to be a comic text means to be *read* as a comic. Each of these two devices highlights a different moment in the historical development of Western reading conventions for comics, and both of them serve as traces of earlier ways of reading, as reminders that the delicate negotiation between sequentiality and simultaneity which we

---

Prepared for this volume and published by permission of the author.

now call "comics" came into being not as the fulfillment of a previously latent formal essence but as the emergence in stages of new ways of perceiving the myriad relationships between word and image on the page. Together they show how the once-unfamiliar reading conventions of the comics audience can eventually come to be both assumed and manipulated by comics creators in the construction of the comics page.

The presence of panel numbers in the comic strips of the first decades of the twentieth century can be puzzling to a latter-day comics reader simply because they often appear to be so unnecessary: why bother to number the panels at all when the normative left-to-right, top-to-bottom relations of a comic page seem to be so perfectly obvious? Yet the convention of numbering individual panels in sequence, usually in a lower corner of each panel, once was an extremely widespread (although by no means universal) feature of American newspaper comic strips. Such numbering was common in the 1890s and the first two decades of the twentieth century, and can be seen in many works by R. F. Outcault, Winsor McCay, James Swinnerton, George Herriman, Rudolph Dirks, and Fred Opper, among others. This numbering generally appears in Sunday strips and very rarely in dailies, and its use even for the Sundays was sometimes intermittent. For example, Sunday installments of George Herriman's *Krazy Kat* might display numbered panels (even for images without panel borders at all) for several weeks, then skip a week or two, only to return to numbered panels. McCay's *Little Nemo in Slumberland* sported numbers for nearly all of its panels, but McCay's contemporaneous *Dreams of the Rarebit Fiend* usually did not. In fact, McCay's habits in this regard seemed to have changed over time, since at first the header image of a Sunday *Little Nemo* containing the strip's logo was not counted as a panel, but starting on July 29, 1906 the header was included in the count.

In any case, the ostensible function of these numbers obviously is to serve as an aid to the reader, to help ensure that the panels are read in the proper order. However, if we assume that by the 1910s newspaper readers were aware that comics panels usually were intended to be read in a left-to-right, top-to-bottom sequence—an assumption supported by the counterexample of the majority of strips which did *not* feel the need to number the panels—the actual purpose of the numbers in any given strip remains somewhat obscure. The possibility exists that they were inserted by editors or by artists at an editor's behest, or that they were inserted in case the panels were rearranged into some format other than that of the original art (as is often done with comic strips today). However, in the case of Herriman the numbers are rendered in the artist's distinctive style, and sometimes they are inscribed within fairly elaborate scrollwork or other decorative devices. Furthermore, many, and indeed perhaps most, characteristic Herriman and McCay Sunday pages are so completely integrated as single-page compositions as to be impossible to reproduce coherently in any other format.

The most logical explanation for the presence of these apparently superfluous indicators of sequence, therefore, is that they are fossilized holdovers included by habit or by waning convention from an earlier stage in the development of what came to be called the comics medium. Although in the Western tradition comics reading conventions have over time become aligned with those of prose, such has not always been the case. David Kunzle's two volumes of pre-twentieth century comic strips show that in the eighteenth and nineteenth centuries many sequential pictorial narratives were published in formats in which the columns are read top to bottom rather than in horizontal tiers, or in which the horizontal tiers continue across two-page spreads, or in which the images are strung out haphazardly across one or more pages, so that the earlier generation of readers accustomed to the variegated formats of the picture sequences in *Puck, Judge, Chat Noir* or other nineteenth-century periodicals would not necessarily assume that pictures in a series, even if separated by borders and organized into a grid, were to be read as a sequence or, if they were perceived as sequential, that they must be read in left-to-right, top-to-bottom order. In fact, reading many such nineteenth-century picture series which are *not* numbered requires careful attention to determine if the operative principle linking the images is narrative sequence or a more general thematic association.

With the standardization of formats for newspaper comics and the codification of their reading conventions, by the 1910s the majority of newspaper strips in America no longer used numbers for their panels; by the 1930s such numbers had disappeared nearly entirely, although they occasionally did crop up from time to time. Even if their primary function had become vitiated by the early decades of the twentieth century, however, they still remained meaningful, albeit slight, compositional elements of the work of many cartoonists, major and minor.

Not surprisingly, George Herriman's *Krazy Kat* manipulated panel numbers in some notably imaginative ways. Most *Krazy Kat* strips, even those with the most complex layouts, are not numbered at all, while the numbers on many pages are quite unremarkable. Yet Herriman routinely subjected these numbers to the same transformative logic as all the other elements of his *Krazy Kat* strips, deploying them in an array of methods and visual styles, including simple numerals, circled numerals, outlined numerals, Roman numerals (July 14, 1918), spelled-out words, words enclosed in decorative scrollwork, large words, small words, and words transformed by several kinds of linguistic play. For instance, in the January 4, 1920 strip, the phonetic transformations of the image numbers parallel the habitual metamorphoses of the strip's backgrounds, forming a kind of concurrent action with the strip's familiar triangular plot. Three 1923 strips substitute different double vowel sounds for the normal ones, answering the previously undreamed-of question of what would happen if the central vowels in the words for numbers were replaced by double-o's (August 5, 1923), double-e's (September 16, 1923), and double-i's (September 23, 1923).

This apparently whimsical transformation reminds us that numbers embody the dual nature of the comics form itself, since they can be indicated by two written forms, one verbal and the other at least iconic if not actually pictorial. Herriman's games foreground the moribund nature of the numbering convention, the presence of the numbers reminding readers not so much of the proper order in which to read the panels as insisting that, no matter how spectacular the pages are as overall visual compositions, the images still are to be read as a sequence. In the work of Winsor McCay, Fred Opper, and the other cartoonists of the teens and twenties, the numbers in the panels inherently invoke the concept of sequence, reminding readers of what they already know: that the separate pictures on the page have meaning only as an integrated whole. Thus the historical moment when the reading audience no longer needs the panel numbers to understand that the words and images constitute a sequence helps to demarcate the point at which that mode of sequential pictorial narrative which has come to be called "comics" becomes independent from other, related forms.

If the effect of the panel numbers is to evoke the sequentiality of the comics page, the use of directional arrows serves to temporarily suspend the normal reading process in order to foreground the spatial relations of the panels. Directional arrows seem at first glance to highlight a problem or artistic misstep in the overall construction of the page, functioning as emergency signs which lead readers onto a detour off the high road of the standard reading path. These arrows most often appear on the comics page in a structural environment that we might call the "right-hand vertical," that is, where a panel on the right side of the comics page is elongated vertically to the size of two or more panels. In such a case, as the reader's eye moves from the left side of the page, the elongated panel invites the eye to descend down the right side of the page to the bottom, and thence on to the next page. But such a path leaves out the middle or lower panels of the left side of the page, so some kind of signpost is needed to direct the reading gaze back to the left. In an example from *Batman* #30 (1945), the first two panels are read in the usual order, but the next image to the right is initially narrative dead space, and the reading eye cannot yet be allowed to plunge down the long vertical panel to the bottom right of the page. Thus the arrow swerves the reader's attention back down and to the left. Then, helped by a second arrow (since the vertical panel is still not yet narratively "active"), for three panels the page reads top-left to bottom-left until at last the final arrow authorizes the hitherto delayed movement to the right and up and eventually off the page.

Less commonly an arrow appears when an enlarged panel opens the page in the upper left position, as in an example from the first Human Torch story in *Marvel Mystery Comics* #1 (1939). The spatial relationship of the bottom of the first left-hand panel (or rather the partial circle inset panel, which has an ambiguous narrative relationship to the main panel) suggests that the next panel in reading order is the first of the second tier; therefore the arrow is needed to move the reader's gaze back to the top of the first panel, thus avoiding the orphaning of the two small panels of the top tier.

What is achieved by forcing the reader against the structural grain like this? In order to answer this question, it is necessary to consider in some detail the ways that the arrangement of comics panels create meaning beyond basic linear sequence. In the *Batman* example, the long right-hand panel opens up the physical space of the page, thematically emphasizing the smallness of the heroes against the vast expanse of elevator machinery, and thus heightening the sense of danger. In the second example a longer panel likewise opens Carl Burgos's characteristic extremely cramped—and often confusing—page layout to allow space to show the Human Torch's dramatic action of burning through the top of the automobile as well as the reaction shot in the close-up inset panel.

There is little notable in panels of action being larger than panels of speech or reflection. In fact, the technique of varying the size of the comics panel to fit the action contained within it is one of the fundamental gestures of the comics medium, as in Winsor McCay's famous Befuddle Hall sequence, where the panels stretch and shrink in size as the characters view themselves in a funhouse mirror. Likewise, the overt use of the comics page as an overall visual composition rather than a mere collection of entirely discrete individual panels has a long history, most notably in the work of those cartoonists who emphasize the graphic design of their Sunday pages such as McCay, Herriman, Lionel Feininger, and many others. But the multi-page format of the comic book enabled if not required a profound shift in the conceptualization of the comics page away from even the most sophisticated treatments by newspaper comic strip artists, and the directional arrows of early comic books show creators grappling with a new way of thinking about the organization of space on the comics page.

That is, panels on the page always create narrative meaning both as sequences and as spatial arrangements; this double-text is implicit in all comics forms, but it comes to the fore most fully in comic books. Since a daily comic strip consists of a single tier of only a few panels at most, the cartoonist's scope for the manipulation of the spatial relationships of panels is minimal at best—the panels generally simply come one after the other, and in today's primarily verbal gag strips, those panels must be constructed so that, at the desire of the comics-page editor, they can be printed in a single horizontal tier, or a vertical row, or two short tiers of two or three panels with little effect on the strip's meaning. Yet even a page of discrete strips establishes subtextual visual and thematic connections with its neighbors—most overtly when the syndicated cartoonists jointly agree to espouse a cause or to celebrate a historical anniversary, but also when serendipitous parallels occur from strip to strip. A Sunday strip works in somewhat larger units than do the dailies, and in the heyday of the American newspaper comic strip, creators such as McCay, Herriman, Cliff Sterrett, and Frank King could construct their pages (and later half-pages) with the overall visual effect of the page itself in mind. In the hands of the more graphically oriented cartoonists, such Sunday pages could aspire to be apprehended as compositional *objets* as well as narrative sequences.

The comic book, with its pages upon pages of panels, posed new problems and afforded new opportunities in the construction of longer story units. One less-than-satisfactory although extremely common answer to the question of how to construct multi-page comics stories is the use of an absolutely regular grid structure, a technique sometimes used when sequences of comic strips were reprinted as comic books: panels of identical shape and size are arranged in even tiers across the page. Though extremely economical of space, highly regular grids tend inevitably toward both visual monotony and flatness in narrative action, since each event is given a similar visual weight whatever its importance in the story, so that a panel of mechanical plot exposition looks much the same as the slam-bang climax of the adventure. For example, the penultimate page from the first Human Torch issue attempts to cram twelve identical panels onto a single page, and its efficient construction extracts a steep price in legibility. Given the freedom to design page layouts from scratch in the comic-book format, most artists almost immediately preferred to modify regular grids by eliminating one or more vertical panel borders to form double-or triple width panels, thus varying the visual effect without actually altering the basic dimensions of the basic building-block panels. A modern example of the potential of this approach is Alan Moore & Dave Gibbons's *Watchmen*, which achieves a remarkable range of narrative rhythm using an array of variations on an almost completely regular three-panel-by-three-tier page layout.

Another conservative solution to the twin problems of avoiding visual monotony and creating more flexible narrative emphasis is to simply vary the size of the panels slightly so that the vertical gutters no longer line up perfectly. Like slight variations in poetic meter and rhyme, even this relatively small change in the regularity of the grid mitigates the visual sing-song effect of identically shaped and sized panels. This extremely versatile and eye-pleasing "offset grid" page layout has become one of the standard compositional strategies for the comic-book page; for example it was used with only slight variations by Carl Barks in hundreds of *Donald Duck* and *Uncle Scrooge* stories. Indeed, today it may be the most common style of comic-book page layout.

A more radical solution resulted in what might be called the "high baroque" style of comic-book page layout. Widely used in the comic books of the 1940s, this approach energized the page itself by means of a variety of flamboyant technical gestures, including wavy or jagged lines for panel borders, circular, triangular, or other unusually shaped panels, blackout panels, extreme close-ups (often within circular panels—sometimes called "cameo" panels), and extensive use of figures which appear to emerge from within the panels onto the physical page itself so that the panel becomes only a notional "container" for the action. Pushed to an extreme, this baroque impulse results in what might be called the "gestalt" layout, in which the overall shapes of the panels take on narrative or thematic significance, as in an example from *Wings* comics where a scene set in a airplane in flight is enclosed in a series of panels shaped like an airplane's fuselage. Not surprisingly, the baroque style is typical of the 1940s work of Jack Kirby, where the dynamism of the page design parallels the frenetic pace of the stories being told; rarely in the early issues of *Captain America* is a simple rectangular panel bounded by straight vertical borders.

Even more common in the 1940s than the full-blown baroque style is a layout style which combines simple variations of panel size with some of the graphic flourishes of the baroque, so that a norm of rectangular panels, usually on a slightly irregular grid, is established then embellished with an occasional circular panel or a figure moving beyond the panel border. Directional arrows are common in both the high baroque style and its more sedate variant, since such complex layouts resulting from varyingly sized panels often pose the fundamental navigational puzzle of which panel is meant to be read in which order. In fact, at first glance the baroque style can verge on the narratively incoherent, as in Jack Kirby's early habit of constructing layouts which end at the bottom left rather than bottom right of the page, thus leaving the reader theoretically unable to get out of the page at all.

The baroque style embodies at the level of the entire page the same problem indicated by the local phenomenon of the directional arrow: the reading process of the story is subordinated to an immediate visual effect. The result is often a highly antic mode of storytelling, with the emotional effects suggested by the design of the page disconnected from the tone and atmosphere of the actual story being told. While sometimes such connections between the page and its contents can be extremely close, as when the design of a "gestalt" page echoes or reinforces the story's themes or actions, oftentimes the pages crackle with florid graphic gestures even during relatively sedate narrative passages. Furthermore, the anxiety raised in readers about the proper way to decipher the comics page can run counter to the narrative energy that the baroque style is presumably designed to evoke: readers who are trying to figure out the proper way to read the page are readers who are not immersed in the story.

The baroque style does represent an early response to the new demands of multi-page comics storytelling and acknowledges that the experience of reading a comic is a function not only of what is contained within each panel, but also of the size, shape, and design of the panels themselves as well as the spatial relations among them. Freed to a large extent from the requirement of creating stories which must exist alongside others on the newspaper comics page, the early comic book artists sensed the possibilities inherent in shaping narratives using the page itself as the fundamental unit. As Will Eisner says: "In comics, there are actually two 'frames' . . . the total page, on which there are any number of panels, and the panel itself, within which the narrative action unfolds. They are the controlling device in sequential art" (*Comics & Sequential Art*, 41). The apparent number disagreement in Eisner's last sentence is not a grammatical error at all, but a precise statement of the case: the page and the panels together make up a single narrative device. Eisner's conception of the comics page, therefore, makes the control of the reader's gaze in navigating the comics page a fundamental aspect of the creative art of the medium, and the use of such unsubtle devices as the directional arrow in the early comic book suggests that artists took some time to adapt their practices to the requirements of the longer comics format.

In his discussion of the role of the page, Eisner emphasizes the way layout functions in controlling the tendency of the eye to wander out of proper sequence, the task he calls "reader discipline." Integral to this process is the interaction between the panel breakdowns (that is, the composition of individual panels) and the page layouts to create subtexts (or parallel texts) to the literal level of the narrative within the panels. Some of these interactions have become silent conventions; for example, the habit of placing action which is physically lower in relation to the characters lower down on the page stems from the sense that the panels on a page to some extent exist in space simultaneously with one another.

Contemporary comics display page layout styles and designs fully as complex as the most baroque pages of the 1940s, with concomitant challenges to the reading skills of the audience, but the navigational role once played by the directional arrows has been taken over by more integrated aspects of panel breakdowns and page composition to help guide the reading eye to the proper panel in a sequence. Such devices include the lines of sight of the characters, the physical orientation of figures and objects, and perhaps most commonly, the judicious placement of word balloons to link one panel to the next. Increasing sensitivity to the orientation of the reader through such devices made possible the phasing out of the directional arrow as a serious technical device. The arrow has not disappeared entirely, however; its obsolescence has freed it for use by contemporary creators as a sign of a self-consciously nostalgic comics style, or as in the hands of someone like Chris Ware, as part of the construction of complex page designs which ultimately serve as infernal machines for, in Will Eisner's mildly sadistic phrase, the "discipline" of potentially wayward readers. Both the numbering of panels and the directional arrows remain as traces of the process by which the Western comics reader has been constructed, a reader trained to perceive the comics page as both a linked sequence of separate panels and as a meaningful semiotic field in itself. These devices thus stand as signs pointing back down along the path still trod by readers and creators alike, and they suggest that any given attempt to define some unchanging essence of comics may well find itself undone as reading conventions and textual practices continue to revise each other.

WORKS CITED AND CONSULTED

Eisner, Will, *Comics & Sequential Art* (Tamarac, FL: Poorhouse Books, 1985).

Hayman, Greg, and Henry John Pratt, "What Are Comics?" in David Goldblatt and Lee B. Brown, eds. *Aesthetics: A Reader in Philosophy of the Arts* (Upper Saddle River: Pearson Education, 2005): 419–24.

Harvey, R. C., "More New Historic Beginnings for Comics." *Comics Journal* 246 (Sept. 2002): 115–20.

Horn, Maurice, "100 Years of Comics: An Introduction," in Maurice Horn, ed., *100 Years of American Newspaper Comics* (New York: Gramercy Books, 1996): 11–19.

Horrocks, Dylan, "Inventing Comics: Scott McCloud Defines the Form in *Understanding Comics*," *Comics Journal* 234 (June 2001): 29–38.

Kunzle, David, *The Early Comic Strip: Narrative Strips and Picture Stories in the European Broadsheet from c. 1450 to 1825* (Berkeley: University of California Press, 1973).

———, *The History of the Comic Strip: The Nineteenth Century* (Berkeley: University Press of California, 1990).

Meskin, Aaron, "Defining Comics?" *Journal of Aesthetics & Art Criticism* 65: 4 (Oct. 2007) 369–79.

McCloud, Scott, *Understanding Comics* (Northampton: Tundra, 1993).

The Construction of Space in Comics

PASCAL LEFÈVRE

This chapter seeks to give a concise theoretical overview of the various types of "space" a reader encounters in a comic: diegetic space (the fictive space in which the characters live and act) versus extradiegetic space, visualized versus non-visualized space, etc. Furthermore the aim is to describe briefly how a flat medium can suggest a three-dimensional space and how readers (re)construct the diegetic space of a story. This approach is clearly inspired by research in other domains as visual perception, art history, and film theory.[1]

Before dealing with the various aspects of construction of space, let us recall the several goals of diegetic space in fictional comics (Lefèvre, 1996). In the first place a particular space is necessary to situate the action. Therefore a lot of artists use stereotypical icons (like the Statue of Liberty for New York or the pyramids for Egypt) because such famous buildings or monuments can be easily recognized by the readers. Moreover most buildings can already by their form indicate which function they have (e.g. farms, airplanes, houses . . .). Space can also suggest other meanings: the way a person has decorated or organized his room can suggest something about his personality (orderly or messy, classic or modern, etc.). Furthermore space can express a certain mood or be a symbol for an underlying concept or a scene or even a complete story. For example the rigid, monumental forms of the architecture of Urbicande (in Schuiten and Peeters's *La Fièvre d'Urbicande*, 1984) suggest an authoritarian system that suppresses its inhabitants as insignificant parts. No wonder that the authors found their inspiration in Stalinist and fascistic buildings and in futuristic architectural projects of the early twentieth century. Schuiten and Peeters use this architecture in a metaphorical way in their *Dark Cities* series.

VISUALIZED VERSUS NON-VISUALIZED SPACE

The reader constructs the diegetic space in various ways: both by elements that appear inside the frame of a panel and by elements that remain unseen (in French called *hors champ*). This non-visualized space does not only refer to the virtual supposed space outside the frame (in French called *hors cadre*) of a certain panel, but also to the supposed

---

Reprinted by permission from *Image and Narrative* 16 (February 2006; www.imageandnarrative.be).

"hidden" space within the borders of the panel itself (in French called *hors champ interne*): for instance figures can overlap one another and hide parts from the eye of viewer. While some elements may not be visualized, they can be suggested by direct and indirect means: an element can directly indicate its presence outside the visualized space (e.g., a shadow or a balloon inside the frame that indicates the presence of someone outside the frame), or indirectly unexpected elements can pop up in a later panel: e.g. while the first panel shows us a close-up of a person, the second panel by enlarging the frame can show that this close-up is just of photograph on a wall and not an acting character in this scene (for example in the opening sequence of *City of Glass* the first telephone we see, turns out to be a drawing on a telephone directory). The artist has thus a powerful tool, namely framing, at his hands: by limiting the scope for the viewer and therefore the available information, the artist can cause a reader to make wrong inferences.[2]

Furthermore not all comics rely on the same amount of visualized space: in funny comic strips (e.g., *Peanuts* or *Garfield*) the backgrounds are quite minimal or even absent, while in adventure stories (e.g., *Tarzan*) lavish backgrounds of exotic places can be prominent and detailed.

THE CONSTRUCTION OF SPACE IN SEPARATE PANELS

The construction of space is a dynamic process, not only for each individual panel, but also for sequences and the complete comic. Several cues can help or obstruct the reader in this process. In the first place every flat image has to deal with its fundamental two-dimensional aspect: the picture can try to deny the flatness by suggesting an illusionary depth or, on the contrary, can accentuate this flatness (like Trondheim's *Bleu*, 2003). In most comics a two-dimensional composition represents a three-dimensional space in which the action occurs. In the course of history visual artists have developed several means to suggest a voluminous space on a flat surface. Spatial relations between figures or objects in a picture can be described by projection systems. Willats (1997) following Booker (1963) defines projection systems in terms of primary and secondary geometry. Primary geometry is viewer-centered and describes pictures in terms of projection rays: "The geometry of projection of lines or rays from objects in the scene and their intersection with the picture plane to form an image or picture." (Willats, 1997: 369). Most technical drawings can be described by primary geometry, but other formal projection systems as the reversed perspective cannot be described by primary geometry. In those cases an object-centered system is needed, like secondary geometry, which Willats (1997: 369) like Booker (1963) defines as: "The two-dimensional geometry of the picture surface, obtained without recourse to the idea of projection." From the Renaissance till the end of the nineteenth century, linear and aerial perspective was the most used projection system in European art, but in other periods and other places other projection systems were used: for example the reversed perspective in Byzantine and Russian icons (Willats, 1997: 12) or the forty-five degree oblique in East Asian paintings and drawings. Each method has its possibilities and limitations, so the choice of a certain projection system has many consequences. While linear perspective offers only one possible view on an object, object-centered projection systems can offer various views on the same object (e.g., cubist effects) or respect the relative distances (e.g., forty-five degree oblique). The intrinsic qualities of the object to represent can play a role in the choice of the projection system (Palmer, 1999: 370). Objects that appear on a flat surface can never show the complete reality of such three-dimensional objects. The flat and unmoving image can only use monocular cues to suggest depth: interposition or overlapping, convergence, relative size, density gradient. Not all depth cues were everywhere and in all times used (for an historical overview see Solso, 1994: 192).

While various depth cues can lead to the same conclusion, sometimes they can contradict each other, which can cause tension (Arnheim, 1971: 126).[3]

A drawer does, of course, a lot more than just deliver depth cues: the style of his drawing is also of paramount importance in the construction of space. A drawer does not only depict something, but expresses in his drawing at the same time a philosophy, a vision: implicit in every drawing style is a visual ontology, i.e., a definition of the real in visual terms (Rawson, 1987: 19). Consequently the form of the drawing does influence the manner the reader will experience and interpret the image: the viewer cannot look at the object-in-picture from another point of view than the one the picture offers; he is invited to share the maker's mode of seeing, not only in the literal, but also in the figurative sense (Peters, 1981: 14).[4]

Furthermore, the visualized space appears within the borders of a single panel, which itself can have various sizes, dimensions, and locations on a page. All these aspects can be important for the construction of space: for instance a high vertical panel is of course better suited to represent a tall building, while a long horizontal panel can be ideal for a landscape.

CONSTRUCTION OF SPACE IN A SEQUENCE

In general the reader expects that the diegetic space of a comic is sufficiently coherent: he expects—in analogy with daily life—a consistent space, because he tries on the basis of cues (given in the panels) to form a global image of the complete space. Some authors such as the French François Bourgeon dedicated great attention to the (re)construction of a diegetic space: for his story about the Middle Ages, *Le Dernier Chant des Malaterre* (1989), he even built scale models and drew plans of his locations (Thiebaut, 1992: 57–68).

The reader knows the cues to construct a space: he recognizes the linear perspective depth cues, he is conscious of the unseen but virtual space outside the panel borders, and to link the fragments together, the reader is looking for overlaps. Without the necessary overlaps, the readers can only guess that the various fragments belong to the same and consistent space. By and large, readers will not check every diegetic space in all its details for its degree of contingency: he knows that the diegetic world is not completely the same as his daily reality and he has to accept the existence of fictive worlds with their own rules and principles (e.g., imaginary worlds as cities on other planets). Some contradictions of the diegetic space remain unnoticed; usually the suggestion that the various fragments belong together is sufficient for the reader. Scores of comics suggest a coherent diegetic space without giving sufficient proof. Seldom in a sequence are all the corners of one room shown or is a global view of the space presented. The reader's expectation of a consistent diegetic space is often wrong. Berthomé (1990: 44) argues that the décor changes according the needs of the moment, and he gives the example of the Asterix village (the same houses occupy different locations in various stories of the series). Also Donald Duck's fictional city Duckburg is not a stable place but can change fundamentally from one story to another.

One has to make a distinction between changes that do not affect the illusion of a consistent diegetic space and those changes that weaken this illusion or belief. Readers accept that not in each panel every detail of the décor is repeated: the décor might disappear temporally from the reader's view to accentuate the actions of the characters. By and large, readers do accept these codes; they are not surprised that elements disappear and reappear. Aside from these temporal disappearances of the décor, there may be also more unexpected changes in the diegetic space that affect the represented space intrinsically. Even in series like *The Dark Cities* (*Cités Obscures*) an attentive reader may notice such inconsistencies: for instance, in *La Fièvre d'Urbicande* (1983) the big world map (on the wall of Robricks office) changes; in *Brüsel* (1991) the same window of Wappendorf's house is drawn with different numbers of panes (51 and 54); also Wappendorf's invention, the *solenoïde* (52–53), does not carry always the same number of rings.

Such inconsistencies do not have to surprise us, because unlike in cinema there is no camera that registers a material décor or existing place, in comics every panel has to be composed again on the blank page. Characters and décor can only exist in comics if they are represented in some way or another. Even if panels seem to offer the same view on a certain space, everything that is not drawn again will be absent. Small changes will not obstruct the reading, because they are not considered as radical inconsistencies of the represented world (Baetens and Lefèvre, 1993: 31–32). Usually these are details of lesser importance and their visibility may depend both on the comic and the reader: if a comic pretends to be a realistic depiction of our world, the reader will expect a sufficient degree of consistency. In a humorous drawn comic the reader will accept more voluntary inconsistencies in the representation of the diegetic space. In some comics the changes are a little more visible, but even then they mostly remain unnoticed by the average reader. Not only in more experimental comic strips as *Krazy Kat*, but also in mainstream comics (e.g. Duckburg in *Donald Duck* or Captain Haddock's castle of Moulinsart in *Tintin*) the décor can be volatile. The characters themselves never do notice the bizarre changes of their space: for them their environment seems to be stable and consistent—but the attentive reader knows otherwise. If such a very attentive reader notices these inconsistencies, he may both become frustrated that his realistic expectations were fooled and delighted because he found some "mistakes."

EXTRADIEGETIC SPACE

In addition to the diegetic space every comic has also an extradiegetic space, namely the space outside the fictive world of the comic. The extradiegetic space is the material space that surrounds the individual panels: not only the whites between the panels, but also the real space in which the reader is located. Of course characters are not expected to be aware of this space; only in self-referential exceptions characters deal with that aspect: for instance the frame of a panel crumbles upon Little Nemo, and in Martin Vaughn-James's *The Cage* (1975) the white is used as a kind of mat placed over the drawings (Baetens and Lefèvre, 1993: 35–36). Furthermore the extradiegetic space can be integrated by means of a character seemingly looking the reader straight in the eyes and addressing the reader in his speech balloon; but the extradiegetic space can never be directly represented in the comic—except when a real mirror would be pasted on the page.

The space of the page is essential in comics because it is the space where various panels are organized in a layout and related to each other: from a strict grid pattern (as in *Peanuts*) to a very loose organization (as in many *shojo* manga). Usually the order of the panels respects the normal reading direction in a culture (from left to right in the U.S.A. and Europe, from right to left in Japan).

The (white) extradiegetic space between the panels can be used in various ways: in the past artists used a regular and constant distance between the panels, but an artist can vary these distances to various effects. For instance Chester Brown in *I Never Liked You* (1994) does not only use black for this extradiegetic space, but he also plays with the distances between the panels: by placing sometimes only one (relatively small) panel on a black page, he accentuates that panel. Also various Japanese authors, especially in *shojo* manga, are using extradiegetic space very creatively.

Moreover, the size (small versus big) and the form (upright, oblong, square) of the page's space can be of importance. In *Le Triangle Rouge*, the oblong format is well suited for the drawings of the horizontally extended building inspired by Frank Lloyd Wright.[5] Another example is Fantagraphics reformatting of the tenth *Love & Rockets* collection in the square format (and a six-panel grid) to imitate the look of a record cover (originally it was published in the traditional format of a nine-panel grid).

Space in comics can thus exist in many various shapes (types of representation) and levels (diegetic vs extradiegetic). Each reader is confronted with a particular extradiegetic space of the comic book itself, with a particular organization of the space on each page, and with a particular representation of the fragmented diegetic space in a series of panels. During his reading process the reader tries to cope with these various aspects of space and to make meaning of it all.

NOTES

1. This is a revised and expanded version of the article published in *Image and Narrative* 16 (February 2007), which was already based on parts of my Ph.D. dissertation, *Willy Vandersteen's* Suske en Wiske *in the dailies (1945–1971): A Theoretical Framework for the Formal Analysis of Comics* (originally written in Dutch in 2003), and on some earlier publications in Dutch and French such as *Het hors champ in de strip* (Lefèvre, 1989), *Pour une lecture moderne de la bande dessinée* (Baetens and Lefèvre, 1993), *Architecture dans le neuvième art* (Lefèvre, 1996).

2. Leaving elements outside the frame is regularly used in cliffhangers.

3. An author can deviate from the normal proportions between the figures or objects: in the Middle Ages the most important figures like Christ or Maria were painted a lot bigger than the other figures. Also in comics disproportions are often used: for instance to make a character more visible in a car his body and head can be enlarged in comparison to the car.

4. Nevertheless the reader is not just a passive agent: he or she looks at images with prior knowledge and activates the images. The individual context is thus also of considerable importance.

5. Andreas (Lacroix and Sohet: 43) explains that the idea of the oblong format came from an oblong book with drawings of Frank Lloyd Wright.

WORKS CITED

Arnheim, Rudolf, *Art and Visual Perception: A Psychology of the Creative Eye* (Berkeley: University of California Press, 1971 [1954]).

Baetens, Jan, and Pascal Lefèvre, *Pour une Lecture Moderne de la Bande Dessinée* (Bruxelles: Centre Belge de la Bande Dessinée, 1993).

Berthomé, Jean-Pierre, "Décors, décors" in *CinemAction: cinema et bande dessinée* (Paris: Corlet-Télérama, 1990), 41–47.

Bordwell, David, *Narration in the Fiction Film* (London: Methuen, 1986).

Lacroix, Yves, and Philippe Sohet, eds., *Andreas. Une Monographie* (St. Egrève: Mosquito, 1997).

Lefèvre, Pascal, "Het hors champ in de strip," *Andere sinema*, no. 6, 1988: 41–42.

———, *Architecture in de negende kunst/Architecture dans le neuvième art* (Arnhem: NBM-Amstelland Bouw BV, 1996).

———, *Willy Vandersteen's* Suske en Wiske *in de krant (1945–1971): Een theoretisch kader voor een vormelijke analyse van strips* (Leuven: Doctoraat Sociale Wetenschappen, Katholieke Universiteit Leuven, 2003).

Palmer, Stephen E., *Vision Science: Photons to Phenomenology* (Cambridge: MIT Press, 1999).

Peters, Jan-Marie, *Pictorial Signs and the Language of Film* (Amsterdam: Rodopi, 1981).

Rawson, Philip, *Drawing* (Philadelphia: University of Pennsylvania Press, 1987 [1969]).

Solso, Robert L. *Cognition and the Visual Arts* (Cambridge: MIT Press, 1994).

Thiebaut, Michel, *Dans le sillage des sirènes: Autour des Compagnons du Crépuscule de François Bourgeon* (Tournai: Casterman, 1992).

Willats, John, *Art and Representation: New Principles in the Analysis of Pictures* (Princeton: Princeton University Press, 1997).

The Acoustics of Manga

ROBERT S. PETERSEN

Sound in comics is not a stylistic trait or a feature of a particular genre of comics, but is endemic to all comics due to the multimodal way words and pictures are formed and combined. Some comics exploit the dimensions of sound more effectively than others, and none is more effective than the Japanese manga. The reasons for the exuberant nature of sounds in Japanese manga are in part due to the features of the Japanese language and script that make it ideally suited to explore the aesthetic possibilities of sound in comics. Another important factor is the cultural history of storytelling in Japan, which has long explored the rich possibilities of sound and visual spectacle. But perhaps the most important is the artistic exploration of the manga artists (*mangaka*) themselves; who, through intense competition, have labored to create some of the most extravagantly popular comics in the world; comics that have found the means to make full creative use of the intrinsic dynamics of sound in comics. By examining the use of sound in Japanese comics, I will identify some of the range of possibilities that sounds can have in comics and later discuss why sounds in manga defy easy translation.

Being able to read is a prerequisite to both comics and books, but there is an important shift in the nature of the medium of comics that draws the reader into the sound of the action. Comics utilize word/pictures and pictured/words, where the way something is written visually informs sound qualities in narrative action. Such exaggerated onomatopoeic words commonly appear in comics as hybrid word/pictures, which convey the essence of lived sensations by using the sound-like experience to fuse the sign/icon into a single sensation. Visual clues, such as scale of words indicating volume and the way the visual character of the speech balloons conveys emotion, have been shown to be comprehensible to even a preliterate audience (Yannicopoulou, 2004). This is not to say that the multimodal strategy is somehow a faster or more efficient way to communicate; such mixed communicative modes are often redundant or conflicting streams of information that complicate and slow down comprehension, work against meaning. Indeed the purpose of sound in comics is to represent sensations at the speed they would be actuated in the narrative.

Comics are read as if aloud; where the speech of the characters and the noise of the action is an essential component of the aesthetic experience; more so than most literature and perhaps even more so than the written dialogue of a play, where the indications of

Reprinted by permission from the *International Journal of Comic Art*, vol. 9, no. 1 (Spring 2007), 578–90.

sound remain, like other written works, in the abstract realm of words and line breaks. For this reason, comics resist speed reading because the information is not uniform and regularly spaced across the page. The eye must move back and forth, up and down to sort through the conflicting streams of information to assemble the visual verbal code. The combination of visual and written clues accentuates the sound experience by requiring the reader to slow down to get the full effect. Thus, comics are ideally read at the speed of sound, whereas books are read at the speed of sight.

Walter Ong has written extensively on the nature of oral traditions, people, and cultures that rely predominantly on oral transmission of knowledge, and has commented on the importance of sound, and especially rhythm, for defining and organizing narrative experiences. Sound, according to Ong (1989), allows the audience to become immersed in the narrative experience to a greater degree. The audience is no longer merely witness to the narrative, but it becomes an extension of themselves. The reason for sound, rhythm, and meaning to mimic one another is due to the need for communicative channels to reinforce one another so that the information will be remembered and effectively transmitted from one generation to the next. When there is no self-obviating text that is independent of the speaker, the story must be transmitted through being embodied, and to ensure we pay attention to these lessons, the human brain has developed so that it derives pleasure from patterns of sound. Mnemonic mechanisms help us to learn to read, and thereafter, the mechanism for oral learning does not go away; it is hard wired into our genes, and it is that mechanism that provides the basis for the sensual dynamics of narrative sound.

Comics exploit this sound dynamic though subvocalization, which is a natural habit of readers to imagine the sound through the inaudible speech movements of the lips and throat. It is a useful tool readers use for reinforcing meaning in written works. Subvocalization eventually diminishes in its intensity as readers become more proficient in reading at speeds above 300 words per minute, but it never entirely goes away. In comics the reader is encouraged to sound out the narrative as they read; the words are often not complete words but an assortment of consonants and vowels that approximate sound. The lack of possibility in interpreting the sound onomatopoeic word as an actual word with specific meaning makes the sound of the word the only meaning the word has to convey in the comic. In essence, the reader is performing the comic for themselves, just as a ventriloquist might bring a voice to a puppet while acting as witness to the character he/she manipulates, Steven Conner's cultural history of ventriloquism, *Dumbstruck*, speaks eloquently to the way the art of ventriloquism exploits the ambiguous nature of sound, which emanates from us as it also resonates within us. By inviting the reader to experience the sound of an action or place is to encourage embodiment of the space, and give an animating force to the actions. Conner argues that sound is not the "sign of this animation, it is the very means by which animation is accomplished" (2000: 10). The oral learning mechanism triggers in us the impulse to make the sound we see. Readers desire that sensual internal sound of the comic, and give it an undeniable life force, because they share their own vocal presence to make the comic resonate.

My approach to sound in comics in general, and manga in particular, is based on this notion that the auto-oral sound of the reader creates a dynamic presence. This is an aesthetic presence similar to what Hans Gumbrecht (2004) has described as temporal, ephemeral, often violent actualization, a desirable experience, which lies outside the everyday and the mundane. Such sensations are often attractive and desirable just because they are momentary and considered outside everyday, more mundane sensory experiences. The audience allows these temporal moments to happen, because a precondition of the aesthetic experience is that it is bounded and outside ordinary time and circumstances. My term *narrative erotics* is an application of Gumbrecht's notion of presence within a narrative structure. Narrative erotics are those moments when the narrative becomes embodied through a sensual presence. Most units of narrative are concerned with meaning that establishes temporal or causal relationships between events. Narrative erotics do not move the plot forward more than allow the action to be realized or actuated. Susan Sontag wrote about the need to look beyond meaning to the erotics of art, how art is embodied with emotional force and presence that cannot be entirely reduced to meaning. Narrative erotics create an animated interior for the story to live within, allowing it to become more evocative and memorable. This presence is not in opposition to meaning; rather it creates a space for meaning to accrue. The subject here is not the meaning of the sounds in the narrative, but how the presence of the sound creates a potentiality or potency within the narrative. A presence that defies interpretation and when contemplated often has absurd signification; but, taken in context, sounds in comics have a startling power and hold remarkable grace.

Even a casual comparison between United States comics and Japanese manga clearly shows that sound in manga is far more prevalent and with a greater range and variety than is found in U.S. comics. In U.S. comics, some genres, such as adventure comics like Harold Foster's *Tarzan* and *Prince Valiant*, and some serious graphic novels, Spiegelman's *Maus* and Moore's *Watchmen*, do not use onomatopoeic sound at all. In contrast, all genres of Japanese manga employ the use of onomatopoeic sound to some degree, and the sheer range of sounds is far greater than any other comic tradition in the world. Japanese manga use certain features in Japanese language that give the sounds in manga exceptional dynamic expression. Mack Horton argues that oral features in Japanese are more prominent because writing came relatively late in its cultural development (fifth to sixth century CE) and written language did not wholly supplant story recitation; rather, the auditory qualities of the language were maintained, as early fiction, such as Lady Murasaki's *Tale of Genji*, were commonly read aloud.

The logographic Chinese model used to develop writing in Japan was cumbersome and awkward to the way Japanese language was traditionally spoken, such that several alternate syllabaries developed to accommodate the differences, which represent certain vowel and consonant/vowel sound combinations. Unlike Chinese characters, which largely represent ideas, the separate sets of syllabary characters represent sounds that can be strung together or stand alone. Repetition of sounds, like a dying echo, can be achieved through the use of the tsu syllabary sound, which when added into a word or sound drops its own sound and mimics the preceding sound. Also, lines are commonly used at the end of a string of syllabary characters to extend the final vowel sound of the character. Some English-style punctuation, such as exclamation points and question marks, are fairly common but none matches the frequency of the ubiquitous ellipses marks (typically rendered as a vertical row of dots), which further extends the realm of sound to such barely audible expressions such as gasps of awe.

Master of the comic medium, Osamu Tezuka, fully exploited the dimensions of sound as seen in a page from *Phoenix* (*Hinotori*) Volume 8, where the sound of wind (*cho cho cho*) has been added to a realistic rendering of mountains in order to establish the scene and give a feeling for the passage of time. Such sound might appear redundant because seeing the mountains one might expect to hear some wind. But the strategy to include sounds is not intended to produce redundancy, rather to slow the reader down and create greater visual depth and texture to the scene. The character of the lines used to describe the sound appear more like brush strokes, which is distinctly different from the character of lines used to render the scene. This allows the expression to stand outside the rendered world. It is also interesting to note the direction of the syllabary characters is arranged, from top left angled toward down right, which is opposite from the way Japanese would naturally be read from upper right to lower left. These differences in character of line and reading direction disrupt the reader's ability to take the whole scene in all at once and allow time for subvocalizing the sound.

Sounds appear across the densely drawn pages of manga punctuating the flow of the page and creating visual patterns that unify and add complexity to the composition. Tauyou Matsumoto's surreal science fiction adventure, *Number 5*, uses sounds to break up the space on the page and reinforce the momentum of actions across panels, even where the actions cannot be seen. The marching of feet carries across the entire page even though the actual action of marching is shown only once. Similarly, Matsumoto has the sound of a barking dwarf hippo persistently scattered across the page, though the creature appears only once. Aware of the commonly abused convention of ellipses in manga, Tauyou Matsumoto gives ellipses to the non-sequitur image of a pigeon in a tree. Even absurd sounds in nonsensical images function to produce the idea of a sound that slows the reader down.

The shape and placement of sound in manga is not incidental to the narrative sweep of the manga, but in an important way reflects the larger dramatic movement of the story. Take for example Samura Hiroki's *Heroes of the Western World: "Emerald,"* which when shrunk down so the whole story can be seen at once, the soundscape reveals some fascinating parallels between the dramatic development and the visual placement of sound. By tinting the location and size of the sound on each of the pages, it is possible to record how sounds develop over the course of a manga and see the whole manga like a musical composition where the appearance of sounds (mostly gunshots) grow in size and frequency as the action of the plot develops. The loudest and most dramatic sounds are reserved for the most climactic scene, but they also appear growing in frequency and size as the story develops. The sounds do not create the dramatic action; rather they provide time for the intensity of the action to develop. The presence of sound gives force and dimension to the dramatic action.

The reason sounds in manga are so rich and varied is also in part due to the nature of the Japanese language that has a much wider range of onomatopoeic expressions than most languages. Japanese has a whole host of words for things that typically make noise, but even events, actions, and feelings that do not naturally produce sounds are given onomatopoeic expression. *Noro noro* for moving quietly and *peko peko* for bowing humbly are two such sounds, but there are sounds which are used to describe some real sound such as a heart beat, *doki doki waku waku*, but that can be cropped short to simply *doki*, to create the impression that someone's heart has skipped a beat in surprise. The Japanese recognize two different kinds of onomatopoeic *giseigo* or *giongo*, which are words that mimic real sounds and *gitaigo* which are words that mimic psychological states and non-auditory sounds. While onomatopoeic words abound in every language, non-auditory sounds (phenomimes and psychomimes) are much rarer. Most onomatopoeia sound effects in Japanese spoken language function as adverbs modifying actions. They enter daily discourse with much greater frequency than other languages, and they have played an important role in storytelling traditions in Japan.

Sound in storytelling has transmuted into sound in manga through the history of Japanese performing arts, which has found ways to exploit aural dynamics of the language for dramatic effect. Popular storytelling with pictures, also called picture recitation, has a long tradition in Japan that dates back to the tenth century CE where it was instrumental in propagating the legends surrounding Shōtoku Taishi, the founder of Japanese Buddhism. Buddhist nuns and monks gave sermons (*etoki*) while holding up a painting of a Buddhist *mandala* that depicted Buddhist vices and virtues along with their corresponding punishments and rewards. The *Kumano Kanjin Jikkai* mandala was one such painting that was accompanied by rhythmic chanting designed to appeal to popular tastes.

Most famous of the storytellers, Takemoto Gidayu (d. 1714), was so influential in defining the craft of storytelling that his name, Gidayii, is synonymous for storytelling itself. Numerous amateur groups practice this art for each other, but the tradition is best known for its part in the traditional puppet theatre of Japan, *bunraku*. The chanter Takemoto Gidayu was the first to add puppets to his storytelling tradition, and it was he who first enlisted the aid of Japan's premiere playwright of the Edo period, Chikamatsu Monzaemon (1653–1724) to write plays for the puppet theatre. Chikamatsu excelled in the use of sounds and challenged the chanters with plays that included opportunities for ever more outrageous displays of virtuoso chanting. Take for example his play *Love Suicides at Amjima* where the opening narration begins with a long series of nonsensical sounds. Scholars have pondered the possible meaning of this text, but it seems that Chikamatsu had no other intent than to create a soundscape that imitated the hustle and bustle of the Edo city. At the same time the storytelling traditions were developing in bunraku, the popular woodblock prints, *ukiyo-e*, also began to include a rich variety of sounds in the pictures. This can be found especially in the shunga art prints of lovers where it is possible to see onomatopoeic words for heavy breathing (*süsü*), kissing (*chüchä*), along with copulating noises (*pichapicha*) (Klompmakers, 2001: 17).

The genesis of manga derives directly from the storytelling tradition through the performance of the *kami-shibai*, who were itinerant storytellers who traveled through city parks and the countryside giving picture recitation performances off the back of a bicycle. The kami-shibai performers had sets of illustrated stories set inside a frame, and they would reveal one picture after another as they told their story. Kami-shibai performers were most numerous just following World War II and prior to the arrival of television in 1953, when it was estimated as many as 10,000 performers did more than five million performances a year (Kinsella, 2000: 24). Kami-shibai achieved its remarkable popularity by filling a void left during the war when paper was scarce and almost half of all print

Yutaka Asô, *Nonki na Tôsan*, 1923.

publications ceased to exist. Following World War II, as manga became popular, many of the publishers and artists who made the drawings on cards for the kami-shibai moved into the new manga industry. Hence, manga was derived from the experience of story-telling tradition of kami-shibai.

The influence of the storytelling tradition can be seen in early Japanese manga, which, though they were heavily influenced by American newspaper comics, were very innovative about the way they represented sound. "Easygoing Daddy" (*Nonki na Tōsan*) from 1923 by Yutaka Asō, often characterized as an imitation of George McManus's *Bringing Up Father*, attempted some innovative use of sound. The father figure, uncle Nonto, took on a variety of odd jobs that made him gently suffer the indignities of the modern middle-class world. At one of Uncle Nonto's jobs as a radio announcer, a woman sings into the microphone and her song appears as pictures within a jagged speech bubble. The first picture is of squeaking wheels of a rail car and another is of a demon hurling thunderbolts. Nonto tries to escape the noise, but is stopped by the station owner for leaving the show mid-broadcast. The picture within a speech bubble is used to graphically characterize the nature of her song and give it visual expression. The use of pictures within speech bubbles is an adaptation of a convention in Chinese and Japanese popular prints which depicted dreaming by placing the dream vision within a balloon shaped frame with a tail that pointed to the dreaming figure. Sound as pictures brings the expressive nature of the lines in comics into focus and provides an example how pictures alone can communicate sounds.

The influential Rakuten Kitazawa was well known for his carefully rendered British-style illustrations, but later in his career, he used a looser more expressive style painted with a brush. This can be seen in his "Tonda Haneko" from 1928, which vibrantly captures the young girl, Haneko, dancing the charleston to the shock and honor of her traditional minded elders. The noise of the dance is represented in twenty-two katagana characters with thirteen different sounds. The range and complexity of the dance sounds creates the needed energetic excess that drives the humor and enlivens the action. Kitazawa's looser

Rakuten Kitazawa, *Tonda Haneko*, 1928.

style of drawing carries over into the character of the calligraphy. Haneko is made of the same kinds of energetic lines that make up the sound of her dance.

A humorous scene from Suihô Tagawa's "Black Stray" (*Norakuro*) beautifully dramatizes the use of sound in the way he contrasts the satisfying *ei-i* of the sword in Hiragana, but then uses Katagana to give a startling *pochin* to the sound of the sword breaking. The code switching between Hiragana and Katagana remains to this day an important dynamic in manga sounds. Hiragana is most often employed to suggest internal noises that are sensual and of a personal nature, such as chewing, breathing, and the sound of heart beats, whereas katagana is used to suggest the harsher external world of sounds that bombard us. The katagana is also written differently in larger block letters. This follows one of the most widely used multimodal codes, whereby the larger the type the louder the sound.

Type differentiation in Japanese manga has greatly expanded, exploiting the inherent differences in the two syllabaries. Katagana is more angular than Hiragana and this has been further exaggerated over the years, such that the Katagana characters become abstract shapes that break the composition and create visual complexity without disrupting the overall visual effect of the action. Digital production has allowed for ever more complex layering of words and pictures. But the general aesthetic distinctions between sounds and the images they are related to is that they constitute a separate set of lines that are often in contrast to the quality and character of the lines that make up the rest of the drawing.

As manga began to be translated, it was evident that one of the complex issues in the translation was the translation of sound effects. The challenges of translation underscore the differences in culture and language between U.S. and Japanese comics. The first major translation of a Japanese manga was Katsuhiro Otomo's *Akira*, which was translated and colorized by Marvel comics in 1988 and later in the original black and white by Dark Horse in 2004. In the Dark Horse translation, the sound of the pipe striking the motorbike *doya-a* is translated into "glang." The translation follows the standard U.S. comic idiom of large, overlapping, and interconnected sans serif letters that cut across the action. The chief difference in the translation is the way the Japanese sound text appears far back in the picture, radiating against the speedlines and the English text does quite the opposite by resting in the foreground between the two front figures. Otomo's use of sound is more economical in its use of lines and while it is clearly present, it has integrated with the original drawing more effectively by emphasizing the action of the pipe.

One of the main problems in sound representation in U.S. comics is that all of the sounds seem to have equal weight and emphasis, making them appear equally loud. In the original *Akira*, by contrast, the katagana sound characters alternately complement and contrast the forms in the composition to create different degrees of sound presence which gives the impression of louder or quieter sounds. Katagana speaks for itself visually. More recently, Hayao Miyazaki's *Nausicaä from the Valley of the Wind* has been translated and rather than ignore the sounds entirely, volume one includes a glossary of 481 sounds listed by page and frame. The manga is only 127 pages long so each page has on average 3.7 sounds per page! While leaving the sounds untranslated retains much more of the visual integrity of the original, it is our loss that there is no effort to create such a richly textured soundscape in U.S. comics. Even those comics that attempt to imitate the manga style, called "Amerimanga" or more commonly now "OEL Manga" (Original English Language Manga) do not attempt to imitate the manga soundscape with the same degree of complexity or frequency. Like most manga translations, OEL manga have not attempted to create sounds that describe the action rather than just tell of the action.

When comparing languages and cultures, it is important not to fall into the trap of the Whorf Hypothesis; saying that, because the Japanese language has certain characteristics by default, Japanese manga has them as well. The relation between language and culture is more complex and there seems to be a great deal of the way comics communicate ideas visually that transcends culture and even reading ability (Yannicopoulou, 2004). However, it is evident that the character of Japanese language has helped mangaka create new and exciting uses for sound in their manga. The effective use of sound in manga produces a drama and vitality to the work where the reader not only subvocalizes the sounds, but also becomes more attune to silences. Even though the English language does not have the same onomatopoeic features, it would be well worth the effort of translators and English comic artists not to shy away from exploring the auto-oral presence of visual sound in comics.

WORKS CITED

Connor, Steven, *Dumbstruck: A Cultural History of Ventriloquism* (New York: Oxford University Press, 2000).

Gumbrecht, Hans Ulrich, *Production of Presence: What Meaning Cannot Convey* (Stanford: Stanford University Press, 2004).

Kinsella, Sharon, *Adult Manga: Culture and Power in Contemporary Japanese Society* (Honolulu: University of Hawai'i Press, 2000).

Klompmakers, Inge, Harunobu Suzuki, and Koryusai Isoda, *Japanese Erotic Prints: Shunga by Harunobu & Kory Usai* (Leiden: Hotei, 2001).

Matsumoto, Taiyou, *Number 5*. Vol. 2.4 (Tokyo: Big Comic Ikki, 2002).

Miyazaki, Hayao, *Nausicaä of the Valley of the Wind*, Vol. 1.7 (San Francisco: VIZ Media, 2004).

Ong, Walter J. *Orality and Literacy: The Technologizing of the Word* (New York: Routledge, 1989).

Samura, Hiroki, *Heroes of the Western World: "Emerald."* Online at www.dragonvoice.org.

Schodt, Frederik L., *Manga! Manga!: The World of Japanese Comics* (Tokyo: Kodansha International, 1983).

Suiho, Tagawa, *Norakuro*, Vol. 3, reprinted 1975.

Tezuka, Osamu *Hi No Tori*. Vol. 8: Kadokawa Shoten, 1992.

Yannicopoulou, Angela, "Visual Aspects of Written Texts: Preschooler's View of Comics," *Educational Studies in Language and Literature* 4 (2004): 169–81.

CULTURE, NARRATIVE, IDENTITY

Comics were born in the age of mass culture. Without modern printing technology and the distribution networks that allow for mass dissemination, comics as we know them would not exist. As an offshoot of mass culture, comics are a rich source for social analysis. Using comics for social analysis can take the form of looking at how comics portray issues of identity (including issues of race, nationality, generational location, and gender). Equally fruitful is to examine not just the content of comics but also how readers interpreted the comics they read. As we saw in the second section, elements of a reader-response approach are implicit in certain types of formalist analysis. But formalism focuses on how the individual deals with particular comics. A more wide-ranging way of addressing the question of reader response is to situate the production of comics within a social network that includes satisfying multiple audiences. The essays in this section are united by the fact that they look at comics as a social phenomenon to illuminate issues of culture, narrative, and identity.

Roger Sabin examines the social dimension of comics through the prism of Ally Sloper, an endearing fictional tramp that flourished in the British popular press of the late nineteenth and early twentieth centuries. Sloper was one of those characters who took on a life of his own outside his original habitat on the printed page. Endlessly reproduced on advertisements and on the music hall stage, he personified an unlikely set of national attitudes: fecklessness, individuality, and patriotism all combined. Sloper's iconic status and rapport with his vast audience, Sabin suggests, was created by a canny use of "synergistic marketing techniques involving a range of advertising campaigns and reader-response devices such as competitions." Sloper's rise to celebrity status took place "as part of the same drive that led to the establishment of mass-market leisure industries in the last decades of the nineteenth century." In examining the marketing of Sloper in detail, Sabin establishes that early British comics were an integral part of the social matrix of an emerging mass culture.

The issue of reader-response to comics produced by mass culture is also central to Martin Barker's essay "*Jackie* and the Problem of Romance," dealing with British love comics. Barker strenuously argues with the view propounded by earlier scholars who claimed that these comics taught girl readers to passively adhere to traditional gender roles. For Barker, this view of love comics is premised on an implicitly elitist belief that mass culture is inherently simple-minded and manipulative, a viewpoint that is supported by a crude a priori analysis of the comics themselves which ignores narrative complexity and the existence of "tensions and clashes" within particular stories. The burden of Barker's rebuttal is to look at the love stories in *Jackie* with a fresh eye attuned to conflicting and shifting narrative strategies. The goal of this rereading is not just to rehabilitate the comics themselves, but also to suggest that the audience for these comics had a complex, interactive, and dialectic relationship with what they read. As readerly expectations changed, so did the comics. Readers were not simply passive but were agents in the making of mass culture.

Anne Rubenstein poses similar questions for Mexican *historietas*, using them as a window into the longstanding Mexican cultural debate over tradition and modernity. Rubenstein's work is notable for the range of sources she brings to bear in situating the *historietas*, demonstrating the seemingly lowly comics were organically tied to much larger debates in Mexican society. As with Barker, Rubenstein is careful not to oversimplify the stories she reads and wants to call attention to the internal tug-of-war within narratives. Whereas Barker shows that seemingly conservative romance stories also included themes of female empowerment, Rubenstein demonstrates that soap opera comics that were widely considered modernist drew on a storehouse of traditionalist themes. As Rubenstein notes, "even as comic books were elaborating on this discourse [of modernity and urbanity], the stories they told often agreed with and added to the discourse of conservatism. And when members of the audience got the chance to describe themselves, they chose the words, veiled assumptions, and values of 'tradition.'" Taken together, Barker and Rubenstein can both be seen as arguing for narrative readings that emphasize the existence of conflicting discourses in seemingly simple comics and for a greater attention to the interaction between the producers of mass culture and their audience.

The very popularity of comics as a mass medium and the existence of readerly expectations can be a problem for artists who are trying to create work that is more personal and less bound by genre convention. Bart Beaty examines the dilemma of French cartoonists of the last thirty years, who have had to carve out a space for autobiographical work against the background of a genre-dominated publishing industry. Looking at the emergence of autobiographical comics as a genre among aesthetically ambitious cartoonists, Beaty places this development in the context of a market where fantasy-based comics enjoyed overwhelming popularity and cartoonists lacked cultural capital vis-à-vis high art. Against this social context, Beaty suggests that one part of the appeal of the autobiographical genre is that it "offers the most explicit promise of legitimizing cartoonists as authors."

Adam Kern and Fusami Osi focus on Japanese comics from two very different periods. Kern gives the historical background to the *kibyōshi*, satirical prints that flourished during the Edo period (1603–1868). While the *kibyōshi* provide a vivid window into the politics and culture of pre-modern Japan, they have been largely ignored by scholars until recently when they have been reclaimed as ancestors of manga. Kern challenges this genealogy by stressing the differences between *kibyōshi* and manga, seeking to situate both in their particular social and historical contexts. But he does conclude that they have one important similarity; both emerged in periods of social crisis. As Kern concludes, "the visual-verbal imagination in Japan achieves its greatest inspiration during moments of intense technological, economic, and social upheaval that challenge fundamental notions of visuality."

Shoujo manga (comics aimed at a female audience) provides fascinating material for examining the representation of gender in Japanese comics. In her essay, Fusami Osi looks at how *shoujo* in the 1980s dealt with the emergence of the AIDS. A popular genre of *shoujo* often presents love stories involving gay men. In confronting the AIDS crisis, ambivalent attitudes towards homosexuality came to the fore, as some stories replicated the stereotype of AIDS as a "gay disease" while other stories used gay characters to parody and challenge conventions of heterosexual courtship.

In keeping with the other contributions to the section, Osi avoids a one-dimensional reading in favor of an approach that seeks to tease out narrative complexity. The existence of genre conventions does not preclude multiple and conflicting meanings, particularly when reader-response itself adds another layer of complexity. "*Shoujo* manga as a category acts like an item of clothing which anyone can wear, but the way of wearing it produces in each case an original individuality and sometimes works as subversion, a process which never lets the person look the same as before," Osi argues. The same could be said of many other comics genres, especially when they are viewed as part of a social matrix.

Ally Sloper: The First Comics Superstar?

ROGER SABIN

The extraordinary Ally Sloper appeared in British "funny papers" and comics between 1867 and 1916 and periodically thereafter.[1] Today, few people have heard of him outside of comics scholarship, but a century ago it is no exaggeration to say that his visibility in U.K. popular culture would have been comparable to that of any blockbuster Hollywood creation. He was a Victorian hero—or anti-hero—and entered the public consciousness to the point where he set the template for a new kind of comedy. There has never been a British fictional character like him since.

My intention is not to emphasize the quality of the Sloper publications' artwork or writing, or indeed their possible interpretations. Instead, I want to explore the less well-known narrative of how the character was marketed. For it was through a combination of what we would now call synergistic marketing techniques involving a range of advertising campaigns and reader-response devices such as competitions that the profile of the character was consolidated to become an everyday icon. So much so that he was jokingly considered "real" by a proportion of the readership and that he developed a life outside the comics. His fame was capitalized upon by music hall and later by the movie industry, while at the same time he became the star of less "authorized" entertainments such as street theatre and village parades. The "bootleg" Slopers of such events, along with unofficial merchandising, were then commented upon, and indeed sometimes (re)capitalized upon, by the Sloper papers and comics themselves.

Thus, I want to suggest that a complicated circuit of mutually promoting manifestations of Sloper was created, and further that this was the first time in history that such a circuit could have come into existence. This is because we can think of Sloper's rise as part of the same drive that led to the establishment of the mass-market leisure industries in the last decades of the nineteenth century—music hall, cigarette smoking, organized sports (especially football), large circulation newspapers and "penny publications" ("dreadfuls" and their heirs), and to an extent, seaside holiday culture. Sloper—or his publications—commented upon all of these, and in some cases was intimately related to them, as we shall see. For these new industries ("new" in the sense of being "mass") to flourish there needed to be certain preconditions, and it was only in the late Victorian and Edwardian eras that such preconditions could come together: namely, a mass

Reprinted by permission from *Image and Narrative* 7 (October 2003; www.imageandnarrative.be).

working-class audience with money and time to spare, a rising level of literacy, urban growth and concentration, an efficient transport system (to reach those urban centers), and the inclination to use advertising and new technologies (especially with regard to printing). Whether Ally Sloper was the first comics character per se to be exploited in terms of these conditions is a subsidiary theme of the paper.

For the uninitiated: who was Sloper? He was essentially a conman and a drunkard—the illustration shows him holding on to a lamppost for stability—and was often drawn with a bottle sticking out of his back pocket. As his character evolved, he would become involved in all kinds of schemes and would be joined by supporting characters, among them his wife and children and his "good friend" Ikey Mo (sometimes "Iky Mo"), a Jewish stereotype. His name, "Ally Sloper," is a pun on sloping off up the alleyway to avoid the rent collector. His environment was essentially London, but as we shall see, he went on excursions to other parts of the U.K. and also abroad—the purpose of which was primarily to make fun of foreigners.

In terms of starting to think about how the character was promoted, it is useful to turn to the work of British historian Martin Barker, who while investigating comics of a more recent vintage built on aspects of literary theory to argue for the idea of a "contract." Barker states: "A 'contract' involves an agreement that a text will talk to us in ways we recognize. It will enter into a dialogue with us. And that dialogue, with its dependable elements and form, will relate to some aspect of our lives in our society" (Barker 1989: 261). In other words, the media are only capable of exerting power over audiences to the extent that there is a contract between texts and audiences, like a silent conversation, which relates to some specific aspect(s) of the audiences' social lives. Ideology is thus dialogical (an idea that is close to the work of some European scholars, notably Jan Baetens and his studies of Philippe Marion; for example, see Baetens 2001). In terms of Sloper, how the nature of this contract was first shaped by commercial factors and then by the barreling momentum of the creation itself is most conveniently explored in chronological fashion.

Sloper's origins were in the pages of *Judy*, in 1867, though he had appeared previously elsewhere in prototype form.[2] *Judy* was a less politically orientated companion to the more famous *Punch*, and by the 1890s advertising had become a major form of revenue, to the point where it swamps everything else on the cover. Sloper was created by Charles Ross, formerly a writer of penny dreadfuls, though his wife Marie Duval soon took over cartooning duties and was certainly important in developing the character. Sloper was possibly influenced by Dickens's Mr. Micawber and maybe certain characters in *Punch* (e.g. the cockney "Arry"), but soon developed his own conniving charm and became the most popular feature of the publication.

The Sloper stories were then filleted out from *Judy* to be published discretely in collected books, a process that began in 1873 with *Ally Sloper: A Moral Lesson*. These smaller format books were responsible for consolidating Sloper's reputation as a star in his own right, and it is fair to date his cult status to around this period. The *Judy* spin-offs, none of which were as illustration/strip orientated as *A Moral Lesson*, numbered seven in all (see Gifford 1984: 39f).

One book from 1878 illustrates the possibilities for advertising. *Ally Sloper's Guide to the Paris Exhibition*, in part a parody of the tourist guides then popular, was the fourth of the *Judy* line. The cover depicts Sloper being kicked out of the Exhibition by a gendarme for bad behavior.

Inside we have a story, told in text with illustrations, in which Sloper enters a restaurant because he thinks he can get a very cheap meal. The cost is thirty-two sous, but because the bread is free, Sloper goes to town and stuffs himself. The waiter brings loaf after loaf and gets increasingly disgruntled. It's a good joke, and eventually Sloper is ejected from the establishment with his tail between his legs. But if we look closely at the script that accompanies the second drawing, we can see that in the background there is an advert for "Brand and Co's Own Sauce." This is curious because in the first drawing the sign on the window is in French, and, after all, we are supposed to be in Paris.

All becomes clear, however, when we flip to the back of the publication and survey the advertisements. Sure enough, there it is at the top of the page: "Brand and Co's Own Sauce." The text reads: "An excellent relish for all kinds of soups, meats, fish, entrees, etc." You have to wonder: could this be the earliest example of a publication starring a comics character in which "subliminal advertising" plays a role? Indeed, did the device originate in popular publishing?

There is one final twist to the story, because some time between 1870 and 1910 bottles of sauce were manufactured with Sloper's image embossed into them. They are usually colored green, are about ten inches tall, and have an image of Sloper holding a bottle and jumping in the air with the legend "Ally Sloper's Favourite Relish." We can speculate that the sauce was very popular owing to the number of such bottles that are in circulation today in U.K. antique shops and on Ebay.

Whether or not the Sloper bottle does appear in the 1878 book, the point is that the "contract" between Sloper and his readers is being extended into areas of everyday consumerism. Direct endorsement of products by the character in his funny papers/comics from the 1873–1916 period would include offers of goods in which the manufacturer's name was not mentioned, e.g. cigars ("Ally Sloper's Torpedoes") and pills ("Sloper's Pills . . . cure liver complaint, headache and stomach troubles"), as well as adverts for those of named producers, e.g. bicycles, neck-ties, magic lanterns, and melodeons—the latter with an image of Sloper in the advert itself ("My favorite musical instrument").[3] These were products for adults—or at least, mainly teenagers and adults—and show that advertisers believed that potential purchasers would be willing to enter into the spirit of "the game of Sloper." In other words, he was transcending his role as a vehicle for humor and becoming associated with, in particular, the rise of leisure consumerism. Importantly, then, Sloper was developing as a "brand," and as ever the cultural role of brands was to respond to the *zeitgeist*.[4]

By 1884, it was clearly time that Sloper had his own publication, and the historically important *Ally Sloper's Half Holiday* marked the next step in his evolution. The title was a reference to the "half holiday" given to workers on a Saturday afternoon, and signposted the idea that the focus of the comic would be on working class leisure. (This did not necessarily mean that the readership would be solely working class, however, as Bailey has shown; see Bailey 1983: 17 and 27.) Sloper appeared on the cover in almost every issue, and the publication was therefore unusual in that it featured a continuing character (there had been recurring characters before, but never promoted with quite such gusto).[5] Published for most of its existence by the Dalziel Brothers and edited by one Gilbert

Dalziel, *ASHH* was a mix of cartoons, strips, and text stories and had a galvanizing effect on the way funny papers and comics were marketed and guided editorially.

What was particularly interesting about *ASHH* was that it extended the contract between Sloper and the readers still further. This was a deliberate policy, largely masterminded by Gilbert Dalziel (who was simultaneously the editor of *Judy*). In the words of a retrospective of *ASHH*'s history (*ASHH*, December 23, 1922), Gilbert was ". . . a splendid businessman, keen, enthusiastic, brainy . . . and brimful of ideas for 'stunts' for making his papers go . . ." ("Chats at 'The Cheese,'" 10). This business acumen would be increasingly in evidence as time progressed.

Thus, the endorsing of products by Sloper continued in the back pages, along with regular adverts (including for other Dalziel products such as books of prints), but towards the front of the comic a space was created for reader interaction—competitions, readers' letters, and so on. This also included the opportunity for readers to actually "create" their own comic by way of sending in jokes, limericks, puns, and sketches.

A random example from January 2, 1904, included the following:

- Offer of £150 to the "the next of kin of any Man, Woman, Boy or Girl . . . who shall happen to meet with his or her death in a Railway Accident . . . *provided* a copy of the current issue of *Ally Sloper's Half Holiday* be found upon the Deceased . . ." [Evidently this was not meant to be a joke. *ASHH* was seen as "railway literature," i.e., sold from railway kiosks and intended to be read between stops. Crashes were frequent—as the grotesque "11 Claims Already Paid" would indicate.]
- A competition: "A Fifty Guinea Diamond Ring" is offered to the "handsomest actress of them all," voted upon by readers.
- "Circulation Competition": "A prize of five guineas will be given to the reader who induces the greatest number of people to purchase the *Half Holiday* during the week . . ."
- "A shilling pocket knife . . . To every reader who sends us Twelve signed Coupons of this week's issue."
- "A silver watch will be given for the best original joke."
- "A silver watch will be given for the best funny sketch."
- "A silver watch will be given for the best pun."

This looks like an extravagant list. But in the period leading up to the First World War there were numerous other examples of reader rewards, including razors, tobacco jars, and clay pipes. In the early issues of *ASHH* such items were given away for free—readers merely had to send in their address or a set of cutout coupons. But towards the end of the nineteenth century, as competitions became the craze of the moment, so "free gifts" gave way to "prizes." The high point of this phenomenon can be dated to an article in *ASHH* for February 11, 1899, entitled "Our Prizes," which announced that thenceforward, ". . . prizes of some kind will be given away every week regularly . . ."

No doubt rivalry from other funny papers post-1890, especially those published by the Amalgamated Press, lent urgency to the craze. Usually such competitions would be on inane topics (perhaps the most amusing was 1899's "Sloper Potato Competition" in which a one pound prize was given "For the tuber most like Ally"), but occasionally they

Ally Sloper cast iron doorstop, circa 1880.

would be more orientated towards current affairs, such as an example from 1902 which asked when various sieges throughout the world would end, and another from 1904 which invited readers to count the number of British battleships in an illustration—with hindsight, a poignant reference to the arms race that would contribute to the outbreak of war a decade later.

It would be wrong to suggest that such schemes were unique to *ASHH*. Other publications from the period were going in a similar direction (including *Judy*), and the fad for competitions spawned at least one example devoted entirely to them (*Competitions Weekly*). It would also be erroneous to argue that the policy didn't have its occasional problems—as a "Law Report" from the *Times* in 1909 attests: ". . . The action was brought by Miss Gertrude F. J. Jenkins against the proprietors and publishers of *Ally Sloper's Half Holiday* to recover damages for breach of contract . . . [involving] what is known as a Limerick Competition . . ." (Report for June 10, anon., *Times*, June 11).

Also, it didn't take long for others not involved with *ASHH* to come up with the idea of producing "prizes" that didn't have to be competed for. Bootleg merchandising undoubtedly originated in the *Judy* period but reached a peak at around the turn of the century. Products never advertised in *ASHH*, for example, included paperweights, mugs, door stops, walking sticks, bits of treen, vesta cases, tie pins (sold, possibly exclusively, by Gamages store), vending machines, crested china busts, puppets, and a number of games.[6] Indeed, the comic itself sometimes made reference to the "illicit" Sloper industry.

But in general, it is clear that the addition of competitions was a great success, and gave *ASHH* a significant lift. The lists of winners and their addresses were proof that distribution of the comic was penetrating the furthest corners of the Kingdom (thanks to the recent expansion of the railways) and even of the Empire. And the number of competition entrants was huge: the *Times* report above states that 17,621 people had entered the limerick contest—a staggering figure even by today's standards. Moreover, *ASHH* had an advantage over its rivals in the person of Sloper himself. So although in one sense the "game of Sloper" was being extended to "the game of *ASHH*," nevertheless he could be called upon in cartoon form to "present" and display prizes, announce competitions, etc. (For the example of the "fifty guinea diamond ring," given to "the handsomest actress," in the issue mentioned above, Sloper was depicted in several subsequent issues parading the glittering piece of jewelry.) In short, when people competed for prizes, they were also competing for Ally's favors.

But Gilbert Dalziel had other stunts up his sleeve. Perhaps the most imaginative was the creation of a Sloper fan club. "All you have to do is send in twelve coupons from twelve consecutive issues . . . you will receive a splendidly designed diploma . . . You can then use the letters MOSC (Member of Sloper's Club) after your name . . . You will also receive the Sloperian Token. . . ." This is the first example of a club of its kind that I am aware of and is clearly a precursor to the much better known comics clubs for titles such as *Eagle* in the U.K. and Marvel comics in the U.S. Clearly, the sheer longevity of the character meant that it was possible to generate and sustain a devoted fan base on this level, something that no other publication from the period was in a position to consider.

Other gimmicks were less about direct engagement with the readers than about the publication's producers expressing the imagined sentiments of those readers. So, for instance, the "Friend of Sloper" (F.O.S.) Awards of Merit were bestowed upon people that Ally estimated were worthy of the honor. Often these would be popular music hall performers, but occasionally more eminent personalities would be named. When Prime Minister Gladstone was made F.O.S., it did not need to be made explicit that this was in recognition of his reputation as "the friend of the working class": Gladstone in turn made capital out of the award and had the certificate of merit framed and put on his wall in his Scottish home (whether this was a sincere expression of his liking for the comic, or more a political gesture—like Tony Blair shaking the hands of members of Oasis—can only be speculated upon). Similarly, there were "Lifesaving medals," given by Sloper to members of the public who had performed outstanding acts of bravery—a surprisingly sober addition to the comic.

In summing up this main part of the paper, we can say that during the period of *ASHH*, the "contract" that Martin Barker has written about was solidified. The idea of reader participation essentially ensured that the comic became people's "friend" and that they would come back to buy it week after week. They invested in the comic, and it in turn gave the illusion of investing in them. The arrangement had all the appearance of being a "dialogue"—it was the point at which, perhaps, the silent conversation became audible—and was an essential ingredient in making *ASHH*, in its own words, "The Biggest Selling Penny Paper in the World."

This was a lesson well learned by the publishing trade in general. Other funny papers followed suit, as we shall see in a moment, and so too did the nascent women's magazine industry. Historians of the latter have been keen to point out the emphasis on reader-generated content. *My Weekly*, launched by DC Thomson in 1910, was conceived with

THE CORONATION OF THE KING OF COMICS.

The Coronation of King Edward VII. has partially eclipsed an event which would, at any other time, have stirred the earth from Pole to Pole, namely, the Coronation of ALLY I., King of the Comics, which ceremony was successfully performed at Mildew Court on the same day. Special artists being laid on for the occasion, we are enabled to present ALLY THE FIRST in his Coronation robes, together with several implements of the Regalia, etc. : (1) The Sloper Standard, borne by the roof of Mildew Court.——(2) The Crown and Sceptre (signboard), kindly lent by the proprietor of the establishment.—— (3) Alexandry, Master of the Horse, bearing the (Judson's) Gold Spur.——(4) The Spur. ——(5) The Horse (Skunk), in his Collar.——(6) Iky Moses, Esq., Master of the (ward) Robes, in his Hats of Maintenance.——(7) The Coronation Spoon, pinched for the occasion by Iky Moses, Esq.——(8) The Sword of State, borne by Jubilee, the King's Champion. ——Orders of the Garter : (9) Evelina,——(10) Mrs. Sloper.——(11) Tootsie.——(12) Aunt Geeser.

Ally Sloper, the king of comics.

"a personal relationship" with readers in mind, and by the time of *Woman's Own*, the market leader in 1950, the rule that one fifth of the content should be reader generated had become a set formula (see Braithwaite 1995).

But before leaving this notion of the contract, it is important to note that it had political boundaries. At a basic level, these were set by the parameters of capitalistic exchange. In other words, Sloper and his comics had to conform to a certain kind of politics in order not to offend advertisers (and to a lesser extent readers). Thus, although Sloper was "degenerate," in the terms of the period, in the sense that he was a drunkard and a trickster, it is also made clear that he is pro-Royal, anti-the unemployed, and pro-Empire. On one cover he is seen kissing Queen Victoria's hand; on another he's dressed in policeman's garb, fighting off a mob of the unemployed. There are many other examples.

In other words, Sloper is a loyal working-class citizen, a bit rough around the edges, but not likely to revolt. This is an image of working class masculinity that became more and more prevalent in the music hall as the nineteenth century progressed, an area of entertainment that Sloper was intimately involved with, as we shall see, and has been interpreted as an imaginative effort to allay middle class fears of revolution (see Jones 1974). Indeed, according to Bailey, the cartoonists and writers on *ASHH* were themselves middle class. This innate conservatism was certainly out of tune with the rising discontent that led to the workers' riots of 1887 and the connected spread of socialist ideas (it was the British working class, after all, that had provided the model for Marx's and Engels's thinking on capital).[7]

But it served a purpose, and in terms of a modern "Chomskyian" analysis of the press, it is logical to argue that Sloper only became as famous as he did because he stayed within certain limits.[8] The advertisers had to be satisfied that this was the kind of character they could happily be associated with, and therefore the politics of the stories were never likely to stray into controversy. Sloper was both made by a certain kind of ideology and a transmitter of that ideology. This was the underlying nature of the dialogue that Martin Barker has outlined: though how far readers negotiated the text and offered interpretations of their own can only be imagined.

All of this goes some way to explaining Sloper's fame, but perhaps not entirely his place in British culture, his "superstar" status. For the years 1867 to 1916 were notable for the way in which he developed a life of his own. In order to explore this, the role of music hall is unavoidable. For the same forces that allowed for the rise of Sloper—a working class with growing leisure time and more income—were also responsible for the explosive expansion in the number of music halls in the period. The crossover between the two was significant from the start.

According to an article in a 1922 *ASHH*, referring to events of several decades previously, "As the 'only Jones' of *Judy*, Ross was one of the best-known first-nighters of his day . . . theatrical criticism then-a-days compared very favorably with these buttery times when the only honest criterion of a play is the box office . . ." It goes on to say: "Ross himself was manager of the Surrey, Strand, and Princess's theatres, and toured several companies, including an Ally Sloper Comedy Drama, and, with our mutual friend Gus Harris, arranged for a character called 'Ally Sloper' played by Victor Stevens, to be introduced into the D. L. Panto of the 'Forty Thieves' . . ." ("Chats at 'The Cheese,'" anon., *ASHH*, Christmas Cattle Show Day, 1922, 9).

Ross was thus clearly very important in recognizing Sloper's crossover potential from the start. We know that music halls would vet acts in advance, so it seems fair to speculate that a "safe brand" such as Sloper—moreover one with wide recognition among the public courtesy of his comics—would have a significant advantage (see Horrall 2001, especially 1–6). Theories on the increasing political conservatism of the halls would seem to reinforce this (see above). Ross, for his part, positioned himself very cannily: he owned the copyright to Sloper until he sold it to the Dalziels, and as a theatrical (music hall) impresario could make the best use of it.

But as well as these "authorized" performances, Sloper also became the star of street theatre. For example, a variety of ventriloquist dummies and automata have survived from the period, as well as smaller puppets of Sloper plus wife which are believed to have taken over from "Punch and Judy" in sideshows. There are also photographs of village parades in which Sloper appears, courtesy of huge papier-mâché heads that would fit over the heads of the paraders. (Quite possibly these heads were pantomime masks.) Clearly, much of this activity would have been amateur in nature, though it is true that professional performers from the music hall would also perform in the street as a ploy to attract punters to the regular shows. Whether these less official Slopers were any more radical in a political sense than their music hall and funny paper/comics counterparts must remain a mystery.

Thus, by 1896, in the words of one newspaper, Sloper was the most famous fictional character in the country: "He stars in a full fifty per cent of our pantomimes and hops it with the best at sixty per cent of our fancy dress balls." (*Brighton Society*, November 21, 1896.) He was, in other words, an entertainment phenomenon, and as such a character that just about anybody could have a go at mimicking. The "game of Sloper" had become a national obsession.

ASHH under Dalziel was crucial in feeding this obsession. The publication promoted music hall ceaselessly. Sloper was often pictured on the cover either on stage performing or in the audience, and inside would often "interview" top performers of the time. Song sheets hymning his praise were also common—the first being given away as a supplement in 1886—and music and lyrics for other songs increasingly occupied space in the publication itself. The "Friend of Sloper Award of Merit" was given to magicians, singers, ventriloquists, and of course comedians. The paper would also carry listings of music hall shows and occasional reviews, and Tootsie was given a regular column to recount her adventures as a chorus girl at "The Friv" (Frivoli Theatre). She was something of a sex symbol and fashion model, and the column was written by Ross's son. Finally, it is almost certain that routines were "borrowed" from the comic by performers, and vice versa—though establishing which and when is near impossible.

When the fledgling cinema industry started to look for subjects at the turn of the twentieth century, Sloper was a natural choice.[9] The music hall and comic papers gave inspiration to many of the first film comedy shorts, and although unfortunately the Sloper movies do not survive today, there are records of two being released in 1898 and two in 1900 (see Barnes 1983). It is quite possible that these were screened as an "amusement" in a music hall setting, as well as being distributed to cinemas per se. Other skits from *ASHH* may also have been purloined as the basis for film comedies, although—again—it is usually very hard to tell their origins.[10]

Cartoon from cover of *Ally Sloper's Half Holiday,* February 27, 1896. Art by W. G. Baxter.

THE "UNEMPLOYED" AT SLOPER'S.

Movie stars, too, owed a debt to Sloper. Biographers of Charlie Chaplin have made much of the fact that he went on record saying that the comics he read as a child in London were the inspiration for his "Little Tramp" character. W. C. Fields is speculated to have taken his act more directly from Sloper: Fields fancied himself as a cartoonist in the early 1900s and traveled widely in Europe at that time. Although evidence is sketchy, Fields' stage routine from 1915 onwards featured the similarly big-nosed comedian in a top hat, and cut-away coat and collar, and carrying a cane. In the movies, Fields was an automatic choice for the role of Mr. Micawber, who, as we have seen, may have been an inspiration for Sloper.

But although Sloper's legacy lived on, the great man himself could not last. From 1890 onwards, he was faced with heavy competition from other comic papers and from new cartoon stars. Alfred Harmsworth, proprietor of the Amalgamated Press, decided to launch a line of comics that would sell for half the price of *ASHH*. This "halfpenny revolution" encouraged other publishers to join the fray, and ushered in such Sloper-influenced characters as "Weary Willie and Tired Tim" (*Illustrated Chips*), "Nobbler and Jerry" (*Funny Cuts*) and "The Three Lodgers" (*Larks!*)—many of whom would themselves become the stars of stage and screen.

Harmsworth's ruthlessness made him a fortune, on which he established a newspaper empire, becoming Lord Northcliffe in the process. There is evidence that at one point he tried to buy *ASHH*, but by that time he had nothing to fear (his comics were sharper and more modern-looking than *ASHH*, which remained stuck in a stylistic rut, and his cut-price tactics were ever-popular). Dalziel tried to fight back with his own half-penny Sloper spin-off (*Ally Sloper's Ha'porth,* Jan.–Mar. 1899), but it was to no avail. In 1916, *ASHH* ceased publication, and although it was revived fitfully thereafter never regained its former prominence.

But Harmsworth/Northcliffe had learned much from *ASHH*, and not just about what makes a funny comic. He was clearly impressed by Dalziel's marketing stunts and especially the way that links had been made between the publication and music hall, and latterly cinema. Thus, Harmsworth developed a business strategy that exploited comics as merely one part of his empire. Other aspects, in addition to his newspapers, would come to include theatre productions, advertising, and the publication of song sheets. These could then be cross-fertilized to maximize profits. William Randolph Hearst did much the same in the U.S. (starting an animation company to capitalize on the strips in his papers). It is here, I would argue, that we can see the template for the policies of multimedia conglomerates today. From Ally Sloper to AOL-Time-Warner is perhaps not such a distance to travel.

This chapter is called "Ally Sloper: The First Comics Superstar?" But why "first"? In many ways, it was a provocation. But please note that question mark at the end. For whenever you say something is "first" it becomes a problem. For example, the idea that Ally Sloper is the earliest of anything relies on a set of criteria that may not be universally shared. Most obviously, there is an assumption that Sloper was a comics character, and by implication that the *Judy* spin-offs and *Ally Sloper's Half Holiday* were "comics." If a comic is something that is print based, mass-produced, stars a continuing character and contains as a significant part of its content strips and cartoons, then maybe these publications fit the bill.[11] But such defining characteristics are not "givens" by any means.

Recently, for example, other definitions of a comic have taken hold that emphasize an approach rooted in aesthetics. This allows a wide range of sequential image narratives to be included—everything from Egyptian hieroglyphics through medieval emblems to modern web comics.[12] In Europe, some commentators have extended this idea further, seeing the continuing graphic narrative formats of the nineteenth century as seamlessly connected to other kinds of cultural outputs—illustrations, games, magic lantern shows, "Punch and Judy" shows, etc.[13] With the rise of such competing perspectives, it has become ever more difficult for historians to reach agreement.

Nevertheless, the fact remains that the majority view among academics and serious commentators on comics up until now is that the Yellow Kid was the first comics superstar. Here is a quote from the latest in a long line of studies: "The Yellow Kid has been accepted by several generations of comic strip historians as a pivotal creation in the history of the comics." One of the main reasons for this is because, it goes on: "The Yellow Kid was the first comic strip character to inspire widespread merchandising and licensing, and [to inspire] theatrical productions . . ." (Couch, in Varnum and Gibbons 2001: 74).[14] The problem with the assertion excerpted here (and it is an excerpt: the rest of the essay is excellent) is a very simple one: The Yellow Kid did not appear until 1894. By that time Ally Sloper had been a superstar for over twenty years. The evidence, as we have seen, is unambiguous. With due respect to the various (very valid) arguments around the definition of comics, it would be ideal if any future reprints of such books could be modified in this small but important regard.

NOTES

1. The difference between a "funny paper" and a "comic" is a matter for some debate, as will become clear. For a full Sloper timeline, see Gifford 1984: 37–43.

2. According to a reminiscence by "Sloper" in the "Gas House Opening Day," 1922, edition of *Ally Sloper's Half Holiday*, ". . . Ross used to say . . . 'I think it was about 1860 I wrote a book about Sloper's adventures

for messrs. Ward and Lock calling him "The Great Gun," and before this introduced the character into a romance I wrote called "Dead Acres!" . . .'" (Anon. "Chats at the Cheese," 10).

3. By the Nov. 5, 1922, *ASHH*, Sloper and Tootsie were endorsing McKenzie motorcycles ("because it is equally suitable for either Lady or Gentleman . . .").

4. Sloper also commonly advertised other Sloper publications. One cartoon from *The Eastern Question Tackled by Ally Sloper* (1878) has him attaching a banner for *Ally Sloper's Comic Kalendar* to an Egyptian pyramid.

5. Others might include broadsheet heroes "Tom and Jerry" (1822), and "Brown, Jones, and Robinson" in *Punch* (1850).

6. I am indebted to Frank Nelson, a long time Sloper collector, for information on some of the odder spin-offs.

7. Though Sloper can perhaps be read as the embodiment of Marx's "lumpenproletariat."

8. Chomsky"s arguments about the conservatism of the U.S. press are best articulated in *Manufacturing Consent: The Political Economy of the Mass Media* (New York: Vintage, 1995).

9. It is also worth noting that Sloper had previously appeared in magic lantern shows, and as a subject for stereoview cards (with impersonators in papier mâché "panto mask" heads).

10. Some gags are perhaps too obvious to have been "invented" by any source in particular. For example, there is a recurring skit in the Sloper comics where either he or some other unfortunate gets squirted in the eye by a hosepipe. This same gag was repeated in U.S. comics (notably in the first strip to star "The Katzenjammer Kids") and in Europe, and was the subject for one of the earliest movies (in France). Other gags are less obvious. For example, one British movie short from 1898 described by Barnes as being about a portrait sitter sticking his head through a canvas could well have had its origin in the *ASHH* strip entitled "Pouter's Portrait" from October 16, 1886.

11. Denis Gifford (Gifford 1984) was arguably the first to recognize the significance of Sloper to nineteenth-century popular culture and has written about him extensively in various histories (although he favored *Funny Folks* as his "first comic"). Sloper is still very often cited as "the first comics character" by academics, commentators, and librarians (e.g., the British Library catalogue).

12. This expanded definition has been associated with Scott McCloud in recent years and in particular his two books *Understanding Comics* (London: HarperCollins, 1994) and *Reinventing Comics* (New York: DC Comics, 2000).

13. For a flavor of the complexities of the debate, see the exchange between Belgian scholar Thierry Smolderen and various American and British respondents on PlatinumAgeComics@yahoogroups.com, the on-line discussion list for those interested in the origins of comics (see "archive," circa January 13, 2003).

14. For more detailed information on the commercialization of the Yellow Kid, a trajectory that echoed that of Sloper fairly closely, see also Gordon 1998. For a fuller discussion of the disputed nature of the Yellow Kid as "first," see Harvey 1996: 113–15.

WORKS CITED

Baetens, Jan, "Revealing Traces: A New Theory of Graphic Enunciation," in Robin Varnum and Christina Gibbons, eds., *The Language of Comics* (Jackson: University Press of Mississippi, 2001).

Bailey, Peter, "Ally Sloper's Half Holiday: Comic Art in the 1880s," *History Workshop* (1983) 16: 4–31.

Barker, Martin, *Comics: Ideology, Power and the Critics* (Manchester: Manchester University Press, 1989).

Barnes, John, *Pioneers of the British Film* (London: Bishopsgate Press, 1983).

Braithwaite, Brian, *Women's Magazines: The First 300 Years.* London: Peter Owen, 1995).

Couch, N. C. Christopher, "The Yellow Kid and the Comic Page," in Robin Varnum and Christina Gibbons, eds., *The Language of Comics* (Jackson: University Press of Mississippi, 2001).

Gifford, Denis, "Ally Sloper: The Legendary Cartoon Character Celebrates the 100th Anniversary of his Comic 'This Year,'" *Book and Magazine Collector* 3 (May 1984): 37–43.

Gordon, Ian, *Comic Strips and Consumer Culture 1890–1945* (Washington, DC, and London: Smithsonian Institution, 1998).

Harvey, R. C., "More Firsts Than the Garden of Eden," *Comics Journal* 189 (August 1996): 113–15.

Horrall, Andrew, *Popular Culture in London c. 1890–1918* (Manchester: Manchester University Press, 2001).

Jones, Gareth Stedman, "Working Class Culture and Working Class Politics in London, 1870–1900: Notes on the Remaking of a Working Class," *Journal of Social History* 7 (Summer 1973–74).

Kunzle, David, "Marie Duval: A Caricaturist Rediscovered," *Woman's Art Journal* (Oxford), Spring/Summer 1986.

Jackie and the Problem of Romance

MARTIN BARKER

On the U.K. alternative comedy show *Saturday Live* in 1987 a comedian stepped to the microphone. She launched into a series of jokes about how women are led to look at their own bodies, how terrified they can be about getting overweight. But of course, she laughed (and the audience laughed with her), we all know why—we all read *Jackie*, didn't we? That explains everything. "Everyone knows" that magazines like *Jackie*, but perhaps that one especially, have done long-term damage to girls' psyches. These magazines have subtly preached at girls about boys, romance, beauty, boys, fashion, their bodies, their desires, boys, everything in fact that will help fit them for a future as worried but passive women, everything "right" to think and think about.

That joke crystallises the topic of this chapter. "Everyone knows" these things. This view is remarkably ingrained. This makes it very hard to challenge without simply inviting the wrath of women who are rightly concerned to identify those things which are influencing girls into a "feminine career." Nevertheless I do want to challenge this radical commonsense about *Jackie*, which has been expressed in a thousand jokes, a hundred articles, and quite a few academic analyses. I don't wish to present the magazine as a source of hidden virtues. Simply, I think it is far more complicated than the critics have made out. My worry has several aspects. First their methods of understanding how an "ideology of femininity" might be embodied in such magazines are grossly unsatisfactory. Second, there are politics implicit in their accounts, tightly related to those inadequate methods. And third all the accounts I have looked at just cannot account for the enormous changes that *Jackie* has undergone. There is a total absence of history in all the varieties of feminist work on teenage romances—and that is both disturbing and revealing.

My way of working has been, in each case, to revisit the particular issues of *Jackie* (or other magazines) discussed, to see how critics' methods make them work on the texts. But doing so has brought to the surface two major problems. First, typically, critics do not bother to give proper references when they criticise popular materials of this kind. Yes, we will find a nice list of academic secondary sources. But all too frequently I have had to hunt through many months' editions in order to locate, say, a small piece of dialogue

Reprinted by permission and adapted from Martin Barker, *Comics: Ideology, Power and the Critics* (Manchester University Press, 1989), 134–59.

presented as decisive evidence. I had thought of simply footnoting a rude remark on this. But I now think it is of quite critical importance since it reveals a cavalier attitude to the material—as though it hardly matters since "we all know" what dangerous junk it is. Then, almost invariably I would find that a story was either only retold in part or, if fully recounted, was done in a way that already fitted it to the assumptions of the critic. But that would be all we had to go on. There was no way to check whether the evidence really did support the critique being (usually) so powerfully expressed. We are thus very dependent on the manner of retellings.

This double dependence has effects. Since we only get fragments of stories, we tend to "fill in" what they must be like to qualify for the critics' outraged response. Here, we are told, is a story which restricts girls, or stereotypes them, or enforces a powerful ideology of femininity, tells them that a boy is the only important thing in life and other girls are never to be trusted. Very well then, let's play that game. In researching these chapters, I sample-read one month of every year of *Jackie* since its start in 1964. I was able to identify some fairly typical story-openings. I have chosen two and I invite you, my readers, to complete the stories so that they become attempts to "stereotype" girls, restrict them to feminine careers, enforce an ideology of romance on them. My characters Jane and Peter are now grown up a little and of course (in the light of what they might get up to) not sister and brother.

Our story opens with Jane wondering what she should do. She is in love with Peter, but . . . (flashback) Peter is a wild one. He drives a fast motorbike, dangerously (we see them in one frame swerving down the road, with Jane hanging on unhappily). Then we see them in a café, and he is planning a wild holiday for just the two of them—they can go picking grapes in the South of France. Next frame shows Peter impulsively leaning over the table and kissing Jane. A thought balloon ascends from her head: "This is what I love him for . . . Mmmm. At times like this I think I couldn't live without him." But then we learn that Peter has had to go away for a time, because of his job. This ends the flashback, for now Jane is expecting Peter's return . . .

How should this continue and end? I have constructed this opening as a collage from some fifteen years of *Jackie* stories. Please note I am not asking how it ought to end. Indeed, therein lies a problem. I often feel, when reading critics' accounts, that they begin from a model of what ought to happen in stories for girls—the kind of anti-sexist messages that they want put across. Anything that does not conform to that is then accused of doing the opposite.

I offer my second unfinished story in a different way: first, the opening, and then, a list of possible completions, for you to decide which you might object to, and why:

It is mid-summer's eve. The story opens with a picture of Jane standing under an old tree, beside a river. She is thinking to herself where did our love go? How did we come to lose it? Again we go into flashback, and we see that this is where, a year ago, she first met Peter. She had been sitting on the bank, sad, and he had come and comforted her. Gradually, they had got to know, then fallen in love with, each other.

They had had wonderful times together, wild free times which had made them both ecstatically happy. But then . . .

What went wrong? And how was it dealt with? How did the story continue, and end? Here are some possible versions:

1. Though they go on meeting, Jane becomes unhappy because she feels they are living in a dream. She tries to make Peter see that they must come out into "reality"—and so, one day after their meeting by the river, she follows him home—to find him working in a grotty café, tied by feelings of guilt to a girl whom he evidently doesn't like. Next time they meet in the woods, she tells him what she now knows, and that they can't go on in "dream-style." Peter suddenly asks her to wait—he has to go home to sort out something he should have done years ago. The story ends with Jane waiting, wondering will he return? Will he manage to sort out his life at home, and come back so that they can build a real relationship, not just a dream one?
2. As Jane stands there, she suddenly hears Peter approaching—with another girl! Slipping behind a tree she hears them talking about why Peter likes coming here, to remember Jane whom he used to love. But she went away to London, and there was killed in a road accident. Now all he has left is the memory. The new girl says he mustn't worry—she isn't jealous. She is just glad that Jane once made him happy. At the end we see that Jane is fading away like a ghost, saying to herself as she goes: Now I can rest happy . . .
3. Jane recalls that they began arguing over little things, and the arguments got out of hand—like, her being late for dates, or because she once kissed another boy. Peter had got upset, and she hadn't seen why she should apologise. So, at a disco, they had a terrible row, and Peter walked out on her. They had both been terribly unhappy—Jane had cried herself to sleep at nights—but neither would apologise. Now a strange figure appears at the "haunt" and tells her a parable about how she had lost someone she loved by being too proud. Jane suddenly understands, and we last see her rushing off to find Peter to apologise.
4. In the "present" of the story we see Jane has a letter in her hand, but she can't bring herself to read it. Why? We go into flashback again—to learn that Jane had spent a lot of time encouraging Peter in his ambitions, to become a fashion designer. Eventually he had succeeded, and had grabbed at a chance to go to America. But his letters tailed off, and now at last the promised one had come to say whether he was coming back. She opens it . . . he's not coming. It's all over. Now the story ends with her thinking to herself. I encouraged him in his dreams, and look where that got me. Can I find the courage to go and realise my own dreams?

Four possible endings. Which ones do you find objectionable, and which ones do you think actually appeared in *Jackie*? So that your eyes can't slide ahead before you have thought it out for yourself, I have sneakily put the answer to the second question in the notes.[1] Now return to the first "opener." Here are two examples of how *Jackie* actually completes such a story-form. Are they anything like the endings you thought out?

While he is away, she realises that, however strong her feelings for him, she can't just carry on with him the way he is. When he comes back, she tries to tell him, but he won't ever keep still to listen. She gets swept along again for a while, until the day when—doing his daredevil bit again—he almost kills an old man. Peter laughs it off, assuring her he had it all under control. Anyway, he says, you can't go through life never taking risks. She now tells him he'll have to go his way, while she goes hers. They just are too different. "I don't understand you," Peter says to Jane in the final frame. "That's why it's over,' she replies. (See *Jackie*, no. 104, January 1, 1966: "He Mustn't Guess My Secret")

The next frame shows Jane reading a letter, and remembering, in flashback, all their good times together—the fun, the kisses, the adventure. Above, a narrator's comment tells us that they had promised to write to each other. We see some of their good times together, and how good they were for each other—each one introduced as something that's recalled in a letter he has written her. But after these frames, we see that she is crying; and now we learn that this letter is from a friend, to tell her that Peter has been killed in a motorbike accident. Jane is left, weeping at her loss. (See *Jackie*, no. 678, January 1, 1977: "Tell Me You Love Me")

Whatever we might want to say about such stories, they do not simply fall into a class called "ideology-purveyors." If critics insist they do, they lose the distinction between these and, for example, endings which work straight to a moral point. Suppose, for example, Jane had met a nice "boy-next-door" type while Peter was away, and discovered that this was True Love compared to her earlier infatuation . . . or suppose she had written to Peter saying it was "all over" unless he agreed to sell his motorbike and he had come home and promised—reformed by the "love of a good woman" . . . or suppose Peter had come back, and despite promises to herself, she had gone on going out with him and someone had been killed, perhaps Peter, too—and we saw Jane in the last frame condemning herself for not sticking to her principles. All these would have their moral points printed on their faces. Real stories are rarely so self-evident. In order to extract their meaning, we need subtle and cautious research instruments, able to grasp the flow and stresses of these stories to bring out the manoeuvres and moments of decision that make the stories meaningful.

I say this because I am puzzled. The most striking thing about the over two hundred stories I sampled was how many of them seemed almost wholly unmotivated. Yet it is in that, in the end, that I think their significance lies. They were unmotivated in the sense that the incidents in them were not causally or purposefully connected with each other. They just occurred. Take the following example, from *Jackie*, no. 107, January 22, 1966: "A Kiss, A Dream, A Bunch of Roses." It's wedding day. The story opens with our seeing the heroine/narrator worrying how she will cope with the day. Why? We see, in her flashback, how she fell in love with David while she was in London. David was a married man, with a wife and child whom he had left. But just because of them she couldn't stay with him. She had left and had now met someone else whom she was about to marry. As the moment to commit herself approaches she is haunted by memories, and wonders if she is free of him. In the excitement of getting ready, her mind is temporarily cleared. But as they are setting out for the church a large bunch of yellow roses is delivered—just the same as he once bought her in London. Immediately she understands their meaning. They are saying "Be happy. Forget me. I am happy." Now she can go unreservedly to Simon, her new love, to "create new memories."

The striking thing about this story is just how unconnected the events are—with one crucial exception. We're given no reason why she should suddenly remember, even be obsessed by David. She just does, and is. We're not told why he should have sent her the roses or, indeed, how he knew she was getting married. They just arrive. In a story where things just seem to happen in a sequence, one transition stands out, and everything else seems to assemble round it. It is the point where, having (how did she do it?) immediately "understood" the message of the flowers, the story can say "*Now* she could go to Simon . . ." What seems to happen is a releasing, a transformation of the emotions. One might even say that the rest of the story is given its point by this moment. Realising something, she is able to change herself, modify her emotions. A moment before she was still half in love with David. Now understanding his message, she can instantly redirect that love to its "proper object," Simon. But there is something particular here which we mustn't lose. She "understands the meaning" of the roses. Fine. But it is very easy to see other possible "understandings." David could have been saying, "Don't do it. I love you still. Here is my token." Or he could have been saying "You'll never be happy with anyone else. You know you love only me. Remember . . . remember . . ." The endings would have had to be quite different in each case, and certainly neither would let her just go off to Simon, purified of her past. We have to agree to see her as a particular young woman in order to restrict the interpretation of the roses to what she "instantly" sees in them. This is why I think that the research instruments used by other investigators have been mallet-like. They haven't so much opened up the stories, as crushed them. They have found morals in the stories by treating individual characters as instant moral fables. They have looked on the stories as no different from parables. I hope you can begin to see that they are not obviously like that.

To extract their meaning, we need fine grained analysis. Most of the time, leading characters retain their individuality and are not simply lessons for readers. In that case, we need to make a collage of many individuals' stories. We need to glean from each one its vital motivated element. Often, I shall argue, this turns out to be some transformation of emotions. Where can this get us? Consider a story which certainly is offering a very traditional, conservative picture of women, from the very first edition of *Jackie* (no. 1, January 11, 1964: "The Fifth Proposal"). The story begins with Julia announcing that she has already had four proposals of marriage. She is an air hostess whose pilot—a classic handsome type—keeps proposing to her. Very tempted, she promises she won't keep him waiting long for an answer. But she is suddenly asked to crew an emergency flight to Monte Carlo—where she is approached in a casino by the bewitchingly rich Paul Roget who courts her furiously. He flies back to London with her, hoping for an answer to his proposal. Still worrying whom to accept, she goes off on a visit. In a hospital we see her talking to a young doctor, Neil, who is so glad she has come back. He had encouraged her to go off, but only because she said she wanted "glamour" in her life. A struggling hospital doctor can't give that. Suddenly she realises that it is him she will marry. The pilot and Paul only want her because she "fits" their wishes. But Neil is different. Now she loves him—"because he needs *me.*"

This is a thoroughly reactionary story. Not because she ends up preferring a hospital doctor to an airline pilot or an arrogant French man—that is the level of particularity in the story. It may be a bit homely, but it is not intrinsically wrong—especially if the other two are, as presented, so very selfish. No, the reactionary element lies in how the story reaches its solution. Julia doesn't judge whom to marry by her own emotions. She reorganises her own emotions in the light of the situation. It is almost strategic. Because Neil is a "nice guy," and needs her, immediately it is him she loves. It is this element, and this alone, that once again lifts it out of being merely a story of one woman. Without that self-transformation the story just seems arbitrary. To identify the ideological elements in such stories, we must start from how sequences of incidents, otherwise disconnected, relate to kinds of emotional self-realisation in their women characters.

With these points in mind, I want now to discuss the main critics of *Jackie*. Each is representative of a way of analysing such texts to determine their "ideological significance." There are in fact many discussions of girls' romance comics, almost all hostile.[2] They share several features. Foremost, all our critics assume that these comics form a unity: in two senses. The comics include fiction, editorial chat, readers' letters, a lot of information about pop and fashion. The critics take it for granted that somehow all the various parts accumulate and form a pattern to make up a single kind of influence. If there are tensions and clashes, they are of small significance compared with the overwhelming pressure of their "ideology of femininity." Second (though one or two of the critics might demur), there are really no important differences among the various comics which have been on offer now for around thirty years. Of course superficial differences can be found; but the underlying message, it seems, is unaltering: "being a proper woman means preparing yourself, making yourself attractive and suitable to finding and keeping a mate." We will need to question these assumptions.

It is also common to think that there is something disturbing, even devious, about these comics' singleminded interest in "love." Frequently, this is expressed as a belief that the concentration on romance is a systematic exclusion of all else—a way of saying to young girls that nothing else matters in life. This is how Hollings expresses this view: "The outstanding thing about the portrayal of women in romance comic strips is not really what is shown so much as what is not shown."[3] Hollings is saying that the comics are not just narrow, but therefore dangerous. Much the same view is expressed by most of the other investigators. I find this view strange, and I will try to show why.

Another shared assumption is that the audience for these comics is particularly vulnerable. Toynbee, for example, calls the magazines' readers "impressionable."[4] Girls in the typical age-range of twelve to sixteen are pictured as "incomplete." They are still forming their sexual and personal identities, it is suggested; and this makes them prone to absorbing the image of themselves offered by these magazines. I don't so much want to reject as refine this argument. I think there is an important grain of truth in these ideas; but it does not lead to the kinds of conclusion which the critics reach.

Still for all the things they agree on, the critics also differ. And more than any other, *Jackie* has given me a chance to review a number of different approaches to how the media might influence their audiences. Therefore I want to consider each approach in turn. I will be looking at each theory in its own right, and at how it leads them to "read" particular stories.

IT'S ALL SIMPLY MASS CULTURE

The earliest work to note is Connie Alderson's.[5] Alderson starts by assuming that the main romance comics of her time, *Jackie, Valentine*, and *Trend* are effectively identical. The fact that they have very different backgrounds and traditions doesn't matter to her because they all are simply pieces of "mass culture." There is an unspoken criterion in her account measuring the comics against what they ought to be doing. So these comics are bad-for-girls because they are "amoral" ("The heroines of the stories are never really involved in a moral decision" [26]), "anti-intellectual" ("Studying is definitely equated with having no social life and not being available for constant dating" [27]), and "emotionally immature." The language is constricted, and so confuses thought; it is banal, simple and hackneyed. The plots use simple psychology ("Just one feeling motivates action: 'The wedding's off. No girl keeps me waiting'" [67]). They create "a world of simple dualities—boys vs girls; like vs dislike; homely vs sophistication; free vs tied down; boy-next-door vs boy in an exciting way-out job" (70). And each of these is obviously damaging. No girl should be possibly allowed to think like that.

She suggests their tattiness is all a function of "Big Business." It is all just a device for selling goods to girls and young women. The "businessmen and promoters who lurk behind them are selling their wares through the very nature of the magazines" (106–7). The picture she gives us of romance comics is of dull, repetitive, motiveless crap, narrow in conception and routine in performance. The wonder is that girls could be got to keep reading such pathetic stuff. And predictably, at this point, an "explanation" enters. Woman are encouraged like mad to "identify" with these magazines: "All stories contain strong reader-identification" (11).

> The stories contain positive and negative elements in common. Reader-identification has been mentioned, and this is a common denominator. There are certain forbidden subjects which are never mentioned. These are common to the romantic stories in the cheaper women's weekly magazines, but the boundaries in the teenage magazines are even narrower. Anne Britton and Marion Collin, who have both been fiction editors of women's magazines, advise in their guide to would-be writers of Romantic Fiction that reader-identification is the most important aspect of women's magazine stories. They point out that most women like a story with an escapist quality, yet the plots must not exceed the realms of possibility. (13)

There are two elements in this account. First, "identification" means that the comics reflect the narrowness of women and their lives, and don't "broaden" them. These magazines ought to educate, but don't:

> (T)he allegiance that girls and women give to women's magazines is pernicious. It is because they are magazines for women that they are pernicious. . . . In our machine age it is vital for women to keep up the traditional arts of being able to run a home well, be able to cook and sit down and make a child a fancy dress. But if women are not to be second-class citizens, and looking at the figures for women's entries into the universities and the professions it is plain that women are underprivileged in this

respect . . . they must be able to play their part in the community and to be in a position to voice their own special needs and those of their children. (108)

Alderson is criticising the comics for not doing what she wants. She is one of those who
think that women must be prepared for the double work of being wives and mothers and also public people. Because the comics are not readying women for that, they
are bad. In her scheme of things, not to be doing this is to be actively blocking it. If
Alderson accuses the comics of setting up "simple dualities," she is not above those herself. So, education and broadening the mind is opposed to "escapism." Odd things do
appear under the "broadening" heading: for example, "False as they may have been, the
romantic pulp magazines of pre-war days did introduce their readers to the 'enchanted
East,' but the identification level in teenage magazines is kept within tight and narrows
bounds" (13). So narrow dreams are more insidious than far-flung fantasies: "the harm
from this kind of literature is the persistent encouragement to 'dream' rather than to
'do' or to participate." Apparently, dreaming about the East is at least partly educational
(not a lingering relic of imperialist fantasies about exotic natives), whereas dreaming
about a boy in a café is dreadfully dangerous.

This argument only makes sense because she assumes young women are anyway prone
to this kind of dreaming. The sin of *Jackie*, in other words, is to connect too successfully
with women's natural tendencies. It should have fought against them; women should be
"forced to be free." Hence the citation from the Newsom Report: "All children, including those of very limited attainments, need the broadening experience of contact with
great literature" (2). And of course great literature and *Jackie* are mutually exclusive. The
former is unquestionably good for you. You may be bored by it. You may feel it is irrelevant to your life. That is a problem to be overcome. *Jackie* is unquestionably bad for
you. You may enjoy it. You may feel it helps to answer problems you are having. That is
another problem to be overcome. Readers of these things are so "emotionally and mentally unformed" (41) that they are incapable of sensible judgements for themselves. There
are even suggestions that they will lose touch with the "real world." "Values of the real
world do not exist. The background of the girls working in offices is monotonous. The
reader is seldom told the type of industry" (17). Now that would be exciting! And would,
of course, begin the transformation of readers' lives! If only they had known that Helen,
the heroine, worked in a solicitor's office . . . typing, filing, running errands, they'd begin
to understand that "doing" is better than "dreaming." It is hard not to pour scorn on the
appalling elitism in her argument. Education = good (where education feels like a combination of government schemes plus travel brochures); fantasy = bad (and especially so
when it stays close to their lives).

The second element in her notion of "identification" is the "story-devices" that make
the reader feel part of the story. So, the majority of stories are "written from a woman's
angle" (16). This has the power to convert what would be boring pap into an addictive
drug. How otherwise do we make sense of this paradoxical argument? "The effect of the
thin, superficial structure of the stories with a choice of two endings, either catching the
right boy or of being resigned to tears until the right boy comes along, is one of frustration and leads to the desire to read to another story in the hope that it might prove more
interesting" (23). If so boring, why not throw the bloody thing away? Ah, because of

"identification." It ensnares them. They are caught, unable to make any critical response. The "less educated, the less articulate and the unprivileged" will thus be confirmed in their unfortunate stupidity—thinking their office job dull, not thinking about what industry they work in, not knowing about the mysterious East.

What picture do we get of the individual stories? We have already seen the main components: amorality; anti-intellectualism; rejection of complexity, plus that "the word 'love' is thoroughly debased in the context of the stories" (11). (What undebased love is like, we can only guess . . .) But as we've seen, all these depend on external criteria about what the stories ought to do, but don't. Let us then consider a story she does cite as evidence: "Time To Say Goodbye" (no. 99, November 27, 1965). It is one of the few of her *Jackie* references I have been able to track down. The story opens with narrator Judy standing uncertainly by her door. She is thinking: what will she say to Bill when she opens it? She'll tell him she won't be seeing him again . . . but when she opens it, in he rushes and sweeps her off her feet, insisting on taking her for a fast drive. ("Life's never dull with him, but I wish . . .") At the coast they go for a swim. He lifts out of the water on to a rock and tells her he'd like to keep her there, safe, forever, just loving him. Love him? Oh yes, but that doesn't help her—she must give him up. After a good day, they drive slowly home, savouring each other's company. As she gets out of the car, he promises to be round tomorrow. She doesn't say goodbye . . . "and now I never will say it because tomorrow I'm going away . . . tomorrow he'll find this note telling him." She'll be gone for two years.

Why must she go? Think what you would expect, given Alderson's picture of "amorality." Again, I've "hidden" the answer in the footnotes, so you can think it for yourselves first.[6] When you have looked, you will see that there is a real problem. The story expresses the early deep conservatism of *Jackie*. But that took the form of urging women to be too moral, dismissing their own desires and goals for others. The problem is not simply that Alderson is wrong. Rather, in measuring such a story by her external criteria she judges without understanding. Because the decision isn't moral in her sense of the word, it isn't moral at all.

In one sense Alderson is atypical, her politics are so markedly pre-feminist. Yet she is still frequently cited, no one having thought to go back and check her readings of the stories. Those who refer to her tend to dismiss her "mass culture" theorizing on its own as though it wouldn't have affected her interpretation of the stories themselves. It's not at all that she wants women returned to the home—far from it. True, they must have those "home-making skills." But they also need to be broadened; they must get out into the world of men, run a home, bring up the children, read great literature, go to university, learn about the worlds of intellect, politics, and work. With all this to do, there simply isn't time for diversions like romance. I am not caricaturing, only spelling out what she has left implicit. If the resultant picture is awful, that is her problem, not mine.

Subsequent analysts of romance comics have been much more influenced by the arguments of the women's movement. They share Alderson's dislike of *Jackie* and its equivalents and judge their influence baleful. But Alderson's insistence on women keeping their home-making skills now becomes part of the problem—to which *Jackie* contributes.

SEMIOLOGICAL ANALYSIS

Surely the most influential analysis of girls' romance comics has to be Angela McRobbie's. Published originally in 1979, then updated by a further discussion in her co-edited *Feminism for Girls* (with a report of her research on *Jackie* readers in between), it is often seen as the definitive study of *Jackie*. Only the first piece is explicitly semiological in orientation; but the difference is hard to detect. The first study sees Jackie as mapping out the feminine career "in such all-embracing terms, there is little or no space allowed for alternatives" (1, p. 3). In the third piece, she writes of all other ideas being "eliminated" (3, p. 120), of readers being "denied any choice" (3, p. 123), "allowed no time off from" romance (3, p. 124). Romances are "the only attachments worth forming"; any other kind "don't find a place" (3, p. 119): "Instead of having hobbies, instead of going fishing, learning to play the guitar, or even learning to swim or play tennis, the girl is encouraged to load all her eggs in the basket of romance and hope it pays off" (3, p. 118). Once again, the language of "limits" leads to the language of "restriction" leads to the language of "exclusion." It would be easy to show that this is actually untrue. *Jackie* does encourage its readers to have other interests; it regularly advises girls that romance is not the only thing that matters in their lives. But to reply thus would only suggest that McRobbie has overstated her case a bit. We need to look at how she uses a theory and a method to reach these conclusions.

McRobbie combines a semiological way of looking at meanings with a view of young girls' especial marginality and vulnerability. So, *Jackie* is popular: not because it furnishes its readers with any positive self-image, not because it encourages them to value themselves and each other, but because it offers "its exclusive attention to an already powerless group, to a group which receives little public attention and which is already, from an early age, systematically denied any real sense of identity, creativity, or control" (3, p. 128). I don't want to deny this. Young girls, particularly young working class girls, are marginalized in our society. But that doesn't necessarily mean that they are more vulnerable to media influence. McRobbie thinks it does: "*Jackie* is so definitive about its dealing with youth and femininity, it's so authoritative (in the friendliest way), it implies ultimately that it's all 'sewn up,' all dealt with here. This makes it difficult for readers to imagine alternatives" (3, p. 115). Ironically, the period she samples is one in which the magazine was losing confidence in its own view of romance. But let that wait. I am interested in her bracketed reference to *Jackie*'s friendly tone, a point repeated from the first study. By comparison, earlier magazines were much more preachy and dictatorial. *Marilyn*, for example, one of its immediate predecessors, used to run a strip-column headed "Mum Knows Best" which gave direct instructions on behaviour. It looks very much as though in McRobbie's theory *Jackie* is more dangerous since it is friendlier than the older overtly conservative magazines. She could be right, but we need to know how she reaches this conclusion. To understand, we need to consider the theory of semiology.

Semiology is an approach to understanding how meanings are generated and communicated; it derives ultimately from the work of the Swiss linguist Ferdinand de Saussure. I will only state the theory briefly here, enough hopefully to make clear how it is used on *Jackie*. Semiology argues that while language is clearly the most important system of meanings, it is not unique. There are many other equivalent systems, for example, clothing, food, furniture, gestures, and facial expressions. We don't wear clothes only to keep warm, or eat food only to satisfy hunger; we choose clothes to convey a self-image, a social status; our choice of foods expresses all kinds of social ideas. They are all rich in meanings, are "languages" in their own right. Thus all of them share certain features.

1. Any "language" is composed of signs: road-signs, at one extreme, which exist purely for the sake of conveying a message. At the other extreme, a car, a pet, a jacket, a hairdo all also convey meanings; but they do other jobs as well. In each case, though, we have a sign. Signs, say semiologists, are a combination of two elements: a signifier—whatever is used to convey the meaning; and the signified—this is the concept conveyed. This is an important step in their argument. The signified of "dog" is not the animal. It is the concept of a dog. When we name something we are assigning it to a category, saying what kind of thing it is. If not, we couldn't make any sense of the following. I go into a house, and I see two orange boxes upturned and side by side. Someone asks me to put something on "the table," and points to the boxes. "That's hardly a proper table," I think—and thus I reveal that "table" is a category with criteria to be met before something is assigned to it. My concept of a table was offended by the boxes. But the implication is that words do not directly depict the world; they cut it up into categories.
2. No single unit of a "language" can produce meaning on its own. Each unit, says semiology, gets its meaning by being different from the other units surrounding it. An example: "woman" is a concept with many associations. To call someone "womanly" is traditionally to think of them as supportive, motherly, attractive. But to call a man a "woman" would be an insult, implying lack of proper qualities. He is being called weak, emotional, dependent, and so on. To call a woman "manly" is more equivocal, suggesting strength and independence, but perhaps "not properly female." The point the semiologists want to make is that the meanings of "woman" can't be understood except through its difference from/relation to "man." They define each other by their differences. Thus language is a system of differences.
3. A sign then has two elements. It also does two jobs. It denotes—that is, it points towards those things in the world which fall under it. But it also connotes—that is, it links the things it denotes by association with other things. A standard example is "rose." "Rose" denotes a range of flowers. But in our culture, it has taken on connotations of romance. Other flowers have taken on different connotations, though few quite as definitely: "buttercups" with innocence and childhood, "orchids" with luxury. The important thing is that connotations reflect cultural ideas and practices. It is here we begin to see why semiology can have political implications.

Let us try out its distinction on a more significant example. Take the word "democracy." In our culture, "democracy" occupies a very special place in our "system of differences," somewhat like this:

				TYRANNY		
DEMOCRACY	=	GOOD	Versus	AUTOCRACY	=	BAD
				TOTALITARIANISM		

Democracy is clearly a good thing—but what kind of a good thing is it? It is a state of affairs, a political arrangement. It is good, almost by definition, to live in "a democracy." But compare "Western democracy," or "political democracy" which sound right, with "school democracy" or "industrial democracy" or "prison democracy." The last three sound awkward. "Democracy" is not simply a term which depicts clearly, and adds on a glow of rightness; it is rather complicated. It is a good state of affairs within certain spheres. And it has other implications, too. The following was a news trailer on Radio 4 during 1986: "Today the Queen visits China, the country which tried to step from feudalism to socialism without going through democracy. Today, it is trying to mend its ways."[7] Democracy is apparently a good in itself. It is a "system" without which societies can't achieve anything, apparently.

This has not always been so. Consider the following quotation from a nineteenth-century essay prompted by concerns over the newly enfranchised working class, and their penchant for "Dreadful" reading matter:

> The penny novelette has probably much more effect on the women members of the working classes than the newspaper has on the men. . . . In the majority of instances the objects held up to the derision of the people are the aristocracy, the plutocracy, and sometimes even the monarchy itself. . . . Capital and birth are the two themes on which the democratic journalist never tires of expatiating. By deriding the governing classes he hopes to arouse the enthusiasm of the public. He is, however, victim of the delusion that the democracy is primarily moved by enmity towards the aristocracy."[8]

Here "democracy" is not a state of affairs. It is a definite group of people, a dangerous, unpredictable mass; and they stand opposite aristocracy, security, rationality. Try inserting that meaning of "democracy" into Brian Redhead's comments on China, and it looks decidedly odd. Or try to talk of a "property-owning democracy" in the nineteenth-century meaning. It becomes a contradiction in terms! In any "language," then, units get their meaning from their difference from/relation to all the other elements around them.

4. We don't just see differences, we see relationships. If a "language" cuts up its world, it also puts it back together again to form a system. Meanings form patterns. So, we don't just see women as different from men, but as having particular kinds of relationships to them. To be a "woman" in our society's main cultural definition is to stand in particular relationships to men, to children, to politics, to work, to nature, and so on. When I was a child, I well remember learning an expression for when everyone significant was at some gathering: we said "all the world and his wife were there" . . . Think about it. This reassembling in distinct patterns is what is meant by the semiological terms "code" and "myth."

5. The next element is the separation of "langue" and "parole." "Langue" is language as a system, pre-existing any individual who may use it. A child learning to speak misstates the past tense of "come" as "comed." It is corrected. Its use (parole) of the language is measured against certain rules which make up the "langue." People of course do both make mistakes and deliberately break the rules. But you can only make mistakes

and break rules if there are rules to be broken. This is (crudely) the distinction between "langue," the system of words and their meanings at any time; and "parole," the way an individual uses (or misuses) that system.

6. Lastly comes the element in semiological thought that is surely the most important for its theory of ideology. It is also the most troublesome. This is the "arbitrariness" of languages. "Language is an arbitrary system of differences with no positive term," wrote Saussure. This is not the place for a full discussion of this. But some discussion is necessary. First, it has more levels of meaning than are usually acknowledged. Normally, commentators discuss only two meanings of "arbitrary":

   a. The choice of signifier is arbitrary. It does not matter what sound is used to signify four-legged, hooved animals used for riding. The fact that the English language uses "horse" whereas French uses "cheval" is irrelevant—each works equally well as signifier. The only (partial) exceptions are onomatopoeic words, like "hiss," where (perhaps) a sound may have evolved as signifier because of its similarity to the concept it is depicting. This notion of arbitrariness poses no problem, as far as I can see.

   b. The relation of signifier to signified is arbitrary. In English we separate the concepts of "tree" and "bush." French does not—but it does distinguish (as Jonathan Culler points out) between rivers flowing to the sea, and those that flow into lakes. The argument of the semiologists is that there are no self-evident classifications which impose themselves on language. Language carves up the world, not the other way round. This is a highly contentious claim, but one which I am not discussing directly in this book. I note it particularly because it connects with a third meaning of "arbitrariness," one that is relevant to how we should understand "ideology." This third meaning is missing from most discussions of semiology.

   c. The "system of differences" that is a "language" imposes itself on us in arbitrary fashion. The best way to understand this is to see what is excluded by it. There are in theory plenty of reasons why we might accept a claim about the world. It could be because it is the only view we have ever come across, or because it seems to make sense of our experience, or because, after evidence and arguments, it seems the most plausible. It could be enforced on us, by fear or threat, or because the ideas have some pleasing quality. None of these is necessarily innocent. But the mode of persuasion, as we might call it, is quite different in each case.

Now semiology is not only a theory dealing with how meanings are produced. It already contains a theory of influence. Language is a system governed by rules before we use it. The world only falls into categories of meaning because language imposes them on it. Because of these ideas, semiology has to assert that any "language" works on us by imposing itself on us, in effect, by gridding us. Of course semiologists say that we can and do resist this influence. But their theory already tells them how that influence must work. It tells them what sort of effect it must have. Put crudely, their idea is that we do not accept ideas because they make sense of our world for us; they make sense of our world because we have been influenced by them. We do not accept them because they appear to us rational and intelligible; they appear rational and intelligible because we have been moulded in that system's image. The theory of ideology implied by semiology is a grossly anti-rational one.

It was Saussure who coined the term "semiology" for a future science of meanings. This science would encompass all sign-systems, including language. But Saussure's particular view of language would have made it hard for him to have applied his ideas to systems like fashion, or cars. This was because he thought of each "language" coinciding with the boundaries of a natural language. French was a "langue," so were English, Dutch, Arabic. It was hard on such an account to make much sense of dialects or local variations. It was still harder to be able to think of ideologies. For to think about ideology in his way, you need to be able to think of a "local system." This might then "belong to" or "fit the interests of" some social group. It took Barthes' reworking of Saussure's ideas to make that possible. He dropped the assumption that we "already know" the boundaries of a sign-system; that became a problem to be solved.

But that left him in a difficult situation. Saussure could perhaps not deal adequately with social difference within a language. But at least his approach made it clear how we would know the boundaries of a system. Look at a dictionary. But once stop identifying the system with natural language, and the problem arises: how do we identify the limits of a system? And if we are doing research, how do we know when we have a sample that will enable us to grasp the whole system? We do need to know if we are going to investigate, say, *Jackie*. For semiology requires us to look for a complete "system" in it. How exactly are we to do this? What in fact happens is that these Saussurean assumptions change into something just as worrying. They become methodological commands. I want to show what these are, and then illustrate their workings on *Jackie*.

1. The surface features of a cultural object like *Jackie* must be understood as expressions of an underlying pattern or structure. Semiology says meanings are created in systems. But systems are not apparent on the surface of a culture. We have to look beyond the surface to the way all the elements interrelate. But straightaway this command sets up a problem. Which surface elements should we focus on? A concrete case: during the 1960–70s DC Thompson, publishers of *Jackie*, became dependent for much of their artwork on Spanish artists. This had effects on how the characters looked. They tended to be highly idealised, postdated copies of images from other British media. Long after Twiggy and Jean Shrimpton had left the advertising scene, their lookalikes graced the pages of *Jackie*. How should we interpret this? On one interpretation this is an accident of the production history of the magazine, a curious but not very revealing fact. It might even be seen as a barrier to what *Jackie* was trying to say. When in 1978/9 DC Thomson adopted photostrip techniques, perhaps that was a solution to the problem of having to use overseas artists.

   Another interpretation favoured by both McRobbie and Sharpe is that the drawings by the foreign artists expressed the comic's fundamental ideology: an idealisation of romance, a highly selected range of physical and personality types, narrowing the possibilities for self-images. How should we decide between these? Following the methodological command, we have to go for the second explanation. The command "treat surface features as expressive of a deeper pattern" means that in principle we must treat every single surface feature as part of the "system." Drawing styles, print styles, paper quality, size, format, price, sectioning, editorial matter, quizzes, stories, references to the "stars" (and perhaps a schematism of metaphorical connection between "stars" (= horoscopes) and "stars" (= pop idols) could be built . . . ?), letters, and so on ad infinitum. Everything must count. There can be no principle for distinguishing relevant from irrelevant surface features. Everything is equally meaningful. The result is that the decision about what to attend to, must be a function of the investigator's own prejudgements. Because of the other methodological commands, it can only confirm her or his hunches. It can never challenge them.

2. Look for a system, a unified system of differences. Here further aspects of the first command come to light. First, *Jackie* for example must be a complete system. This is how the problem of the adequacy of a sample comes back as practical problem. It must be enough just to look at the comic by itself. That alone should reveal the "system of differences." Second, *Jackie* must be coherent. If there are contradictory elements, they must be simply differences within the (unified) system. The methodological command to find a system of differences turns into a command to carry on researching until we have found a complete, coherent system. We will know when our research is complete, by the "discovery" of a system. Afterwards we might want to look at how people use it. But that is a separate study. And you can't even begin on that until you have met the third demand.

3. Explore how the system works to impose itself. This command comes out of Barthes' modification of Saussure's theory. On Barthes' view a system can embody a socially inflected view of the world. To do this effectively, it must disguise its own origins. Recall Barthes' claim that if something is disguised, it will be more effective in persuading us than if it reveals its nature; and this leads to some curious claims about disguises. McRobbie for example claims that *Jackie* is somehow concealing its nature as commodity:

> One of the most immediate and outstanding features of *Jackie* as it is displayed on bookstalls, newspaper stands and counters, up and down the country, is its ability to look "natural." It takes its place easily within that whole range of women's magazines which rarely change their format and which (despite new arrivals which quickly achieve this solidness if they are to succeed) always seem to have been there! Its existence is taken for granted. Yet this front obscures the "artificiality" of the magazine, its "productness" and its existence as a commodity. It also obscures the nature of the processes by which it is produced. (1, p. 11–12)

I always find myself wanting to ask silly questions when confronted with claims like this: like, would it be hiding or revealing its existence-as-commodity more if the price was covered up? I honestly do not know what is meant by this kind of claim that "appearing natural" is a disguise for the processes of production. What would have to change to make it untrue? It seems to me a simple confusion between something being recognizable and being naturalized. Just because *Jackie* looks like other magazines, I can see no reason why this should make us confused about how or why it is produced.

The problem is the way semiologists know what they must find. It is a game of Hunt-the-Thimble where you know there must be one. Keep looking long enough, and eventually, something will be found that you can call a thimble. In McRobbie this goes one stage further. She not only knew in advance that there must be a unified system in *Jackie*, she also knew what kind of system it must be and what jobs it would do. This is because the take-up of semiology in the 1970s was not "innocent." It was taken up because it offered a way of investigating "culture" that fitted the needs of post-1968 radical suspicions. Disappointed hopes led to a search for the villains who were restraining workers, women, black people from radical action. One of the main blackguards had to be the media. People had been bought off mentally as well as materially. The most recent phase of capitalism (now also called patriarchal) was one that "positioned people as consumers"; it produced the goods and pseudo-goods to sell to its populace; it produced pseudo-leisure in which to use those goods; and it produced the pseudo-ideas to tie us into consuming. To understand it all, we had to give particular attention to the processes of masking and directing our wishes. At the macro-level the arguments of Louis Althusser told of the "construction of the subject" as an essential stage of the reproduction of labor.

Semiology neatly dropped into place in this explanation; we "already know" that consumerist capitalism depends on our willing self-subjugation to being used in certain ways. Now we could show how this was done. This is how McRobbie can begin her essay on *Jackie* with her conclusions: that *Jackie* is involved with consumerist capitalism at three levels. It is a product (but "hides" the fact); it sells products: and it sells an all-consuming involvement with leisure which is the necessary ideology to maintain the other two. These between them construct *Jackie*. And though McRobbie insists (1, p. 2) that hers is not a conspiracy model, that denial sits uneasily with claims like the following: "a concerted effort is . . . made to win and shape the consent of the readers to a particular set of values" (ibid).

NOTES

1. In fact all these endings are based on stories found in *Jackie*, from various points in its history. They are based on the following stories: (1) "The Girl with Green Eyes," no. 470 (January 6, 1973); (2) "Forever and Ever," no. 681 (January 22, 1977); (3) "Throwaway Love," no. 473 (January 27, 1973); "Take Me in Your Arms," no. 158 (January 14, 1967).

2. See Connie Alderson, *Magazines Teenagers Read* (London: Pergamom Press, 1968; Elizabeth Frazer, "Teenage Girls Reading *Jackie*," *Media, Culture and Society* 9 (1987); Sandra Hebron, "*Jackie* and *Woman's Own*: Ideological Work and the Social Construction of Gender Identity," unpublished paper, Sheffield City Polytechnic, 1983; Julie Hollings, "The Portrayal of Women in Romance Comic Strips, 1964–1984," unpublished paper, University of Reading, 1985; Angela McRobbie, Jackie: *An Ideology of Adolescent Femininity* (Birmingham: Center for Contemporary Cultural Studies, 1978); Angela McRobbie, "Working Class Girls and the Culture of Femininity," in *Women Take Issue* (London: Hutchinson, 1978); Angela McRobbie, "Just like a *Jackie* Story," in Angela McRobbie and Trisha McCabe, *Feminism for Girls: An Adventure Story* (London: Routledge, 1981); Gillian Murphy, "Media Influence on the Socialization of Teenage Girls," in James Curran, Anthony Smith and Pauline Wingate, eds., *Impacts and Influence: Essays on Media Power in the Twentieth Century* (London: Methuen, 1987); Judith O'Connell, "Sexist Images in Children's Comics and Television," unpublished paper, University of Sheffield, 1982; Jacqueline Sarsby, *Romantic Love and Society* (Harmondsworth: Penguin, 1983); Sue Sharpe, *Just Like a Girl: How Girls Learn to Be Women* (Harmondsworth: Penguin, 1976).

3. Julie Hollings, "The Portrayal of Women in Romance Comic Strips," 78.

4. Polly Toynbee, "The Magazines Preach a Stultifying Message," *Guardian*, October 30, 1978.

5. Connie Alderson, *Magazines Teenagers Read.*

6. "Time to Say Goodbye" in fact ends as follows: realizing that she is endangering his career as a successful accountant (he's spending too much time romancing with her, not studying for his exams), she takes the hint from his parents that she is doing him no good. And so she just goes away, miserably, to save him from himself. As a say, hardly a lack of morality, rather a self-sacrificial excess.

7. Brian Redhead, Radio 4, 8 pm, October 12, 1986.

8. Edward Salmon, "What the Working Classes Read," *The Nineteenth Century* (July 1886).

Home Loving and Without Vices

ANNE RUBENSTEIN

What is Mexico's national culture? This question has been at the center of political and scholarly debate for most of the twentieth century. Indeed, beginning in the 1920s, it was the explicit project of at least some of Mexico's leaders to create a modern national culture by supporting mass media and high culture, controlling education, construct- ing a revolutionary mythos, and intervening into aspects of everyday life from cuisine to transportation. Although proponents emphasized the newness of such revolutionary enterprises, these projects also continued late-nineteenth-century positivist efforts to bring progress and order to Mexico—through urban planning, hygiene, architecture, and state control of poor people's behavior. Planners and politicians, both Porfirians and revolutionaries, claimed to be bringing a new nation into existence, thereby imply- ing that before them there had been no nation at all except in the strictest legal sense.

Scholars of the 1940s through the 1960s more or less agreed that no single Mexican national culture existed. Some anthropologists—notably Robert Redfield—saw two static Mexican cultures, both presumably with deep roots in the past: one urban and modern, the other rural and traditional. Other scholars, like historian Luis Gonzalez y Gonzalez and anthropologist Guillermo Bonfil Batalla, have insisted on a Mexico of many near-independent regions, each requiring study on its own terms. These regional- ist scholars tend to see national culture as an imposition from outside—if they see any national culture at all. To them, "deep" Mexico is Mexico state by state, or town by town; from their point of view, to look for cultural continuities at the national level is to participate in a process of state formation that may well be inimical to the interests of a particular region.

More recently, historians have begun looking for spatial and chronological continu- ities again. As Steve Stern puts it, the irony of the "many Mexicos" model is that, in the end, we start to notice "language and experience in common," among Mexico's regions, that is, "many Mexicos." Alan Knight suggests that these commonalities did not arise from the revolutionary attempt at creating a national culture, which he believes generally to have failed, but from the subsequent rise of a modern national culture created by the new consumerism that was another prominent feature of Mexican life after 1920.[1]

Reprinted by permission of the publisher and adapted from Anne Rubenstein, *Bad Language, Naked Ladies, and Other Threats to the Nation* (Duke University Press, 1998), 41–68.

From the vantage point of consumer culture and mass media, there is yet another answer. A new national culture did develop after the Revolution, but it had two faces; one might even say it was comprised of two discourses. One was the set of ideas, arguments, attitudes, and metaphors related to modernity, progress, industrialization, and urbanity. The other was a discourse of tradition, conservatism, rural life, and Catholicism. Both of these discourses were equally rooted in the past, both were equally new, and both of them changed over time. Both were deployed by representatives of the government, and their opponents, at various times and for various purposes. These discourses developed in dialogue with each other over gender, work, and nation. "Tradition" did not precede "modernity" any more than modernity displaced tradition. Each required the other. And both were aspects of a single national culture that was developing throughout this period.

These discourses run through mass media in the postrevolutionary period and through the political debates that mass media inspired. Many commentators assumed that comic books—along with movies and radio—must be a modernizing force, and the language and imagery of progress certainly did figure prominently in *historietas*. Journalistic and scholarly descriptions of the comic book audience, too, came to rely on the language of modernity and urbanity. At the same time, even as comic books were elaborating on this discourse, the stories they told often agreed with and added to the discourse of conservatism. And when members of the audience got the chance to describe themselves, they chose the words, veiled assumptions, and values of "tradition."

THE EXPERTS EXAMINE THE AUDIENCE

The comic book audience was a subject of controversy almost from the moment it came into being. Mexican conservatives presumed that the *historietas* had a terrible effect on their readers, and in 1944 the Mexican state implicitly agreed by setting up a censorship office. Four decades later, critics Adriana Malvido and Teresa Martinez Arana wrote that this controversy had reinforced assumptions about the identity of comic book readers and the effects that mass media had on them: the "contempt that the majority of journalists, writers, students, researchers, art critics and government officials profess for this medium . . . leads to an underestimation of the readers, millions of Mexicans," and the image of the audience as "semiliterate."[2] This picture of the audience drew, as well, from an academic discourse that both lamented modernity and took for granted its inevitability as it described postrevolutionary city life.

Oscar Lewis (with Redfield, perhaps the most influential of all ethnographers of Mexico) saw a "culture of poverty" when he started to study Mexico City working-class life in 1943. He recorded the memories of two generations of a "typical" poor family in his 1961 *The Children of Sanchez*, noting that they had moved from the countryside—"a Mexico without cars, movies, radios or TV"—to a place and time formed by "post-Revolutionary values . . . individualism and social mobility." According to Lewis, however, these new values had destroyed the prospects of the family's second generation, for while the hardworking patriarch had "managed to raise himself out of the depths of poverty," his children had sunk back into it.[3] These new values were carried by the mass media, and comic books—alongside radio and cinema—were prominent in Lewis's account. He cites the fond memory of Sanchez's shiftless son, Roberto, that "my father had always brought copies of the comic magazines for Elena [the stepmother] and for us kids," thus unwittingly setting them up for corruption.[4] In the case of daughter Marta, whom Lewis depicts as having ruined her life through early promiscuity, her troubles began in her "tomboy" childhood when she took Tarzan as a hero.[5]

Following Lewis, other ethnographers, essayists, psychologists, journalists, and travel writers picked up on the theme of comic books as a corrupting force of modernization or, at the least, a defining trope of urban poverty. In 1984 a reporter for the *New York Times* repeated the received wisdom of liberal sociology when he presented a grim picture of comic book readers as innocent peasant girls newly arrived in the big city, working as maids, corrupted by mass media "exposing them . . . to different standards of morality," thereby rendering them vulnerable to premarital pregnancy and subsequent abandonment by family, employers, and lovers.[6]

More serious and sympathetic scholars, such as Larissa Lomnitz, drew less extreme conclusions; still, in 1977 she asserted that the "comics, photo-romances, [and] sports sheets" that she had seen everywhere in the "shantytown" she studied were "carriers of the values, norms, and aspirations of urban national culture."[7] Similarly, Jonathan Kandell connected urbanity, modernity, and media when he wrote of the growth in Mexico City's population between 1940 and 1970:

> Migrants were pulled toward Mexico City by the communications revolution . . . reaching into the most isolated rural zones—that evoked an advanced, renumerative, and exciting way of life as an alternative to the static poverty of the countryside.[8]

In the 1970s, other scholars—influenced by the Chilean literary critic Ariel Dorfman— took up a new modulation of the older view of comic books as part of a modernizing wave of consumer culture, that is, as cheerleaders for capitalist materialism. They added that comic books were a form of counterrevolutionary political brainwashing. These sociologists, anthropologists, and critics identified capitalism with the United States and, thus, resistance to capitalism with nationalism.[9] For example, Dick Reavis described a migrant to Mexico City whom he encountered in 1977. This man had been a peasant activist when he lived in San Luis Potos and, in a particularly dangerous moment, had drawn courage from imagining himself doing "what Kalimán [a popular comic book character at the time] would have done." Reavis records his own disappointment that this heroic man did not take "Fidel or Che" as a model instead.[10]

This position required some explanation, as the most popular *historietas* in Mexico were not the Disney comics that Dorfman studied in Chile but rather locally produced and descriptive, in their own way, of local conditions. Irene Herner, whose valuable 1979 study of the comic book and photonovel industries was informed by this anti-cultural-imperialist perspective, got around the difficulty by explaining that "the imperialist offensive" against Mexican sovereignty had found "native allies [in] Mexican private enterprise" who were helping to inject foreign values into the "spiritual and intellectual formation of the people."[11]

Such qualitative accounts had quantitative counterparts. Two surveys from mid-century participated in the academic construction of the comic book audience: in 1950, a Universidad Nacional Autonoma de Mexico economist, Lazlo Radvayi, studied "readers addicted to comicbook magazines"; and a professor of education at the Instituto Nacional de Pedagogia, Herculano Angel Torres Montalvo, surveyed "the literary tendencies of Mexican adolescents" in 1956.[12] Neither survey says much of interest about the audience for comic books and related periodicals, but both reveal a great deal about standard academic assumptions of the time. Both took teenagers as representative of the comic book audience as a whole while also being an especially problematic or endangered group, and assumed that mass media consumption was an urban phenomenon: so the surveys used Mexico City adolescents as the sample group to stand in for the entire audience. Both assumed that *historieta* readership would be inversely related to education, and expressed surprise when their results did not show any relationship at all. And both relied on hierarchical relationships, sending university students out to examine (generally) poorer and (always) younger subjects, while the oldest, most authoritative men designed the questions and interpreted the answers.[13]

In sum, the experts who examined and described comic book readers were all participating in a broader project: the development of a critique of Mexican modernity from within the discourse of modernity. These scholars and journalists viewed Mexico's industrialization and urbanization as inevitable, and beneficial overall, but they highlighted progress by pointing out what they viewed as its darker effects: the increasingly visible misery of poor people in the cities. At the same time, the experts sought to displace the blame for such misery from modernity itself or from modernity's beneficiaries (a group to which they belonged, after all). Instead, they moved back and forth between ascribing urban poverty to poor people's values and behavior (in this case, their passive willingness to consume too much cheap entertainment) and blaming the troublesome values and behavior on the cheap entertainment.

THE MODERN GIRL

In comic books, as in Mexican cinema and recorded popular music in this era, the discourses of modernity and tradition formed primarily around the representation of women. The contrast between the (invented) past and the (imagined) future was played out in stories that valorized either *chicas modernas* or traditional women, but displayed both. The stereotypical traditional women stayed at home, preferably in rural areas. They subjected themselves to their husbands, fathers, and sons—or if necessary, they used deceit and manipulation to maintain the appearance of subservience. They never directly expressed a desire and avoided presenting themselves as sexual objects. *Chicas modernas*, on the other hand, obeyed nobody—except, perhaps, an employer. They were up-to-date consumers who tried to appear desirable and expected companionate marriages. They were impatient and could speak bluntly, but were honest, chaste before marriage and faithful afterward.

Mass media deployed both stereotypes as they participated in the development of both lines of cultural argument. After 1940, however—the year that marked the transition from the administration of Lázaro Cardenas, which had relied heavily on the language of progress, to the Avila Camacho administration, which used both languages—the picture of this modern girl painted by most forms of media grew pro-gressively uglier, while the traditional woman's portrait gained a far rosier tint. Only a few forms of popular culture (certain song genres, burlesque and variety theater, and to a certain extent, *Pepín*) resisted this trend. An editorial in *El Hombre Libre* recognized the survival of the *chica moderna* in lyrics when it complained that "songs like *Adelita*," the most popular of all revolutionary ballads, "must result in moral and intellectual retardation."[14] In this period, *historieta* narratives invariably presented traditional wom-anhood in a flattering light. Yet they also continued to offer stories valorizing the *chicas modernas*.

It was well known that the ranks of comic book producers included some real-life *chicas modernas*, who wore suits to their offices, competed with men, and sometimes even went on working after marriage. The single most successful author of comic book scripts, Yolanda Vargas Dulché, was one such modern type. Her astonishing narrative gift lifted her from poverty to riches, beginning when—still a teenager—she submitted her short stories to newspapers. Among the many *historietas* she created were two of the most popular ever—*Memín Pingüin* and *Lágrimas, Risas y Amor*; she wrote scripts for hugely successful radio dramas, films, and *telenovelas*; and her work made her husband's comic book business, Editorial Argumentos, into one of Mexico's largest publishing companies (it is now directed by their sons).[15] Vargas Dulché also pushed the boundaries of female propriety, not only by working well past marriage and the birth of her children but also by leaving the country, as a young woman, to try her luck as a nightclub singer in Cuba.[16] Usually, the heroines of Vargas Dulché's narratives—good wives and mothers, downtrodden servant girls, hardworking clerks, and the like—did not lead lives as daring as their creator's own. For the most part, she reserved such adventures for her wonderful villainesses, like Raratonga, "a jungle queen . . . equally comfortable on her island and at the corporate headquarters of her transnational empire."[17]

The *chica moderna* as heroine was an important trope in *historietas* almost from their inception, especially in the work of *Pepín*'s most prolific writer, José G. Cruz. Whether or not Josefina was directly responsible for it, José Cruz's work in the 1930s and 1940s por-trayed independent, active, powerful women as attractive and moral characters. Readers eavesdropped as they thought out loud about pressing gender questions.

In Cruz's "Adelita y las guerrillas," the *chica moderna* Nancy (the character who was born in Mexico City) often made the case for the pleasures of life as a modern girl while sometimes requiring rescue by the slightly more circumspect title character, Adelita. In a 1941 episode, the two friends discuss Nancy's romantic prospects in Adelita's luxurious Mexico City apartment as they prepare for an evening out on the town. Nancy criticizes her new beau:

I never could fall in love with a man like him. . . . This man dreams of the classic peaceful home: to arrive at night after work and to glimpse from afar the tranquil form of his wife waiting for him in a white robe, with the newspaper ready for him in one hand and his slippers in the other. . . . He thinks of love the way my grandfather did, he is a gentleman and he will be the ideal man for it but . . . *I don't want it!* I dream of love, but in another way, with a man with modern, advanced ideas. The rhythm of the times requires that everything moves along with it; even matrimony itself, though still preserving some of its old characteristics, shows us new facets and a certain undeniable modernity.

Adelita replies:

It could be that you are right in some ways, above all because you are a girl with ultra-modern ideas and character.
    Nancy continues: If you knew where he takes me (sigh). . . . He takes me to visit his relatives!!
    Adelita: I can't believe it! What for?
    Nancy: I don't know . . . maybe so that they can approve his choice. . . . His relatives asked me, no less, when I made my first communion and if my mother and father were legally married. . . . And now we are going to visit Aunt Carmela.
    Adelita: B-but you won't go, will you? . . . So what will you tell [him]?
    Nancy: That I want to go to the wrestling matches, even if I have to pay for the tickets."[18]

Here, José Cruz (perhaps with the help of his sister Josefina) envisions a marriage based on shared activities, sexual attraction, and emotional attachment, a marriage made solely in the interests of the couple involved. To this "ultra-modern" idea, the author opposed the "classic" picture of a marriage made to benefit the entire extended family, with the pleasure of the husband and wife being of much lower priority than the respectability and social status of everyone involved. The passage even implies some disdain for traditional womanhood, in the form of the man's snoopy relatives—though they stay out of sight. In this story, a woman can earn and spend her own money, present herself as a sexual object (throughout the scene, Adelita and Nancy are applying makeup, fixing each others' hair, and picking out fancy evening clothes), and speak disrespectfully of the older generation without feeling ashamed, losing her dignity, or suffering some horrible fate in the final chapter. In fact, the entire narrative, not only this passage, presents the case for this new picture of Mexican womanhood and new style of heterosexual pair bond: Nancy does indeed reject her old-fashioned swain.

The modernist content of *Adelita y las guerrillas* should not be exaggerated. Some of the strip's other female characters acted in more traditional ways. Adelita and Nancy were clearly portrayed as being at the far end of a spectrum of acceptable female behavior. Furthermore, they never appear to be frustrated by the limited possibilities open to women of their time and place, nor seriously annoyed by male behavior or attitudes; they enjoy being girls. And the narrative logic behind their endlessly drawn out engagements appears to have been the unexpressed idea that, when they finally married, they would have to stop having their fabulous adventures.

Yet, even with all these limits, it is easy to see how shocking the Adelita stories might have been, particularly since the pictures told the audience how attractive these new women could be, while the text constantly underlined their new, modern, antitraditional stance. Adelita also shared her name with the most famous song of the Mexican Revolution. Cruz meant her to be seen as profoundly Mexican, playing roles that other Mexican women had enacted before her, and connected to the most important events of the Mexican past. Her name told fans and critics alike that Adelita could not be dismissed as a foreigner.

Adelita and Nancy were not unique. Other popular comic and dramatic serials also presented continuing female characters who were pleasure-seeking rather than long-suffering, including the extremely successful Gabriel Vargas comic book, *La Fanilia Burrón*. Ten years after Nancy and Adelita held the conversation reproduced above, Vargas wrote a scene in which the middle-aged housewife, Doña Borala, mother of the comic-book Burrón family, proudly listed the priorities she shared with her teenage daughter: "We modern girls, *first* we learn to dance, flirt and smoke and then later to cook, to sew and to embroider."[19]

Comic book stories sometimes presented the modernist critique of urban poverty—characterizing the lives of poor people in the cities as chaotic, pleasure-seeking, and aimless—though not precisely in the scholarly mode of sociology and anthropology. A 1942 serial in *Pepín* showed a man infecting his girlfriend with an unspecified venereal disease through a single kiss, supposedly, although everyone in the story behaves as though this kiss stood for a sexual relationship. The couple dies, but the woman goes to heaven because she was "innocent" and "faithful."[20] This is an extreme case; comics rarely mentioned sexually transmitted diseases. Premarital pregnancy, however, was so common a plot device that it appears in perhaps half of all romance or true-life-story *historietas* after 1950.

Whether they emphasized the pleasures or dangers that modernity held for Mexican women, comic book narratives helped to define what modernity meant. Like movies and radio dramas, theater and dance music, and tabloid journalism and women's magazines, *historietas* showed readers how "modern girls" looked and acted, what might be expected of them, and what they might expect from the world. But even as they were elaborating on this image, the comics were also participating in the construction of a counter-narrative of "tradition."

OLD STORIES AND NEW

The experts' negative assessments of comic book readers came from within the Mexican discourse of modernity. But the comic books themselves were considerably more complex in the assumptions they made about their own audience. They spoke both the language of tradition and modernity; in fact, they often managed to deploy both discourses in a single story. This can be seen in a close reading of a single serial from mid-century: *El Viejo Nido* (The old nest), printed in *Pepín* in brief daily installments between Sunday, July 24, 1949, and Tuesday, December 20, 1949.[21]

El Viejo Nido was drawn by a longtime contributor to *Pepín*, Guillermo Mann; it was written by Fernando Casillas V., whose name never appeared in the comic book before this serial began publication. Nothing distinguished *El Viejo Nido*: no contests were associated with it, no advertisements mentioned it, and it was featured on *Pepín*'s cover only eight times in the fifty issues in which it was published. Nor was it exceptionally titillating: there were no shocking sex scenes and violence consisted merely of punches and slaps, mostly in a boxing ring. *El Viejo Nido* was as close to typical as any of the hundreds of serialized narratives published in the daily comic books between 1934 and 1950.

Much of the serial's content was dictated by its form. Like the other serials running in *Pepín* at the time, *El Viejo Nido* appeared in daily episodes of five to seven pages, most divided horizontally into two panels. Each episode, therefore, rarely contained more than twelve panels. This allowed room for a maximum of twenty lines of dialogue per installment, and often far less.[22] The story had little space for verbal flourishes; instead, the pictures had to convey the nuances. Mann's illustrations informed the audience of the characters' personalities, explained what the social status of each household was, and announced the precise location of every scene. The words of *El Viejo Nido* might be pared down to a dry minimum, but its rich visual detail more than made up for any deficiencies.

El Viejo Nido tells a complex tale. Its complications include a large number of characters: two protagonists, eight important secondary figures, and innumerable "bit players."[23] Moreover, several secondary characters abruptly switch from being virtuous to evil (or vice versa) in the course of the action. The number of locations adds to the difficulty. The pace of the story, too, can be confusing: sometimes the events of a single day occupy several installments and sometimes months of fictional time seem to have passed in the gap between two episodes.

But in other ways, *El Viejo Nido* is quite simple. The visual and verbal language has been stripped of all complexity. The script, while perfectly grammatical, employs the most basic Spanish. It avoids subjunctive and compound tenses and uses a sharply limited vocabulary.[24] The pictures, as well, contribute to the ease with which the story may be followed. They never show one thing while the script talks about another. The artist uses a few readily understandable icons—hearts, question marks, flying drops of sweat—but otherwise eschews abstraction. The human figures and inanimate objects in *El Viejo Nido* are realistically proportioned, and drawn with the proper perspective and shading to give them a solid, believable appearance. Like the words, the pictures require very little effort (or experience with reading comics) to be understood.[25]

The plot structure of *El Viejo Nido*, too, is not complicated. Readers learn of events in the exact order in which they are supposed to have happened. There are no flashbacks, flash-forwards, or dream sequences. There is scarcely a "meanwhile."[26] Yet the story of *El Viejo Nido*, though told in an easily comprehensible form, is convoluted and long. At the same time that the style betrays a certain anxiety over the naïveté of the audience, the length and richness of the story reveal great faith in the readers' patience and memory.

These omissions and inclusions, simplifications and convolutions, were absolutely typical of the comic book serials that were so popular in mid-century Mexico. What do they say about the audience? The creators of *El Viejo Nido* produced a tale for unskilled readers and viewers, who had some experience at listening to long stories. And the serial (which carefully incorporated scenes of settled domestic life and youthful passion, boxing matches and fashion shows, life in high-rise office buildings and rural shacks) reached for an audience that stretched across lines of age, class, and sex.

The drama of *El Viejo Nido* revolved around a series of family crises caused by a move from country to city, a transition that nearly everyone involved in the periodical industry at this time had made. Writers, artists, entrepreneurs: all lived and worked in Mexico City, though few had been born there; all were struggling upward from poverty toward middle-class status or even the riches that a few of them attained; and all, as the industry was so new, were engaged in a different business from that of their parents.[27] The men and women who produced Mexican comic books encouraged their readers to identify with the characters and producers of *historietas*, but such identification ran in the other direction, too: to some extent, they told the stories they knew.

Three issues—gender relations, representations of modernity, and anxieties over migration—are central to *El Viejo Nido* (and, by extension, to all comic book tales from this period). Readers should come to these topics with a clear understanding of how heavily they weigh in the story as a whole. Therefore, a recounting of much of the plot of *El Viejo Nido* is in order here.

The serial begins in a small town. Other locations will be carefully specified, but this fictional place remains merely "a village [*pueblito*] in the interior of the Republic," which might be any reader's hometown.[28] Outside the front door of a tiny house surrounded by identical houses, José—a handsome young man in a suit—is making his farewells to his parents and home, as his "adventurous character" has impelled him away.[29] His grayhaired parents bless him, warn him against bad companions, and exhort him to behave well. José's mother, Julia, complains that he was the last of their children to leave—"Alvaro is there at the university in Mexico City. . . . Elvira got married"—while her husband, Marcial, reassures her that, at least, "every day we love each other more."[30]

El Viejo Nido, however, does not revolve around José's story; readers will not see him again until the final crisis of the plot. Instead, the next episode introduces Don Refugio Suarez, a banker "with a heart of stone."[31] He will foreclose on the old couple's house unless Alvaro begins sending money home to repay the debt his parents incurred in financing his education. At the banker's house, Julia meets his beautiful, virtuous daughter, Consuelo. Consuelo, who immediately befriends the visiting debtor, asks her father to forgive the loan; he shouts back, "Get to the kitchen!"[32]

The next day, Marcial comes home with a young man named Luis. He tries to explain what Julia has already guessed:

Neither in my youth nor when I entered adulthood was I any kind of saint. I had many faults which I am not going to try and excuse, as these are things that now have no cure. . . . I met a woman and—I don't know if I loved her or not but—the fact is that Luis . . .[33]

Julia interrupts: she knows Luis is his son. She has been feigning ignorance for years in order to avoid "embittering our lives."[34] Marcial wants to introduce his son into their household, since the young man's mother has died; Julia is dubious but accedes graciously to her husband's wishes.

Luis immediately alarms them by announcing that he intends to earn his living as a boxer. Once again, however, *El Viejo Nido* defies expectations: it does not become a story about generational conflict, it does not require Luis to defy his family in pursuit of his dream. Instead, the young man quickly finds work to help support Marcial and

Julia, and he does more than his share of the work at home, too. By contrast, the married daughter Elvira visits only to complain about her own children and her servants. She tells her father that Luis is "a son of yours but not a brother of mine."[35] Her visiting brother Alvaro adds, "If you were to recognize all the children you have had, I suppose that this house would not have room for them all."[36]

When a doctor warns Marcial that too much hard work will kill him, Julia takes a job as a seamstress while Luis cooks the meals at home and works in a shoe factory. One night, the dutiful but ambitious young man sneaks out of the house to enter a boxing match. He meets the local boxing promoter, Chato, and with his advice, first beats the local champion and then a professional in a nearby town. Chato greets him on his triumphant return, insisting that he take to the road as a traveling boxer. Luis, indecisive, returns to his house, only to find that Marcial has died.

Elvira and Alvaro argue over who will take charge of their mother now. Julia wants to stay in her house with Luis. Alvaro, however, tells Luis to go.

Outside, Luis encounters Consuelo, who tells him that she will not enter the little house. She fears Alvaro, whose attentions she has already rejected. Alvaro and Elvira finally depart; although Consuelo reunites Julia and Luis, he decides to take up Chato's offer of a boxing tour. Consuelo bids him farewell with a tender kiss.

Luis wins bouts all over Mexico. Alvaro remains in the village with his broken-hearted mother, who believes that Luis has forgotten her. (In fact, Luis sends money and letters, but Alvaro intercepts them.) Elvira abruptly moves to Mexico City when her husband finds a job there, happy to "leave this filthy little town."[37] Her mother admits tearfully, "If I were to leave this town, I would die." Alvaro retorts, "You wish that everyone else would stay here too; but . . . there must be progress."[38]

Alvaro, too, plans to go, but he hopes first to marry Consuelo. He drunkenly tries to kiss her in front of a group of his male friends. She slaps his face and his friends laugh. Swearing revenge, Alvaro bets his friends that he can spend the night with her. He forges a note from Julia, saying that she is ill. Consuelo, defying her father's orders, rushes to Julia's house, but she is away for the night. Alvaro locks Consuelo in and hides on the patio to await his friends' arrival at dawn, in time to see her run out. Soon, the whole town believes that Consuelo has disgraced herself. Alvaro departs for Mexico City to begin his career as a lawyer, leaving his mother to face the wrath of banker Suarez, Consuelo's father.

The banker calls in Julia's debt, selling her home and forcing her to move into his house as a servant. There, she is humiliated and starved. But Consuelo assures her that Luis has not forgotten them. Even though Luis has not contacted Consuelo, fearing that to do so would anger her father, the young woman believes his promise that once he has earned a world championship (and his fortune), he will return. Julia finds consolation in religion, but she grows so hungry that she begs food from the neighbors. Someone hands her meat wrapped in an old newspaper; too tired to read it, she misses the photograph of Alvaro, with a pretty blond member "of the most distinguished metropolitan society" on his arm.[39] The family's fragmentation is now complete.

Luis, meanwhile, concentrates on his career. Since Julia never received his letters, she has not written back. Assuming that she "prefers to forget me," Luis trusts that Alvaro has remained with Julia to take care of her.[40] Thus, Luis is infuriated when Alvaro visits him in Chato's Mexico City gym. When Alvaro flees, Luis finds his office address in the phone book and confronts him. Alvaro claims that he supports Julia. He teases Luis about Consuelo's ruined reputation, giving Luis a version of the story that leaves out his own part in the matter. Luis refuses to believe it, but his ruined concentration leads him to lose boxing matches.

Chato traces his boxer's decline to the encounter with Alvaro and returns to the village to discover the truth. He finds Julia, by chance, on the street. She is delighted to hear about Luis's career, and reassures Chato of Consuelo's virtue and loyalty. Wishing not to worry Luis on the eve of his championship bout, she also claims that Alvaro is supporting her and that she is living comfortably in her old house. Chato repeats all this to Luis, who decides not to visit them until he has gained the championship.

Back in the city, Alvaro is arrested for extorting money from "unwary people" in his law practice.[41] Reading this in the newspaper, Luis rushes to the jail to bail him out. Alvaro, shamed by the goodness of Luis, confesses to his half brother that all the gossip about Consuelo was only the result of his trickery. He also accepts Luis's money to give to Julia. Luis goes away satisfied, but Alvaro thinks, "Luis believes that I am going to change, but I am not very sure. Even I myself don't know yet."[42]

Meanwhile, Julia collapses from overwork. As she lies near death, the evil banker orders his daughter, Consuelo, to "throw her out on the street."[43] Consuelo arranges for an ambulance and sends a letter begging Luis to return. Her outraged father chases the ambulance down the street through a rainstorm, then returns home and knocks Consuelo unconscious. He is suddenly stricken with pneumonia, however, brought on the doctor explains—by rage and wet clothing. Suarez dies soon after, but torments Consuelo even from the grave: his will disinherits her, and she is left penniless and homeless.

In New York City, Luis wins his championship bout. Afterward, Jose, the half brother whose departure set the whole story in motion, visits Luis in his dressing room, simply to congratulate someone from his distant hometown. Jose is ignorant of all that has happened since his departure, but the two men soon realize their connection and form a friendship. Back in his hotel room, Luis finds Consuelo's desperate letter. He insists on their immediate departure, bringing Jose with him despite his protest, "I have a job here."[44]

On returning to Mexico City, Luis punches Alvaro in the head as punishment for his failure to support Julia. Then Luis sends Alvaro to collect Elvira. At last, all three of Julia's children, along with Luis and Chato, take the train back home, where—to their horror—they find their old house boarded up and for sale. Julia, meanwhile, wakes in the hospital to discover that her illness has passed. Regretful, she asks, "Oh God, why did you not take me to you? I will only suffer again."[45]

Suddenly, her three children appear to promise her, in Alvaro's words, that "all the sufferings that I caused you, I will change to happiness—I will never be separated from you again!"[46] Luis, having repurchased Julia's home, joins the happy family in the hospital. He announces that soon Julia will have another daughter as well, and Julia replies that Consuelo, too, already "has treated me as if she were my child."[47] Alvaro assures his mother that both Luis and Consuelo have pardoned him, thus resolving her last anxiety: "I see that you have repented," Julia says.[48]

At the doorway of the family home, Consuelo and Luis kiss passionately. The last frame of the serial pulls away from the happy couple to a shot of the whole house with a sunrise behind it and the caption, "Once again there was warmth in *the old nest*."[49]

THE AUDIENCE DEFINES ITSELF

Of all the groups of people who argued about the dangers, pleasures, and profits of comic books in Mexico, the audience had the least audible voice. They spoke, for the most part, only with their centavos and pesos. Little remains of the contemporary responses of these consumers. Comic book companies appear not to have bothered with market surveys nor to have preserved reader letters.[50] Traces of the readers, however, can be found in the comic books themselves: in the readers' photos, drawings, and stories *de la vida real* that helped to fill so many pages. And when we turn to the one space in comic books where readers did speak directly to each other, we find them telling some very dramatic (if radically simplified) tales about themselves.

Readers were often given the chance to publish lonely hearts or pen-pal advertisements in their favorite periodicals. The truthfulness of their voices need not concern us. The underlying values and habits of thought that were expressed—even in such a mediated form—clearly and consistently speak through the discourse of tradition that Mexican media helped to invent in this era. The discourse of modernity was not the one that readers chose to use in describing themselves and their world.

Lonely hearts advertisements first appeared around 1945 in a women's magazine, *Confidencias*, that also sometimes ran photonovel-style romances. They entered the comics in 1948, in *Paquito Grande*, a *historieta* that specialized in romantic serials. Free to both advertisers and respondents, they were a bargain as well for the publishers, as they provided a page of interesting filler in every issue for only the price of setting type and forwarding mail. And, in some cases, they must have engendered intense reader loyalty, for they occasionally helped to create happily married couples (the magazines would, of course, print wedding photos and even anniversary pictures), and in at least one instance, they really did reunite long-estranged family members—oddly enough, the "Sanchez" family studied by Lewis was brought together with some Veracruz cousins thanks to an ad in *Pepín*.[51]

Such pages of personal ads have been one of the most popular and enduring features of Mexican comic books. The appeal of the ads in *Paquito Grande* can be seen in the prominent place that the lonely hearts page held for at least three and a half years: the inside front cover. During and after the era of *Paquito Grande*'s greatest popularity, similar features ran in *Historietas* (1954–55, under the title "My Heart in an Envelope") and many other comic books. They can still be seen today, on a greatly reduced scale, in *Libro Semanal, Libro Pasional*, and other romance comics.

Lonely hearts advertisers sometimes shaped their brief texts into chapters from the romance serials. They represent themselves, but they also represent stock characters; they tell pieces of their life stories, but they also retell tales that they and their readers have read many times before. Here is one:

I am Mexican, white, average height, of ordinary cultivation, 20 years old and without vices. I find myself locked up in the Mexico City penitentiary, and to remake my life I need the hand of an understanding little lady who would send me a little letter to fill me with courage and spirit.[52]

And another:

I am looking for a friendly heart who could relieve my hours of loneliness. I am a young man but I have failed in life. If there is a reader who feels the same need for a soul like her own, write me, you will not regret it. I come from the state of Puebla.[53]

And a third:

I want to establish a correspondence with a gentleman no older than 38, it would not matter if he was a widower with one or two darling little children as long as he had no vices, was moderately cultivated, hardworking and honest. I am 25 and not pretty, but I am friendly and have a jovial, sincere nature. I want the gentleman who writes to have the aim of forming a firm household, which is what I pray for. I ask for your absolute sincerity and am not looking for adventures.[54]

These writers seem to be hoping to turn their lives into *historietas* as much as, perhaps more than, they yearn for companionship.

Moving beyond individual cases, the aggregate of the personal ads contains equally suggestive evidence about the mentality of the comic book audience. Between 1949 and 1952 (the years for which some issues can be found in the Hemeroteca Nacional's archive), *Paquito Grande* ran ten to twenty such advertisements in every issue, producing a completely new page twice a week. The tens of thousands of resulting advertisements cannot be taken as unvarnished fact, of course.[55] Moreover, the advertisers were a self-selected group of unattached readers, unlikely to be completely representative of the entire comic book audience. Still, these advertisements do offer a blurry collective self-portrait. Their language reveals what the advertisers, as a group, believed desirable traits to be in men and women.[56] Almost all the ads followed a strict formula and used a limited vocabulary. (This rigid form is all the more remarkable since the ads were unedited and cost nothing.) Looking at the words that advertisers choose to describe themselves and their ideal mates, certain conclusions about their values, ambitions, and worldviews become inescapable.

Religion mattered deeply; 58 percent of the ads displayed this concern by either announcing that the advertiser was Catholic or requesting that the respondent be, or both (the percentage is slightly higher for women and lower for men). Of course, far more than 58 percent of the Mexican population was Catholic at mid-century; anyone reading the advertisement could have been assumed to be Catholic. The point for these advertisers was not simply to state the obvious, but to show that they took their religion seriously—despite their involvement with comic books. The leaders of the Catholic Church had long since created a connection in the public discourse between reading comic books and various forms of sinfulness. The advertisers who called themselves Catholics, or were looking for Catholic partners, knew that and were trying to disassociate themselves from such a connection.[57]

Moral character, along with religious affiliation, was the most important descriptive category to advertisers. "Formal"—that is, capable of behaving within the bounds of propriety—was a desirable trait for 43 percent of both males and females in describing either themselves or a mate. Other moral concerns were expressed in highly gendered language. An attractive man would be "without vices" (*sin vicios*) (61 percent of the men described themselves in this manner, while 54 percent of the women sought this in their ideal partner), and "hardworking" (*trabajador* or *muy trabajador*) (similarly, this was a self-description for 41 percent of the men and a desirable trait in a mate for 28 percent of the women). Some women (16 percent) also hoped for a "gentleman" (*caballero*). All of these terms had an economic dimension: for instance, men *sin vicios* were men, very specifically, who did not smoke or drink, and therefore, could be trusted not to waste family money.

Women's moral character mattered, too, although, the terms that described them or that they picked to describe themselves had no economic implications. Women were supposed to be "simple" (*sencilla*) (a self-description for 22 percent of the women and a trait in an ideal partner for 35 percent of the men), and "home-loving" (*hogeña*) (again, 24 percent of the women described themselves this way and 24 percent of the men described a desirable respondent as such). A few men hoped to find a "kindly" (*amable*) (6 percent), "agreeable" (*agradable*) (12 percent, with 19 percent of women describing themselves), and "affectionate" (*cariñosa*) (13 percent) mate.

Words that indirectly suggest social status overlapped the category of words dealing with morality and religion. An astonishing total of 78 percent of the female advertisers and 60 percent of the males specified their degree of education by employing some version of a phrase with strong connotations of social class: 68 percent of the women and 48 percent of the men presented themselves as "cultivated" (*culto/a* or *de buena cultura*); 12 percent of the men and 10 percent of the women advertised themselves as "not too cultivated" (*poco culto/a*). Similarly, the 18 percent who described themselves as "well-mannered" (*educado/a*) were matched by the 28 percent who called themselves or their perfect mate "humble" or "from humble beginnings" (*humilde* or *de cuña humilde*). Two percent of all respondents went so far as to label themselves *pobre*, and all of them were also looking for a "poor" mate. Advertisers, as a group, seemed less concerned about inflating their status than they were with finding a match neither too far above nor too far beneath them socially.

Advertisers in *Eslabones Espirituales* (Spiritual Bonds) cared about looks only to the extent that appearance reflected class. Twenty-nine percent of them either felt themselves to be, or wanted someone who was, "presentable" (*bien parecido/a*), while only 9 percent called themselves or their dream date "beautiful" or "handsome" (*guapo/a*). Three percent of the men even described themselves as "ugly" (*feo*); similarly, 13 percent of the women said that they were "neither pretty nor ugly" (*ni fea ni bonita*). Their concern here seemed to be maintaining modesty while still providing potential mates with some identifying information. The fine details of skin and hair that place Mexicans in their precise spot on the racial map frequently appear in these ads, as with the 11 percent who reveal their hair texture and the 30 percent who use some variation of "brown-skinned" (*moreno/a*) to portray themselves. Another indication of the class status of most *Paquito Grande* readers is that only 9 percent of the men and 7 percent of the women called themselves "white," and a mere 2 percent of both sexes hoped for a "white" mate.

Kinship and marital status had a less consistent vocabulary than other important descriptive categories found in these personal ads; still, roughly a third of the ads referred to children or previous spouses in some way. Nineteen percent of the women announced that they wanted a man "without other ties" (*sin compromisos*), but only 5 percent of the men described themselves that way. Six percent of the men identified themselves as "unmarried" (*soltero*), but less than 1 percent of the women used the feminine form, *soltera*, with its connotation of spinsterhood, to describe themselves. Two percent of the men and 1 percent of the women said that they were widowed. Three percent of the women said that they already had children, while only 1 percent of the men announced that they wanted a childless mate. Conversely, 4 percent of the men specifically requested a "widow or divorced woman." A small number sought to reassure potential mates of their good intentions: 4 percent of the men and 3 percent of the women wrote that they were "not in search of adventures," with a specifically sexual connotation, while 3 percent of the men and 2 percent of the women declared their goals in placing the advertisement to be "serious" or "matrimonial," and another 3 percent of the men and 1 percent of the women said that they wanted "to form a home" with a new mate.

Choice of profession or leisure activity mattered little to this group. Unlike descriptions of appearance, education, or behavior, words referring to work or play did not seem to serve the secondary function of implying social class. Fewer than 10 percent of the men and 4 percent of the women mentioned what they did for a living. (Another 4 percent of the men and 1 percent of the women said that they were students.) The range of employment mentioned was quite wide, however, from small business owners and factory workers to lawyers and accountants. Hobbies and recreation mattered even less to advertisers. Only 3 percent mentioned an interest in movies; another 2 percent said they liked to dance; and 4 percent enjoyed sports. Not a single advertiser said that he or she read comic books.

This collective self-portrait should be read against the stories that *Paquito Grande* published, narratives from other comic books (such as *El Viejo Nido*), and the criticisms of comic books that were raised during the first censorship campaign. The central objection to the pepines was that they contributed to the corruption of the nation by showing sexually active women as well as romances that broke the bounds of propriety in various ways. *Paquito Grande* did describe such behavior, in its decorous and moralistic manner. Premarital pregnancies, usually involving secondary characters, often advanced the plots of its serials. The motor of many stories in the comic book was a relationship between inappropriate people, such as employees and employers, who insisted on making a life together despite opposition from society in general and their families in particular. Female characters often held jobs, ranging from domestic work and clerical work to factory work, waitressing, and teaching. Such comic book romantic narratives might be read as valorizing economic independence for women, affectionate relationships based on shared interests, and romantic love and sexual pleasure even for poor women, as well as across class and race lines.

The readers of *Paquito Grande* who placed lonely hearts advertisements, to judge by their own words, had absorbed none of these values. Instead, they clung to the moral code underpinning such apparently racy serials, the moral code that structured the plot of *El Viejo Nido*: they believed in a firm set of hierarchies—based on kinship, class, and gender—that organized their world no matter where they found themselves. The advertisers evidently were not looking for "adventures," sexual freedom, or the thrill of vice; nor were they searching for companionate, egalitarian unions. They distinguished clearly between acceptable traits for men and women, while believing that both men and women should conform to religious and social expectations appropriate to their carefully delineated class and kinship positions.

Advertisers were willing to look for love outside their own locality; relations that began in the pages of *Paquito Grande* lacked the implicit approval of family or community. To that extent, they were as untraditional, or "corrupt," as the anti-comic-book crusaders feared. Yet most advertisers placed no importance on shared interests with a potential romantic partner, and they did want him or her to be of the appropriate social status. They did not care much about sexual attraction; thus, they did not emphasize their own or their partners' looks beyond what was necessary to ensure that no socially awkward mismatch would occur. Questions of character and morality within marriage deeply concerned them.

The men and women who advertised themselves in *Eslabones Espirituales* presented themselves as, and desired to marry, people who had avoided the vices of modernity and the big city. Perhaps we cannot believe what the advertisers said about themselves. Probably, though, we can assume that what they said represented what they wished were true and believed ought to be true. If so, to judge by this, the fears of the anti-comic book campaigners were groundless: like the *historietas* themselves, their audience upheld deeply conservative values and patterns of life in the face of all the pressures of urbanization, migration, and industrialization. What, then, motivated some Mexicans to express profound hostility toward the comics and to fear their power to corrupt readers?

NOTES

1. See Robert Redfield and Milton Singer, "The Cultural Role of Cities," *Economic Development and Social Change* 3 (1954), and *Tepoztlan* (Chicago: University of Chicago Press, 1930); Luis Gonzalez y Gonzalez, *Invitación a la microhistoria* (Mexico City: Secretaria de Educacion Publica, 1973); Guillermo Bonfil Batalla, *Mexico profundo* (Mexico City: Secretaria de Educacion Publica, 1987); Steve J. Stern, *The Secret History of Gender: Women, Men, and Power in Late Colonial Mexico* (Chapel Hill: University of North Carolina Press, 1995), 309; and Alan Knight, "The Peculiarities of Mexican History," *Journal of Latin American Studies*, suppl. (1992), and "Revolutionary Project, Recalcitrant People: Mexico, 1910–1940," in *The Revolutionary Process in Mexico*, ed. Jaime Rodriquez O. (Berkeley: University of California Press, 1990).

2. Adriana Malvido and Teresa Martinez Arana, "La historieta en Mexico: un mundo ancho y ajenjo," *Casa del tiempo* 42 (July 1984): 19.

3. Oscar Lewis, *The Children of Sanchez* (New York: Random House, 1961), xxiii.

4. Ibid., 44.

5. Ibid., 133.

6. Quoted in Alan Riding, *Distant Neighbors* (New York: Knopf, 1984), 354–55.

7. Larissa Adler Lomnitz, *Networks and Marginality: Life in a Mexican Shantytown* (New York: Academic Press, 1977), 182.

8. Jonathan Kandell, *La Capital* (New York: Random House, 1988), 506.

9. Ariel Dorfman and Armand Mattelart, *How to Read Donald Duck: Imperialist Ideology in the Disney Comic*, trans. David Kunzle (New York: International General, 1975).

10. Dick Reavis, *Conversations with Moctezuma* (New York: William Morrow, 1990), 213.

11. Irene Herner, *Mitos y monitos* (Mexico City: Editorial Nueva Imagen, 1979), xi.

12. These are the only statistical analyses of the audience that I could find, except for those published by Herner, *Mitos y monitos*, and Harold Hinds Jr. and Charles Tatum, *Not Just for Children: The Mexican Comic Book in the Late 1960s and 1970s* (Westport: Greenwood Press, 1992).

13. The broad conclusions of these surveys are worth reporting, if only because they agree, generally, with data collected a quarter century later (Herner, *Mitos y monitos*, 111–33); Hinds and Tatum, *Not Just for Children*, 16–20): roughly a third of the population admitted to reading at least one comic book per week, and the audience was split more or less evenly between men and women.

14. "Que puede esperarse de una Juventud a la que se ha procurado prostituir?" *El Hombre Libre* 2053, June 18, 1944, 1.

15. Lágrimas, Risas y Amor, and Memín Pingüín began publication in the 1950s and lasted until 1997, placing them among the most durable narratives in Mexican media. Yolanda Vargas Dulché's first book of short stories (1944), two of her radio drama scripts (1943, 1946), and a film script (1944) can all be found in Archivo General de la Nación, Propierdad artística y literaria, files 731-543, 646-14101, 703-15676, 1178-9. These florid early works already exhibit the author's gift for engaging audiences and building suspense through the use of working-class characters and sentimentality.

16. Hinds and Tatum, *Not Just for Children*, 54, 66; Beth Miller and Alfonso Gonzalez, *26 autres de Mexico actual* (Mexico City: B. Costa-Amic Editor, 1978), 375–84; and Angelina Camargo Brena, "De escritor a editor: entrevista con Guillermo de la Parra de Editorial Argumentos," *Libros de Mexico* 5 (1986): 17–20.

17. Hinds and Tatum, *Not Just for Children*, 59.

18. *Pepín*, no 865, July 26, 1941, 12–19.

19. *La Familia Burrón*, no. 16231, July 11, 1955, 21. Conflict between the mother and the father of the Burrón family over their daughter's behavior has provided an infallible comic plot device for the four decades of the comic book's existence.

20. "Ocasa," *Pepín*, no. 1141, April 28, 1942, 12.

21. I picked this narrative as the subject for a close reading almost at random and, in part, for reasons unconnected to the purposes of this essay: its cartoonist had a particularly clear and comprehensible style, its author used relatively few extraneous subplots in constructing the story (at least by *Pepín*'s standards), and the story itself was quite concise (again, by *Pepín's* standards). Most important, the entire run of issues that included chapters of the story—numbers 3779 to 3928—were available in the Memeroteca Nacional.

22. The episode in *Pepín*, no. 3849, October 2, 1949, contained the least amount of dialogue (eight lines), while the episode in *Pepín*, no. 3843, September 26, 1949, contained the most (twenty lines).

23. On the other hand, many secondary characters fill two or more functions in the narrative, such as Chato, who acts as both a small-town boxing promoter and big-city boxing trainer (as well as the hero's best friend) at different points in the plot. This strains credulity, but it reduces the number of characters a reader must keep track of over a six-month span.

24. The installment in *Pepín*, no. 3843, which, as noted above, has more lines of dialogue than any other episode, contains 305 words. Still, it uses only twenty-four nouns, four adjectives, thirty-five verbs, and four adverbs (in various numbers, genders, and tenses), supplemented with pronouns and prepositions, and augmented by an enormous degree of repetition.

25. See Scott McCloud, *Understanding Comics* (Northampton: Tundra, 1993), 24–137.

26. This radically simplified form of narrative has come to dominate comic book plot design in Mexico, but in the first decade of the industry's existence (1934–1944), more complex modes of storytelling were common.

27. There is little evidence available on the people involved with the comic book industry during this period other than the descriptions they themselves sometimes included in their work and the testimony some of them gave before the Comision Califorcadora de Publicaciones y Revisitas Illustradas.

28. *Pepín*, 37799, July 24, 1948, 2.

29. Ibid., 5.

30. Ibid., 6.

31. *Pepín*, no. 3780, July 25, 1949, 11.

32. *Pepín*, no. 3784, July 29, 1949, 36.

33. *Pepín*, no. 3790, August 4, 1949, 34–35.

34. Ibid., 36.

35. *Pepín*, no. 3799, August 12, 1949, 21.

36. *Pepin*, no. 3802, August 16, 1949, 12.

37. *Pepín*, no. 3790, August 4, 1949, 43.

38. Ibid., 49–50.

39. *Pepín*, no. 3902, November 24, 1949, 26.

40. *Pepín*, no. 3893, November 15, 1949, 16.

41. *Pepín*, no. 3911, December 3, 1949, 30.

42. *Pepín*, no. 3913, December 5, 1949, 7.

43. *Pepín*, no. 3916, December 8, 1949, 26.

44. *Pepín*, no. 3924, December 16, 1949, 32.

45. *Pepín*, no. 3926, December 18, 1949, 5.

46. *Pepín*, no. 3927, December 19, 1949, 8.

47. *Pepín*, no. 3928, December 20, 1949, 16.

48. Ibid., 17.

49. Ibid., 20.

50. There is a single exception: Elena Poniatowska, in "Gabriel Vargas y su Familia Burro," *El Gallo illustrado: suplemento dominical de El Dia* 33 (February 10, 1963): 2, refers to a collection of letters that Vargas received, mostly containing suggestions for modifications of his long-running humor series. Cited in Hins and Tatum, *Not Just for Children*, 31.

51. Lewis, *Children of Sanchez*, 44, 81.

52. *Paquito Grande*, no. 2034B, July 5, 1950, 2.

53. *Paquito Grande*, no 2016, June 7, 1950, 2.

54. *Paquito Grande*, no 2034, January 11, 1950, 2. The phrase "not looking for adventures" here means that the writer is emphatically denying an interest in sexual adventure, rather than rejecting the possibility of romantic excitement.

55. Some statistics can be extracted from the lonely hearts page; they contain few suprises. Although *Paquito Grande* appears to have been aimed at women, 53 percent of the advertisers were male. All advertisers used the magazine as a mail drop, so there was no requirement to locate themselves. But of the 54 percent who gave an address, only a quarter lived in Mexico City. Another 23 percent had addresses in four other major cities—Guadalajara, Tampico, Tijuana, and Veracruz—but the rest were scattered evenly across the country, in small towns and rural areas. Seven percent lived outside the country, mostly in Quatemala and Texas. The median age for male advertisers was twenty; for female advertisers, seventeen. Yet, since this was a group of readers looking for marriage partners, the statistics say little about the comic book audience as a whole. The range of ages represented in the advertisements may provide a better clue: the youngest advertiser was fourteen and the oldest was fifty.

56. Both the facts and the linguistic analysis here were extracted from a database that contains approximately 600 of the ads published in *Paquito Grande* between 1949 and 1952. *Paquito Grande* actually contained about 3,600 such advertisements, but I only entered the ads from one issue in every six into the database, because the process was so time-consuming and the advertisements seemed so consistent.

57. The importance of Catholicism to readers was perceived, too, by the creators of comic books. In the introduction to a serial with the provocative title "Blasphemy," writer Antonio Gutierrez carefully explained to his audience that he was not advocating heresy: "do not judge [the story] until we get to the end. We believe it necessary to offer this warning, given the delicacy of the theme, taking into account that 90% of our readers are Catholic" (*Pepín*, no. 2752, September 9, 1946, 17).

Autobiography as Authenticity

BART BEATY

A three-page short story by Lewis Trondheim published in *Lapin* #26 outlines the stakes at play in contemporary autobiographical comics. Trondheim's autobiographical essay, "Journal du journal du journal," is a peculiar *mise-en-abyme*. Trondheim begins by depicting himself reading Fabrice Neaud's autobiographical novel *Journal (III)* (1999). On that page, Neaud depicts himself reading Dupuy and Berberian's autobiographical novel *journal d'un album* (1994). At that point in *Journal d'un album*, Philippe Dupuy depicts a momentous intersection in his personal and professional life. Having chosen, with his partner Charles Berberian, to undertake an autobiographical comic book detailing the creation of the third book in their *M. Jean* series, Dupuy shows a number of early pages to his colleagues in L'Association. Their assessment of the work is rather tough, noting that the work seems to have lost its rhythm and that it could be done more concisely. Returning home, he falls into a despairing dream before being awakened by a phone call from his father informing him that his mother has passed away. The following page encapsulates his mother's life in just six images, recalling the advice that Trondheim offers in the story: "You could do it in one page."[1]

Reading this passage in *Journal (III)*, Neaud is impressed by Dupuy's work, but finds himself enraged by the comments offered by the members of L'Association. He suggests that their inappropriate remarks may be a displacement of their inability to be interested in the lives of other people. Visually, through the use of a non-diegetic intercut, he associates the intemperate observations of the L'Association artists with the dismissive commentaries on his own work that are leveled at him by his close friend and love interest, Dominique, thereby casting aspersions on their motives.

Trondheim's essay is an exact replica of Neaud's page, drawn in Trondheim's style. Visually, the page's seven-panel grid is recreated, and the figures are placed in identical positions. Further, Trondheim duplicates the narration, shifting the details slightly from Neaud's commentary on Dupuy and L'Association, to Trondheim's commentary on Neaud's commentary on Dupuy and L'Association. Where Neaud was shocked at the opinions offered by L'Association on Dupuy's work, Trondheim is shocked that Neaud would make such basic judgments about their roles as editors and publishers. On the

Reprinted with permission of the publisher from Bart Beaty, *Unpopular Culture: Transforming the European Comic Book in the 1990s* (University of Toronto Press, 2007), 138–51.

second page of Trondheim's essay, which again visually reiterates Neaud's page, he re-reads his own first page and finds himself shocked that he would make such a rash judgment of Neaud's work. The work potentially recedes to infinity as Trondheim comments on his own commentary regarding Neaud's commentary on L'Association's comments about Dupuy's self-reflexive work. The game is in play; the text is never finished but always ripe for reinterpretation.

Clearly, Trondheim approaches the question of the autobiographical essay in a satiric and toying manner, playing with the similarities between the titles of the books and the closeness of the content initiated by Neaud. At the same time, however, his work contains a few barbs that suggest it is something more than mere whimsy. Where Neaud depicts Dominique dismissing all autobiographical writing with the phrase " *The Diary of Anne Frank*, that pisses me off. I find it badly written,"[2] Trondheim reacts to L'Association president Jean-Christophe Menu's dismissal of the mainstream genre comics of Jean Van Hamme this way: "*XIII*, that pisses me off. I find it badly written."[3] This transition re-centers the discussion away from the concerns of autobiography to those of the small press. This is an entirely apt displacement. Since the beginning of the 1990s, autobiography has become an increasingly prominent genre within the small-press and independent comics scene, with strengths in a number of European nations. Indeed, autobiography has become the genre that most distinctly defines the small-press comics production of Europe in its current revitalization. Specifically, a number of cartoonists have made the narrativization of comic book production a central signifier of authenticity in the contemporary European small-press scene.

Central to the study of autobiography has been the project of defining it as a genre distinct from biography and fiction. Philippe Lejeune's often-cited definition of the genre is widely regarded as normative: "Retrospective prose narrative written by a real person concerning his own existence, where the focus is his individual life, in particular the story of his personality."[4] Lejeune's definition has, of course, opened up number of challenges, and the policing of the boundaries of autobiography in relation to other literary forms has become a major undertaking. Indeed, it is fair to say that the study of autobiography is dominated by inquiries into the particular traits of autobiography and comparisons between autobiography and other literary forms.[5] Paul de Man, writing in 1979, indicated how these assumptions had driven the study of autobiography down a dead end:

> The theory of autobiography is plagued by a recurrent series of questions and approaches that are not simply false, in the sense that they take for granted assumptions about autobiographical discourse that are in fact highly problematic. They keep therefore being stymied, with predictable monotony, by sets of problems that are inherent in their own use. One of these problems is the attempt to define and to treat autobiography as if it were a literary genre among others.[6]

For de Man and others, theories of psychoanalysis, post-structuralism, and feminism have called into question the self-evident nature of the subject and knowledge. Post-structuralism in particular had deposed the unified subject of autobiography by positing discourse as preceding and exceeding the subject, calling the very basis of the genre's distinctiveness into question.[7] Nonetheless, the study of autobiography continues to dwell upon the questions that de Man sought to vacate, often complicating notions of "truth" and "self" in light of current theorizing, but proceding with that work of definition all the same.

Two ideas predominate in the study of autobiography: the relation of the text to historical truth and the relation of the text to the conventions of biography. Timothy Dow Adams, for example, argues, "a promise to tell the truth is one of autobiography's earliest premises."[8] He suggests that autobiography is an attempt to reconcile one's life with one's self and that therefore the core of autobiography is not historical accuracy but metaphorical truth. Philippe Lejeune identifies the "referential pact" as central to the process of autobiography:

> As opposed to all forms of fiction, biography and autobiography are *referential* texts: exactly like scientific or historical discourse, they claim to provide information about a "reality" exterior to the text, and so to submit to a test of verification. Their aim is not simple verisimilitude, but resemblance to the truth. Not "the effect of the real," but the image of the real. All referential texts thus entail what I will call a "referential pact," implicit or explicit, in which are included a definition of the field of the real that is involved and a statement of the modes and the degree of resemblance to which the text lays claim.[9]

This focus on the issue of truth—whether metaphorical or historical, simple verisimilitude or "resemblance to the truth"—fundamentally deadens the instrumentality of autobiography study. As critics have narrowed the debate to the precise definition of genre, it has become trapped in merely formal questions. The creation of autobiographical works, particularly in terms of how the form has been understood and mobilized by contemporary European comic book producers, is better thought of as a social process. Autobiography, with its implicit claims to replicate the "real world," stands in stark contrast to a European comic book heritage that has celebrated adventurous boy reporters, wisecracking Gaulish adventurers, cowboys, astronauts, and other heroes of escapist literature. Indeed, the central issue relating to the use of autobiography in contemporary comics is not whether it can be demonstrated that L'Association actually criticized Dupuy's comics or that Neaud reacted violently to reading these critiques, but rather how various authors have adopted autobiographical work as a distinctive device that sets them apart from the normative elements of the comics market. The importance of autobiography in the field of contemporary comic book production stems at least in part from the renewed importance of the genre in the field of French literature in the 1970s and 1980s. Indeed, autobiographical comics derive much of their importance from their insertion of modes of visuality into an increasingly legitimated literary genre. Writing about autobiographical tendencies in contemporary French painting, Monique Yaari suggests that the turning point for autobiography—which had been devalorized by modernism—occurred in 1975 with the publication of *Roland Barthes par Roland Barthes*, Georges Perec's *W*, and Philippe Lejeune's *Pacte autobiographique*. Subsequent years saw the release of Michel Beaujour's *Miroirs d'encre* (1980) and autobiographies from noted French intellectuals Marguerite Duras and Alain Robbe-Grillet. Similarly, in the field of painting a number of shows using on the self-portrait also helped to revitalize the genre in the 1970s.[10] Thierry Groensteen has argued that French autobiographical cartoonists drew inspiration from this revitalization of the self-portrait and the auto-biography, as well as from innovative forms of autobiographical cinema, such as those by Jean-Luc Godard, Nanni Moretti, and Cyril Collard.[11] If autobiography was in the air—and, more importantly, in the art schools—in the early 1990s, what did the new generation of cartoonists hope to achieve by adopting its form? Of all the neglected liter-ary forms, why autobiography?

In the first instance, autobiography is the genre that offers the most explicit promise of legitimizing cartoonists as authors. The death of the author pronounced by Roland Barthes in the 1960s was confirmed in the decades that followed, as Janet Staiger has pointed out, by the prevalence of post-structuralist criticism and the ubiquity of a mass-mediated marketplace of ideas.[12] According to Michel Foucault, the author-function continued to exist to the extent that the concept upheld bourgeois sensibilities about art.[13] For cartoonists, this assertion functioned as a promise. If cartoonists could assert their own identities as authors by conforming to these sensibilities and meet the expec-tations placed on artists in other fields, their social position could be improved. For cartoonists an important precursor in this regard was cinema, a medium in which the development of an auteur theory had created the social conditions under which film could come to be regarded as a legitimated art form.

At the same time, however, cartoonists were arriving late to the party, and the pos-sibility existed that these doors had already closed. From this standpoint, cartoonists occupied an aesthetically marginal space in much the same way that certain social groups were—and are—marginalized politically. As Nancy Hartsock has noted, "Why is it that just at the moment when so many of us who have been silenced begin to demand the right to name ourselves, to act as subject rather than objects of history, that just then the concept of subjecthood becomes problematic?"[14] Similarly, Julia Swindells points to the way in which autobiography itself has served as a liberating space for oppressed peoples:

> Autobiography now has the potential to be the text of the oppressed and the cultur-ally displaced, forging a right to speak both for and beyond the individual. People in a position of powerlessness—women, black people, working-class people—have more than begun to insert themselves into the culture via autobiography, via the as-sertion of "personal" voice, which speaks beyond itself.[15]

Swindells's notion of the culturally displaced inserting themselves into culture might seem particularly appealing to comic book artists of the 1990s seeking to have their work valorized as serious or important. I do not intend to claim that cartoonists belong in the same category as those who are socially and politically marginalized based on race, class, or gender. However, in terms of artistic production and the processes of legitimation, and because their chosen métier has so long been regarded as a devalued subculture intended for children, the adoption of an autobiographical tone can be seen as empowering.

Autobiography, therefore, becomes a mode which foregrounds both realism (as op-posed to the traditions of fantasy) and the sense of the author as an artist demanding legitimacy (in contrast to the view of the cartoonist as a cultural hack slaving away to turn out mass-mediated product). In the field of contemporary comic book production, autobiography holds a promise to elevate the legitimacy of both the medium and the artist. Far from propounding the death of the author, as de Man would have it, autobiography in comics holds the possibility of giving the author birth for the first time.

Arguably the most important forerunners of the recent surge in European cartooning come from the American underground comics movement of the 1960s and 1970s. Harvey Pekar is probably the most representative figure, although the importance of Robert Crumb and Justin Green as innovators should not be minimized. Pekar's *American Splendor* series began in the 1970s and is often regarded as a major departure point for realist comics production, although Pekar is not particularly widely translated in Europe. The best-known—and best-regarded—autobiographical comic in Europe to have come out of the American underground comics movement was Art Spiegelman's *Maus*. Part autobiography, part biography of his parents, Spiegelman's work dealt with the personal legacy of the Holocaust, and in particular with his parents' experiences of Auschwitz. Combining cartooning and the Holocaust allowed Spiegelman to develop a "personal voice" within the comics idiom, and his book is widely regarded as the most important "serious" comic book ever published, earning a Pulitzer Prize in 1992. The success of translated editions of *Maus* in Europe in the 1980s and 1990s was suggestive of the possibilities afforded to both autobiographical and non-conventional comic books. What the American underground demonstrated to European cartoonists was the possibility of creating comics that were primarily addressed to questions of personal subjectivity. The American underground movement was at once both a liberatory, personalizing visual aesthetic as well as a working model of authorial independence that favored personal expression above all else. The insertion of the self into the aesthetic and business practices of the underground movement suggested new possibilities for the promotion of the field of comics as an art movement, possibilities that played out in Europe in a different manner.

In the 1970s a number of cartoonists—such as Marcel Gotlib and Moebius—had begun to place their self-images into their work, often in an ironic fashion. Gotlib, for instance, frequently portrayed himself in *Rubrique-à-brac* (1970) as a megalomaniacal, beret-wearing "artiste" character. Other than such satirical efforts, however, straightforward autobiographical comics were rare in the 1980s. Readers could speculate about the relationship between the life histories of artists like Barn and Yves Chaland and the protagonists of seemingly autobiographical fiction such as *Quequette blues* (1984) and *Le Jeune Albert* (1985), but neither of these books explicitly signaled an "autobiographical pact." Their work pointed towards the viability of an autobiographical approach within the traditional full-color album format, but it did not mark the type of fundamental shift in perspective that is represented by the current generation. The precursor of that transition was Edmond Baudoin.

Baudoin helped to launch the field of autobiographical comics with his work in the 1980s for Futuropolis. *Passe le temps* (1982) and *Couma Aco* (1991) were central to the reputation of Futuropolis for publishing serious-minded, non-genre, and artist-driven works. In terms of delving into real situations and people rather than fantasies and adventure, Baudoin signified a growing sense of maturity in French cartooning, both in terms of audience expectations and personal aesthetics. With the death of Futuropolis as a publishing house in 1994, Baudoin moved much of his artistic output to L'Association, where he continued to produce autobiographical works like *Éloge de la poussière* (1995) and *Terrains vagues* (1996). His autobiographical output largely frames the possibilities inherent in the genre for a number of European cartoonists. It is important that Baudoin is not merely chronicling the passage of his life. His works are framed within poetic narratives complemented by a very loose rendering style. As such, Baudoin primarily offers meditations on his life and his personal relationships, often with women, rather straightforward accounts of his activities and reminiscences. His books contain roughly equal parts eroticism and philosophy.

In 2002 Baudoin began a new project that is typical of his interests in autobiography. *Le Chemin de Saint-Jean* is an oversized (27 x 37 cm) black-and-white book that tells of Baudoin's connection to a mountain near his childhood home in Nice. The book is structured as a series of sketches of the mountain drawn at various points in Baudoin's life. There is no narrative as such, simply a series of notes regarding the feelings and memories that the metaphorical road of the title evokes in the artist. Further, the book—like so much of Baudoin's autobiographical work—is not fixed. Because Baudoin anticipates returning to this material throughout the rest of his career, the book is described as being in "permanent elaboration."[16] The first edition of the book was given a relatively small print run of two thousand copies. Each subsequent reprinting of the book will contain new material as Baudoin develops it, allowing the text to mutate over time in much the same way that memories themselves develop and recede. Indeed, the second edition of the book (2004) was expanded in page count, but reduced to the more traditional size of the French album in L'Association's Collection Éperluette. Baudoin's poetic approach to the representation of his own memories and relationships marked a decidedly different approach to autobiographical cartooning than could be found in the work of previous European cartoonists, throwing open the door to contemporary autobiographical comics in Europe.

While Baudoin represents the most important precursor of European autobiographical comics, Marjane Satrapi better represents the critical and financial importance of autobiographical comics as a movement in Europe. Satrapi, termed the "Persian comics star" by the French daily *Libération*,[17] is among the most commercially successful of the new generation of European small-press cartoonists. Her four-volume autobiographical comic book, *Persepolis*, has been translated into numerous European languages, and an English-language edition was published by Pantheon—the publishers of *Maus*—in two volumes (2003, 2004). The French editions of her book, published by L'Association, have sold more than 100,000 copies.[18] Moreover, the third volume of the series was prepublished in the pages of *Libération* in the summer of 2002, giving the work the same kind of national media exposure that a famous novelist or essayist might expect.

Persepolis is the strictly chronological story of Satrapi's life from childhood to young adulthood. Born in Tehran to middle-class parents, Satrapi evokes the hardships that her family suffered under the Islamic revolution that swept through Iran when she was ten years old. The series recalls her efforts to circumvent the strict religious teachings in the devastation wrought by the Iran-Iraq war of the 1980s, her schooling in Vienna, and her return to art school and a brief marriage in Iran. Satrapi's books, which are presented with a spare, stripped-down visual aesthetic, define for many the contemporary autobiographical comics movement. The wide exposure of her work, and its warm reception beyond the confines of the traditional comics reading public, has served to reinforce the association between serious subjects in contemporary comics and autobiography. Indeed, by dealing with her youth in autobiographical manner rather than through fictionalization, Satrapi's work draws upon common assumptions about autobiography and truthfulness for much of its power.

While Satrapi has achieved the greatest commercial success in the autobiographical genre, her work is by no means normative. The visual aspects of autobiographical approaches within contemporary European comics are remarkably heterogeneous and plural despite evidence of considerable overlap within the thematics of the movement. Moreover, because the narrative content of so many autobiographical comics is roughly analogous, it is primarily through the processes of rendering and visualization that these works differ from each other. In 1996, for example, Thierry Groensteen identified a number of traits common to the narrative component of autobiographical comics. The two most prevalent of these were recollections of childhood and a recounting of intimate or sexual encounters.[19] These categories clearly encompass the work of Baudoin and Satrapi but also incorporate a large number of practitioners working in different contexts. Jean-Christophe Menu, whose own *Livret de phamille* (1995) is a central early text in the autobiographical comics movement, foregrounds his familial relationships—particularly to his wife and children—in his work. Swedish cartoonist Asa Grennvall details her relationship with an extremely demanding and insensitive mother in *Det känns som hundra år* (1999), as well as her relationship with an emotionally and physically abusive boyfriend in *Sjunde våningen* (2002). Maaike Hartjes portrays her quotidian life and her personal fears in *Maaikes GrotDagboekje* (2002). The 381-page Finnish anthology *Sarjakuvapaivat* (2001) features twelve artists—including Kati Rapia, Katja Tukianinen, and Johanna Rojola—recording their diaries for a month apiece in comics form. Each of their pieces foregrounds the intimate in a very direct and highly personal manner. Frederik Peeters's 2001 book *Pilules bleues* addresses his romantic involvement with an HIV-positive woman and her young HIV-positive son. While each of these artists utilizes a different visual approach—Menu's loose cartooning, Hartjes's minimalist quasi-stick figures, Peeters's highly symbolic figures within a traditional page design—the intent behind their projects bears a considerable degree of overlap. Indeed, the social and narrative concerns of contemporary European autobiographical cartooning have been codified, even across national borders.

The most notable of all autobiographical comics publishers is France's Ego Comme X. Begun as an anthology publisher in 1994, Ego Comme X was started by students from the Atelier Bande Dessinée at the Ecole Regionale des Beaux-Arts d'Angoulême. Their stated desire was to highlight the importance of "the real" in contradistinction to the dominant comics aesthetic of escapist fantasy. While various other publishers had pushed autobiography to the forefront of the new comics scene in the 1990s—particularly L'Association and Cornélius—Ego Comme X was the first to make autobiographical comics something of an imperative. Writing in the first issue, Thierry Groensteen argued: "Still, at one time, the full-color adventures of irreproachable heroes were rolled out on glazed paper. They neglected reality, preferring to turn to any elsewhere, provided that it was synonymous with escape, and the promise of entertainment. But all that is finished!

The comic book has changed."[20] The artists published by Ego Comme X—Aristophane, Xavier Mussat, Fabrice Neaud, Frédéric Poincelet, Frédéric Boilet, Matthieu Blanchin, Pauline Martin, among numerous others—share a common concern with detailing their intimate personal relationships, and often recollections of their childhoods, in the comics form.

Loïc Nehou and Poincelet take this tendency to the extreme in *Essai de sentimentalisme* (2001) in which Poincelet illustrates explicit stories of Nehou's sex life. The doubled disclosure that this effort entails—Nehou's openness to Poincelet, the artist's frankness with the reader—is unusual in the field and pushes the portrayal of the intimate to its logical extreme. Poincelet's visual approach is perhaps the least conventional in the field of autobiographical comics. Coming from a fine arts and painting background, Poincelet uses no traditional panels, and his pages are mostly composed of white space. Indeed, his work is an obvious bridge between the autobiographical comics movement and the avant-garde tendencies of Frémok (he published a book, *Livre de prieres*, with Amok in 1998).

If Poincelet's work is proof that, as Groensteen suggested, the comics had changed as a result of these formal and, more accurately, thematic lulls, it is also evidence of an increasing concretization of opposition to the heteronomous comics market. Autobiography, as a largely untapped genre offering the opportunity to speak directly for one's self as an author, represented to the new generation of creators a credible alternative to the fantasies that comprised the majority of European comics production. The diverse approaches that autobiography accorded the comics form served as a reinforcement of the idea, as another editorial in *Ego Comme X* 1 indicated, that "a comics that reflects, wonders about its means, realized by authors conscious of being able to express themselves differently with a great deal of accuracy, becomes a language of its own."[21] At the same time, however, autobiography risked calcifying into a genre that was as formalized and structured as those that it sought to reject, becoming the small-press genre par excellence. The tension between the heteronomous regimes of fantasy comics publishing in Europe and the more autonomous sector of artist-driven autobiography is highlighted in a number of books published by Ego Comme X and L'Association. Specifically, the work of David B., Dupuy and Berberian, and Fabrice Neaud offers concrete assessments, within an autobiographical form, of the shaping of an independent or alternative European comics culture rooted in personal psychodynamics.

In outlining the common tropes in autobiographical comics, Thierry Groensteen suggests that a distinctively French aspect of the movement is a focus on "the chronicle of the professional life, the *mise-en-scène* of the author's trade in comics."[22] In the case of David B.'s six-volume *L'Ascension du Haut Mal* (1996, 1997, 1998, 1999, 2000, 2003), the author combines his childhood recollections, the history of his family, and his own growth as a cartoonist in order to place his life story in dialogue with his other comics work, genre-based fantasy comics. In an interview, David B. defined his particular approach to autobiography, which extends far beyond recollections of his own life:

> Often, people in autobiographical comics tell their life. Period . . . Me, I try to tell another thing, I tell what has happened to my family. I also tell memories of my grandparents, of the things which I heard told, a kind of family mythology, memories

of grandparents, great-grandparents. For example, the war of 1914 in the case of my great-grandfather, things like that. And then, I try to tell, parallel to that, the construction of my imagination and the influence that all that I lived could have on this imagination.[23]

Indeed, the strong family element in David B.'s autobiographical comics is suggested when he says, "Of course, it is not a work that I undertook all alone, egotistically. It is a work that I make for my sister as well, for my parents and my brother."[24] The sense of producing comics not only for one's self, but for an entire family, is highlighted by the content of the books themselves. David B. has used *L'Ascension du Haut Mal* as a sort of explanatory text that provides insight into the mind that has created some of the most offbeat genre comics in recent publishing history. From this standpoint the distinction between autobiographical and fictional work in contemporary European comics production is revealed as more fluid than defenders of the genre might otherwise claim. It is clear, in fact, that autobiography is simply one strand of a complex web of possibilities that constitute the contemporary field of European comics production, albeit a strand for which particularly ideological claims have been regularly made.

NOTES

1. Fabrice Neaud, "Résponses a huit questions sur l'autobiographie," *9e Art* 1 (1996): 80.
2. Philippe Dupuy, "Lundi 23 Août 1993," *Journal d'un album*, Philippe Dupuy and Charles Berberrian (Paris: L'Association, 1994), n.p.
3. Fabrice Neaud, *Journal (III)* (Angouleme: Ego Comme X, 1999): 241.
4. Lewis Trondheim, "Journal du journal du journal," *Le Rab de lapin* 26 (2001): 33.
5. Philippe Lejeune, *On Autobiography*, trans. Katherine Leary (Minneapolis: University of Minnesota Press, 1989): 4.
6. William C. Spengemann, *The Forms of Autobiography: Episodes in the History of a Literary Genre* (New Haven: Yale University Press, 1980): 207.
7. Paul de Man, "Autobiography as De-Facement," *Modern Language Notes* 94 (1979): 919.
8. Linda Anderson, *Autobiography* (London: Routledge, 2001): 6.
9. Timothy Dow Adams, *Telling Lies in Modern American Autobiography* (Chapel Hill: University of North Carolina Press, 1990): 9.
10. Lejeune, *On Autobiography*, 22.
11. Monique Yaair, "Who/What Is the Subject? Representations of Self in Late Twentieth-Century Art," *Word and Image* 16.4 (2000): 363.
12. Thierry Groensteen, "Les Petites Cases du moi: L'autobiographie en band dessinée," *9e Art* 1 (1996): 65.
13. Janet Staiger, "Authorship Approaches," *Authorship and Film*, ed. D. A. Gerstner and Janet Staiger (New York: Routledge, 2003): 27.
14. Michel Foucault, "What Is an Author?" *The Foucault Reader*, trans. Josue V. Harari, ed. Paul Rabinow (New York: Pantheon, 1984): 107.
15. Nancy Hartsock, "Foucault on Power: A Theory for Women?" *Feminism/Postmodernism*, ed. Linda J. Nicholson (New York: Routledge, 1999): 163–64.
16. Julia Swindells, *Victorian Writing and Working Women* (Cambridge: Polity Press, 1985): 7.
17. "Elaboration permanente," *L'Association Catalogue* (Paris: L'Association, 2004).

18. "Instantane," *Libération*, February 12, 2003: 7.

19. "La lutte des cases," *Liberation*, January 23, 2003: 11.

20. Groensteen, "Petites cases," 66.

21. Thierry Groensteen, "Petit Manuel d'introspection graphique," *Ego Comme X* 1 (1994): 2.

22. Thierry Leprevost, "Edito," *Ego Comme X* 1 (1994): 2.

23. Groensteen, "Petites cases," 66.

24. "Interview David B.: *L'Ascension du Haut Mal*" (2000). http: //www.bdparadisio.com/intervw/davidb/ intdavid.htm.

Manga versus *Kibyōshi*

ADAM L. KERN

The *kibyōshi* and the manga share much in common. They certainly seem to be similar media, which is to say they bear certain resemblances in format, modes of production, and reception. In terms of the first of these, the *kibyōshi* and the modern manga are inherently visual-verbal narratives. Both employ a number of similar pictorial conventions, and both seem visually associated with other forms of culture by virtue of their role as meta-media, parts of a larger network of closely aligned genres, commercial goods, and advertising mechanisms comprising virtual industries unto themselves.

In terms of production, the *kibyōshi* and the modern manga are mass-fabricated in assembly-line-like processes that exert vaguely similar pressures on authors and artists to produce, often to the point that earlier material—the material of one's competitors—is, in one form or another, recycled. Both rely on the availability of disposable income in a capitalist society in some stage of industrial development. Both the *kibyōshi*, by virtue of the woodblock printing process, and the modern manga, by virtue of the modern printing press, are products of mechanical reproduction, even if the former was powered by hand and the latter by electricity.

In terms of reception, the *kibyōshi* and the modern manga have enjoyed a comparable degree of broad-based appeal, gripping the popular imagination in ways that at the time of their emergence must have felt genuinely unprecedented. A case could be made that the majority of readers of both forms tended or tend to consist of "middle-class" men in their twenties and thirties. And if the modern manga industry has made significant headway in diversifying its readership, the same might be said of the *kibyōshi*, which over time seems to have broadened its own base to the point that it lost some of its unique qualities. Indeed, if the *kibyōshi* was one of the top-selling genres of its day, so too is the manga at present. One is hardly surprised to see the proverbial impeccably attired middle-aged businessman on the Tokyo subway briskly thumbing through the latest issue of *Young Magazine*, or a schoolgirl in the far-flung fishing village of Noboribetsu, Hokkaido, poring over *Nakayoshi*, one of several "comicbooks for girls" (*shōjo* manga). "Japan is the first nation in the world," Schodt notes, waxing idealistic only slightly, "to accord 'comic books' . . . nearly the same social status as novels and films."[1]

It is therefore natural to draw comparisons between the *kibyōshi* and the modern manga. It is also understandably tempting for those with a vested interest in overcoming the conservative cultural criticism of the latter to argue for an historical continuity with the former. Still, political agendas aside, the *kibyōshi* and the modern manga would seem to share a number of superficial similarities owing to the nature of the comicbook medium itself, rather than to any direct causal or historical link between the two forms or between their corresponding visual cultures. If the *kibyōshi* and the modern manga can be said to emanate from a common ground of Japanese visual culture, they do not emanate from the same wellspring.

The visual regime of the *kibyōshi* seems to derive primarily from the representation of the popular stage in woodblock prints, whereas the visual regime of the modern manga derives primarily from Western genres like the comicbook and the cinema. Any apparent similarity or overlap between the two is, more often than not, coincidental, an epiphenomenal effect of the comicbook medium itself that one might just as easily observe in comicbooks appearing in isolation anywhere around the world, not evidence that the *kibyōshi* poured continuously into the modern manga. Both are types of comicbooks, to be sure, though their respective visual idioms are just about completely unrelated. In the final analysis, the *kibyōshi* and the modern manga are similar media but different genres. Thus, many of the putative similarities between the two turn out to be flukes, hardly educing a more profound cultural homology, or common origin, let alone a verifiable direct influence. At a deeper level, dissimilarities become glaringly apparent.

BUBBLES ON THE SURFACE

One example of such a superficial similarity that turns out to have sharply different origins and even uses is to be found in the example of the text "balloon" or "bubble." When this device appears in the modern manga, as in the Western comicbook, it generally tends to encapsulate text representing the speech or thoughts of a character. The *kibyōshi* makes frequent use of the bubble, too, though almost never in this same way. Such text typically gets positioned near the figure of the character without being demarked by enclosing lines, as though simply hovering in the ether. Rather, the *kibyōshi* uses the bubble to enclose scenes, replete with figures of characters and perhaps some written narrative text, that are most often associated with some other realm, particularly that of dreams. The *kibyōshi* has dream bubbles, in other words, not speech or thought bubbles.

The bubble in the *kibyōshi* and other genres of illustrated Edo literature can also sometimes convey a fictional character from one realm to another. In one of Akinari's ghost stories from *Tales of Moonlight and Rain* entitled "The Dream-Inspired Carp" (*Muō no rigyo*), published during An'ei (1772–1780) though not a *kibyōshi*, the Priest Kōgi returns from an underwater kingdom in a wisp of smoke emanating from a fish about to be sliced open and devoured. Similarly, in one of Santō Kyōden's (1761–1816) *kibyōshi*, a courtesan trapped in the underworld appears before her lover within billows of incense. The bubble functions this way in other *kibyōshi* too.

Furthermore, the tail of the bubble sometimes points toward some spot "offstage"—or "offpage"—completely outside the pictorial frame, as though to indicate that the bubble's contents are conveyed telepathically or supernaturally or spiritually from the Beyond. More frequently, the tail emanates from a character's midsection. This reflects the longstanding popular belief in Japan that the soul is reposed in the center of the body, just below the navel. However, by the twentieth century, the locus of individuality in the modern manga had shifted to the head—which would seem to suggest direct influence from the Western comicbook as opposed to the *kibyōshi*.

There are two major theories about the origins of the bubble convention in premodern Japanese visual culture. The first holds that the bubble derives from the folk belief that a departed soul can appear as a vision within graveside incense fumes (*hangonkō*).[2] To the extent that the actual fumes of such incense appear to connect earth and heaven visually, its appropriation as a pictorial device to connect earthly and otherworldly realms could hardly have been more apropos. The *kibyōshi* scenario just cited is a case in point. Ultimately, this convention probably traces back to the Chinese pictorial trope of Emperor Wu (approx. 141–87 BCE) gazing upon the image of his departed wife Li who appears before him within incense billows.

The other major theory holds that the bubble derives from the pictorial convention of representing dreams within a mist band (*suyarigasumi*), a kind of stylized cusped cloud with pictorially narrative weight, apparently a practice connected to the tropic rendering of the Buddha's dreamlike visitation to mortals. Although the use of the mist band as a pictorial device goes back to Heian-period picture scrolls, if not earlier, and can be spotted throughout premodern Japanese visual culture, it seems as though it is only during the early Edo period (1600–1868) that the mist band is made to convey dreams: the "earliest known unambiguous use" of this kind of dream balloon, according to Kenji Kajiya, "occurs in 'The Flute' (*Yokobue*) scene in [the woodblock-printed book] *Illustrated Tale of Genji* (*Eiri Genji monogatari*), published in Kyoto by Yamamoto Shunshō (1610–1682) in 1654. A simplified version of the smoke-shaped outline is used to distinguish the dream from the dreamer."[3] Kajiya maintains that dream-conveying mist bands appear no earlier: "Before the device of balloons was invented in the early Edo period, dream figures are represented in the same scenes, and in essentially the same forms, as humans."[4]

Whichever theory of the origins of the dream bubble to which one subscribes, it must be said that neither one informs the modern manga, which indubitably appropriates its text balloon from the Western comicbook. Needless to say, the Western comicbook probably did not derive its text balloon from premodern Japan. Furthermore, it should be clear that the *kibyōshi's* dream bubble and the modern manga's text bubble fulfill different functions. Therefore, while the materialization of the bubble in both the *kibyōshi* and the modern manga might at first seem to suggest a direct pictorial link, if the premodern bubble reveals anything, it is that the dream of manga culture proponents of direct influence between the two is itself illusory.

Yet it is hard to believe that the use of the bubble in both genres is entirely coincidental. It is possible that the nature of the comicbook engenders a balloon-like device. Once a medium of visual-verbal narrative begins to depict more than a straight or linear progression of narrative time, some kind of narrative pictorial device like the bubble becomes useful. The bubble helps to render temporal complexity pictorially because it is essentially a form of mini-panelization—a smaller panel that can represent one moment in narrative time within a larger panel representing another moment (usually representing the visual if not narrative present). Thus, it is plausible that the bubble is a natural effect of the comicbook medium itself. If so, then this might help explain why various cultures around the world seem to have invented something like the bubble device independently—as a function of the medium, not because there was some kind of synchronized global cabala of comicbook creators. Surely there is no direct causal link among the Jewish *tefillin* (phylactery), the American balloon, and the early Edo-period mist band.[5] It is by virtue of the comicbook medium itself, then, that the Japanese have their incense fumes and the Italians their *fumetti* (puffs of smoke).

Mention of the bubble as a form of mini-panelization raises the issue of panelization itself, which, although present in both the modern manga and the *kibyōshi*, upon closer inspection also turns out to be a superficial similarity. The modern manga customarily employs multiple panels on each page, allowing for moment-to-moment transitions of the sort one might find in a comic strip or on the movie screen. The *kibyōshi* as a rule tends to take the page as its primary panel, engendering transitions that are almost always scene-to-scene. Granted, it could be argued that the dream bubble, the corner picture (*komae*), and other sorts of mini-panelization in Edo-period visual culture each are a form of multiple panelization, though these certainly do not amount to the primary unit of visual-verbal narrative as the multiple panel is in the modern manga. Absent moment-to-moment transitions, which can be said to facilitate if not actually to encourage the depiction of physical movement, there was little if any need for the *kibyōshi* to develop expressionist or synaesthetic lines, which figure prominently in many modern manga. Furthermore, the absence of multiple panels on the typical *kibyōshi* page precludes the cinematographic technique one not infrequently finds in the modern manga of the "bleed," a panel that hemorrhages into timeless space.

The third and last example here of a superficial similarity in a pictorial convention may be provided by a kind of expressionist line, in fact, the so-called speed line, which the Japanese refer to as the motion line (*dōsen*). Although it appears ubiquitously in the modern manga and only sporadically in the *kibyōshi*, the more significant difference resides in the type of action conveyed with it. In the modern manga, the motion line covers a vast range, from characters ripping off each other's clothes, through the emphasis of well-endowed body parts, to facial expressions of rapture. In the rare instances in which the motion line is used within the *kibyōshi*, according to Natsume Fusanosuke in his study of the subject, it is restricted to the conveyance of water, wind, light, and little else.

This is surprising since motion lines had been used in Japan prior to the *kibyōshi* in a way more in keeping with the modern manga. One finds them in earlier picturebooks (*ehon sōshi*) and picture scrolls, where they might animate a toy wheel rolling down a hill, carriage wheels spinning round, a halberd being twirled, even the slapping down of a token in the game of travel Parcheesi (*sugoroku*).[6] What this quick survey suggests, then, is that if modern manga artists discovered the motion line in their native tradition rather than in Western comicbooks, they did not do so in the *kibyōshi*. And even if they did,

A spoof of a double-suicide scene from the kabuki stage. The playboy wannabe Enjirō and his courtesan Ukina stumble home after their attempt at a fake double suicide is botched when desperadoes strip them half naked. From *Playboy, Roasted à la Edo* (*Edo umare uwaki no kabayaki*), a *kibyōshi* by Santō Kyōden published in 1785.

they must have applied it to a wider range and different order of action than can be found there. In the case of the motion line, then, the modern manga bypassed the *kibyōshi*.

It should be observed that for each superficial similarity between the *kibyōshi* and the modern manga, there are probably many more profound differences. During the century or so dividing the two forms, the nature of the socioeconomic infrastructure in Japan changed dramatically. The remarkable transformation from a proto-bourgeois economy into one of advanced capitalism—a transformation that arguably has had its most conspicuous manifestation in the postwar Japanese "economic miracle"—could not but affect the nature of visuality, since the technologies of mechanical reproduction, delivery, and consumption were themselves completely transformed. It was not simply a matter of the modern printing press displacing woodblock printing, in other words, but new kinds of media that changed the way people looked at the world.

Generalizing grossly, the *kibyōshi* derived its visual idiom from the then-available woodblock-printed representation of the kabuki stage, whereas the modern manga has so far found its visual idiom in radically new forms of foreign media unknown during An'ei-Tenmei (1772–1789), such as the Western comic strip, the Western comicbook, the animated film, the photographic frame, the silver screen, the small screen, the computer screen, even the videogame screen. This is not to imply that the modern manga has *completely* disregarded premodern Japanese visual culture. However, compared to these new media, premodern modes of visuality pale badly. How, then, could the visual regime of the modern manga not but differ paradigmatically from that of the *kibyōshi*?

To refine this slightly, the modern manga can be described in the main as a kind of visual analogue of film, since the serial nature of its multiple panels within each page either takes its inspiration from, or else closely resembles, the sequential unfolding of frames on the celluloid spool. One might generally view the modern manga as a sequence of images that, were the gaps only *slightly* filled in, would effortlessly amount to an anime or some other kind of movie. The multiple panelization on the average page allows the manga to pan wide, zoom in, flash back, fade out, all in accordance with the cinematographic storyboard. The anime is less an animated film in this sense than it is an animated manga, though both ultimately are indebted to motion pictures. And as one would expect, many manga are closely linked to anime, which according to Napier, draws upon "worldwide artistic conventions of twentieth-century cinema and photography."[7]

The *kibyōshi*, which cannot be described as a serial narrative in quite the same way since its basic panel tends to be the single page, takes most of its visual cues from representations of the popular theater in theatrical texts, which is to say both woodblock-printed books as well as pictures. Being a woodblock-printed genre itself, and its artists being woodblock print artists themselves, the *kibyōshi* naturally obeys—or at least plays off—many of the visual conventions of the woodblock print in general, not just those concerned with the stage; for instance, scenes in some *kibyōshi* resemble maps, board games, encyclopedia pages, and so forth. That said, the *kibyōshi* is particularly beholden to the kabuki theater as manifested in such things as the actor picture (*yakushae*), the kabuki star portrait (*nigaoe*), the beauty picture (*bijinga*), the illustrated playbook (*eiri kyōgenbon*), and theatrically inflected works in earlier genres of comicbooks, principally the blackbook.

The moment-to-moment transition between panels in the modern manga, then, suggests an affinity with the cinema, whereas the scene-to-scene transition of the *kibyōshi* suggests an affinity with the *mise-en-scène* of the kabuki stage as represented in some form of woodblock-printed theatrical text. Thus, the *kibyōshi*, like the theatrical text, positions the reader in the perspective of the audience member with respect to the stage and its actors, which is to say at the bottom of the page looking up. In fact, when a *kibyōshi* depicts a fictional audience, it tends to be situated this way, as evidenced by the depictions of the Dutch-style peepshow in *Those Familiar Bestsellers* (*Gozonji no shōbaimono*, 1782) and the freakshow in *The Unseamly Silverpiped Swingers* (*Sogitsugi gingiseru*, 1788). Furthermore, the *kibyōshi*, like the theatrical text, represents the stage chanter's narrative (*ji*) and the stage character's dialogue (*kotoba*) by laying out these utterances on different parts of the page, which is to say at the top and near the figures below, respectively, since the chanters and actors are analogously separated on stage.

The few apparent similarities between the *kibyōshi* and the modern manga surveyed here—as well as the tendency mentioned previously of both genres to include commercial tie-ins, product placement, and mass marketing—would seem to be flukes, only superficially related, products of the comicbook medium as it was conceived and produced in isolated moments in time, rather than indicative of some putative historical continuity. Phenomenal advances in the technology of mechanical reproduction and in capitalism itself fundamentally changed the nature of visuality and continue to separate the visual regimes of the *kibyōshi* and the modern manga. Thus, contrary to the intimations of the proponents of manga culture, the modern manga was *not* the inevitable culmination of the *kibyōshi*. Nor did the *kibyōshi* entail the manga. The modern manga would have come into existence even without the *kibyōshi*. Furthermore, even if it could be demonstrated that the modern manga borrowed this or that convention or style or trope from the *kibyōshi*, the *kibyōshi* cannot be meaningfully described as a major influence, let alone as the direct progenitor. A distant, even long-lost uncle, perhaps. Certainly not the father.

The most that can be said of premodern influence, then, is that the *kibyōshi* provided the precedent of a vastly popular comicbook for adults—conceivably even a comicbook that was close to reaching its potential as a medium of visual-verbal narrative. One may be able to track adult comic books over time from the *kibyōshi*, into the multivolume (*gōkan*), through Meiji satirical prints, up to the modern manga, in other words, not in terms of visual-verbal conventions, artistic styles, literary tropes, let alone stories or their *auteurs*, but in terms of an adult readership. In this sense, it is possible that this precedent of an adult comicbook in An'ei-Tenmei Edo may have helped predispose the Japanese to the eventual reception of the modern Western comicbook.

No diary or record or other evidence has come to light, to the best of my knowledge, demonstrating that a *kibyōshi* author or artist became involved in the production of the modern manga. Nor could there be, of course, for too much time separates the two. Since the *kibyōshi* as a phenomenon more or less ended in 1806 (though individual works continued to be issued for a couple more decades), even if one defines the manga liberally, placing its origins in 1895 instead of the 1900s, upwards of ninety years separate the *kibyōshi's* demise and the manga's rise.

Still, one suggestive correlation between the *kibyōshi* and the modern manga is that both seem to have attained phenomenal popularity at crucial technological turning points in cultural history: the *kibyōshi*, during the transition from a handwritten manuscript culture to a woodblock print culture that was also tied up with the decline of the *ancien régime* in Kamigata and the rise of a centralized culture in Edo-Tokyo; and the modern manga, during the transition from woodblock-print and even print culture to an electronically driven, fast-paced, modern culture under the spell of Western influence.

Visuality itself, it might be suggested, was being challenged in fundamental ways in the heyday of both genres. As Screech and others have argued, it was during the mid-Edo period when Japanese proponents of Western science (*Rangaku*—literally "Dutch Studies") helped introduce the microscope, the telescope, even the *optique*, to the public, and this not only radically altered how many Japanese artists literally saw the world, but how the popular imagination visualized the world as well.[8] This is evident in the way that Kyōden in his book of mock-designs, *The Latest Word on Fine Patterns* (*Komon-shinpō*, 1786) microscopically enlarged the common flea to the scale of artistic visibility—the first time anything like this had been done, I would hazard to guess, in the history of Japanese visuality. This is also evident in the way that one of Andō Hiroshige's (1797–1858) woodblock prints would, decades later, reveal the world from the perspective of an eagle soaring high over the landscape, shrinking human beings to the minuscule scale of insects.[9] When technological advances and paradigmatic shifts in society alter the way people look at the world, it is only natural for people to look to visual genres to assess the new and to reassess the old scopic regimes.

Thus, it is possible that the meaning of the superficial similarities between the *kibyōshi* and the modern manga is not merely that the efforts of the proponents of manga culture to demonstrate influence are insupportably overstated. That much seems obvious. Rather, the visual-verbal imagination in Japan achieves its greatest inspiration during moments of intense technological, economic, and social upheaval that challenge fundamental notions of visuality.

NOTES

1. Frederik L. Schodt, *Dreamland Japan: Writings on Modern Manga* (Berkeley: Stone Bridge Press, 1996), 9.
2. See Natsume Fusanosuke, "Kibyōshi o manga kara miru," pp. 196–97. In Tanahashi Masahiro, ed. *Edo gesaku zōshi* (Tōykō: Shōgakukan, 2000), 196–205.
3. Kenji Kajiya, "Reimagining the Imagined: Depictions of Dreams and Ghosts in the Early Edo Period," *Impressions* 23 (2001), 91.
4. Kajiya, "Reimagining the Imagined," 89.
5. There is some speculation that in Europe the bubble developed from the Jewish prayer practice of strapping leather cases (*tefillin* in Hebrew) containing written law to the forehead.
6. Natsume draws these examples from *Shigisan engi emaki* (twelfth century), *Heiji monogatari ekotoba* (thirteenth century), *Ishiyamadera engi emaki* (tenth century), and *Haseo sōshi* (thirteenth-fourteenth century), respectively. In Natsume, "Kibyōshi o manga kara miru," 198–200.
7. Susan J. Napier, *Anime from Akira to Princess Mononoke: Experiencing Japanese Animation* (London: Palgrave Macmillan, 2001), 4.
8. For more on this, see Minezo Tani, *Asobi no dezain* (Tōkyō: Iwasaki bijutsusha, 1984).
9. For more about the influence of the Western regime of visuality on Japanese art, see Timon Screech, *The Western Scientific Gaze and Popular Imagery in Later Edo Japan* (Cambridge: Cambridge University Press, 1996).

Beyond *Shoujo*, Blending Gender

FUSAMI OGI

Shoujo (girls) manga (Japanese comics) was at first a gender-specific category that assumed a female world for both readers and authors. Once *shoujo* manga began to incorporate male homosexuality as a subject in the 1970s, however, this female world was subverted in several ways. When male characters made their appearance, they introduced a new vision of sexuality by giving *shoujo* a vantage point through which to explore female desires without overtly acknowledging them. This essay begins by exploring the construction of a sexual subjectivity for *shoujo* through manga's representation of male homosexuality. It then explores the ways *shoujo* manga have expanded their scope to include such topics as HIV/AIDS.

Until the 1970s, the word *shoujo* in *shoujo* manga usually referred to the readers or main characters, not to the authors. *Shoujo* were first positioned only as objects in the discourse of *shoujo* manga. However, as a number of women writers began writing, *shoujo* manga gradually came to signify manga which *shoujo* wrote as well, in that most women writers were in their teens—the same age as *shoujo* they wrote for.

The most interesting aspect that becomes apparent in the 1970s is the theme of sexuality. Sexuality could not be a central theme in the world of the *shoujo* who are not yet thinking of marriage and should be sexually innocent. At the very moment when writing that concerned sexuality appeared under the category of *shoujo* manga, the writing revealed itself as a "failure" of the traditional meaning of *shoujo*.

Since a certain group of women writers, later called the *Hana no 24 nen gumi*,[1] such as Takemiya Keiko and Hagio Moto, began to write, *shoujo* manga have displaced their traditional settings and have changed the materials which the category dealt with. Instead of showing a *shoujo* dreaming of romance with a boy, they showed boys and focused on boys' love. In other words, not presenting texts for *shoujo* but showing the absence of *shoujo*, the texts have changed the position of women subjects and subjects of interest to women into the one which subverts the traditional concept of women. The women writers effectively differentiated the fixed form of heterosexual love and, in addition to having male characters, added other themes to the text and displaced the theme of love as the principal concern of the text, taking on more social and political issues, which conventional *shoujo* manga rarely took an interest in. That made for a sharp contrast to the

Reprinted by permission from the *International Journal of Comic Art*, vol. 3, no. 2 (Fall 2001), 151–60.

Yamagishi Ryoko, *Hi izuru tokoro no tenshi* 7, 90–91.

other type of *shoujo* manga, which mainly focused on the emotions and minds of women characters and their lives.

Most critics claim that a *shoujo* is not present in the narrative because her body is oppressed under and within the current social code. In other words, they have assumed that a shoujo's body is "nothing" under the current ideology. Even the feminist sociologist Ueno Chizuko points out that "the number of *shounen ai* (boys' love) dramas might not increase if *shoujo* could gain another way to present their sexuality by using their own sex" (Ueno, 1998: 153, my translation).

However, even after a genre which included female sexuality, called *ladies comics* was born in 1980, the theme of male homosexuality remains one of the major themes in the field of shoujo manga. In the 1990s some commercial magazines for this genre called boy's love emerged. Importantly, *shoujo* manga, without the *shoujo*'s own body, can be a sign which suggests that one can separate from the sexed body to which one is born. I would submit that boys' bodies instead of girls' in *shoujo* manga show such a potential, as well as unveiling the imagined inferiority of *shoujo*.

The first half of the 1990s has been recognized as a gay culture boom in Japan; gay people came out of the "closet" in Eve Sedgwick's sense. *Shoujo culture*, including *shoujo* manga, seems to have encouraged their coming out. However, *shoujo* manga writers as well as critics often insist that the *shoujo*'s fictional world has no connection to actual male homosexuality.

In fact, other pioneer writers on the theme of male homosexuality of *shoujo* manga also share this assumption. Yamagishi Ryoko, who is regarded as a member of the *Hana no 24 nen gumi*, makes an interesting comment in terms of sexuality. Unlike other writers in the 1970s, who exclusively presented male homosexuality, she introduced both male and female homosexuality in 1971 when Yamagishi wrote *Shiroi heya no futari* (Two in a White Room) about a girl's love for another girl. In an interview in 1978, Yamagishi was asked, "Which do you prefer, gays or lesbians?" She answered, "Gays, because I am a woman" (Yamagishi, 1978: 69). This question and answer may confuse us. Yet they well signify bafflement and ignorance about the concept of homosexuality. Yamagishi was not the only writer who answered like that.

The theme of male homosexuality in the world of *shoujo* manga has been emphasized by many writers and critics as a result of a heterosexual woman's desire for a man. In an interview in 1992, Yamagishi looked back at her earlier view of sexuality, regarding one of her most popular works, *Hi izuru tokoro no tenshi* (A Prince of the Nation from Which the Sun Rises),[2] in which one of the most historical male figures in Japan is portrayed as homosexual. The ending of this work presents the break up of a love affair between two male characters. The arrangement of the two characters in this scene indicates that the male protagonist's love is destined not to be accepted by the other male character. Yet in the interview, Yamagishi says that now she can also imagine their story without ending their love. She did not understand homosexuality in a positive sense at that time, although she thought she did. She used to claim to have a positive attitude about homosexuality, but in fact, she did not understand it (cited in Sato, 1996: 168).

Male homosexuality in *shoujo* manga has been regarded as a substitute for a heterosexual relationship for women who could not face their own sexuality under the male dominant discourse. As heterosexual women, most female writers and readers enjoy men (Kakinuma, 1995: 171) and subgenres of *shoujo* manga for the theme of male homosexuality create a myth of a heterosexual couple for a heterosexual woman (Mizoguchi, 2000: 197). Moreover, as Yamagishi admits later, this preference for male homosexuality does not mean a public affirmation of homosexuality. Rather, their representations of homosexuality, which rarely show male characters' love affairs ending happily, may convey a negative message to homosexuals.

The theme of male homosexuality created a *shoujo*'s narrow fantastic space called *yaoi*. The term *yaoi* is a combination of three Japanese words: *yama nashi*, *ochinashi*, and *iminashi*, which mean without climax, without ending, and without meaning. However, there is, in fact, some meaning in their representations regardless of their nametag, and this term now covers this genre of male homosexuality rooted in *shoujo* manga, although there is some debate about it. Only *shoujo* as heterosexual females seem to pertain to the world of *yaoi*, and do not see how *yaoi* could perform as a genre, which would also affect its non-target readers. However, I want to explore another view of *yaoi*. The genre *yaoi* is interesting in terms of gender, not only because it provides *shoujo* with a tool to see their own sexuality, but also because the representation itself at once holds multiple views of gender and makes it possible to present social and political issues in relation to gender, not just the single gender of *shoujo*.

To introduce several examples of the multiplicity of gender in *shoujo* manga, I use the case study of one *shoujo* manga entitled *TOMOI* by Akisato Wakuni, written in the 1980s, which has also been regarded as *yaoi* by some readers. This work focuses on homosexual characters and their problems, including the homophobic reactions they face, AIDS, and their "coming out." This work is important to analyze in terms of the multiplicity of themes in *shoujo* manga, especially considering how *shoujo* manga can be political.

TOMOI started in 1985. The events it depicts take place between the years of 1982 and 1984. This work was written for *shoujo* manga when AIDS and homophobia were becoming serious issues. Discrimination against homosexuals became unveiled in public, in relation to the problems of AIDS, from the late 1980s to the beginning of the 1990s (Vincent, 1997: 47). The first Japanese AIDS patient, officially reported March 22, 1985, by the Welfare Ministry, was a gay man living in the U.S. At that point, however, 2,000 people with hemophilia were already infected with HIV because of the distribution of non-heated blood products imported from the U.S. (Ochiai, 1998: 33–34; Feldman, 1998: 217). In accordance with the spread of AIDS, an assumption which regarded AIDS as a "disease of homosexuals" had been constructed in the 1980s in Japan, just as AIDS was at first regarded as a "gay disease" and preserved the virtue of heterosexual "victims" in the U.S. (cf. Grover, 1987: 21, 27: Treichler, 1987: 42). In the middle of the 1980s in Japan, prostitutes and homosexuals were labeled as high risk groups, but later, that was proved inaccurate after people found AIDS spread among those who did not belong to the minority groups (Kawaguchi, 1999). *TOMOI* deals with the days when such discrimination against homosexuals began to draw more people's attention and reinforced the ideological equation of AIDS and homosexuality.

TOMOI is about a young Japanese man, Tomoi Hisatsugu. He becomes a doctor and goes to New York City to do his residency at a hospital. There, his sexuality gradually awakens. An older German doctor, Richard Stein, is the first man with whom Hisatsugu falls in love. In this relationship, where younger Hisatsugu looks more immature than Stein, Hisatsugu seemingly often plays a highly feminine role. Hisatsugu appears to care about Stein's ex-lovers and seems to believe in a predestined love relationship like a *shoujo* who believes in her future prince in *shoujo* manga, while the German doctor enjoys his multiple love affairs with different men. There are some scenes which also remind readers of *shoujo* through Hisatsugu's attitude toward Stein. However, every scene introduces some twists into the concept of heterosexuality, which may disturb readers' preconceived notions of it. For example, when Hisatsugu feels as if he is a shy girl who cannot even eat in front of her first love, he says to himself, "I could be a virgin, if an anus had a hymen." This scene carries a comical tone in spite of the character's serious facial expression, but at the same time, his line, which delineates the attitude of a nervous girl, reminds readers of female sexuality, although this is a story about gay men. However, flowers on the table in this scene convey images of gay men, as well as those of *shoujo*, for roses allude to gay men, especially in *yaoi*'s context. Their relationship goes well and Stein's son accepts Hisatsugi as his father's partner. But when Stein finds that one of his former lovers died of AIDS, he suddenly decides to return to Germany. Throughout this story, AIDS appears as a "weird disease only gay men get infected with," because of Hisatsugu's ignorance. He has only known the term AIDS for two weeks at this point. Informed of Stein's departure, Hisatsugu gets upset and cries, "I cannot be a gay without being afraid of the weird disease." It appears to Hisatsugu that Stein tries to avoid AIDS despite being a doctor. Swearing not to let him go, Hisatsugu goes to the airport, but when he faces Stein, Hisatsugu only asks him to say, "I loved you," in Japanese and lets him go. The

TOMOI, 66–67.

story never tells us the exact reason for Stein's leaving. His only word to Hisatsugu is "Mike was dead because of AIDS."

As I suggested, throughout the story, the representation of Hisatsugu reminds us of *shoujo*, which may emphasize his femininity and passivity. Yet his images gradually change from passive to active, especially when we read this first story as his first encounter with the term AIDS, as well as his love story with Stein. Most parts of this story tell that Hisatsugu has no knowledge about AIDS although he is a doctor, which only emphasizes his passivity. However, his future transition from passivity to activity is suggested at the final scene of this first story.

Hisatsugu's lover in the final episode is Marvin, who is married. He hides his gay identity from his wife, who suspects that he betrays her with another woman, while Marvin cannot tell her about his relationship with Hisatsugu. When Hisatsugu met Marvin, Marvin was an AIDS patient. Hisatsugu decides to marry him, swearing to be together and sharing his death. The wedding scene shows Marvin in white clothing, which may signify the color of a female wedding dress and may reinscribe heterosexual values. However, interestingly, this scene also suggests that it is not a simple imitation of a heterosexual marriage, because of the roses on the right, which imply gayness.

Finally, Marvin is shot by his wife, who finds out her husband has deceived her. She shoots him not because he has betrayed her by having another lover but because he has hidden his sexual identity from her. When she thought that Marvin might have another women, she did not have an urge to murder. Marvin in his last moments asks Hisatsugu not to kill himself. After Marvin's death, Hisatsugu goes to Afghanistan, as if he were

TOMOI, 306.

placing himself in a situation where he might be killed. At last, he dies in the war in 1984.

This story begins to give more information about AIDS from a doctor's calm and unemotional point of view after Hisatsugu finds Marvin to be an AIDS patient. Hisatsugu asks a doctor directly to explain AIDS-related symptoms. A U.S. critic of manga, Frederik L. Schodt, remarks: "Most impressive is the way she (Akisato) is able to deftly weave information on the symptoms and causes of AIDS into her story, even at such an early stage of the epidemic" (Schodt, 1996: 195–96). Until then, as I suggested before, the information which Hisatsugu hears about AIDS has been totally unreliable. Hisatsugu is first informed about AIDS by Stein's son in the first episode, who refers to AIDS as "a weird disease among gay men." From this moment until Hisatsugu himself actively collects information about AIDS, this story continues to show Hisatsugu's passivity in regard to AIDS. His ignorance and passivity may remind readers of the very beginning of the AIDS epidemic, when gay men were much more likely to become HIV-positive than heterosexual men and women. This way of representing AIDS in *TOMOI* may function as a message which says that it is crucial to our understanding of AIDS not to take risks and to shatter the myth of the epidemic. Hisatsugu's and Marvin's deaths might create another romantic myth of gay men in *shoujo* manga, however, regarding the gay relationships which *TOMOI* presents. Schodt mentions the following: "Akisato's depiction of relationships among gays seems (to me at least) both uncontrived and sensitive"

(Schodt, 1996: 195). According to Wim Lunsing, an anthropologist of gay culture in Japan, "while the endings of relationships with partners dying are typical of Japanese drama, the story is quite plausible and realistic, except for the rather farfetched end, when Tomoi dies in an air raid in Afghanistan where he, disillusioned after his second lover left, went to work as a physician for the Mujahedin" (Lunsing, 1997: 273).

According to Akisato, the author of *TOMOI*, she gained readers in their twenties after this story began (Akisato, 1984: 15). Akisato mentions in an interview in 1984 that most readers seriously seem to try to understand the story. We may not know whether this story could gain more serious readers than other *shoujo* manga, yet, by introducing the theme of AIDS. *TOMOI* suggests how *shoujo* manga, one gender-specific genre, could destabilize its own existing way of idealizing a homosexual character's death as beautiful and feminine.[3]

What has been replaced with the prevailing notion of the beautiful death of homosexuals in *shoujo* manga is ignorance to AIDS and the myths about it. This story does not offer the actual death from AIDS. However, *TOMOI* repeatedly presents how human assumptions can prove fatal to our understanding and practice, and how they might actually have killed people in the period when AIDS had been seriously regarded as a "gay disease" in Japan. Depicting how the relation of AIDS to gay men has been reinforced at the earlier stage of AIDS in the 1980s, *TOMOI* disturbs *shoujo* to identify themselves with the two homosexual characters' death as part of their dream. Gay men in the story, who face AIDS as part of their lives, belong to the reality where young girls live also, rather than to their dream world where young girls can enjoy their sexuality through male bodies as secure substitutes for female bodies under the male dominant society. AIDS is not gone, even after both Marvin and Hisatsugu die.

The theme of male homosexuality at first was constructed as a narrow space of women by women, but it has expanded itself by disrupting its existing style as *shoujo* manga. Not only presenting male bodies to fulfill women's desire, but also questioning its relation to gender issues, *shoujo* manga with the theme of male homosexuality questions and challenges the existing gender system. Parodying the system, not portraying heterosexual characters, and seeking women's desire by rewriting *shoujo* manga means that diverse processes are generating one category of *shoujo* manga, which is always finding ways to challenge the genre. Despite being a gendered category, *shoujo* manga uses multiple dimensions of gender and provokes the creation of new categories of writings, questioning *shoujo* manga's conventionality in terms of gender. *Shoujo* manga as a category acts like an item of clothing which anyone can wear, but the way of wearing it produces in each case an original individuality and sometimes works as subversion, a process which never lets the person look the same as before.

NOTES

1. Fujimoto Yukari translated "hana no 24 nen gumi" as "Magnificent 24's." The group got its name because they were all born about 1949, the twenty-fourth year of the *Showa* period.
2. *Hi izuru tokoro no tenshi* was published in *Monthly Lala* from 1980 to 1984. *TOMOI* appeared in *Petit Flower* from 1985 to 1986. Throughout my analysis, I am using this *Petit Flower* version, collected in one

book in 1996. *TOMOI*'s former versions, "Kibun wa seihou kei" and "Manhattan Syndrome," were published in *Weekly Shoujo Comic* in 1983.

3. A homosexual character's death like that of Gilbert, a beautiful boy with a feminine figure who dies young in *Kaze to ki no uta* (Song of Breeze and Lice), a pioneer work in terms of male homosexuality in *shoujo* manga, written by Takemiya Keiko and published in 1976.

WORKS CITED

Akisato, Wakuni, "Interview: Akisato Wakuni," *Pafu* 10:6 (Tokyo: Seisui sha, 1984), 7–15.

———, *TOMOI* (Tokyo: Shogakukan, 1996).

Feldman, Douglas A., and Julia Wang Miller, eds., *The AIDS Crisis: A Documentary History* (Westport: Greenwood Press, 1998).

Fujimoto, Yukari, "A Life-size Mirror: Women's Self-Representation in Girls' Comics," *Review of Japanese Culture and Society* Vol. IV (Saitama, Japan: Center for Inter-Cultural Studies and Education, Josai University, 1991), 53–57.

Grover, Jan Zita, "AIDS: Keywords," *October* 43, 1987, 17–30.

Kakinuma, Eiko, "Ai' wo tsukuridasu shoujo manga ka tachi." *Imago* 6:4 (Tokyo: Seitosha, 1995), 170–78.

Kawaguchi, Kazuya, "Homophobia in the Times of AIDS Epidemic—An Analysis of 'Gay Street Youth,'" *The Liberation of Humankind: A Sociological Review* 13 (Kyoto: The Japanese Association of Sociology for Human Liberation, 1999), 27–52.

Lunsing, Wim, "Gay Boom in Japan: Changing Views of Homosexuality?" *Thamyris: Mythmaking from Past to Present* 4:2, 1997: 267–93.

Mizoguchi, Akiko, "Homophobic Homos, Rapes of Love, and Queer Lesbians: An Analysis of Recent Yaoi Texts," *Queer Japan* 2 (Tokyo: Keisoshobo, 2000), 193–211.

Ochiai, Keiko, and Itou Satoru, *Jibun rashiku ikiru: douseiai to feminism* (Kyoto: Kamogawashuppan, 1998).

Sato, Masaki, "*Shoujo* Manga to Homophobia," *Queer Studies '96* (Tokyo: Nanatsumori shokan, 1996), 161–69.

Schodt, Frederik L., *Dreamland Japan: Writings on Modern Manga* (Berkeley: Stone Bridge Press, 1996).

Sedgwick, Eve, *Epistemology of the Closet* (Berkeley: University of California Press, 1990).

Treichler, Paula A., "AIDS, Homophobia, and Biomedical Discourse: An Epidemic of Signification," *October* 43, 1987, 31–70.

Ueno, Chizuko, "Gay to feminism wa kyoutou dekiruka?" (Can Gay Men and Feminists Fight Together?). *Hatsujou souchi* (The Erotic Apparatus) (Tokyo: Chikuma shobou, 1998), 241–58.

Vincent, Keith, Kazama Takashi, and Kawaguchi Kazuya, *Gay Studies* (Tokyo: Seitosha, 1997).

Yamagishi, Ryoko, *Hi izuru tokorono tenshi*. Vol. 7 (Tokyo: Hakusensha, 1994).

———, "Tokushuu Yamagishi Ryoko" (Special Topic of Yamagishi Ryoko), *Dakkusu* 4:4 (Tokyo: Seisui sha, 1978), 17–76.

SCRUTINY AND EVALUATION

While previous sections treated comics in terms of their historical evolution, their formalist properties, or their social role, this section is devoted to analysts who give more detailed attention to particular cartoonists and stories. If comics are a language, as formalist critics suggest, it remains true that different artists deploy this language with varying degrees of skill and aesthetic agendas. The essays in this section use many of the analytical tools we have seen in earlier parts of the book: Ariel Dorfman certainly places Chilean comics in their social and historical context and Gene Kannenberg is attentive to the formalist innovations in Chris Ware's book; what distinguishes this section, however, is the closer attention paid to the oeuvre of particular artists, rather than broader categories like genres or styles.

Ariel Dorfman's essay examines the serialized stories of the characters Mampato and Ogú, written and drawn by cartoonist Themos Lobos, setting them against the background of the counter-revolution that overthrew the democratically elected government of Chilean president Salvador Allende in 1973. Using his own memories of Chile during this crisis when he was actively involved in governmental affairs, Dorfman links the plots of these stories to stirred up fears against pro-socialist policies that led to the coup. "The comic strip does not portray the truth of what happened in Chile in those months but rather the version that the Chilean ruling class would have given, and gave, of those events," Dorfman argues. "Mampato is the dream, the self-justifying, idealized way, the best possible account they could have presented to their children, and to themselves, of the destruction of democracy in their land." The strength of Dorfman's reading is the close connection he draws between the seemingly disparate realm of the children's comics and high politics.

Dorfman's essay can profitably be read in conjunction with Thomas Andrae's "The Garden in the Machine," which offers an alternative interpretation of the same type of children's comics. In the years after World War II, Carl Barks (1901–2000) won an enormous audience for his comic book stories about Donald Duck and his extended clan (including three nephews and his miserly Uncle Scrooge). Among the most beloved of all American comic books, they have also had their share of critics. In their famous book *How to Read Donald Duck: Imperialist Ideology in the Disney Comic* (1975), Dorfman and co-author Armand Mattelart argued that Barks's stories inculcated neocolonial messages, showing the civilized and successful ducks as explorers profiting from the wealth gained through jaunts into third world countries.

Rereading the Barks oeuvre with care, Thomas Andrae argues these animal fables carried a gentler message, one of tolerance for other cultures and environmental awareness.

For Andrae, Barks was a pastoralist critical of modern society, and the lands the ducks visited were meant to be utopian alternatives to the depredations of modern life. "Barks was an anti-historicist who critiqued the First World's illusions of economic and technological progress as a model of development for underdeveloped nations," Andrae contends. "His story lays bare the dysfunctionality of the commodification of indigenous culture by American imperialism and satirizes the neocolonialist myths that legitimated it."

Cartoonist Bernie Krigstein (1919–1990) had a relatively brief career in comic books, running from 1943 to 1957. But during those years he brought a rare level of formalist concern to the stories he was asked to illustrate, particular when working for EC comics. John Benson, David Kasakove, and Art Spiegelman provide a panel-by-panel analysis of "Master Race" (1955), one of the most famous stories Krigstein illustrated. This essay highlights the dense layer of visual allusions in the story as well as Krigstein's care in fusing the breakdown of the page with the unfolding of the story.

This essay shows the strengths of what can be called a "close reading" approach, that is to say one that scrutinizes a relatively brief work with attention to minute details. Part of the authors' argument is that Krigstein's value as an artist is reflected in the fact that his work can withstand and reward such microscopic attention. In praising Krigstein they are seeking to clearly delineate his particular stylistic achievement: "In fact, much of the power that Krigstein brings to the story is due to his choice of a style which is the antithesis of standard comics storytelling. Instead of employing the exaggerated visual comic book phrases usually used to clearly denote action and emotion (speed lines, large beads of sweat, etc.), Krigstein uses a much more objective standard of delineation. Instead of frequent close-ups, an often used technique to get 'close' to a character's feelings, Krigstein keeps a physical distance from the characters. Instead of using 'dramatic' motion picture type lighting effects, Krigstein uses patterns of dark and light in much more abstract ways. Instead of a humanizing use of free shapes, Krigstein concentrates on using sharp angles and straight lines wherever possible."

Words and pictures work together in comics to tell a story: often true but not always. In Chris Ware's "Thrilling Adventure Stories" (1991) the pictures present a superhero tale while the words unfold a painful coming of age story. The story presents a formalist challenge that Gene Kannenberg, Jr., takes up with exegetical cleverness. As with the essay on Krigstein, Kannenberg approaches comics through an intensive, focused scrutiny in order to calibrate a cartoonist's particular aesthetic strength. "Through deliberate manipulation of the appearance and placement of text within—and surrounding—his comics pages, Ware exploits the graphic nature of printed comics text in ways few other cartoonists have attempted," Kannenberg argues. "In so doing, he takes full advantage of comics' innate ability to create complexity through the multivalent interpretive possibilities engendered by the form's presentation of structured text/image combinations."

Comics normally exist on the page but there has long been a parallel tradition of paracomics, whereby cartoon images are used as part of a stage performance. Among the classic cartoonists, Winsor McCay gave "chalk talks" to make comics come alive. The writer Alan Moore is a more recent example of an artist interested in making performative comics. In her essay on Moore and his occasional collaborator Eddie Campbell, Annalisa Di Liddo not only explores these performance works (and their adaptations into print comics), she demonstrates that they cast light into the very nature of comics as a medium. In

Di Liddo's essay we see that a close reading of comics is shown to be an activity that can move beyond rigid formalist boundaries. To appreciate Campbell's adaptation, Di Liddo argues, it "must not be read as an attempt to substitute the performance, but as an alternative and just as effective way to convey the multi-sensory experience of the live act."

Art Spiegelman's *Maus* (1991) is one of the most lavishly praised of all comics. Yet most of the attention that this groundbreaking work receives has focused on the contents (a story of surviving the Holocaust). Spiegelman's skills as a storyteller make this literary approach feasible, which has the unfortunate effect of leading commentators to avoid dealing with Spiegelman's art. In her essay "History and Graphic Representation in *Maus*," Hillary Chute works to counteract this tendency by focusing on "the specificities of reading graphically, of taking individual pages as crucial units of comics grammar." Reading graphically means teasing out the layers of meaning in Spiegelman's drawings and relating them to the thematic concerns of the work.

What distinguishes these essays is the way they use the array of analytical tools developed by comics scholars, applying in various measures historical context, social analysis, and formalist readings to the examination of particular comics. As such, they point towards the increasing success of comics scholars in synthesizing a range of approaches to gain a more integrated view of comics.

The Innocents March into History

ARIEL DORFMAN

In Santiago de Chile, every Wednesday on my way home, I used to buy a children's magazine called *Mampato*, and each evening, before putting my six-year-old son Rodrigo to bed, I would read it to him. It was 1973. The Allende government was fighting for its life. We were fighting for ours. There wasn't an instant to spare. Nonetheless, I always managed to keep that Wednesday appointment.

In the repetition of this act there was undoubtedly a sense of despair. To cling to a pattern or a schedule, some landscape untouched by violence, when things are falling apart, is to make believe that a semblance of normalcy remains somewhere, awaits us someplace. It is possible, however, that I was doing more than indulging in a family ritual on the brink of disaster. There may also have been a pinch of intellectual curiosity in my reading activities.

On the surface, there was nothing special about the magazine. It contained all the usual material of a semi-educational sort: nature studies, little vignettes on Chilean history, cutouts, puzzles, mazes, jokes, some comic strips from abroad, do-it-yourself sections. But *Mampato* was not only the name of the magazine. It was also the name of a boy, a character whose feats—to be eternally continued in the next issue—occupied four central full-color pages, as he and his friend Ogú, a primitive, overgrown caveman, ventured into the far future to battle the tyrant Ferjus. It was this story, drawn exclusively in Chile itself, which began to interest or should I say to obsess me.

As we read, each Wednesday, it began to dawn on me that what I was reading in the comic mirrored what was happening in the streets of Santiago. While Mampato and his friends went about the business of overthrowing a tyrant in the year 4000, Salvador Allende, the democratically chosen president of the real Chile, was being similarly branded "tyrant" by rather less fictitious forces seeking to oust him.

For a person who had already written books and essays on mass subliterature for children, and on the childish aspects of the adult media, this was a unique opportunity: to watch a comic strip intervening directly, albeit covertly, in history. I had assumed, and still do, that such fictional forms influenced people, especially youngsters, through a code of half-hidden values, which helped them adapt to reality by blurring out, or perhaps by falsely acting out, its dilemmas. I had therefore focused my attention primarily on the covert structure of the work itself—how it functioned, its meaning, and how it established certain formulas for success which could be popularized and incorporated into other versions and variations. I felt it was important to denounce the dominant model behind mass culture, the techniques, precepts, implicit educational views that shaped the consumer's imagination and dissolved his critical faculties. Although such a model was useful, displaying the invisible ideas that inform our everyday mythology, it was itself no more than a construction. Once this model has been inferred from the texts and frozen into a common denominator applicable to so many other media representations, it was easy to forget how it operated in reality: reacting to threats, defending the status quo, absorbing and reinterpreting the latest problems in neutral terms, trying to offer explanations for a seething, conflicting stream of troubles. By concentrating on the finished product, and trying to discover the ideological foundations behind it, I had separated it from the historical movement and matrix where it was produced and received by living human beings.

It was clear that behind each individual work there lurked, if we are allowed such melodramatic verbs, a consciousness industry. The owners of the economy and the State were also, of course, the owners of the means of definition, transmission, and reception of culture. They were a class. But I had not asked myself specifically how emotion and intellect came together, and under what circumstances, to spawn such works; what people, under what particular strains, with what degree of clarity or blind intuition produced mass subliterature. Nor had I explored how the chain of command and persuasion, economic and political interests, could obtain such results.

I told myself—and it was right to do so—that what I cared about were the effects on the readers. Mass media fiction, as opposed to art, leaves hardly any space for interpretation by the audience. With less leeway for participation, the passive consumer was restricted to certain foregone avenues and conclusions. So the reader I had in mind was not a real person who, with all his or her contradictions, must deal with that vision, accommodate it, modify it, fight it, succumb to it. My reader was, in a way, an idealization, an objective possibility that could be deduced or was implicit in the text itself.

A sociology of art, an examination of culture as an interplay between real readers and real producers, was not then, and is not now, my main intention. But the *Mampato* case gives us an opportunity, if not to answer questions about how such processes work in reality, at least to ask them. By observing a mass media production for children unfolding in particularly vivid historical circumstances, we can not only enrich the conclusions we have already reached but clarify some of the issues which have been, so far, left out of our perspective.

Mampato, accompanied by Ogú, has journeyed into the far future in order to visit his girlfriend Rena, who typifies everything a young lady should be according to upper-class Chilean standards: white-skinned, blond, green eyes, slim, wearing the latest fashions. She and the other inhabitants of her land are peaceful, beautiful telepaths who are technically very advanced (because here "all minds think in a united way") without having lost their naturalness and charm. Unfortunately, they are unable to defend themselves against their neighbors, "malign beings" out to "dominate the earth." Ferjus, the tyrant of that other country, can read minds, just like Rena. She, however, does not abuse this power ("It's not nice to invade private thoughts without asking permission"), while he uses it to subject and destroy his victims.

Each of these countries seems to be, in different ways, a recognizable metaphor for Chile. If Rena's land has the same topography (high mountains, cultivated valleys, the same sort of trees and birds), the despot's has the right shape. He reigns over a mammoth tree, as elongated and slender as Chile, its different floors or regions interconnected by elevators. If Rena's country is the utopia Chile might someday become (or, with its bucolic tranquility, what it supposedly once was), the realm of Ferjus projects the more contemporary and infernal image of a house ferociously divided against itself. Those responsible for such a sorry state of affairs are clearly "foreigners." Disciples of Ferjus, they are yellow-skinned usurpers of power who have many of the physical characteristics normally associated with villains: Dracula teeth, advanced prognathism, small heads on overmuscular bodies. To these features, which—as usual—seem to caricature the working class, may be added two which are typically Chilean: a certain Indian-like look; and helmets which are, in point of fact, the hard hats used by construction crews and identified with Allende's followers. Except for Prince Sicaliptus the First, the "stupid, cruel and lazy" son of Ferjus, there are no children or women among them.

These parasites have enslaved a hardworking, pacific, diverse-colored little (mutant?) people who, able of hand and nimble of wit, manufacture goods and till the land. They have done so with the help of spying rat-men, whose thoughts are so repugnant that Rena cannot even register them, and with the threat of the "Anthroposaurus," a prehistoric monster of colossal strength, with a hankering for slaves. Ferjus does not, however, need to call often on such extraordinary allies, for he can count on his armed forces, a mutant race of warrior giants, a good but befuddled lot who, time and again, with their confused leader, Gor, save the tyrant whenever somebody questions his authority.

Mampato leads the little people and their families in a protracted, desperate struggle for freedom. Time is running out. Previously, Ferjus had two kinds of weapons: primitive spears that he first used to conquer the tree, and more modern hand-held paralyzers which the little people have been producing against their will. Now he is forcing them to build an immense paralyzer with which to subjugate Rena's civilization and, eventually, the entire planet. Mampato's plan is to trick Ferjus. The little people will supposedly agree to his plan, while giving themselves time to plan a mutiny. Mampato is found out, taken prisoner, and is able to escape the tree only when one of the peaceful little mutants decides to use a gun to free his friend, overcoming his own disgust at the use of violence.

Outlaws (babes?) in the woods, they discuss the strategy.

"Those who have not accepted the rule of Ferjus are many. But [Ferjus is] very powerful. The only thing we know how to do is work."

"That's it," exclaims Mampato. "That will be our weapon."

In the next episode, one of the most surprising events in the history of mass media comics occurs. In none of the subliterature we have examined would such an incident be possible. In fact, I can't remember a strike ever having been shown favorably in children's mass fiction. And yet, it is a general strike that brings the tree to a standstill. The "yellow" men yawn and complain. "There are no slaves to milk the cows. Nobody is collecting fruit. The elevators aren't working." It is this last factor that is decisive, both in the strip and, as we shall see, in Chile itself. All vertical communication in such a long country has been cut off.

The rat-men offer a truce, a dialogue, though their intentions are to spy on the patriots. "Peace and friendship," they murmur, brandishing a dirty white banner. They offer the little people their assistance but would like to keep some of their slaves. They are given the boot.

Ferjus then sends the giant Cor on a surprise attack. He is to exterminate those who head the insurrection. But he's beaten by Ogú. As he's retreating, he's captured by a Zorko, a vegetable mutant that "surrounds and devours its victims." The rebels decide to help their enemy, and they set him free. Before he departs, shamefaced, he's taught a lesson in good manners by Mampato. "Gor, the mutants have saved your life. Remember that you are one of them. In spite of that, you serve the tyrants who have enslaved your people. Now you may leave."

As the titan withdraws, he looks at his ex-adversaries tenderly. It is clear that, during the future confrontation, he will line up with them.

We interrupt this story to bring the reader a special announcement. The issue that carried this heartwarming reconciliation went on sale at newsstands around the country on September 5, 1973. Before the next Wednesday's adventure appeared, the Chilean armed forces—on Tuesday the 11th of September to be precise—had staged one of the bloodiest coups in the history of Latin America.

Meanwhile, back in the forty-first century, our friends have fallen into a trap Ferjus sets for them. He has given the Anthroposaurus the go-ahead signal, and that beast is about to cannibalize Mampato and company. Fortunately, Gor and the other giants have had a change of heart and turn on their former masters. "We are also slaves and have been used against the other mutants."

Without military support, Ferjus and his last comrades take refuge at the top of the magnificent tree. They swear that they shall "overcome them, enslaving them in worse conditions than before." (Once again, a word from our sponsors: I have used the translation "we shall overcome," which has a progressive and activist coloring, to render "*los vencerernos*," which was the key phrase of the left in Chile, the one slogan publicly identified with the Allende regime from 1970 to 1973.)

The little people repudiate emigration as an alternative and decide to fight. "This is our land and we'll fight for it. The yellow race has come to enslave us and must go." While the enemy is alive, "there will be danger." An ingenious solution is arrived at: The tree has been "mined by the tunnels that the rat-men have burrowed." The mutants begin to "weaken the roots of the giant tree. Ferjus and his cronies will have to surrender."

But Ferjus won't get the chance. A devastating tempest knocks the tree down, extirpating it. Even though not intended by the good mutants, and not directly shown, the yellow race and the rat-men die. It is nature itself that has impersonally meted out justice. The brutality of this ending is somewhat mitigated by the fact that there were no women or children involved. Ferjus has, in a way, chosen the crazy path of self-elimination, punished by his own evil.

Now, "the tempest is over and the sun shines." Mampato says good-bye, while the little people, perched on the shoulders of the repentant giants or on the exposed roots of the tree, listen. "Mutant friends! The tyranny is at an end. You shall never more be slaves. Now you must all work together: the little people, the giants, the peasants and the rat-men. All the mutants laboring united will obtain a prosperous, free, and happy future!"

The end.

The end? Not quite.

We have just read a comic that, between May 1973 and October of that same year, week after week, has been telling the story of how an oppressor has been overthrown by an industrious and peaceloving populace. To those who reject the possibility that infantile literature can have political implications, the fact that the very story people were reading in a magazine was also being enacted in the streets may be no more than a surprising coincidence. But it is not enough to point an awed finger as if it were a "That's Incredible" situation. The parallels between the story and the history in which it was produced are simply too striking to be dismissed.

Allende was not ousted in a week. It took the ruling class almost three years of social mobilization, coupled with an economic blockade from abroad and sabotage from within, plus many errors and divisions inside the Popular Unity parties, to recover the executive branch. When the military finally intervened, it was because major shifts had already taken place in that society. Allende had lost all the potential allies that he needed in order to carry out his program and liberate his land, allies on whose tolerance, at the very least, he counted when he began his period in office. From any point of view—economic, political, ideological—the working class, which was the main motor of the revolution, had become increasingly, dramatically isolated; the middle classes, the Christian Democrats, the Christians, in short all those forces necessary to create a national front for such a transformation and preserve the democratic process, had gone over to the other side.

To achieve these ends, those who controlled the media and the cultural machinery in Chile waged a campaign in which Allende was portrayed as if he were Ferjus, and the Chilean people as if they were the mutinous mutants.

Nobody attempts a coup d'etat in the name of foreign companies that desire their mines and factories back, large industrialists who have lost their banks and monopolies, or a feudal aristocracy that has watched illiterate and impoverished peasants taking over its land. A coup d'etat is always carried out in the name of morality, freedom, and the fatherland, eternal values undermined by corruption and international communist conspiracies. The crusade of ethical surgery that will be painstakingly executed declares itself at the service of the "silent" people, the little folks, the peaceful and humble inhabitants of all social sectors who yearn for the "good old times" when they could work together without the artificial hatred imported from abroad by "aliens." An elected government, which jailed and tortured nobody, which stimulated total freedom of the press, which obeyed all judicial orders even when most of them were decreed by judges defending private interests and twisting the meaning of the law; a government which staged all scheduled elections and won most of them, was labeled illegitimate, unjust, and vindictive—in other words, a dictatorship.

The owners of Chile's economy, the perennial owners of its institutions, scrambled back into power by projecting the image of a noble country and a pure race besieged by malignant anti-Chileans bent upon taking over the world in conjunction with satanic international forces. These antipatriotic villains combined primitivism and modernity, stupid brutality with devious calculations. Public opinion was constantly being reminded of the terrors that the future held; the tremendous monster inside the working class which, once unleashed, would provoke a bloodbath and the end of civilization. This primeval force, which had been waiting in the darkness of the land and of the heart for an opportunity to attack an innocent population, could be defeated only by a miraculous intervention of the army, the navy, and the air force, the sole institutions left with the ability to safeguard the nation's continuity and identity.

The only way to deal with cancer is to cut, doctor, cut deep, and never mind the patient's screams. Allende's downfall, when it came, was seen by many not as a counter-revolution which would abolish democracy, not as the result of "destabilization" cooked up by Kissinger, but as the consequence of his own blind obstinacy or of tragic forces unchained from beyond, from the "very nature of things."

The adventures of Mampato in the forty-first century must be read in the context of this ideological war, whose presuppositions and thrust it shares. The comic strip does not portray the truth of what happened in Chile in those months but rather the version that the Chilean ruling class would have given, and gave, of those events. *Mampato* is the dream, the self-justifying, idealized way, the best possible acount they could have presented to their children, and to themselves, of the destruction of democracy in their land. Their own actions cannot appear under a more favorable light, nor advertise more honorable and disinterested objectives.

But *Mampato* is special not only because it is the scenario for the aspirations and the fears of a class that is reconquering power with the most drastic means at its disposal, but because it lets its protagonists use exactly the same tactics, and in the same order, as those that were actually used against Allende. Even more startlingly, *Mampato* often anticipated the stages of the uprising against Chile's leader. We can even summarize the strategy for both sequences with the same words, although we must adopt an uncomfortably neutral and dispassionate posture to do so.

A government that has a transitory monopoly on military strength has to be deposed. Insubordination begins weakly and doubtfully at first. Passive civil disobedience is followed by appeals to the authorities to mend their ways. Negotiations with the government allow time for the revolt to spread. Next come partial confrontations which the government can surmount due to the loyalty of the military. A strike paralyzes the country with the transport workers in the forefront. The government's call for a truce is rejected. Finally, after invocations of unity, liberty, and the fatherland, the armed forces break with their superiors and go over to the other side. The insurrection is successful, and those who caused the problem have not only disappeared but their very roots have been eradicated. The head of state's efforts to avert that outcome are useless: Each week finds him more alone, abandoned. He believes himself more powerful than he is, threatens everybody with an untapped, monumental force he has kept in reserve until now, accuses his armed forces of betrayal, takes refuge in a last sanctuary, refuses to surrender, and is wiped out with his faithful followers by a whirlwind of sudden violence.

We have just listened to the story of Ferjus; it is also the story of Allende.

Once a young reader, or an older one, has identified the two, at a subconscious, involuntary level, he is ready to interpret from the point of view of the plotters what is happening in his everyday life in those months, the prolonged and bitter struggle to oust Allende.

That sort of identification is furthered by a series of hints and overt parallelisms: the word *Venceremos* in the overlord's mouth; the speeches given by Mampato (almost verbatim renditions of many antisocialist slogans of the day); the description of the presidential guard in terms that remind us of the caricature of the Popular Unity partisans in the Chilean right-wing press. We could go on and on, showing how an element in one structure has dynamic counterparts in the other. But such an exercise, for those unfamiliar with the details of Chilean history, is a boring and, moreover, useless undertaking. To note that when, in an early October issue, Ferjus calls his giants "traitors" and retires to his treetop, he reminds us of Allende going to die in La Moneda, the presidential palace, ordering the women to leave, and transmitting a defiant message, we are not really adding essential data. Once the good little mutants are surreptitiously identified as the people of Chile, and the yellow-skinned parasites discharge the role of evil foreigners who have come to enslave them, all the other equivalents either fall into place, or are incessantly adjusted so that they will.

These similarities between corresponding structures are not so surprising. After all, Chile itself was being modeled by the same forces that were generating the magazine. The reader's first basic and vague intuition that the rebels are good and the government bad will be increasingly confirmed by an ongoing struggle in the streets, the barracks, and the banks. Chilean reality was being changed, managed, driven, manipulated—and children's literature was a zone of that reality—by a class that also, of course, accompanied its actions and interventions with a social consciousness, an indispensable, almost automatic set of ways of interpreting and understanding what is being done. If we can assert that Chilean history causes *Mampato*, we can also announce the reverse: Allende's downfall was orchestrated by countless acts such as the writing of this scenario. Story and history overlap and mutually reinforce each other.

These observations have some bearing on the discussion of the genesis of the adventures. It is tempting to surmise that we are in the presence of a juicy and full-fledged conspiracy to brainwash children and make a bloody putsch look like a patriotic endeavor. The arguments for such a view are persuasive. *Mampato* was brought out by the Lord Cochrane Company, the same enterprise that published *El Mercurio*, the most important newspaper in Chile. Since its foundation in the nineteenth century, *El Mercurio* had not only defended the ruling class's foreign and domestic interests but had always been the ideological counselor behind all Chile's governments, an "organic intellectual" in Gramscian terms if there ever was one. Let us add that Lord Cochrane is owned by the Edwards family, perhaps the most powerful oligopoly in Chile, connected to many multinationals. (Agustín Edwards was even international vice-president of Pepsi-Cola for some years.) *El Mercurio* not only received funds from the CIA during the Allende period, but its media blitz against the left was, it has been stated, directed by North American propaganda experts, specialists in graphic design and disinformation. What could be more natural than to cover all the bases by inventing a fable that would win the minds of the children?

Such suspicions are further enhanced by a strange incident. In late July, instead of continuing Mampato's adventures in the future, the readers were suddenly presented with a single-issue, self-contained episode involving Ogú in prehistoric times (supposedly due to "numerous solicitations"). It had nothing to do with current events. Such a bizarre and unprecedented interruption could always be attributed to technical difficulties or delays. However, there is another, more sensible interpretation for this lull. A few days before the issue was scheduled to come out, the Chilean cardinal, Raúl Silva Henríquez, called for national reconciliation and a dialogue between the Christian Democrats and the left to avoid civil war. The effort did not succeed, but there were rumors that a hefty sector of the opposition would enter a national-unity government. Under these circumstances, the publishers of Mampato's sortie against tyranny may have wanted to wait before committing themselves further to a strategy that might have to be modified.

Although this theory of a conspiracy is attractive, I feel it to be flawed. It is not just that we have no way of proving or disproving it, no way of researching the subject at the North American or the Chilean end, or even of listening to what we must conjecture would be the heated denials of Themos Lobos, the man who has written and drawn these adventures. This is not to say that I would be astonished to find out someday that it all was part of a preconceived campaign. I've long ceased to wonder at what the human mind—especially when the body is cornered, the life-style imperiled—can concoct. So many actions—among them a number that could be said to have no immediately verifiable political resonances—have turned out to come from conscious and rational planning, that this children's story might well be one of them. But such an explanation is, ultimately, no explanation at all. It is too easy and reductive, almost intellectually slothful, to suggest that each ideological action, each cultural creation, each set of new ideas and emotions comes from some entity—Machiavellian, all-powerful, and calculating—which programs our lives down to their last detail. It is true that some planning is always involved, particularly if we are dealing with the mass media, which spring from a complex chain of production, but this does not necessarily mean overt and unremitting control over the contents of its products. It is nearer the truth if we consider stories such as *Mampato* as the automatic answer by artists, already equipped with mechanisms of expression and set interpretations of the world, to new conflicts that they are living along with their readers, by which means they work out their dilemmas and make them comprehensible to others. Indeed, the purported freedom to create stories without "interference" from above is essential to the survival of such a system. The less the author feels himself a pawn in a strategy he does not control, the better his performance will be. The more his relationship to unbridled power is cloaked and velveted, the easier it will be for him to develop his ideas and characters without restraint. And meet the deadlines.

The person who conceived these episodes of *Mampato* was not that different from millions of other Chileans. They all were confronted by an intolerably tense situation, a day-by-day instability of emotions, painful and confusing contradictions which did not seem to permit the usual outlets. At such moments, many tend to fall back on the most traditional, reassuring, and therefore dominant solutions. There is comfort in conservation. Someone who works in the media has at his disposal means with which such reactions (in many senses of the word) can be objectified and communicated to others. What the creator of *Mampato* did with his fiction and his imagination others were doing in a myriad of different ways. His creation was inserted in a mesh of dread and hope which by innumerable channels, simultaneously, was germinating in Chilean society. He might have been copying reality, as when he translated the October 1972 truckers' strike against Allende into the elevator-operator strike of the mutants against Ferjus, or he might have been anticipating what was going to happen, as when he predicted, the week before the government was crushed, the change in sides of the armed forces.

What is difficult and perhaps futile to estimate is the intentionality of the author. He may or may not have been aware of his work as a political instrument for altering the state of mind of his audience. The final effect of his words and drawings does not depend on his consciousness of what he is doing.

We can illustrate this by studying two other *Mampato* adventures published in 1973. Both were of normal length, that is, half the Ferjus episode. The first extended from January to March, and recounted the capture of Ogú's tribe. A "red monkey-man," who is more "civilized and cruel" than Mampato's friend, has taken over Ogú's magic stick, the instrument and symbol of his power. Even though Mampato scolds him ("Forget your stupid superstition and remember that it is your obligation to liberate your people"), Ogú feels helpless, unable to reconquer his birthright. He has lost faith in his own capacity to "overcome" an adversary. As he wanders through the jungle, lamenting his loss, his son, disobeying his father's injunctions, secretly trails him. When the boy is finally captured and is about to be devoured by (that's right, here we go again) a gigantic primeval serpent, Ogú leaps into the fray and is victorious. "You don't need your magic stick," Mampato tells Ogú. "If I'm this strong without it," counters the caveman, "imagine what I'll do now that I have it back." (You don't need to imagine. Just ask the Chilean people.) Mampato comments, "Nothing is too difficult if you love your children."

This episode appeared during the summer of 1973, in the midst of the parliamentary elections that the right wing was confident of winning. They hoped to dominate the new Congress and, from there, impeach the President: a comfortable way of avoiding the embarrassment of a military takeover. In the previous months the country had been shaken by turmoil, with heavy student mobilization against the government. The story seems to be saying that it does not matter if the country has been occupied by "red" barbarians, who have usurped the executive, the very instrument with which power had been wielded up to that instant. Youngsters, by going out onto the streets to protest, are showing the way. There's no need to be downcast. Soon we'll have our "instrument" back.

However, the next episode, from March to May, is filled with panic. Because Allende did not lose the election. On the contrary, gainsaying the trend—in Chile, as in so many other countries—whereby the government voting percentage invariably declines in its first congressional test, the left took forty-five percent of the parliamentary vote, up more than nine percent from the presidential totals of 1970. This popular backing of Allende's policies—although the economy was in a deep crisis—engendered an atmosphere of despondency among his opponents. It is this climate that prevails in Mampato's odyssey in Atlantis, of all places. A volcano is about to erupt, while other minor cataclysms beleaguer the natives, and all that Mampato and some other inhabitants can think of is escape. A story of this sort, where the hero is defeated by natural catastrophes and hounded by the fear of apocalypse, is uncommon, not to say nonexistent, in children's mass literature, where some kind of triumph is always depicted.

Clearly, the Atlantis episode was suddenly substituted for the Ferjus story, whose advent had already been glowingly announced in the last Red Ape Man number. Coming next week: Mampato against Ferjus, villain of the forty-first century. . . . In other words, the editors had planned, as their post-election issue, a struggle against a dictator in the year 4000. Having reconquered a tribe in the far past, Mampato and Ogú would now assault a tyranny of the future.

Instead, we get a story which howls that everything is lost. Paradise is about to be ravaged by fire. It is better to abandon the sinking ship and emigrate. We seem to be confirming the conspiracy theory.

But there is a slight problem. This episode corresponds to the mood but not to the interests or the intentions of the Chilean ruling class. I do not think it is correct to understand the Atlantis story as a mere attempt to adjust the reader's experience to prevalent beliefs. Instead, we must explore it, just as with any other aesthetic phenomenon, as a symptom of a contemporary crisis, a mirror for problems that are inscribed or reflected unconsciously in its structure. This is another sort of function, which goes beyond simple instrumentality.

All these examples, and particularly the last one, make it seem plausible that the man who was writing the script and drawing the characters, rather than being caught up in a conspiracy, was caught up in the mood of the times, fluctuating according to the social winds and undercurrents. More than part of a plan, his stories seem to have been part of a larger collective effort in imagining, foreclosing, even exorcising the future. In this lies, precisely, the strength of the dominant system. It enables each person to react to different situations, to adapt their thoughts and views in certain safe, preordained, sanitized directions. Nobody is commanding that they think or feel or interpret in this way.

Control over each idea and emotion is not required, because powerful political and economic interests hold sway over a more crucial link, or bottleneck, of the process of communication: They can select the messages, retain those that coincide with their positions, and prevent and discard those that are critical or doubtful. One only has to imagine what would happen if the story of Ferjus were to appear in Chile today. It would be relatively incoherent, and might not fit as snugly as it did in 1973. There is, for instance, no truckers' strike against Pinochet (at least not yet), and the president's thugs are far from being construction workers. But in spite of certain inconsistencies, most of the population would deem it an attack on the current dictatorship. That is exactly why it would never be published. The owners of the magazine, or the people they have put in charge of it, would see to that. When a product deviates beyond a tolerable frontier, when it jars the existing web of beliefs and cannot be rewritten or accommodated, only then does the real power, the real ownership pattern, emerge from the shadows.

This sort of intervention, however, tends to be unnecessary. The less visible and purposeful it is, the more successful, if self-censorship does not do the trick, the genre itself, its techniques, perceptions, practices, and traditions oversee and influence the producer, keep him within limits. Let us not forget that, in general, these stories do not betray a direct, causal relationship with society. To go against the grain is political; to flow with it is entertainment. That is how the cards are stacked.

This reminds us that we could, after all, treat *Mampato* as we have treated Donald Duck or the Lone Ranger: We could watch the variations on a model which we have already established. Mampato and Ogú, for instance, continue in the tracks of the heroes we have examined. One of them represents the child-as-savage, the dominated social and psychological zones of life, while the other is the child-as-adult, acting out the predominant values with total responsibility, both of them working together to reestablish an order that has been menaced by chaos and "injustice." Or we could observe that Rena's people, like Babar's, have solved the tension between civilization and wilderness, between city and country, between science and the simple life, by embodying a *Reader's Digest* utopia where modern technology coexists with natural virtue. These, and so many other structures, would be found in most other mass media products for children and for adults in the Western world.

Because these formulations are disguised, or mediated, one needs considerable intellectual stamina and some mischievous malice, as this book proves, to disentangle their political genesis, unmasking the different stages in the manufacture of consciousness, the routes by which true problems are given false solutions. These forms of fiction cannot but exhibit themselves as fun, denying (and indeed erasing) any links to more serious issues or interests. What is fascinating about *Mampato* is that, along with the role of strategic defender of the status quo which it shares with other comics, it has been forced by history to assume a different role—a tactical one. This new function, in which infantile literature becomes instrumentalized in a political confrontation, is added to its previous and simultaneous existence as a guardian of "eternal" values and procedures, the very guidelines and storylines that the consumer has a taste for, has been led to expect. When a crisis of such dimensions as the Chilean one shakes the foundations of society, threatens to overturn and revolutionize prevailing conditions of power and property, the media tend to abandon their "neutrality." They divest themselves of the autonomy they normally need to operate without becoming suspect. At times such as these, the connection between culture and society becomes more manifest and can be laid bare. In this case, the permanent manipulation that has always been the invisible law behind *Mampato* is more effortlessly revealed, because the magazine itself has drifted—we cannot tell whether on purpose—into the arena of everyday conflict.

Our analysis of *Mampato* has an advantage over our preceding explorations: It has zeroed in on the specific, giddy moment in which a whole chain of mass-art production has been forced to adapt dynamically and change according to pressing challenges and requirements. This alteration under the stress of history is not unique. What *Mampato* performs with such urgent transparency is repeated constantly, almost mechanically, but on a different scale, in a different, slower rhythm, by other mass media products around the world. Each of them has been flexibly produced in a situation as solid, material, and full of uncertainties as the one that gave birth to *Mampato*, but because they were not responses to emergencies, their intricate, immediate relationship with society is not so easily uncovered. As if they were orphans·set loose in the universe, nephews without a father, their origins have been lost, and it is an arduous, thankless, often impossible task to pinpoint and reconstruct the source from which they arose.

It is enough to understand, as we have done, I hope, the ways in which they link up with trends in society and forces in history, their inception in the prevalent ideological and cultural models. Our analysis of *Mampato*, however, affords us a vision of some of the richness we may be losing by not being able to ground these products in daily circumstances, where they could acquire added significance; and where, indeed, burrowing into the hidden turmoil of a period of social gestation, we might see how critical elements are dealt with as they emerge, and are answered by a system in unceasing evolution. Who does not dream of a "natural history" of cultural forms?

But just because the parenthood of Mampato's 1973 adventures is unquestionable, just because we have found out who his father really is (or is it only his stepfather?), does not mean that such an enterprise is, in itself, devoid of methodological risks. Even if we could operate in a similar fashion for each work we have studied, we would still have many pitfalls to hurdle. To prove, for instance, that the offensive of Mampato and his mutants is parallel to that of Allende's rivals, one must have established beforehand a periodization, stages in the attack, and a framework for the comprehension of Chile's recent history. Have we then discovered in the work only what we had already surreptitiously analyzed into it? Have we disinterred only those structures that we wanted revealed in the first place?

Indeed, there are many who would not only reject my premises as absurd (children's literature has nothing to do with social issues, unless it is propaganda and intentional), but would also refuse to agree with the way in which I have dissected the struggles of the year 1973. A different viewpoint on that society might yield other results. Such an approach, an observer would assert, is not exclusive to *Mampato*. Indeed, mass fiction of this sort can be denounced as limiting people's capacity for understanding the world and transforming it, because the author has decided, before he began to write, that there was such an entity as a dominant system, and a manner in which it functioned and persuasively victimized its members. The conclusions of such a study would therefore be suspect, because they derive from a construction, an ideological position that leads the critic to detect, perhaps even to reconstruct, in the works he is researching a similar architectural configuration.

These sort of accusations hold enough truth to worry me. I feel that my observations on children's literature and on the childlike aspects of adult mass media production reveal the essence of their ultimate effects; but I also believe that I have not gone far enough into the complexities of the incestuous association between culture and society, nor have I taken sufficiently into account the fact that those who scrutinize these matters are themselves a product of what they are studying, occupy a mobile place both in history and in the field of knowledge. It is outside the range of this essay—and, indeed, far from my current interests—to engage in an exploration of the sociology of culture, that elusive, all-encompassing scientist's apprentice. But that does not mean that I am unable to recognize that these methodological questions have implications for my conclusions and, in a perplexing manner, limit their impact.

I am also troubled by another aspect of this debate. By stating that the works I am studying are inimical to the freedom and humanity of those who read them, I am probably scaring off the very people I would like to reach. Although it is important to deepen the discussion with those who would concur with my belief that the present economic and political structures generate a culturally repressive situation, I would prefer to journey, as I stated in the first chapter, beyond the circle of the preconvinced and the already initiated. But, of course, to those who devour mass media products with all the innocence available to them, plucking specimens from the tree of fun, my reinterpretations of their reality from a radically diverse perspective will seem not only a disgusting and biased exercise but a threatening one. The only answer to this is that I am a historical subject, as much a product of history as *Mampato* or Babar or the *Reader's Digest* is. As much as the readers or nonreaders of these pages. As much as an author who would read these works from a supposedly neutral point of view, purely as archetypes, myths, entertainment, or psychoanalytical manifestations.

To recognize this condition, and make it part of the perspective from which we seek to comprehend our circumstances, to be wary of our own preconceptions and correct ourselves, is vital. There can be no retreat, however, from holding a position. For me, the only way in which it becomes possible to open the closed shutters of reality, the only way to break the idols and the icons and unlock their secrets, is to bring to them a view which is, in a sense, alien and blasphemous. To the general feeling of being an outsider, a rebel against the status quo, I add my coming from a continent which is in itself outside the mainstream of events. To be politically committed may affect the outcome of research, but it is also an instrument with which the surface placidity of things can be disrupted, whereby the object can reveal its innards, its skeleton, its truth.

There is, I think, no other way to advance our knowledge.

The case of *Mampato* shows us a breed of readers who lived history as it was sketched in a story, readers who acted as if reality were identical to what they were imagining through adventures in a faraway century. They were being subtly told that the death of Chilean democracy, the massacre of thousands, the denationalization of the economy, the assassination of the President, was in fact an epic struggle for justice and freedom. They did not even realize that they were being indoctrinated; because, just like millions all over the world who consume other mass media messages of less obvious origins, they cannot entertain the notion that their innocence, and that of their characters, is profoundly fraudulent.

If they were willing to risk the destruction of that innocence, they might be able to see that it is Mampato who helped plan the coup, Ogú who is pulling the trigger, Rena who is cleaning and absolving us all.

It would change them beyond their softest dreams.

But that, of course, would be another story.

Or do I mean another history?

The Garden in the Machine

THOMAS ANDRAE

To heighten his critique of modernity, the Disney artist Carl Barks (1901–2000) invoked an imaginary world of lost races and societies. These tales encompass both satirical portraits of urban civilization and a longing for a utopian transcendence of modern life. They reflect Barks's upbringing on the rural Oregon frontier and portray isolated, agricultural communities uncontaminated by modern life and inhabited by lost races, most typically of elfin little people, who resist the ducks' encroachment into their sanctum sanctorum. These creatures tend to be insular and pacifistic, living in harmony with nature and each other. As such, they offer a striking contrast to the hierarchy, exploitation, and domination of nature characteristic of modern Duckburg.

The notion of a lost city that exists simultaneously with but unknown to contemporary urban civilization has fascinated fiction writers, religious clerics, and philosophers since the Middle Ages. At that time, many people believed that paradise still existed in some far-flung corner of the earth.[1] With imperialism at its height, popular versions of the lost city mythos became prevalent in Anglo-American popular fiction in the nineteenth century, as in the stories of H. Rider Haggard and science fiction authors such as H. G. Wells and Edgar Rice Burroughs and in film adaptations of their books. The image of the lost city also became a major theme in 1930s movie serials such as *The Phantom Empire* and *The Lost City*. Such modern fantasy writers as J. R. R. Tolkien have evolved the mythos into detailed portraits of alternative worlds.

According to Stanley Diamond, primitive societies rest on a communal economic base.[2] This is not to say that everything in such societies is owned in common. Personal property such as tools, weapons, clothes, and so forth exists. However, the material means of group survival either are held in common or are accessible to any individual and therefore need not be owned communally. As a consequence, claims Diamond, class stratification and economic exploitation as they are present in archaic and modern civilizations are absent in primitive cultures. Even when a degree of exploitation exits, as in protostates usually through payment of tribute or labor service—it rarely results in economic ruination of one group by another. Primitive societies have no concept of economic gain: work is for pleasure or use rather than profit. In contrast to modern societies, everyone

---

Reprinted by permission and adapted from Thomas Andrae, *Carl Barks and the Disney Comic Book: Unmasking the Myth of Modernity* (University Press of Mississippi, 2006), 157–86.

receives a guarantee of subsistence, an assurance that Paul Radin calls the "irreducible minimum," the "inalienable right" of all individuals in the community to "food, shelter, and clothing," irrespective of the amount of work contributed by them to the acquisition of the means of life.[3] No one starved unless the whole tribe was starving.

Such societies also lacked political states and their apparatuses of centralized administration, laws, and courts. Consequently, individuals possessed a high degree of personal autonomy bounded by the needs of the group. According to Radin, "If I were asked to state briefly and succinctly what are the outstanding features of aboriginal civilization, I, for one, would have no hesitation in answering that there are three; the respect for the individual, irrespective of age or sex; the amazing degree of social and political integration achieved by them; and the existence of a concept of personal security which transcends all forms and all tribal and group interests and conflicts."[4]

Barks's adventures offer a unique hybrid form combining funny animals in highly realistic settings, imaginary worlds set in authentic, historical cultures. "I always tried to tie my stories in to the locale," he explained in 1975. "It had to be grounded right on the earth of that particular scene. That is, if you're going to the Andes, it had to look like the Andes, the ways of the people, and the ways of nature and the terrain, everything had an effect on the gags and dictated the type of gags that I would use." Although he created imaginary worlds, Barks wanted to infuse them with an aura of realism and believability. "I wanted kids to be able to identify with a place that they themselves could go to, a place that was possible, that they could find in their history books."[5]

While Barks's use of realistic settings stemmed from a desire to make his stories plausible, the imaginary nature of the societies that he created derives from their symbolic and psychological dimensions. The emphasis on little people marks the tales' affinity to fairy tales. Yet Barks's stories do not possess the trappings of fairy tales: they do not deal with kings, princes, or princesses, and there is no hint of magic, a *sine qua non* of most fairy tales. Rather, what Barks's little people stories draw from fairy tales is their utopian dimension.

The rise of the fairy tale coincided with the decline of feudalism and the rise of a bourgeois public sphere. According to Jack Zipes, the middle class originally considered fairy tales immoral because of their implicit and explicit critique of utilitarianism and bourgeois morality. The emphasis on play, alternative forms of living, the pursuit of dreams, and striving for a golden age "challenged the rationalistic purpose and regimentation of life to produce for profit and expansion of capitalist industry."[6] Dominant bourgeois groups considered fairy tales amoral because they subverted bourgeois virtues of order, discipline, industry, modesty, and cleanliness, and these groups regarded the emphasis on imagination as harmful to children. As capitalism and bourgeois morality became more firmly established, the tales began being rewritten and watered down, becoming moralistic and didactic, and began to serve compensatory functions, soothing the public's alienation from the harshness of industrial life by retreating into a realm of pastoral innocence. Conversely, avant-garde artists and writers in the romantic movement utilized the fairy tale as a form of protest against the utilitarian ideals of the Enlightenment. Thus, many tales harbored elements of critique. According to philosopher Ernst Bloch, "the fairy tale narrates a wish-fulfillment which is not bound only by its own time and the appeal of its content."[7] Fairy stories remain vital because of their capacity to harbor unfulfilled wishes in symbolic form and to project the possibility of their realization.

Bloch coined the word *Vor-Schein* (anticipatory illusion) to explain how fairy tales can mirror processes invoked by the imagination that depend on humanity's use of reason to carry through the wishes of fantasy. The fantastic images of such tales can estrange the reader from everyday life, providing a critical reflection on the ways that social and cultural discourses confine us within the parameters of "normal" thought and practice by opening up the possibility that what Bloch called the "little fellows" could recover power and autonomy and take control of their lives. As Alison Lurie observes, in common parlance the little people are not elves but surrogates for children and, before feminism, what we would call the "common man" or the "man on the street." Supernatural powers were claimed for the least powerful among us—that is, children and anonymous, invisible ordinary citizens. In "pixolatry," she claims, this power "was to be found not in great cities, but in out-of-the-way rural locations; in forgotten villages, isolated farmhouses, untidy patches of woods."[8] Barks's comics invoke the same protagonists and the same locales.

Bloch argued that the consciousness of a group or class does not flow directly from the material conditions of its existence. Socioeconomic developments can bring about a certain non-synchronism in people's lives. A group of people may live in the present yet still think in terms of a previous time or behave in terms of ideas and cultural discourses of a past society. Such is the case when social development does not fully resolve the contradictions of a previous social formation. As a result, groups or classes that are marginalized or left out may feel dissatisfied, alienated, and confused and may yearn for the fulfillment of needs and desires that have been overlooked or are no longer considered meaningful or verifiable in the dominant culture. The residual ideologies and social practices that encode these wishes thus can offer alternative or oppositional critiques of the dominant culture. In Barks's stories, not the future but the past offered glimpses of (albeit imperfect) utopian alternatives to modernity.

"Mystery of the Swamp" (*Donald Duck* Four Color #62 [1944]), was Barks's first story about an imaginary society. He explained the story's genesis:

> I had been struggling for days, trying to think of something I could use for a long story plot. There was a whole bunch of company in the house at the time, and I never had time to really sit down and think of anything. Finally, I got to the point where I just ignored the company and did some serious thinking. All of a sudden I got to thinking of the Everglades and what sort of creatures besides alligators would he find in the Everglades. And just like that, I thought of all these weird little people, like little gnomes who lived out there. . . . So I just sat there and let the thoughts pour all over me. When I had gotten enough that I knew I had a story, I joined the party and hoisted a few drinks.[9]

Barks's imagination had been sparked by reading about the Everglades in *National Geographic.*[10] The Florida swamp's untamed environs, flotilla of small islands, and exotic birds and alligators provided the backdrop for a new kind of adventure story—a place of mystery "that no man has ever seen!" as a stranger tells Donald.

The swamp's inaccessible reaches provided a home for the Seminole Indians. In 1819 Spain ceded Florida to the United States, and settlers got the Seminoles to agree to move onto a reservation. The Americans' greed was insatiable, however, and they wanted more territory. In 1830, the settlers got the backing they wanted from President Andrew Jackson, and the U.S. Congress passed the Indian Removal Act, which forced many Indians off their lands. Many died in the march to the Indian Territory infamously known as the Trail of Tears. Only one group of Indians successfully resisted removal— the Seminoles. After a series of wars, around five hundred Seminoles remained in Florida, hiding in the alligator-infested Everglades, where white men dared not venture. Though the draining of the Everglades and the paucity of game have forced the Seminoles into closer contact with outsiders, they remain the only Indian tribe never to have signed a formal peace treaty with the U.S. government.

Donald finds the Gneezles, like the Seminoles, living cut off from the outside world and using the traditional bow and arrow. Like their Indian counterparts, the Gneezles have a long hostility toward civilization. "Go back! Go back!" calls a Gneezle guard. "Gnot for a millyun years has human creeters entered the land of the Gneezles!" Like the Seminoles, the Gneezles are undaunted by their civilized foes, and the ducks are unable to defeat the tribe despite their superior weaponry.

Barks had also been inspired by Disney's animation factory. The portfolio that won him a tryout at the Disney Studio contained two drawings based on the not-yet-completed feature *Snow White and the Seven Dwarfs*. However, while the dwarfs in that film were cute and cherubic, Barks's dwarfs are bizarre and wacky looking and include a backwoods hayseed and ethnic caricatures such as an Irish leprechaun, a Jewish elf, and a parody of Gandhi wearing only a towel. All have the bulbous noses, long beards, and strange hats that would later characterize the Gneezles.

The Gneezles' appearance and the idea of making them gnomes were partly inspired by Barks's desire to depart from Disney's dwarfs and other well-known imaginary creatures. Barks recalled, "I just tried to make them different so they'd look like fairy creatures rather than part of our human world. They had pointy ears and finny feet and wore crazy costumes. They were fairy tale creatures who lived in the area so long they had become swamp Okies."[11] The Gneezles' Okie patois, love of square dancing, and use of the bow and arrow all link them to the agricultural societies of the American frontier. They are rural rednecks, and Barks clearly sympathizes with their hostility toward and retreat from civilization; indeed, the bulbous noses he gave them were a trademark of his self-caricatures.

Barks's portrait of Gneezle Gnob, the Gneezles' city, was his first attempt at rendering an imaginary society, and he created it out of whole cloth rather than grounding it in previously existing societies. Consequently, he was unable to make the elements of his fictional world fully cohere. We are given a pastiche of details from various periods and cultures rather than a unitary world. In the crowd scene, for example, an assembly of elders wears Amish-style hats, while two guards sport Roman helmets and carry medieval halberds adorned by Indian-style feathers. Barks implies that the Gneezles have stolen this mélange of costumes and props over the centuries from groups of invaders. The effect is comic and exotic but gives us little sense of who the Gneezles are. Donald and his nephews escape from Gneezle Gnob only when the Gneezle king allows them to, and he leaves apples spiked with "fergettin' juice" so that they can recall nothing of their adventure. The land of the Gneezles thus remains only an oneiric presence like the fairy tale, an emblem of our fears of civilization and desire to escape.

Barks created his first fully realized imaginary world in "Lost in the Andes" (*Donald Duck* Four Color #223 [1949]). This story had its roots in the Disney films *Saludos Amigos* and *The Three Caballeros*, anthologies of animated shorts dealing with Latin America. Since these films were projects of the U.S. State Department's "Good Neighbor Policy," intended to encourage the two American continents, in Disney's words, to "like one another better," the films had a political purpose. They were aimed at shoring up pan-American unity as a bulwark against Fascism during World War II. They had an economic motive as well: to capitalize on Latin America's cheap, nonunion labor, the U.S. government sought to send film producers like Disney to the country to test the feasibility of setting up Hollywood film production there. Disney had his own economic rationale for the trip to Latin America: having lost most of the foreign market for his films because of the war, he saw South America as a viable new market for his cartoons.

South American scholars have been highly critical of the representations of Latins in these films. Julianne Burton-Carvajal, for example, views *The Three Caballeros* as an allegory of First World colonialism and argues that the film provides a "narrative of conquest in which the patriarchal unconscious and the imperial unconscious insidiously overlap" the most egregious example of which is the lascivious Donald's mad chase after doe-eyed Latina bathing beauties, ripe for conquest.[12] Appropriately originally titled *The Surprise Package*, the film is structured around "gifts" of Latin culture that Donald receives from his new Latin friends. Much in the same way, Disney utilized Latin culture as raw material for his films—to be repackaged, commodified, and sold to American audiences as "authentic" examples of exotic Latinness.

"Lost in the Andes" moves in an opposite direction. Barks was an anti-historicist who critiqued the First World's illusions of economic and technological progress as a model of development for underdeveloped nations. His story lays bare the dysfunctionality of the commodification of indigenous culture by American imperialism and satirizes the neocolonialist myths that legitimated it.

Barks depicts three different civilizations, implicitly inviting us to draw comparisons between them. The first is modern Duckburg, a place of petty hierarchies and alienated labor. Dignity, wealth, and social status are available only to the few at the top. A fourth-assistant janitor at the local museum, Donald longs to be third-assistant janitor and to give rather than take orders. When he enthusiastically jumps at the chance to polish the museum's rare gemstones, he is ignominiously grabbed by the neck and told by the third-assistant janitor to polish a "collection of rubble" instead. Even when Donald accidentally discovers that these "stones" are really "square eggs" he receives no credit for the discovery.

Duckburg functions as an assemblage of isolated teams working separately rather than functioning harmoniously for the good of the community as a whole. A group of scientists and experts examine the rare eggs, trying to classify and categorize them by their physical properties. Barks depicts the scientists as caricatures of instrumental rationality, narrow-minded specialists so concerned with discovering what the square eggs are that they are blind to the ends to which their knowledge will be put. One has whiskers that cover most of his face; another has thick glasses and prune-like wrinkles, symbols of his myopia and desiccated humanity. Duckburg's egg barons are also morally bereft. Barks shows them salivating in anticipation of the mega-profits the square eggs will bring in solving the stacking problem. To maximize profit, the tycoons would bring all nature under their control, making eggs conform to a square shape. Satirizing the capitalists' arrogance, Barks drew them with egg-shaped bald domes that mirror the contours of the globe behind them. The farmers too are enmeshed in the mania. Rather than being close to nature, they dream of crossing square roosters with round hens, blind to the Frankensteinian implications of such tampering. The anxious look on a rooster's face indicates the deformation of nature that would result.

The expedition to Peru is structured like the museum hierarchy. Barks portrays it as a dysfunctional bureaucracy that promotes individual irresponsibility and distorts communication through its chain-of-command structure. Each of the levels sneaks a taste of the professor's omelet, which the nephews, unknown to the others, have made from square eggs. Although each one finds that it tastes rank, he passes it along to his superior, never correcting the original mistake. As a result, everyone from Donald to the professor ends up in sick bay with acute "ptomaine ptosis of the ptummy," in Barks's brilliant alliterative turn of phrase, an illness that causes the stomach to tie itself up into "square knots."

The second civilization is that of the Andean natives of contemporary Peru. Barks parodies the readiness with which they abandon their local culture to produce for the tourist trade. When Donald flashes wads of cash offering to buy any square eggs they can find, the natives crank out fakes using ice trays and a "Ward and Roebuck" cement mixer. Barks's satire shows the way in which a neocolonial system of exchange destroys indigenous cultures to make Third World subjects into avid and dependent consumers in a global capitalist market.

The third civilization Barks presents is of a pre-Columbian Inca city, Plain Awful. Aided by an old vicuna hunter, the ducks tumble through the mists of time to discover a strange square-shaped city hidden beneath the fog. "Sure is a blocky-lookin' place!" exclaims Donald. In one of his most famous splash panels, Barks drew a complete square-shaped city. Barks drew inspiration from images of the idiosyncratic stone architecture of the Inca in the National Geographic, especially those of the lost city of Machu Picchu (Old Mountain), which is famous for its polygonal masonry. Most of the buildings were made of granite blocks fitted together without mortar so perfectly that even the thinnest knife blade could not be forced between them.[13]

Preceded by the corrupt worlds of modern Duckburg and the contemporary native village, the square city might be expected to be a primitive utopia. And to some extent it is. The Plain Awfultonians' "southern hospitality" stands in stark contrast to Donald's demeaning treatment as fourth-assistant janitor in Duckburg. Although he is ignored for his discovery of the square eggs in that environment, the ancient Incas elevate the ducks to high positions for their discovery of the square chickens that lay the eggs that make up the natives' sustenance. "They had so little of anything," muses Donald after leaving the city, "yet they are the happiest people we have ever known!"

However, Barks's portrait of the Inca culture is ambivalent. Although he finds them superior to capitalist modernity, Barks rejects a romantic primitivism that elevates pre-industrial cultures to the status of utopias. Plain Awful, as its name suggests, is radically flawed. It is conformist and shackled by custom. When the nephews blow round bubbles with their chewing gum, the Awfultonians threaten to consign the ducks to a lifetime of hard work in the "terrible stone quarries" as punishment for committing such sacrilege. Only when the nephews learn a trick that enables them to blow square bubbles are they freed. Barks's story implies that primitive societies have a spirit of community and generosity but are so conformist and custom-bound that they lack tolerance and freedom of expression. However, as we shall see shortly, this view stems from a conflation of primitive and archaic cultures.

Plain Awful seems at first to have always been the blocky place we see. But much of its culture has resulted from an earlier visit by another American, Professor Rhutt Betlah of the Birmingham school of English. Barks's wordplay on Clark Gable's character Rhett Butler in *Gone with the Wind* refers to another insular, agricultural society, the Old South.[14] In a bizarre example of the colonizing process, much of the Awfultonians' culture results from this lone American. In a metonymic riff, Barks's story equates South America with the American South. The Awfultonians speak in southern dialect, pride themselves on their southern hospitality, and love to sing "Dixie." Their country even gets its name from the professor and dates its history by his visit. Barks's Plain Awful implicitly parodies the bigotry of the American South: because of their intolerance of difference, the natives perceive Donald as "queer-looking" even though they are square-shaped, subject the ducks to southern lynch-law justice, and threaten to make them lifetime slaves.

The shock of seeing Inca primitives as faux southerners invites a process of reader estrangement, working to defamiliarize and "make strange" to readers assumptions of neocolonialism that are embedded in Eurocentric culture, that are normalized and taken for granted. This approach invites readers to examine how Anglo-Americans have defined native culture for those in the metropolis while eliding indigenous peoples' voices. In political policies such as the Monroe Doctrine, the United States declared its supremacy in the Americas and assimilated Latin America to U.S. interests. Barks's story satirizes this cultural amnesia by making it seem ridiculous.

This estrangement process exposes what Beau Riffenbaugh calls "the myth of the explorer." The explorer had his heyday in the nineteenth and early twentieth centuries. "Men who achieved remarkable feats were more than just popular heroes," Riffenbaugh writes. "They were symbols of real and imagined nationalist and imperialist cultural greatness. Explorers, confirming as they did the heroism, romance, and adventure of empire, were a particularly celebrated genre."[15] With Social Darwinism and the western demand for the conquest of the physical world serving as ideological justification for their actions, explorers opened the way for national expansion by overcoming the challenges of the natural world, defeating "barbarism," mapping the unknown, and establishing trade. Since continued expansion provided a means of achieving or maintaining moral, racial, and national superiority, exploration came to symbolize a nation's collective cultural superiority.

Barks's satire of the western explorer is grounded in the introduction of Machu Picchu to the West. Professor Hiram Bingham from Yale University, who "discovered" the city in 1911, becomes the "Professor from Birmingham." Although other westerners and the Andeans themselves previously knew of the city, Bingham received the credit because of his exploitation of the journey in the media.[16]

Barks's tale is structured around the treasure hunt motif that characterizes the colonial adventure story. The hero typically braves native threats and gains the treasure for a song, returning to civilization in triumph. Barks subverted this ending, opting for an ironic closure. Instead of building the "new breed of super poultry" so assiduously desired by Duckburg's egg barons, farmers, and scientists, Donald mistakenly returns with two square roosters. The corporate scheme to dominate the world is derailed by a revolt of nature that ironically mocks its illusions of grandeur.

"Lost in the Andes" is considered one of the Duck Man's best stories, and Barks himself lauded it for its "technical" perfection and the fact that it was laced together by means of running gags—that is, jokes that recur throughout a story. "It was puffed up in the studio's story department as being a very good gimmick if you could get a running gag going to connect sequences," Barks recalled. "Look how the chewing gum gag holds the Andes story."[17]

Barks's art is denser in this story than in any previous one, displaying a use of "deep focus"—a term in film criticism that denotes a shot's ability to keep foreground, middle ground, and background all in clear view. Backgrounds in the story are highly defined, making the imaginary word come alive. Such high definition creates a feeling of claustrophobia in the reader, evoking fears of confinement that mirror the suffocating uniformity of Plain Awful and its square world.

Nonetheless, Barks was not satisfied with his most spectacular drawing in the story-the splash panel of the city: "I botched up my perspective a little in drawing that; I should have laid out all these squares down here by measuring points instead of from the vanishing point—see how they become diamond-shaped toward the bottom of the panels? When I was drawing it, some neighbor friend dropped in and sat there persistently talking to me, all the time that I was trying to make that big, complicated layout. And I would have to look up and answer, with my thoughts interrupted . . . it's been a problem my whole life: whenever I was up against something on which I had to use my head and do some really deep thinking, somebody would always come along and have to talk about something?"[18] Yet the story marks a high point in Barks's mastery of graphic narrative and one of the medium's greatest stories.

Despite his faithful rendering of its architecture, Barks's portrait of an Inca-like civilization was anachronistic. His attraction to simple, communal societies led him to mischaracterize the Incas as a primitive social order when, in fact, they were a highly sophisticated, imperialistic culture with a far-flung empire that stretched along the Pacific coast from the equator south to Chile. Built by the Inca king Pachacuti between 1460 and 1470, Machu Picchu itself was not a poor, communal city, as Barks portrayed it, but a retreat for the Incan royal family characterized by luxury and spaciousness at a time when ordinary citizens lived in windowless, one-room huts. The hospitality and friendliness of Barks's Incan town stands in contrast to the Incan habit of conducting human sacrifices as part of religious rituals.[19] Diamond classifies the Incas as an archaic society because they possessed a proto-state. Unlike primitive societies, which were proto-democratic and lacked formal governments, the Incas created a centralized, totalitarian government that controlled every aspect of subjects' lives.[20] Although the Plain Awfultonians live a life of ease and contentment, Inca stone architecture was created through slave labor, a fact alluded to, but never developed, in Barks's story when the ducks are threatened with a lifetime of toil in the stone quarries as punishment for breaking the city's taboos against depicting anything not square.

In fact, this taboo did not exist in Incan civilization, whose religion revolved around worship of the circular orb of the sun and the irregularly shaped Andes. Indeed, Machu Picchu's architecture functions as a kind of cosmic clock, the sun and constellations appearing in certain stone windows at specific times of the year. Barks got the idea for creating a world for square people, chickens, and eggs from an unproduced Disney cartoon, The Square World, a satire of Nazi conformity written in the 1940s. Modern conceptions of conformity as squareness, not ancient Andean religion, thus dictated the geometric shapes in his story.

Barks returned to the trope of little people living in a preindustrial utopia in "Land beneath the Ground" (Uncle Scrooge #13 [1956]). However, the story differs from its predecessors in situating its fairy world in a realm that is tied to and affects the everyday one. The geologic realm in literature has come to represent the psychologic, and this story deals with the repressed longings that underlie the civilized psyche.

The underground has always been a mysterious, terrifying place. In ancient Greece, it was called Hades, a shadow world where dead souls went to be washed of their memories before returning to earth. With the arrival of Christianity, the underworld became a place of evil that housed the damned, who suffered eternal punishment for their sins. The meaning of the underground shifted in the late eighteenth century, coming to signify a purely imaginary world that was somehow related to the world above.[21] In modern times, the underground has retained its connotations of menace. The word underground is associated with the poor, criminals, and outcasts, including political countercultures and avant-garde movements in art. It has also come to serve as a metaphor for the unconscious and the wellspring of forbidden thoughts and desires buried deep within the psyche.

Barks drew on these connotations in creating his underground kingdom. The Terries and Fermies are direct threats to Scrooge because they make earthquakes that crack open his money bin, sending all his money underground. San Jacinto, where Barks was living at the time he wrote this story, is riddled with faults, and its propensity for earthquakes was certainly in Barks's mind in inventing this story. However, Carlsbad Caverns provided the inspiration for the look of the nether realm in Barks's drawings. Photographs of a group of pisolites ("cave pearls"), round stones created by dripping water over grains of sand, provided the image of the round, rocklike creatures that inhabit the cavern floor.[22] In fact, their spherical shape became part of the earthquake motif, enabling the creatures to roll like bowling balls, smash into the cavern's pillars, and jolt the upper world.

Like Lewis Carroll's Alice in Wonderland (originally titled Alice's Adventures Underground), which satirized Victorian England, Barks's underworld both reflects and inverts surface life. Scrooge and his cash embody the civilized overground—one might say the superego. The money bin itself is a monument to the Protestant ethic, which teaches that work is toil and that pleasure must be deferred in the service of future gain. For McDuck, life is a business, and his first concern on meeting the local denizens is to ask what work they do: "Are you miners or farmers, or what?" Worst of all, the bowling-ball men reject the most basic principle of Scrooge's world: they find dollars offensive. "We all know how much money is worth!" one cries. "They try to give it away on their radio programs!"

The Terries and Fermies represent the repressed desires that undergird the Protestant ethic, fusing work and play and functioning as emblems of unalienated labor. They initially believe that getting rid of Scrooge's money would be a "lot of hard work": Then they discover that it "needn't be a job of work" transforming the task into "fun" by making it a contest. Indeed, their whole lives are devoted to work that has become play—the creation of earthquakes.

Like Barks's other imaginary creatures, the Terry Fermians espouse values from a preindustrial era. The Greek vase from the year zero that they use as a trophy in their contest marks them an ancient culture, while their cowboy lingo links them to the American frontier. "Cowboy music was popular on the radio in stations in San Jacinto where I lived," Barks explained.[23] Even more than America's rural ancestors, these creatures are one with the earth, appearing like rocks when the ducks first encounter them. The Terry Fermians are also one with each other and, like Barks's portraits of other lost races, are communal beings who think, act, and look alike. In contrast to the hierarchal and exploitive Duckburg, they are eminently democratic: when Scrooge proposes a contest with the vase as prize, the underground creatures must put it to a vote of a worldwide assemblage of Terry Fermians.

At the time that Barks wrote this story, America was witnessing the upheaval of another underground. The romanticization of the juvenile delinquent in films such as *Rebel Without a Cause* and the coming of the so-called Beat Generation prefigured the youth rebellions of the 1960s. Led by writers Allen Ginsberg and Jack Kerouac, the Beats advocated dropping out of the rat race to find a more spontaneous and authentic way of life. Several years later, the hippies and their guru, political philosopher Herbert Marcuse, embraced this ethic, calling for the transformation of work into play. Marcuse sought to annul Freud's equation of civilization and repression, distinguishing between "basic repression" (the degree of repression required by reality testing and social cooperation) and "surplus repression" (the "additional controls over and above those indispensable for any form of human association arising from specific institutions of domination").[24] Capitalism, claims Marcuse, operated according to the "performance principle"—that is, the almost total mobilization of the human body and mind as instruments of alienated labor rather than as a vehicle for pleasure, creative expression, and sensuous enjoyment.

The Terry Fermians can be seen as a kind of dropout, rejecting the money ethic and espousing an unalienated form of life based on the pleasure principle. Indeed, they mark the return of the repressed—the inability of civilization totally to control or even fully to sublimate instinctual needs. The earthquakes that the Terries and Fermies create jolt the surface world, an apt metaphor for the way the rejection of the work/consumer ethic was shaking up modern society. But Barks's response to the Beats was anything but sympathetic. In a 1966 story, he made the obnoxious, work-hating Gladstone Gander one of their number ("The Not-So Ancient Mariner," *Walt Disney's Comics & Stories* #312).[25]

The story's coda contrasts two viewpoints. The geology professor who visits the money bin is a rationalist who believes in material causes: he would attribute earthquakes to "gas that builds up in fissures as the earth shrinks." Scrooge, however, has seen the underground—the realm of play, imagination, and sensual pleasure that we all repress. He may not fully realize what it represents, but he recognizes its power to shake up civilized hierarchies. His final wink to the ducks (and the reader) constitutes both an acknowledgment and a dismissal of that world. We can be certain that he will not give up his asceticism, but his closing comment gives the final word to the Terry Fermians: "He shore ain't been around has he, podners?" Fantasy and imagination remain powerful expressions of utopian longings for the satisfaction of repressed needs whose reality cannot be denied.

"The Secret of Atlantis" (*Uncle Scrooge* #5 [1954]), a story about the lost continent of Atlantis, began as a ten-pager, then expanded. The initial idea came from Barks's editor, Chase Craig, who suggested "a way that Uncle Scrooge could inflate the value of a very common coin by obliterating all but one of a whole issue."[26] The Atlantis material does not begin until well into the adventure, making the story seem like two separate narratives. However, Scrooge's manipulation of the coin market in the first part is central to Barks's characterization of Atlantis.

Economists usually justify the rule of the market by arguing that it creates an equilibrium between supply and demand. However, this story can be read as revealing the way a capitalist elite may inflate the market, thereby creating an artificial scarcity. It describes how finance capital makes money by inflating markets through speculation rather than investment in productive activities by entrepreneurs, inventors, and industrialists.[27]

Barks juxtaposes this artificially created scarcity with the natural abundance of Atlantean civilization. He characterizes Atlantis as an ecotopia ruled by merpeople. They have evolved over the centuries as their continent slipped gradually into the sea, adapting to the rising waters by becoming half human and half fish. Western culture has created an image of humanity that is alienated from nature and supposed to dominate it in the name of progress. Barks's story, conversely, breaks down the traditional western opposition between nature and culture, animal and human, showing how the two can be harmoniously fused.

Atlantis itself serves as an emblem of the symbiosis that can exist between humans and nature. It possesses no machinery and fears modern technology. When the nephews point out a wrecked plane to their teacher, he recoils in terror. Rather, the city is powered by all-natural agencies. It is lit by fish, gets milk from a whale dairy, and receives electricity from electric eels. It is a completely sustainable society with no exploitation or degradation of the environment but in total harmony with it. In contrast, the king derides the surface people's "smoggy world above," echoing Barks's comments about Los Angeles.[28] In the face of such natural abundance, Atlantis views money as worthless, and the king offers to give Scrooge as many of the "rare" coins as he wants.

But like Barks's other preindustrial utopias, Atlantis is flawed. It is a restrictive society that makes the ducks prisoners and denies them freedom to leave because it fears that they will tell the surface world about the underworld's existence. Becoming a citizen is thus compulsory: "You cannot leave!" the king tells the ducks. "You must become one of us! It is the law!" The ducks are thus eager to return to the surface.

Barks most fully developed the myth of the garden in "Tralla La" (*Uncle Scrooge* #6 [1954]). The urge to withdraw from civilization and begin life anew in an unspoiled, natural landscape has been typical of the pastoral since the time of the Roman poet Virgil. The idealization of a simple, rural environment, a "virgin land" uncontaminated by the vices and bigotry of Europe, has been a core belief in American mythology. The pastoral ideal has also been associated with orientalist fantasies of Tibet as a special embodiment of spiritual harmony and enlightenment made famous in 1933 by James Hilton's novel, *Lost Horizon*, and its film adaptation four years later by Frank Capra.[29] Although Barks never read the book, he saw the film and based his story on it. So famous has the name Shangri-La become that it has become a synonym for a utopian place of peace and harmony. Barks intended his story to be a parody of the utopian vision of *Lost Horizon* and the notion of a society so pure that it was purged of all greed, selfishness, and envy.

Besieged by demands for money, Scrooge suffers a nervous breakdown. To find peace, he takes off to find the fabled land of Tralla La, where "there is no money and wealth means nothing." Barks portrays it as an uncontaminated paradise whose terraced fields and fertile crops suggest that "it is really a land of abundance—of milk and honey." Greeted warmly by the high lama, Scrooge is told that, "We Tralla Laians have never known greed! Friendship is the thing we value most!" However, Scrooge's visit turns this paradise into a model of the worst excesses of civilization. When he throws away a seemingly worthless bottle cap, he accidentally creates the cycle of envy, greed, and contentiousness from which he had tried to escape. "Human nature wouldn't allow them to be that good when they got up against the real nitty-gritty," Barks commented. The bottle cap inaugurates a feverish round of buying and selling, with the price of the worthless object going up astronomically. "Instead of putting it in a museum for everybody to look at," Barks explained, a villager's "wife urged him to sell it for the highest price that he could get. . . . Very quickly the profit system was going in Tralla La."[30] Barks satirizes the absurd lengths to which the natives are willing to go for the pride of owning the cap, contrasting its worthlessness with the real worth they are abandoning to possess it. One man offers Scrooge "200 pigs"; another pledges to be his "servant for forty years."

The story ends with Scrooge attempting to solve the problem by ordering a plane to dump a billion bottle caps into the village, hoping to make them so common that they would no longer be objects of contention. However, the plan backfires when the plethora of caps destroy the natives' crops and threaten to flood the city. "I wanted to do a story that had a billion of something in it," Barks explained. "I read about the appropriations that Congress makes of a billion for this, ten billion for that."[31] One can read this conclusion as an expression of Barks's misgivings about intervening in indigenous cultures with programs of massive American aid.

Barks's interpretation of the story implies that a society in which people do not take advantage of each other is only a pipe dream because of humanity's egoistic nature. However, the text's construction of utopianism points to an ambiguity. The valley is corrupted not by human nature but by the arrival of representatives of civilization. The tale can be read as an allegory of the deracinating effects of western imperialism's introduction of money and a market economy into a society based on what Marx called use values (that is, the distinctive needs an object fulfills rather than the market value it has in exchange for other commodities). The story's moral seems to be that one should not ignore the value of wealth such as the bounty of nature, the value of friendship, and the happiness of a heart at peace for the sake of possessing worthless objects such as bottle caps—and, by extension, money.

Many of Barks's stories reveal a longing for a primitive, preindustrial realm free from modern cares and greed, imploring us to be critical of civilization's money fetishism. The ethic of moderation and balance voiced by the people of Shangri-La in *Lost Horizon* resonated with Barks's beliefs and must have made a significant impression on him. The people of Shangri-La seek to avoid excess of any kind, "including, if you will pardon the paradox, excess of virtue itself" explains the high lama's major domo in the film. This philosophy of the "middle way" bears clear resemblance to Barks's ethic of moderation.

This ethos dovetails with that of the myth of the garden. According to Leo Marx, the ideal of the garden was conceived as a "middle state" contrasted both to a romanticized and nostalgic primitivism of raw nature or wilderness and to urban industrial capitalism.[32] The cultivated nature of agriculture offered an alternative to the excesses of both an untamed nature, which was equated with a hellish desert in this mythology, and to the machine technology and "satanic mills" of the factory system. Barks also deployed this type of mythos, contrasting the savage wilderness of tribes in Africa and Australia with the agricultural utopias in Tralla La and Atlantis.[33]

Barks's source material also argues for a more positive view of utopianism in this story. Rather than being inspired solely by fantasy, Barks based Tralla La on the real-life Asian province of Hunza, whose citizens were reputed to live extraordinarily long and healthy lives: "Not only the *National Geographic* had articles on the long-lived people of Hunza and the Himalayas. It was fairly common fare in the media that all us stupid stuffers of junk food and breathers of carbon monoxide were missing the good life."[34] Bordered by Tibet, China, and Afghanistan, Hunza, like Tralla La, lay in a deep valley obscured from view by the towering Himalayas and accessible only by precipitous mountain paths. Hunza boasted a communal economy and a lack of wealth and precious metals. Barks's first closeup shot of the valley, with its lush terraced fields and blossoming fruit trees, was inspired by a similar picture of Hunza in *National Geographic*, and the magazine article supplied other details for Barks's story as well.[35]

Consequently, it is not surprising that Barks later invoked Hunza in another story, this time calling the valley by its real name. In "Go Slowly Sands of Time" the paradisiacal valley of Tralla La is replaced by windswept slopes where a few hardy villages scratch out a meager existence. The parameters of this story are reduced to exploring the requirements for personal rather than social happiness, and the tale deals with Scrooge's desire for longevity. This focus reflects the musings of an elderly Barks about the recipe for maintaining health, happiness, and longevity. "Go Slowly" was originally a story synopsis that Barks gave to a Danish publisher. In 1981, he worked up the idea as a prose fable for an anthology of Uncle Scrooge stories.[36]

In "Tralla La," Barks contrasts two different economies, one based on money, the other on barter and gift giving. In Marcel Mauss's classic study, *The Gift*, archaic economics are founded on the exchange of gifts. Such societies have no notions of profit and no accumulation of wealth and power; everything is given back eventually or right away, to be immediately redistributed. They are marked by "the joy of public giving; the pleasure in generous expenditure on the arts, in hospitality, and in the private and public festival, social security, the solicitude arising from reciprocity and co-operation."[37] The exchange of gifts promotes not only reciprocity and social solidarity but also reconciliation and peaceful relations. As one Bushman put it, "The worst thing is not giving presents. If people do not like each other but one gives a gift and the other must accept, this brings a peace between them. We give what we have. This is the way we live together."[38] From "Lost in the Andes" to "Tralla La" to "Old California," Barks's stories about preindustrial cultures are marked by an emphasis on generosity and giving as a means of establishing felicitous community. Barks's yuletide tales are distinguished by asserting the need to transcend individuals' egocentrism and the commercialization of gift giving as a way of expressing a spirit of generosity and unselfish love of others.[39]

The myth of the frontier is one of America's oldest and most cherished beliefs. The story of an expansion westward and the struggle to carve a civilization out of the wilderness has been thought to be the key to what is most significant in U.S. history. The pioneers' surge west to claim the free land that lay beyond the frontier became an integral part of the symbolism of America as a garden of the world. As Henry Nash Smith notes, the "image of this vast and constantly growing agricultural society in the interior of the continent became one of the dominant symbols of nineteenth-century America." Moreover, according to Smith, "The master symbol of the garden embraces a cluster of metaphors expressing fecundity, growth, increase, and blissful labor in the earth, all centering around the heroic figure of the idealized frontier."[40] However, the myth of the garden and the ideal of the western yeoman could not be brought to fictional expression, nor could the frontier farmer be made into a viable fictional protagonist. His sedentary life and laborious calling stripped him of the glamour needed to become a frontier hero. The picturesque Wild West rather than the domesticated frontier became exploited in popular entertainment.

"The Land of the Pygmy Indians" (*Uncle Scrooge* #18 [1957]) was the final story in which Barks reprised the myth of the garden. It is one of the earliest and most powerful ecological stories in comic books, preceding the rise of a mass environmental movement in the 1970s. The story reveals the contradictions of notions of progress in capitalist modernity. Scrooge wants to leave Duckburg's smog and overpopulation and decides to buy an uninhabited wilderness preserve. At the same time, his commitment to industrial development threatens his pastoral oasis. "I'm through with it—even though I'm the guy that started all those smelly factories!" he admits. Barks uses Scrooge's inability to treat nature other than as a resource to be exploited as a running gag throughout the story. When he visits the pristine wilderness, he cannot help but see it as a source of raw material for his chemical plants, its moose as steaks to be sold by the pound, and its minerals as ores for his factories. Paradoxically, this mentality threatens to create the same environment from which he had sought to escape. Throughout the story, the nephews function as a Greek chorus, pointing out his instrumental attitude toward nature and admonishing him to "leave this country clean and free for the animals and birds!"

"The Land of the Pygmy Indians" features another lost race of little people—in this case, a band of diminutive Indians named the Peeweegahs. In this story, Barks made his fairy creatures smaller than the ducks. "That makes a slight menace out of the ducks," he explained. "They were always pee-wees in comparison with the villains. In order for them to become a menace, they had to come up against somebody smaller."[41] He would keep this size ratio in all the rest of his little people adventures.

Barks's story was inspired by Longfellow's famed poem, "The Song of Hiawatha" (1855), which Barks had discovered in grade school. "About the eighth grade, I had to read it and recite it in school: I thought it was tiresome way of telling a story back then, but the meter lends itself very well to the comments of the Peeweegahs when they talk about what they're going to do."[42] Barks gave a lyrical quality to their dialogue, emulating Native Americans' singsong, mythopoeic ways of speech in Longfellow's poem.

Longfellow was the most important mid-nineteenth-century American writer to articulate the notion of the Indian as "noble savage." His poem about Hiawatha had virtually no connection, apart from the name, to the historical fifteenth-century Iroquois chief Hiawatha. Longfellow followed Henry Schoolcraft's version of a cycle of Chippewa legends, assuming, as Schoolcraft did, that the Chippewa demigod Manibozho was identical to the Iroquois statesman Hiawatha.[43] This misunderstanding of Native American history was intrinsic to the image of the noble savage. At this time the Indian as an opponent of civilization was dead but still lay heavy on American consciences. The image of the noble savage allowed writers to place the Indian in a dim, remote past that kept him outside the march of civilization. He is part of America's childhood, which it must outgrow to attain its maturity. In Longfellow's poem, Hiawatha understands the fate of the noble savage and endorses the missionaries who come, but at night he slips quietly away, traveling westward alone. He can be no part of civilization. The image of the noble savage thus allowed white Americans to romanticize guilt figures while valorizing the march to civilization as a form of inevitable progress. Thus, the image of the noble savage, then and now, legitimates the triumph of western imperialism.

However, the notion of the noble savage can be viewed more positively as containing elements of truth about the viability and accomplishments of Native Americans. The historical Hiawatha, for example, was a follower of Deganwidah, a prophet and shaman who founded the League of the Iroquois. Hiawatha was a skilled and charismatic orator who was instrumental in persuading the Iroquois peoples—the Senecas, Onondagas, Oneidas, Cayugas, and Mohawks—to stop fighting among each other and to accept Deganwidah's vision and band together as a confederacy. (The Tuscarora nation subsequently joined the Iroquois Confederacy, forming the Six Nations.)[44] The league's concept of federalism had a significant influence on America's Founding Fathers. The first person to propose a union of all the American colonies and to propose a federal model for it was reportedly an Iroquois chief, Conassatego, who suggested in 1744 that the colonists make their government into a union of all the colonies in a federal system similar to that of the League of the Iroquois. American political thinkers from Benjamin Franklin to Thomas Jefferson and Thomas Paine were heavily influenced by Native American political notions of liberty, equality, and community.[45] Barks also utilized the concept of the notion of the noble savage in positive terms, not to elegize a vanishing American but as a model of a sustainable relationship the environment.

Barks contrasts the anthropocentric and the ecocentric ethics of the two groups. While Uncle Scrooge embodies a human-centered ethic, the Indians are avatars of a nature-based morality. Scrooge can only envision nature in terms of its utility to humans, while the Peeweegahs believe that nature is intrinsically valuable and has a right to exist independently of the way humans view it. Barks's approach also entails contrasting visions of property and property rights. When Scrooge presents his deed as proof of ownership of their land, the chief replies, "By whom was this token taken? By whose hands these written scratches? Did the *sun* from high above you sell you all these lands and waters? Did the winds that bend the pine trees? . . . [M]e no believe that such a token would be honored by the fishes, by the creatures of the forest, by the birds we call our brothers. . . . None could sign away these woodlands, none could have the *right* or reason, but the chiefs of *all* the brothers in a powwow with the seasons!"

This lyrical speech accurately reflects Native American beliefs with respect to property: that nature is sacred and comprises living beings with the same rights as people. Consequently, nature cannot be bought and sold, as in western concepts of property, which look on the land as a dead object and the flora and fauna as resources for human benefit. In tribal society, property is governed by custom and kinship agreements.[46] The territory as a whole belongs to the nation, with jurisdiction over it held in trust by the chiefs. It is inalienable, and the identity of a nation is inseparable from the land, animals, and ecosystem in which they live. In Amerindian cosmology, the Indian belongs to the land as much as the land to the tribe. When Indians made property agreements with white settlers, they were granting rights to co-use of the land, not rights to the land itself, which could not be sold.

The Peeweegahs' relationship to the environment is one of kinship, and they live in harmony with it. Barks invokes a relationship of reciprocity between the tribe and nature by showing that the Peeweegahs can communicate with the fish and animals, who will come to their aid when the Indians are threatened. When the ducks capture an Indian, he asks the fish for help, and the forest creatures work together to free him. However, Barks does not romanticize nature as monolithically benevolent. The giant sturgeon is an evil creature who eats smaller fish and destroys the Peeweegahs' canoes. When it tries to swallow Donald, he is saved by the nephews and emerges from its mouth like Jonah escaping from the biblical leviathan.

Our growing ecological awareness has transformed the nature of the pastoral. No longer can we take for granted the notion of a bountiful earth and assume its infinite permanence. We are now capable of altering and destroying nature. We have changed the global climate, polluted the air and oceans, decimated wildlife, wantonly destroyed animal and plant species, and clear-cut forests. In the pastoral, wilderness—that is, wild nature—was traditionally looked on as an untenable extreme that had to be transcended, as did the city, by the humanly cultivated nature of the garden. Now, however, wilderness has become a paramount source of value and its preservation one of the *sine qua nons* of the survival of civilization. Barks's story echoes this change. Scrooge is hoisted on his own petard when the Peeweegahs invite him to smoke a peace pipe filled with the same noxious chemicals that he has showed them how to mine. The tale ends on a note of redemption: Scrooge proclaims that he is giving the land "back to the Indians" those from whom westerners originally had expropriated it, and the wilderness is preserved. "Land of the Pygmy Indians" was Barks's last story featuring a preindustrial culture that offered an alternative worldview to our own. Nevertheless, his Junior Woodchuck stories from the 1970s would continue to elaborate an ecological perspective.

NOTES

1. Jean Delumeau, *The History of Paradise* (New York: Continuum, 1995).
2. Stanley Diamond, *In Search of the Primitive: A Critique of Civilization* (New Brunswick, NJ: Transaction, 1987), 106.

3. Paul Radin, *The World of Primitive Man* (New York: Grove, 1960), 106.

4. Ibid.

5. Barks, interview by Ault and Andrae, August 4, 1975.

6. Jack Zipes, *Breaking the Magic Spell: Radical Theories of Folk and Fairy Tales* (New York: Methuen, 1979), 14.

7. Quoted in ibid., 138.

8. Alison Lurie, *Don't Tell the Grown-Ups: Subversive Children's Literature* (Boston: Little Brown, 1990), 43.

9. Barks, interview by Ault and Andrae, August 4, 1975.

10. John O'Reilly, "South Florida's Amazing Everglades," *National Geographic*, January 1940, 115.

11. Barks, interview by Hamilton, September 24, 1983.

12. Julianne Burton-Carvajal, "'Surprise Package': Looking Southward with Disney," in *Disney Discourse: Producing the Magic Kingdom*, ed. Eric Smoodin (New York: Routledge, 1994), 131–47.

13. Barks based his interpretation of the city on photographs in Henry Albert Phillip, "The Pith of Peru," *National Geographic*, August 1942, 167–88.

14. Clark Gable was Bark's favorite male movie star.

15. Beau Riffenbaugh, *The Myth of the Explorer: The Press, Sensationalism, and Geographical Discovery* (London: Belhaven, 1993), 2.

16. Hugh Thompson, *The White Rock: An Exploration of the Inca Heartland* (New York: Overlook, 2001), 79–80.

17. Barks, interview by Ault and Andrae, August 4, 1975.

18. Barks, interview by Hamilton, September 24, 1983.

19. Thompson, *White Rock*, 77–78.

20. Murray Bookchin, *The Ecology of Freedom* (Palo Alto, CA: Cheshire, 1982), 246.

21. Wendy Lesser, *Life Below Ground: A Study of the Subterranean in Literature and History* (Boston: Faber and Faber, 1987).

22. Mason Sutherland, "Carlsbad Caverns in Color," *National Geographic*, October 1953, 499.

23. Barks, *Walt Disney's Uncle Scrooge McDuck: His Life and Times* (Millbrae, CA: Celestial Arts, 1981), 215.

24. Herbert Marcuse, *Eros and Civilization* (Boston: Beacon, 1969), 34.

25. The story's attraction for the counterculture is evident in an underground newspaper's discussion of it with a fake interview with Barks in "Terries and Fermies: Underworld People Cause Quakes," *Bugle American*, February 25, 1971.

26. Notes for *Carl Barks Library*, 1984.

27. David C. Korten, *The Post-Corporate World: Life after Capitalism* (San Francisco: Kuarian and Berrett Koeler, 1999), 51.

28. Barks to Malcolm Willets, April 19, 1962.

29. Peter Bishop, *The Myth of Shangri-La: Tibet, Travel Writing, and the Western Creation of Sacred Landscape* (Berkeley: University of California Press, 1989).

30. Barks, *Walt Disney's Uncle Scrooge McDuck*, 117.

31. Ibid.

32. Leo Marx, *The Machine in the Garden: Technology and the Pastoral Ideal* (New York: Oxford University Press, 1978).

33. See "Adventure Down Under," *Donald Duck* Full Color #156 (1947); "Race to the South Seas," *Boys' and Girls' March of Comics* #41 (1949).

34. Barks to Thomas Andrae, April 30, 1987.

35. Jean and Frank Shor, "At World's End in Hunza," *National Geographic*, October 1953, 485–518.

36. Published with his illustrations in Barks, *Walt Disney's Uncle Scrooge McDuck*.

37. Marcel Mauss, *The Gift: The Form and Reason for Exchange in Archaic Societies* (New York: Norton, 1990), 69.

38. Lorna Marshall, "Sharing, Talking, and Giving: Relief of Tensions among Kung Bushmen," *Africa* 31 (1961): 245.

39. See "Christmas for Shacktown," *Donald Duck* Full Color #367 (1952).

40. Henry Nash Smith, *Virgin Land: The American West in Symbol and Myth* (New York: Vintage, 1950), 138.

41. Barks, interview by Hamilton, September 24, 1983.

42. Barks, *Walt Disney's Uncle Scrooge McDuck*, 170.

43. Roy Harvey Pearce, *Savagism and Civilization: A Study of the Indian and the American Mind* (Berkeley: University of California Press, 1988), 193.

44. Jack Weatherford, *Indian Givers: How the Indians of the Americas Transformed the World* (New York: Fawcett Columbine, 1988), 133–50.

45. Ibid.

46. James Tully, *An Approach to Political Philosophy: Locke in Contexts* (Cambridge: Cambridge University Press, 1993), 154.

An Examination of "Master Race"

JOHN BENSON, DAVID KASAKOVE, AND ART SPIEGELMAN

Bernard Krigstein's "Master Race" is one of the finest stories ever to appear in the comics form. It is a comic book rarity; a story with such density and breadth of technique that it merits a detailed and exhaustive examination on the part of the reader. Partly because of the nature of the industry most comic book stories, even the good ones, contain nothing beyond that which is immediately apparent to the casual reader. But "Master Race" has layers of meaning and detail both in its form and visual content which will yield the alert reader new enjoyment beyond the immediately apparent with each rereading. What follows is not a definitive analysis, but merely the results of one such examination.

Although this article confines its attention to the art, one must bear in mind that the text of "Master Race" was written as it was printed before the artist ever saw it. No one at this date can recall who wrote the original script, but editor Albert Feldstein did enough rewriting for his style to be apparent.

It is a powerful narrative, using the most dramatic events of this century as a backdrop for the brief confrontation of two antagonists. Obviously it was the basic narrative that inspired the artist to make this story the classic that it is. But it is just as obvious that it is the artist's contribution that lifts the story out of the context of the twist-ending comic book story and makes it a memorable artistic experience.

In fact, much of the power that Krigstein brings to the story is due to his choice of a style which is the antithesis of standard comics storytelling. Instead of employing the exaggerated visual comic book phrases usually used to clearly denote action and emotion (speed lines, large beads of sweat, etc.), Krigstein uses a much more objective standard of delineation. Instead of frequent close-ups, an often used technique to get "close" to a character's feelings, Krigstein keeps a physical distance from the characters. Instead of using "dramatic" motion picture–type lighting effects, Krigstein uses patterns of dark and light in much more abstract ways. Instead of a humanizing use of free shapes, Krigstein concentrates on using sharp angles and straight lines wherever possible.

Finally, in opposition to the cartoonist's approach, there is the chilling, aloof, precise, clean rendering which is used throughout the story. In this contrast between the apparently detached style and the extreme emotional content of the story lies the strength of

---

Bernard Krigstein, *Master Race* (1955), reprinted in Greg Sadowski, *B. Krigstein, Volume One* (Fantagraphics, 2002). © William M. Gaines, Agent, Inc. (2008).

Krigstein's interpretation. The distancing allows a perspective that illuminates the events and forces a deeper, more introspective, analysis.

The story is composed of three well-defined sections; an initial confrontation, a long flashback, and the denouement. The first section sets the mood of the story; the depiction of routine city life is coupled with a developing sense of unease.

Page 1 appears simple enough; six panels of equal width show a man purchasing a subway token and waiting on the platform. The panel symmetry reminds one of the opening page of Krigstein's earlier story "Monotony," in which he used the design to satirize the story's title. On a closer look within the panels, however, great differences between the two stories emerge. Though the page structure in both cases denotes order, the "Monotony" panels have a light, airy atmosphere, with simple compositions, while the "Master Race" panels are dark and foreboding, and are infinitely more complex.

In panel 1 the protagonist Reissman is seen from beneath, making his descent from light into the blackness that dominates the panel. The subway locale is an important element of the story, and both the angle and the dominant black are the first signals of Krigstein's vision of the subway as a dramatic cavern. Although the change attendant is the one in a cage, it is Reissman who is seen behind bars and wire in panel 2, his eyes shrouded in shadow, in contrast to the innocently lit attendant. His cold expression is inked with thick blacks, not the more delicate rendering used for the attendant. In panel 3, Reissman's face is still deep in shadow although one can see the full faces of the strangers around him. The composition frames Reissman against a bank of bars with a heavy black mass hanging over his head. Such compositional touches reinforce the text's description of Reissman as a man haunted by memories of horrors.

In panel 4, the rails sweep ahead of the train in a powerful three-dimensional arc, shattering the calm vertical and horizontal composition just as the scream of the wheels "shatter the silence."[1] As Reissman has entered the story alone in the first panel, so the train, an important entity in the story, enters alone in the panel below. In panel 5 the viewpoint shifts to include the platform, so that Reissman and the train are now in confrontation.

JOHN BENSON, DAVID KASAKOVE, ART SPIEGELMAN

MASTER RACE

YOU CAN **NEVER FORGET**, CAN YOU, CARL REISSMAN? EVEN *HERE*...IN *AMERICA*...TEN YEARS AND THOUSANDS OF MILES AWAY FROM YOUR NATIVE GERMANY... YOU CAN NEVER FORGET THOSE *BLOODY WAR YEARS*. THOSE MEMORIES WILL HAUNT YOU FOREVER... AS EVEN NOW THEY HAUNT YOU WHILE YOU DESCEND THE SUBWAY STAIRS INTO THE QUIET SEMI-DARKNESS...

YOUR ACCENT IS STILL THICK ALTHOUGH YOU HAVE MASTERED THE LANGUAGE OF YOUR NEW COUNTRY THAT TOOK YOU IN WITH OPEN ARMS WHEN YOU FINALLY ESCAPED FROM BELSEN CONCENTRATION CAMP. YOU SLIDE THE BILL UNDER THE BARRED CHANGE-BOOTH WINDOW...

TWO TOKENS, PLEASE.

YOU MOVE TO THE BUSY CLICKING TURNSTILES...SLIP THE SHINY TOKEN INTO THE THIN SLOT...AND PUSH THROUGH...

THE TRAIN ROARS OUT OF THE BLACK CAVERN, SHATTERING THE SILENCE OF THE ALMOST DESERTED STATION...

YOU STARE AT THE ONRUSHING STEEL MONSTER...

YOU BLINK AS THE FIRST CAR RUSHES BY AND ILLUMINATED WINDOWS FLASH IN AN EVER-SLOWING RHYTHM...

Master Race. © William M. Gaines, Agent, Inc. (2008).

It is worthwhile noting the differences between panels 4 and 5. In panel 4 both the track and ceiling are curved, a sense of depth is achieved through a careful use of dark shadows, and the side pillars are realistically depicted. While there is some feeling of depth in panel 5, it is composed of straight lines, no blacks, and almost abstract patterns on the wall to the right. There is a feeling of compression in panel 5 due to the fact that the principal perspective line, the edge of the platform, is absolutely vertical. Both panels create a sense of depth, although the methods used are quite different. In panel 4 the reader's eyes are led into the panel, whereas in panel 5, one's eyes are led outside the panel, the forward motion of the train threatening to go beyond the surface of the page.

The two panels are separate pictorial entities, and although they create a strong dual staccato punch, it is caused by an interrelationship that is wholly different and more complex than the standard comics "cinematic" device of repeating an identical scene for two panels, with an object or person moving closer in the second panel.

Krigstein makes a sudden switch from the depiction of depth in panels 4 and 5 to total two-dimensionality in panel 6, wonderfully reconstructing the actual shock a person gets when he views a train approach and subsequently pass directly in front of him.

Though not immediately apparent, the relationship of panel 6 to panel 5 completes the relationship of panel 5 to panel 4. In these three panels Krigstein observes the geometric ratio of the increase in size of an onrushing train (the ratio of the window sizes is 2:5:30). Many artists, though composing the panels differently, might use this geometric increase in size. The interesting element here is that Krigstein has used the same geometric ratio for the sensation of depth—going from a strong illusion of depth, to a slightly more compressed image, to an absolutely flat two-dimensional composition.[2]

The flatness in panel 6 is intensified by the multiple—"unrealistic"—images of the passengers. These multiple images simultaneously serve several other purposes. First, they very successfully reproduce the stroboscopic effect a person gets when standing close to a moving train. Second, having used the device on page one, he is able effortlessly to indicate the slowing of the train in the next panel (page 2, panel 1) by showing only two multiple images. This also creates a strong continuity which bridges the turning of the page. Finally, its distinctive quality is such that the use of the same technique on the last page of the story creates a strong coda. So the multiple images are not merely a flashy device, but serve very practical dramatic purposes.

In panel 2 of the second page, Reissman is again enveloped in shadow, his hunched back and shoulders a mass of black that dominates the panel. The contrast to the affable mild-mannered face of the emerging passenger, seen fully lit from front view, is clear; the passenger is "free," Reissman is not, in spite of his attempts to convince himself otherwise.

It is not until panel 3 that we first see Reissman's eyes, and here his character is shown in another way; a dozing mask hiding the fear that his hunched body and upturned collar can not. The diagonal that is created by his arm pressed to his face subtly suggests the difference between the neutral surroundings and Reissman's own tensions. Here and in panel 5 the panel edges seem to be claustrophobically squeezing in on him.

It should be noted that in these three panels there is the compositional unity of Reissman on the left of panel 1 facing right, in the center of panel 2 facing away from us, and on the right of panel 3 facing left, which suggests the character's movement through the scene.

By placing the images of panels 4 and 5 under a single block of text the artist is able to show two viewpoints simultaneously; Reissman in panel 5 sits reading inside the thundering train of panel 4. The slightly askew ceiling girders suggest the "lurches" mentioned in the text.

The un-Krigstein-like mass of text that follows causes a visually unattractive hole in the center of the page, and is probably the result of the space limitations that were given the artist. Even so, the block of text is a visual reference to the columns of type in Reissman's newspaper in the previous panel. Even the words themselves—"meaningless . . . nothing has meaning . . . nothing . . ."—could be thought of as reflecting what Reissman actually sees as well as being a comment on his thoughts. The most is made of a compromised situation.[3]

The text for panel 7 describes Reissman studying the faces of his fellow passengers, something a man living in fear would be unlikely to do. Krigstein solves this inconsistency in characterization by showing Reissman surreptitiously looking at their reflections from behind his upturned collar. Reissman is walled in by faces, in reflection to his right, in life to his left, trapped as he was by the panel border in panel 3.

The first panel in the last tier, panel 8, is the symmetrical opposite of the previous panel. Due to the switch in viewpoint, we now see the people whose reflections were previously in the window; the man in the cap, the woman in the turban. From panel 8 to panel 9 there is a switch from an objective to a subjective viewpoint, one of the two clearly subjective panels in the story. One knows that the man getting on is important because he is seen through Reissman's eyes. The single line of text similarly isolates the event.

There are other shocks to the eye which establish the importance of panel 9. There is an element of depth between the close view of Reissman and the retreating passengers in the background in panel 8 that sharply contrasts with the single plane of panel 9. This change is reinforced by the contrast of the delineation of roundness of the exiting passenger's coat with the solid flat black of the new passenger. Finally there is the very important contrast between the clutter and sketchiness of panel 8 to the simple austerity of panel 9.

The man who enters is dressed in black, with a face like a skull; the symbol of death. He is framed in a Mondrian-like abstraction of Perfect Order, the certitude of retribution that is soon to fall upon Reissman.

Reissman's reaction to the new passenger, panel 10, is emphasized with the story's first and practically only close-up. His terror-laden eyes are further claustrophobically squeezed between his hat and the newspaper. The exaggerated whites of his eyes, framed with black, heighten the drama and contrast with the narrow slits Reissman had previously used to survey the other passengers.

At this very dramatic moment, Krigstein draws back. The caption of panel 1 on page 3 describes Reissman's mouth twitching, his hands opening and closing, wet with perspiration, yet we are shown only his back unobtrusively placed in the corner of a panoramic longshot. This is not to be the moment of confrontation. Instead, Krigstein establishes the antagonists in their locale, squared off on the opposite sides of a nearly empty subway car, separated by a lone uninvolved passenger who, bored or asleep, is unaware of their private drama. Reissman and the Man are inked in heavy blacks, unlike the antiseptically rendered subway car around them. Krigstein's subway is barren, cold, sterile, not the familiar well-worn garbage-strewn vehicle that we feel comfortable in.[4]

After thus setting the stage, the story embarks on a three-page flashback, with panel 2 serving as the connecting device.

AND THE TRAIN GRINDS TO A HISSING STOP...

YOU MOVE TO THE DOOR AS IT SLIDES OPEN. A PASSENGER EMERGES AND YOU FEEL HIS EYES UPON YOU AND YOU SHUDDER. WHY ARE YOU FRIGHTENED, CARL? THAT WAS A *LONG TIME AGO!* THIS IS *AMERICA.* YOU'RE *SAFE* NOW! YOU'RE *FREE*...

EXCUSE ME...

BUT YOU *ARE* AFRAID, *AREN'T* YOU, CARL? YOU'LL *ALWAYS* BE AFRAID. YOU'LL *KEEP REMEMBERING*... REMEMBERING THE *HORROR*...THE *HATE*...THE *SUFFERING*...AND YOU'LL *STAY* AFRAID. YOU STEP INTO THE ALMOST–EMPTY CAR AND YOU SIGH INTO A SEAT...

THE DOORS SLAM SHUT. THE TRAIN LURCHES AND ROLLS AHEAD, THUNDERING OUT OF THE STATION AND BACK INTO THE BLACK CHASMS TUNNELING BENEATH THE CITY. YOU UNFOLD YOUR PAPER...

YOU TRY TO READ, BUT THE WORDS ARE MEANINGLESS. NOTHING HAS MEANING ANY MORE...NOTHING BUT THE SICKENING SENSATION THAT HAS PLAGUED YOU FOR OVER TEN LONG YEARS. THE CONCENTRATION CAMP HAS LEFT ITS MARK UPON YOU, HASN'T IT, CARL REISSMAN?

YOU LOOK AROUND AT YOUR FELLOW PASSENGERS SITTING ALONE IN THEIR OWN LITTLE WORLDS OF FEAR. YOU STUDY THEIR FACES...THEIR FEATURES...THEIR EYES...LOOKING...ALWAYS LOOKING. WHAT ARE YOU *LOOKING* FOR CARL? WHO *IS* IT YOU'RE *AFRAID* OF?

THE TRAIN GROANS INTO ANOTHER STATION AND JERKS TO A STOP, THE DOORS HUM WIDE. YOU LOOK DOWN AT YOUR PAPER, ONLY *SENSING* PEOPLE GETTING OFF...

...SOMEONE GETTING ON...

AND THEN...DOWN DEEP INSIDE YOU... YOU FEEL THE CHILL...THE COLD CHILL ...THE CHILL OF DEATH, YOU STARE AT THE PAPER ON YOUR LAP, UNABLE TO RAISE YOUR EYES...AFRAID TO SEE WHAT YOU KNOW IS THERE. BUT, AFTER A FEW TERRORIZED MOMENTS, YOU CAN'T STAND IT! YOU *DO* LOOK UP! AND YOU *SEE* HIM...

CHOKE!

Master Race. © William M. Gaines, Agent, Inc. (2008).

Whereas the first section of "Master Race" achieves its suspense through a use of the physical qualities of the art (spatial relationships, the opposition of black and white, flatness and depth, etc.), the second section uses clear-cut visual symbols and metaphors to make unmistakable political and moral statements. In addition, the flashback section is generally arranged like a series of photographs; less importance is placed on continuity. Each panel provides a separate piece of historical information.

Perhaps it is a flaw of the twist-ending plot that this section does not deal directly with the characters. Krigstein has seized upon this impersonality to drive home the universal nature of the conflicts in the story.

It is in this section that Krigstein's cold aloof rendering is most apparent. Here is where long shots are most often used. The horrors described are consistently underplayed in the pictures. This distancing only serves to accentuate and heighten the horror of the events that transpired during the Nazi reign.

In the first panel of the flashback, panel 3 on page 3, Krigstein uses a long shot which emphasizes the crowd's roar echoing the roar of the train, rather than, as the text does, tying Hitler's voice to the screech of the wheels. The long shot of the gigantic rally is a much better image to begin the flashback with than Hitler's face as described in the text. It forcefully establishes the whole sweep of a period of history. Using the blocks of vast crowds and the angular rim of the podium, Krigstein captures the motif of power and massiveness used in the Nazi rallies. The "Sieg Heil" is not enclosed in a standard balloon, but floats over the crowd as a generalized roar.

In panel 4 Krigstein reverses the process, showing a close-up of glassy-eyed faces when the text speaks of "multitudes." He has thus added an element not present in the text, rather than merely illustrating it.

In panel 5, the figures, dwarfed by the towering fascist icons, move stiffly as though hypnotized. The blowing paper proclaims "Work makes life sweet," a phrase which was inscribed over the entrance of Auschwitz and other concentration camps.

Panel 6, one of the panels created by Krigstein's expansion of the story, isolates Reissman from the rest of the crowd. Once again, Reissman is in shadow. Panel 7 compositionally echoes panel 5; both show a group of advancing figures seen from a low angle. The civilians have been transformed into Hitler's Gestapo. When separated by the lone figure of Reissman, the three panels together also hint at Reissman's own transition from a member of the crowd to a Nazi.[5]

The three panels at the top of page 4 form a remarkable triptych encapsuling the universality of the Nazis' brutalizing effect on German life; not only Jews were affected. Because the representation is meant to be universal, the symbols are clear. Labels are applied almost in the manner of a political cartoon. The simian faces of the brownshirts are so exaggerated as to be caricature. Across the top, serving almost as titles for each picture, are the words "Kultur," "Jude," and a crucifix, the three great life-modes that were present in Germany, with Judaism, the one which suffered most, in the center.

Below these titles are dreamlike composite scenes showing violence to various social classes; the intellectual, the shopkeeper (middle class), and the worker. The titles on the books are labels rather than realistic representations; the star of David is certainly a symbol, and the falling man's overall straps are another. That this last symbol was important to Krigstein is demonstrated by the fact that he still recalled and was annoyed that the colorist had mistakenly colored the straps the same as the shirt, eight years after he had last seen the story in color.

Note that panel 2 shows a brownshirt about to strike. Although panel 3 is a different scene, the action is carried through and the blow has been struck. In panel 3, the man's

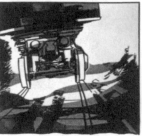

Master Race. © William M. Gaines, Agent, Inc. (2008).

outstretched arms parallel, compositionally and in theme, the crucifix on the wall. The floor tiles are slightly angled, subtly emphasizing the imbalance of the falling man. Note other details, such as the drops of blood from the word "Kultur" in panel 1 and the observer who smiles without compassion in panel 2.

NO ONE COULD STOP THE BOOKS FROM BEING BURNED...

...OR THE SHOP WINDOWS FROM BEING SMASHED AND THEIR CONTENTS RANSACKED...

...OR THE SANCTITY OF HOMES FROM BEING VIOLATED...

IT WAS A MADNESS...A WAVE THAT SWEPT THROUGH YOUR HOMELAND LIKE A PLAGUE...A TIDAL WAVE OF FRENZIED HATE-FEARS AND BLOOD-LETTING AND EXPLODING VIOLENCE...A WILD UNCONTROLLED WAVE THAT SWEPT YOU AND YOUR KIND ALONG WITH IT...

WHAT HAPPENED TO YOU, CARL? WHEN WERE YOU CAUGHT UP IN THIS TIDE? WHEN DID YOU FIRST SEE BELSEN CONCENTRATION CAMP AND THE HUMAN MISERY THAT SOBBED WITHIN ITS BARBED-WIRE WALLS?...

DO YOU REMEMBER, CARL? DO YOU REMEMBER THE AWFUL SMELL OF THE GAS CHAMBERS THAT HOURLY ANNIHILATED HUNDREDS AND HUNDREDS OF YOUR COUNTRYMEN?...

DO YOU REMEMBER THE STINKING ODOR OF HUMAN FLESH BURNING IN THE OVENS...MEN'S...WOMEN'S...CHILDREN'S...PEOPLE YOU ONCE KNEW AND TALKED TO AND DRANK BEER WITH?...

Master Race. © William M. Gaines, Agent, Inc. (2008).

In panel 4 Krigstein again juxtaposes image with text. While the text speaks of a "wild uncontrolled wave" of hate, the picture shows the other side of the coin, everything coldly efficient and orderly, with strict horizontal columns of anonymous soldiers and overpowering vertical pillars of Nazi architecture. The text of the whole flashback section does not describe the extreme regimentation inherent in fascism, an element one must be aware of to understand its nature. Krigstein has added the element here. In fascism the hate and the regimentation are bonded; this panel and its caption successfully portray the bond.

In contrast to the faceless automatons in panel 4, each prisoner depicted in panel 5 has an individual, albeit similar expression, each a different manifestation of suffering. The prisoners seem calm, even tranquil. A part of this picture's power is derived from its inspiration, a historical photograph of camp inmates.

Panel 6 is a view from inside a guard tower, a view that Reissman must have seen many times—another clue that Reissman was one of the oppressors, not a victim. The road in this silent sombre picture suggests a swastika. Again, the scene is orderly, cold flat walls hiding the horror described in the text.

The sombre tones are further emphasized in another view of the gas chambers in panel 7. Here the blacks and greys are so strong as to preclude any color. The ledge of the wall sharply divides the panel, and below it, cleanly rendered Germans go about their business, trying to avoid the stench. The tree reaches into the top half of the panel; its leaves are blackened.

In panel 1, page 5, Krigstein again allows the horror to be expressed in the text, depicting ordinary-looking doctors performing what could be, from the evidence of the picture alone, a beneficial operation. When juxtaposed with the text, the *lack* of horror in the picture is probably more terrifying than a graphic representation of tortures could ever be. Part of the incomprehensible horror of the camps was, in fact, that many who staffed them treated their grisly tasks as everyday jobs.

In panel 2 the innocent-looking lamp dominates the scene. Instead of the office locale the text describes, Krigstein shows us an image of debauched Nazis at their leisure, perhaps to stronger contrast the horrors of the camps. The poses are vaguely reminiscent of George Grosz.[6]

The montage of panel 3 returns us briefly to the present, tying the sweep of history to the drama of the subway. The train's wheels and the pulsating repetition of the Man's face again powerfully call forth the roar of the subway. But the images from Reissman's past literally burn through to the forefront, and the flashback continues.

Panels 4 and 5 appear to depict realistic scenes, yet the extraordinary rendering exudes a dreamlike quality. The bodies appear to float in slow motion down to their common grave. The absence of background and of any delineation of the grave contribute to the unreal effect. Colorist Marie Severin seems to have realized this; she used unrealistic colors, a single solid tone for the figures and another for the backgrounds. Again, note the careful details, such as the baby falling into the pit, and the guard casually lighting a cigarette while standing near the victims' piles of shoes.

Panel 1 on page 6 shows in a visual way what the text states, that the war is over. Both Germany's civilian and military destruction are pictured. In a very effective composition, Krigstein contrasts the destroyed German tank in the foreground with the approaching Russian ones. The text indicates that the Man is in the scene, but Krigstein shows only a landscape to emphasize the close-up in the next panel.

Although the story is told in the second person (a narrative device rare outside of EC), Krigstein all but completely avoids the use of subjective viewpoints, probably because their excessive use becomes a gimmick. Even Krigstein's own experiment with the

DO YOU REMEMBER THE UNMERCIFUL TORTURES...THE SCREAMS IN THE NIGHT...THE PITIFUL WAILING OF THE DOOMED? DO YOU REMEMBER THE MAD EXPERIMENTS WITH HUMAN GUINEA PIGS...THE WANTON WASTE OF HUMAN LIFE?...

...THE BULBS THAT BURNED IN LAMPS ON DESKS IN THE CONCENTRATION CAMP OFFICES...GLOWING THROUGH THEIR HUMAN-SKIN-SHADES?...

LOOK, CARL! LOOK AT THE FACE OF THIS MAN SITTING ACROSS FROM YOU IN THIS NOW DESERTED SUBWAY CAR! LOOK... AND REMEMBER! REMEMBER THE GUARDS THAT GLEEFULLY CARRIED OUT THE SADISTIC ORDERS OF THE MASTER RACE...WHIPPING...KICKING... BEATING!... THE GUARDS THAT EAGERLY DRAGGED THE WOMEN AND CHILDREN TO THE WAITING, SMOKING OVENS!...

REMEMBER THE GUARDS THAT PUSHED AND SHOVED...HEAPING THE HELPLESS CAMP INMATES INTO THE FRESH DUG MASS GRAVES...

...LAUGHING WILDLY AS THEY BURIED THEIR VICTIMS ALIVE...SHOVELING THE DIRT DOWN UPON THEM, MUFFLING THEIR PATHETIC SCREAMS ...MUFFLING THEIR PATHETIC LIVES!...

Master Race. © William M. Gaines, Agent, Inc. (2008).

subjective viewpoint in "You, Murderer" (obviously inspired by another EC second person script), while excellent, definitely has an element of gimmickry that cannot compete with the classic style of "Master Race."

Panel 2 is the second of two clearly subjective panels in the story, and the Man's vengeful stare is directed squarely, not only at Reissman, but at the reader as well. The reader is no longer a detached observer as he has been throughout the flashback; Reissman's guilt is now his guilt.

The flashback, which in 18 or 20 images has presented a remarkably diverse mosaic of the Nazi era, ends with panel 3. The strange perspective in this panel causes the figures lying at the side of the road to look as if they are already underground and buried. Note that the dead are soldiers and the living are civilians. A dog traverses the line dividing the living from the dead—perhaps Cerberus, the hound of Hell.

We are brought back to the present, and Krigstein begins his famous adventure into subjective time. Nearly half the total number of panels in the story are devoted to the next few moments of action, moments which seem like an eternity for Reissman. These moments are the core of the story—in some ways they *are* the story, for until now nothing has occurred other than two people being seated acrosss from each other in a subway. To merely show Reissman's death in one panel, as the original script may have done, would not serve the dramatic purpose of the story.

The third section returns to a strong sense of continuity from panel to panel. But whereas the first section progresses at a regular rhythm, the third section is much more irregular, like the terrified gasps of a running man. The rhythm of the continuity speeds up or slows down, according to the needs of the narrative. Time becomes static.

In the first section, although each panel is the integral part of a strong continuity, each panel individually also contains a great deal of information, given both in the detail and in the technique of presentation. This was natural and necessary because of the expositional nature of the opening sequence.

In the third section the panels are much more closely interrelated to one another, with generally less detail within the panel. The exposition is over and what is important now is Krigstein's creation of different rhythms which draw the reader into the violent climax. Thus the amount of information in each panel is crucial; it must be enough so that the full drama of the sequence is grasped, while at the same time it must not be in such profusion that the rhythm of the panels is lost.

In the last five panels of page 6, there is a progressive expansion of the height of the panel, drawing the reader into the scene, coupled with a progressive contraction of panel width, speeding up the rhythm of these short takes. The change to a diagonal background from panels 5 to 6 also serves to quicken the rhythm.

Panels 4 and 5 work as a couplet. In panel 4 Reissman is a bundle of nerves, hiding behind his paper, his shoulders hunched up, his cheek-bone high and tight on his face. In the next panel a number of subtle changes take place. Reissman finally lets out the tension which has been within him since the beginning of the story. His paper, shoulders, and jawbone all drop down.

In the next two panels, 6 and 7, the viewpoint has been reversed, but the symmetrical balance between the two characters has been maintained. The previous viewpoint was from over the Man's right shoulder; now it is over Reissman's left shoulder.

The changes between panel 6 and panel 7 are also very significant. The major development is the Man's transformation from an undefined lump to an upright angry-faced individual, from victim to attacker. There are other less obvious but equally important changes. Reissman's hat has become lower in the panel, moving closer to his collar; he has shrunk back in addition to throwing up his arm in a gesture of defense.

LOOK AT THIS MAN AND REMEMBER, CARL! REMEMBER HIS FACE... THE LOOK THAT CAME INTO HIS EYES WHEN THE NEWS CAME THAT THE RUSSIANS WERE ONLY A FEW KILOMETERS AWAY! IT WAS OVER FOR YOU, THEN, CARL! THE KILLING AND MAIMING AND TORTURING WAS SUDDENLY OVER FOR YOU!

AND YET IT *WASN'T* OVER, BECAUSE HE LOOKED AT YOU AND *SWORE*...

SOMEDAY, I'LL *GET* YOU, REISSMAN! I'LL *GET* YOU... IF IT'S THE *LAST THING I DO!*

AND THEN YOU WERE *FREE*... RUNNING *PELL-MELL ACROSS EUROPE*, HIDING YOUR *CLOTHES*, LOSING YOURSELF IN AMONG THE STREAMS OF REFUGEES THAT CHOKED THE ROADS AND HIGHWAYS BEFORE THE ADVANCING ALLIED ARMIES...

AND YET YOU *WEREN'T* FREE, CARL! EVEN THOUGH YOU SOMEHOW *GOT* TO AMERICA, YOU *NEVER FORGOT!* YOU NEVER FORGOT HIS *PROMISE!* SO YOU CARRIED THE FEAR *WITH* YOU FOR *TEN YEARS* AND *NOW* IT'S *CAUGHT UP* WITH YOU! HE'S *THERE*... SITTING *OPPOSITE* YOU... FEELING YOUR FRIGHTENED STARING EYES UPON HIM...

AND NOW HE'S *LOOKING* AT YOU. HE'S LOOKING AT YOUR *HAIR*... AT YOUR *LIPS*... YOUR *NOSE*... DEEP INTO YOUR *FRIGHTENED EYES*, AND A SPARK OF *FAR-AWAY, LONG-AGO RECOGNITION* IGNITES HIS FACE...

YOU! CHOKE...

HE RISES SLOWLY, HIS MOUTH SET IN A GRIM TAUT LINE. HIS EYES CLOUD WITH HATE, HIS FISTS CLENCH...

REISSMAN! ...IT'S *YOU!*

NO! NO! GOTT IN HIMMEL!

Master Race. © William M. Gaines, Agent, Inc. (2008).

As were panels 6 and 7 on page 6, the first three panels on page 7 are unified by a single block of text into an analysis, in staccato flashes, of a brief moment. Note, however, that each of the three panels is shown from a slightly different viewpoint.

Once again, it is the changes that occur between the panels that are so interesting. In panel 1, the Man is relatively calm. In panel 2, he has tensed up; his arm is thrown out with

Master Race. © William M. Gaines, Agent, Inc. (2008).

a half fist. The space between his coat and his hat has shortened; he is crouching, ready to pounce. But the door has slid open between panels 2 and 3, allowing Reissman to flee. The tension is deflated. Within the larger chase, Krigstein is creating sub-units of events.

Note the odd cropping of the figures in these and the following panels, which conveys a sense of claustrophobia and confusion. Krigstein's ability to show emotion through

301

the way the characters posture their bodies, of importance throughout the story, is particularly noticeable in this section. In panel 4 he incisively captures the very specific and real gesture of a man squeezing purposefully through a closing subway door. In panel 5 the Man appears to be stalking Reissman as much as chasing him. Reissman's running is feverishly agitated, wild. In panel 6 he is on the right, in panel 7 on the left, giving the swaying sensation of uncontrolled running. The delineation of his shapeless wobbly pantlegs contributes to the effect.

The panoramic view of the deserted station in panel 8 marks the change from the startled beginnings of interaction between the antagonists to the long chase. Not unlike panel 1 on page 3, this sudden distancing at a dramatic moment, this emphasis, with a horizontal long shot, of an antiseptic and unfeeling locale, shifts the reader's perspective of the drama from the personal to the universal. The Man's arms are raised like an avenging angel. The endless pillars and ceiling ridges radiate intensity in an overpowering manner not unlike Munch's painting "The Scream."[7] Indeed, it is this very architectural intensity that recalls the immutability of Fate.

Jack Davis chose the same scene for the cover and it is interesting to compare the two. Davis has created a nice composition in which all the lines focus one's attention on the little man in black; it is a textbook example of the illustrator's art. But Krigstein's panel is infinitely more complex and conveys the ineffable quality of real art.

The close-up of the foot in panel 9 provides balance for the similar close-up at the top right of the page. Reissman has regained his strength; his pants legs are now taut.

Page 7 has been filled with optical shocks: unusual cropping of figures; cuts from close shots to long shots; from small vertical panels to large horizontal panels. Another occurs between panels 9 and 10; movement in depth is juxtaposed with flat, horizontal movement. Time freezes, and one becomes aware of the not quite real nature of the entire situation. The use of scale, the tiny running figures dwarfed by the images of horror, is as important in achieving the effect of nightmare as is the combining of past and present in the same panel.

The last panel of the page begins the denouement. It is now explicit that Reissman was not a prisoner but a commandant, the cause of his present guilt and fear. Reissman is viewed from below, a natural way to depict power; it is also the same angle with which he entered the story. Expressionistic scribbles at the bottom of the panel provide a metaphor for the irrational chaos over which he reigned.

The final page of the story features Krigstein's most famous use of the breakdown technique, the spectacular depiction of Reissman's fall from the subway platform. The very brilliance of this sequence seems to have overshadowed Krigstein's masterful handling of the rest of the story, just as his breakdown technique has overshadowed his other contributions to the comic form.

In panel 1 on page 8, the Man has already stopped running; he knows that Reissman's moment of death is upon him. Reissman desperately tries to keep himself balanced, but one can see from the delineation of the folds of his trousers that he has no footing.

With panel 2 there is a dramatic shift of angle which serves to emphasize both the space into which Reissman will soon fall and the onrushing train which will crush him.

Master Race. © William M. Gaines, Agent, Inc. (2008).

Panels 3 to 6 show four separate images of the actual moment of fall. Strangely, this most famous example of the breakdown technique is uncharacteristic in that each panel shows exactly the same viewpoint. Perhaps the moment depicted is so brief that Krigstein felt it constituted a single visual unit, the four successive heads forming one curve of

descent. Note how Reissman's expression changes from surprise to horror and then determination, and his body posture shifts from formless falling, to tense straining to regain
his balance, to a final hopeless grab for the platform.

The sequence of the next four panels (7 to 10) alternates shots looking along the
tracks at the oncoming train with shots at right angles to the tracks showing Reissman's
fall into the path of the train. This could be considered cross-cutting, but could just as
logically be showing simultaneous occurrences. A more standard method would be to
show the train and Reissman's fall in one single shot, but Krigstein has broken the scene
down into component images. This technique continues the rhythm of the panels that
has been built up, avoids a panel that would be too full of data for a climax, and expands
the final moment before Reissman's death.

Finally, at the point of impact, Krigstein cuts away from the tracks to the platform
(panel 11). The nightmare is over. The panel is square; there is no longer the activity of
the slender panels. The depiction of the rushing train reflects back to the nearly identical
panel on page 1. There is a return to the every day reality that existed before the drama
began.

Krigstein's grasp of the human moment is again evident in his depiction of the passengers flooding from the car in panel 12. The arm of a hurried commuter who doesn't wish
to be involved is seen in the lower left. A woman cranes her head to get a better view.

The Man turns and fades into the darkness from whence he came. The statement
that Reissman was "a perfect stranger" adds a note of ambiguity. The man is probably
lying; indeed, he was seen rushing toward Reissman. But possibly the earlier scenes were
Reissman's subjective understanding of altogether different objective events.

NOTES

1. Krigstein's comment: *I'm glad you've mentioned sound, because to me the whole first section has a strong sound
effect. I was very conscious of the sound of that train coming in. Creating a rhythm, both within the picture and
the rhythm relating one picture to another, was an extremely important element in designing pictures for this
specific story.*

2. Krigstein's comment: *I do remember the sensation of inspiration in panel 5—the crucial transitional unit in
a series of three. I didn't think of the design as flattening out (which it does do), but felt the picture rising up to
the viewer from the deep interior in an accumulating rush, and resolved in panel three. But your analysis is also
quite correct.*

3. Krigstein's comment: *Maybe both things are true. If I had had all the space that I wanted, it would not have
been just text. But because of the limitations of space, I made what for me was a very important decision; to have
a pictureless panel, which was totally contrary to my whole feeling about pictures. And that was the one that I
sacrificed because I could get away with it in a good formal way. It still remained part of the total form. But the
decision was definitely the result of soul searching.*

4. Krigstein's comment: *I wanted the story to appear in a total, clear light. And the more clear and orderly the story,
the more "objectively" done, the more the emotional content of it would have weight. I thought the emotional
intensity of the story was best served by total clarity. In the story, my subway cannot be well worn; the subway is
a great, a tremendous engine.*

5. Krigstein's comment: *You've given this a psychological implication that I'm not aware of. I did not think of him,
or these other people, at that time, transformed into brownshirts. But it's open enough; it certainly could be that,*

and I may have been confronted with that possibility when I drew it. But frequently when I have been confronted with the possibility of interpretation I don't go any further than that single confrontation, and whatever happens afterwards, happens.

6. Krigstein's comment: *The reference to George Grosz would not apply. He is a great artist, but the content of bitter satire is what separates his work from my approach in this story.*

7. Krigstein's comment: *I'm fascinated that you should recall Munch in this context, because he's really one of my favorite artists. I didn't think of the analogy between that particular painting and this panel though.*

The Comics of Chris Ware

GENE KANNENBERG, JR.

Artists like Dan Clowes, Jason Lutes, and myself, are all trying to tell a serious story using the tools of jokes. It's as though we're trying to write a powerful, deeply engaging, richly detailed epic with a series of limericks. I've just tried to expand the possibilities for the [comics] form, just to get in a little more sense of a real experience.

CHRIS WARE (qtd. in Juno, *Dangerous Drawings* 53)

Chris Ware stands as a leading contemporary cartoonist, garnering numerous industry awards and receiving glowing reviews in trade publications and popular magazines alike. With work appearing in various comics anthologies, magazines, and his own comic book series, *Acme Novelty Library*, Ware has worked in a variety of comics genres, from stand-alone gag cartoons to his serialized novel of multi-generational ennui, "Jimmy Corrigan: The Smartest Kid on Earth." Critics have praised Ware's work for its formal complexity, characterized by dizzyingly intricate pages, while marveling at how deftly Ware manipulates traditional comic-book characters (superheroes, cowboys, spacemen) to tell darkly humorous stories that concern acceptance and loss, pain and longing.[1]

This narrative complexity manifests itself in Ware's skilled juxtaposition of disparate narrative and graphic elements, and his sophisticated approach to the use of text plays a vital role in this process. Through deliberate manipulation of the appearance and placement of text within—and surrounding—his comics pages, Ware exploits the graphic nature of printed comics text in ways few other cartoonists have attempted. In so doing, he takes full advantage of comics' innate ability to create complexity through the multivalent interpretive possibilities engendered by the form's presentation of structured text/image combinations.[2]

In this essay I will discuss how Chris Ware's ingenious use of text in comics relates to theories of visual literature in order to demonstrate Ware's unique understanding of the comics form's underpinnings and potential. Text reads as an image in Ware's comics, conflating two sign systems in ways which question the binary text/image opposition. His comics can present simultaneous narrative strands by combining text and image in

Reprinted by permission from Robin Varnum and Christina T. Gibbons, eds., *The Language of Comics: Word and Image* (University Press of Mississippi, 2001), 174–97.

nontraditional designs. In his long narratives, Ware brings together many different strategies of reference between visual elements both within and across comics pages, exploring the narrative potential of the comics form. And his overall book design for his comics shows a kinship with the visual narrative form known as artists' books. Ware's careful attention to the appearance and placement of text in his comics—its visual appearance and its placement upon the page—reveals the nature of comics as the union of story and structure, simultaneously tempering levity with gravity to approximate, in his terms, "real experience."

VISUAL LITERATURE

The detail in Ware's artwork itself reveals his careful attention to the appearance of text. Additionally, Ware himself describes his specific approach to text in his comics in numerous interviews. In his interview from *Comics Journal* 200, Ware notes:

> The way text is used visually in comics seems to me to be so incredibly limited. It's the one avenue in comics that seems to have been more or less completely untouched. I mean, when you have all the tools of visual art at your disposal, then why put words in balloons? (Ware, qtd. in Groth 16: 1)

Although Ware does not define what "all the tools of visual art" might contain, his practice makes clear his familiarity with both high art history as well as the traditions of American publication design—in which word and image both play important roles. In Ware's comics, we see echoes of architectural blueprints, electrical diagrams, maps, and catalogs. Unlike the work of some cartoonists whose sole point of artistic reference seems to be old comic books, Ware's publications reveal an awareness of and appreciation for art and its relation to text in broad terms. Although Ware does not shy from using traditional comics devices like word balloons when it suits him, his work indeed reveals a concerted effort to use text in various, rarely seen fashions.

He notes elsewhere:

> How they [the tools of visual art and design] are patterned and combined is what makes the stuff interesting and emotionally real. By synthesizing the visual mechanics of written language with the effects of seeing, a comic strip "fools" you into the illusion of "theater" by letting you think you're "watching" an event transpire, when you're actually reading it! (Ware, qtd. in Sabin 41)[3]

For Ware, design thus becomes a crucial narrative element. The arrangement of visual elements upon the page creates the illusion of theater, the acting-out of narrative. Unlike theater, however, comics allows for the simultaneous presentation of convergent or divergent information via the arrangement of various visual elements within the unifying space of the comics page. While most comics narratives progress in time from panel to panel, many of Ware's comics pages juxtapose different narrative sequences within a contained space.

In this way, Ware actively explores the tension in comics between word and image in a manner similar to that done in what is known as *visual literature*.[4] Eric Vos has defined visual literature as "the use of visual means of representation in a literary context" (135), a description which immediately calls to mind the image of the comics page, although Vos does not mention comics per se in his discussion.

For Vos, visual literature exists not as a "hybrid" form between literature and visual art, but rather as a system in which verbal and visual symbols retain their traditional denotative functions while affecting each other in complex, form-determined ways:

> [O]ne and the same semiotic procedure underlies the integration of the verbal and the visual. In both cases, that is, we are dealing with not a unilateral referential relationship from sign to referent that we could call iconicity, but with a bi- or even trilateral relationship from the sign to some concept that in turn both refers back to a characteristic of the sign in question and leads us toward contemplating conventions of verbal and literary communication. (141)

This idea yields some important points relating to comics, and Ware's comics in particular. First, symbols in such systems do not lose their denotative function—that is, nothing is lost when symbol systems are combined within the same space, although much can be gained. Thus, the arrangement of word and image in Ware's comics allows us to consider the page itself as a visual-literary totality, a closed system in which the various elements both act in their traditional representative fashions and, through their spatial juxtaposition, participate in creating larger units of meaning.

Second, "the exemplificative elements of this referential complex are the prime factors of the work's aesthetic status and function" (144)—that is, the work's medium and identity are defined precisely by this interplay of sign systems. In Ware's work, layout and design govern visual and thematic complexities, wherein the words and the images are conjoined in such a way that it is not possible to discuss one without considering the other.

Third, "exemplification and complex reference are totally unconcerned with boundaries between media and art forms. As exemplifying symbols, verbal and visual signs function in exactly the same way. This and only this is what allows us to speak of semiotic integration of the verbal and the visual" (144). The semiotic basis of this statement may be questionable; verbal signs, as units of a system of language, clearly follow systems of grammatical rules that images do not. But visual literature's enterprise—to use visual means of representation narratively—asks readers to reconsider the binary opposition between word and image by blurring distinctions between the two. And it is just such a blurring that Ware's work embodies so well.

WORD AS IMAGE

Ware radically questions the binary opposition of text and images in highly structured pages, including those used in the self-contained mini-narratives of Quimby the Mouse and Sparky the Cat from *Acme Novelty Library* 4. The use of text in many of his pages reflects Vos' observations about visual literature quite clearly: text and image enlighten each other without one system dominating the other; the juxtaposition of disparate elements cannot be separated without fundamentally altering the piece; and text is used as a visual element every bit as illustrative as the images, allowing for an integration of verbal and visual narrative.

In the Sparky and Quimby stories, Ware explores the difficulties involved in interpersonal relationships. Quimby the mouse at times loves and at other times hates Sparky, who exists as a disembodied cat-head and therefore requires special care and attention; this tension informs the strips. (In a nod to *Krazy Kat*, George Herriman's ode to unrequited love in which Krazy becomes alternatively male or female, Sparky remains gender-neutral, while Quimby appears to be male.) Like most of Ware's short-form work, each strip runs a page in length and narrates a complete event. Movements from page to page in these collections do not reveal one continuous narrative; rather, these strip collections recall sonnet sequences, in that each page is a single unit and the aggregate whole is more concerned with communicating mood and feeling than in presenting a narrative.

Ware graphically manipulates text in ways which acknowledge cartoonist Will Eisner's dictum that "text reads as an image" (Eisner, *Comics & Sequential Art*, 10). Given the complexity with which Ware approaches his textual elements, it will be helpful in these discussions to speak not simply of a speech balloon or caption, but of lexias. I use *lexia* to describe a distinct textual division in a graphic, not grammatical sense: a block of text which is designed to be read/viewed as a single unit, usually (although not always) a smaller sub-unit in a larger structure such as a panel or page.

In his "Quimby" pages, Ware uses lexias as bold display and design elements, as much a part of the page's composition and structure as the individual panels themselves. As we see in several instances near the top of the page, representations of Quimby interact with lexias as if they represented physical objects in the story-space, not simply text elements on the page. This conflation of "text" and "image" becomes understandable when placed in context with Ware's views on the use of images within his work. He states:

> It [comics] involves two completely different parts of the brain. The part that reads and the part that looks. It comes down to an almost Platonic difference of the specific and the general. You've got a drawing of a car, you can't make it too specific because then it becomes too much of a drawing and then it doesn't work within a circumstance where you're "reading" the pictures. I try to balance that by making the pictures look cold and dead, like typography. (Ware, qtd. in Juno 53)

The comparison with "typography" should not be conflated with comics lettering itself, however, which for Ware is often the most expressive element on his comics pages. And not simply expressive, but structural in the way in which the images and panels themselves are generally understood:

> I've done strips where I've tried to make the words the structure on which the pictures are hung as opposed to the other way around, which is the way comics are

Acme Novelty Library 4 (Winter 1995). Reprinted by permission of the artist.

usually thought of—a series of pictures with the words plopped down on top. (Ware, qtd. in Groth 164)

The "Quimby the Mouse" stories have at their heart (so to speak) a tension between the desire for love and connection and the desire for independence—conflicting though simultaneous emotions. The text design makes this tension explicit through a sophisticated use of color and layout, so that text becomes diagrammatically directive in both *narrative* and *meta-narrative* fashions. By *narrative* I here refer to the way in which the placement of lexias act to guide the reader's gaze across the page in a specific direction in order to read various elements in a particular order. By *meta-narrative*, however, I refer to the ways in which the appearance or placement of lexias on the page serve to reflect thematically on characters or events in the narrative. A third form of textual practice is *extra-narrative*, in which the appearance of the text reflects not on the story proper but rather on the book-object itself; this practice is discussed in more detail below.[5]

In this page's visual narrative, we see Quimby asleep in a chair in his house; he is awakened by a phone call (presumably from Sparky), and he then calls Sparky back. The large lexias serve in some stretches to echo or reinforce the dialogue which Quimby speaks into the phone, at other times to convey the conflicting emotional states that Quimby does not verbally express but which nevertheless inform his hesitant, contradictory replies. Thus text, whether used within a panel in traditional fashion or in bold lexias placed upon the page in atypical ways, provides a simultaneous structural and contextual element that unites the page in both design and theme.

This "Quimby" page begins with an arch of text reading "I'm a Very Generous Person"; the "I" is oversized in comparison to the rest of the line of text, and printed in red, distinguishing it from the inverse blue of the rest of the sentence. The emphasis on the "I" here immediately draws our attention meta-narratively to the self-centeredness of Quimby, our protagonist. Next to the "I" we see an image of Quimby tossing money in a cartoonish emblem of financial "generosity." Here Quimby wears a stovepipe hat which echoes the large "I," creating a sort of eye-rhyme referral between image and text; it also refers to the single other image of Quimby in this hat which occurs in this collection, on the previous page in which he is also "generously" offering a drink (actually symbolizing self-pity) to Sparky.

By buttressing the "n" in "Person" with "But I" in black text, Ware begins narratively to lead the reader's eye back across the page, right to left, to add the sentence "But I Just Can't Stand Being Around You Anymore"; this contradictory reading direction meta-narratively mirrors the contradictory emotional tenor of the two thoughts. Notice that the "T" in "But" also functions as a spike which Quimby is shown striking with a hammer into the "I," symbolizing the pain he is inflicting both upon his love and, paradoxically, himself. The word "Just" drops out of the sentence, offering Quimby a perch upon which to stand as well as a verbal hedge in his painful declaration.

This sentence blends into the following one in an unusual way. By utilizing the opacity of printed ink on white paper, Ware creates a deliberate, legible palimpsest, superimposing conflicting sentences—and conflicting emotions—on top of each other. He thus creates a visual representation of Quimby's inner emotional turmoil, which also meta-narratively reflects the dream state we see illustrated in this panel. The object "You" in the previous sentence becomes the subject in "You Make Me Happy Sometimes, Though. . ." Because words from each sentence occupy the same space on the page, we cannot read one sentence without seeing/reading the other; in this way, Ware makes explicit the conflation of emotions which the story attempts to convey graphically.

Placing "I Guess. . ." in the panel in which Quimby is awakened by the ringing of the telephone reinforces the tentativeness of his emotional state/s; the subtle coloring shift within the letters moves the narrative into the next panel, and into the strip-format of panel-to-panel continuity; the alternating color backgrounds of these small panels further reflect Quimby's changeable attitudes and emotions; a pattern of pulsating visual referral guides the "seeing" eye as well as the "reading" eye.

"Yeah, I'm Sort of Busy Right Now," which runs backwards across the middle of the page, serves narratively as a verbal vector to lead the eye back to the left-hand margin of the page. Of course, it also magnifies, quite literally, the lie which this speech-act represents. Also, referring to the construction metaphor from the top of the page, we see an image of Quimby quite outside the main narrative, struggling to support the asymmetrical house-structure which contains the narrative, a metaphor for the unstable rhetorical framework which his speech represents.

Due to the alternating direction and sloping attitude of the various lexias, we also can find the sentence "I Can't Stand Being Alone" running down the right-hand side of the page. The fact that the word "Alone" stands as a palimpsest over the panel after which Quimby states "I was just thinking about you" emphasizes this sentiment, although the dream-thought makes the reader aware that "I was just thinking about you" is not as positive a statement, perhaps, as it is intended.

"Remember? You Said So Yourself" hangs in the air outside the house with the telephone wire visible, emphasizing the weight of language, the ever-present burden of communication, on the understanding and relationship between these two people. After this, two small scenes are subdivided and pared down even further. Even at this greatly reduced size, the body language of Quimby itself says almost as much as his words do, expressing his unease both with the caller and his own feelings—a way in which Ware attempts to make his drawings more "readable" rather than illustrative. The final panel's tiny, white-upon-black "Look . . . I *Said* I Was *Busy!*"—utterly incomprehensible in light of his apology just four panels previously—speaks as loudly as do the large, multi-colored lexias throughout the page. Quimby has learned nothing; yet we, as readers, have seen his thought process which reveals, however unconsciously, his desire for connection, for communication, for love. As in most of Ware's comics narratives, here we see not only the worst of human nature, but also the conflicting emotional states underlying such actions.

The graphic design of this page, managed via and structured by text placement and visual arrangement, allows for—and, due to its branching and overlapping nature, demands—a reading which must meander, drawing visual, verbal, and thematic connections between the images and various lexias of the page. This page presents a perfect example of Ware's ability to structure the comics page in order to subordinate plot to theme; compositional referral between lexias and non-text images allows for communication on multiple levels simultaneously.

SIMULTANEITY

Ware has a specific goal in mind when creating complementary, co-existing narratives:

> It seems like comics are the perfect place to [. . .] recreate how those words in your mind superimpose or affect the perceived experience. In comics it can be done almost synthetically in a way that's more immediate than writing. You're always at one point in writing. As you read, you can't be simultaneously in two places, the way you can be in a comic, with a word and a picture. (Ware, qtd. in Groth 161–62)

One of Ware's earliest published anthology pieces demonstrates a sophisticated attempt to portray simultaneity in comics—to portray an instance in which perceived experience is colored by intellectual action. "Thrilling Adventure Stories /I Guess," was published in 1991 in *Raw*.[6]

The story presents two apparently unrelated narratives through a clever, disorienting ploy: the pictures, or the visual narrative, illustrate a cliched "superhero vs. mad scientist" story, while the words, or the textual narrative, tell a young boy's first-person reminiscence of the troubles he and his mother have with various men. This textual narrative is broken up and placed, piece-meal, into the visual narrative's word balloons, captions, and sound effects, and other textual elements, presenting two narratives within the same (con)textual space, yielding an instance of what Holly O'Grady has termed "visual polyphony."[7] A careful reading of "Thrilling Adventure Stories" reveals Ware's deliberate, mutually reflective patterning between word and image by conjoining seemingly unrelated verbal and visual narratives; within each panel, and across pages, verbal and visual themes meta-narratively magnify, undercut, or otherwise comment upon each other.

In the top two tiers of the final page of the story, we see the superhero (who has reduced his size) fix a faulty wire within a mad scientist's brain and escape through the scientist's ear. The accompanying textual narrative, four sentences which are broken into six lexias shaped like either narrative captions or thought balloons, describes how the bigotry of the narrator's stepfather upsets the boy's mother so much that she eventually leaves the man. While the images show a superheroic way to re-order a person's unacceptable behavior, the text presents the viewpoint that such problems have few easy solutions but many long-term and difficult consequences.

The middle tier of panels shows the superhero reunited with his love interest, the plucky reporter, as they watch the scientist move from madness to sanity. In his excitement, however, the scientist (accidentally?) steps on a detonating switch. In the text, the narrator describes one of the last times he spent with this stepfather, an uncomfortable and only dimly recalled "sleepover." In terms of the visual narrative, the lexia in the scientist's speech bubble—"Maybe that's what we did, but I don't remember"—could almost function directly as quoted speech. The ambiguity of the textual narrator's recollection of this point, however, is doubled in the ambiguity of exactly why the scientist hits the detonator switch. Perhaps he does not recall "what happened," but perhaps he does; so too, perhaps the narrator simply does not wish to recall the events of the night in question.

In the final tier, the story's Freudian subtext is brought to the fore. Holding the reporter, the hero leaps to the sky, leaving the scientist behind; an explosion occurs, but the

"Thrilling Adventure Stories/I Guess," *RAW* 2.3 (1991), 81. Reprinted by permission of the artist.

final shot reveals a close-up view of our escaped main characters—a look of thanks (and perhaps love?) on the reporter's face, and a grim-set look of self-satisfaction on the hero's visage. The text, however, reads, "But that was okay with me, since I liked things better / When / It was just my Mom and me, anyway." Using the lexia "When" as the sound effect for the explosion (middle panel) creates visual punctuation and allows the final text/image juxtaposition to exist in relative isolation from other action. Throughout the story, the hero figure in the visual narrative has coexisted in uneasy thematic relationships with the various father figures in the narrator's life—his grandfather, his stepfather. At the story's end, however, this "sliding signification" has been transferred to the boy narrator himself—he "like[s] things better" when other male figures have been left behind, so no one can come between him and his mother.

"Thrilling Adventure Stories" is remarkable for its sophisticated blending of two narratives, and all the more so because it ultimately suggests a third field of interpretation. The textual narrative's point of view is that of a young boy who, as the larger story reveals, is enamored with superhero comic books, their costumed heroes as well as their moral and narrative clarity. The events he witnesses in his own life, however, are anything but clear; the nuances of adult interrelationships and the depths of bigotry are concepts which he cannot yet fully understand.

To read "Thrilling Adventure Stories," then, is to experience the conflicting emotional states of the boy himself. The text reveals the events of the boy's life, while the accompanying pictures reveal the limited types of relational and moral reasoning which are at this point available to him, as he tries to make sense of his experiences. The visual narrative's idiom glosses the content of the textual narrative in an attempt to reproduce a psychological state upon the page. In this way, Ware makes good his claim that comics can reproduce on the page conflicting and simultaneous emotional states—to communicate both an event and how that event is experienced, within a contained, coordinating space.

TEXT/IMAGE INTEGRATION ON A GRAND SCALE

A final example will serve to explore the text/image relationships that Ware brings to bear upon longer narratives, wherein page design is used to subdivide one long narrative into smaller portions (as opposed to sagas like "Quimby," above, wherein each page represents a unit of discourse complete in itself). The longest narrative Ware has attempted to date is his serialized novel "Jimmy Corrigan: The Smartest Kid on Earth," appearing in issues 5–6, 8–9, and 11–14 of *Acme Novelty Library*.

This nearly 400-page story centers on Jimmy's family history; while Jimmy's reunion with his estranged father represents the prime story, the idea of family history is felt throughout the narrative. Flashbacks make up a good deal of the novel, reaching back to the 1893 Chicago World's Fair and the death of the mother of Jimmy's great-grandfather William; these events are shown to have repercussions in both the past and present. Similar situations of familial loss, or other forms of abandonment, figure prominently over the narrative's course. Throughout the novel, characters strive for, but rarely attain, stable relationships; they often seek substitutes for comfort, such as mass-produced entertainment or the acquisition of material goods, but even at the best of times, such panaceas are ultimately revealed to be merely powerless placebos.

"Jimmy Corrigan" utilizes several highly distinctive and effective narrative methods, and text usually plays a decisive role in these strategies. Narration itself is at times limited to nothing more than conjunctions writ large: lexias such as "And." or "But." are placed within panels of their own or are printed large and in color atop or alongside panels, providing graphic, relational referral between illustrated events. In such instances, the picture narratives convey brief incidents, and the conjunctions demonstrate the relatedness of such incidents to each other. Unlike typical comics narrative blocks which float at the top of panels and which form only part of a larger omniscient narrative voice, these conjunctions serve as striking, graphic punctuation on the narrative level, linking not verbal sentences but illustrated events.

Another form of narration that Ware uses in the series' flashback sequences is a third- or first-person narrative voice, presented in cursive handwriting, which "floats" in unadorned lexial units amongst panels on the page. This voice "speaks" haltingly, at times using complete sentences within a panel, at other times presenting only phrases or single words within a panel. In such latter cases, entire sentences or thoughts can be spread across one or several pages, portions appearing in only selected panels. Readers need to "assemble" a sentence over a long series of non-contiguous panels which may be interspersed with scenes of dialogue as well. This narrative technique mandates a non-linear reading strategy that once again demonstrates Ware's use of comics to describe events from multiple points of view in the same space.

One good example of this narrative technique may be found in *Acme* 2, which takes place before the death of William's mother, young James' grandmother. Here we can see how Ware's design differs from previous examples. The initial two lexias on this page complete the phrase begun on the previous page: "The sound of One Lung / filling with water / drowned out by wave after wave / of a million buzzing insects / an invisible chorus / that only knows how to sing / the last letter of the alphabet." This elaborate way of highlighting the insects' onomatopoetic "Zzzz" brings to mind the referential nature of the alphabetic letter without printing it on the page; it also anticipates the page's focus on the letter "M" to follow.

In the visual narrative, young James (Jimmy's grandfather) climbs into a tree overlooking the construction site of the 1893 Chicago World's Fair; Lake Michigan lies at the horizon. The text continues: "Up here he can see all the way / to The Ocean." Note that the lexia "to The Ocean" is printed along the same horizontal line as the Lake Michigan horizon, conflating via design the text and the picture to create a meta-narrative idea about the boy's perceptions, much as in "Thrilling Adventure Stories." Of course, Lake Michigan is not an ocean at all, but to the young boy, the technical distinction is slight at best. As one of the Great Lakes, Lake Michigan is an ocean-like mass of water lying in the middle of North America; and the next lexia on the page seems to echo this fact: "In the middle" read the letters, in an inverse white upon red text field. This lexia also stands in approximately the middle of the page, a visual blockade ensuring narratively that the first column of panels are read together as a whole unit. These words also begin the narration which draws our attention to the letter "M" in the dictionary which young James has brought with him.

In the middle of the dictionary, which by its nature contains all stories, lies a picture of James' mother, who died in childbirth and whose absence James feels ever more acutely now that his paternal grandmother also lies dying. As this sequence of sixteen panels develops, note how each small panel contributes to the revelation of the book's contents. In the first nine panels, which eventually reveal a complete textual sentence,

Acme Novelty Library 11 (1998). Reprinted by permission of the artist.

lexias are usually placed in panels featuring close-ups of James and his incidental actions. The other panels in the sequence, while "silent," reveal contextual details. Through a combination of visual and verbal variation, the panels gradually reveal the narrative situation; specific close-up views gain importance through the referral made possible by the continued return to the contextual image of James in the tree.

The end of the sixteen-panel sequence reveals the presence "of a girl's hair," perhaps the boy's mother's, also in the book. Earlier in this chapter, James has fantasized about a magic lantern's beam of light resembling a human hair, a metaphor for life which continues its journey into the heavens, occasionally interrupting and simultaneously illuminating outside phenomena, until it is finally extinguished; the chapter will end striking a similar, though more forlorn, note. Here, "in the middle" of the chapter, the metaphor is recalled obliquely; the juxtaposition of the silent panel showing the strand of hair and the next panel, containing the lexia "to which he clings like a rope," calls to mind the hair as a symbol of escape—from the tree in which he sits, and from his young life which is, so far, governed by whims of family and fate.

The arrival of the ambulance carriage in the final two panels—which also include the tree in which James sits—serves to reinforce this powerlessness. The positions of the lexias within these two panels are themselves narratively significant. "These private summer daydreams" occur, quite literally, within the dark safety of the tree, and exist "away from the critical scrutiny of paternity" via their separation within the frame. The "scrutiny of paternity" is replaced with a perhaps more terrifying image, the specter of death, in the final panel, as that scrutiny is replaced physically with the ambulance—which "abruptly end[s]" by being cut off by the panel border to end the page. This meta-narrative visual referral allows the text and the image to each comment on the text to illuminate the theme of the scene.

Ware uses color itself as a compositional reference. One page, for example, is dominated by pale burgundy tones which elsewhere in this story are used when the grandmother's failing health dominates James' thoughts, as opposed to those slate gray tones that color passages about the forward-thinking, progressive World's Fair or the deep gray tones that suffuse the pages upon which James runs away from home to avoid confronting death.

All of these elements together—color, composition, textual placement (or absence)—create complex and overlapping systems of referral over the course of the narrative. While each of these elements plays a substantial role, the text itself becomes an anchor to which Ware returns again and again. In his comics, wherein the images themselves take on an air of familiarity (due to Ware's precise drawing style which attempts to render images as instantly recognizable shapes *à la* words themselves), the deliberate design of the text—in grammatical reference as well as the reference invoked by placement and appearance—allows for ever-expanding possibilities for text/image relationships upon the comics page.

FROM COMIC BOOK TO ARTIST'S BOOK

"Jimmy Corrigan" and "Sparky and Quimby" are but two of the story types Ware includes in his *Acme Novelty Library*; other stories use traditional comic book staples like cowboys, spacemen, and superheroes. When used in traditional comic books, these character types have served as tools for telling simple, genre-based stories. Through his use of such stock character types, Ware invokes genres which he can then by turns embrace and alter in service to larger thematic issues, as we have already seen with Quimby and the superhero from "Thrilling Adventure Stories"; the received and preconceived ideas which underlie such characters paradoxically contribute to the depth of the stories which Ware creates. Yet for all its indebtedness to comic book conventions, *Acme* exhibits a peculiar design sense all its own; it does not look like a traditional comic book. In fact, Ware's insistence on treating each issue of *Acme* as a unified design space, characterized by the use of expressive typography as well as his tight integration of text and image in his comics pages themselves, places the series more in line with "artists' books" than with comic books as such.

We may think of artists' books as carefully crafted books in which every detail—from illustration to prose, from binding to typeface—is controlled by the artist toward some thematic end. In *The Century of Artists' Books*, Johanna Drucker offers a potential definition of the form—which by its very nature is hard to describe definitively:

> It's easy enough to say that an artist's book is a book created as an original work of art, rather than a reproduction of a preexisting work. And also, that it is a book

which integrates the formal means of its realization and production with its thematic or aesthetic issues. (2)

Quick to qualify all of these terms, Drucker notes, for example, that some artist's books have in fact been created for reproduction. Yet the most important aspect, for Drucker, is that an artist's book is "almost always self conscious about the structure and meaning of the book as a form" (4). Ware's attention to detail and overall design in the Acme series certainly meets this criterion. While his comic books are published by Fantagraphics Books, Ware himself designs the entire contents of each issue anew, including the publishing indicia.[8] No publisher-decreed insignias or even standard UPC code boxes violate the integrity of Ware's intended vision. The format of individual issues varies; physical size corresponds to content, from the small issues of the serialized novel, "Jimmy Corrigan, Smartest Kid on Earth" (1/4" x 6") to the "Book of Jokes" issues (3/4" x 18").

The design of these periodicals makes these booklets appear to hail from a century past, dimly remembered yet fondly recalled. Faux art nouveau detailing on the covers, hyperbolic editorials, ironic advertisement pages, and even paper models and games all contribute to the books' overall impact. The design of such pages and the typefaces used on them extra-narratively recall early-twentieth-century magazine and catalog designs, as well as grant an overall visual identity to each individual issue. While these text designs do not contribute to the comics' narratives in a direct sense, these extra-narrative associations identify each comic book as a unique object. These associations also create a semblance of nostalgic innocence, a context of comfort which serves ironically to amplify Ware's stories' often harsh themes.

The cover to *Acme Novelty Library* provides a bold example of Ware's often baroque design sensibility, a tendency to crowd his display spaces with a variety of superficial artistic flourishes, densely ornate compositions, and verbose slogans. Immediately, the reader notes the bold, cartoony figure of young Jimmy Corrigan as scientist, giant, shrunken boy, and—startlingly—self-surgeon. The text, while mostly given to absurd hyperbole, also professes a deep cynicism, e.g. "An Indefensible Attempt to Justify the Despair of Those Who Have Never Known Real Tragedy" and "Where Art and Avarice Share the Same Telephone Line." These arch labels serve to critique the nostalgic impulse which the pictorial style apparently embraces, a tension similar to the strategies we have seen in Ware's work thus far.

Throughout each book, the extra textual material itself contains additional illustrations by Ware, often containing the same characters and situations found within the comics "proper." The text pieces are by turns humorous and abrasive, and oftentimes both at once. The design and diction of the advertisements not only recall the past; they often, as Daniel Raeburn notes, draw explicitly upon material found in the 1900 Sears, Roebuck & Co. Catalog and the Johnson Smith & Company Catalog, infamous for its variety of items including live alligators, "whoopee cushions," X-Ray Spectacles, and the like (Raeburn 14–15).

Ware's parodic concerns, however, extend beyond specific goods. Items "for sale" in *Acme* speak to the bleakness of existence or the horrors of modern life; typical consumer goods include "Certainty," "The Noose," or "Happy Family *Appliqués*." Within these advertisements, the carefree joys of nostalgia are humorously debased with the deadening

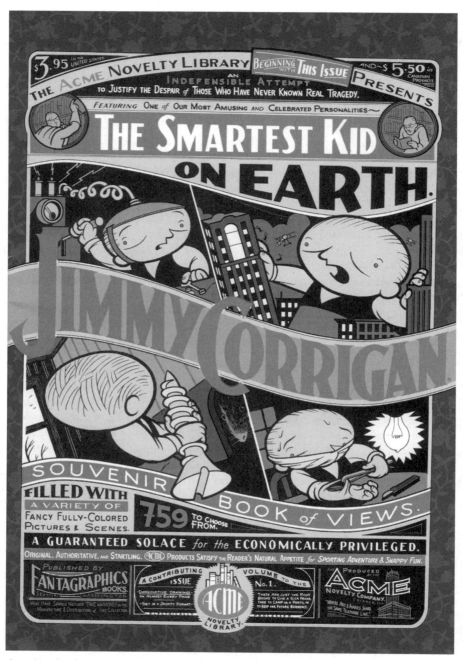

Acme Novelty Library 1 (Winter 1993), cover. Reprinted by permission of the artist.

effects of modern life. In the books' hyperbolic editorial matter, often concerning the hypothetical "Acme Novelty Library Corporation," century-old diction combines with the bleakest of "goal-oriented" corporate progress to ensure readers that they have purchased a quality product:

> Under these conditions it is not surprising that in addition to sudden illness among employees we have an outrageous number of accidents each day. We have been particularly fortunate, however, since we opened this grand facility, in that we have incurred very little in the way of legal pursuit. (Ware, *Acme* 3: 37)

In both the advertisements and editorial material, Ware simultaneously embraces and undercuts the American consumer culture, and the entertainment industry which is part and parcel of that culture, as a utopian ideal. Richard Dyer, in his essay "Entertainment and Utopia," notes that entertainment has at its core an attempt to communicate the idea of utopia:

> Entertainment offers the image of "something better" to escape into, or something we want deeply that our day-to-day lives don't provide. . . . Entertainment does not, however, present models of utopian worlds, as in the classic utopias of Sir Thomas More, William Morris, *et al.* Rather, the utopianism is contained in the feelings it embodies. It presents head-on as it were, what utopia would feel like rather than how it is organized. (373)

Ware himself sees at least a tendency toward utopianism, or at least comforting humanism, in early-twentieth-century advertising and design matter. He notes his affinity for the style's visual appearance:

> Design in the period between the turn of the century and the Depression has a quality I like. I enjoy the typography and the general look. It feels much more human and warm to me, than the current slick, sophisticated design. It's more inviting. It has a certain dorky "join the party" quality, whereas design today has a maybe-you-can-be-like-us-if-you-want quality. (qtd. in Juno 42)

Ware's text design on the level of the book-object, then, can be seen as an active critique of the twentieth century's utopian optimism. Entertainment and advertising, from various sources, mix in the popular magazine format; Ware's comic books, products of a single aesthetic viewpoint, conjoin advertising and entertainment forms with specific content which questions their utopian pretensions. In so doing, Ware demonstrates the cultural path which has led so many of his stories' characters to their downtrodden lives: society conditions these responses by building unrealistic utopian goals which cannot be fulfilled by the products and services which are produced and advertised to do just that. By utilizing what he sees as "human and warm" design elements in his own work, Ware tempers the bleakness of his thematic concerns, but in a way which paradoxically reinforces them, as well.

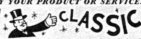

Acme Novelty Library 10 (Spring 1998), 9. Reprinted by permission of the artist.

The "party" his ads and editorials ask readers to "join" seems, in his view, ironically to lessen the quality of life. Through employing designs, rhetoric and publishing conventions of the past to construct his books, Ware produces a nostalgic veneer which, like the comics genre characters he uses in his stories, appears to embrace the ideals of a bygone era. However, the comics narratives themselves demonstrate that the "good old days" were hardly ever that. In fact, the problems of the present (an absent father, an emotionally distant mother, an inability to maintain friendships or sexual relationships) have their mirrors—and often their roots—in the actions of the past. The tragedy in the search for connection found in so many of Ware's stories thus lies not entirely within the characters themselves, but rather is symptomatic of the culture which these characters inhabit. In presenting his comics stories in the context of self-designed book packages in which textual content and form serve in various ways to reinforce and amplify the stories' own themes, Ware's practice can be seen as analogous to the artist's book, which, Drucker states, "has to have some conviction, some soul, some reason *to be* and *to be a book* in order to succeed" (10–11, emphasis Drucker's).

CONCLUSION

More than perhaps that of any other modern cartoonist, Ware's work is highly contextualized and thematized through its publication design. Not only has Ware created a series of artists' books in the form of comic books; he has, further, created an all-encompassing reading experience—the entire *Acme* series—which is united in terms of visual design, narrative themes, and characters, by one guiding artistic and aesthetic principle. And while Ware actively uses genres and print traditions which initially call to mind simple pleasures, he uses those elements to fashion a narrative which rises above the humor and nostalgia which color it, calling the values embodied by those forms into question.

Through combining text and images in mutually expressive ways, and by exploring how the appearance of his text can affect both his comics narratives and his comic books as a whole, Chris Ware makes a significant contribution not just to comics but to visual literature as a whole. Ware takes the traditional elements of comics—panels, word balloons, sound effects, narration, and page design—and combines them in startling, sophisticated ways, emphasizing the materiality of text on the comics page as a visual element and using it to fashion complex, polyvalent narrative structures. In his comics pages, text is often used quite specifically in a narrative function, directing the reader's gaze across, through, or around intricately designed pages, pages in which panels progress in decidedly non-linear fashions. Text faces and placement also serve *meta-narratively* to reflect thematically on his stories. His use of text for display purposes reveals an *extra-narrative* tendency to use the appearance of text—and therefore, the publication—which resonate throughout each comic book issue as information does within artist's hooks.

Aaron Marcus observes, "[V]isual literature begins where language leaves off; it extends mankind's abilities to identify, describe, analyze, evaluate and extol the ineffable" (19). In his various textual/aesthetic practices, Ware provides a compelling example of comics which—however apparently familiar, funny, or frustrating they might at first appear—also use concrete textual and visual means to address the ineffable. Chris Ware's use of text in his comics narratives demonstrates a formidable grasp of the properties and potentialities of this plastic and eloquent means of artistic expression.

NOTES

1. See, for example, Roger Sabin, Jean-Christophe Menu, and Benoît Peeters.

2. Ware's goal to tell sophisticated stories is of course shared by many alternative cartoonists and their underground forebears, who believe that comics need not be relegated to telling juvenile fables or adolescent power fantasies as in the so-called mainstream comic books.

3. For an illustration of this idea, see *Acme* 6, 16, a wordless deconstruction of a single action interpreted as both reading and theater; for an analysis of this illustration, see Raeburn 11.

4. While most comics do include text, a strong tradition of wordless comics exists around the globe; Ware's own comics often contain wordless sequences, and the comics in the third issue of *Acme Novelty Library* are almost all completely wordless.

5. I define this terminology in more detail in Kannenberg, "Graphic Text, Graphic Context."

6. The story is listed in the book's Table of Contents as "Thrilling Adventure Stories," but the first page of the stories uses the lexia "I Guess" as if it were the story title. Given the story's conflation of two very different narratives, the fact that the story apparently has two titles makes a certain sense.

7. In discussing John McClurg's visual novel *Sperry*, O'Grady writes: "Words and images are used to form a literary polyphony. The verbal narrative forms one line of the polyphony while the drawings, photographs and other visual elements create related yet independent voices throughout the book. Thus, McClurg is able to overlap narratives keeping several story lines concurrent with each other" (O'Grady 157). While the specific formats of *Sperry* (a book of text and drawings) and "Thrilling Adventure Stories" (a comic) differ, their verbal/visual rhetorical strategies operate in similar fashions.

8. Ware does, however, use assistants from time to time, usually for mechanical tasks such as computer color separating. Kim Thompson of Fantagraphics Books, listed as "editor," usually edits only for grammar, not for content. Acknowledgments are found in each issue of *Acme Novelty Library*.

WORKS CITED AND CONSULTED

Drucker, Johanna, *The Century of Artists' Books* (New York: Granary Books, 1995).

Dyer, Richard, "Entertainment and Utopia," in Simon Durning, ed. *The Cultural Studies Reader* (New York: Routledge, 1999), 372–81.

Groensteen, Thierry, "Historie de la BD muette," *9e Art* 2 (1997): 60–75 and *9e Art* 3 (1998): 90–105.

Groth, Gary, "Understanding Chris Ware's Comics [interview]," *The Comics Journal* 200 (December 1997): 118–71.

Juno, Andrae, *Dangerous Drawings* (New York: Juno Books, 1997).

Kannenberg, Gene, Jr., "Graphic Text, Graphic Context: Interpreting Custom Fonts and Hands in Contemporary Comics," in Paul C. Gutjahr and Megan L. Benton, eds., *Illuminating Letters: Typography and Literary Interpretation* (Amherst: University of Massachusetts Press, 2001).

Marcus, Aaron, "Literature and Vision," in Richard Kostelantez, ed. *Visual Literature Criticism* (Carbondale: Southern Illinois University Press, 1993).

Menu, Jean-Christophe, "*La prodigieux projet de* Chris Ware." 9e Art 2 (1997): 44–57.

O'Grady, Holly, "Sperry: A Verbal/Visual Novel," in *Visual Literature Criticism*, 157–60.

Peeters, Benoît, *La Bande dessinée* (Paris: Flammation, 1993).

Raeburn, Dan, *Chris Ware* (New Haven: Yale University Press, 2004).

Sabin, Roger, "Not Just Superheroes," *Speak* 6 (September 1997): 38–45.

Spaulding, Amy, *The Page as a Stage Set: Storyboard Picture Books* (London: Scarecrow Press, 1995).

Witek, Joseph, "From Genre to Medium: Comics and Contemporary American Culture," in Ray B. Brown and Marshall W. Fishwick, eds., *Rejuvenating the Humanities* (Bowling Green: Bowling Green State University Press, 1992): 71–79.

Transcending Comics

Crossing the Boundaries of the Medium

ANNALISA DI LIDDO

The aim of this chapter is to discuss some aspects and recent developments in the work of Alan Moore. These involve in particular his mixed media performance works, two of which—*The Birth Caul* (1995) and *Snakes and Ladders* (1999)—have been released on CD, and additionally interpreted and turned into comic books by Eddie Campbell. While Moore's "magical" and performative turn has been widely investigated in review articles and interviews, in relation to his overall opinion on the creative process, to the well-known series *Promethea*, or to the general ideas underpinning his live acts, the comic book adaptations of the performances have always been mentioned but, at the same time, they have also been dismissed as minor results (with the exception of Marc Singer's comprehensive study of *The Birth Caul*; see Works Cited). On the contrary, my purpose here is to demonstrate how, in those adaptations, the approach to magic at the core of Moore's performances brings about some interesting outcomes as regards the uses of the comics medium. The chapter will focus primarily on *Snakes and Ladders*, performed on April 10, 1999, in London and published as a comic book by Eddie Campbell in 2001. But before moving on to a brief analysis of some aspects of this work, it is necessary to make some preliminary remarks about the key concepts of magic, psychogeography, and performance.

MAGIC, PSYCHOGEOGRAPHY, PERFORMANCE

More than ten years have passed since Alan Moore declared himself a magician in November 1993. He asserts that the process which led him to allow for the existence of magic was triggered by the realization of a series of odd coincidences and concurrences between his art and his life and by the necessity of answering questions as to the nature of consciousness and inspiration (Campbell, 2002: 3). He claims to have established first contact with the irrational while writing the character of Dr. William Gull in *From Hell* and having him say that, "The one place Gods inarguably exist is in our minds

Reprinted by permission from the *International Journal of Comic Art*, vol. 7, no. 1 (Spring/Summer 2005), 530–45.

where they are real beyond refute, in all their grandeur and monstrosity" (Moore and Campbell, 2000: ch. 4, 18). This sentence forced him to come to terms with the idea that what seems to lie beyond the boundaries of human rational thinking is nothing but the product of human thinking itself—therefore, in the ultimate analysis, fiction. After resuming and refashioning Aleister Crowley's notion of magic as "a disease of the language" and integrating it with this concept, Moore now considers magic as an essentially "linguistic phenomenon" (Campbell, 2002: 4) and has elaborated a complex theory that branches out to include the Tarot deck and the Kabbalah as related to fractal mathematics and genetics, and that eventually identifies magic with imagination and creativity. If magic is a linguistic system, then, it will provide us with a vocabulary to read and interpret the world surrounding us:

> The world is kind of pregnant with revelation if you're somebody who comes equipped with the right kind of eyes and the right kind of phrase book . . . for decoding. Magic is, in a sense, a kind of language with which to read the universe (Babcock 2002).

This acknowledgment leads directly to the concept of "psychogeography," defined by Moore as "a means of divining the meaning of the streets in which we live and pass our lives (and thus our own meaning, as inhabitants of those streets)" (Campbell, 2002: 7). In Moore's production, the traces of this process date back as far as 1990: in the first issue of *Big Numbers*, Mr. Slow, a history teacher, is shown while explaining to his students the importance of recognizing Hampton's—a fictional equivalent of Moore's own native Northampton—historical and cultural substratum in order to understand their own place in society (Moore and Sienkiewicz, 1990: 28–29). Psychogeographical practice is common to other artists, above all to British writer and director Iain Sinclair.[1] By means of walking and of researching places, the psychogeographical writer becomes not an author as much as a channel for the cultural legacy of place to emerge through the mass of historical coordinates and anthropological memories he gathers from the geographical—often urban—experience; therefore, he uses physical space as a palimpsest for outlining a path on a subjective and yet universal fictional map in which the reader can recognize his own identity and cultural references. The same approach also lies at the core of the novel *Voice of the Fire* (1996), in its attempt to cover a span of 5000 years of British history through the fictional voices—including Moore's own—of characters located within ten miles of Northampton. However, the best-known example of psychogeographical writing by Alan Moore is certainly chapter 4 in *From Hell*, which depicts Dr. Gull and coachman Netley's route through the streets of London in search of evidence of the city's Masonic structure, where the historical reminiscences of places overlap with Gull's own perception of reality (Moore and Campbell, 2000: ch. 4, 4–38).

The interest in psychogeography, together with ritual and magical practice, evolved into the idea of mixed media performances, designed with the aid of musicians and collaborators Tim Perkins and David Jay. The reason for the choice of performance as a form of expression is the will to convey the considerable amount of information accumulated in the ritual/shamanic process through creating a multi-sensory experience, which is supposed to overwhelm the senses of the audience, thus involving it in the experience itself. The declaration of intent Moore wrote in his short explanatory essay about *The Birth Caul* can apply to all of his performance acts:

> I've attempted to construct a process and a context for performance art and po-
> etry that builds on and makes use of the shamanic worldview to direct the audience
> through a structured mental landscape to a predetermined level of awareness. Each
> performance that emerges from this process is considered a unique event to be per-
> formed on one occasion only, at a specified location that is felt to be appropriate
> to the intention of the work, on a specific date considered to be equally significant
> (Moore, 2001).

Again, as in the case of psychogeography, performance has proved to be an old concern of Moore's: in the early 1970s, when he was about seventeen, he spent a period of
artistic apprenticeship at the Northampton Arts Lab, an experience he has defined as
seminal in his intellectual development, not much in terms of acquiring high technical
skills, as in those of adopting an open attitude towards the potential boundlessness of
artistic practice. The activities of the Lab included performance poetry readings, independent theater, music, and multimedia installations, and it was through the Lab that
Moore had the chance to meet "Principal Edward's Magic Theatre," an experimental
band based in a Northampton commune whose live acts mixed music with stage performance and dance (Khoury, 2003). Even though there is no trace of any precise theoretical point of reference on the part of the Lab, it is reasonable to trace its approach
to artistic creation back to the influence of thinkers and directors such as Peter Brook,
Jerzy Grotowski, and Eugenio Barba, who all tried to bring theater back to its original
collective and ritual status, and whose pervasive effect was strongly felt in most militant
theatrical groups and institutions in the 1970s.

In his 1968 collection of essays, *The Empty Space*, Peter Brook advocates a return to
Antonin Artaud's notion of theater as a site for magic and totemic evocation, and the
idea of "a cry from the womb" (Brook, 1978 [1968]: 54), clearly referring to the attempt
to evoke the audience's prenatal consciousness, seems to foreshadow the conception of
Moore's *Birth Caul*. Jerzy Grotowski's *Towards a Poor Theatre* (1968) is even more radical
in reasserting the nature of the stage act as a vehicle for spiritual knowledge; the Polish director maintains that the ideal theatrical performance is a communal psychic experience in
which the audience's mental blocks are removed by means of the actors' formal discipline,
and of the control of the structure of the act, resulting in a universal, mythical experience
which allows each partaker to acquire a higher perception of his/her own personal awareness.[2] This view very palpably tallies with the notion Moore expresses in the essay about
The Birth Caul quoted above, with the difference that, in Moore's works, the "structured
mental landscape" (Moore, 2001) perceived by the audience comes not so much from the
actors' use of the body, as from the web of psychogeographical references woven by the
author throughout the stage act. Therefore, Moore's performances can be seen as a part of
what is now a well-established theatrical tradition; in addition to this, Moore himself has
appealed to some performative magic rituals of the past, particularly to those by Aleister
Crowley, MacGregor Mathers, and—back in the sixteenth century—John Dee, and then
again to Claudio Monteverde and the origins of opera (Beaton, 2003).

Being the fourth of the five performances carried out so far,[3] *Snakes and Ladders* was staged at Conway Hall, Red Lion Square, London, UK, on April 10, 1999; the psychogeographical suggestions of the London Holborn area, mainly concerning Oliver Cromwell, the Pre-Raphaelites, and most of all *fin de siècle* fantastic fiction writer Arthur Machen, provided the leitmotifs for a five-part reflection on life, place, and the function of art. The CD recording of the performance was made available only later, after the appearance of Campbell's comic book adaptation, published in 2001. Obviously excluding the possibility of attending the performance, there remains for most of us a threefold possibility to approach *Snakes and Ladders*, i.e. 1) listening to the recording; 2) listening to the recording and, with Moore's voice as a guide, following Campbell's adaptation in print; 3) reading the printed version only. Due to the scarce availability of the limited edition CD, the easiest way to access this work is the volume, which is the element I am going to focus on to demonstrate how, while reading an adaptation is unquestionably different from attending a live act and cannot substitute the whole multimedia experience, the comic book proves effective in itself and opens the way for some useful remarks.

FROM PERFORMANCE TO COMICS

In the essay about *The Birth Caul* quoted above, Moore explains that "the energy of the performance . . . is undiluted by all subsequent or previous repetitions, standing as a singular event with its initial force intact" (Moore, 2001): it may thus be argued that transferring a one-off event into comic book form is a questionable choice. The unrepeatability of the performance is taken here as an essential feature which comics, permanently fixed on paper and allowing as many readings as one wishes, can only fail to represent. Nevertheless, there are various reasons why Campbell's adaptation can be considered worthwhile. First of all, if on the one hand the printed version loses the element of uniqueness and instantaneousness, on the other, it noticeably gains another aspect, i.e. the possibility for the reader to dwell upon details and to delve deep into the text and pictures. Secondly, the medium of comics engages all of the reader's senses and requires a very high level of interaction on his/her part (McCloud, 1994 [1993]: 88, 92); as a consequence, it gets close to the sort of strong personal involvement and synaesthetic experience which, through the stimulation of various sensory faculties at a time, Moore sets as the goal of his performative experiments (Campbell, 2002: 9–10; Beaton, 2003).

Moreover, as Alasdair Watson has remarked, some artists achieve interesting results "when they're working against some kind of imposed limitation, as they try and find ways to work with it and around it" (Watson, 2001); such is the case of landmark genre fiction, to quote a pretty straightforward example. As a consequence, the choice to represent the impact of the live performance and to convey the core of Moore's esoteric experience has compelled Campbell to devise some interesting visual strategies in his adaptation. Therefore, the following analysis will focus on the most relevant issues connected to the manipulation of the medium in each section of *Snakes and Ladders*.

One of the crucial features in determining the visual layout of *Snakes* is the narrating voice's continuous, non-linear movement from personal to collective experience and backwards: hence Campbell renders the free flow of words by means of very loose page layouts, where there is no precise panel framing but mostly a juxtaposition of images which differ in size and arrangement. In the first section, "The Gate of Tears" (Moore and Campbell, 2001: 2–11), the first three paragraphs of the monologue conjure up a dark vision of the end of the twentieth century—a century filled with "the smoking wrecks of ideologies" (2), compared to smashed cars with broken-down wheels and shattered radios, and seething with clammy, muddy filth percolating through the fissures in the once-solid soil of the collective certainties of Western civilization. The background of pages 2 and 3 is an entirely grey area that seems stained by an undefined organic matter, on top of which, on page 3, Campbell has pasted a reworking of a photograph—its edges tattered as if it were torn off a newspaper page—of the Berlin Wall, cracked and covered with faded graffiti announcing the "Millennium" and pleading for "Freiheit" (freedom); in front of the wall lies a pile of wrecked cars, while in the heap of junk that occupies the foreground, a copy of *Vogue* magazine with Lady Diana Spencer on its cover stands out, emblematically exposing massive commodification of misfortune as a sign of last century's ideological decadence. In these same paragraphs, Moore intertwines this all-inclusive view on turn-of-the-century anguish with the time-specific, site-specific nature of the performance:

It's 1999. . . . It's April 10; we find ourselves in Red Lion Square . . . caught in the crosshairs of geography and time like sitting ducks. . . . Fluttering attention pinned to where we are and when and who we are. The honey-trap of our personal circumstance, of our familiar bodies restless in these chairs (2–3).

Campbell aptly represents the simultaneous presence of universality and spatial/temporal specificity by placing a panel depicting Moore addressing his audience onto the "organic" background of page 2, and by completing page 3 with a view of Red Lion Square. The narrative movement continues on pages 4 and 5, this time starting again from personal experience:

From this complex lace of moment, all our strands of individual information stretch away towards their different points of origin, through how we got here, winding back to where we're from. In my case, that would be Northampton, an unprepossessing blur on the Ml halfway to Birmingham.

Moore goes on to weave a network of references to Oliver Cromwell, Arthur Machen, and Francis Crick, who all spent some time in Northampton or in its surroundings, and whose connection to the Holborn area will be revealed through the monologue's psycho-geographical journey. But the narrating voice, seemingly not knowing which reference to start from, decides to "start with the basics. Best make sure we're all on the same page," and therefore moves again to the universal dimension, rising to speak about the origin of the cosmos and then descending once more to locate Red Lion Square, to expand on the history of its construction and on the characters who inhabited it through the centuries, mostly focusing on Cromwell and the Pre-Raphaelites. In his attempt to reproduce the multiplicity of references and factual correspondences which crowd Moore's script, Campbell makes a substantial use of collage, placing his own drawings side by side with photographs, portraits, and maps (4–5, 7) or reproductions of Pre-Raphaelite paintings

(9). In order to represent the shift to the cosmic plane, he makes use of a splash page where the words are set in a column and three quarters of the space is occupied by a starry sky which, with its vastness, overhangs a small building.

Another interesting example of Campbell's treatment of the performance material is the second section, "Stars and Garters" (12–23). The section opens with a reproduction of a pamphlet, fully designed and written in nineteenth-century fashion, inviting the audience to attend the performance by Mr. Moore and his collaborators. The setting of the following pages is a late Victorian or Edwardian stage where a woman—according to the monologue, the incarnation of imagination—carries out a dance with a puppet snake steered by a hooded figure. As the snake—which, in the performance, was a prop moved by Frank Ryan (see the CD booklet for credits)—appears on page 16, the narrating voice starts to list creation legends and stories involving the serpent, eventually connecting it to the DNA. The words wind on the page in a single line that loops in a spiral around the head of the reptile, thus visually symbolizing the coils of the snake's body and the rhythmic curls of the narration in its persistent shifting from past to present and from singular to universal. The dance with the snake puppet was originally performed by Paula van Vijngaarden; Campbell reproduces the act in his adaptation, being careful to emphasize not only the thread tied to the reptile's head but also the machinery on stage and the presence of the people who operate it (22–23), thus clearly reasserting Moore's theory about magic as a purely fictional product of the human mind, and also referring to Moore's own tongue-in-cheek worship of the fake second-century Roman snake divinity Glycon.[4] The same topic appears again in section three where, with further irony and self-referentiality, Moore himself enters *Snakes and Ladders* as a character and meets the occultist John Constantine from *Swamp Thing*,[5] who reveals the secret of magic to him: "Any %#@& could do it" (31).

Campbell brings his visual strategies to further expansion in the "Baghdad" section (24–31), where the use of the collage technique is made even more significant and where the simple juxtaposition of visuals is often placed side by side with the superimposition of images. Baghdad is the name Machen gave to the imaginary lunar landscape he claimed to have visited in the nightmarish state of mind that followed his wife's death. Moore identifies it with "Yesod" (27), which he associates with the descent into the unconscious and into the realm of dream, the dark repository of images and fantasies underlying any act of creation—hence underlying art, thought, and life. Moore elucidates the topic of the connection between the lunar territory of Yesod, death, and imagination in his magical manifesto *Promethea*, where, in Issue 14 ("Moon River"), Promethea crosses the Styx, the river that leads to the underworld, and reaches the Moon. Charon, her guide, immediately tells her that "the Moon governs the dreams and the unconscious. The unconscious, in a way, is the underworld" (Moore, Williams, and Gray, 2002: 32). Before observing the lunar citadel (46–47), whose clock towers and little bridges slightly resemble those of Campbell's Baghdad (Moore and Campbell, 2001: 26–27), Promethea reads the word "Yesod" carved into the archway at the entrance, and exchanges the following views with Charon:

[Promethea] It's a Hebrew word, meaning Foundation. I guess it implies that spirituality is founded in imagination.

Alan Moore and Eddie Campbell, *Snakes and Ladders* (2001), 9. Used by permission of the artist.

Snakes and Ladders, 16. Used by permission of the artist.

Snakes and Ladders, 31. Used by permission of the artist.

[Charon] Naturally. Before journeying to higher spheres, man must first reach the Moon. From here, armed with imagination's vision, man need only look up (Moore, Williams, and Gray, 2002: 46).[6]

This is the same progression Machen goes through in *Snakes and Ladders* as, after crossing Baghdad, he ascends to the enlightened state of "Syon" (Moore and Campbell, 2001: 38–48). But let us go back to Campbell and to his representation of Baghdad and its inhabitants: page 38, by means of a dense collage of images in various styles, conveys the sense of marvellous vision and of a plunge into collective imagination in both its beauty and horror. The pictures range from a watercolor depicting an exotic, monstrous elephant-like creature to a series of photographs of actresses such as Marilyn Monroe and Brigitte Bardot, rising in the form of soap bubbles blown out of a pipe. A sketch of Vlad Tepes, the historical figure at the root of the legend of Count Dracula, and of his victims, here impaled on flowers, is placed not far from a lifelike portrait of nineteenth-century British fairy painter Richard Dadd, and from a freeze frame from George Meliès's *Voyage dans la Lune* (1902). Then, the monologue reaches a decisive turning point in connecting imagination with life, and thus with genetics:

Everyone knows this Moontown, that has ever dreamed or wondered. In our reveries we windowshop at its emporiums and in our fevers ride wild, steaming horses down its avenues. . . . Machen and Morris, Burne-Jones and Rossetti. J. D. Watson, co-discoverer with Francis Crick of the dual helix, dreams of interwoven stairwells and the structure of the DNA is suddenly made clear. These are not tourists in the moonsoaked mews of the unconscious, but explorers (28–29).

It is at this point, on page 29, that Campbell portrays the common root of all creation by superimposing Edward Burne-Jones' angels walking down the steps in his 1880 painting *The Golden Stairs* onto the pattern of the DNA dual helix. In the upper part of the picture, a further image overlaps with these two, i.e., a line of tiny black silhouettes representing the characters quoted in the text: one holds a painting brush, another a pen, and the bent silhouette we identify as Watson is picking up the DNA pattern, seemingly fallen from the windblown tie of Crick, who appears wearing a tie with that same pattern on page 4. Last but not least, the bottom right corner of the page is occupied by a small reproduction of a panel from Winsor McCay's "Little Nemo in Slumberland," thus highlighting again the theme of dream and reminding the reader that comics have the right to be included in the field of artistic creation.

Moreover, it might be worth remarking that in 1914, Winsor McCay used his first animated sequence for "Gertie the Dinosaur" for performing in a vaudeville stage show, where he pretended to interact with the animal on the screen, eventually even pretending to walk into the very film.[7] For this reason, we could consider the reference to "Nemo" as a homage not only to one of the fathers of comics and animation, but also to a distinguished predecessor in connecting comic art and performance, although of a different kind.[8] The surface of the following page is occupied by other superimposed visuals, as the narration focuses here on Machen's meeting with the characters from his own work *The Three Impostors* (1895): "In Baghdad, Machen . . . is engaged in conversation with his own creations. . . . The written page becomes too frail a barrier. Things start to tear their way from the other side" (30). Campbell represents the crossing of the blurred border between fiction and reality by reproducing a torn fragment of a page from the *Impostors* and overlaying it with the figure of Machen and of the other characters enumerated by Moore's voice.

Section 4, "Art" (32–37) goes on in its development of the reflection on imagination to prepare the audience and the reader for their—and Machen's—final ascent to artistic ecstasy and the golden reign of Syon. This part of the monologue is centered on the difficulty of reaching the semi-divine, orgasmic state of mind to be identified with Syon, a state that can be attained only when silver and gold, i.e., lunar imagination and vision, and solar determination and radiance—also standing for traditional representations of the feminine and masculine principles—are intertwined and then totally blended into each other. The six pages which form this section are characterized by a peculiar layout: much of the available space is left empty and white, the drawings are bigger in size and this time there is no collage, no visual barrage as it often happened in the previous sections; this compensates for the increasing complexity and lyrical intensity of the script, and paves the way for the moment when "we step out in the white-hot streets of Syon. And in their radiance, we know ourselves" (37). Each page is occupied by a single image, which not only relates to the monologue, but which also expands and elaborates on the theme presented in the previous page. The section opens with a reproduction of the Tarot card for "Art" designed by Lady Frieda Harris: the card depicts a two-faced woman whose dress is embroidered with snakes, as she bends over a goblet, side by side with a lion and an eagle (32).[9] The next page follows the monologue's reflection on man's imperative to rise and go beyond his earthly condition through imagination, inspired by the

Snakes and Ladders, 29. Used by permission of the artist. *Snakes and Ladders* and *The Birth Caul* are reprinted in Alan Moore and Eddie Campbell, *A Disease of Language* (Knockabout, 2006).

endless spiral of the DNA, and shows us two snakes, inextricably coiled as in Promethea's caduceus. Campbell fills the space between the coils with three images: the bars of the terrestrial prison in the lower part, the moon in the middle, and the sun in the higher part. Page 34 resumes the theme of the spiral and represents it in the form of a gold-and-silver chain—again, Sun and Moon—accompanied by the figures of the lion and the eagle; "the burnished chain of difficult ideas our shaking ladder has become" (34) represents man's path towards Syon, and it becomes an actual ladder on page 35. As a consequence, pages 36 and 37 depict a small Machen, who finally reaches Syon after going through all the ups and downs of his existence—visually, after climbing a ladder on a huge Snakes and Ladders board, while the narrating voice, in accordance with the pattern it has followed throughout the work, reminds its audience that this abstract, universal experience is also *their* personal experience, taking place in *that* precise moment:

> It's April tenth . . . all of us dragged from the vaults of earth to see the sun again. . . . We remember what we are. . . . We are each other, are the dead and the living. We are Arthur Machen. . . . We are Dante Gabriel Rossetti. And it is Now, and we are by this heat distilled, and it is Now forever (36–37).

The final "Syon" section (38–49) brings the movement between universality and historical/geographical specificity to its apex and conclusion. The initial description of the heavenly city is accompanied by an illustration which covers two full pages. The skyline of Syon, made both of historical and of industrial buildings rising on "a pavement of York stone" (38), is silhouetted in the distance against a white sky. The only characters on the pavement are a flower-girl and a customer, quoted in the monologue (39), and a reproduction of Botticelli's *Venus*, which can be seen as a symbol of birth, art, and creation. The massive shape of an insect stands out on the stone paving, probably the ant mentioned in the script—an obscure reference we might interpret as referring to the mythological figure of the ant as capable of communicating with the gods, as in Aztec and Tagalog cultures, or as the first human being, as in Hopi creation myths, which are but two of the many symbolic implications ascribed to insects throughout myth and history (Cherry and Kritsky, 2000). Finally conflating timelessness and history, the narrating voice then moves on to an overview on a space-time where "decade and distance are collapsed to a magnificent carnelian of Here and Now" (Moore and Campbell, 2001: 40), thus placing Cain and Abel in contemporary London, evoking the Roman empire together with Dresden, Carthage, and Nagasaki, and finally shifting to King George the Fifth's funeral procession, which took place in Holborn in 1936 (40–41), to move on to a reflection on the Christian symbol of the cross and of the sacrifice of Christ, which in Western culture personifies the ultimate emblem for the fusion of the divine and the human, and for the path that reaches ecstasy through sacrifice (42–43).[10] These issues, once again, are visually rendered through the juxtaposition of panels in different styles and through the employment of photographs, while in the last pages of the book, Machen's progression towards mystic awakening after his descent into hallucination is mirrored by the gradual increase of white areas and by the respective decrease of words. The process culminates in the very last page, which contains neither words nor pictures, but only a blurred photograph of Red Lion Square—in color, so as to finally bring the reader back to his own time and reality (49) and to complete the audience and the reader's psycho-geographical journey into man's existence.

The examples discussed in this short survey do not wholly account for the extreme complexity and density of *Snakes and Ladders*. However, they hopefully give some hints as to the main features of this comic book. Campbell's adaptation, therefore, must not be read as an attempt to substitute the performance, but as an alternative and just as effective way to convey the multi-sensory experience of the live act. Comics in *Snakes and Ladders* are really "transcending"; and, just like *Snakes and Ladders*, the title of this paper encompasses different layers of meaning. Reaching the apex of a long development which began in comics, with his reflection on psychogeography as related to identity, Moore has come to *transcend* the matter of much of his previous production, crossing the boundaries of storytelling to move into the field of narrative as connected to ideas and magic. He has then *transcended* the form of comics by shifting to the multimedia sphere; and *Snakes and Ladders*, thanks to Campbell's skillful interpretation, has moved back to comics, where after assimilating the multimedia experience, the medium is stretched, altered, and made to cross the borders of its formal conventions to try out its newly professed capabilities. *Snakes and Ladders*, therefore, can be seen as an example of Moore and Campbell's unflagging commitment to the expansion and innovation of the expressive potential of comics.

NOTES

1. The reference to Iain Sinclair is particularly relevant, because he and Moore have now been acquainted for a long time and their interests often seem to run on parallel tracks. Moore has apparently drawn inspiration from Sinclair's *White Chappell, Scarlet Tracings* (1987) to outline Dr. Gull's route across London in *From Hell*. Moreover, Sinclair comes from a multimedia background in experimental filmmaking, and he has professed a deep fascination with the figure of Arthur Machen (Pilkington and Baker, 2001)—both features that connect him once again to Moore, as the following part of this essay will show.

2. Other interesting details on theater as an all-absorbing practice emerge from the theories elaborated by Eugenio Barba during his work with the Odin Teatret in Holstebro, Denmark. My reference, on this occasion, has been Taviani's *Il Libro dell'Odin: Il Teatro-Laboratorio di Eugenio Barba*; as an alternative, as there is no English translation of this volume, I would recommend Ian Watson's *Towards a Third Theatre: Eugenio Barba and the Odin Teatret* (see Works Cited).

3. Besides the two performances I have already mentioned, the others are *The Moon and Serpent Grand Egyptian Theater of Marvels* (1994), *The Highbury Working* (1997), and *Angel Passage* (2000). Additional information appears in the detailed bibliography to be found in the collection edited by George Khoury (2003: 202–21).

4. For additional information on Moore's ironic cult of Glycon, see Campbell (2002: 5).

5. Moore's legendary run of *Swamp Thing* went from 1983 to 1987 and is now published in collected volumes by DC Comics.

6. Of course, both these representations are part of a longer, older tradition of fantastic lunar journeys, starting with Lucian of Samosata's (AD 120–180) account of his *Trips to the Moon*. Lucian and other authors appear on the houseboat by the Moon citadel in *Promethea* Issue 14 (Moore, Williams, and Gray, 2002: 44).

7. An excellent resource on Winsor McCay's (1869–1934) animation movies and art is the DVD *Animation Legend: Winsor McCay* (see Works Cited).

8. There is a long tradition of contacts between comics and performance, going from McCay through the "chalk talk" comic artists to experimental groups such as the Chicago-based *Live Action Cartoonists* (see Works Cited).

9. Lady Frieda Harris (1877–1962), a friend and collaborator of Aleister Crowley, designed and painted for him the set of Tarot cards known as the "Thoth deck."

10. Again, *Promethea* provides us with useful reference. In Issue 17, Promethea and her travelling companions witness the crucifixion and comment on Christ's sacrifice: "Crucifixion, it wasn't just, like, executin' somebody. It was something you'd do to a dog. . . . That's us up there, man" (Moore, Williams, and Gray, 2002: 133). This same idea resonates, in more lyrical terms, in *Snakes and Ladders*—"In Syon, every incident is symbol, every symbol is immediate and real. . . . The symbol of divinity within mankind is crucified, a dog's death. . . . Oh Christ. Oh Christ in all of us" (Moore and Campbell, 2001: 42–43).

WORKS CITED

Babcock, Jay, "The Rational Shaman," *LA Weekly* (2002), www.laweekly. coni.

Beaton, Frank, "Snake Charmer: An Interview with Alan Moore," Part 1 & 2, *NinthArt* (2003), www .ninthart.com.

Blackton, Stuart, dir., *Animation Legend: Winsor McCay* (DVD: Lumivision, 1997).

Brook, Peter, *The Empty Space* (New York: Atheneum, 1978 [1968]).

Campbell, Eddie, *Egomania* (2002) 2: 1–32.

Cherry, Ron, and Gene Kritsky, *Insect Mythology* (New York: Writers Club Press, 2000).

Crafton, Donald, *Before Mickey: The Animated Film, 1898–1928* (Cambridge: The MIT Press, 1984 [1982]).

Grotowski, Jerzy, *Towards a Poor Theatre* (London: Methuen, 1975 [1968]).

Khoury, George, ed., *The Extraordinary Works of Alan Moore* (Raleigh: Tomorrows, 2003).

Live Action Cartoonists, "Have Markers, Will Travel: Live Action Cartoonists in the Age of Multimedia Performances and Online Comics," *International Journal of Comic Art* (Spring 2003): 355–65.

McCloud, Scott, *Understanding Comics: The Invisible Art* (Northampton, Tundra, 1993).

Meliès, George, "Voyage dans la Lune," *The Movies Begin Vol. 1: The Great Train Robbery and Other Primary Works* (Kino Video, 2002 [1902]).

Moore, Alan, *Voice of the Fire* (London: Gollancz, 1996).

———, "The Birth Caul," *Locus* (2001), www.locusplus.org.

Moore, Alan, and Eddie Campbell, *From Hell* (London: Knockabout, 2000).

———, *The Birth Caul: A Shamanism of Childhood*, originally staged at the Old County Court, Newcastle, UK, November 18, 1995.

———, *Snakes and Ladders*, originally staged at Conway Hall, Red Lion Square, London, UK, April 10, 1999.

Moore, Alan, and Tim Perkins, *Snakes and Ladders* (Audio CD: Re: Records, 2003).

Moore, Alan, and Bill Sienkiewicz, *Big Numbers* 1 (Northampton: Mad Love, 1990).

Moore, Alan, J. H. Williams III, and Mick Gray, *Promethea: Book 1* (La Jolla: America's Best Comics, 1999).

———, *Promethea: Book 2* (La Jolla: America's Best Comics, 2001).

———, *Promethea: Book 3* (La Jolla: America's Best Comics, 2002).

———, *Promethea: Book 4* (La Jolla: America's Best Comics, 2003).

Pilkington, Mark, and Phil Baker, "City Brain: Iain Sinclair Interview." *Fortean Times* (2001), www.forteantimes .com/articlesf147_iainsinclair. shtml.

Singer, Marc, "Unwrapping the Birth Caul," in smoky man and G. S. Millidge, eds., *Alan Moore: Portrait of an Extraordinary Gentleman* (Leigh-on-Sea: Abiogenesis, 2003), 41–46; and in *International Journal of Comic Art* (Spring 2004): 236–49.

Taviani, Ferdinando, ed., *II Libro dell'Odin: Il Teatro-Laboratorio Eugenio Barba* (Milano: Feltrinelli, 1975).

Watson, Alasdair, "Camera Obscura: Charming the Snake," *NinthArt* (2001), www.ninthart.com.

Watson, Ian, *Towards a Third Theatre: Eugenio Barba and the Odin Teatret* (London: Routledge, 1993).

History and Graphic Representation in *Maus*

HILLARY CHUTE

Because I grew up with parents who were always ready to see the world grid crumble, and when it started feeling that that was happening here and now, it wasn't a total surprise. . . . I think the one thing I really learned from my father was how to pack a suitcase. You know? It was the one thing he wanted to make sure I understood, like how to use every available centimeter to get as much stuff packed into a small space as possible. The ice might be thinner than one would like to think.

ART SPIEGELMAN (qtd. in D'Arcy, 3)

In *In the Shadow of No Towers*, his most recent book of comic strips, Art Spiegelman draws connections between his experience of 9/11 and his survivor parents' experience of World War II, suggesting that the horrors of the Holocaust do not feel far removed from his present-day experience in the twenty-first century.[1] "The killer apes learned nothing from the twin towers of Auschwitz and Hiroshima," Spiegelman writes; 9/11 is the "same old deadly business as usual." Produced serially, Spiegelman's *No Towers* comic strips were too politically incendiary to find wide release in the United States; they were largely published abroad and in New York's weekly Jewish newspaper the *Forward*. *In the Shadow of No Towers* powerfully asserts that "the shadow of a past time [interweaves] with a present time," to use Spiegelman's own description of his Pulitzer-prize winning two-volume work *Maus: A Survivor's Tale* (Spiegelman qtd. in Silverblatt, 35). In one telling panel there the bodies of four Jewish girls hanged in World War II dangle from trees in the Catskills as the Spiegelmans drive to the supermarket in 1979.[2]

The persistence of the past in *Maus*, of course, does figure prominently in analyses of the text's overall representational strategies. We see this, for instance, in Dominick LaCapra's reading of the book's "thematic mode of carnivalization" (175), Andreas Huyssen's theorizing of Adornean mimesis in *Maus*, and Alan Rosen's study of Vladek Spiegelman's broken English.[3] Most readings of how *Maus* represents history approach the issue in terms of ongoing debates about Holocaust representation, in the context of postmodernism, or in relation to theories of traumatic memory. But such readings do not pay much attention to *Maus*'s narrative form:[4] the specificities of reading graphically, of taking individual pages as crucial units of comics grammar. The form

Reprinted by permission from *Twentieth-Century Literature*, vol. 52, no. 2 (Summer 2006), 199–230.

From page 79, *MAUS II: A Survivor's Tale/And Here My Troubles Began* by Art Spiegelman, copyright © 1986, 1989, 1990, 1991. Used by permission of Pantheon Books, a division of Random House, Inc.

of *Maus*, however, is essential to how it represents history. Indeed, Maus's contribution to thinking about the "crisis in representation," I will argue, is precisely in how it proposes that the medium of comics can approach and express serious, even devastating, histories.[5]

"I'm *literally* giving a form to my father's words and narrative," Spiegelman observes about *Maus*, "and that form for me has to do with panel size, panel rhythms, and visual structures of the page" (Interview with Gary Groth 105, emphasis in original). As I hope to show, to claim that comics makes language, ideas, and concepts "literal" is to call attention to how the medium can make the twisting lines of history readable through form.

When critics of *Maus* do examine questions of form, they often focus on the cultural connotations of comics rather than on the form's aesthetic capabilities—its innovations with space and temporality.[6] Paul Buhle, for instance, claims, "More than a few readers have described [*Maus*] as the most compelling of any [Holocaust] depiction, perhaps because only the caricatured quality of comic art is equal to the seeming unreality of an experience beyond all reason" (16). Where Michael Rothberg contends, "By situating a nonfictional story in a highly mediated, unreal, 'comic' space, Spiegelman captures the hyperintensity of Auschwitz" (206), Stephen Tabachnick suggests that *Maus* may work "because it depicts what was all too real, however unbelievable, in a tightly controlled and brutally stark manner. The black and white quality of *Maus*'s graphics reminds one of newsprint" (155). But all such analyses posit too direct a relationship between form and content (unreal form, unreal content; all too real form, all too real content), a directness that Spiegelman explicitly rejects.[7]

As with all cultural production that faces the issue of genocide, Spiegelman's text turns us to fundamental questions about the function of art and aesthetics (as well as to related questions about the knowability and the transmission of history: as Hayden White asserts, "*Maus* manages to raise all of the crucial issues regarding the 'limits of representation' in general" [42]). Adorno famously interrogated the fraught relation of aesthetics and Holocaust representation in two essays from 1949, "Cultural Criticism and Society" and "After Auschwitz"—and later in the enormously valuable "Commitment" (1962), which has been the basis of some recent important meditations on form.[8] In "Cultural Criticism" Adorno charges, "To write poetry after Auschwitz is barbaric" (34).[9] We may understand what is at stake as a question of betrayal: Adorno worries about how suffering can be given a voice in art "without immediately being betrayed by it" ("Commitment" 312); we must recognize "the possibility of knowing history." Cathy Caruth writes, "as a deeply ethical dilemma: the unremitting problem of *how not to betray the past*" (27, Caruth's italics). I argue that *Maus*, far from betraying the past, engages this ethical dilemma through its form. Elaborating tropes like "the presence of the past" through the formal complexities of what Spiegelman calls the "stylistic surface" of a page (*Complete Maus*),[10] I will consider how *Maus* represents history through the time and space of the comics page.

In the hybrid form of comics, two narrative tracks never exactly synthesize or fully explain each other.[11] In "their essence," Spiegelman says, comics

> are about time being made manifest spatially, in that you've got all these different chunks of time—each box being a different moment of time—and you see them all at once. As a result you're always, in comics, being made aware of different times inhabiting the same space. (qtd. in Silverblatt, 35)

Comics are composed in panels—also called frames—and in gutters, the rich empty spaces between the selected moments that direct our interpretation. The effect of the gutter lends to comics its "annotation" of time as space.[12] "Time as space" is a description we hear again and again from theorists of comics. However, it is only when one recognizes how *Maus* is able to effectively approach history through its spatiality that one appreciates the form's grasp on nuanced political expression. Emphasizing how comics deals in space, as I do here, highlights how this contemporary, dynamic medium both informs and is informed by postmodern politics in a productive, dialogical process. Space, Fredric Jameson contends, is the perceptual modality of postmodernity (*Postmodernism* 154–80); and where the dominant rhetoric of modernism is temporal, Susan Stanford Friedman argues, postmodernism adopts a rhetoric of space—of location, multiplicity, borderlands, and, I would add, boundary crossings.[13]

In the epigraph to this essay, describing how his father taught him to pack a suitcase to "use every available centimeter to get as much stuff packed into a small space as possible," Spiegelman alludes to his father's experiences in wartime Poland. Yet the historical lesson also shapes Spiegelman's formal preoccupations. Throughout *Maus* he represents the complicated entwining of the past and the present by "packing" the tight spaces of panels. He found an "architectonic rigor . . . necessary to understand to compose the pages of *Maus*," he explains (qtd. in Silverblatt, 33), and has commented: "Five or six comics on one piece of paper . . . [I am] my father's son" (Spiegelman, Address).[14] It is to this effect that *Maus* exploits the spatial form of graphic narrative, with its double-encodings and visual installment of paradoxes, so compellingly, refusing telos and closure even as it narrativizes history. In this light, I will analyze a range of sections of the book: some that have been treated comparatively little in *Maus* criticism, such as the multitemporal panel in the embedded comic strip "Prisoner on the Hell Planet" and the double epitaph of the book's last page, and some that have not been treated at all, such as the scene that centers on a timeline of Auschwitz.

BLEEDING AND REBUILDING HISTORY

The first volume of *Maus* is subtitled, significantly, *My Father Bleeds History*. The slow, painful effusion of history in this "tale," the title suggests, is a bloodletting: its enunciation and dissemination are not without cost to Vladek Spiegelman (indeed, it is his headstone that marks, however unstably, the ending of *Maus*). In suggesting that the concept of "history" has become and is excruciating for Vladek, the title also implies an aspect of the testimonial situation we observe over the course of *Maus*'s pages: the fact that, as Spiegelman reports, his father had "no desire to bear witness" (Interview with Joey Cavalieri et al., 192). Indeed, throughout much of the book, Vladek would clearly prefer, we see, to complain about his rocky second marriage. Towards the end of the second volume of *Maus*, Vladek protests to Artie, "All such things of the war, I tried to put out of my mind once and for all. . . . Until you *rebuild* me all this from your questions" (98).[15] Vladek's bleeding is his son Artie's textual, visual (as well as emotional) rebuilding. Spiegelman as author is distinctly aware of Artie the character's shades of vampirism, however well intentioned. And the idea of "bleeding" history (at the demand of a son) acquires further poignancy when one realizes—as transcripts of the taped interviews between Vladek and Art Spiegelman on the CD-ROM *The Complete Maus* reveal—that Vladek and his wife, Anja Spiegelman, never spoke to each other in detail about their (literally unspeakable) experiences in the camps.[16] This "bleeding" of history is not an easy process; Anja's diaries, for instance, as Vladek explained, were too full of history to remain extant after her death: "I had to make an order with everything. . . . These papers had too many *memories*. So I *burned* them" (*Maus I*, 158). Art Spiegelman's narrativization of his parents' history, then, as many critics have pointed out, is also his *own* making "an order with everything." He reconstructs history in his own language—comics—in frames and gutters, interpreting and interrupting as he rebuilds.[17] Comics frames provide psychic order, as Spiegelman recently remarked about 9/11: "If I thought in page units, I might live long enough to do another page" (Gussow).

Maus's chapter 1, "The Sheik," zooms into history. In the middle of its second page is a panel packed with signifiers of the past and present, jammed together in a long rectangular frame, only an inch high, that spans the width of the page. In a space that was once Artie's bedroom (a pennant proclaiming "Harpur," Spiegelman's college, is still pinned to the wall), Vladek, his camp tattoo visible for the first time, pumps on an Exercycle. Not moving forward, he is literally spinning his wheels. This suspension is also indicated by the fact that a full view of his body, locked into position, appears across frames on the page: his head in panel four, his torso in panel five, his foot in panel seven. The wide berth of his arms frames Artie, who sits and smokes, looking small. A framed photo—of the dead Anja Spiegelman, we will later find out—is propped on a desk to the right of both men, representing both an object of desire and a rebuke. In a speech balloon on the left that echoes the photograph and tattoo on the right, as if the past—articulated (spoken), inscribed (tattooed), documented (photographed)—were flanking both men, closing in on them, Vladek proclaims: "It would take *many* books, my life, and no one wants anyway to hear such stories" (12).

From page 12, *MAUS I: A Survivor's Tale/My Father Bleeds History* by Art Spiegelman, copyright © 1973, 1980, 1981, 1982, 1984, 1985, 1986. Used by permission of Pantheon Books, a division of Random House, Inc.

From page 45, *MAUS I: A Survivor's Tale/My Father Bleeds History* by Art Spiegelman, copyright © 1973, 1980, 1981, 1982, 1984, 1985, 1986. Used by permission of Pantheon Books, a division of Random House, Inc.

From the start, Spiegelman crams his panels with markers of the past (the camp tattoo, prewar photographs) and the ultimate marker of the present: Artie Spiegelman himself, framed by his father's body, his parents' postwar child, born in Sweden after the couple lost their first son to the Nazis. And while the horizontally elongated panel implies a stillness—its page-spanning width eliminates any gutter, where the movement of time in comics happens—it yet registers Vladek's first moments of dipping into the past. While Vladek verbally refuses to offer "such stories," the panel below, an iris diaphragm depicting his dapper young self ("really a nice, handsome boy" [13]) in the early 1930s, pushes up into the rectangular panel of the present, its curve hitting the handlebars of Vladek's Exercycle between his grasping hands.[18] This protruding circular frame can be figured as the wheel to Vladek's Exercycle. Spiegelman points out, "You enter into the past for the first time through that wheel" (*Complete Maus*).

The visual intersection of past and present appears throughout in the architecture of panels. In chapter 3 of *Maus I*, "Prisoner of War," Artie sprawls across the floor of his father's Rego Park, Queens, home, pencil in hand, notebook open, soliciting stories (45). Artie's legs span decades. Looking up at his sitting father, facing forward toward the direction of the unfolding narrative, Artie's legs are yet mired in the past: they conspicuously overlap—indeed, unify—the panel depicting 1939 and the one depicting the conversation in 1978. Artie's body, then—in the act of writing, of recording—is visually figured as the link between past and present, disrupting any attempt to set apart Vladek's history from the discursive situation of the present.

The connection between past and present in this chapter is also emphasized by verbal parallels. Vladek, for instance, describes a grueling POW work detail, in which a German soldier demands that a filthy stable be spotless in an hour. Interrupting his own recollection, Vladek suddenly bursts out, "*But look what you do, Artie*! You're dropping on the carpet cigarette ashes. You want it should be like a stable *here*?" (52). Joshua Brown points out that this incident—which he identifies as one of many "interstices of the testimony"—suggests that "Vladek's account is not a chronicle of undefiled fact but a

345

constitutive process, that remembering is a construction of the past" (95). And the ways in which the past invades the present recollection, or vice versa, gradually grow more ominous: in the beginning of *Maus* comparisons may involve issues like cleanliness, but by the second volume, Spiegelman will draw Artie's cigarette smoke as the smoke of human flesh drifting upward from the crematoria of Auschwitz (*Maus II*, 69).[19]

INHERITING THE PAST, PACKING A PANEL

The most striking instance of representing past and present together in *Maus I* is the inclusion of the autobiographical comic strip "Prisoner on the Hell Planet: A Case History" (1972) in the text of *Maus*. Breaking the narrative flow of *Maus*, interrupting its pagination, style, and tone, "Prisoner on the Hell Planet" enters into the story, it would seem, from outside, registering confrontationally—and materially—the presence of the past. First published in an underground comic book, *Short Order Comix* 1, it narrates the immediate aftermath of the 1968 suicide of Spiegelman's mother, Auschwitz survivor Anja Spiegelman, at his family's home in Queens.

Readers are introduced to the existence of "Prisoner on the Hell Planet" at the same time that a calendar is first made conspicuous in *Maus*, in the panel in which his stepmother Mala startles Artie by mentioning "that comic strip you once made—the one about your mother" (99). This calendar appears in five of eight panels preceding "Prisoner" and in eight out of the nine panels on the page directly following it, but this representation of the linear movement of time is disrupted by the intrusion of "Prisoner," which does not seamlessly become part of the fabric of the larger narrative but rather maintains its alterity. Featuring human characters, it is clearly distinct from the rest of *Maus* in its basic representational methodology; its heavy German Expressionist style is an unsubtle analog to the angry emotional content of the strip. *Maus*'s page numbers stop while "Prisoner" unfolds: and the older strip's pages are set against a black, unmarked background, forming what Spiegelman calls a "funereal border" that stands out as a thick black line when the book is closed (*Complete Maus*).

"Prisoner" is Artie's earliest testament to what Marianne Hirsch persuasively describes as "postmemory" ("Projected Memory," 8), a now oft-cited term that she first conceived of in relation to *Maus*.[20] And while this visual and narrative rupture of the text suggests what and how the past continually means in the present I want to focus in particular on one packed panel on "Prisoner's" last page. Like the volume in which it is embedded, "Prisoner" spatially depicts multiple temporalities in single visual-verbal frames. If Spiegelman claims that he feels very much like his "father's son" when he draws five comics on one page, here we see five different moments in one panel, criss-crossed by text that alternates sentiments corresponding with the frame's accreted temporalities: We get "Mommy" (the past) but we also get "Bitch" (the present); we get "Hitler Did It!" (the past) but we also get "Menopausal Depression" (the present) (103). Approaching the past and the present together is typical for someone considering narratives of causality, but here Spiegelman obsessively layers several temporalities in one tiny frame, understood by the conventions of the comics medium to represent one moment in time. Artie's childhood bedroom is contiguous with a concentration camp; Anja's disembodied arm, ready-

From page 103, *MAUS I: A Survivor's Tale/My Father Bleeds History* by
Art Spiegelman, copyright © 1973, 1980, 1981, 1982, 1984, 1985, 1986.
Used by permission of Pantheon Books, a division of Random House, Inc.
Reprinted by permission.

ing for her suicide, floats out from the body of the youngster Artie, its thumb just about
touching the leg of the adult Artie, who sits in despair on what looks like her casket.

This frame, smaller than 2 inches by 2 inches, depicts several images from different
time periods: Anja's dead body in the bathtub; a heap of anonymous dead bodies piled
high underneath a brick wall painted with a swastika; Anja reading to the child Artie;
Anja cutting her wrist, her tattooed number fully visible on her forearm; the young man
Artie in mourning, wearing the same Auschwitz uniform he wears even as a child, happily listening to his mother read. "Prisoner," then, posits that Artie inherited the burden
that the uniform represents, in a natural transfer of pain that wasn't consciously accepted
or rejected but seamlessly assumed.[21] He earned his stripes at birth.

MAUS II: MAKING AN ORDER

In *Maus II: And Here My Troubles Began* Spiegelman's self-reflexivity is a strategy specific to representing the Holocaust. By explicitly centering portions of the text on its own enunciative context, he offers his doubts as to his adequacy to represent the Holocaust, as a secondary witness and as a cartoonist. He assiduously explores his feelings about *Maus I* in *Maus II*, whose subtitle, after all, refers not only to Vladek's statement made after he left Auschwitz ("Here, in Dachau, my troubles began" [91]), but also to Spiegelman's own success with *Maus I* ("things couldn't be going better with my 'career,' or at home, but mostly I feel like crying" [43]). The most metafictional section in the volume is the "Time flies" episode (41–46). While "Prisoner" represents a retextualization and resignification of a past narrative into a newer, yet still provisional one, "Time flies" works as a projection forward, a meditation on the viability of the present project.[22]

The double voicing of *Maus*—Artie's voice and his father's—presents a view of narrative generally and testimony specifically as a polyvalent weave.[23] Testimony and memory here are collaborative procedures generated by both speaker and listener. Further, the play of voices in *Maus* is complicated in light of Spiegelman's position that comics provides a "visual voice in the artist's hand" (qtd. in D'Arcy, 2). In this Holocaust representation, the artist's hand is the visibilized link between the personal voice of the primary witness and its translation, the voice of the secondary witness: as such, Spiegelman's hands are frequently pictured in *Maus*, and his "artistic hands" are the subject of conspicuous conversation between him and his father. The comics medium, as Spiegelman makes us aware, is not only *dialogic*—able to represent the competing voices of autobiography and biography in one layered text—but cross-discursive, as when Spiegelman draws against his father's verbal narration, turning what he calls the "cognitive dissonance" between the two of them into representational collision (Silverblatt, 32). (One prominent example of the son battling his father's verbal testimony with his own visual medium is Spiegelman's drawing of an only just visible orchestra playing as prisoners march out of the gates of Auschwitz, contradicting Vladek's firm vocal insistence that no orchestra was present.)[24]

Both Artie and Vladek want to order historical narrative. But Vladek's order—poignantly, understandably—involves a *de*gridding. He wants to dismantle, to destroy in order to forget ("I had to make an order with everything. . . . These papers had too many memories. So I burned them" [*Maus I*, 159]), even as his account is teased out by his son over a period of years. While Vladek's order is a defenestration, Artie wants to build windows, to resurrect; Spiegelman's language is that he "materializes" Vladek's words and descriptions in *Maus* (qtd. in Brown, 98). In the introduction to his 1977 collection *Breakdowns*, which contains the three-page prototype for *Maus*, Spiegelman attaches the concept of narrative to the spatial, "materializing" work of comics:

> My dictionary defines COMIC STRIP as "a narrative series of cartoons . . ." A NARRATIVE is defined as "a story." Most definitions of STORY leave me cold . . . Except for the one that says "A complete horizontal division of a building . . . [From Medieval Latin HISTORIA . . . a row of windows with pictures on them]" (Spiegelman's brackets)

And Spiegelman speaks of the act of ordering a comics narrative in frames as a kind of necessary reckoning: "The parts that are in the book are now in neat little boxes. I know what happened by having assimilated it that fully. And that's part of my reason for this project, in fact" (qtd. in Witek, 101). Working with his father's slippery, strange, non-linear, incomplete testimony, Spiegelman is drawn to the concept of imposing formal order.[25] It comes as no surprise, then, that at one point he was drawn to a high modernist ethic of representation for *Maus*; he thought he should compose the book "in a more Joycean way" (qtd. in Brown, 94). Yet finally, Spiegelman ceded the structure of a *Ulysses* for the mere structural containment of "neat little boxes," a description that evokes both a hopeful (if impossible) burial of the past in coffin-panels, and the full, packed suitcases that are his father's history lesson for the present.

The difference in the way Vladek and Artie each "order" history registers clearly in a crucial scene in which Artie's attempt to chronologically account for Vladek's time in Auschwitz provides the basis for disagreement. While Artie emphasizes Vladek's time there, Vladek insists on the space of his Auschwitz experience. Appropriately, then, in the chapter "Auschwitz (time flies)," *Maus* presents a timeline of 1944 which is the only explanatory diagram not part of the authorial purview of Vladek. (Diagrams are a recurring subject, a mode of representation, and a collaborative textual practice in *Maus*, where, with this exception, they are organic to Vladek's narrative thread.) This diagram represents a disagreement; the son is "imposing order" while the survivor, caught up in his testimony, resists that historiographic impulse.

Artie wants to present a lucid and chronological narrative of his father's months in 1944, but Vladek resists Artie's accounting: "In Auschwitz we didn't wear watches" (68). When Artie draws a diagram for *Maus*, then, he draws it as the site of a father-son battle. Spiegelman presents his own desire for linear order and Vladek's resistance to that kind of order in an especially complex fashion. The diagram pierces three rows of frames. It begins at the end of the page's first tier, where it blocks a corner of Vladek's speech balloon, interrupting a first-person sentence. "I—" Vladek starts, before our eyes run up against a black-rimmed timeline, its corners sharp (68).

The timeline begins in March 1944 and continues down vertically, representing Vladek's Auschwitz activity: quarantine, tin shop, shoe shop, black work. It does not occupy the furthermost space of the page however, but is recontextualized, if only teasingly, by the shrubs poking messily out from its right margin. Moreover, while the diagram cuts off Vladek's speech in the first tier and his shoulder in the second tier, in the third tier it is itself interrupted by Artie's wife Françoise's speech balloon—"YOOHOO! I was looking for you." We have, then, the present layered thickly by the past, framed tentatively by the present, layered again by the past, and interrupted by a present-day exclamation, a burst of the banal: lunch time. Directly under the timeline, Françoise calls attention to the tangle of temporalities in a comment as applicable, in the haunting abstract, to Vladek's months in Auschwitz as it is to the length of Artie's stroll around the bungalows: "I was worried. You were gone a long time" (68).

Superimposed over the frames, the timeline makes the sort of historiographic gesture that the overall narrative, shuttling rapidly back and forth from past to present, does not attempt, and that Vladek cannot offer. As Spiegelman puts it: "The number of layers between an event and somebody trying to apprehend that event through time

From page 68, *MAUS II: A Survivor's Tale/And Here My Troubles Began* by Art Spiegelman, copyright ©1986, 1989, 1990, 1991. Used by permission of Pantheon Books, a division of Random House, Inc.

and intermediaries is like working with flickering shadows" (qtd. in Brown, 98). He thus represents the accreted, shifting "layers" of historical apprehension not only through language but also through the literal, spatial layering of comics, enabling the presence of the past to become radically legible on the page.

THE QUESTION OF CLOSURE

Pointing to *Maus*'s specific argument about temporality and the representation of history, one anecdote is particularly telling about the political work *Maus* accomplishes. Spiegelman acted as a catalyst to get a show about Bosnia at the Holocaust Museum in Washington, DC—"a show which, to me, was a justification of that museum's existence," he says. (Spiegelman had rejected the idea of having a show about *Maus* there: "The Holocaust Museum didn't need *Maus*, and *Maus* didn't need the authority of the Holocaust Museum to make itself understood") (Interview with Andrea Juno, 16).[26] Spiegelman wanted to call the Bosnia show "Genocide Now." The museum drew back. As Spiegelman narrates the museum's objection:

> "Does it have to be called Genocide Now? Got a better one? Can't we just talk about the atrocities in former Yugoslavia?" Well, if the situation looks and smells like genocide, it probably is. They were still against the title, and the best alternative I could come up with was: "Never Again and Again and Again." They didn't like that title either, and that was about the time I checked out. (Interview with Andrea Juno, 16)

This insistence, "Genocide *Now*," is a refusal to see "the past" as past, which is an adamant, ethical argument that *Maus* undertakes through the temporal and spatial experimentation that the narrative movement of comics offers. "Genocide Now" is blunt, grim, unflinching. But even its lesser incarnation, "Never Again and Again and Again," expresses the continuousness of history as "what hurts" (as Jameson puts it), as our nondivorce from the traumatic events of the past, the impossibility of rejecting horror as ever completely "behind us" (102). This title strongly recalls Spiegelman's own choice of an internally repetitive title for his recent collection of work, *From Maus to Now to Maus to Now*, which itself posits the historical trauma represented in *Maus* as unending. Spiegelman insists on the persistence of trauma—in his choices of titles, in his textual practice of spatial intrusion, overlaying, and overlapping—in order to show how memory can be treated as an ongoing creative learning process, rather than something anchored in insuperable trauma. On the pages of *Maus*, Spiegelman shows us the violation and breaking of the "world grid" in both senses of the term—phenomenologically and literally on the page. Spiegelman's overtly political suggestion—which he registers in literal, graphic frame-breaking—is that the past is present, again and again and again: *Maus* questions the framework of everyday life that is taken for granted. As Robert Storr asserts of the obscene mouse-head corpses "piled like crumpled wastepaper" under Artie's feet in the section "Time flies" while he sits at his drawing board, contemplating his project: "this is not a sick joke but evidence of the heartsickness that motivates and pervades the book: it is the gallows humor of a generation that has not faced annihilation but believes utterly in its past reality and future possibility" (28). *Maus*'s enmeshed temporalities suggest a line of thinking that indeed stems from such a worldview. In his latest work, Spiegelman admits to having an "existential conviction that I might not live long enough to see [*In the Shadow of No Towers*] published."

The effect of visually, spatially linking the past and the present as *Maus* does is to urgently insist on history as an "untranscendable horizon" (Jameson, 102). "Instead of making comics into a narcotic, I'm trying to make comics that can wake you up, like caffeine comics that get you back in touch with things that are happening around you," says Spiegelman (qtd. in Silverblatt, 31). Indeed, *Maus*'s challenging multivocality, cross-discursivity, and the thick surface texture of its pages demand a reading process that engages the reader in an act of consumption that is explicitly anti-diversionary.

In "Collateral Damage," a *PMLA* editor's column introducing an issue that explores visuality and literary studies, Marianne Hirsch focuses crucial attention on *In the Shadow of No Towers* and on the form of comics generally.[27] She asks: "What kind of visual-verbal literacy can respond to the needs of the present moment?" (1212). As Hirsch shows in her analysis of *No Towers*, certainly Spiegelman's work is one important place to go. Spiegelman himself expresses strong views about the literacy that comics require and hone: "It seems to me that comics have already shifted from being an icon of illiteracy to becoming one of the last bastions of literacy," he has said (Interview with Gary Groth, 61). "If comics have any problem now, it's that people don't even have the patience to decode comics at this point. . . . I don't know if we're the vanguard of another culture or if we're the last blacksmiths."

Historical graphic narratives today draw on a popular form once considered solely distracting in order to engage serious political questions. We see in *Maus* faith in "making hopeful use of popular forms," to use a phrase of Neil Nehring's (36)—the (post)utopian impulse evident in Spiegelman's earlier work such as *Raw*, the magazine that declared it had "lost its faith in nihilism" (*Raw* 3, July 1981). Charles Bukowski wrote Spiegelman in the late 1970s, "Ah, you guys are all ministers in Popeye suits" (qtd. in Silverblatt, 36). To the allegation of masking high moral seriousness with "the popular," Spiegelman responded, "Most of the artists in *Raw*—I won't say every single one of them—are moving forward from a moral center. As a result, it seemed to me to be interesting to be able to make ethics hip."

Indeed, the graphic narrative is a contemporary form that is helping to expand the cultural map of historical representation. Its expansive visual-verbal grammar can offer a space for ethical representation without problematic closure. *Maus* is a text inspirited with an intense desire to represent politically and ethically. But it is not a didactic text pushing moral interpretations or solutions.[28] An author "moving forward from a moral center" is not the same as an author presenting an authoritative morality tale of history—a concept that Spiegelman's text vehemently rejects.[29] *Maus* defines itself against morality tales as Gertrud Koch describes them: narratives that "endeavor to convince us of their own moral qualifications and blur the dark and destructive future the past often presents to its victims" (406). As its stunning last page makes apparent, *Maus* eschews the closure implied by the concept of a moral text, offering instead multiple layers representing time as space; an unstable interplay of presence and absence; and productive, cross-discursive collisions.[30]

As Spiegelman notes, *Maus*'s last page "just keeps ending" (*Complete Maus*). It both suggests the ethical value of narrative and insists that no voice could or should have the last word, thus suggesting the work of memory as a public process.[31] Through a form that "folds in on itself in order to get out," the ending of *Maus* moves beyond the particularity of its "tale," inviting the reader to join in a collective project of meaning-making (*Complete Maus*).

As its grim ending so clearly reveals, *Maus* does not offer—with sincerity—the narrative closure that would seal a traditionally moral story. *Maus*'s last page breaks the frame because it is innovative in its spacing, ontologically suggesting that there is no closure, no "ending," no telos.[32] Unsurprisingly, the last page of *Maus* does not have a page number; it is not stamped with a linear logic of progression. In a way, Maus does end the most traditional way a narrative can: with a literal claim of "happy ever after." And it ends the most literal way a biography can: with the death of its subject. But like so much postmodern fiction, *Maus* offers, exploits, and undercuts the most traditional of happy endings (romantic reunion; family romance). And, like so much biography, it offers and undercuts that most traditional of structural principles: life dates.

The last page of *Maus* is charged with movement: the narrative accelerates and decelerates—if one can call it that—rapidly. The page offers six panels, two on each row, and each pair of frames works off of an opposition. The first tier moves from outside to inside, from the open Sosnowiec street to a close view of the Jewish Organization building (a speech balloon juts out from its closed window). The second tier moves from a position of graphically stark apartness (Vladek, dressed in white, and Anja, dressed in black, face each other disbelievingly across a room) to a position of dramatic togetherness (Vladek and Anja embrace in front of an iris diaphragm). In the third tier's first panel, Artie sits as if anchored to his father's bed, and in the second panel, Artie stands, leaving; in the first panel Artie is Art, and in the second, his father names him Richieu (the name of his long dead brother, who did not survive the war); in the first panel Vladek faces Artie—and the reader-and in the second he rolls over and turns away, bending his arm over his face. Essentially, for the readers of *Maus*, in that last moment he dies, for the next image Spiegelman presents is his tombstone, balanced exactly in the middle of the two last frames, its Star of David shooting up the gutter. The Spiegelman tombstone rises up into this bottommost tier of frames, splitting the two panels symmetrically. The literally central presence of the tombstone's Star of David on the last page of *Maus*, then, is a key affirmation of Judaism, for this prominently placed symbol resignifies: Spiegelman recalls the Star as a mark of hatred and oppression on the Nazi-enforced badges that are so prevalent in the first volume of *Maus*, reversing the "mark" to attest to the enduring survival of Judaism and Jews.[33]

Immediately we notice that balanced below the headstone, marked with the upper-case "SPIEGELMAN," is a lowercase echo, a reply to this death—Art Spiegelman's signature, and the dates he worked on *Maus*: "art spiegelman 1978–1991." The narrative argument of this page is in its spacing, its echoes and replies, its gulfs and repetitions, what it buries and what it at once engenders. Narrative closure (death, marriage) is often, especially in postmodern fiction, questioned by epilogues.[34] Spiegelman's signature—shaggy, stylized, undercase—and the tombstone that he places exactly in the center of a symmetrical page, is that very questioning "epilogue." As ever, Spiegelman competes with

From page 136, *MAUS II: A Survivor's Tale/And Here My Troubles Began* by Art Spiegelman, copyright © 1986, 1989, 1990, 1991. Used by permission of Pantheon Books, a division of Random House, Inc

his father's narrative while at the same time faithfully representing it. Spiegelman's signature—not an extra-narrative detail or flourish but part of the (post-plot) narrative itself, does not represent closure or finality. The Spiegelman signature, echoing the engraving on the Spiegelman parental tombstone, marks the narrative's awareness of the falsity of *Maus*'s patently unhappy "happy ending." Vladek and Anja did not live "happy, happy, ever after," as Vladek claims in the narrative voiceover that accompanies their reunion embrace. The doubled inscriptions, epitaphic and autographic, *show* us that Spiegelman does not intend to let his father have the "last word" (even as he might desire the incredible delusion behind the inaccurate "happy ever after"). The last spoken words in *Maus* are Vladek's: "It's *enough* stories for now . . ." (emphasis and ellipses in original). The "story" suggested by the tombstone, though, is one that Vladek does not himself narrate (Anja's suicide), but of which readers of *Maus* are aware. The traumatic stories, *Maus* implies, go on after its last image and will continue to come in the future; in this way, *Maus*, while a "survivor's tale," is not a morality tale. *Maus* rather exploits and resists the happy ending that punctuates a morality tale. In *Maus*'s last page, Vladek and Anja reunite after Auschwitz, and *Maus* completes its family romance. "V-Vladek!" cries Anja. "Gasp," manages Vladek. In his narrative voiceover to Artie, Vladek describes that "It was such a moment that everybody around us was crying together with us." In the next panel the couple embrace as in an old Hollywood movie, in the center of a dramatic iris diaphragm, their faces buried in each other's shoulders. Vladek narrates: "More, I don't need to tell you. We were both very happy, and lived happy, happy ever after." The intra-textual reference for *Maus*'s last page is a page in *Maus I*'s Chapter Two, "The Honeymoon." In this scene, which takes place before the war breaks out definitively, the dressed-up Spiegelmans dance closely with each other (at Anja's sanitarium) in front of an iris diaphragm, in six separate frames (35). Vladek tells Anja, as the two dance, an amusing story about his father's pillow; which the elder Spiegelman had retrieved at great peril when the family fled the 1914 war (in *Maus*'s last page, Vladek Spiegelman will place his arm, in a gesture of exhausted finality, across his pillow, almost like a child settling down to sleep). In this page's final panel, when Vladek completes the punchline, about his father's safe return but horse-sore behind, Anja—in the same posture as in *Maus*'s dramatic final page—embraces Vladek, her arms around his neck. "I love you, Vladek," she says. Vladek's voiceover narration, in a box below the image—as in *Maus*'s ending—is as follows: "And she was so laughing and so happy, so happy that she approached each time and kissed me, so happy she was" (35).

This repetition of "happy" three times is echoed in *Maus*'s conclusion, which correspondingly, unbelievably repeats "happy" three times: "We were both very happy, and lived happy, happy ever after." Of course, however, although they embrace as if in a melodramatic film still at the end of Vladek's testimony, readers of *Maus* know that the Spiegelmans' narratives do not end happily. Instead, *Maus*'s last sequence shows, as Gertrud Koch puts it, the "endlessness of sadness" (403). Anja did not live "happy ever after": even if the text had not earlier referenced her suicide, the tombstone punctuating the page clearly shows she died fourteen years before Vladek, at age fifty-six. And Vladek, as we well know, devastated by Anja's death, in ill health, was often estranged from his only son and unhappy in his second marriage.

On one hand, the doubling of nomenclature (a representation of engraving, the "SPIEGELMAN" inscribed in stone—and its mimicry, the representation of authorial "voice" and performance, the "art spiegelman" inscribed in ink below, the drawn grave) indicates Spiegelman's attention to the idea of text as a social space, here particularly as a collaborative fabric created by father and son (and absent mother) that produces no single master of enunciation, but several interacting enunciators. It is clear that *Maus* subverts, even as it installs, the singularity and originality implied in signature (*Poetics* 81). But here Spiegelman's narrative (implied in the open-endedness that his signature unexpectedly delivers) also competes with his father's narrative of closure. Terms like "polyphonic" or "dialogic" come to mind, but the page, intermixed in its "conversation" with different media, is more complicated than a rubric like dialogism indicates, since Spiegelman responds to his father's verbal narrative *visually*, by drawing his gravesite and drawing his own signature. Reading this page, one is reminded, as Felman points out, that testimony often functions as signature. Here Spiegelman's literal signature competes with the signature of Vladek's testimony. Spiegelman is here, as ever, doing (more than) two things at once, contradictorily preserving and questioning his father's narrative. Spiegelman's visual post-dialogue epilogue is at once oppositional (calling our attention to the stories told on the tombstone as a rejoinder to his father's "ever after" conclusion), *and* commemorative, a tribute to his parents, a supplement to Vladek's testimonial signature that he marks with his own literal signature: a deferring, lowercase inscription.

If life dates are the most traditional way to narrate a biography, Spiegelman offers us his parents' life dates in *Maus*'s final page, gesturing towards the most basic, simplistic form of life narrative. Drawing their shared headstone as the penultimate punctuation of *Maus*, he officially immortalizes his parents in text (of course, their names are already preserved elsewhere, engraved in stone): "VLADEK Oct. 11, 1906–August 18, 1982" and "ANJA Mar. 15, 1912–May 21, 1968." Directly below, his signature, followed by the dates he worked on *Maus*—"art spiegelman 1978–1991"—suggests several different meanings. We assume that the dates clearly indicate the "life" of *Maus*'s enunciation, the process of researching, drawing, and composing this work. Echoing the inscription of nomenclature on his parents' gravesite, then, his signature implies his desire to put *Maus* to rest; or rather, it defines the life of the project as its procedure. Another way to read this line—if one were keyed to the power of visualizing the literal, as Spiegelman prompts us to do throughout the text—is as Spiegelman's own life dates: indeed, this option makes the most graphic sense, even as we know these dates to be false as those marking his biological lifespan.

By placing his signature directly below his parents' grave—indeed, in the space of the ground below—Spiegelman figures himself as buried by his parents' history. (Indeed, we can recall his strongest response to his status as a member of the "postmemory" generation: his accusations of murder to both parents). But Spiegelman's signature is also a way to read the book backwards: his signature may be figured as generative, growing the text upwards from the space of the buried, repressed, and "entombed" where it appears to end. *Maus*'s ending, then, *spatially* marks itself as a "working through" (the spaces and enclosures of panels and gravesites and ground), which is that documentary/testimonial imperative that does not give into closure.[35] From a graphic perspective, the movement of the page strikingly travels *upwards* (and backwards, then), suggesting the engendering of the narrative we have just read. Grass grows, somewhat wildly, up from the Spiegelman gravesite; the headstone is positioned as an arrow shooting up through the gutter into the grid of the page—and, it is implied, back through the narrative we have just completed. The Eternal Flame that is engraved on the stone, which represents Jewish persistence and permanence in the face of oppression and death, points up through the dead center of the page, aligned with the straight white line of the gutter. Thus positioned, the Eternal Flame—spiritually and graphically—signals the unending of life and narrative. This marks a continuousness rather than a closure, as with *Maus*'s double epitaph, which resists the teleological and the epitaphic. Because of the complexity of *Maus*, the defining example of this politically invested aesthetic form, graphic narratives are now part of a postmodern cartography, with new work such as Marjane Satrapi's *Persepolis* charting childhood in revolutionary Iran, and Joe Sacco's *Palestine* and *Safe Area Gorazde* mapping the frontlines of Palestine and Bosnia. Epitomizing the possibilities of the new comics form, *Maus*, interlaced with different temporalities whose ontological weave it frames and questions through spatial aesthetics, rebuilds history through a potent combination of words and images that draws attention to the tenuous and fragile footing of the present.

NOTES

1. Laura Frost recently argued that this connection is a weak point of *No Towers*. In my reading, however, the most interesting and politically useful, if risky, aspect of the book is its willingness to analyze a world-historical stage as opposed to keeping 9/11 local and specific, as Frost urges.

2. *In the Shadow of No Towers*, like the groundbreaking *Maus*, makes attention to interlacing temporalities part of its very form: Spiegelman's twenty-first-century comic strips are followed by reprints of old newspaper comic strips from the turn of the twentieth century. Spiegelman's own ten strips are followed by seven plates, lavish reproductions of the historical strips. *No Towers*, then, like *Maus*, offers no end that implies recovery or transcendence. Working specifically against any metanarrative of progress, it argues, through its narrative grouping of original and historical material, that the "end" is in fact a return to the old. Spiegelman says in an interview that the confusion that the combination of new and old work might induce is "exactly the point of the book" (qtd. in Dreifus).

3. Other authors also note the persistence of the past in *Maus*. See for instance Sara Horowitz, Michael Rothberg, James Young, and Andrea Liss.

4. The work of Marianne Hirsch and Michael C. Levine are two important exceptions. In "Family Pictures: *Maus*, Mourning, and Postmemory" and in "Collateral Damage," Hirsch discusses how the comics form "performs an aesthetics of trauma" ("Collateral Damage," 1213). Levine discusses bleeding as the hemorrhaging of visual images that break out of frames (71). I disagree, however, with Levine's explication of the grammar of comics in terms of film language; dismissing comics on its own terms, he cites "Spiegelman's art of the slow motion picture" (72). Deborah Geis also notes the "filmic" style of *Maus* (2). While *Maus* does make cultural references to fun, I believe its form is best understood as specific to comics. For instance, as Scott McCloud points out about the crucial space of the gutter, comics' structural element of absence, "what's between the panels is the only element of comics that is not duplicated in any other medium" (13).

5. Rildiger Kunow is correct to point out that "a self-reflexive awareness of the limits of representation has become not only a specific problem germane to the Holocaust but more generally a *conditio sine qua non* of all representations in theory, history, and cultural texts" (252).

6. Erin McGlothlin thoroughly dissects *Maus*'s temporalities through identification of its three diegetic levels and Genette's tripartite narrative classification system, but she does not consider the aesthetic issue of how time is represented spatially on the comics page.

7. Spiegelman rejected a certain woodcut style for *Maus* because it made the text "like a political cartoon" ("Jewish Mice," 116). He rejects the notion of a "graphic approach" as "a visual analog to the content" (Interview with Andrea Juno, 10).

8. See Shoshana Felman and Don Laub's *Testimony*, especially the chapter "Education and Crisis"; and W. J. T. Mitchell's "Commitment to Form."

9. Felman rightly believes this statement "has become itself (perhaps too readily) a cultural cliché, too hastily consumed and too hastily reduced to a summary dismissal" (33). This reading is affirmed by "Commitment," in which Adorno demands that art strive to resist the judgment of its uselessness in the face of suffering.

10. Spiegelman claims, "The page is the essential unit of information" and "I've considered the stylistic surface [of the page] a problem to solve" (*Complete Maus*).

11. While many critics invoke *Maus*'s "hybrid form" (Miller, "Art of Survival," 99) or "hybridized status" (LaCapra, 146) when elaborating the destabilizing work that the text performs, few analyze the graphic form of *Maus* that creates this hybridity. Although LaCapra goes beyond other critical invocations of *Maus*'s hybridity by explaining that "blurring and hybridization should not be conflated although they may at times be very close" (146 n.14), his frequent use of the term warrants further discussion: see 145, 146, 147, 149, 151, 152, 153. See also Huyssen, Orvell, and Young for unexplicated invocations of *Maus*'s hybridity. My own understanding of this term as apposite to comics is premised on the fact that in comics, the images do not necessarily illustrate the text but can comprise a separate narrative thread; verbal and visual narratives do not simply blend together. This notion of hybridity is clarified in Lyotard's discussion of the *differend*: necessarily set into play by the nonunity of language, the *differend* represents the impossibility of bridging incommensurate discourses.

12. Annotation is Spiegelman's term for the procedure of comics; he describes comics pioneer Bernard Krigstein as "a philosopher of how time could be made visible and annotated in space" ("Krigstein"). For important theorizations of framing generally see Derrida, *The Truth in Painting*; Goffman; and Malina.

13. Friedman discusses location on page 20, multiplicity on page 24, and borders on 27–30. See also Mitchell, "Space, Ideology, and Literary Representation."

14. Spiegelman refers here to his dense comic strip "A Day at the Circuits," collected in his book *Breakdowns*. This obsession for packing and gathering took a more virulent form in Spiegelman's youth, when, reportedly, he hoarded string while hospitalized for a mental breakdown, as he knew Vladek had done at Auschwitz (Gerber, 168).

15. All emphases in quotations from *Maus* are Spiegelman's. I call *Maus*'s artist character Artie (as his father does) and the text's author Art Spiegelman.

16. The second volume of Spiegelman's 1980s magazine *Raw* evokes *My Father Bleeds History* in its subtitle, *Open Wounds from the Cutting Edge of Commix*. This connection emphasizes the extraction implied in Spiegelman's father "bleeding history" for his son's medium.

17. There is an important body of criticism that explores this rebuilding in terms of the absent mother, Anja Spiegelman. See Hirsch, "Family Pictures"; LaCapra; Levine; and Miller, "Cartoons of the Self" and an expanded version, "The Art of Survival."

18. *Maus* makes frequent use of the iris diaphragm, a technique often used at the end of silent films when the scene is viewed as if through a binocular and the image gradually diminishes into the darkness. This description is in Koch, 401.

19. Smoke also figures the presence of the past in *In the Shadow of No Towers*, where Spiegelman draws Art's cigarette smoke as the smoke coming from Ground Zero on 9/11. Art connects his father's inability to describe the smell of the smoke of bodies in Auschwitz with his own indescribable olfactory experience in Lower Manhattan in 2001, all the while himself smoking, as in *Maus*, Cremo brand cigarettes.

20. Hirsch writes: "I use the terms postmemory to describe the relationship of children of survivors of cultural or collective trauma to the experiences of their parents, experiences that they "remember" only as the stories and images with which they grew up, but that are so powerful, so monumental, as to constitute

memories in their own right" ("Projected Memory," 8). See also Hirsch's "Family Pictures," "Surviving Images," and "Family Frames."

21. Artie's therapist Pavel even suggests that Artie is "the *real* survivor." *Maus II* 44.

22. Spiegelman sees "Prisoner" and "Time flies" as sequences that exist outside of the already complicated narrative structure of *Maus*. But, he notes, they "pull the narratives taut in different temporal and spatial directions" (qtd. In Silverblatt, 35–36). Notably, Spiegelman's language here suggests a loose flow of historical narrative that is made more lucid—instead of more slack—by a complicating self-reflexivity.

23. The CD-ROM *The Complete Maus*, in which we hear portions of Vladek's narrative, suggests Spiegelman's attempt to represent Vladek's literal voice. It also shows how Spiegelman edited his father's speech to fit the format of *Maus*.

24. Spiegelman, while allowing his father's rejection of this "very well documented" fact, lets readers know which "version" is correct. *Maus II*, 54.

25. As Felman points out, testimony is composed of "events in excess of our frame of reference," and does not offer a completed statement, a totalizable account (5).

26. *Maus*'s representational ethic firmly rejects aesthetic mastery as inappropriate to Holocaust representation. Spiegelman says: "I wanted [the drawing in *Maus*] to be more vulnerable so that it wouldn't be the master talking down to whoever was reading" (Brown 102). This methodology would seem to figure itself against the mastery of subject implied in the project of an institution like the Holocaust Museum. Liliane Weissberg writes, for instance, that the Holocaust Museum is problematically "an object fully mastered by its creators" (19). For more on the Holocaust Museum and *Maus*, see Landsberg.

27. "Collateral Damage" is the first literary analysis I have read of any Spiegelman text besides *Maus*. Hirsch's cogent reading reinforces and clarifies my claim that the same fascinating formal procedures (the architectural structure of pages and the complex, layered panelization therein) drive both *Maus* and *In the Shadow of No Towers*.

28. See also Koch and Rothberg. Hungerford reads *Maus* as a fundamentally strong moral text, claiming it seeks to "build a Jewish identity around the Holocaust" (93) and imagine a "healthy, true relation to the past" (94)—ideas that I read *Maus* as rejecting. Spiegelman comments on the question of Jewish identity in "Looney Tunes."

29. Fascinating work, however, is just now being published on historical comic books exactly because of their persuasive and didactic impulses. See Hansen.

30. *Maus* also eschews the idea of an instructional morality by offering no model characters, refusing to sentimentalize or sacralize either the survivor or the artist.

31. Two points are worth mentioning: first, Spiegelman came up with fifty to sixty ideas for the ending of *Maus*; therefore, we may understand that he wanted to make a significant, particular (graphic) point on this last page (*Complete*). Second, Spiegelman purposefully designed the last page to go right up against the endpapers: there is no white page following the conclusion. The contiguity of text and endpapers that Spiegelman presents—achieved by rejecting the spatial format of traditional books—underscores my point that Spiegelman did not want this ending to mark itself as a definitive "end."

32. I use "breaking the frame" after Felman, and after Hirsch's "Family Pictures." *Maus*'s few photographs, such as one of Anja and Artie in *Maus I*'s "Prisoner," and *Maus II*'s souvenir snapshot of Vladek in a concentration camp uniform, also literally, spatially break the frame by tilting out of their tiers at diagonal angles (*Maus 1* 100, *Maus II* 134).

33. It is in a broad, affirmative sense that Spiegelman foregrounds the Magen David so powerfully on the last page of *Maus*. It would be incorrect to read the graphic prominence Spiegelman bestows the Magen David as a statement about Israel. Arguing that the world itself has become "the Diaspora Jew," Spiegelman was attached (before 9/11 compelled him to reconsider himself as a "rooted cosmopolitan") to the notion of the "rootless" and "ruthless" cosmopolitan, and also to the concept of the Diaspora Jew: "For me the romantic image of the Jew is . . . the pale, cosmopolitan, alienated, half-assimilated, International Stateless outsider Jew" ("Looney Tunes," 16). In *Maus II*, Spiegelman jokes that he would draw Israeli Jews as

porcupines, and his attitude about Israel is ambivalent and evasive: "I am not anti-Zionist. I am Agnostic . . . maybe Israel was a bum steer, a quick-fix salve for the world's guilt that was in all-too-adequate response to the urgent and profound questions Auschwitz should have raised" (16).

34. See, for instance, Hutcheon, 121.

35. Friedlander's gloss (52).

WORKS CITED

Adorno, Theodor, "After Auschwitz: Meditations on Metaphysics" *Negative Dialectics*, trans E. B. Ashton (New York: Continuum, 1973): 361–65.

——, "Commitment," in Andrew Arato and Eike Gebhardt, eds., *The Essential Frankfurt School Reader* (New York: Continuum, 2000): 300–318.

——, "Cultural Criticism and Society," *Prisms*, trans. Samuel Weber and Sherry Weher (Cambridge: MIT Press, 1981): 17–34.

Brown, Joshua, "Of Mice and Memory," *Oral History Review* 16.1 (Spring 1988): 91–109.

Buhle, Paul, "Of Mice and Menschen: Jewish Comics Come of Age," *Tikkun* 7.2 (1992): 9–16.

Caruth, Cathy, *Unclaimed Experience: Trauma, Narrative, and History* (Baltimore: Johns Hopkins University Press, 1996).

D'Arcy, David, narr., "Profile: Art Spiegelman's Comic Book Journalism." Transcript, NPR Weekend Edition, June 7, 2003: 1–3.

Derrida, Jacques, *The Truth in Painting*, trans. Geoff Bennington and Ian McLeod (Chicago: University of Chicago Press, 1987).

Dreifus, Claudia, "A Comic-Book Response to 9/11 and Its Aftermath." *New York Times*, August 7, 2004, B9.

Felman, Shoshana, and Don Laub, *Testimony: Crises of Witnessing in Literature, Psychoanalysis, and History* (New York: Routledge, 1992).

Friedlander, Saul, "Trauma, Transference, and 'Working-Through' in Writing the History of the Shoah," *History and Memory: Studies in Representations of the Past* 4.1 (Spring-Summer 1992): 39–59.

Friedman, Susan Stanford, "Locational Feminism: Gender, Cultural Geographies, and Geopolitical Literacy," in Marianne DeKoven, ed. *Feminist Locations: Global and Local, Theory and Practice* (New Brunswick: Rutgers University Press, 2001): 13–36.

Frost, Laura, "The Twin Towers of Auschwitz and Hiroshima: Art Spiegelman, 9/11, and the Limits of Analogy," Address. Modern Language Association Annual Convention (Washington, DC. December 28, 2005).

Geis, Deborah R., "Introduction," in Deborah R. Geis, ed. *Considering Maus: Approaches to Art Spiegelman's "Survivors Tale" of the Holocaust* (Tuscaloosa: University of Alabama Press, 2003): 1–11.

Gerber, David A., "Of Mice and Jews: Cartoons, Metaphors, and Children of Holocaust Survivors in Recent Jewish Experience: A Review Essay," *American Jewish History* 77.1 (September 1987): 159–75.

Goffman, Erving, *Frame Analysis: An Essay on the Organization of Experience* (Cambridge: Harvard University Press, 1974).

Gussow, Mel. "Dark Night, Sharp Fears: Art Spiegelman Addresses Children and His Own Fears," *New York Times*, October 15, 2003: E1.

Hansen, Bert, "Medical History for the Masses: How American Comic Books Celebrated Heroes of Medicine in the 1940s," *Bulletin of the History of Medicine* 78.1 (2004): 148–91.

Hirsch, Marianne, "Collateral Damage," *PMLA* 119.5 (Oct. 2004): 1209–15.

——, *Family Frames: Photography, Narrative, and Postmemory* (Cambridge: Harvard University Press, 1997).

——, "Family Pictures: Maus, Mourning, and Postmemory," *Discourse* 15.2 (Winter 1992–93): 3–30.

————, "Projected Memory: Holocaust Photographs in Personal and Public Fantasy," in Mieke Bal, Jonathan Crewe, and Leo Spizer, eds., *Acts of Memory: Cultural Recall in the Present* (Hanover: University Press of New England, 1999): 3–23.

————, "Surviving Images: Holocaust Photographs and the Work of Post," *Yale Journal of Criticism* 14.1 (2001): 5–37.

Horowitz, Sara R., *Voicing the Void: Muteness and Memory in Holocaust Fiction* (Albany: SUNY Press, 1997).

Hungerford, Amy, *The Holocaust of Texts: Genocide, Literature, and Personification* (Chicago: University of Chicago Press, 2003).

Hutcheon, Linda, *A Poetics of Postmodernism: History, Theory, Fiction* (New York: Routledge, 1988).

Huyssen, Andreas, "Of Mice and Mimesis: Reading Spiegelman with Adorno," *New German Critique* 81 (Fall 2000): 65–83.

Jameson, Fredric, *The Political Unconscious: Narrative as a Socially Symbolic Act* (Ithaca: Cornell University Press, 1981).

————, *Postmodernism or the Cultural Logic of Late Capitalism* (Durham: Duke University Press, 1991).

Koch, Gertrud. "'Against All Odds' or the Will to Survive: Moral Conclusions from Narrative Closure," *History and Memory* 9.1 (Spring-Summer 1997): 393–408.

Kuno, Rudiger, "Emotion in Tranquility? Representing the Holocaust in Fiction," in Gerhard Hoffman and Alfred Hornung, eds., *Emotion in Postmodernism* (Heidelberg: Universitätsverlag, 1997): 247–70.

LaCapra, Dominick. "'Twas the Night Before Christmas: Art Spiegelman's *Maus*," *History and Memory After Auschwitz* (Ithaca: Cornell University Press, 1998): 139–79.

Landsberg, Alison, "America, the Holocaust, and the Mass Culture of Memory: Toward a Radical Politics of Empathy," *New German Critique* (Spring–Summer 1997): 63–86.

Levine, Michael G., "Necessary Stains: Spiegelman's *Maus* and the Bleeding of History," in Deborah Geis, ed., *Considering Maus: Approaches to Art Spiegelman's "Survivor's Tale" of the Holocaust* (Tuscaloosa: University of Alabama Press, 2003): 63–104.

Liss, Andrea, "Between Trauma and Nostalgia: Christian Boltanski's Memorials and Art Spiegelman's *Maus*," *Trespassing through Shadows: Memory, Photography, and the Holocaust* (Minneapolis: University of Minnesota Press, 1998): 39–68.

Lyotard, Jean-François, *The Differend: Phrases in Dispute*, trans. Georges Van Den Abbeele (Minneapolis: University of Minnesota Press, 1988).

Malina, Debra, *Breaking the Frame: Metalepsis and the Construction of the Subject* (Columbus: Ohio State University Press, 2002).

McCloud, Scott, "Understanding Comics," in *Comic Book Rebels: Conversations with the Creators of New Comics* (New York: Fine, 1993): 3–15.

McGlothlin, Erin, "No Time Like the Present: Narrative and Time in Art Spiegelman's *Maus*," *Narrative* 11.2 (2003): 177–98.

Miller, Nancy K., "The Art of Survival: Mom, Murder, Memory," in *Bequest and Betrayal: Memoirs of a Parent Death* (New York: Oxford University Press, 1996): 97–125.

————, "Cartoons of the Self. Portrait of the Artist as a Young Murderer." *Meaning* 12 (1992): 43–54.

Mitchell, W. J. T., "The Commitment to Form; or, Still Crazy after All These Years," *PMLA* 18.2 (Mar. 2003): 321–25.

————, "Space, Ideology, and Literary Interpretation," *Poetics Today* 10.1 (Spring 1989): 91–102.

Nehring, Neil, *Popular Music, Gender, and Postmodernism: Anger Is an Energy* (Thousand Oaks: Sage, 1997).

Orvell, Miles, "Writing Posthistorically: Krazy Kat, *Maus*, and the Contemporary Fiction Cartoon," *American Literary History* 4.1 (Spring 1992): 110–28. Rpt. and expanded in *After the Machine: Visual Arts and the Erasing of Cultural Boundaries* (Jackson: University Press of Mississippi, 1995): 129–46.

Rosen, Alan, "The Language of Survival: English as Metaphor in Spiegelman's *Maus*," *Prooftexts: A Journal of Jewish Literary History* 15.3 (Sept. 1995): 249–62.

Rothberg, Michael, *Traumatic Realism: The Demands of Holocaust Representation* (Minneapolis: University of Minnesota Press, 2000).

Silverblatt, Michael, "The Cultural Relief of Art Spiegelman," *Tampa Review* 5 (1995): 31–36.

Spiegelman, Art, Address on *In the Shadow of No Towers*, Barnes & Noble, Union Square, New York, September 23, 2004.

———, *Breakdowns* (New York: Nostalgia, 1977).

———, *The Complete Maus*, CD (New York: Voyager, 1994).

———, "A Day at the Circuits," *Breakdowns: From Maus to Now: An Anthology of Strips by Art Spiegelman* (New York: Nostalgia, 1977).

———, Interview with Joey Cavalieri, Gary Groth, and Kim Thompson, in Gary Groth and Robert Fiore, eds., *The New Comics: Interviews from the Pages of the Comics Journal* (New York: Berkley, 1988): 185–203.

———, Interview with Gary Groth, *The Comics Journal* 180 (Sept. 1995): 52–106.

———, Interview with Andrea Juno, in Andrea Juno, ed., *Dangerous Drawings: Interviews with Comix and Graphix Artists* (New York: Juno, 1997): 6–27.

———, *In The Shadow of No Towers* (New York: Pantheon. 2004).

———, "Jewish Mice, Bubblegum Cards, Comics Art, and Raw Possibilities," Interview with Joey Cavalieri, *The Comics Journal* 65 (August 1981): 98–125.

———, "Krigstein: A Eulogy by Art Spiegelman," *The Comics Journal* (February 1990): 13. Rpt. *From Maus to Now to Maus to Now: Comix, Essays, Graphics, and Scraps* (Palermo: La Centrale dell'Arte, 1998): 90.

———, "Looney Tunes, Zionism, and the Jewish Question" *Village Voice*, June 6, 1989: 20–21. Rpt. *From Maus to Now to Maus to Now: Comix, Essays, Graphics, and Scraps* (Palermo: La Centrale dell'Arte, 1998): 14–16.

———, *Maus I: A Survivor's Tale: My Father Bleeds History* (New York: Pantheon, 1986).

———, *Maus II: A Survivor's Tale: And Here My Troubles Began* (New York: Pantheon, 1991).

Storr, Robert, "Art Spiegelman's Making of *Maus*," *Tampa Review* 5 (1995): 27–29.

Tabachnick, Stephen, "Of *Maus* and Memory: The Structure of Art Spiegelman's Graphic Novel of the Holocaust," *Word and Image* 9.2 (April–June 1993): 154–62.

Weissberg, Liliane, "In Plain Sight," in Barbie Zelizer, ed. *Visual Culture and the Holocaust* (New Brunswick: Rutgers University Press, 2001): 13–27.

Weschler, Lawrence, "Art's Father, Vladek's Son," *Shapinsky's Karma, Boggs's Bills* (San Francisco: North Point, 1988): 53–68.

White, Hayden, "Historical Emplotment and the Problem of Truth," in Saul Friedlander, ed. *Probing the Limits of Representation: Nazism and the "Final Solution"* (Cambridge: Harvard University Press, 1992): 37–53.

Witek, Joseph, *Comic Books as History: The Narrative Art of Jack Jackson, Art Spiegelman, and Harvey Pekar* (Jackson: University Press of Mississippi, 1989).

Young, James, "Art Spiegelman's *Maus* and the After-Images of History," *At Memory's Edge: After-Images of the Holocaust in Contemporary Art and Architecture* (New Haven: Yale University Press, 2000): 12–41.

CONTRIBUTORS

Thomas Andrae teaches sociology at California State University, East Bay. He is co-founder and senior editor of *Discourse: Journal for Theoretical Studies in Media and Culture*. His most recent books are *Carl Barks and the Disney Comic Book: Unmasking the Myth of Modernity* and *Masters of Comic Art*.

Martin Barker is professor of film and television studies at Aberystwyth University. He has researched widely, moving from comic books into films, covering their histories, textual forms, controversies, and—more recently—their audiences. He was director of the 2003–2004 international *Lord of the Rings* audience research project. Most recently he has conducted research for the British Board of Film Classification into audience responses to screened sexual violence.

Bart Beaty is associate professor of media studies at the University of Calgary. He is the author of *Fredric Wertham and the Critique of Mass Culture*; *Unpopular Culture: Transforming the European Comic Book in the 1990s*; and, with Rebecca Sullivan, *Canadian Television Today*. His articles on European comics have been published in numerous magazines, and he publishes regularly on this topic for ComicsReporter.com.

John Benson, who has been writing about comics for over fifty years, is the editor of *Squa Tront*, a magazine about EC comics. His interview with Bernard Krigstein in 1962 (with Bhob Stewart) was the first in-depth interview with a comics artist. His recent book, *Confessions, Romances, Secrets, and Temptations*, published by Fantagraphics, is a historical and critical perusal of the St. John romance comics.

David Carrier has published books on the methods of art history, on Poussin, on the abstract painter Sean Scully, on Baudelaire's art criticism, and on the art museum. And he writes art criticism. His *A World Art History* is forthcoming from Penn State University Press.

Hillary Chute is a junior fellow in literature at the Harvard Society of Fellows. Her essays about comics have appeared in or are forthcoming in *Twentieth-Century Literature*, *MFS: Modern Fiction Studies*, *Women's Studies Quarterly*, *American Periodicals*, and *PMLA*. In 2006 she and Marianne DeKoven coedited a special issue of *Modern Fiction Studies* on graphic narrative. Hillary is currently working with Art Spiegelman on his book project *MetaMaus* (Pantheon), and on a study of contemporary graphic narratives by women.

Peter Coogan wrote his dissertation on "The Emergence of the Superhero Genre in America from Daniel Boone to Batman." In addition to serving as the writing specialist for the Kinkel Center for Academic Resources at Fontbonne University, he is the cofounder and co-chair of the Comics Arts Conference, held annually at the San Diego Comic-Con International.

Annalisa Di Liddo completed her Ph.D. at the University of Milan after extensively researching comics, popular culture, and contemporary literature in the U.K., U.S., and Canada. Her thesis explores the work of Alan Moore. Dr. Di Liddo has taught at the universities of Milan, Como, and Trento. Her papers encompass works by Angela Carter, Alan Moore, Art Spiegelman, and Chester Brown; the publication of her monograph about Moore is forthcoming. She currently works as an editorial consultant and a literary translator.

Ariel Dorfman is a Chilean writer who teaches at Duke University. He is the author of *Death and the Maiden*, a prize-winning play that was made into a film by Roman Polanski, and the coauthor (with Armand Mattelart), of *How to Read Donald Duck: Imperialist Ideology in the Disney Comic*. His other books include *The Empire's Old Clothes: What the Lone Ranger, Babar, and Other Innocent Heroes Do to Our Minds*; *Widows: A Novel*; and *Heading South, Looking North: A Bilingual Journey*.

Thierry Groensteen has written and edited more than twenty books about the history, semiotics, and aesthetics of comics, including in-depth studies on Tardi, Herriman, Caran d'Ache, Schulz, Hergé, and Baudoin. He has curated the Angouleme Comics Museum from 1993 to 2001, and been chief editor of the journals *Les Cahiers de la bande dessinée* and *Neuvième Art*. He now works as a publisher for Actes Sud and teaches at the Ecole supérieure de l'Image.

Robert C. Harvey has been writing about cartooning for well over a quarter of a century, beginning with a column in the *Menomonee Falls Gazette* in the fall of 1973. A one-time freelance cartoonist, Harvey is a member of the National Cartoonist Society (NCS), an associate member of the American Association of Editorial Cartoonists (AAEC), and a member of the Comic Art Professionals Society (CAPS). He has authored several books about cartooning, including *The Art of Comics*, *The Art of the Funnies*, and, most recently, *Meanwhile: A Biography of Milton Caniff*.

Charles Hatfield is associate professor of English at California State University, Northridge. He is the author of *Alternative Comics: An Emerging Literature*, and his essays on comics have appeared in *Inks*, *ImageTexT*, *Children's Literature Association Quarterly*, the *Comics Journal*, and elsewhere.

Jeet Heer is writing a doctoral thesis on the cultural politics of Little Orphan Annie at York University (Toronto). He is coeditor, with Kent Worcester, of *Arguing Comics: Literary Masters on a Popular Medium*. With Chris Ware and Chris Oliveros, he is editing a series of volumes reprinting Frank King's *Gasoline Alley*, three volumes of which have been published by Drawn and Quarterly under the umbrella title *Walt and Skeezix*. He is the editor of Clare Brigg's *Oh Skin-nay* and is writing the introductions to a multivolume series reprinting George Herriman's *Krazy Kat*. His essays have appeared in *The Virginia Quarterly Review*, the *Literary Review of Canada*, the *Boston Globe*, the *Guardian*, Slate.com, and many other publications.

M. Thomas Inge is the Robert Emory Blackwell Professor of English and the Humanities at Randolph-Macon College. His books include *Comics as Culture*; *Charles M. Schulz: Conversations*; *Handbook of American Popular Literature*; *The Humor of the Old South*; and *Anything Can Happen in a Comic Strip*. In recognition of his contributions to the field, the M. Thomas Inge Award for Comics Scholarship was created in 1996 under the aegis of the Comic Art and Comics Section of the Popular Culture Association.

Gene Kannenberg, Jr., has presented and published widely on comic art, including his Ph.D. dissertation from the University of Connecticut in 2002. He has chaired both the Comic Art & Comics Area of the Popular Culture Association and the International Festival of Comic Art. A freelance writer and editor, he lives in New York's Hudson Valley along with his wife, author and academic K. A. Laity; visit his website at ComicsResearch.org.

David Kasakove is a litigation partner at the international law firm of Byran Cave LLP.

Adam L. Kern is associate professor of Japanese literature at Harvard University. His noteworthy experiences in Japan include a stint as a newspaper reporter for *The Kyoto Shimbun*, an internship in the editorial offices of the manga weekly *Young Magazine*, and the day student radicals set the roof of his house on fire.

David Kunzle is professor of art history at the University of California–Los Angeles. He has published widely on popular, political, and public art, such as murals and comic strips, and the revolutionary art of Latin America. He is the author of *inter alia*, *The History of the Comic Strip*; *From Criminal to Courtier: The Soldier in Netherlandish Art 1550–1670*; and an updated edition of *Fashion and Fetishism: A Social History of the Corset, Tight-lacing and Other Forms of Body-sculpture in the West*.

Pascal Lefèvre worked successively as a researcher at the Belgian national broadcasting corporation and the Belgian Centre of Comic Strip Art. Since 1998 he has been lecturing on comics and visual media at two Flemish university colleges of art (in Brussels and Antwerp).

John A. Lent is professor of communications at Temple University and the founder and editor of the *International Journal of Comic Art*. He is the author of numerous books and articles on comics and animation, including *Pulp Demons: International Dimensions of the Postwar Anti-Comics Campaign*; *Animation in Asia and the Pacific*; and *Illustrating Asia: Comics, Humor Magazines and Picture Books*.

W. J. T. Mitchell is Gaylord Distinguished Service Professor of English and Art History at the University of Chicago. He is the editor of *Critical Inquiry*, and the author of several books on theories of images, including *Iconology*, *Picture Theory*, and *What Do Pictures Want?*

Amy Kiste Nyberg is associate professor of media studies in the Department of Communication at Seton Hall University in South Orange, N.J. She is the author of *Seal of Approval: The History of the Comics Code*, which analyzes the rise of comic book censorship and industry self-regulation. She earned her doctorate from the University of Wisconsin-Madison.

Fusami Ogi is associate professor of English language and literature at Chikushi Jogakuen University in Fukuoka, Japan. She is the author of numerous conference papers and has published articles on different aspects of manga.

Robert S. Petersen is an assistant professor in the Departments of Art and Theatre at Eastern Illinois University where he teaches a course on the history of graphic narratives. Petersen received a Fulbright scholarship to Indonesia and has published on art and theatre in Japan, India, and Southeast Asia.

Anne Rubenstein is associate professor of history at York University in Toronto. She is the author of *Bad Language, Naked Ladies and Other Threats to the Nation: A Political History of Comic Books in Mexico* (recently published in Mexico under the title *De los Pepines a los Agachados* by *Fondo de Cultura Económica*), and the coeditor of *Fragments of a Golden Age: The Politics of Culture in Mexico Since 1940*. Her current research concerns the history of movie going and fans in Mexico and elsewhere.

Roger Sabin is the author of several books on comics, including *Adult Comics: An Introduction* and *Comics, Comix and Graphic* Novels. His current focus is on the nineteenth-century origins of the form, and in 2006 he was the co-winner of the Franco Fossatti Award for his research into Ally Sloper. He teaches at Central Saint Martins College of Art and Design, University of the Arts London.

Gilbert Seldes first achieved prominence as a critic with his 1924 book *The Seven Lively Arts*, which argued for greater critical acceptance of popular culture. Seldes published widely in opinion magazines such as the *New Republic*, *Esquire*, and the *Saturday Evening Post*. He also wrote plays (for theatre and radio) and served as the first program director for CBS Television.

Art Spiegelman is the author of *Maus*, which received a special Pulitzer in 1992, as well as *Breakdowns*, *The Wild Party*, *Jack Cole and Plastic Man*, and *In the Shadow of No Towers*. With his wife, François Mouly, he launched and edited the influential comics magazine *Raw*, and subsequently the *Little Lit* series. In 2005, *Time* magazine listed him in the top 100 "of the world's most influential people."

Fredric Wertham was a German-American psychiatrist whose controversial writings on violence, comics, and public health made him an international figure. His best-known book, *The Seduction of the Innocent*, published in 1954, helped fuel an anti-comics movement. He had already established himself in the medical profession with his first book, *The Brain as an Organ*. His other books include *A Sign for Cain* and *The World of Fanzines*.

Joseph Witek is professor of English at Stetson University, where he has taught courses on comics since 1989. He is the author of *Comic Books as History* and numerous essays on comics. His latest book is a collection of interviews, *Art Spiegelman: Conversations*.

Kent Worcester is the author of *C. L. R. James: A Political Biography* and the coeditor, with Jeet Heer, of *Arguing Comics: Literary Masters on a Popular Medium*. He is a regular contributor to *The Comics Journal*, and a member of the Board of Trustees of the Museum of Comic and Cartoon Art (MoCCA). He teaches political theory at Marymount Manhattan College.

INDEX